If practice makes perfect, imagine what *better* practice can do . . .

MyWritingLab is an online learning system that provides better writing practice through progressive exercises. These exercises move students from literal comprehension to critical application to demonstration of their ability to write properly. With this better practice model, students develop the skills needed to become better writers!

When asked if they agreed with the following statements, here are how students responded:

97%
The MyWritingLab Student-user Satisfaction Level

"MyWritingLab helped me to improve my writing." **89%**

"MyWritingLab was fairly easy to use." **90%**

"MyWritingLab helped make me feel more confident about my writing ability." **83%**

"MyWritingLab helped me to better prepare for my next writing course." **86%**

"MyWritingLab helped me get a better grade." **82%**

"I wish I had a program like MyWritingLab in some of my other courses." **78%**

"I would recommend my instructor continue using MyWritingLab." **85%**

Student Success Story

"The first few weeks of my English class, my grades were at approximately 78%. Then I was introduced to MyWritingLab. I couldn't believe the increase in my test scores. My test scores had jumped from that low score of 78 all the way up to 100% (and every now and then a 99)."

—Exetta Windfield, *College of the Sequoias* (MyWritingLab student user)

If your book did not come with an access code, you may purchase an access code at

www.mywritinglab.com

Registering for MyWritingLab™...

It is easy to get started! Simply follow these steps to get into your MyWritingLab course.

1) **Find Your Access Code** (it is either packaged with your textbook, or you purchased it separately). You will need this access code and your course ID to join your MyWritingLab course. Your instructor has your course ID number, so make sure you have that before logging in.

2) **Click on "Students"** under "Register or Buy Access." Here you will be prompted to enter your access code, enter your e-mail address, and choose your own login name and password. After you register, you can **login under "Returning Users"** to use your new login name and password every time you go back into MyWritingLab.

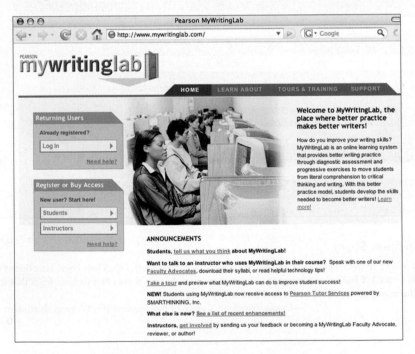

After logging in, you will see all the ways MyWritingLab can help you become a better writer.

www.mywritinglab.com

The Homepage ...

Here is your MyWritingLab HomePage.
You get a bird's eye view of where you are in your course every time you log in.

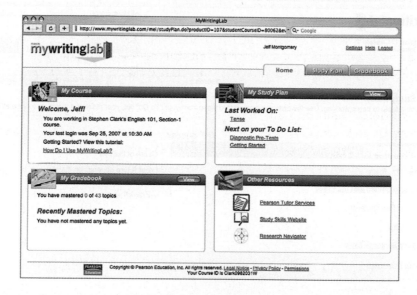

Your **Course** box shows your class details.

Your **Study Plan** box shows what you last completed and what is next on your **To Do** list.

Your **Gradebook** box shows you a snapshot of how you are doing in the class.

Your **Other Resources** box supplies you with amazing tools such as:

- **Pearson Tutor Services**—click here to see how you can get help on your papers by qualified tutors . . . before handing them in!

- **Research Navigator**—click here to see how this resembles your library with access to online journals for research paper assignments.

- **Study Skills**—extra help that includes tips and quizzes on how to improve your study skills

Now, let's start practicing to become better writers. Click on the Study Plan tab. This is where you will do all your course work.

www.mywritinglab.com

The Study Plan . . .

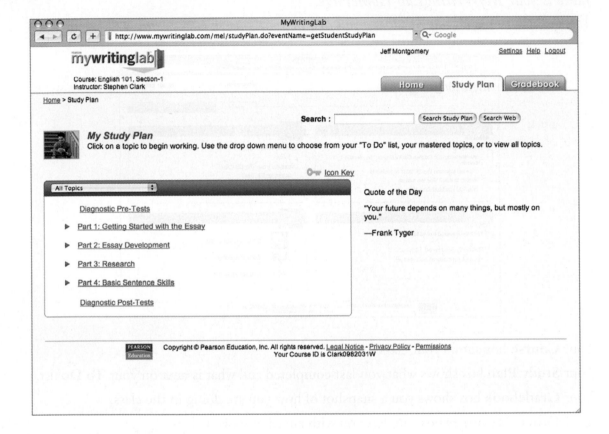

MyWritingLab provides you with a simple Study Plan of the writing skills that you need to master. You start from the top of the list and work your way down. You can start with the Diagnostic Pre-Tests.

www.mywritinglab.com

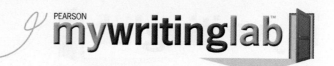

The Diagnostic Pre-Tests . . .

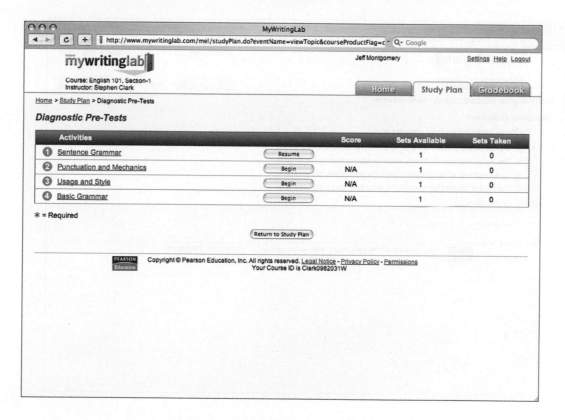

MyWritingLab's Diagnostic Pre-Tests are divided into four parts and cover all the major grammar, punctuation, and usage topics. After you complete these diagnostic tests, MyWritingLab will generate a personalized Study Plan for you, showing all the topics you have mastered and listing all the topics yet unmastered.

The Diagnostic Pre-Tests ...

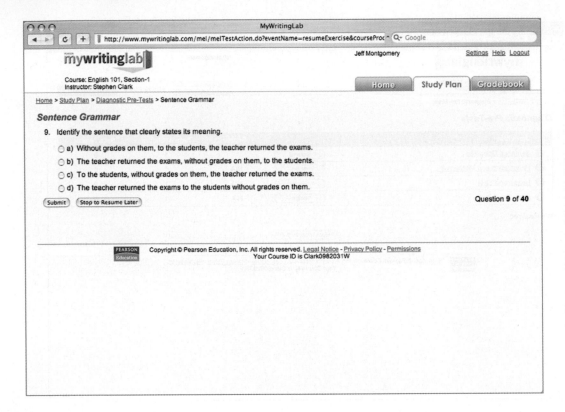

The Diagnostic Pre-Tests contain five exercises on each of the grammar, punctuation, and usage topics. You can achieve mastery of the topic in the Diagnostic Pre-Test by getting four of five or five of five correct within each topic.

After completing the Diagnostic Pre-Test, you can return to your Study Plan and enter any of the topics you have yet to master.

www.mywritinglab.com

Watch, Recall, Apply, Write . . .

Here is an example of a MyWritinglab Activity set that you will see once you enter into a topic. Take the time to briefly read the introductory paragraph, and then watch the engaging video clip by clicking on "Watch: Tense."

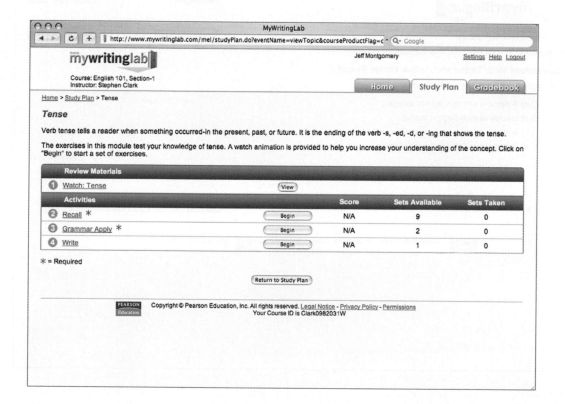

The video clip provides you with a helpful review.
Now you are ready to start the exercises. There are three types:

- Recall—activities that help you recall the rules of grammar
- Apply—activities that help you apply these rules to brief paragraphs or essays
- Write—activities that ask you to demonstrate these rules of grammar in your own writing

www.mywritinglab.com

Watch, Recall, Apply, Write . . .

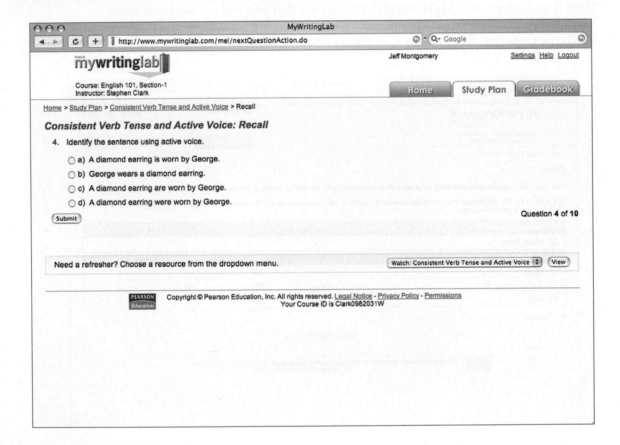

Recall questions help you recall the rules of grammar and writing when you complete multiple-choice questions, usually with four possible answers. You get feedback after answering each question, so you can learn as you go!

There are many sets available for lots of practice. As soon as you are finished with a set of activities, you will receive a score sheet with helpful feedback, including the correct answers. This score sheet will be kept in your own gradebook, so you can always go back and review.

www.mywritinglab.com

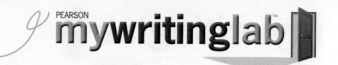

Watch, Recall, Apply, Write . . .

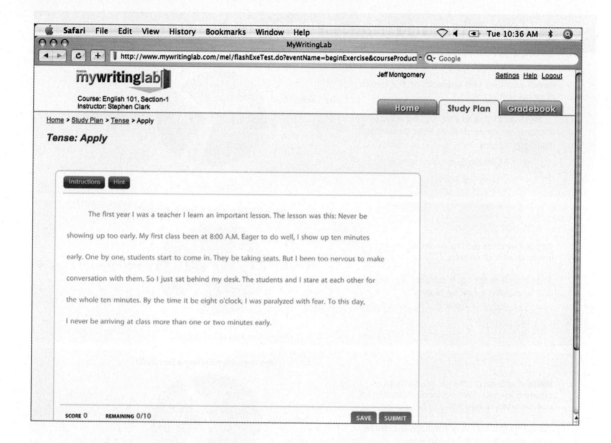

Apply exercises help you apply writing and grammar rules to brief paragraphs or essays. Sometimes these are multiple-choice questions, and other times you will be asked to identify and correct mistakes in existing paragraphs and essays.

Your instructor may also assign **Write exercises,** which allow you to demonstrate writing and grammar rules in your own writing.

Helping Students Succeed ...

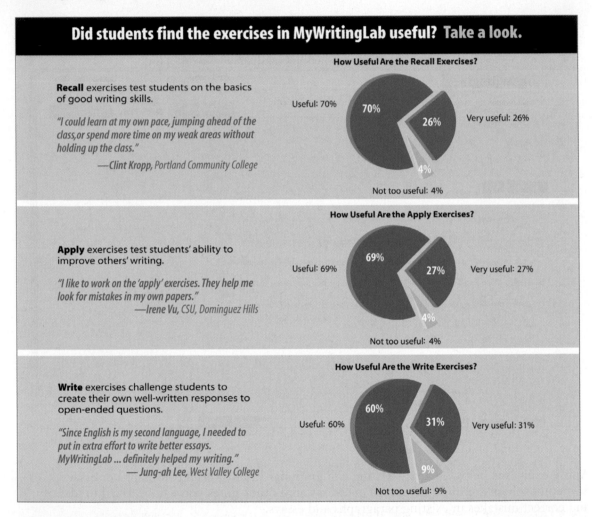

Did students find the exercises in MyWritingLab useful? Take a look.

Recall exercises test students on the basics of good writing skills.

"I could learn at my own pace, jumping ahead of the class, or spend more time on my weak areas without holding up the class."

—*Clint Kropp, Portland Community College*

How Useful Are the Recall Exercises?

Useful: 70%
70%
26% Very useful: 26%
4%
Not too useful: 4%

Apply exercises test students' ability to improve others' writing.

"I like to work on the 'apply' exercises. They help me look for mistakes in my own papers."

—*Irene Vu, CSU, Dominguez Hills*

How Useful Are the Apply Exercises?

Useful: 69%
69%
27% Very useful: 27%
4%
Not too useful: 4%

Write exercises challenge students to create their own well-written responses to open-ended questions.

"Since English is my second language, I needed to put in extra effort to write better essays. MyWritingLab ... definitely helped my writing."

— *Jung-ah Lee, West Valley College*

How Useful Are the Write Exercises?

Useful: 60%
60%
31% Very useful: 31%
9%
Not too useful: 9%

Students just like you are finding MyWritingLab's Recall, Apply, and Write exercises useful in their learning.

www.mywritinglab.com

The Gradebook ...

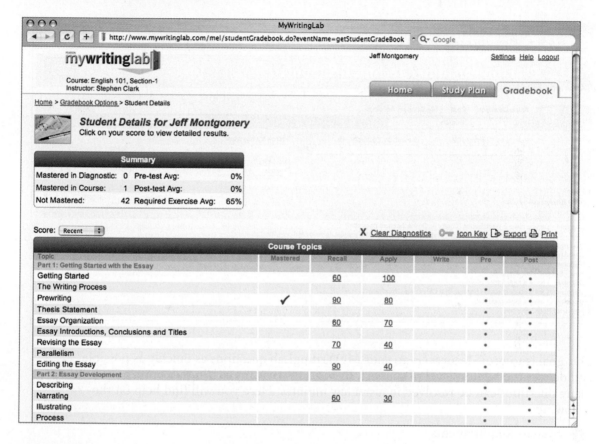

Let's look at how your own on-line gradebook will help you track your progress.

Click on the "Gradebook" tab and then the "Student Detail" report.

Here you are able to see how you are doing in each area. If you feel you need to go back and review, simply click on any score and your score sheet will appear.

You also have a Diagnostic Detail report so you can go back and review your diagnostic Pre-Test and see how much MyWritingLab has helped you improve!

www.mywritinglab.com

Here to Help You . . .

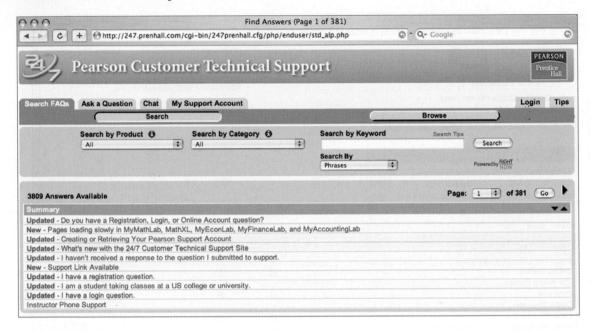

Our goal is to provide answers to your MyWritingLab questions as quickly as possible and deliver the highest level of support. By visiting **www.mywritinglab.com/help.html**, many questions can be resolved in just a few minutes. Here you will find help on the following:

- System Requirements
- How to Register for MyWritingLab
- How to Use MyWritingLab

For student support, we also invite you to contact Pearson Customer Technical Support (shown above). In addition, you can reach our Support Representatives online at **http://247.pearsoned.com**. Here you can do the following:

- Search Frequently Asked Questions about MyWritingLab
- E-mail a Question to Our Support Team
- Chat with a Support Representative

www.mywritinglab.com

The WRITE STUFF

Thinking Through Essays

MARCIE SIMS

Upper Saddle River, New Jersey 07458

Library of Congress Cataloging-in-Publication Data

Sims, Marcie.

   The write stuff : thinking through essays / Marcie Sims.

      p. cm.

   Includes index.

   ISBN-10: 0-13-194295-6

   ISBN-13: 978-0-13-194295-0

1. English language—Rhetoric—Study and teaching (Higher)   2. Critical thinking—Study and teaching (Higher)   3. College readers.   4. Academic writing—Study and teaching (Higher) I. Title.

   PE1408.S533 2008

   808′.042—dc22

                                        2008035332

VP/Editorial Director: Leah Jewell
Editor-in-Chief: Craig Campanella
Acquisitions Editor: Blair Zoe Tuckman
Editorial Assistant: David Nitti
Executive Marketing Manager: Megan Galvin-Fak
Marketing Manager: Tom DeMarco
Marketing Assistant: Patrick Hume
Assistant Vice-President, Editor-in-Chief Development: Rochelle Diogenes
Development Editor: Gillian Cook
Director of Market Development: Maureen Prado Roberts
Text Permission Specialist: Robyn Renahan
Senior Operations Supervisor: Sherry Lewis
Operations Specialist: Christina Amato
Project Manager: Maureen Benicasa

Manager, Design Development: John Christiana
Interior & Cover Design: Kathryn Foot
Manager, Cover Visual Research and Permissions: Karen Sanatar
Manager, Rights and Permissions: Zina Arabia
Manager, Visual Research: Beth Brenzel
Image Coordinator: Vickie Menanteaux
Full-Service Production and Composition: Pine Tree Composition
Full-Service Project Management: Karen Berry, Pine Tree Composition
Printer/Binder: Courier Companies
Cover Printer: Coral Graphics

This book was set in 11/13 Goudy.

Credits and acknowledgments borrowed from other sources and reproduced, with permission, in this textbook appear on appropriate page within text (or on page 724).

Pearson Education LTD., London
Pearson Education Singapore, Pte. Ltd
Pearson Education Canada, Inc.
Pearson Education–Japan
Pearson Education Australia PTY, Limited

Pearson Education North Asia, Ltd., Hong Kong
Pearson Educación de Mexico, S.A. de C.V.
Pearson Education Malaysia, Pte. Ltd.
Pearson Education, Upper Saddle River, New Jersey

**Prentice Hall
is an imprint of**

www.pearsonhighered.com

10 9 8 7 6 5 4
ISBN-13: 978-0-13-194295-0
ISBN-10: 0-13-194295-6

Brief Contents

iv

Contents

PART III WRITING AND CRITICAL THINKING IN THE MODES 125

7 Narration 128

8 Description 151

12 Example and Illustration   239

13 Cause and Effect   261

PART VI   SENTENCE CONSTRUCTIONS AND COMMON SENTENCE ERRORS   503

To the Instructor

The Write Stuff: Thinking Through Essays is an all-in-one writing text designed for upper developmental and beginning-level composition courses. *The Write Stuff* provides all the information students need to build their analytical reading and writing skills, as well as the information and practice they need for doing so using correct grammar and an appropriate style. Most beginning composition texts do not provide the basic instruction and exercises needed while at the same time developing more difficult to grasp analytical skills: interpretation and analysis. This text not only provides students with the basic tools for writing well organized and developed essays that are grammatically and mechanically correct, but it also focuses on teaching students the critical thinking skills they need to interpret and analyze information and express their ideas clearly and logically in writing. Critical thinking provides the theme that integrates the instruction throughout the text.

Students in developmental and entry-level composition courses need detailed instruction on how to write paragraphs and essays; how to spot and correct their spelling, usage, and sentence-level errors; and how correctly to include quotes from other writers. They also need instruction on how to interpret what they read, how to go deeper into the topics they've chosen to write about, how to choose the best approach for communicating their ideas to their target audience, and how to pull all of these aspects together into a meaningful purpose for writing. *The Write Stuff* encourages students to engage in an active critical thinking process during all stages of reading and writing and helps them to move beyond defending the obvious in their understanding of others' ideas as well as their own.

The tone and level of *The Write Stuff* speaks to students who are on the cusp of college-level reading and writing. The user-friendly tips and exercises help students develop the tools they need to succeed in reading and writing, and the critical thinking focus throughout the book helps them move past rote learning and summary into true interpretation and analysis of what they are reading or what they are writing about.

CRITICAL THINKING IN *THE WRITE STUFF*

Critical thinking, the unifying theme of *The Write Stuff*, is defined in Chapter 1, which also includes clear explanations of the meaning and function of specific critical thinking terms and tools that are used in almost every chapter of the book. These terms include *purpose, ideas, support, assumptions and biases, conclusions, point of view,* and *analysis.*

Critical thinking terms may be unfamiliar to many students and seem abstract and hard to grasp. In order to make explicit the connection between these terms and their application to writing essays that clearly articulate and support ideas and arguments, the concept of a critical thinking toolbox is used. Each of the terms listed above is linked to a specific tool icon. The idea is to provide students with visual cues that identify critical thinking tools they can use whenever they embark on a writing or reading assignment. For example, blueprints and drafting tools are used to represent purpose, and beams to represent the main ideas expressed in topic sentences to support a thesis. Nails are used to represent the support (examples, details, facts) a writer uses to underpin ideas, while a magnifying glass represents the importance of looking closely at and analyzing the elements of an argument, an essay, or even an individual sentence.

These icons are used consistently throughout the text to make explicit to students the connection between the critical thinking tools they have learned about in Chapter 1 and their application to real-world writing. The icons work not only on a visual identification level, alerting students that a specific tool is being used, but on a subliminal level, so that students begin automatically to connect the icons with important critical thinking concepts. As they progress through the text, students will become increasingly familiar with these critical thinking concepts and tools and develop confidence in using them in their writing assignments.

CONTENT

The Write Stuff focuses on upper developmental writing, reading, and analysis skills, and it works well for both developmental and entry level composition classes. It includes the following features:

- **Critical thinking skills defined and applied** with critical thinking pointers, prompts, and exercises throughout the text

- **Critical reading and analysis techniques** for reading college-level assignments, including visual aids
- **Applying Critical Thinking boxes** that either briefly define the critical thinking tools relevant to specific sections of these chapter and explain in concrete terms how students can apply them, or demonstrate practical applications of these tools
- **Critical thinking icons** that keep terminology and tools discussed in Chapter 1 fresh in students' minds, integrating them into the ongoing instruction, and showing them to have practical use in all aspects of essay writing
- A review of the basics for writing paragraphs
- Thorough coverage of the basics for writing essays
- Separate chapters on each of the modes, including argument
- Professional reading selections, with writing prompts, for analysis
- Annotated student essays that provide achievable models for student writers
- Two chapters that cover how to find, evaluate, summarize, analyze and cite sources, and how to use MLA documentation style
- A section on sentence construction and common sentence construction errors with ample practice exercises
- A handbook that provides information and helpful tips on correct use of grammar, spelling, vocabulary, and style, plus plentiful sentence and paragraph length exercises
- A chapter on analyzing visuals
- Instructor resources for setting up a course and successful in-class and out-of-class tasks
- An appendix on writing about stories

ORGANIZATION

Part I introduces students to the concept of critical thinking, defines important terms, and outlines critical thinking skills and how they apply to reading and writing.

In Part II, students are given a review of how to write expository paragraphs and essays. They learn about paragraph and essay structure, and how to generate ideas, clarify their purpose for writing, assess their audience, and customize their approach to a topic. They are introduced to the essay writing process, shown how to organize and provide details and support for their essay's purpose, and learn about the importance of order, unity, and coherence.

In Part III, students learn about various modes, or essay types, including narration, description, process, classification, definition, example/illustration, cause and effect, comparison and contrast, and argument and persuasion, as well as how to combine them. Each chapter contains critical thinking pointers, specific instruction on how to write in a particular mode, an annotated student essay that provides a realistic and level-appropriate model, an annotated professional sample of the mode with exercises, and tips for possible mode combinations depending on essay purpose and assignment. The section ends with a chapter that provides tips on writing timed essays and essay exams.

In Part IV of *The Write Stuff*, students learn how to write from sources including readings, articles, literature and visuals, as well as how to summarize, paraphrase, and analyze other writers' work. They learn how to find sources to support their own ideas (research), how to evaluate these sources, and how to cite them correctly in their own writing (MLA citation format).

In Part V, students learn how to write about visual forms of communication, including paintings, photos, and sculpture, as well as film, TV, and advertisements. Moreover, they get a selection of readings for analysis with comprehension and critical thinking questions and writing prompts. The essay modes chapters (7–15) provide annotated sample student essays as well as professional reading selections (also in Chapter 21) for students to practice their critical reading skills. All of the reading selections have exercises and writing prompts that emphasize critical thinking and encourage deeper understanding and analysis by students.

Part VI provides a review of sentence parts and common sentence construction errors, and contains tips and exercises for avoiding sentence fragments, run-ons, and comma splices.

Part VII, a grammar handbook, covers the following topics and provides a wealth of sentence and paragraph level exercises for each:

- Punctuation
- Common shift and construction errors (with tips for spotting and fixing them)
- Spelling and mechanics
- Tone, style, diction, and usage
- ESL tips
- Tips for building vocabulary and using context clues to figure out unfamiliar words
- Typing and word processing tips

There are two appendices. Appendix A provides detailed guidance on how to write essays about professional stories, articles, and essays. Appendix B includes additional practice for nonnative speakers of English.

There are also resources for the instructor. The Instructor's Guide is the last 41 pages of the Annotated Instructor's Edition. This guide includes multiple strategies for integrating critical thinking into the classroom, sample syllabi, and a detailed essay on meeting the needs of nonnative speakers.

In addition, Pearson is pleased to offer an Instructor's Resource Manual, complete with chapter summaries and quizzes, as well as PowerPoint slides for every major topic. Print copies of the manual can be ordered by using ISBN 0-13-294299-9, or can be downloaded online from our Instructor's Resource Center at www.pearsonhighered.com <http://www.pearsonhighered.com/>.

Hopefully, you and your students will find that this text provides *the right stuff* to help them develop critical thinking abilities and learn how to apply them in every aspect of writing and reading.

ACKNOWLEDGMENTS

I am grateful to all of my students, colleagues, friends, and family who have helped in the process or given me their support in the process of writing *The Write Stuff: Thinking Through Essays*.

First, I would like to thank my editor, Craig Campanella, for his support, vision, and encouragement throughout the development of this text. I would also like to thank Gillian Cook, my development editor, for her guidance, meticulous and brilliant editing, and her ongoing sense of humor through our multiple revisions and the whole process of producing *The Write Stuff*. Kudos to Karen Berry for her careful and valuable copy editing. Thanks also to Rochelle Diogenes, David Nitti, Tom DeMarco, and all the editorial assistants, design staff, and marketing support at Pearson/Prentice Hall.

I am grateful to all my colleagues who helped review chapters or preliminary versions of this text and those who adopted preliminary versions in their composition classes. Special thanks to Hank Galmish, Julie Moore, Lisa Trujillo, Brad Johnson, Walter Lowe, Jaeney Hoene, Sandy Johanson, Jennifer Whetham, Erin Mommer, Abby Biggerstaff, Heather Pundt, Liz Petersen, Anna Nelson, Jeb Wyman, and Douglas Cole. Thank you to my colleagues at Green River Community College for their support and encouragement as I wrote this text, and thanks for the acknowledgments and pride in this project from President Rich Rutkowski, Executive Vice President April Jensen, and Dean Judy Burgeson. Moreover, this text benefited greatly from the feedback and suggestions from reviewers.

Another thanks to the artists and photographers who let me feature their beautiful visuals in this text: I am especially indebted to Douglas T. Cole,

Cindy Small, Patrick Navin, Tim Schultz, Gary Oliveira, Lily Ning, Paul Metivier, Hank Galmish, Douglas L. Cole, and the other artists features in this book.

I am extremely grateful to my students, past and present, who have inspired me in the classroom and who inspired me to begin writing textbooks in the first place. Thank you also to those students who have given me permission to use their work and to those who provided their feedback on this text and its exercises. *The Write Stuff* would not be if not for you.

Finally, I want to thank my family for their patience and support as I worked on this text. Special thanks to my sons, Marcus and Thomas; to my mother, Delores Sims; to my brothers and sister and their families, Nick, Charlie, Dolly, Diana, Jerith, Mathew, Krysta, and Ashley Sims; and to the rest of my family: Sharon Thornton, Fumitaka Matsuoka, Doug and Nancy Cole, Traci Cole, David and Rachel Haygood, and all of my extended family across the country.

Preface to the Student

USE THIS TEXT AS A RESOURCE

Phương pháp - phg sách
tài nguyên

The Write Stuff is a tool, so remember to use it in a way that best serves your purpose. You don't need to read the chapters in order. Read them in the order assigned by your instructor, but don't forget to use the index to look up what you need help with in your own writing and to answer questions that arise as you study. Throughout the book, notes in the margin will direct you to where you can find related information or expanded explanations for specific topics.

The Write Stuff weaves critical thinking practice throughout the sections. You will learn about the basic components of critical thinking in Chapter 1. In Chapter 2, you'll learn how to apply critical thinking skills to reading. Then, in the chapters on writing essays, the chapters related to reading and analysis skills, and in the reading selections themselves, you will find critical thinking questions and writing prompts to hone your analysis skills as you read. There are critical thinking tips and icons in every chapter to motivate and guide you in your critical thinking.

The critical writing and reading skills you learn here will help you do better in courses you will take throughout your college career (not just in English or writing classes).

ORGANIZATION

The Write Stuff is designed to provide the basic skills you'll need for successful college writing, reading, and critical thinking—skills you will continue to use after college, in your career, and beyond. Throughout the text, you will find helpful Applying Critical Thinking boxes and visual icons to help you apply critical thinking skills in your reading and writing.

Part I of *The Write Stuff* provides an overview of critical thinking skills, including a definition of critical thinking and of the specific tools and terms you can use to apply critical thinking analysis to your own writing and the writing of others. It also provides step-by-step instruction in how to engage your critical thinking skills and read analytically.

Part II of the text provides a review of writing paragraphs, a general introduction to the writing process, and step-by-step guidance through the process of writing expository essays.

Part III introduces different modes or types of essays and discusses how to choose which mode to use, when to use one mode over another, and when to use a combination of two or more modes. It provides the tools you need to write a clear argument and to read and evaluate the arguments of others.

In Part IV, you will learn how to paraphrase and summarize what you read as well as additional techniques for writing about what you read. You will find out how to evaluate and use outside sources in your writing, and be introduced to the MLA (Modern Language Association) format for documenting sources correctly and avoiding plagiarism. Part V of this text includes a chapter that describes techniques and critical analysis skills for writing about visuals, and provides a selection of professional and student sample readings for analysis, critical thinking, and writing tasks. Part VI focuses on sentence construction and common sentence errors, and Part VII features a grammar, mechanics, and style handbook with user-friendly explanations of the most common grammar and usage, tone, and style errors with exercises for practice. This part of the text also has a chapter on how to build your vocabulary and how to figure out words you don't know from their context in a reading. This last part of the text provides tips for typing and word processing.

This all-in-one textbook provides what you'll need to succeed in your college writing and reading tasks. The appendices include detailed guidance and techniques for how to write essays about other stories, articles, or essays that you read, and a summary of the process for peer evaluation of your essays and a self- and peer-critique form for essays.

STUDENT SUCCESS TIPS

In order to do well in any course, not just an introduction to writing course, it helps to know some basic tips for succeeding as a college student.

Before Your Course(s) Begins

1. **When registering for courses, first check with an advisor and/or research your campus's college catalog (usually available online).** You want to make sure the courses you are registering for are the correct ones for your intended degree or certificate, and to make sure you have satisfied all prerequisites for the course.

2. **Locate your classroom(s) before the first day of class so you won't get lost and be late on your first day of classes.** First impressions are important, and it is a stressful experience to be late to class.

3. **Get to your campus bookstore and purchase all of your course textbook(s) at least a week before classes begin.** If you order your books online or from another source, then be sure to check with your instructor(s) first to get the exact book information you need, including the edition number, and allow time for delivery.

4. **After you have purchased your textbooks, review them before classes begin** to familiarize yourself with the material you will be learning and to get a sense of the purpose and direction of your courses.

5. **Research on-campus tutoring facilities.** Visit your campus writing center or tutoring locations to see what is available to you once your classes begin. Visit your campus library to get a sense of the tools and resources available to you. Research any other on-campus resources that may help you with particular needs: the financial aid department, the career center, student programs, the women's center, the advising and counseling center, the disabled students resource center, and so on. Depending on your circumstances, you could be eligible for additional support, which often is free.

The First Week of Class

1. **Review the course syllabus** (the handout that is an overview of the course, usually distributed on the first or second day of class) carefully for each class you take. Be sure you understand all of the learning objectives and requirements for the course as well as the grading policies. The course syllabus is like an agreement—a contract—between you and the instructor. If you stay in the course, you are agreeing to the terms of this contract.

2. **Make a connection with at least one other student from class.** Exchange phone numbers and email addresses (if you choose to). Later, if you miss a class, you can get information and notes from your contact, and vice versa.

3. **Create a calendar of due dates for papers, projects, and exams.** Post the calendar in your room or place it in the front of your notebook so you are aware of these dates and won't procrastinate. You should arrange your work and outside schedules carefully, especially on the days that come before a major test or due date for an essay assignment.

Throughout the Class

1. **Find a "study buddy" or, even better, form a study group with three or more classmates.** Be careful, though, not to share homework or writing assignments. Do your own work. Study groups are for studying together for tests or special projects. When it comes to individual homework or essay assignments, they must be done on your own. You

can, however, peer critique each other's work afterwards or go to the on-campus tutoring or writing center for help in reviewing your drafts. Studies have shown that when students form connections with other students on campus, it increases their chances of being successful, and they are more likely to stay and complete their degree.

2. **Complete your work on time and submit it in a professional format.** You're in college now, so be sure that the quality of your work reflects that. You are responsible for knowing due dates and assignment requirements and accomplishing them on time.

3. **Keep copies of all the work you submit.** It is your responsibility to be able to reproduce any lost or misplaced work. Also, keep all graded work turned back to you until you have received your final grade. Even the most organized instructors can make a mistake in their grading records and miss recording, or record incorrectly, a score for an assignment or essay.

4. **Take notes in class.** Many students don't take notes during class, yet this is an integral part of student success and leads to increased comprehension and retention of material.

5. **If you need to communicate with your instructor, make an appointment.** Do not assume that an instructor is "on call" at all times, either in person, by phone, or via email. Instructors usually teach around 70–150 students per quarter or semester, so be respectful of their time and request an appointment if an issue or question arises that can't be answered by another classmate. Do not approach your teachers to ask for something at the beginning of class, or worse, to say "Did I miss anything?" if you missed the previous class. Of course you missed something! Get the information from a classmate first; if you need a handout from an instructor, approach him or her after class to get that handout, or see the instructor during scheduled office hours to get missed handouts.

6. **Take care of yourself.** College is stressful, so be sure to eat well, exercise, and remember to get enough sleep. Even the most conscientious students can't succeed if they become ill and can't make it to class or do their work.

7. **Keep a positive attitude and keep your goals in mind.** Remember why you are in college in the first place. These college years are ones that you will most likely look back upon fondly later, so keep your goals in mind and be proud of your accomplishments. Keeping a sense of humor helps too. Remember, you learn from mistakes, so do what you can to remedy them, and, most important, learn the lessons that they give you and grow as a result. After all, some of the best learning in college doesn't come out of lectures or assignments. It comes out of life experiences and working with others.

Critical Thinking in Reading and Writing

1

THINKING CRITICALLY

Look at the picture above. Then answer the questions that follow.

1. On first glance, what do you think this image is? What do you see?

_____

_____

2. Now take a closer look, paying attention to each detail of the photograph. Answer these questions:

What perspective is this picture taken from? Was it taken outside in the open air or inside a building? How do you know?

_____

_____

3. The picture was taken from the ground floor inside an office building looking up through the glass roof of the first floor. Was your first *assumption* about the picture correct? Did your *conclusion* hold up when you carefully examined the evidence?

The italicized terms above are critical thinking terms: Look for detailed explanations of them in this chapter.

CRITICAL THINKING

Critical thinking is a term you will hear quite a bit in college because it refers to the kind of thinking you'll be asked to do in your courses and later in your career. You'll be happy to know that you are already a critical thinker! You engage your critical thinking skills every day. Whenever you make a decision, solve a problem, or prioritize tasks, you are using critical thinking. For instance, when you choose your classes each term, you have to think carefully about your schedule: What classes are open this term? Which classes count toward your degree or certificate goals? How many classes can you take in one term and still be successful? Which classes are most important for you to take first? Engaging in the process of making these decisions, weighing the choices, and prioritizing all involve critical thinking. Even on a day-to-day basis, you engage your critical thinking skills. When you shop for groceries, when you decide which bills you should pay first on a limited budget, when you work out problems and arguments between you and your friends or you and your coworkers, you are being a critical thinker.

This chapter will define critical thinking in the context of using critical thinking skills to perform college tasks. It will provide you with tools and tips designed to help you read and write analytically (to read looking for answers to questions and to draw some conclusions about your topic) and to evaluate your own reading and writing processes. The skills involved in thinking critically are essential to effective reading and writing. Good thinking and good writing go hand in hand.

Critical thinking in society and education is not a new concept. The process of evaluating one's own thinking process has been around since human history began. Critical thinking was an essential part of ancient cultures, including the Egyptian (3150 BC), Sumerian (2900 BC), and Babylonian (2300 BC) cultures, and later was an integral skill and focus for the ancient Greek philosophers. Socrates (469–399 BC) is known for teaching his students how to analyze their critical thinking processes. In fact, the word *critical* comes from the Greek word *kritikos*, meaning to question or to analyze.

Various experts define critical thinking differently, but critical thinking is always a process that involves actively thinking through and evaluating all the steps in your own thinking process or the thinking process of others. Many teachers and experts emphasize the importance of critical thinking in college courses. Richard Paul is one of today's most well known scholars of critical thinking skills. According to Paul, critical thinking involves a "mode of thinking—about any subject, content, or problem—in which the thinker improves the quality of his or her thinking by skillfully taking charge" of each step in the process of thinking and the conclusions reached as a result of that thinking (Foundation for Critical Thinking, **www.criticalthinking.org**).

The bottom line is that you must be aware of your own thoughts and how they affect your conclusions. There are different skills and tools you can use to improve your thinking process as you read and write. You can use these critical thinking skills to understand and evaluate the writings of others and to discover the strengths and weaknesses in their reasoning or arguments. As you learn these skills, your own thinking and writing skills will improve. Develop the habit of a step-by-step process of thinking about each part of an argument or idea. Critical thinking skills are essential for clear, fair-minded, analytical writing as well as for good analytical reading. Once you get hooked on the power that comes from using your critical thinking skills, you may not be able to stop—you will find yourself using them everywhere: while reading the newspaper, listening to the radio, reading a novel, even watching a movie.

Think of each step in the critical thinking process as a domino in a long line of dominoes set up to fall in a certain pattern and to end in a specific place. Knock over one domino, and it will knock over the next. But if one domino is out of place, it will keep all the others that follow it from falling correctly. In the same way, one error in your reasoning can throw off your whole chain of thinking and interrupt the flow and logic of your ideas. So line up each step in your critical thinking process carefully: Weigh each piece of evidence you provide, think about your reasons and conclusions, and make sure no point you make is out of line. Otherwise, your chain of thought and evidence will be thrown off and your end result will be derailed. You want your dominoes to fall into place perfectly, one idea sparking the next: a perfect process.

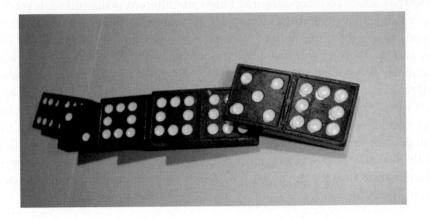

CRITICAL THINKING TOOLS

The following critical thinking tools—terms and elements of argument—are used throughout this textbook to help you evaluate your thinking, reading, and writing processes; to explore your ideas, arguments, and conclusions; and to analyze the arguments and writing decisions of other writers. The icons (pictures) that accompany these key critical thinking tools will alert you to when they are being used in the text and remind you when to use them yourself as you read selections and practice your writing skills.

CRITICAL THINKING TOOLBOX

Icons	Critical Thinking Terms		Definitions	Writing Terms
(BLUEPRINTS/PLANS)	Purpose	⟷	What you want to say about your topic: the point(s) you are making. The purpose is the plan or blueprint for what you want to say in your essay.	Thesis statement
(SUPPORT/BEAMS)	Ideas	⟷	The foundation for your argument: Ideas develop your purpose. They form the structure of your overall sentences (beams), develop your thesis (plans), and hold up your conclusion.	Topic sentences
(NAILS)	Support	⟷	Examples, details, and evidence illustrate the ideas you use to support your purpose. They provide support (nails) for the ideas (beams) that support your purpose.	Major and minor details
(WRENCH)	Assumptions and Biases	⟷	Assumptions (information you take for granted) and biases (personal beliefs you have about particular topics) can be a helpful tool or they can throw a wrench into your thinking if they are not valid. Always evaluate them when making an argument.	
(FINISHED HOUSE)	Conclusions	⟷	The results of your argument or purpose. The result of carefully building your argument (using plans, beams, and nails) is a well-thought-out conclusion (house).	Conclusion
(GOGGLES)	Point of View	⟷	How you see the subject you are discussing.	
(MAGNIFYING GLASS)	Analysis	⟷	Breaking down an idea and working out the meaning of the individual parts and how they relate to the whole: you look at the overall meaning and the connections between the parts.	

These critical thinking terms are essential to the critical thinking process, but they are also the tools of argument. In some ways, *most college writing contains some level of argument:* you always have a purpose to put forth to your readers.

Now read the following more detailed explanations of each of these terms and consider the questions related to them that you should ask yourself as you read and write in order to think more critically and analyze more thoroughly.

1. **Purpose.** When you write, your purpose—the point(s) you want to make—should be clear and consistent from the beginning to the end of your essay or paragraph. Everything you include should develop that purpose. This is the argument you put forth to your readers.

   When you read, ask yourself:

   What is the author's purpose for writing?

   What argument(s) is the author putting forth?

   What *direct or implied questions* is he or she addressing?

   When you write, ask yourself:

   What is my purpose in this writing assignment?

   What is my argument for this topic?

   What conclusion(s) have I reached related to it?

   How will I argue this conclusion or these conclusions?

2. **Ideas and Information.** You develop your purpose using your own ideas, personal knowledge, and information. Your ideas and background information are specific branches of the tree that forms your purpose—they expand upon it. Later, you develop these individual ideas, or branches, using examples, ideas, details, and commentary.

   When you read, ask yourself:

   What ideas does the author include to support his or her purpose?

   What background information does he or she provide?

When you write, ask yourself:

What ideas do I want to include to support my purpose?

What background or personal information can I use to help develop the purpose?

3. **Support.** You need to provide information to support your purpose, ideas, and conclusions on a subject. You can draw on your personal experiences or those of others, use facts and statistics you have researched if your instructor allows research for the particular assignment you are working on, provide examples and specific details, or supply information provided by your instructor to support your reasoning. Always evaluate the information provided by other writers. Include commentary about the examples and details you provide.

When you read, ask yourself:

What evidence or examples is the author using to support his or her reasoning?

Are the examples and support believable and clearly explained?

Do they adequately support the author's purpose?

When you write, ask yourself:

What evidence or examples can I provide to back up my ideas?

Are they believable and clearly explained?

Do they support my purpose?

4. **Assumptions and Biases.** Be sure that the assumptions you or another author make about a topic or idea are not flawed or based on misinformation. Check for any errors in ideas resulting from an unfounded bias in your thinking process or that of an author. Any mistakes in the concepts or ideas that your reasoning is based on can cause problems in your argument. So, although assumptions and biases are helpful tools, they can throw a *wrench* in your thinking if they are unfounded.

When you read, ask yourself:

Is there an error in the idea the author is explaining?

Does the author include assumptions or biases that are flawed or unfair?

When you write, ask yourself:

Is there an error in the idea I'm explaining?

Are the assumptions I make or the biases I brought into thinking about my topic based on false information?

5. **Conclusions, Implications, and Consequences.** A conclusion is the final point in your argument, the place you reach after discussing the ideas that support your purpose, your argument. Consequences *are the results* of a point you have argued. Implications are more subtle: They are the possible results of an argument that you have inferred (or an author has implied). Be sure to look at all the possible consequences of your argument. For instance, if you argue that the music program should be cancelled at your school and the money should be used to add more parking spaces at your campus, be sure to address all the implications and consequences of canceling the music program. You need to be aware that you are implying that having more parking spaces is more important to your school than having a music program. The consequences could be a loss in the artistic identity of your school, fewer students who wanted to focus on music would apply to your college, and so on.

When you read, ask yourself:

What are the implications of the author's ideas in this reading?

Are the consequences of his or her arguments acceptable?

When you write, ask yourself:

What are the implications of my ideas in this paper?

Are the consequences of my ideas acceptable and clearly thought out?

Back to the domino idea again: Think of the concluding argument in your writing not as the last domino falling over in the chain but as one near the end. The consequences of your argument are the last few dominoes that follow that one. They might not be directly stated in your paper: You'll have to imagine those last dominoes falling and what they mean. For instance, will the canceling of the music program lead to a decrease in enrollment and hurt the overall budget at the school and the quality of the education provided?

6. **Point of View.** Your point of view is your perspective on a topic. Be sure to check the assumptions your point of view is based upon and whether your point of view is unreasonably biased.

When you read, ask yourself:

What point of view does the author have on his or her topic?

Did he or she consider other points of view that might be relevant?

Is the point of view one-sided or biased?

When you write, ask yourself:

What is my point of view on the topic?

Have I considered other points of view that might be relevant?

Is my point of view too biased for my intended audience?

7. **Analysis.** Analysis involves breaking down an idea and working out the meaning of the individual parts and how they relate to the whole. It is an in-depth look at every detail of an idea or argument, like using a magnifying glass to examine something up close and carefully.

When you read, ask yourself:

What is the author saying?

Does the author develop his or her ideas well using specific ideas, support, and analysis?

When you write, ask yourself:

What am I saying, and how can I explain it?

Do I develop all the ideas well using specific ideas, support, and analysis?

Using the critical thinking tools for reading and writing will help you focus on the basic parts of your written arguments. With practice, these skills will become an automatic and natural part of your reading and writing processes.

CRITICAL THINKING CHECKLIST

The critical thinking skills defined in this chapter can help you get into the habit of analyzing and evaluating the ideas and techniques you and other writers use to present arguments. Throughout this book, you will see critical thinking questions based on the concepts covered here. Be sure to use the general Critical Thinking Checklist below to evaluate your critical thinking process or the process of another writer.

CRITICAL THINKING CHECKLIST

PURPOSE

1. What is the *purpose* of this piece of writing? Is it clear?

_____

_____

IDEAS

2. What *ideas* and *background information* are provided to support the purpose of this piece of writing?

_____

_____

SUPPORT

3. What *evidence and examples* are used to explain and develop the ideas that support the argument made in this piece of writing? Are the evidence and examples provided sufficient?

_____

_____

ASSUMPTIONS BIASES

4. Are there unfounded *assumptions* or unreasonable *biases?*

_____

_____

CONCLUSIONS

5. Are all of the *conclusions, implications,* and *consequences* of the argument (the results of the argument taken to their furthest extreme) considered?

_____

_____

6. Is the *point of view* clear and consistent, and have other points of view been considered?

_____

_____

7. Using these critical thinking tools, *analyze* the overall structure of this essay and the strength of the author's argument, ideas, and support. Was the author successful in accomplishing the purpose? Why or why not?

_____

_____

CRITICAL THINKING IN ACTION

In order for these tools to become second nature, you need to practice using them in your own writing and when you read others' work. Practice these skills on the following reading.

Activity 1-1   Using the Critical Thinking Checklist

Directions, Part 1: *Review the critical thinking terms, and read the article "Nirvana Is Just a Click Away." Then, answer the seven questions in the Critical Thinking Checklist after the article.*

READING

"Nirvana Is Just a Click Away"

Christopher John Farley

You know that feeling you get when you walk into Blockbuster and there are racks and racks of videos but you can't seem to settle on a single one? Multiply that experience a couple thousand times, and you've got a fairly accurate picture of music on the Internet. A lot of musical acts are concerned about how they'll make money in the Age of the Download. But there's another question that merits attention—one of particular importance to consumers. With hundreds of thousands of songs floating around the Net, how does the ordinary fan sort out all the junk in order to get to the good stuff? Off-line, finding music is straightforward: you hear about new bands from friends or critics, see them on Leno or Letterman and buy their CDs from the stacks of new releases that are placed right up front in most record stores.

Online, however, the degree of difficulty goes up. There are innumerable independent bands on the Web that aren't being written up in the mainstream press and aren't getting played on TV or radio. There aren't enough hours in the day for a single listener to get a handle on all these microbands. Unless you've got rabbit-quick dsl service (most ordinary folks have relatively tortoise-like 56K modems), downloading a song can take half an hour or more. Given that there are many more songs online than there are at your local record store, who has the time—or the bandwidth—to listen to it all? That's where talent-scout websites come in. A growing number of sites on the Web specialize in finding unsigned bands. Among the best such sites are Riffage, iCAST and Jimmy and Doug's Farmclub.com. They all feature more than just new music. iCAST, for example, has news stories, chat rooms and other services. Most important, however, they offer guidance in locating low-profile, high-quality performers (also, the downloads these sites serve up are done so with the artists' permission). For fans exhausted by the frat rock/tot pop dominating the charts, these online destinations are an exciting alternative. "The Internet is like cable television," says Ken Wirt, founder and CEO of Riffage. "Music that appeals to a smaller niche audience can still exist, so bands that are the equivalent of Comedy Central or Animal Planet can flourish."

Every day Riffage presents a featured artist, offering up downloadable songs from a performer who's usually unsigned or on a tiny, independent label. The acts are chosen by Riffage staff members (they draw from music submitted to the site), and Riffage's users rate the music and post reviews. Last week one of the showcased acts was a San Francisco–based country group called The Court and Spark (a user named Rodco called the band "supercool mood country"). Using a 56K modem, it took a mind-numbing 2 hr. 20 min. to download the band's track "Sugar Pie in Bed" (this critic was able to have a buffet lunch, shop at Barnes & Noble and listen to the new Papa Roach CD in the interim). Still, the track, with its gently curmudgeonly vocals and drowsy guitar, was worth the hassle. Well, maybe 1 hr. and 45 min. of it.

iCAST also has a "track of the day" (a recent pick by the alternative-rock duo Tegan and Sara was particularly good). In addition, the site held a "Land Your Band" contest in which groups were rated by iCAST users, with the highest-rated act (the rock group Laughing Colors, based in Annapolis, Md.) winning meetings with major-label executives. "I kind of laugh at all this Napster stuff," says Laughing Colors lead singer Dave Tieff. "At our stage, offering free tracks makes sense. We're trying to get noticed, and promotions like this are a tool." Tieff says sales of the group's independently released CDs (available via the band's website) have risen more than 50% since it won iCAST's contest last month. Of course, Laughing Colors has sold just over 27,000 CDs in all, which is about a tenth of what Britney Spears sells in a typical week.

Talent-scout sites are exerting a small but growing influence off-line. Farmclub.com has a weekly TV series on USA Network. The site (which also has a record label) has signed three artists it discovered online to recording deals. "The Internet has made more people interested in music," says Jimmy Iovine, CEO of Farmclub.com and co-chairman of Interscope Geffen A&M Records. "With more people getting into music, you'll find that there are more people capable of becoming great artists and having great ideas." The Web hasn't produced the new Kurt Cobain yet, but—who knows?—Nirvana could be a click away.

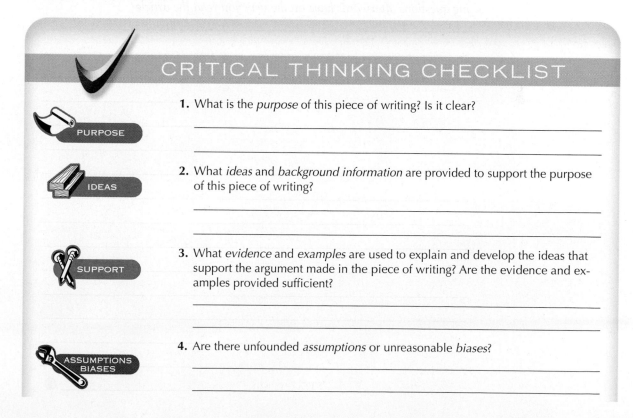

CRITICAL THINKING CHECKLIST

PURPOSE

1. What is the *purpose* of this piece of writing? Is it clear?

_____

_____

IDEAS

2. What *ideas* and *background information* are provided to support the purpose of this piece of writing?

_____

_____

SUPPORT

3. What *evidence* and *examples* are used to explain and develop the ideas that support the argument made in the piece of writing? Are the evidence and examples provided sufficient?

_____

_____

ASSUMPTIONS BIASES

4. Are there unfounded *assumptions* or unreasonable *biases*?

_____

_____

5. Are all of the *conclusions, implications,* and *consequences* of the arguments (the results taken to their furthest extreme) considered?

_____

_____

6. Is the *point of view* clear and consistent, and have other points of view been considered?

_____

_____

7. Using these critical thinking tools, *analyze* the overall structure of this essay and the strength of the author's arguments, ideas, and support. Was he or she successful in accomplishing the purpose? Why or why not?

_____

_____

_____

Part 2:   *What effect did knowing that you would have to answer critical think-ing questions afterwards have on the way you read the article?*

_____

_____

_____

_____

_____

_____

_____

_____

_____

_____

_____

_____

_____

Activity 1-2   Checking Your Critical Thinking Skills

Directions; Part 1:   *Read the article below, and draw icons from the Critical Thinking Toolbox in the left or right margin next to the places where the writer uses those tools. Don't worry about your drawing skills.*

READING

Business School Makes PowerPoint a Prerequisite

Justin Pope,
Seattle Times Online, July 31, 2007

Chicago business-school administrator Rose Martinelli says PowerPoint presentations permit potential students to demonstrate creativity that might not come through in traditional applications. At business meetings the world over, PowerPoint-style presentations are often met with yawns and glazed eyes.

But at one of the world's top business schools, such slide shows are now an entrance requirement. In a first, the University of Chicago will begin requiring prospective students to submit four pages of PowerPoint-like slides with their applications this fall.

The new requirement is partly an acknowledgment that Microsoft's PowerPoint, along with similar but lesser-known programs, has become a ubiquitous tool in the business world. But Chicago says so-called "slideware," if used correctly, also can let students show off a creative side that might not reveal itself in test scores, recommendations and even essays.

By adding PowerPoint to its application, Chicago thinks it might attract more students who have the kind of cleverness that can really pay off in business, and fewer of the technocrat types who sometimes give the program a bad name. "We wanted to have a free-form space for students to be able to say what they think is important, not always having the school run that dialogue," said Rose Martinelli, associate dean for student recruitment and admissions.

Online applications are already the norm, and it's not uncommon for colleges to let students submit extra materials such as artwork. Undergraduate and graduate applications also are beginning to ask for more creative and open-ended essays. Partly that's to better identify the students with a creative spark. Partly it's to fend off the boredom of reading thousands of grinding, repetitive responses to "Why is University X right for you?" But asking for four electronic slides appears to be a new idea.

Chicago's new requirement may provoke groans from some quarters. It could be called corporate America's final surrender to a technology that, in the name of promoting the flow of information, often gums it up by encouraging bureaucratic jargon and making colorful but useless graphics just a little too easy to produce.

Nonetheless, PowerPoint has become the lingua franca of business meetings worldwide. Its 500 million copies are used (or misused) in 30 million presentations per day, Microsoft has estimated.

Technology isn't a hurdle for most University of Chicago applicants, but "other schools might have to think about that," said Nicole Chestang, chief client officer for the Graduate Management Admission Council, a worldwide group of management programs that oversees the GMAT entrance exam.

It's also business schools that traditionally have the most boring essays, focusing on workplace accomplishments rather than passions or unusual talents, which are increasingly interested in creativity. Michael Avidan, a second-year Chicago MBA student, predicts some applicants will be turned off by the requirement but says it's an opportunity for clever students whose test scores and other application materials might not stand out to shine.

Part 2:   *Write a few sentences about what effect looking for these specific critical thinking tools had on the way you read and understood this article.*

_____

_____

_____

_____

_____

Part 3:   *On a separate sheet of paper, answer the seven Critical Thinking Checklist questions for this article.*

Glossary of Critical Thinking Terms

Here is a glossary of critical thinking terms to help you in your reading and writing. Some of these terms have already been covered in the chapter, and some of them are new but will also help you in using your critical thinking skills.

Analysis: Analysis involves breaking down an idea and working out the meaning of the individual parts and how they relate to the whole. For example, if you were asked to analyze a paragraph or a poem, you would go through each line or sentence and figure out what each individual part is saying; then you'd look at the overall meaning and the connections between the parts. Think back to the Thinking Critically opener for this chapter: The picture may not have been completely clear until you carefully analyzed each part of the image and put together all the evidence.

Argument: In most college writing, you are making some type of argument(s) and presenting a conclusion about a topic using reason and evidence to convince your readers of your point. Arguments in writing can be casual and entertaining (such as arguing for the best place in town to go for a first date), or they can be more formal and structured (such as arguing for the need for a new science building on your campus).

Cross Reference
See Chapter 15 for information on writing argument essays.

Assumptions: An assumption is a belief or claim that you take for granted or that society, particular people, or an author you are reading takes for granted without providing or asking for evidence or proof to support the idea. Almost everything you believe and do is based on assumptions; for instance, you assume the sun will rise each morning and set each evening. Some, however, are more individual assumptions that you take for granted but that not everyone would agree with. It is important to learn to separate the assumptions that have a basis in fact from ones that don't. For instance, if you based an argument for a new school playground on the assumption that children like to play, that's a good assumption. However, if you based an argument for building it on the assumption that the school has extra money to spend for a new playground, you would have to research your assumption to make sure it is true. When reading other people's writing, look carefully for the assumptions, the ideas they take for granted, and consider whether these are an undeniable truth.

Bias: Bias is a particular viewpoint that you or an author has about an idea or a topic. All ideas or opinions reflect a bias. Sometimes you (or an author) are conscious of the biases in your ideas, and sometimes you are not. Having biases is not necessarily a bad thing (it is inevitable), but when one's biases are founded on misinformation or unrealistic assumptions they can get in the way of good critical thinking.

Conclusion: A conclusion is the end result of an argument. It is the main point you make in your paper and should be the logical result of the reasons you provide to support your argument. For example, if you had to write a paper on the subject of canceling or adding more funding to your campus basketball team, your choice—the opinion you reach on the debate—would be your conclusion, and you would back up your conclusion with reasons and support. When you read an author's argument, you are looking for their conclusion about the topic they have chosen and how well they have developed it using reasons, examples, and details as support.

Evaluation: Evaluation is looking at the strength of your reasoning, support, and conclusions (or those of another writer) and how well those ideas are developed and explained. For example, if you were writing an argument paper taking a stand on an issue such as gun control, you would want to evaluate the arguments you put forth and how well you supported them with examples, reasons, and details. Also, you would need to consider the counter-arguments—what people who argue for a different stand might say against your conclusion on the issue—and evaluate how well those arguments are constructed.

Imply/implication: To imply means to hint that something is so, to say it indirectly. For instance, if your aunt visits you and says, "My, aren't you looking *filled out* these days!" she may be implying, or hinting, that you need to go on a diet.

Inference: Inference involves tapping into your ability to read between the lines and figure out, or infer, what someone means based on clues in what they say or write. For instance, in the example above, your aunt has *implied* that you are getting fat, and you, in receiving those clues from her language, have *inferred* her meaning.

Interpretation: Interpretation involves decoding an idea so you understand its meaning. When you interpret an author's idea, you decode it using your own words. You need to interpret and understand an author's ideas before you can analyze their meanings and evaluate them.

Opinion: Your opinion is what you (or another writer) believe about an idea, question, or topic. Opinion involves thinking about an idea or question and coming to your own conclusions about it. An opinion is based on weighing information and deciding where you stand on a question.

Point of View: Point of view in critical thinking refers to the perspective you are coming from in your reasoning and writing (or the perspective of the author you are reading). Be aware of your own point of view and the biases, assumptions, and opinions that make up that point of view, and be prepared to think of potential points of view that differ from yours (or from the views of the author you are reading).

Purpose: The term purpose refers to the reason you are writing a piece in the first place. What have you (or the author you are reading) set out to explain or prove to your readers? Sometimes the purpose of your writing is directly stated, as in a thesis statement, and sometimes it is implied by the arguments and reasons you provide throughout your writing.

Synthesis: Synthesis involves pulling together your ideas, and sometimes the ideas of others, in order to make or support an argument. Often, in writing, synthesis involves pulling together ideas from different authors that connect on a particular subject or argument to give a bigger picture. For instance, if you were writing an essay that compared two or more readings on a similar theme, you would synthesize the ideas that overlap to help develop your purpose in that piece of writing—like putting pieces from different puzzles together to make a new image.

Activity 1-3   Critical Thinking Review and Practice

Directions: *Answer the following questions.*

1. Reread the definition for critical thinking on page 2. Then write a definition of critical thinking using your own words:

   _____

   _____

   _____

   _____

2. List three assumptions you had about college before you began. Then write a line or two about whether each assumption ended up being valid (true) or invalid (not true or unfounded).

   Assumption 1: _____

   _____

   _____

   True or unfounded: _____

   Assumption 2: _____

   _____

   _____

   True or unfounded: _____

Assumption 3: _____

_____

_____

True or unfounded: _____

3. List two benefits you predict you will gain from learning and applying the critical thinking tools and terms explained in this chapter.

1. _____

_____

_____

2. _____

_____

_____

Activity 1-4   Critical Thinking Terms and Tools

Directions: *Answer the following true/false, multiple choice, and matching questions to test your understanding of the terms and concepts discussed in this chapter.*

1. T/F _____ Critical thinking is a new concept from the last ten years or so.

2. T/F _____ We engage critical thinking skills in college and also in our day-to-day decisions in life.

3. T/F _____ It is always a bad idea to have a *bias* in your ideas or views of a subject.

4. T/F _____ An assumption that you have as the foundation of your thinking can be an accurate assumption or a false assumption.

5. T/F _____ *Inference* means the ability to read between the lines and figure out what an author means using clues in the text.

6. T/F _____ *Synthesis* means adding supporting examples.

7. _____ Which of the following critical thinking terms **best** matches the term thesis statement?

a. bias

b. support

c. purpose

d. point of view

Matching Terms to Definitions: *Draw the tool icon (for example hammer, nails, and so on) for each term on the line provided next to it. Then, match each term to its definition.*

_____ **8.** Analysis   _____

_____ **9.** Bias   _____

_____ **10.** Support   _____

_____ **11.** Ideas   _____

_____ **12.** Conclusion   _____

_____ **13.** Purpose   _____

_____ **14.** Point of view   _____

_____ **15.** Assumption   _____

a. Looking at the individual parts closely to assess the whole purpose or argument

b. The end result of an argument

c. A belief or claim one takes for granted without providing or asking for evidence or proof to support the idea

d. The perspective you or the author is coming from in his or her reasoning and writing

e. A particular viewpoint that you or an author has about an idea or a topic

f. Personal knowledge and information (specific branches of the tree that form your purpose)

g. The reason you are writing a piece in the first place; what you (or the author you are reading) set out to explain or prove to the readers

h. Personal experiences or those of others, facts and statistics you have researched, examples and specific details to develop your purpose

IN SUMMARY

Be sure to refer to the critical thinking terms and tools provided in this chapter whenever necessary as you work through different sections of this text. You will see these tools and terms used in different places throughout the book (watch for the icons), and you will need to use some or all of them in the writing assignments, reading selection activities, and grammar exercises. Also, critical thinking skills are essential to developing good *arguments* in paragraphs and essays. Finally, you'll need to engage critical thinking skills to evaluate the writing of others: classmates, professional authors you read for class, and any sources you consult. As with any new language, the language of critical thinking gets easier with familiarity and practice. Training yourself to use critical thinking skills is challenging, but using these skills will significantly improve your reading and writing abilities, and it may become a treasured, lifelong habit.

Critical Thinking and Reading Techniques

"Sign on a Fence at Ground Zero," New York City, 2002.

THINKING CRITICALLY

Look at the picture above, and read the words on the sign. Then answer the questions that follow.

1. Based on the title of this picture and what the sign says, what is the message and purpose of the sign? To what specific historical event and place does this sign refer?

_____

_____

2. How do the words and photograph work together?

_____

_____

3. What message(s) or emotions do the words on the sign and/or the photograph create?

_____

_____

CRITICAL THINKING AND THE READING PROCESS

The critical thinking tools discussed in Chapter 1 can help you go beyond basic comprehension of what you read. If you get into the habit of asking critical thinking questions as you read a selection, you will be able to understand it better and reach deeper analytical conclusions. Not only will you be able to assess the arguments an author is making in a story or essay, you will also be able to recognize the writing techniques used and the ideas the author is building arguments and conclusions upon. You can also check to see if the author makes any errors in the introduction or conclusion to the piece.

ACTIVE READING

In order to become a better reader, you must engage in active versus passive reading. Developing active reading habits helps you read critically and engage in thoughtful analysis as you read. The difference between _passive_ and _active_ reading is like the difference between _hearing_ and _listening_. You can hear what someone says without listening to the words, and you can read words passively without actively engaging in understanding what they mean. Good listening takes concentration and so does active reading. Active reading involves communication between you and the text: It's a dialogue, not a monologue.

Once you develop a system for reading actively that works for you, use it regularly. Many of the assigned readings you'll have in college require you to think critically and analyze the ideas and arguments, the techniques, and the reasoning of the author. Try out the following active reading systems to see which one works best for you, or combine and customize these techniques into a system of your own. As with developing any new habit, it takes a commitment up front, but the time you spend pays off in a more thorough understanding of what you read and an increased ability to remember what you have learned.

Applying Critical Thinking

Here are some questions you can ask as you read to help you think critically about what an author is saying.

1. What is the author's **purpose** or **goal** in this reading selection? What does he or she set out to explain, argue, or prove?

2. What are the **implied** or **stated** questions being addressed in this reading selection?

3. What **ideas** and **support** (evidence, data, experience, or facts) does the author use to develop a purpose or goal for the reading? Is the support adequate? Convincing?

4. Does the author present alternative **points of view** when needed?

5. What **assumptions** does the author make in this reading selection? (Assumptions are ideas or reasons the author takes for granted, and upon which he or she bases judgments or develops his or her reasoning.) Are the assumptions valid?

6. What are the **implications** or **consequences** of the author's reasoning and/or ideas and arguments (direct or implied) in this selection? What **conclusions** does the author reach?

SIX STEPS TO ACTIVE READING

Use the following six steps to turn your reading process into an active engagement between you and the text instead of a passive process that leaves you bored or keeps you from understanding and remembering what you read. First buy a notebook to keep as your Reader's Log. For each textbook chapter, article, or essay you read, follow the six steps below and record them in your Reader's Log. Start each entry in your log with the date, title of the chapter or article, and the page numbers of the reading. The entries in the sample student log that follow are based on the reading "A Whole Lot of Cheatin' Going On," by Mark Clayton on page 432.

> **Reading Log**
>
> **Date:** 10-8-08
>
> **Reading:** "A Whole Lot of Cheatin' Going On" by Mark Clayton, pp. 432–436.

Step One: Preview the Reading

Previewing what's coming in a chapter or article helps increase your retention as you read—it's like glancing at a whole picture before you study its individual parts.

Preview the entire chapter or article before you begin reading it, and be sure to do the following:

1. Read the chapter or article title and any subtitles.
2. Read the introduction (or at least the first paragraph of the chapter or article if there is no formal introduction).
3. Read the first sentence of each paragraph. In textbooks, this is often the topic sentence and will tell you the main point of the paragraph.
4. Look for text that is in boldface or italic font, underlined, or presented in a bulleted or numbered format. Key words that are defined in the text are often in boldface, and authors use italics or underlining to emphasize important information.
5. Look at any photographs, graphs, charts, diagrams, or other visual aids, as these are included to provide additional information that supports and illustrates the text.
6. Read the summary at the end of the chapter or article (if there is no summary, then read the last paragraph).

Step Two: Think About What You Already Know About the Topic

After you have previewed the reading, *ask yourself what you already know about the topic.* Chances are you have heard or read some things about it before reading the piece. What can you tap into in your memory or knowledge that will help you better understand this new reading? If you don't know anything about the specific topic, what do you know about related topics, subtopics, or ideas within the article? For instance, if the article is about how to fly fish successfully, but you've never fly fished, have you fished with a rod at all? Have you seen someone fish with a rod on TV? What do you know about fishing in general? Even a little bit of background helps you feel more comfortable and retain new information better, so take a moment to scan your knowledge about the topic itself or background information related to the topic.

Reading Log

Date: 10-8-08

Reading: "A Whole Lot of Cheatin' Going On" by Mark Clayton, pp. 432–436.

Prior knowledge/background: I know that cheating is a problem that has gotten worse in both high schools and colleges and that many schools are trying to crack down on cheaters. I also know that the Internet makes it easier to cheat and even has lots of sites devoted to getting papers written by other people (to copy).

Step Three: Create Questions to Begin Your Dialogue with the Text

Creating questions keeps you active and engaged in your reading as you look for answers. Turn the title and subheadings into questions before you read, and then look for answers to them as you read the whole selection. This active process will help you build a more detailed picture of the reading. Write the questions that you create from the title and subtitles in your Reading Log and leave space beneath your questions to fill in your answers after you read (Step Four).

Then, create a few more questions of your own that come to mind based on your preview of the chapter or article (e.g., What is osmosis? Why do volcanoes erupt? How does the American jury system work?) and write them in your log.

Reading Log

Date: 10-8-08

Reading: "A Whole Lot of Cheatin' Going On" by Mark Clayton, pp. 432–436.

Prior knowledge/background: I know that cheating is a problem that has gotten worse in both high schools and colleges and that many schools are trying to crack down on cheaters. I also know that the Internet makes it easier to cheat and even has lots of sites devoted to getting papers written by other people.

Questions made from title and subtitles:

1. Why is a "whole lot of cheatin' going on"?
2. How are "colleges watching more closely"?
3. How is technology contributing to both the problem and the solution?
4. What does the "expectation of honesty" mean?

Step Four: Read in Blocks

Either read from one subtitle to the next or, if there are no subtitles, read one or two paragraphs at a time, and then, after each section, complete Step Five.

> **Note:** Reading in blocks instead of straight through a chapter without stopping keeps you focused and careful. It helps prevent the "I just read the whole chapter or article, and I have no idea what I read" syndrome.

Step Five: Write in Your Reader's Log

Write the following in your Reader's Log for each of the blocks of text you read:

1. **A two- to three-sentence summary of the main ideas from each section** or one or two paragraph block(s) as you finish it.
2. **The answers to the questions from Step Three** as you discover them— or amend your questions if you find your questions were off track.
3. **Any vocabulary words** from each block that you don't know. If you can't figure out their meanings by the end of the block, then look them up after finishing the block (not understanding a key word or term can sabotage your understanding of that section).

Once you are sure you have understood the section you have read, place a check mark at the end of it and move on to the next one.

Reading Log

Summary of Section 2: This section explains the kinds of technology students are using to cheat, such as sites like cheater.com where they can download essays. Also, it talks about how librarians are using technology to spot the downloaded essays by collecting examples and using a database that stores these lifted essays.

How are "colleges watching more closely"?

They are using technology and special programs to spot plagiarized work.

> **How is technology contributing to both the problem and the solution?**
>
> Students are using the Internet to cheat, and librarians are keeping track of the sites available and using software that detects stolen work.
>
> **Vocabulary:** There were no words in this section that I didn't know.

Step Six: Review and Answer

When you've finished reading the article or essay and writing your summary statements, answers, and new vocabulary for each block of the chapter or article, go back and read (review) them all.

Next, in your Reader's Log, review all the questions and your answers from Step Three without looking at the chapter or article or your notes from Step Five. If you can't remember the answers easily without looking, or if you are unsure of your answers, then review your Step Five notes and, if necessary, the relevant sections of the reading selection.

> **Final note:** If you follow all these steps, you will have engaged in an active reading process. Also, you will have notes for review to use later for class discussions, tests, or writing assignments. At first, The Six Steps for Active Reading will take longer than passively reading straight through a chapter or article. However, with practice, you will be able to go through these steps quickly, sometimes doing Steps One, Two, and Six completely in your head as you get into the habit of reading as a dialogue. Finally, this process can actually *save you time* by preventing you from having to reread whole chapters or articles because you didn't understand or retain information.

Example of the Six Steps in Action

Read through the excerpt below from an article in the *Christian Science Monitor* about the icecaps melting and global warming, and see how the Six Steps process works for one student.

> **Reading Log**
>
> **Step One:** I have previewed the entire article and read the title, introduction, first sentence of each paragraph, and the last paragraph.
>
> **Step Two:** I already know that the nations of the world are competing for the limited supply of oil in the world and that there are restrictions on where nations can drill. I also know that global warming has contributed to melting of the icecaps and a changing environment in the Arctic.

As Icecaps Melt, Russia Races for Arctic's Resources

By Fred Weir
The Christian Science Monitor, July 31, 2007

MOSCOW — As global warming makes exploration of the Arctic sea floor possible for the first time, Russia has launched a massive expedition to help secure the region's vast resources.

In the next few days, two manned minisubs will be sent through a hole blasted in the polar ice to scour the ocean floor nearly three miles below. They will gather rock samples and plant a titanium capsule containing the Russian flag to symbolize Moscow's claim over 460,000 square miles of hitherto international territory — an area bigger than France and Germany combined in a region estimated to contain a quarter of the world's undiscovered oil and gas reserves. ✓

The issue of who owns the North Pole, now administered by the International Seabed Authority, has long been regarded as academic since the entire region is locked in year-round impenetrable ice. But probably not for much longer.

The area of the Arctic Ocean covered by ice has been shrinking since the early 20th century and the change has accelerated in the past decade, according to the U.S. National Oceanic and Atmospheric Administration. Some scientists blame the shrinkage on the effects of human-driven climate change. ✓

As the Arctic's ice recedes, its waters are becoming more navigable — and its riches more accessible to a resource-hungry world. "The No. 1 reason for the urgency about this is global warming, which makes it likely that a very large part of the Arctic will become open to economic exploitation in coming decades," says Alexei Maleshenko, an expert with the Carnegie Center in Moscow. "The race for the North Pole is becoming very exciting." ✓

The U.S. Geological Survey estimates that 25 percent of the world's undiscovered oil and gas reserves lie beneath the Arctic Ocean. Experts at the Russian Institute of Oceanology calculate that the saddle-shaped territory that Russia is planning to claim may contain up to 10 billion tons of petroleum, plus other mineral resources and vast, untapped fishing stocks.

The 1982 Law of the Sea Convention establishes a 12-mile offshore territorial limit for each country, plus a 200-mile "economic zone" in which it has exclusive rights. But the law leaves open the possibility that the economic zone can be extended if it can be proved that the seafloor is actually an extension of a country's geological territory. In 2001, Russia submitted documents to the United Nations claiming that the Lomonosov Ridge, which underlies the Arctic Ocean, is an extension of the Siberian continental shelf and should therefore be treated as Russian territory. The case was rejected.

Step Three, Question 6: Is it attached to Russia?

✓ **Step Four:** I went through the article and read in blocks (see checkmarks)

Reading Log

Step Five: Summary: This section of the article is about the Arctic icecap beginning to melt, which will make it easier for humans to explore and have access to its resources. Russia is exploring the area now in an attempt to get the oil. There are questions about whether or not Russia or anyone else can claim the area exclusively.

Answers, Question 1: Global warming is melting the icecaps in the Arctic, and Russia is racing against other nations to get the oil that is under the ice there. **Question 2:** So far, Russia is the first country to explore getting the oil from there. **Question 3:** There is not yet a process for deciding who owns the North Pole, but now that it is reachable, there may be a battle coming. **Question 4:** Human-driven climate change has made the icecaps melt, and the melting will begin a battle over who owns the North Pole and its resources. **Question 5:** It looks like it will be collectable, billions of gallons. It is not clear yet who owns it. **Question 6:** So far, the United Nations has rejected Russia's claim.

Vocabulary words: titanium, impenetrable, accelerated.

Step Six: My answers to the questions were accurate, so I will review them. Vocabulary words mean (1) titanium: a type of metal, (2) impenetrable: unable to get through, (3) accelerated: sped up.

Activity 2-1   Six Steps Practice

Directions, Part 1:   *Apply the Six Steps method to the next section of the icecaps article. Write your questions in the margin of the reading; place check marks after each section after you have read and understood it; and write the answers to your questions, your summary, and any unfamiliar vocabulary words in your Reader's Log or on a separate sheet of paper.*

As Icecaps Melt, Russia Races for Arctic's Resources (*continued*)

But a group of Russian scientists returned from a six-week Arctic mission in June insisting that they had uncovered solid evidence to support the Russian claim. That paved the way for the current expedition, which includes the giant nuclear-powered icebreaker Rossiya, the huge research ship Akademik Fyodorov, two Mir deep-sea submersibles—previously used to explore the wreck of the Titanic—and about 130 scientists.

The subs were tested Sunday, near Franz-Joseph Land in the frozen Barents Sea, and found to be working well. "It was the first-ever dive of manned vehicles under the Arctic ice," Anatoly Sagelevich, one of the pilots, told the official ITAR-Tass agency. "We now know that we can perform this task."

The upcoming dive beneath the North Pole will be far more difficult, and involve collecting evidence about the age, sediment thickness and types of rock, as well as other data — all of which will be presented to the United Nations Commission on the Limits of the Continental Shelf (a body of scientists chosen by parties to the Law of the Sea Convention) to support Russia's claim to the territory.

The longer-term goal, Sagelevich says, is to get used to permanently working in that environment. . . . Nations that border the Arctic are concerned about security as well as energy. The U.S. Navy and Coast Guard co-sponsored a symposium in Washington this month titled "The Impact of an Ice-Diminishing Arctic on Naval and Maritime Operations." . . .

Some experts fear the potential for conflict over Arctic territory and resources, and the Russian media highlighted reports of a "U.S. spy plane" that allegedly shadowed the North Pole expedition this week. But others say existing international law is adequate to enable boundaries of influence to be negotiated between the key players as global warming unlocks the north's treasures.

"I don't see why this issue should worsen relations between Russia and other countries," says Pavel Zolotaryov, deputy director of the official Institute of USA-Canada Studies in Moscow. "We can solve our differences on the basis of information. And after this expedition, Russia will be able to say that we've been there and conducted the research" to bolster Russia's claims in the region.

Part 2   *Write a few sentences describing the effect using the Six Steps for reading actively had on the way you read the section and on your understanding of it.*

_____

_____

_____

_____

Activity **2-2**   More Six Steps Practice

Directions: *Pick an article or essay from the reading section of this textbook, from outside of class, or from a chapter in a textbook from one of your other classes, and apply the Six Steps method. Explain below what effect this process had on the way you read the chapter, article, or essay, and your understanding of its content.*

_____

_____

_____

_____ ●

THE T-KED METHOD FOR MARKING TEXTBOOKS AND ARTICLES

To be a good reader, you also need to know how to annotate (mark, highlight, and make notes) throughout your assigned reading. The T-KED method is a system designed to help you mark your text as you read. It gives you codes you can use, in addition to highlighting and using regular symbols (see examples on p. 36). It works best for nonfiction articles, textbook chapters, or essays. The process involves marking the **thesis** (**T**) or main point of the article or essay; the **key ideas** (**K**) in each body paragraph, the **examples** (**E**) that provide major support for those key ideas, and the minor **details** (**D**) that support those examples. By marking these elements as you read, you will increase your comprehension and your ability to distinguish main ideas and arguments from major and minor supporting examples and details.

T = Thesis

The **thesis** is the main idea, argument, or point of an article or essay. It is the purpose statement of a piece. A thesis can be one sentence, or it can be a few sentences, depending on the length and complexity of the piece. Usually, the thesis is located in the first or second paragraph of an article or essay, but sometimes it is stated at the end.

On rare occasions, the thesis is never stated and is only implied by a series of arguments and examples. In an implied thesis, the author doesn't directly state the final conclusion or argument he or she is making in a sentence in the introduction, though it sometimes is stated fairly clearly in the conclusion. Instead, the author will provide many ideas, examples, and details about a subject that will lead you to a conclusion about the topic.

The author provides hints through the kind of examples and information given about the subject and leads you through the article or essay in a way that makes you come to the desired conclusion on your own. If you find that the thesis is implied instead of directly stated in an article you read, write a sentence of your own that explains what the main idea or argument of the reading is *after* you have read all the information and examples (as clues).

Try this: After reading the first two paragraphs of an article or essay, **circle** the one to three sentences that you think state the main argument. **Mark a T** in the left margin next to the sentences you have circled as the thesis statement.

> **Note:** As you read through the article or essay, you may find you were wrong about the thesis statement and will have to mark the correct one. Or, if it turns out the thesis was implied, you might have to write it in yourself.

K = Key Idea

For each paragraph of the article or essay, **underline** the one- to two-sentence key idea for that paragraph. **Mark a K** in the left margin next to each underlined key idea. The **key idea** is the *topic sentence* for the paragraph.

Try this: As you read the article, underline the key idea (topic sentence) in each paragraph.

> **Tip:** Read the entire paragraph before you underline the key idea. Often the key idea or topic sentence for a paragraph is the first or second sentence of the paragraph, but sometimes it's in the middle or even at the end of the paragraph.

E = Examples

In each paragraph, **put an E** over each sentence or part of a sentence that provides a **major supporting detail** or **major example to support** the key idea or topic sentence of that paragraph.

D = Details

In each paragraph, **put a D** over any **minor detail that supports** a major detail or example used to support the paragraph's key idea or topic sentence.

T (again!)

Double check your T (thesis) to make sure it still works as the main idea of the article or essay. If not, circle the real thesis or write in the implied thesis of the article.

> **Tip:** What was the essay or article trying to explain or show through implied ideas or prove though evidence? The answer to that question is the thesis.

ANNOTATE AS YOU READ

Whether or not you choose to use one of the specific active reading systems discussed earlier when you read, you need to get in the habit of using highlighting or underlining, codes, and other annotating methods.

Highlighting and underlining are ways to separate the main ideas from the rest of the sentences in a reading. Use highlighting or underlining on the thesis, topic sentences, and major ideas for each section. You can also use a highlighter to mark words you don't know and then fill in their definitions in the margins.

Be sure to use the margins to write notes to yourself throughout the reading. You can use the margin spaces for the following purposes:

1. To write what you already know about the subject or any insights that you have as you read
2. To number subpoints or examples given in support of the main idea of a paragraph or of the reading as a whole
3. To write in definitions of unfamiliar vocabulary words you've marked
4. To write in questions you have as you read
5. To make comments about illustrations
6. To make comments when you notice an author's biases or assumptions
7. To add codes (see some suggestions below)
8. To note any other reminders to yourself that will help your understanding when you review later

Codes You Can Use

You can customize your own list of symbols and codes to use to annotate text as you read. Here are a few common symbols or codes you can use:

?   Use a question mark whenever you don't understand a term or a concept in a particular section. It will remind you later to doublecheck that part to increase your understanding.

□   Use boxes around key words—you can write the definitions for those in the margins.

O   Or, use a circle around key terms and add the definitions in the margins.

1, 2   Use numbers to indicate listed points that are not already numbered, or use numbers to mark the numbers of examples given for each main idea.

☆, *, ☺   Use symbols such as stars, asterisks, or smiley faces to indicate important points or sections you particularly enjoyed.

Example of Using T-KED, Highlighting, and Codes as You Read

Note the codes, highlighting, and T-KED notations in tan and blue in the following excerpt from Mark Clayton's "A Whole Lot of Cheatin' Going On" (p. 432) with the thesis, a key idea, an example, and a detail noted.

Sitting in the glow of his computer screen at 2 a.m. on Oct. 26, 1998, John Smolik, a University of Texas freshman, fires off an e-mail message to an online debate over academic cheating on the Austin campus.

Many of the 100-plus student messages argue that cheaters only hurt themselves. Not so says Mr. Smolik's missive, labeled "reality check!" ☺ "Cheating is an answer," he writes. "It might not be a good answer, but nonetheless it is an answer."

Actually, Smolik "disagrees with cheating" and was simply playing devil's advocate, he said in a recent interview. But he allows that his provocative message put forward a widely shared view. And researchers agree.

T   Across America, college students and college-bound high-schoolers appear to be cheating like there's no tomorrow, student surveys show. **

K   Whether copying another student's homework, cheating on a test, or plagiarizing an essay, cheating is limited only by imagination—and

E   technology. Some program their calculators with formulas, but rig them to show an empty memory if an instructor checks.

Mr. Krouse taps adult behavior as a factor. "Because adults and role models in society do it, some students may have used those examples to rationalize cheating," he says.

D   In a survey conducted in 1997–98, he also found that 66 percent of the parents of these top students said cheating was "not a big deal."

Activity 2-3 Using T-KED, Highlighting, or Underlining, and Codes

Directions: *Now try out the T-KED method and codes on the following excerpt from Chapter 1. Highlight right over the text and write your codes and comments in the text or in the margins. Then explain what effect this process had on the way you read the excerpt and your understanding of it.*

Excerpt from Chapter 1 on Critical Thinking

Critical Thinking

Critical thinking is a term you will hear quite a bit in college because it refers to the kind of thinking you'll be asked to do in your courses and later in your career. You'll be happy to know that you are already a critical thinker! You engage your critical thinking skills every day. Whenever you make a decision, solve a problem, or prioritize tasks, you are using critical thinking. For instance, when you choose your classes each term, you have to think carefully about your schedule: What classes are open this term? Which classes count toward your degree or certificate goals? How many classes can you take in one term and still be successful? Which classes are most important for you to take first? Engaging in the process of making these decisions, weighing the choices, and prioritizing all involve critical thinking. Even on a day-to-day basis, you engage your critical thinking skills. When you shop for groceries, when you decide which bills you should pay first on a limited budget, when you work out problems and arguments between you and your friends or you and your coworkers, you are being a critical thinker.

This chapter will define critical thinking for you in the context of using critical thinking skills to perform college tasks. It will provide you with tools and tips designed to help you read and write analytically (to read looking for answers to questions and to draw some conclusions about your topic) and to evaluate your own reading and writing processes. The skills involved in thinking critically are essential to effective reading and writing. Good thinking and good writing go hand in hand.

Critical thinking in society and education is not a new concept. The process of evaluating one's own thinking process has been around since human history began. Critical thinking was an essential part of ancient cultures, including the Egyptian (3150 BC), Sumerian (2900 BC), and Babylonian (2300 BC) cultures, and later was an integral skill and focus for the ancient Greek philosophers. Socrates (469–399 BC) is known for teaching his students how to analyze their critical thinking processes. In fact, the word *critical* comes from the Greek word *kritikos*, meaning to question or to analyze.

Various experts define critical thinking differently, but critical thinking is always a process that involves actively thinking through and evaluating all the steps in your own thinking process or the thinking process of others. Many teachers and experts emphasize the importance of critical thinking in college courses. Richard Paul is one of today's most well-known scholars of critical thinking skills. According to Paul, critical thinking involves a "mode of thinking—about any subject, content, or problem—in which the thinker improves the quality of his or her thinking by skillfully taking charge" of each step in the process of thinking and the conclusions reached as a result of that thinking (Foundation for Critical Thinking, **www.criticalthinking.org**).

The bottom line is that you must be aware of your own thoughts and how they affect your conclusions. There are different skills and tools you can use to improve your thinking process as you read and write. You can use these critical thinking skills to understand and evaluate the writings of others, and to discover the strengths and weaknesses in their reasoning or arguments. As you learn these skills, your own thinking and writing skills will improve. Develop the habit of a step-by-step process of thinking about each part of your arguments and ideas. Critical thinking skills are essential for clear, fair-minded, analytical writing as well as for good analytical reading. Once you get hooked on the power that comes from using your critical thinking skills, you may not be able to stop—you will find yourself using them everywhere: while reading the newspaper, listening to the radio, reading a novel, even watching a movie. ●

Activity 2-4   More T-KED Practice

Directions: *Pick another chapter from this text, an article from outside of class, or a chapter from a textbook from one of your other classes, and read and apply the T-KED method to it. Then explain what effect this process had* *on the way you read the chapter or article and your understanding of the chapter or article.*

_____

_____

_____

_____

USE THE CRITICAL THINKING CHECKLIST

Remember to apply the questions from the Critical Thinking Checklist in Chapter 1 to all the articles you read for a class. You can weave these questions into your active reading process by asking and answering them when you have completed The Six Steps for Active Reading or the T-KED Method to make sure you are reading with a critical mind.

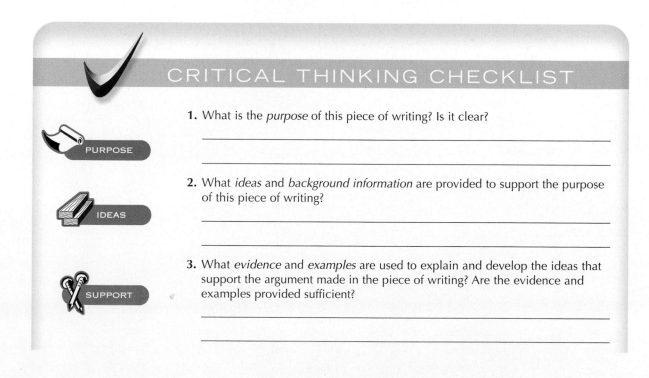

CRITICAL THINKING CHECKLIST

PURPOSE

1. What is the *purpose* of this piece of writing? Is it clear?

_____

_____

IDEAS

2. What *ideas* and *background information* are provided to support the purpose of this piece of writing?

_____

_____

SUPPORT

3. What *evidence* and *examples* are used to explain and develop the ideas that support the argument made in the piece of writing? Are the evidence and examples provided sufficient?

_____

_____

4. Are there unfounded *assumptions* or unreasonable *biases*?

_____

_____

5. Are all of the *conclusions, implications,* and *consequences* of the arguments (the results of the arguments taken to their furthest extreme) considered?

_____

_____

6. Is the *point of view* clear and consistent, and have other points of view been considered?

_____

_____

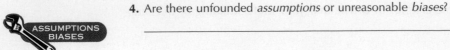

7. Using these critical thinking tools, *analyze* the overall structure of this essay and the strength of the author's arguments, ideas, and support. Was he or she successful in accomplishing the purpose? Why or why not?

_____

_____

Writing Expository Paragraphs

3

Green Man, Stained Glass, Hank Galmish.

THINKING CRITICALLY

Look at the picture above. Then turn the book over and look again. Then answer the question that follows.

When you first looked at the picture, were you immediately aware of the face within the green leaves, or did you see the face only after you turned it over?

_____

_____

Writing a paragraph involves putting the parts in order so that you can effectively communicate your point to your intended audience. Just like the parts of a face, the parts of a paragraph should not be arranged in a random order or your readers will be disoriented and have difficulty understanding your point.

41

Applying Critical Thinking

PURPOSE   IDEAS   SUPPORT   ASSUMPTIONS BIASES   CONCLUSIONS   POINT OF VIEW   ANALYSIS

In this chapter you will use critical thinking to determine your **purpose** for writing a paragraph, the **argument** you want to make, the **support** you will provide, and the **conclusion** you will reach. To write an effective paragraph, you will need to consider the following:

- What is your **point of view**? What do you think or believe about the topic?
- What are your **assumptions** or **biases**? What do you take for granted about the topic? Is your point of view based on correct information?
- What is your **analysis** of the topic? Have you broken the topic down so that you understand it? Have you examined your argument to make sure it is clear and based on solid evidence?

PARAGRAPH TO ESSAY

It is essential to understand the structure of a paragraph in order to understand how to write essays. The major components of a paragraph are also present in an essay. Both feature a statement of purpose. Both include examples, details, and analysis to support and develop the purpose statement, and both include a conclusion that reiterates the purpose and wraps up the topic.

The Paragraph Format

Topic sentence (topic + purpose)

Support (examples and details)

Analysis and interpretation

Concluding sentence

Paragraph to Essay: Pattern Similarities

As you can see in the following chart, both the paragraph and the essay begin with an introduction that sets up the topic and purpose. They both include supportive examples, details, and analysis and interpretation of those examples and details. Both use transitions between major points to maintain flow and coherence, and, finally, both have a conclusion that reiterates the statement of purpose and provides a closing remark or idea for further thought.

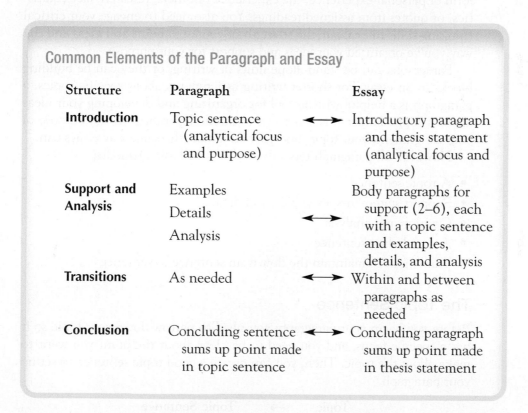

Common Elements of the Paragraph and Essay

Structure	Paragraph	Essay
Introduction	Topic sentence (analytical focus and purpose)	←→ Introductory paragraph and thesis statement (analytical focus and purpose)
Support and Analysis	Examples Details Analysis	←→ Body paragraphs for support (2–6), each with a topic sentence and examples, details, and analysis
Transitions	As needed	←→ Within and between paragraphs as needed
Conclusion	Concluding sentence sums up point made in topic sentence	←→ Concluding paragraph sums up point made in thesis statement

WRITING EXPOSITORY PARAGRAPHS

The word *expository* is derived from a Latin term meaning "to explain." So, an **expository paragraph** always has a purpose or message that it tries to explain. Therefore, you need to engage your critical thinking skills and use the critical thinking tools described in Chapter 1 to make sure that your writing has something meaningful to explain. Even if you are writing an essay in which you describe something that you witnessed, you usually have a critical point you want to make about that experience, something you want to convey to your readers. Many expository paragraphs contain an **argument**, a point the writer is putting forth to readers, that needs evidence and support to back it up.

Since in your expository paragraphs you are attempting to persuade readers to see the conclusions you've come to on your topic or to buy into your opinion, you need to provide evidence and support for your arguments in order to develop your paragraphs. The **evidence** you use can come in the form of personal experience, the experience of others, research, facts, statistics, or quotes from assigned readings. You also need to engage your critical thinking skills to evaluate the strength of your arguments and ideas and the way you've organized your ideas and support for your purpose.

Paragraphs can be stand-alone units of writing, or they can be building blocks in an essay. For shorter writing assignments about specific topics, a paragraph is a helpful writing tool for organizing and developing your ideas about a topic. Paragraphs can be customized, depending on the purpose of your assignment, your topic, and your audience, the same way essays can.

However, all paragraph types share the same basic elements:

- A topic sentence
- Support statements, examples, and details
- Opinion and analysis
- A concluding sentence
- Transitions to maintain the flow from sentence to sentence

The Topic Sentence

Before you begin your paragraph, you need to narrow down your topic so it has a specific focus, and you need to be clear about the point you want to make about the topic. Then, you can create a good topic sentence to set up your paragraph.

Topic   →   Topic Sentence

The **topic sentence** is the *controlling idea* of a paragraph: It establishes the paragraph's topic and purpose. Ask yourself, "What point do I want to make about this topic? What opinion do I want to put forth about this topic?" Your topic sentence should be more than just a fact or detail: It should be a conclusion you've reached related to the topic. Your topic sentence should state your opinion about your topic, and the goal of your paragraph should be to convince your readers of the truth or validity of your opinion by supporting it with examples and details that prove your point.

A topic sentence is *too broad* if it is too generalized or too large in scope to develop and support in one paragraph. A topic sentence is *too narrow* if it is just a fact or detail and not an opinion that can be supported and developed. For instance, if your topic is tennis, you need to think of something you want to say about the sport. If you begin with a topic sentence that is too broad, like "Tennis is a popular sport," it will be hard to make a specific point in the space of a paragraph. What aspect of tennis are you going to address? How popular is it as a spectator sport? How many people like to play tennis as a leisure activity? How many young people take it up in school and college? Make sure your topic sentence isn't too narrow or limited, either. You don't want just to state a fact or detail, like "One common stroke in tennis is the forehand," because then there is nothing else for you to discuss in the paragraph. Try to come up with a focus and an opinion that needs to be developed through examples and details. For instance, *Tennis is a sport that requires both physical and mental training.*

Topic Sentence Revision:

> **Too Broad:** Tennis is a popular sport.
>
> **Too Narrow:** One common stroke in tennis is the forehand.
>
> **Just Right:** Tennis is a sport that requires both physical and mental training.

> **Too Broad:** Weather is important.
>
> **Too Narrow:** Storms usually bring rain.
>
> **Just Right:** Assessing weather conditions is an important factor in driving safely.

> **Too Broad:** There are lots of choices of what to drink in the morning.
>
> **Too Narrow:** Coffee is a breakfast beverage.
>
> **Just Right:** People have different favorites for the right morning drink, including coffee, tea, and juice.

Activity 3-1 Creating a Good Topic Sentence

Directions: *Mark the following topic sentences as TB (too broad), TN (too narrow) or TS (good topic sentence). If a topic sentence is too broad or too narrow, rewrite it on the line provided so that it makes a specific point you can support in the space of a paragraph.*

> **Example:** TV is entertaining.

> TB: Cartoon Network is a network dedicated to entertaining children and adults alike by providing 24-hour-a-day cartoons.

_____ 1. Sports are part of our culture.

_____

_____

_____ 2. One piece of equipment needed for soccer is shin
             guards.

_____

_____

_____ 3. Skiing is an expensive hobby.

_____

_____

_____ 4. Snowboarding is a popular sport.

_____

_____

_____ 5. Snowboarding and skiing have strong similarities.

_____

_____

_____ 6. A warm hat and gloves are helpful when skiing.

_____

_____

_____ 7. Soccer is usually called "football" in Europe.

_____

_____

_____ 8. Soccer requires speed and agility.

_____

_____

_____ 9. Baseball represents American values.

_____

_____

_____10. A baseball game usually has nine innings.

_____

_____

Support and Analysis

You need to provide support and analysis to develop your paragraph's purpose and topic sentence. You can use your own knowledge about and personal experience with your subject to provide support, and you can use examples from other people or writers (major supporting details). Examples are most convincing when you include specific minor details about them that further demonstrate your point. If you use quotes or facts from a source, be sure to acknowledge that source (see Chapter 19). After you provide examples and details, explain what purpose they serve. *Analyze* their significance in proving the point you set out to make in your topic sentence.

Support → Examples → Details → Comments/Analysis

For instance, if you state that tennis strokes are some of the most important elements of the game, you want to give some examples of the different types of strokes and some details that explain what they are and how they work. In the excerpt from a paragraph on tennis that follows, the writer provides examples of the kinds of strokes a player needs to learn (serve, volley, backhand, and lobs), details about the serve, and then analysis of what the player must do to gain these skills. Finally, you need to use transitional words or phrases between one example and the next to keep your paragraph flowing smoothly from sentence to sentence, example to example.

Cross Reference
See pp. 118–119 for examples of transitions you can use.

> The most important physical skills tennis players must learn are the serve, the volley, forehand and backhand strokes, and the lob. The serve, for example, has several components such as the toss, form, speed, and technique. Therefore, tennis players must work on their technical skills in order to improve their game. Moreover, besides the physical demands of tennis, players must work on their mental game to become great at the sport. So much of tennis is psychological.

Notice how the sentences in the excerpt build on each other to provide support (examples and details) and analysis, and see how transition words such as *also, for example,* and *moreover* help move the reader from one point to the next smoothly.

Activity 3-2 Providing Support: Examples, Details, and Comments/Analysis

Directions: *Provide a specific example to illustrate each of the topic sentences below. Then, provide at least one detail about the example and one comment analyzing the significance of the example and detail.*

Example:

Topic Sentence: Severe weather can cause many problems with traffic.

Specific example/s: *For instance, extremely cold temperatures after a lot of rain can cause particularly dangerous road conditions.*

Concrete detail/s: *One of the most dangerous effects of cold after rain is black ice on the roads.*

Comment analyzing the significance of the example and detail provided to support the topic sentence:

Ice on roads, particularly hard-to-see black ice, causes some of the worst conditions for drivers and leads to many car accidents due to loss of control.

1. Most holidays feature some sort of special food that is served in celebration.

   Specific example: _____

   _____

   Concrete detail/s: _____

   _____

   Comment analyzing the significance of the example and detail provided to support the topic sentence:

   _____

   _____

   _____

2. Fruit is nutritious, but it is also a great choice because of its variety of textures and flavors that appeal to the senses.

   Specific example: _____

   _____

   Concrete detail/s: _____

   _____

   Comment analyzing the significance of the example and detail provided to support the topic sentence:

   _____

   _____

3. Cats make great house pets for several reasons.

   Specific example/s: _____

   _____

   Concrete detail/s: _____

   _____

   Comment analyzing the significance of the example and detail provided to support the topic sentence:

   _____

   _____

4. Music is often closely tied to special memories.

   Specific example/s: _____

   _____

   Concrete detail/s: _____

   _____

   Comment analyzing the significance of the example and detail provided to support the topic sentence:

   _____

   _____

5. College helps provide career opportunities for students who graduate.

   Specific example/s: _____

   _____

   Concrete detail/s: _____

   _____

   Comment analyzing the significance of the example and detail provided to support the topic sentence:

   _____

   _____

The Concluding Sentence

A paragraph ends with a **concluding sentence** that re-emphasizes the topic
sentence's focus and *purpose*. Be careful not to just restate your topic sentence. Instead, end with a closing thought related to your topic sentence but

with an idea for further thought on the topic. Be careful not to introduce a completely new argument or purpose in your concluding sentence that changes the focus of your original topic sentence. Sometimes, the concluding sentence in a paragraph can serve as a transition to the next paragraph if you are writing several paragraphs or an entire essay. In the case of the tennis paragraph, a good concluding sentence might be, "Indeed, tennis is a sport that requires players to have both physical and mental discipline in order to be at the top of their game."

Activity 3-3   Creating a Good Concluding Sentence

Directions: *For each of the five topic sentences in Activity 3-2, create a concluding sentence that connects to the topic sentence; highlights the examples, details, and comments you added; and leaves the reader with an ending thought.*

Example:

Topic sentence: Severe weather can cause many problems with traffic.

Concluding sentence: *As you can see, bad weather has disastrous effects on the roads and consequently also on the drivers who face dangerous conditions and slower traffic.*

1. _____

_____

2. _____

_____

3. _____

_____

4. _____

_____

5. _____

_____

Model Paragraph

Here is the full paragraph on playing tennis. It has been annotated to show all the elements of an effective paragraph: topic sentence, support (examples, details, and analysis), and concluding sentence. Transitions are highlighted in blue.

Tennis is a sport that requires dedication. To begin with, tennis requires a player to be in good shape. Tennis demands speed and agility. For instance, a player must be able to run from the baseline to the net very quickly. He or she must also learn the most important physical skills such as the serve, the volley, forehand and backhand strokes, and the lob. The serve, for example, has several components such as the toss, form, speed, and technique. Therefore, tennis players must work on technical skills to improve their games. Moreover, besides the physical demands of tennis, players must work on their mental game to become great at the sport. So much of tennis is psychological. If a player loses mental focus during a match, his or her strokes and techniques begin to fall apart. For example, if a player loses mental focus while serving, the first skill to go is the toss. Then it's easy for the player to begin double faulting. A double fault is when the server misses both serves and loses that point. *Indeed, tennis is a sport that requires the players to have discipline and dedication in order to be at the top of their game.*

Topic sentence
Supporting example
Specific detail
Supporting example
Specific detail
Supporting example
Supporting example
Supporting example
Supporting example
Specific detail
Concluding sentence

PARAGRAPH STRUCTURE

The classic paragraph form is often shown as an inverted triangle: The topic sentence comes first; the middle provides examples, details, and analysis; and the end features the concluding sentence. In most cases, this pattern will be your best bet when writing an individual paragraph or a couple of paragraphs. It is also the most common pattern for body paragraphs within essays.

Sample Paragraph

Reality TV is really more about escaping reality than capturing it. The whole point of reality TV is supposed to be capturing real life on screen. However, most people watch reality TV to escape from the reality and predictability of their own lives. My friends tell me they watch reality TV to "chill," to get away from the day-to-day activities of their normal lives. The "real" people in reality TV shows are put into artificial situations and are

Topic sentence

Supporting example

Supporting example

Specific detail

Supporting example

Concluding sentence

supposed to act normally. But who could act normally in such extreme conditions? One reality show, for instance, focuses on people surviving for a month on a remote island, living off their wits and the land. Some of the contestants resort to eating bugs, strange plants, and anything that will help them get the nutrition they need. But with camera crews filming every move, how could the people on the show ever be real or natural? Maybe they could ask the camera crew for a sandwich! Other reality shows feature artificial living situations where extremely diverse personalities are forced to live together. For instance, a show might feature a German sports star forced to live with a rapper from New York City. Again, with the cameras rolling, no one is acting as he or she would in normal life. So why do people watch these unrealistic reality shows? *They watch them because they provide a brief escape from their very real lives and so they can indulge in a false reality.*

However, there are a couple of variations in the placement of the topic sentence that are available as alternatives to the classic pattern.

Variation One

Instead of the topic sentence being at the beginning of the paragraph, it comes at the end. The paragraph starts out with general information or a personal story to set up the purpose; then it builds to the controlling idea (topic sentence). The topic sentence, then, serves double duty, as the concluding sentence as well. This variation on the typical pattern is best represented by the triangle below.

Sample Paragraph: Variation One

Supporting example
Supporting example
Specific detail
Supporting example

Specific detail

There are many different types of toys on the market today. There are still many action figures that let children use their imagination to role play. For instance, superhero figures still spark the imagination. Spiderman is an example of an action figure that many children like to use to "save the day." Also, many puzzle games and strategy board games are still popular and help children build their math and logic skills. For example, the classic game Battleship is available in peg form and electronic form: Both forms build prediction and math skills. Another popular type of toy is one

that lets children construct shapes and objects. For instance, Legos are
more popular than ever. They even have Star Wars–based Legos that allow
children to play out Star Wars stories. Legos also help children build their
analysis and hand–eye coordination skills. *Overall, there are many toys on
today's market that help build children's imagination and physical and intellectual skills.*

Specific detail

Topic sentence

Variation Two

In this pattern, the topic sentence comes in the middle of the paragraph.
The paragraph begins with a more generalized and elaborate setup for the
main purpose. Then, in the middle, the topic sentence states the paragraph's
controlling idea or purpose. Finally, the paragraph moves into broader examples and analysis again. There may or may not be a specific concluding sentence in this pattern. This variation is best represented by a diamond shape.

Sample Paragraph: Variation Two

There are many different types of toys on the market today. There are
still many action figures that let children use their imagination to play
roles. For instance, superhero figures still spark the imagination. Spiderman is an example of an action figure that many children like to use to
"save the day." Also, many puzzle games and strategy board games are
still popular and help children build their math and logic skills. For
example, the classic game Battleship is available in peg form and electronic form: Both forms build prediction and math skills. *In fact, there are
many toys on today's market that help build children's imagination and
physical and intellectual skills.* Another popular type of toy is one that lets
children construct shapes and objects. For instance, Legos are more
popular than ever. They even have Star Wars–based Legos that allow children to make stories from the Star Wars stories and also help them to build
their analysis and hand–eye coordination skills.

Supporting example
Supporting example
Specific detail
Supporting example

Topic sentence

Supporting example
Specific detail

Applying Critical Thinking

| PURPOSE | IDEAS | SUPPORT | ASSUMPTIONS BIASES | CONCLUSIONS | POINT OF VIEW | ANALYSIS |

You need to engage your critical thinking skills to check the parts of your paragraph to ensure you have developed your **purpose** and provided enough **ideas**, **support**, and **analysis**. Here are some tips you can use to help you write effective paragraphs.

Tip One: Avoid awkward announcements. Don't announce what you are going to write about: Just say it.

Announcement: In this paragraph I will show that shopping can be an addiction.
Revised: Shopping can be an addiction.

Tip Two: Delete *It seems*, *I think*, or *I feel* statements in paragraphs. They weaken your voice and argument.

I think **statement:** I think credit card companies should be monitored more closely.
Revised: Credit card companies should be monitored more closely.

Tip Three: Avoid the common pitfalls of introducing a new idea or contradicting yourself in the conclusion: the "shoot yourself in the foot" effect.

"Shot in the foot" conclusion: Another addiction that's worse though is food addiction.
Revised conclusion sentence: Shopping can, in fact, be a serious addiction with negative consequences.

Tip Four: Choose the appropriate paragraph length based on your topic and purpose. The number of sentences in a body paragraph varies depending on the topic sentence and its scope. The length of a paragraph is also affected by how many support examples and details are needed to develop the purpose. On average, most body paragraphs range from four to fifteen sentences. Decide carefully how much support and how many examples your purpose and topic will need.

Tip Five: Be sure to check that you have provided enough support, using examples and details, and that you have framed your examples with analysis and interpretation when needed.

Tip Six: Make sure you provide transitions to keep your sentences flowing smoothly from one to the next.

SELF AND PEER ASSESSMENT

Self and peer assessment of drafts allows you to evaluate the effectiveness of your writing and to go through, step by step, and look at the separate elements that contribute to the success of your paragraph. Think of these elements *before* you begin an actual draft and use the following self-assessment checklist to make sure you have addressed them well. Then you can have your peers (classmates, friends, or tutors, even) use the peer-assessment checklist to critique your paragraph. Check to make sure critical thinking tools were used in your writing and used to assess the writing of others too.

PARAGRAPH CHECKLIST

Self-Assessment Version

| PURPOSE | IDEAS | SUPPORT | ASSUMPTIONS BIASES | CONCLUSIONS | POINT OF VIEW | ANALYSIS |

_____   Do you have a topic sentence (**idea**) for your paragraph that develops your **purpose** and includes an opinion and not just a fact or detail?

_____   Did you make sure that your topic sentence is not too narrow for your goal or too broad to accomplish in a paragraph?

_____   Do you provide adequate **support** for your topic sentence (examples, details, and analysis)? Review the critical thinking skills in Chapter 1 for deeper **analysis**.

_____   Do you have a **concluding** sentence for your paragraph that supports your topic sentence and pulls together the examples and details for that paragraph? Did you avoid bringing in a new idea?

_____   Do you include transitions between sentences when necessary (either at the end of one or the beginning of the next) to help lead the reader smoothly from one support idea to the next?

_____   Did you proofread, edit, and revise your paragraph for organization, style, unity, sentence variety, grammar, and spelling?

Other problems or needs you noticed that need attention in the next draft:

_____

_____

_____

_____

PARAGRAPH CHECKLIST

Peer-Assessment Version

PURPOSE   IDEAS   SUPPORT   ASSUMPTIONS BIASES   CONCLUSIONS   POINT OF VIEW   ANALYSIS

_____ Does the writer have a topic sentence (**idea**) for the paragraph that develops the **purpose** and includes an opinion and not just a fact or detail?

_____ Is the topic sentence too narrow or too broad to accomplish the goal of the paragraph?

_____ Did the author provide adequate **support** for the topic sentence (examples, details, and analysis)? Review the critical thinking skills in Chapter 1 for deeper **analysis** suggestions.

_____ Does the **concluding** sentence support the topic sentence and pull together the examples and details for that paragraph? Did the author avoid bringing in a new idea?

_____ Did the author include transitions between sentences when necessary (either at the end of one or the beginning of the next) to help lead the reader smoothly from one support idea to the next?

_____ List suggestions for improvement in organization, style, unity, sentence variety, grammar, and spelling.

Other comments for the author:

_____

_____

_____

_____

Activity 3-4 Paragraph Practice

Directions: *Choose one of the following topics and narrow it down to a focused topic you can write a paragraph about. Then, using the steps outlined below, create a paragraph one element at a time.*

Topics

- Grocery shopping
- Downloading music from the Internet

- Marriage
- Funerals
- Holiday rituals

Step One: Choose one of the topics above, and write a list of three to five possible focus topics on the subject.

Topic: _____

Focused topics: _____

_____

Step Two: Create a **topic sentence** that is neither too broad nor too narrow and includes an opinion about the topic.

_____

_____

Step Three: Provide a **supporting example and a detail** to illustrate that example.

Supporting example (one or two sentences):

_____

_____

Detail to illustrate and develop the example (one or two sentences):

_____

_____

Step Four: Provide a **second supporting example and detail**. Be sure to include a **transitional word or phrase** to move smoothly from the first example to this one.

Transitional word or phrase and supporting example (one or two sentences): _____

_____

Detail to illustrate and develop the example (one or two sentences): _____

_____

Step Five: Provide a **concluding sentence** that pulls your ideas together and/or leaves the reader with further thought on the topic. Remember to avoid bringing in a completely new opinion or idea.

_____

_____

Step Six: Review and revise what you have written. Read the entire paragraph and see if you need to fix the language or add transitions between the parts to make sure your writing flows smoothly from one point to the next. You should now have a solid draft of a complete paragraph. ●

Activity 3-5   More Paragraph Practice

Directions: *Choose one of the topics below to write a paragraph about. Be sure to include the essential elements of a paragraph and choose the best paragraph structure (see pages 51–54) for your narrowed topic. Be sure to have a clear topic sentence, specific examples and details to illustrate your points, transitions when needed, and a concluding sentence.*

Topics

- Equipment needed for camping
- Taking care of a family pet
- Learning to ride a bicycle
- Preparing for a job interview
- The funniest show on TV

Paragraph: _____

_____

_____

_____

_____

_____

_____   ●

THINKING CRITICALLY

Look at the picture. Then answer the questions that follow.

What objects do you see in this picture?

_____

_____

How do the different objects and parts in the image contribute to the whole impression of the photograph?

_____

_____

Essays have particular building blocks that can be put together to make a coherent whole.

EXPOSITORY ESSAYS

An **expository essay** has a specific format that allows you to focus on your topic and the point you want to make about it. Like a paragraph, it has a clear statement of purpose (thesis statement); is developed using examples, details, and analysis; has a strong conclusion; uses an organized pattern to convey information; and includes clear transitions to maintain the flow of ideas from sentence to sentence and paragraph to paragraph.

First, you need to know the audience for your essay, and you need to know your subject; then you need to narrow that subject to a manageable topic. The **subject** is the general topic you are writing about, which you need to focus into a manageable topic for the length of your essay. The **purpose** is what you want to explain or prove related to that topic, so your thesis is a statement of purpose of your overall goal. Your **audience** is the intended reader(s) of your essay—who you are addressing—so you'll need to customize both your tone (casual, informal, or more formal and academic) and the amount and types of information you include depending on the intended audience.

An expository essay includes an **introductory paragraph** (or paragraphs, depending on the length and style of the essay); **body paragraphs**, which develop the thesis statement (purpose); and a **concluding paragraph**, which restates the purpose and adds closing remarks.

The number of paragraphs in an essay varies depending on the scope of your topic and the goal(s) of your thesis statement. Most essays have at least four paragraphs and can have as many as needed to achieve the established goals of the topic and purpose. Let your topic, goals, and the guidelines of your instructor's assignment set the length and number of paragraphs you will need. Do not rely on a formula with a set number of paragraphs that might limit your ideas and the goals for your essay.

Writing any type of essay involves using a general format and organizational pattern, and all essays benefit from the writer engaging in some form of writing process to achieve the best results. The process for writing an essay is covered in Chapter 5. Many assignments will require you to blend the skills of two or more essay modes (particular types of essays with a specific expository purpose or approach). For instance, you might combine three modes: argument with comparison/contrast and narration in an argument/persuasion essay on which car to buy as a college student. Rarely does an essay feature one mode only, though there are exceptions (such as a process essay for a biology lab class that provides a report on the steps in an experiment and its results). Most essays use a combination of modes, often with one dominant, for example argument or description. Specific modes and their elements are covered in detail in Chapters 7–16.

Use the following essay format as a guideline.

Cross Reference

See Chapter 5 for information on generating ideas, assessing audience, and narrowing topic.

THE ESSAY FORMAT

Introductory Paragraph

Opening Line/Attention Grabber: Designed to draw in your readers

General Background for the Topic: The set up

Thesis Statement (or Statement of Purpose): Your **thesis statement** states the purpose of your essay. It outlines what you plan to explain to your readers about your subject; it's the conclusion you've reached about the topic.

Ask yourself these questions to get to a strong thesis statement:

- *What* am I writing about?
- *How* will I demonstrate my purpose? What is my plan of development?
- *So What*? What is the main conclusion I've reached on my topic? What do I want my readers to know?

Body Paragraphs

Topic Sentence: Main idea for the paragraph and develops the thesis.

Support: Backs up your topic sentence idea with a statement of support, fact, or opinion (1-3 support statements per body paragraph)

- **Examples:** One or two examples to illustrate each idea
- **Details:** One or more details to illustrate and explain each example
- **Analysis/Commentary:** Analysis and commentary on the importance of the supporting examples and details and how they illustrate the topic sentence
- **Concluding Sentence:** Sums up the main idea from the topic sentence, and/or provides ideas for further thought, or serves as transition to next paragraph.

Include these elements in each body paragraph in your essay. You should use transitions at the end of one

body paragraph or at the beginning of the next to make your essay flow smoothly.

Concluding Paragraph	**Re-emphasizes your essay's thesis without re-stating it:** Reminds your reader of your thesis and sums up your main points
	Sums up your analytical conclusions
	Ends with closing ideas for further thought
	Note: Do not introduce any contradictory ideas in the concluding paragraph (ideas that go against your previous opinions or purpose)

A well written essay has **coherence:** It flows smoothly from one point to the next, and from one paragraph to the next. To achieve good coherence in your essay, make sure that your ideas are developed in a logical order, that you provide support and examples in the best order possible, and that you use transitional words or phrases that move your readers smoothly from one idea or paragraph to the next. **Transitions** are discussed in depth on page 68.

THE BUILDING BLOCKS OF AN EXPOSITORY ESSAY

Following is a detailed description of the basic building blocks of an essay: The title, the introduction and thesis, the body paragraphs, and the conclusion. The sample topic is parking problems on campus.

ESSAY TITLE

The title for your essay is the key to introducing your topic and drawing in your reader. Try for titles that are clear, yet interesting. You can start with a working title before you begin writing your essay, or you may not come up with a title until you have finished your first draft. Either way, the title is an important part of drawing in your reader when your essay is finished.

Example: Pesky Parking Problems at Our Campus

Title Format

Your title should be centered with no extra spaces (stay in double-space format throughout your essay). Do not use a larger font than you do in the body of your paper. Do not use bolding, underlining, or quotation marks (unless you have a quotation within your title). If you have a title with a subtitle, use a colon between the two parts.

Cross Reference
See Chapter 31 for details of typing format for essays.

> **Example:** Too Many Students, Not Enough Spaces: The Parking Problem at Our Campus

Activity 4-1   Creating Catchy Titles

Directions: *For each of the following statements of purpose for an essay, come up with a working title that would help draw the interest of your audience.*

1. College students easily fall prey to fad diets.

   Working title: _____

2. Traveling to another country is a great way to learn about one's own culture.

   Working title: _____

3. Standardized testing in elementary school causes several problems.

   Working title: _____

INTRODUCTORY PARAGRAPH(S)

The purpose of your introduction is to draw in your reader, establish your topic, and explain the purpose you want to develop—the argument or "take" on the subject you want to communicate. Your introduction establishes the style and tone of your essay and the kind of language and "voice" you will use. To create a successful introduction, include the following elements.

Opening Line(s)/Attention Grabber

The first sentence or two of your essay should intrigue your readers, draw them in, and introduce the subject of your paper. Here are some techniques for accomplishing this goal:

1. Begin with a rhetorical question:

> **Example:** "When was the last time you spent over 20 minutes trying to find on-campus parking?"

Note: Usually, it is best to avoid second person ("you") point of view in an essay, but opening an essay with a rhetorical question is a widely accepted exception.

2. Begin with a declaration:

> **Example:** "Campus parking has gotten out of hand."

3. Begin with a definition, a statistic, or a quotation: Define a key term, present a powerful statistic related to your topic, or use an intriguing quotation to hook your readers.

> **Example:** "There is one parking spot for every ten students at our campus."

> **Note:** If you use a definition, statistic, or quotation from a source, you must cite it (see Chapter 19 for help).

4. Begin with a poignant detail or example:

> **Example:** "Most students at our campus wait at least 20 minutes for a parking space if they arrive between the hours of 9:00 AM and noon."

> **Note:** If it is a detail you learned through research, you'll have to cite your source.

5. Begin with a creative scenario or anecdote:

> **Example:** "Imagine your first day at a new college. You pull into the main parking lot 15 minutes before your first class is scheduled to begin. However, as soon as you enter, you see at least 20 cars circling the very full lot."

Again, remember to be cautious with using the second-person point of view—"you"—in your essay.

> **Note:** Avoid using a generalized dramatic statement for your opening line. For instance, "All people feel the need to drive their own cars." You may be wrong, and this statement is too broad. Also avoid formulaic introductory sentences like "In today's society" or "Throughout history . . ." or "According to the dictionary . . . ."

General Background on the Topic

Provide some general information about your topic. Begin narrowing down to your focused thesis statement. Sometimes you need to provide background information about the problem or subject for your audience and give a brief history of the issue to give context for the point you want to make. For instance, if you were writing about the parking problem at your campus for an audience from your campus only, you may need just a little background, more of a reminder really, of the parking problem itself. However, if your audience is the general public, with many readers who don't attend your campus, you'd have to give specific details and background history on the growth and severity of the parking issue at your campus.

Thesis Statement

A good thesis statement establishes the narrowed scope of your topic, provides at least one controlling idea or analytical purpose it will develop, and gives a basic "map" to let your readers know how you will structure and develop your ideas.

You want to write a thesis statement that explains exactly the purpose for your essay. A thesis statement has a message to convey: It is making a claim. A thesis always involves your opinion, not just facts or details. Your thesis statement is the conclusion you've come to about your topic; therefore, it is what you most want to convey to your readers. *It is what you want them to understand about your topic.*

Applying Critical Thinking

PURPOSE   IDEAS   SUPPORT   ASSUMPTIONS BIASES   CONCLUSIONS   POINT OF VIEW   ANALYSIS

Engaging your critical thinking skills will help you develop a **purpose** or **blueprint** for constructing your essay. Your purpose should be clear and consistent from the beginning to the end of your essay. Everything you include should develop that purpose. Knowing what you want to say will help you write a clear, precise thesis statement. Ask yourself these questions to determine your purpose for writing:

1. What is my **point of view**? What do I think or believe about this topic? What do I want to explain or prove to my reader?

2. What **assumptions** or **biases** do I have about the topic? What ideas do I take for granted? Is my point of view based on correct information?

3. Have I **analyzed** the topic so that I understand it?

4. Do I have a clear **point** or **argument** to make about the topic?

Most thesis statements for essays that range from one to four pages in length will be one sentence. Generally a good thesis statement will address the following questions:

1. *What* is the purpose of my essay?

2. *How* will I develop it?

3. *So what* do I want to explain or prove to my readers through this essay?

Asking and answering these questions forces you to create a specific and well developed thesis statement that addresses *what* the purpose of your essay is, *how* the essay will be developed (plan of development or essay map), and *so what*—the main point you want to prove. Here is a thesis statement that includes the answers to the *what*, *how*, and *so what* questions:

> **Example:** [*What?*] "Our campus has a serious parking problem [*How?*] since we have far more students than spots, [*So what?*] so our campus needs to build a second parking lot."

Remember, though, that your thesis statement should not be a question or a series of questions; it should be your *answers* to the questions you want to address on the topic. Also, avoid awkward announcements like "In this essay, I will attempt to show you that parking is a serious problem at our campus." Instead, jump right to your point: "Parking is a serious problem at our campus." In fact, throughout your essay, delete all statements that begin with *I believe, I feel, I think*, or *I will explain* and weak statements like "It seems that . . . ," etc. You can use "I" in expository essays, but use it only when you are giving a personal example for support. For instance, "I once drove around the parking lot for over 30 minutes."

Also, your thesis needs to be narrow enough to be developed thoroughly in the essay, but it cannot be too broad to be covered in sufficient detail.

Activity 4-2   Thesis Practice

Directions: *Create a thesis statement that is neither too broad nor too narrow and that provides an opinion and purpose to pull together the three supporting points listed for each of the following thesis statements.*

Example:

Thesis: *Small breed dogs share many characteristics with their larger breed counterparts.*

   a. Chihuahuas may be tiny, but they tend to form packs like bigger dogs.

   b. Miniature greyhounds are fast, like their larger version breed.

   c. Toy poodles, like the standard poodle, are dogs with strict rules for breeding.

1. **Thesis:** _____

   a. Mexican food features lots of cumin and fresh cilantro.

   b. Italian dishes often include fresh oregano and basil.

   c. Indian cuisine is rich with coriander, hot chilies, and star anise.

2. **Thesis:** _____

   a. Tennis provides an excellent source of cardiovascular activity.

   b. Playing basketball gets the heart pumping and the blood flowing.

   c. Skiing burns calories and provides a great workout.

3. **Thesis:** _____

   a. Japanese anime is a specialized cartoon style that was first popular in Japan.

   b. Now, Americans have become huge anime fans, both watching and creating their own versions.

   c. Anime often features both male and female protagonists who strive to become better individuals. ●

BODY PARAGRAPHS

The function of body paragraphs is to develop the purpose and arguments set up in your introduction and thesis statement. Each body paragraph has a subtopic or idea derived from the thesis that it develops and supports with examples, details, and analysis. The purpose of the body of your paper is to provide the evidence to back up the arguments in your thesis. The number of sentences in a body paragraph varies depending on the topic sentence and its scope; on average, most body paragraphs range from four to fifteen sentences in length. The number of body paragraphs in an essay varies based on the topic, your purpose, your plan for development or essay map, and the

tasks and page requirements of your writing assignment. Be sure that your body paragraphs provide the following:

Cross Reference
See Chapter 6 for more about unity, development, coherence, and transitions.

- **Development:** Elaboration on your purpose, ideas, and analysis
- **Support:** Ample examples and evidence for and analysis of your ideas
- **Unity:** Each sentence helping to support the topic sentence
- **Coherence:** The sentences and ideas flowing smoothly from one to the next with a logical order and appropriate transitions between sentences, if needed, and between body paragraphs

Transitions are words, phrases, or sometimes even complete sentences that help move the reader smoothly from one point to the next. They point the reader in the direction you want to take them. Transitions are necessary both *within* paragraphs and *between* them. When a transitional word, phrase, or sentence is used to connect one paragraph to the next, the transition can come at the end of the previous paragraph or at the beginning of the next, whichever works best for your purpose and organization.

Activity 4-3   Improving Coherence

Directions: *Read the following list of sentences about starting an on-campus club. Next, arrange the list of sentences into the most logical order, and then create a paragraph with those sentences using transitional words and phrases when needed to help the flow.*

1. Create officer positions with clear job descriptions.

2. Find a faculty advisor.

3. Find out if other students are interested in starting up the club with you.

4. Write a mission statement and/or definition of vision for your club.

5. Create and post fliers to recruit more members.

6. Plan activities for the year.

7. Have an election to choose officers for your club after you have created the descriptions of duties.

8. Find a meeting time that works for all members and set a regular time.

_____

_____

_____

_____

_____

_____

Topic Sentence

The topic sentence is the **main idea** for each body paragraph. It is like a mini-thesis for that paragraph. Like a thesis statement, a topic sentence should involve an _analytical point_ that you want to make, not just a fact or detail. It is the blueprint for that paragraph's purpose. Therefore, the topic sentence provides not only your topic for that paragraph but the opinion, argument, or analytical point you plan to make about that topic.

> **Example:** "To begin with, due to a growth in student enrollment, we have more students than we have parking spaces, and this imbalance has caused many problems."

The part about more students than spots would be just a detail or fact, but as soon as your opinion about this imbalance and its effects are added, you have set up an idea that you will demonstrate throughout the paragraph with support and analysis.

Activity 4-4   Topic Sentence Practice

Directions: _Create three topic sentences for each of the thesis statements provided below._

Example:

Thesis: Traveling to foreign countries calls for an open mind and sense of adventure.

Topic sentence 1: _To begin with, you may have to learn the basics of another language and be willing to sound silly trying it out._

Topic sentence 2: _Also, you may be exposed to new and unusual food as you travel._

Topic sentence 3: _You may experience differences in customs and behavior that require an open mind and a good sense of humor._

1. **Thesis:** Getting along well with one's neighbors requires a conscious effort.

   Topic sentence 1: _____

   _____

   Topic sentence 2: _____

   _____

   Topic sentence 3: _____

   _____

2. **Thesis:** There are several ways one can work on remembering important events.

   Topic sentence 1: _____

   _____

   Topic sentence 2: _____

   _____

   Topic sentence 3: _____

   _____

3. **Thesis:** Limiting the amount of television children watch provides several benefits.

   Topic sentence 1: _____

   _____

   Topic sentence 2: _____

   _____

   Topic sentence 3: _____

   _____

Support for Your Topic Sentence

After you have set up your paragraph's purpose with a topic sentence, you will need to support your topic sentence idea. Engage your critical thinking skills to choose the best supporting ideas and examples for your purpose. You can support your topic idea with the following:

1. **Examples:** Give two to four specific examples to support your topic sentence.

> **Example:** Over the past 40 years, since the existing parking structures were first built, our campus enrollment has nearly doubled.

2. **Details:** Give a concrete detail or two to support each of your examples.

> **Example:** According to our campus's *New Student Handbook*, we have over 10,000 students; however, we have only 5,000 parking spaces.

3. **Analysis:** After you have given examples and details to support your topic sentence, be sure to *interpret the significance* of your examples and details with an analytical statement. Don't assume that the facts will speak for themselves: Most readers need and want commentary from you that explains the significance of the details and examples you've provided and their relevance to your argument.

> **Example:** When we look at the numbers, we can see that the growth of our campus has created the current parking crisis: We simply have not kept up with the pace of population growth.

Concluding Sentence

The concluding sentence sums up the purpose and main idea of a body paragraph. It pulls all your ideas and purpose together in a finished product. It may also include a transition to your next body paragraph, although usually the transition appears at the beginning of the next paragraph.

> **Example:** As you can see, the current parking situation has gotten out of hand at our campus.

Sometimes the concluding sentence in a body paragraph is a way to move to the next idea you want to develop: a sentence doing double duty as a close for one paragraph and idea and an introduction to the next example, idea, or concept you want to discuss.

Providing Support in the Best Way

Be sure to engage your critical thinking analysis skills as you provide meaningful support for your ideas.

Cross Reference
See Chapter 20 for more on
the ice cream sandwich.

Creating an Analytical Ice Cream Sandwich

An ice cream sandwich has two chocolate cookies that surround an ice cream filling. Think of the facts, examples, or details you include in your paragraphs as the ice cream filling. You need to surround that filling with two cookies to hold it together. The top cookie is your topic sentence, which sets up the point you want to make in the paragraph, and the bottom cookie is your concluding sentence, which frames your examples with interpretation and analysis.

The Analytical Ice Cream Sandwich

Top cookie: Topic sentence (controlling idea of paragraph)

Ice cream filling: Facts, examples, or details (support to develop the topic sentence)

Bottom cookie: Concluding sentence (interpretation and analysis of the examples and details and how they support the topic sentence)

Ice Cream Sandwich Example:

Top cookie: The parking problem has gotten worse due to the growth of student population.

Ice cream filling: Over the last five years, the student population has grown by over 3,000 students.

Bottom cookie: This large increase has put an unmanageable burden on existing parking lots and parking staff.

Activity 4-5 Ice Cream Sandwich Practice

Directions: *Choose one of the topic sentences you created in Activity 4-4 and create a full ice cream sandwich to support that topic sentence.*

Top cookie: _____

_____

Ice cream filling (example/detail): _____

_____

Bottom cookie (concluding sentence—interpretation and analysis): _____

_____

_____

Concluding Paragraph

The concluding paragraph sums up the main purpose of your essay, re-emphasizing your thesis (without repeating it word for word) and providing an overall sense of conclusion. Most successful concluding paragraphs are at least three sentences long, but they can be several sentences longer than that, depending on the scope of the thesis and assignment. Regardless, they should be succinct and end with a "Ta Da!"—an overall sense of wrapping up with a bang and reiterating your essay's purpose.

> **Note:** Be sure to avoid the common pitfall of introducing a new idea or contradicting yourself in the conclusion: the "shoot yourself in the foot" effect.

> **Example:** As you can see, the parking problem at our campus is bad, but the lack of class offerings at night is an even worse problem.

Ouch! You just shot yourself in the foot and belittled the importance of the topic you chose and developed throughout your essay by introducing a whole new topic out of the blue.

PUTTING IT ALL TOGETHER

Once you are familiar with all the building blocks of an essay, you can put them together in the best possible way to develop your purpose and engage your audience. After you have written a complete draft of an essay, use the following checklist to make sure you have included all the necessary building blocks.

CHECKLIST FOR THE BUILDING BLOCKS

PURPOSE	IDEAS	SUPPORT	ASSUMPTIONS/ BIASES	CONCLUSIONS	POINT OF VIEW	ANALYSIS

Title

_____   Did you provide a title for your essay that is interesting and provides a clue to the essay's topic and/or **purpose**?

_____   Is your title formatted correctly (centered, no boldface type, no quotation marks, no underlining, no large font, and a colon used between title and subtitle if you have both)?

Introductory Paragraph(s)

_____   Do you have an interesting opening line and attention grabber?

_____   Do you provide general background and setup for your topic and **purpose**?

_____   Do you have a thesis statement that explains *what* is the **purpose** for your essay, *how* you will develop that **purpose**, and the significance or **conclusion** reached for your topic (the *so what*)?

Body Paragraphs

_____   Do you have an analytical topic sentence for each body paragraph that develops your **purpose** and follows your plan of development or essay map?

_____   Do you provide adequate **support** for your topic sentence (examples, details, and analysis)? Review the critical thinking skills in Chapter 1 for deeper **analysis**.

_____   Do you have a **concluding** sentence for each body paragraph that reiterates your topic sentence and goal for that body paragraph?

_____   Did you include a transition between each body paragraph (either at the end of one or the beginning of the next) that helps lead the reader smoothly from one support idea to the next?

Concluding Paragraph

_____   Does your **concluding** paragraph sum up the main ideas and purpose of your essay and re-emphasize the thesis statement?

_____   Does your concluding paragraph avoid adding any new ideas or contradictions?

Now that you know the basic parts, or building blocks, for an expository essay, Chapter 5 will guide you through the process for generating a polished essay, from ideas to final product. For specific types of essays or approaches, see Chapters 6–15.

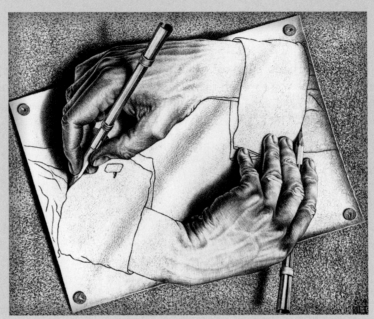

M.C. Escher's "Drawing Hands"

THINKING CRITICALLY

Study this famous drawing by M. C. Escher. Then answer the questions that follow.

What is the artist's message (or thesis)?

_____

_____

How does this image connect to the writing process?

_____

_____

The writing process involves self reflection and active engagement of your analysis and revision skills.

PLANNING AND WRITING EXPOSITORY ESSAYS

Writing an expository essay involves a process in which you engage your critical thinking skills and develop your ideas in stages. Basically, the writing process includes five major stages:

1. **Prewriting:**   Generate ideas and your paper's purpose.
2. **Organizing:**   Develop a plan for presenting your purpose and ideas.
3. **Drafting:**   Create a first draft of your essay based on your plan and the pattern(s) of organization you have chosen; develop support for your essay's purpose.
4. **Revising:**   Reassess the draft for content, development, organization, and support (examples and details).
5. **Editing:**   Check for sentence-level effectiveness, style, diction, grammar, and spelling errors.

This process will be broken down in detail later in this chapter. To begin, though, you must figure out your assignment and decide on your subject, purpose, and audience. From these three elements, you will develop a more specific topic, thesis, plan for development, and appropriate tone and style for your essay. Remember that you can change the order of these steps—this process is a tool—and decide what works best for you in each writing task.

Most writers figure out what writing process works best for them and which steps of the writing process they can switch, modify, or even skip completely. You may modify the process differently from assignment to assignment; however, until you have developed a writing process that works for you and produces fully developed, well organized, well written essays, try this traditional approach to the stages of the writing process. The key is to be actively involved in the process of thinking critically about your ideas and how best to develop them in your essay.

SUBJECT, PURPOSE, AND AUDIENCE

Once you have determined the *subject* you will write about (based on an assignment or your own subject choice), you must narrow your subject to a manageable topic, come up with a *purpose* for writing about it, and adjust your approach and overall tone to suit your intended *audience*.

Use the flow chart on page 78 to help you move from *subject*, *purpose*, and *audience* to *topic*, *thesis*, and *tone* and *approach*.

Subject, Purpose, and Audience

Subject

A broad subject that you chose or is assigned to you.

For example: "Music"

Purpose

What do you want to *explain* or *prove* about your topic?

What point do you want to make? What is your opinion on the topic? What will you argue?

Audience

Who is your target audience? Instructor? Classmates? Other?

Modify your approach (tone, style, ideas, and support) so it is appropriate to the target audience.

Topic

A narrowed aspect of your subject, e.g., "Lipsyncing at Concerts"

Thesis

What is your point?

How will you develop it?

So what? What is the significance of your conclusion or argument?

Tone/approach

Modify your tone and your approach based on your audience.

Narrowing Subject to a Topic

Use your critical thinking tools to figure out a good topic that is narrow enough for the scope of your essay's purpose. Before you can write well on a subject, you need to narrow your topic to a sufficiently specific focus that you can develop well in a short essay. For instance, if you begin with a broad subject such as "parks in our city," then you need to figure out what aspects of parks (size, location, amenities) or what kind of parks (theme parks, recreational parks, green zones) you want to focus on before you come up with exactly what you want to say (purpose).

If you have a subject assigned to you, or if you come up with a subject out of an interest of your own, you need to narrow the focus of your essay's scope and purpose before you begin writing. If your subject is too broad (the scope is too big), you won't be able to cover the nuances of the topic in depth, and your essay will stay too general and gloss the surface instead of delving deeper into the topic. For instance, the topic of "baseball" is too broad: Can you imagine trying to cover everything about this game in one essay? You could narrow this broad topic down to the idea of free agents in baseball. If your topic is *too narrow*, it will not be a big enough issue or question to address in your essay, so make sure your proposed topic is not a detail or fact that doesn't need development. For instance, if your topic was "the baseball is a specific kind of ball used in the game," it would be very hard to come up with enough description and information for a full essay.

Applying Critical Thinking

| PURPOSE | IDEAS | SUPPORT | ASSUMPTIONS BIASES | CONCLUSIONS | POINT OF VIEW | ANALYSIS |

Ways to Narrow a Broad Subject to a Manageable Topic

Here are a few techniques that can help you move from a broad subject to a narrowed topic. They include brainstorming, which is a way to get your ideas flowing, and asking questions that help you **analyze** the subject—break it down into its different parts. The more you think about a broad subject and analyze what it is about, the better able you will be to narrow it down to a workable topic.

The subject of *volunteering* is used here to demonstrate how you can narrow a subject to a topic that would work well for a focused expository essay.

Broad Subject: Volunteering

1. Brainstorm a list of issues related to, ideas about, or types of volunteering.

   Volunteering: community service, Girl Scouts, tutoring, cleanup in neighborhood, school aide, hospitals, nursing homes, types of volunteering, benefits of volunteering

2. Ask yourself why you thought of this topic in the first place—why is it interesting or important to you?

   School aides: I am sad and surprised that local schoolteachers are not getting the support they need to help our children learn.

3. Generate a question or several questions related to the topic you chose.

   How can I get teachers at my son's school the help they need to provide successful classroom experiences? How can I get more people in our community to volunteer their time for our schools?

4. Start with a problem related to the topic.

My son's third-grade class has not been able to go on field trips or have arts and crafts time because there is only one teacher and 30 students.

5. Start with a point or purpose in mind.

I want to convince the other parents from my PTA that we need parents to get involved in the classrooms and take a more active role in helping our teachers.

Activity 5-1   Narrowing Your Topic

Directions: *The following subjects are too broad to develop into successful thesis statements. Use one or more of the techniques given to create two more focused subtopics for each broad topic listed.*

Example:

Topic: Television

Subtopic 1: *The unrealistic side of reality TV*

Subtopic 2: *Television as an addiction*

1. Topic: Sports

Subtopic 1: _____

Subtopic 2: _____

2. Topic: Movies

Subtopic 1: _____

Subtopic 2: _____

3. Topic: Transportation

Subtopic 1: _____

Subtopic 2: _____

4. Topic: Music

Subtopic 1: _____

Subtopic 2: _____

5. **Topic:** Pets

  Subtopic 1: _____

  Subtopic 2: _____

6. **Topic:** Education

  Subtopic 1: _____

  Subtopic 2: _____

7. **Topic:** Travel

  Subtopic 1: _____

  Subtopic 2: _____

8. **Topic:** Nutrition

  Subtopic 1: _____

  Subtopic 2: _____

9. **Topic:** Politics

  Subtopic 1: _____

  Subtopic 2: _____

10. **Topic:** Cities

  Subtopic 1: _____

  Subtopic 2: _____

Purpose and Approach

Sometimes, just narrowing your topic using one of the techniques listed in the Critical Thinking box will lead you to your essay's purpose, and you'll be able to create a thesis statement effortlessly. Otherwise, once you have narrowed your subject to a manageable topic, the next step is to come up with your essay's purpose (what you want to explain to your readers about your topic) and how you will approach it. In order to do this, ask yourself the following questions.

Cross Reference
Review pages 65–66 of Chapter 4 on creating a good thesis statement.

1. What is my *purpose* or *goal* for writing an essay on this topic?
2. What *questions* do I want to address in the essay?
3. Is there a *problem* (or problems) I want to solve in the essay? If so, what is it?

4. What *evidence* (support) can I use to back up my ideas and purpose (for example: personal experience, facts, outside evidence or research)?

5. What point of view (perspective) do I have about the topic, and what assumptions or biases do I have about it?

Activity 5-2   Identifying Your Purpose and Approach to a Topic

Directions: *Choose one of the narrowed topics you came up with in Activity 5-1. Answer the following questions to go deeper and develop a sense of what your purpose would be for writing about the topic and how you would approach it. (Refer to Chapter 1, if necessary, for a review of the critical thinking process.)*

1.   Based on the narrowed idea you chose from Activity 5-1, what would be your *purpose* or *goal* if you wrote an essay on this topic?

_____

_____

_____

2.   What *questions* would you attempt to address in the essay?

_____

_____

_____

3.   Is there a *problem* (or problems) you'd attempt to solve or address in the essay? If so, what are they?

_____

_____

_____

4.   What *evidence* (support) could you use to back up your ideas and purpose (for example: personal experience, facts, outside evidence, or research)?

_____

_____

_____

5. What point of view (perspective) would you be coming from in the essay, and what assumptions or biases do you already have related to the subject?

_____

_____

_____ ●

Once you have thought about your purpose and approach for an essay on your chosen topic, come up with support that will illustrate and explain your purpose. Can you provide any personal examples that would help illustrate your ideas? Are there examples from your community or your knowledge of culture that would support your ideas? Should you provide some data and facts to support your ideas? (Be sure to check with your instructor before conducting and using research.)

Review your answer to question 4 above, then complete the next activity.

Cross Reference
Review Chapter 4 for more information about including support in your essay.

Activity 5-3   Developing Support for Your Topic

Directions: *Using the same narrowed topic you chose for Activity 5-2, provide some examples you could use for support.*

1. Example 1: _____

    _____

2. Example 2: _____

    _____

3. Example 3: _____

    _____ ●

Assessing Your Audience

Another aspect you should consider before writing your first draft is the audience for your essay:

Who are you writing it for?

What do you want them to understand?

Once you have identified your audience, you can make choices about the best approach to take and how much background information or explanation to include about your topic. For instance, if you are writing about ceramics for a general audience, you would have to add more definitions and in-depth explanations. If your audience is academic, your tone and vocabulary should be more formal. An academic audience would also expect supporting evidence, definitions, and examples to back up your arguments. If your audience is specialized—for example, if you were writing an essay about ceramics for other artists who work in the field—your tone would be semiformal and your vocabulary could get specialized. If you are writing an essay for another group of students on a whimsical or humorous topic, then your tone and vocabulary can be more informal.

Cross Reference
See Chapter 30 for help in choosing the right tone and style to match your audience.

Types of Audience

General—all types of people

Academic—college students and faculty

Specialized—specific to a certain field or background, such as nursing students or the instructor for a content class you are taking

Ask yourself which is the target audience for your essay. Then use the answer to assess how much background information on the topic you will have to provide, what level of vocabulary you will use (and how much you'll need to define specialized terms), what approach and tone (more serious/formal, casual/playful, or somewhere in between) would work best, and how much evidence you'll need to provide to persuade your readers.

Activity 5-4   Adjusting Your Approach for an Intended Audience

Topic: *Increasing violence on college campuses*
Audience 1: Other college students
Audience 2: Parents of college students
Audience 3: State legislators

Directions: *How would you need to adjust your tone, approach, inclusion of background information, and even purpose for these three different audiences? Be sure to look at Chapter 30 for more detailed information about style and tone if you need help with this exercise.*

_____

_____

_____

_____

_____

After you have determined the target audience for your essay, choose an appropriate tone, and choose sentence structures and vocabulary that match it.

Activity 5-5   Finding the Right Tone

Directions: *For each of the topics given, determine a suitable audience. Then explain the type of tone you would use (formal or informal), and briefly explain why.*

Example:

Topic: Lack of hospitals in our state

Potential target audience: *The state legislature (senators)*

Best tone choice: *Formal, because I would be making a formal proposal to lawmakers and need to be taken seriously*

1. **Topic:** The need for a new stop sign in your neighborhood

   Potential target audience: _____

   Best tone choice and reason: _____

   _____

2. **Topic:** How to treat an infection

   Potential target audience: _____

   Best tone choice and reason: _____

   _____

3. **Topic:** Tips for downloading songs onto your iPod

   Potential target audience: _____

   Best tone choice and reason: _____

   _____

4. **Topic:** The need to expand the campus bookstore's hours of operation

   Potential target audience: _____

   Best tone choice and reason: _____

   _____

5. **Topic:** The best dog-friendly parks in our city

Potential target audience: _____

Best tone choice and reason: _____

_____

Once you have a topic, know your purpose, have identified your audience, and know what you want to say about your topic, you are ready to craft your statement of purpose—your **thesis**. A thesis statement should be a complete sentence that narrows the topic and provides your opinion about that topic. It is what you want to explain or prove about your topic: The argument you put forth. Make sure your thesis statement is broad enough that it can be developed but not so broad that it can't be developed well in a short essay.

Cross Reference

See Chapter 4, pp. 65–66, for how to write a strong thesis.

Activity 5-6   Writing Your Thesis Statement

Directions: *Choose two of the topics from Activity 5-5 for which you assessed an audience and write a one-sentence thesis statement in a tone that is appropriate for that audience.*

1. Thesis: _____

_____

_____

2. Thesis: _____

_____

_____

You are now ready to start the process of writing an essay, going from prewriting to a final, polished paper. Here is a ten-step guide to the writing process. Some writers use every step, some use some of the steps, and some change the order of the steps. Try out the process and figure out what works best for you. Be sure to use your critical thinking skills throughout the process to make the best choices about your subject, your purpose for writing about it, and the audience you want to reach.

A TEN-STEP GUIDE FOR WRITING AN EXPOSITORY ESSAY

These steps are designed to break the writing process down into manageable stages. Feel free to change the order and continually test what works best for you and your individual learning style. Sometimes your needs change depending on an individual assignment. Remember, all formulas and step-by-step processes are tools designed to help you achieve the standards required for expository essays. Don't let the tools control you: Use them, customize them, and abandon them if you need to for your own needs and purpose.

Applying Critical Thinking

PURPOSE   IDEAS   SUPPORT   ASSUMPTIONS BIASES   CONCLUSIONS   POINT OF VIEW   ANALYSIS

Your critical thinking skills should be engaged in all stages of the writing process. As you go through these ten steps, be sure to keep in mind your **purpose**, the information (**ideas**, **support**) you will need to develop that purpose, the implications of your ideas and arguments, the **assumptions** you make, the **point of view** you are expressing, and the audience you are writing for.

Let's say you choose to write an essay on the topic of adopting versus buying a pet: You could use the following steps to develop your ideas, outline an organizational plan, identify your audience, and clarify your purpose for writing the essay.

GENERATE IDEAS AND PREWRITE

Step One: Generate Ideas

You can use several techniques to generate ideas, narrow your topic, determine your purpose, and organize your ideas. The techniques include thinking about your topic, freewriting, mapping, brainstorming, clustering, and journaling. Everyone's writing process develops individually; try these techniques and figure out which ones work best for you. Some people prefer to do their prewriting on paper using a pen or pencil, and some prefer to use their computer to type brainstorm lists or rough outlines. Others like to use the columns function in their word processing program to create categories and brainstorm directly below the separate categories. Discover what works for you. You may want to change the order or skip some steps, which is fine: These are tools, and you are the essay's carpenter.

Thinking and Talking

As soon as you get your assignment or choose your topic, begin thinking about it. Some prewriting happens in your head before you even put pen to paper. Talk it out with a classmate or friend if you can. Ask yourself, "What do I want to accomplish in this paper?" "What do I have to say about this subject?" "What aspect of this subject am I most interested in, and how do I want to narrow it down to a manageable topic?" "What are some questions or issues I can address related to this subject?"

Freewriting

Freewriting is a popular technique for generating ideas and narrowing your topic. When you **freewrite,** you just put pen to paper and let the ideas flow out of you without worrying about spelling, grammar, or "dumb" ideas. When you freewrite, turn off your inner editor and just let the ideas flow out of you. Later you can sort through the good and the bad stuff.

> **Example:** I know I want to write about adopting an unwanted pet instead of buying one at the pet store . . . let me see . . . I have lots of reasons why I feel this way . . . hmmm some of them include all the unwanted animals that get put down or go without companionship, oh yeah, also, the money for adopting pets goes into spaying and neutering cats and dogs so there are not even more unwanted pets created

Mapping

Mapping is a way literally to map out your essay plan and how you will structure your essay. You can map using boxes and arrows, a flow chart, or whatever works best for your style.

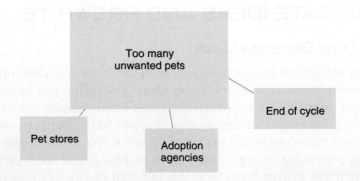

Tip: Computer software designed for generating ideas and mapping is available on most college campuses.

Brainstorming

Brainstorming is a free-flowing, free-association list of words or ideas that you crank out on paper to get the ideas flowing. As in freewriting, you need to turn off your inner editor and just storm your brain for as many ideas and details or even associations as you can related to your subject or assigned writing prompt.

> **Example:** Unwanted pets, pets for profits, unspayed or neutered pets, animals put to sleep, dogs, cats, rabbits, hamsters, rats, mice, ferrets, adoption agencies, pet stores, choosing to get pets from rescue centers over pet stores, ending the cycle

Clustering

Clustering is another way to represent your ideas visually. You can circle your main subject and then draw lines and add further clusters or circles around connected ideas or subtopics that you generate.

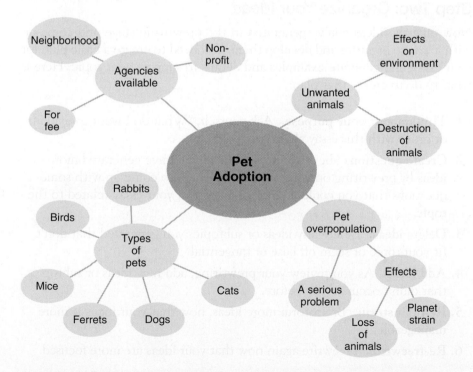

Journaling

Journaling involves writing your thoughts down in a journal. Some instructors will require you to keep a writer's journal for jotting down ideas and recording the steps in your writing process. Or you can start a journal on your own to write ideas as they come to you—that way, your thoughts can be collected in one place as they come to you in bits and pieces over the course of a few days.

Activity 5-7   Generating Ideas

Directions: *On a separate sheet of paper, practice using the prewriting techniques described to generate some ideas and subtopics for the topics provided.*

1. Tips for new college students
2. Finding information for your courses (research)
3. Shopping for food
4. Clothes and personalities
5. Modes of transportation

Step Two: Organize Your Ideas

Now take the ideas you've generated in the prewriting stage and come up with a way to organize and develop them. You need to create a basic plan for your essay, and generate examples and details to support your topic. Here is what to do to create that plan:

1. **Think about your purpose.** Ask yourself, "What do I want to explain or prove with this essay about my topic?"
2. **Create questions about the topic.** After you have generated more ideas by prewriting on your subject, use them to come up with some questions that you could address or answer in your essay related to the topic.
3. **Delete ideas.** Delete any ideas or subtopics you generated that don't fit your topic or seem off base or tangential.
4. **Add ideas.** As you review your prewriting, add new ideas or subtopics that didn't occur to you before.
5. **Re-brainstorm.** Brainstorm more ideas, now that your focus is more manageable.
6. **Re-freewrite.** Freewrite again now that your ideas are more focused.

Now you are ready to create a rough outline of your ideas and subtopics to see how they could be put together in a first draft. Here is an example of a rough outline that is based on the previous prewriting about the advantages and disadvantages of getting a pet from a pet store or a shelter.

Example Rough Outline:

Topic: Adopting pets vs. buying in a pet store

I. Disadvantages of pet stores
    A. For profit—therefore do not always have the best interests of pets in mind
    B. Encourage the creation of more pets for profit
    C. Favor pedigreed breeds over mixed-breed pets
II. Advantages of adoption
    A. Spaying and neutering is guaranteed
    B. Saves the lives of unwanted animals
    C. Discourages creating pets for profit
    D. Helps stop the cycle of unwanted pets

Note: Your campus may have software available for help in creating outlines.

Cross Reference
See Chapter 6 for detailed explanation of outline format.

Activity 5-8   Creating a Rough Outline

Directions: *Choose one of the topics you did prewriting for in the earlier activities, and generate a working thesis. Then on a separate sheet of paper, write a rough outline for an essay based on your thesis using the numbered list above.*

Step Three: Establish Your Topic, Purpose, and Audience

Now you need to determine the purpose for your topic, the audience you are writing for, and how you want to approach it. (Refer to pp. 81 and 83, if necessary, where these concepts are explored more fully.) Remember these elements:

1. **Narrow your topic:** Use the strategies on pages 78–80 to narrow your subject into a focused, manageable topic.
2. **Purpose:** Be clear about what you want to explain, show, or prove in your essay.
3. **Audience:** Think about your target audience. What approach and tone should you use to best address it?

Activity 5-9   Topic, Purpose, and Audience

Directions: *Using the rough outline you created in Activity 5-8, answer the following questions:*

1. What is your *narrowed topic*—the specific question or idea you will be addressing?

    _____

    _____

2. What is your *purpose* for writing this essay? What do you intend to explain or prove to your audience?

    _____

    _____

3. Who is your intended *audience?*

    _____

    _____

WRITE A FIRST DRAFT

Step Four: Start Your First Draft

Just dive in. Although this step is often the one where many students begin in their writing process, you shouldn't write an actual draft until you have accomplished the three steps above. Otherwise, you run the danger of wasting a lot of time and effort figuring out your purpose or rambling through the first page (or even longer) of your essay. Also, while writing your first full draft, don't worry about spelling and grammar: You will only lose your train of thought and become derailed from the points you are making. Instead, check grammar and spelling later in the editing stage.

Activity 5-10   Write a First Draft

Directions: *Use the ideas you generated from prewriting, your rough outline, and your answers to Activity 5-9 to write a rough draft of your essay (1 1/2 to 2 pages), and give it a working title.*

REVISE

Step Five: Reorganize for Order, Unity, Coherence, and Sentence Variety

Revision is the most crucial stage of the writing process, yet the one that more students try to skip than any other. Few writers are such naturals that they crank out perfect essays and sentences in a first draft. Most writers need several drafts to accomplish a well designed, well written, and well supported essay. Many students mistakenly confuse the term "revision" with "edit" or "proofread." Revision focuses on organization, style, and content while proofreading and editing, which will be explained in the next stage, focuses on fixing grammar and spelling errors.

Engage your critical thinking tools as you revise: Essay writing is recursive (a process of going back and reworking what you have written): Revision is the key to excellence in content and delivery. During revision, check the order of your paragraphs and the details within them; move things that need to be moved, and delete things that don't belong. Make sure your paragraphs have enough support from examples and details to develop their topic sentences. Check that each paragraph develops the thesis of your paper and each sentence in each paragraph develops the topic sentence. If it doesn't, get it out of there. Ensure your essay flows smoothly by adding appropriate transitional words or phrases where needed, and check to make sure that you have varied your sentence lengths and sentence types.

Cross Reference
See Chapter 6 for more information on order, coherence, unity, and sentence variety.

Use the following checklist to make sure you revise all the elements of your essay.

Revision Checklist

1. Restructure paragraph order, if needed.

2. Delete unnecessary words, sentences, ideas, or details.

3. Add more support (examples and details) to fully develop your topic sentences.

4. Add transitions between paragraphs and between sentences where needed (see Transitions and Coherence, Chapter 6)

5. Check for sentence variety (see Chapter 23)

Activity 5-11   Revision

Directions: *On a separate sheet of paper, revise your essay draft using the Revision Checklist in Step Five.* ●

Step Six: Fine-Tune Thesis and Topic Sentences

Make sure that your thesis statement is analytical, with a clear opinion or argument that you want to explain or prove. Check to make sure that your topic sentences are also ideas and not just facts or details, and make sure that they support and develop your thesis statement.

Step Seven: Provide Support—Add More Examples, Details, and Analysis

Be sure that each body paragraph has at least two statements of support for the idea set out in the topic sentence. Include examples to illustrate your point, as well as corresponding details and analysis of the examples and details in relation to your essay's purpose.

Activity 5-12   Providing Supporting Examples

Directions: *Come up with at least one new example to provide support for each of the topic sentences in your essay draft.*

Supporting example for topic sentence 1: _____

_____

Supporting example for topic sentence 2: _____

_____

Supporting example for topic sentence 3: _____

_____

Supporting example for topic sentence 4: _____

_____

Activity 5-13   Supporting Details

Directions: *Come up with two supporting details or facts to further define, illustrate, or explain the examples you created in Activity 5-12.*

1. Detail 1: _____
   Detail 2: _____
2. Detail 1: _____
   Detail 2: _____

3. Detail 1: _____

Detail 2: _____

4. Detail 1: _____

Detail 2: _____ ◉

Activity 5-14 **Creating Ice Cream Sandwiches for Your Examples**

Directions: *Choose a topic sentence from your essay draft and use it to create a full ice cream sandwich.*

Top cookie: Your original topic sentence. _____

_____

Ice cream filling: Provide at least one supporting example and one detail to illustrate that detail.

Example(s): _____

_____

Supporting detail(s): _____

_____

Bottom cookie: Provide a sentence that interprets the importance of the examples and details and what they illustrate.

_____

_____ ◉

Cross Reference
See Chapter 4, pp. 72–73, for more about ice cream sandwiches.

PROOFREAD AND EDIT

After you have revised for style and content, you need to proofread your essay for grammar and spelling errors. Turn on your inner editor at this stage of the writing process. Many students fall into the procrastination trap and run out of time to proofread and edit their drafts. It is important to turn in professional quality work; don't let minor errors and typos sabotage the thought behind your ideas, arguments, and support. It helps if you can put your final essay draft aside for a day before you complete this stage; that way you can spot those simple errors and typos that are invisible to your brain for the first few hours after you finish your paper (because you just wrote the sentences and know what they are *supposed* to say). Also, be sure to have your textbook and a dictionary handy as you go through your essay. Remember this rule of thumb as you proofread: When in doubt, look it up.

Step Eight: Check Spelling

Cross Reference
See Chapter 29 for commonly confused words.

Use a dictionary or spell-check to check the spelling of any words you are unsure about and also check for words that you might have used incorrectly.

Activity 5-15   Check Spelling

Directions: *Check the Commonly Confused Words list on pages 628–639 to see if you have committed any of these common mistakes in word choice. Then, use a dictionary or spell-check to doublecheck your spelling—when in doubt, look it up.*

Step Nine: Check Word Usage, Word Choices, Tone, and Style

Cross Reference
See Chapter 31 for help in all of these categories.

Use a thesaurus to find synonyms (words that mean the same thing) to keep you from overusing particular words. Check for slang, gender-biased language, clichés, and inappropriate tone or changes in tone.

Activity 5-16   Check Usage and Tone

Directions: *Go through your essay draft and make sure you have used a consistent and appropriate tone throughout. Also, check word choices and revise any inappropriate dialect, slang, or clichés.*

Step Ten: Check for Sentence-Level Errors

1. Check especially for fragments, run-ons, and comma splices (see Chapter 25).
2. Check for incorrect comma usage, point of view shifts, pronoun agreement, subject–verb agreement, pronoun reference fault errors, semicolon and colon use, apostrophe use, faulty parallelism, dangling or misplaced modifiers, and unnecessary passive voice constructions (these common errors are covered in the handbook section of this text).

Activity 5-17   Grammar Review and Final Revision

Directions: *Go through your essay and check for the common sentence-level grammar errors summarized in Step Ten. Correct any errors you find. Then use the following Revision Checklist to evaluate the basic elements of your essay.*

REVISION CHECKLIST

_____   Check for a clear and interesting title in correct format.

_____   Check for an interesting introductory paragraph that sets up your purpose and leads into your thesis.

_____   Check for purpose and a clear thesis statement.

_____   Check that you have used appropriate vocabulary, tone, and approach for your target audience.

_____   Check to make sure that you have organized your paper logically, with clear topic sentences in the body paragraphs and transitions.

_____   Check to make sure you have maintained unity—all sentences and paragraphs help develop your purpose and thesis.

_____   Check to make sure you have included enough support in your essay to develop your purpose. Do you need more examples and details?

_____   Check to make sure that your sentence structure and your vocabulary choices are varied and interesting.

_____   Check for a strong concluding paragraph that sums up the analytical conclusion (purpose) established in your thesis.

_____   Check for complete sentences (eliminate fragments, run-ons, or comma splices).

_____   Check for correct punctuation throughout the paper (commas, semi-colons, colons, other punctuation marks).

_____   Check for mechanics (spelling, capitalization, underlining, italics, abbreviations, numbering) using the grammar section of this text and a dictionary.

A SAMPLE ESSAY: MODELING THE PROCESS

It helps sometimes to see another student go through a draft and revise an essay in stages. As the student goes through various drafts of her paper on the following pages, look at the annotated changes in the drafts.

Step One: Prewriting

Student: I've been assigned to write something about the city I live in. Hmmm. I live in Seattle; there's so much to say about it. Maybe I'll begin with a brainstorm list to narrow my topic. I'll remember to let everything just flow here and list everything that comes to mind without any judgment or editing at this point. Let's see . . .

Topic: Seattle

I'll just brainstorm a list of what comes to mind on this topic:

Rain, trees, Space Needle, Mt. Rainier, ferries, coffee, music, grunge, restaurants, people, diversity, fish, the aquarium, the Waterfront, downtown, Woodland Park Zoo, University of Washington, community colleges, rhododendrons, parks, beaches, Alki, Golden Gardens, flannel, tourists . . .

OK, OK, I'll stop here. I already have plenty of topic ideas.
I'll pick Seattle's downtown Waterfront as my narrowed topic, and next, I'll do a cluster to generate ideas for an essay on this topic:

Narrowed Topic: Seattle's downtown Waterfront

Step Two: Organizing

OK, next, I'll develop the categories/subtopics I've developed in the cluster above.
First, I'll create a rough outline for my paper based on my cluster.

Seattle's Waterfront

    I. Restaurants
        A. Casual/affordable
        B. Fancy/pricey
    II. Shopping
        A. Cheap or tourist-based
        B. Expensive/exclusive/specialized
    III. Activities
        A. Entertainment
        B. Activities/attractions
    IV. People
        A. Tourists
        B. Locals
        C. Street performers

Note: Here the student could go back and brainstorm again for each subcategory to develop additional examples and ideas. Check your campus for helpful software available for creating outlines in correct format.

Cross Reference
See Chapter 6 for outline format and outline critique form.

Step Three: Drafting

OK, let me see, my *audience* is my classmates and my instructor. My *subject* is narrowed to the *topic* of Seattle's downtown Waterfront. What is my *purpose?* What do I want to explain, show, or prove about Seattle's Waterfront?

Looking at my categories and my rough outline, I can see that I will be focusing on what to do and see on the Waterfront. So maybe my working thesis or statement of purpose will be something like: *There are many things to do on Seattle's Waterfront.*

OK, here goes my first draft . . .

Seattle's Waterfront

    There are so many things to do in the Seattle area. One of my favorite places to go in Seattle is its downtown Waterfront. I always take visiting relatives there too. I like the variety of choices I have when I go there. Seattle's Waterfront offers many things to see and do.

First, there are lots of good restaurants on Seattle's Waterfront. If you don't have a lot of money and want a casual experience, try good old McDonald's. Also, there is a hotdog stand that is open all year. There are lots of places that sell fish and chips to go for not very much money. If you want to go fancier, then there's a great range, there's a Red Robin with a medium priced menu that offers anything from hamburgers to salads. If you want to go even fancier, try one of the many nice Seafood restaurants along the piers. For instance, Elliott Bay Fishhouse or Ivar's.

There is great shopping at the Waterfront. If you want a great spot for souveneers or little trinkets, go to Ye Olde Curiousity Shoppe. It's also a very entertaining place and kind of a tourist attraction all on its own. You can buy anything from candy, shells and "Seattle" pens and cups to strange stuff that will amaze your friends—even gag gifts. If you want a nicer gift, there are many clothes and gift shops that offer nicer gifts, there are also art galleries that sell to the public.

There is also the aquarium, with all kinds of fish and sea animals. There is the Cinemax/Omni theater that shows movies. There is also an arcade with all kinds of games and prizes, and even a carousel. There are lots of street performers too, musicians, comedians, jugglers, etc. You can take a ferry ride or a boat cruise from the pier.

There are lots of people at Seattle's Waterfront. There are tourists from all over the United States and even all over the world. But not only the tourists come to the Waterfront, locals like it too. You can see whole families out for some fun on the pier or in the arcade. You can see couples strolling along the walkway after a

romantic dinner for two. You can also see local musicians and street
vendors trying to make some money.

So, next time you go to downtown Seattle, be sure to visit it's
waterfront. There is so much to do including great restaurants,
shopping, activities and people to see.

Step Four: Revision

1. Reorganize for unity, coherence, and sentence variety.

I need to check whether every sentence or example in my body paragraphs
belongs there—are they in the right spots? Does anything need to be deleted?
Do I need transitions? Do I have sentence variety? I'll work on making these
changes in the next draft.

2. Fine-tune thesis and topic sentences.

Ok, I can see that both my thesis and my topic sentences could be improved. Let me go back to the Building Blocks advice from Chapter 4 on thesis statements and topic sentences.

Thesis—Let me use the *what, how,* and *so what* questions.

What is the purpose of my essay: Seattle's Waterfront offers many
things to see and do (my existing thesis works perfectly as a "what").

How will I develop it: The waterfront has a great variety of restaurants, shopping, activities, and types of people. (I used my categories to create a plan of development, a map for how I will
develop my thesis.)

So what is the main point I want to prove: Therefore, the waterfront is an ideal place to spend a full day in Seattle, as it provides
anything you could want in a perfect Seattle experience.

Topic Sentences: OK, when I look at my topic sentences, I see that
they are a bit broad and don't offer any real point or main idea.
They should be more of an opinion than just a fact or detail. Let
me try to rewrite each of them with more of an analytical message
and a bit more focus.

Topic Sentence 1: First, there are lots of good restaurants on Seattle's Waterfront.

Revision: To begin with, Seattle's Waterfront offers a variety of restaurants to suit any palate and any budget.

Topic Sentence 2: There is great shopping at the Waterfront.

Revision: Also, there are several great shopping opportunities on the Waterfront, from kitsch to classy.

Topic Sentence 3: There is also the aquarium, with all kinds of fish and sea animals. (This is not really a topic sentence since it is not the main idea for my paragraph; it's an example with details to support an idea for things to do. I'll change it.)

Revision: The Waterfront is a great place to go for activities and entertainment.

Topic Sentence 4: Finally, there are lots of people at Seattle's Waterfront.

Revision: Finally, Seattle's Waterfront provides the best people watching in the city.

3. Add more support, examples, and details.

In this draft I'm going to add my new thesis statement and topic sentences and see where I can provide more supporting examples and details.

Note: Changes made by the student in the second draft, including reorganization for unity, coherence, and sentence variety, a new thesis and topic sentences, have been underlined and annotated. Transitions are highlighted in blue.

Seattle's Waterfront

There are so many things to do in the Seattle area. For instance, one of my favorite places to go in Seattle is its downtown Waterfront. I always take visiting relatives there too since I like the variety of choices I have when I go there. No matter what you want, Seattle's Waterfront offers many things to see and do. <u>The waterfront</u>

has a great variety of restaurants, shopping, activities, and types of people. *Therefore, the waterfront is an ideal place to spend a full day in Seattle as it provides anything you could want in a perfect Seattle experience.*

TS   *To begin with, Seattle's Waterfront offers a variety of restaurants to suit any palate and any budget.* If you don't have a lot of money and want a casual experience, try good old McDonald's. McDonald's offers many full-meal options for under five dollars. For instance, you can get a Big Mac, fries, and a Coke for less than five dollars. Also, there is a hotdog stand that is open all year and has great dogs and Polish sausages for under three dollars, and there are lots of places that sell fish and chips to go for not very much money. Ivar's is the most famous place to get fish and chips to go. You can get a full order of fish and chips for six dollars or less. If you want to go fancier, then there's a great range, there's a Red Robin with a medium priced menu that offers anything from hamburgers to salads. Most burgers there, along with unlimited French fries, cost less than eight dollars. They also have a full range of desserts and the best two-dollar shake in town. If you want to go even fancier, try one of the many nice seafood restaurants along the piers. For instance, Elliott Bay Fishhouse, which has fresh salmon and other grilled fish entrées, ranging from thirteen to twenty dollars and has a fancier atmosphere with candles and white tablecloths or Ivar's, the indoor restaurant which serves the full entrée and salad plates for about the same range. Both of these restaurants are a more romantic atmosphere with higher-priced and more elaborate menus. The Waterfront has any type of dining experience you could want.

TS   Also, there are several great shopping opportunities on the Waterfront, from kitsch to classy. If you want a great spot for

Margin annotations:

Thesis statement

Supporting example
Supporting detail
Supporting example

Supporting example
Supporting detail

Supporting example
Supporting detail

Supporting example

Supporting detail
Supporting example
Concluding sentence

souvenirs or little trinkets, go to Ye Olde Curiosity Shoppe. It's also a

very entertaining place and kind of a tourist attraction all on its

own. In this shop, you can buy anything from candy, shells and

"Seattle" pens and cups to strange stuff that will amaze your

friends—even gag gifts. For instance, you can get soap that turns

your friends' hands black when they use it and disappearing ink.

If you want a nicer gift, there are many clothes and gift shops that

offer nicer gifts, for instance, there are art shops with beautiful

Native American carvings and paintings there are also art galleries

that sell to the public, most of these feature local artists and include

paintings, carvings, and glassworks. It's a place where you can find

anything.

Moreover, the Waterfront is a great place to go for activities

and entertainment. There is the aquarium, with all kinds of fish and

sea animals. You can see seals and otters, and you can touch live sea

urchins in a touching tank. There is also the Cinemax/Omni theater

that shows movies, an arcade with all kinds of games and prizes, and

even a carousel. The carousel is a refurbished, old-fashioned carousel

with elaborately painted and decorated horses. There are lots of

street performers too, musicians, comedians, jugglers, etc.

Furthermore, you can take a ferry ride or a boat cruise from the pier.

Some of these cruises include dinner and dancing as you cruise the

Puget Sound. There are even formal Summer Concerts at the Pier

concerts that feature famous R&B and rock artists such as BB King

and the Indigo Girls. As you can see, there are lots of entertaining

attractions on the waterfront.

Finally, Seattle's Waterfront provides the best people watching

in the city. There are tourists from all over the United States and

even all over the world. On any given day in the summer, you can see

---

Margin labels:

Supporting example

Supporting detail

Supporting example

Concluding sentence

TS

Supporting example

Supporting example
Supporting detail

Supporting example

Supporting detail
Concluding sentence

TS

Supporting example

tourists from the Midwest, from Japan, China, Africa, India, and many other countries from around the world. But not only the tourists come to the Waterfront, locals like it too. You can see whole families out for some fun on the pier or in the arcade; also, you can see couples strolling along the walkway after a romantic dinner for two. You can also see local musicians and street vendors trying to make some money. Some musicians play solo, usually with a guitar or a drum, and some musicians include complete bands, with a singer and sometimes even a whole sound system. All types of people like the waterfront.

    So, next time you go to downtown Seattle, be sure to visit it's waterfront. There is so much to do including eating at great restaurants, shopping, doing activities and watching people.

Supporting example

Concluding sentence

Concluding paragraph

Step 5: Editing

1. Check spelling.

I'm a pretty good speller. But I've been burned by spell-check before. I'll just doublecheck the words I'm not one hundred percent sure of with a dictionary. Also, I'm going to glance through the Commonly Confused Words section of my text (Chapter 28) to see if I have misused any of those.

2. Check word usage, word choices, tone, and style.

I see that I have repeated some words a lot and that some of the words are slang terms. The tone is also too informal. I'll check a thesaurus for synonyms I can use. I used the second person ("you") too much in my essay, so I'll change the point of view to third person. I have quite a few "There are" or "There is" statements or "is" and "has" verbs so I'll try and make them into more active verb constructions. Also, I think now that the title is too broad, so I'll add a subtitle.

3. Check for sentence-level errors.

Now I'll go through the whole paper checking for each of the common errors listed in Step Ten of "A Ten-Step Process for Writing an Essay." (See p. 96.)

The Final Version

Note: All of the changes in this final version have been underlined and annotated.

Allegria 1

Debra Allegria

Professor Edelstein

English 095

23 May 2008

Seattle's Waterfront: Fun and Adventure for All

The Seattle area is full of great things to do. For instance, one of my favorite places to go in Seattle is its downtown waterfront. I always take visiting relatives there too since I like the variety of choices I have when I go there. In fact, Seattle's waterfront in particular offers many things to see and to do. The waterfront offers a great variety of restaurants, shopping, activities, and types of people. *Therefore, the waterfront is an ideal place to spend a full day in Seattle as it provides anything one could want in a perfect Seattle experience.*

Thesis statement

To begin with, Seattle's Waterfront offers a variety of restaurants to suit any palate and any budget. If a person does not have a great deal of money to spend and wants a casual experience, he or she can go to reliable McDonald's on the waterfront. McDonald's offers many full-meal options for under five dollars. For instance, a

Topic sentence

Allegria 2

shopper can get a Big Mac, fries, and a Coke for less than five dollars. Also, the waterfront boasts a famous hotdog stand that is open
all year and has great dogs and Polish sausages for under three
dollars. Moreover, several places along the waterfront sell fish and
chips to go for not very much money. Ivar's is the most famous place
to get fish and chips to go. A hungry visitor can get a full order of
fish and chips for six dollars or less.

If a person wants to go to a fancy restaurant on the waterfront,
then there's a great range. Red Robin features a medium-priced range
menu that offers anything from hamburgers to salads. Most burgers
there, along with unlimited French fries, cost less than eight dollars.
Red Robin also offers a full range of desserts and the best two-dollar
shake in town. If one wants to go even fancier, he or she can try one
of the many nice seafood restaurants along the pier. For instance,
Elliott Bay Fishhouse has fresh salmon and other grilled fish
entrees, ranging from thirteen to twenty dollars, and has a nicer
atmosphere with candles and white tablecloths. Also, Ivar's provides
an indoor restaurant that serves full entrée and salad plates for
about the same range. Both of these restaurants boast a more
romantic atmosphere and feature higher-priced and more elaborate
menu options. Indeed, Seattle's waterfront has any type of dining
experience one could want.

Also, Seattle's waterfront offers great shopping opportunities
with all kinds of merchandise, from kitsch to classy. If a visitor wants
a great spot for souvenirs or little trinkets, he or she can go to Ye
Olde Curiosity Shoppe, a very entertaining place and kind of a
tourist attraction all on its own. In this shop, one can buy anything
from candy, shells, and "Seattle" pens and cups to strange stuff that

[New paragraph started]
Topic sentence

Concluding sentence

Topic sentence

Allegria 3

will amaze one's friends—even gag gifts. For instance, one can get soap that turns friends' hands black when they use it and infamous disappearing ink. If a shopper desires a nicer gift, many clothes and gift shops offer nicer gifts; for instance, the waterfront sports art shops with beautiful Native American carvings and paintings and art galleries that sell to the public; most of these feature local artists and include paintings, carvings, and glassworks. Truly, the

Concluding sentence

waterfront is a place where experienced shoppers can find anything.

Topic sentence

Moreover, the waterfront is a great place to go for activities and entertainment. In the Seattle Aquarium, with all kinds of fish and sea animals, guests can see seals and otters and can touch live sea urchins in an open tank. Also, the Cinemax/Omni Theater shows movies and features an arcade with all kinds of games and prizes, and even a carousel. The carousel is a refurbished, old-fashioned merry-go-round with elaborately painted and decorated horses. Street performers frequent the waterfront too: musicians, comedians, jugglers, etc. Furthermore, one can take a ferry ride or a boat cruise from the pier. Some of these cruises include dinner and dancing as they cruise the Puget Sound. Finally, the summer weather brings Summer Concerts at the Pier, which feature famous R&B and rock artists such as BB King and the Indigo Girls. As you can see, several

Concluding sentence

entertaining attractions exist on the waterfront.

Topic sentence

Finally, Seattle's waterfront provides the best people watching in the city. Tourists from all over the United States and even all over the world visit the waterfront. On any given day in the summer, one can see tourists from the Midwest, from Japan, China, Africa, India, and many other countries from around the world. However, not only

Allegria 4

the tourists come to the waterfront; locals like it too. Whole families come out for some fun on the pier or in the arcade; also, couples regularly stroll along the walkway after a romantic dinner for two. Moreover, local musicians and street vendors are prominent on the waterfront. Some musicians play solo, usually with a guitar or a drum, and some musicians include complete bands, with a singer and sometimes even a whole sound system. All types of people like the waterfront, making it the best spot to be seen and do some people watching.

Concluding sentence

    As you can see, Seattle's waterfront offers the best of all possible spots to squeeze in a full day of activities. No other spot can offer so much in one place, including a wealth of great restaurants, shopping, activities, and people to see.

Restatement of thesis

Each person will have a different experience using the ten-step process, which can also differ from assignment to assignment, but following it will help you write an effective essay and ensure that it contains all the elements of a good essay.

Activity 5-18   More Practice Writing an Essay

Directions: *Choose from the following broad topics, or choose one of your own, to practice using the Building Blocks (Chapter 4) and ten steps to writing an essay.*

Topic choices:

1. Music in advertising
2. Uses for the Internet
3. Traveling to a foreign country
4. Finding a good apartment

5. Riding subway versus riding the bus

Topic of your own: _____

SELF- AND PEER ASSESSMENT OF WRITING

Self and peer assessment of essay drafts lets you evaluate the effectiveness of your writing and go through, step by step, and look at the separate elements that contribute to the success of your essay and achieving your purpose. If you know the criteria used by instructors for grading essays *before* you begin an actual draft, you'll be sure to focus on those elements as you write it; then you can self-assess to see if you addressed those elements well. Finally, you can have your peers (classmates, friends or tutors) critique your essay using the checklist on p. 97.

Essays: Order, Unity, and Coherence

6

THINKING CRITICALLY

Consider the image above and the poem titled "The Blind Men and the Elephant." Then answer the questions that follow.

American poet John Godfrey Saxe (1816–1887) based this poem on a popular fable from India.

The Blind Men and the Elephant

It was six men of Indostan
To learning much inclined,
Who went to see the Elephant
(Though all of them were blind),
That each by observation
Might satisfy his mind.

The First approached the Elephant,
And happening to fall
Against his broad and sturdy side,

At once began to bawl:
"God bless me! but the Elephant
Is very like a wall!"

The Second, feeling of the tusk,
Cried, "Ho! what have we here
So very round and smooth and sharp?
To me 'tis mighty clear
This wonder of an Elephant
Is very like a spear!"

The Third approached the animal,
And happening to take
The squirming trunk within his hands,
Thus boldly up and spake:
"I see," quoth he, "the Elephant
Is very like a snake!"

The Fourth reached out an eager hand,
And felt about the knee.
"What most this wondrous beast is like
Is mighty plain," quoth he;
"'Tis clear enough the Elephant
Is very like a tree!"

The Fifth, who chanced to touch the ear,
Said: "E'en the blindest man
Can tell what this resembles most;
Deny the fact who can
This marvel of an Elephant
Is very like a fan!"

The Sixth no sooner had begun
About the beast to grope,
Than, seizing on the swinging tail
That fell within his scope,
"I see," quoth he, "the Elephant
Is very like a rope!"

And so these men of Indostan
Disputed loud and long,
Each in his own opinion
Exceeding stiff and strong,
Though each was partly in the right,
And all were in the wrong!

1. In your own words, what is the main message of this poem (the moral to the story)?

   _____

2. Can you think of any examples from your own life where your perception has limited the way you have seen the truth of an event or issue? How does this poem and your own experience of perception vs. truth relate to writing an essay?

   _____

   _____

   _____

When writing an essay, it is important to have all the "parts" in the right order. Each element of an essay is like each individual part of the elephant in the poem above: The parts, put together in the right order, create the whole, and you must know each part and see its place in the whole picture to have a full perspective on your ideas and your plan for presenting them.

TYPES OF ORDER

Think about the best order pattern for your purpose. There are several ways to organize an essay. It's important to choose an order of development that best suits your purpose. The order pattern you choose to organize your essay helps your readers follow your ideas and your support for those ideas.

Here are a few of the most effective essay order patterns and some suggestions for when to use them.

Time Order

Cross Reference

See Chapters 7 and 9 on how to write narration and process essays.

Time order, also called *chronological order*, is most often used in narration and process essays. This order pattern is used to tell what happened in the order it happened (narrative) and to explain how to do a step-by-step process (process).

> **Narration time order example:** Yesterday, I went to the store. Then, after the store, I had to stop and get gas for my car. Next, I stopped at the post office to pick up my mail . . .

> **Process time order example:** To make chocolate chip cookies, first you will need to gather all the necessary ingredients. After you have assembled the required ingredients, measure the butter and sugar in a large glass bowl. Next, cream together the sugar and butter to make a smooth paste . . .

Order of Importance

Cross Reference

See Chapters 7, 13, 14, and 15 for descriptions of each of these essay types.

Order of importance is most often used in description, narration, cause and effect, comparison/contrast, or argument essays when the writer wants to emphasize *the most to least important ideas* or *the least to most important ideas*.

> **Most to least important order example:** When we get to Disneyland, there are several rides we just have to ride. We should start with the best so we have enough time to ride our favorites. First, we have to ride the Pirates of the Caribbean. After all, it is the best ride in the park. Next, we should go straight to The Haunted Mansion. Following that, we should go to Space Mountain . . .

> **Least to most important order example:** There are several important things to keep in mind when buying a house. First, find a real estate agent you like. Also, set up tours of the houses you like the look of from the real estate website. It's very important to set up an inspection of the house you are interested in to make sure it is safe and in the condition the seller says it is. Finally, and most important, check that the houses are in your price range by figuring out your finances and loan possibilities before you start looking seriously for a new home.

Note: Refer to the transitions section later in this chapter (p. 117) for more information on how to make your order flow more smoothly.

Spatial Order

Spatial order is used when you are describing a place, like a town, city, or room in your house. Using spatial order helps you describe what something looks like: a messy room, a float in a parade, a neighbor's garden. Spatial order helps create a mental picture for your reader of the space you are describing. For instance, if you were describing your room, you could start from front to back, top to bottom, or side to side. One part at a time, describe the space to give a whole picture.

> **Spatial order example:** Gill's garden was beautiful. Front and center was a pool with a fountain in the shape of a little boy in the middle surrounded by water lilies. Immediately behind the pool was a dark green hedge with a wooden bench in front of it. Rising behind the hedge was a line of graceful willow trees whose long drooping branches brushed the top of the bench.

Cross Reference

See Chapters 7–15 for customized forms of order and patterns of development designed for particular essay types and purposes.

Activity 6-1   Patterns of Order

Directions: *Which order pattern would you choose for each of the following essay topics? Some topics may work with more than one order pattern; if so, pick the best one for this topic.*

1. Finding your way around campus _____
2. Steps for making a peanut butter and jelly sandwich _____
3. How to get the most out of college _____
4. A typical morning for a college student _____
5. The many skills of a great teacher _____
6. How to train a new pet _____
7. The health risks of smoking _____
8. Steps for changing your car's oil _____
9. Reasons we need a stop sign on our street _____
10. A description of our house _____

UNITY AND THE ART OF ACHIEVING COHERENCE WITH TRANSITIONS

Good writing flows smoothly from one point to the next with nothing out of place. When writing an essay, it is important to maintain both **unity** (every detail belongs) and **coherence** (smooth flow from one point to the next). Transitional words, phrases, or sentences provide the bridges needed to keep the flow smooth from sentence to sentence or paragraph to paragraph.

Unity

Unity means that each sentence you've included in your essay helps develop the point you have set out to make. In order to achieve unity, each paragraph must support and develop your essay's thesis statement. Also, within the paragraphs, each sentence must develop or support the topic sentence or controlling idea of that paragraph. For example, which sentence in this paragraph does not belong?

> (1) Italian food is comfort food. (2) To begin with, most Italian food is loaded with carbohydrates, which are fundamental for that feeling of comfort from food. (3) Pasta, a main staple in Italian food, is full of carbohydrates and is satisfying and delicious. (4) Spaghetti, for instance, is one of the most famous Italian pasta dishes. (5) Moreover, lasagna is a delicious pasta dish, and it satisfies the cheese lover too. (6) Enchiladas, though a Mexican dish, are a great comfort dish too. (7) Also, ravioli, one of my favorite Italian specialties, is an excellent comfort food choice. Indeed, most pasta dishes fulfill the belief that Italian food equals comfort food.

Did you spot the sentence that didn't belong in this paragraph? The sentence that does not support the topic sentence (and interferes with the unity of this paragraph) is sentence number 6. Enchiladas are a Mexican dish, and, therefore, this sentence does not support the idea of Italian food as comfort food. Not all unity errors will be this easy to spot. Sometimes, you will find you have changed direction or switched focus in a very subtle way during the process of writing your first draft.

Activity 6-2   Test for Unity

Directions: *Read the following paragraph and underline the two sentences that do not belong (do not directly support and develop the topic sentence). Then explain briefly, on the lines provided, why they don't belong in this paragraph.*

> (1) Taking classes online provides the opportunity for students who work full time or are stay-at-home parents to complete their educational goals. (2) Before distance learning and online class offerings, students had no choice but to physically attend college classes or try to find limited choices for old-fashioned correspondence courses. (3) With the ar-

rival of the Internet age, students with limited schedules or children at home have more opportunities to attend college. (4) For instance, students who work full time can sign up for an online class and "attend" the course on their own schedule. (5) Employers will be happy too with more flexible scheduling hours. (6) Moreover, online classes give parents at home more chances to take college courses without worrying about expensive daycare costs. (7) Stay-at-home moms and dads can take the college courses they need while still being home with their children. (8) Some fathers even choose to be the main at-home parent. (9) The Internet and distance-learning opportunities have made scheduling classes for students who work or who are parents much easier.

Sentences that don't belong: _____

Explain why: _____

_____

_____ ⬤

To check your own writing for unity, go through your entire first draft to make sure that each sentence belongs in each particular paragraph and in the essay as a whole. To help you accomplish this task, ask yourself the following questions:

1. Does every sentence in each paragraph specifically support or develop the topic sentence?

2. Does each paragraph in my essay support my thesis?

3. Are there any sentences in this draft that don't develop my thesis statement?

If you answer no to any of these questions, go back to your essay and revise or delete the sentences and/or paragraphs that don't directly support your thesis or topic sentences.

Coherence and Transitions

Coherence means that every sentence in each paragraph, and each paragraph in an essay, flows smoothly from one point to the next. Coherence relates to the order of development you choose for your paragraph or essay and involves the use of transitions between key sentences and between paragraphs in an essay. **Transitions** are words, phrases, or sometimes even complete sentences that help move the reader smoothly from one point to the next. They point the reader in the direction you want to take them. Transitions are necessary both *within* paragraphs and *between* them. When a transitional word, phrase, or sentence is used to connect one paragraph to the next, the transition can come at the end of the previous paragraph or at the beginning of the next, whichever works best for your purpose and organization.

Here is a list of transitional words or phrases categorized by type for easy use in paragraphs and essays.

TRANSITIONS TO SHOW ADDITION OF ANOTHER POINT

again	but also	in addition	nor
also	equally important	last	plus the fact
and	finally	lastly	secondly
and then	first	likewise	then too
another	further	moreover	thirdly
besides	furthermore	next	too

TRANSITIONS TO SHOW CONTRAST OR A CHANGE IN IDEA

although	even though	instead	on the other side
anyhow	for all that	nevertheless	otherwise
at the same time	however	notwithstanding	regardless
but	in any event	on the contrary	still
despite this	in contrast	on the other hand	yet

TRANSITIONS TO SHOW A COMPARISON

in like manner	in the same way	likewise	similarly

TRANSITIONS TO SHOW SUMMARY OR REPETITION

as has been noted	in closing	in other words	on the whole
as I have said	in conclusion	in short	to conclude
in brief	in essence	in summary	to sum up

TRANSITIONS TO ILLUSTRATE OR GIVE EXAMPLES/SPECIFICS

a few include	essentially	in particular	the following
an example	for example	let us consider	specifically
especially	for instance	the case of	you can see this in

TRANSITIONS TO STRENGTHEN A POINT

basically	indeed	truly	without a doubt
essentially	irrefutably	undeniably	without question

TRANSITIONS TO SHOW RESULT AND/OR CAUSE/EFFECT RELATIONSHIPS

accordingly	consequently	since	therefore
as a result	for this reason	so	thereupon
because	hence	then	thus

TRANSITIONS TO SHOW PURPOSE

all things considered	for this reason	to accomplish	with this in mind
for this purpose	in order to	to this end	with this objective

TRANSITIONS TO SHOW PLACE (USUALLY PREPOSITIONS)

above	beside	inside	outside
across	between	nearer	over
adjacent to	beyond	nearly	there
below	farther	next to	through
beneath	here	opposite	under

TRANSITIONS TO SHOW TIME

after	before	in the meantime	not long after
afterwards	between	later	soon
at last	first	meanwhile	then
at length	immediately	next	while

TRANSITIONS TO SHOW AMOUNT

a great deal	less than	most	smaller
few	many	over	some
greater	more than	several	under

Activity 6-3   Provide Transitions

Directions: *Choose transitions from the tables above, or use a transition of your own, to fill in the blanks below and help this paragraph flow more smoothly.*

Advertisements often convey messages that negatively affect women's self-esteem. _____, advertisements in magazines often depict women as extremely thin. _____, the message is women must be thin to be beautiful. _____, television commercials often depict women in the home using some form of cleaning product. _____, one commercial has a woman dancing romantically with her mop in a perfectly clean kitchen. _____, the message to men and women is that women should do the cleaning. _____, they should enjoy the cleaning. _____, many magazine and television ads push cosmetics and hair products and feature glamorous, heavily made-up women. _____, women feel pressured to buy these products to match the images of the women in these ads. These forms of advertising, _____ , convey messages to women that can hurt their self-worth and perception of themselves. ●

PERFECTING YOUR ESSAY'S ORDER OF DEVELOPMENT

One of the best ways to ensure a well organized essay and an order of development that best illustrates your essay's purpose is to write an outline of your essay. Some writers begin with a rough outline of their paper before they've written a draft. However, even if you didn't *start* with an outline, it is a powerful tool to use *after you have written your first draft* to check and revise the organization and structure of ideas.

Outline Format

An outline helps you to order your thoughts: It creates a plan for your essay's development. It's like a table of contents for each component of your essay. Outlines allow you to order your main ideas and supporting examples and details in the most logical way and, therefore, most effectively develop your essay's purpose.

An outline has a consistent format, with the main ideas placed closest to the far left margin. Then the subpoints, examples, and details used to develop those main ideas are indented; the farther right your ideas are placed, the more specific or detailed the support they provide. If you have four main sections to develop in your essay, you'll have four main ideas. Then you can add as many subpoints, examples, and details as needed for each section to fully develop those ideas. Here are some guidelines for writing an outline.

Guidelines for Writing an Outline

1. Write your thesis statement at the top of the outline, but do not include the general introduction that will come before your thesis statement.

2. List the main ideas (concepts for each topic sentence) that will be developed in the body paragraphs of your essay using Roman numerals (I, II, III, and so on). Use a phrase of just a few words to explain each

main idea, not a complete sentence. Think of these instead as titles for each paragraph of your paper. The main ideas are formatted at the left margin.

3. List the subpoints you will use to support the main idea/topic sentence of each paragraph using capital letters A, B, C, and so on. Use short phrases to represent each subpoint. These subpoints are formatted one tab right from the left margin.

> **Note:** you must have at least two subpoints: If you have an "A," then you must have at least a "B." If you have only one subpoint, then combine it with the main idea phrase or develop a second subpoint.

4. List supporting examples and details below each subpoint. The next level of detail is labeled with numbers (1, 2, 3, and so on). If you have details to illustrate these examples, they are labeled with lowercase letters (a, b, c, and so on). If you have even another level of details to develop those, label them with numbers followed by a single parenthesis [1), 2), 3), and so on]. Each level of detail progressively tabs right.

> **Note:** You must have at least two of each supporting level of information, so if you have a "1," you need at least a "2"; if you have an "a" detail under "1," then you also need a "b." If you don't have a second detail at the same level, create one or wrap the single detail into the previous example.

5. Provide a brief statement of conclusion at the end of your outline.

> **Note:** Check your campus for helpful software that is available for creating outlines in the correct format automatically. These tools and programs make your job easier and ensure that your format is correct.

Sample Outline

Debra Allegria

Professor Edelstein

English 095

20 May 2008

Thesis: Seattle's Waterfront is an ideal place to spend a full day in the city since it provides everything one could want to do for a perfect Seattle experience.

I. Seattle's Waterfront: Restaurants

   A. Affordable restaurants

      1. McDonald's

         a. extra value meals

         b. several meals under $5

      2. fish and chips shop

         a. full meal under $5

         b. outdoor seats/no tipping

   B. Fancy/higher budget restaurants

      1. Red Robin

         a. medium to higher price items

         b. good comfort food

      2. Elliot Bay Fishhouse

         a. higher priced seafood entrees

         b. full view

      3. Ivar's Restaurant

         a. higher priced seafood items

         b. full view

II. Waterfront shopping

   A. Ye Olde Curiosity Shoppe

      1. gags

         a. magic tricks

         b. gag/joke gifts

      2. artwork

         a. carvings

         b. Native American paintings

   B. Street vendors

      1. T-shirts

      2. Seattle mementos

III. Activities and Entertainment

   A. Seattle Aquarium

      1. sea animals

      2. gift shop

   B. Street performers

      1. musicians

      2. comedians

      3. jugglers

   C. Summer concerts

IV. People watching

   A. Tourists

      1. U.S. tourists

      2. International tourists

   B. Local artists and musicians

Conclusion: The waterfront offers the best of all possible spots to squeeze in a full day of activities.

Here are some questions you can ask as you develop your outline to ensure you have thought critically about what you want to say and how you want to say it.

CRITICAL THINKING QUESTIONS TO ASK AS YOU DESIGN YOUR OUTLINE

PURPOSE

1. What is the main point or conclusion I've made about my topic? What **purpose** do I want to convey to my readers? (In the above outline, it would be where to go to experience the full Seattle experience.)

IDEAS

2. What are the main **ideas** and **support** I will use in my paper, and in what order do I want to present them? Which evidence and examples are main examples and which are supporting details?

3. Do I have any claims that may need more support to convince my readers of my point?

4. How will I order my reasons for support and main body paragraphs? What is the best order of development to successfully argue my conclusions and present my evidence?

5. **Analyze** to see if there are there any parts that need to be deleted, expanded upon, or re-arranged.

Finally, use the Outline Critique Form below to self-review or peer review your outline.

Outline Critique Form

1. Does the outline start with a thesis statement?   _____

2. Is the thesis statement an idea or opinion that can be developed through examples and details? Is there a clear message or point being made?   _____

3. Did the author use correct outline format (see the format above for outline rules)?   _____

4. Are the subtopics/sections/categories clear and explained with a short phrase?   _____

5. Are the categories and subpoints detailed enough to be clear but not overly detailed?   _____

6. If there is a "1" or an "A" in a category or subpoint, is it followed by at least one more point ("2" or "B," and so on)?   _____

7. If secondary sources are included in the outline, can you tell how they will be used as support?   _____

Comments and suggestions for revision:

_____

_____

_____

_____

_____

THINKING CRITICALLY

Look at the picture above. Then answer the questions that follow.

1. *Describe* this photograph in your own words using as many specific, descriptive words as possible.

   _____

   _____

2. *Narrate* a short, one-paragraph story about this altar; use your imagination.

   _____

   _____

3. *Argue* for or against whether "Dia de los Muertos" (Day of the Dead) altars such as this one should be created at public schools.

_____

_____

_____

_____

_____

ESSAY MODES

Essay **modes** are types of essays designed to address specific purposes. You can use different modes, or specific patterns of writing, to write about the same topic: It all depends on your purpose and your intended audience. Some essays will benefit from the use of a specific mode or pattern, while others will benefit from a combination of several different modes, and some will do better with no formal structure at all. The dominant mode you choose, the choice to combine modes, or the decision to reject using a specific mode, depends on the purpose of your writing. Engage your critical thinking skills and carefully assess your topic, purpose, and audience to make the best choice.

Whether you choose to use a single mode, combine modes, or not to use mode structures at all will be based on several key factors:

1. Your instructor's assignment or specific request for a mode essay
2. The purpose of your essay and decisions you make for how to structure it in the most efficient way
3. Your intended audience and the best combination of modes to illustrate and develop your intended purpose

CHOOSING THE RIGHT APPROACH

All essays should have an **expository purpose,** a point they wish to explain. You have a choice in how you structure your essay, and there are specialized modes you can use or combine to do this. Review the critical thinking tools in Chapter 1 to figure out your essay's purpose and to choose the best way to organize and develop that purpose. Although each mode explained in the following chapters has a specialized purpose and format, they can all be used to make an *argument* or *analytical point*. Many professional essays feature a dominant mode approach but also tap into one to three other modes to develop their purpose. For instance, in "Supersize Me," on pages 456–459, the author uses example and illustration as the dominant mode, but he also uses narration, cause and effect analysis, and argument to develop his purpose. There are nine commonly used essay modes:

Narration:	Telling a story using narrative details and description (see Chapter 7).
Description:	The art of using vivid details to paint a picture with words (see Chapter 8).
Process:	Describing a step-by-step process or a series of steps one must take to accomplish a task (see Chapter 9).
Classification:	Sometimes also called "classification and division." Categorizing people, things, or concepts into particular groups in order to draw conclusions about them (see Chapter 10).
Definition:	Defining an item or a concept (see Chapter 11).
Example and illustration:	Providing examples in order to illustrate an idea or set of ideas (see Chapter 12).
Cause and effect:	The relationship between causes (reasons) and effects (results) (see Chapter 13).
Comparison and contrast:	Similarities and differences between two subjects or among several subjects (see Chapter 14).
Argument or persuasion:	Persuading an audience to agree with a particular viewpoint or arguing for a change in the status quo (see Chapter 15).

Some essay assignments will call for one of the above modes, and some will require you to use a combination of modes to complete your purpose. Many times your essay will have a dominant mode, a particular approach such as argument, but will still tap into several other modes for support, such as narration, examples, comparison and contrast, and so on. All the essay modes follow a simple template for developing a purpose:

Cross Reference
Review Chapters 4–6 for a detailed review of basic essay structure.

1. They begin with an introductory paragraph that introduces the topic and presents the purpose of the essay in an analytical thesis statement.
2. They develop the thesis statement with body paragraphs using clear topic sentences and supporting examples and details.
3. They end with a concluding paragraph that restates or sums up the main purpose and sometimes comments on it.

THINKING CRITICALLY

Look at the photograph above. Then on a separate piece of paper, write a brief story explaining what is going on in the picture. Use your imagination, and include as many specific details about the situation and the children as you can. Answer the questions that follow.

1. What did you focus on when you wrote the story?

   _____

   _____

2. What effect did looking at a concrete (actual) image have on the way you wrote your story and the details you included?

   _____

   _____

NARRATION ESSAYS

In a **narrative essay,** you recount an event, story, or series of events in order to explain some insight or truth gained from an experience. Although some narration essays are less formal and involve a straightforward telling of a story or event, most narrative essay assignments include a more analytical purpose: They have a point, a plot, a lesson, or a message to impart to the reader through telling a story or recounting an event and framing it with analysis.

Critical Thinking and Narration

It is the *inclusion of a lesson* that distinguishes the expository narrative essay from a merely narrative description of events. Expository narrative essays feature a lesson or clear message, implied or directly stated, that is conveyed to the reader through the recounting of events. This analytical purpose is stated in the first paragraph of the essay in the *thesis* (or *purpose statement*). This lesson or message is then restated in the conclusion as well.

Because analytical, or expository, narrative essays have a more intentional purpose, they require more thought than an essay that merely recounts an event. You must engage your critical thinking skills and figure out what

Applying Critical Thinking

PURPOSE   IDEAS   SUPPORT   ASSUMPTIONS BIASES   CONCLUSIONS   POINT OF VIEW   ANALYSIS

In order to determine your **purpose** for writing—the message you want to convey in your narrative essay—use the following questions to help you clarify what you learned from the experience you are writing about and what point you want to convey based on what you learned:

1. What is my **analysis** of the story? What have I learned or what do I want my readers to learn from the story I am telling?

2. What is my plan for my narrative? What point do I want to make through telling this story? How will I convey that message in my essay?

3. What **ideas** will I include? What **support** (facts, examples, evidence) can I include to illustrate and explain the point of my narrative?

you want to say about the event, how you want to say it, how you'll organize your ideas, and how you'll weave in analysis and commentary about the actual event.

BEFORE WRITING A NARRATIVE ESSAY

Before you begin to write a narrative essay on an assigned topic, or one you have chosen, start by asking yourself these questions:

1. What did I learn from the experience?
2. What do I want my readers to learn or understand after reading about the event I experienced or witnessed?
3. How can I re-create the event vividly in my readers' heads? What examples and details should I use to re-create the story?
4. How should I organize my paragraphs after my introduction and thesis, and how can I move smoothly from one event or detail to the next?
5. What's the best way to conclude my essay?

Answering these questions will lead you to an expository thesis statement, help you decide which examples and details to include for support, and give you a general idea of how you want to organize and conclude your essay.

Activity 7-1   Outlining a Specific Event

Directions: *Think of an event you witnessed or a specific happy or sad event in your own life. Then, answer the following questions about that event.*

1. What happened? (Describe briefly in one paragraph.)

_____

_____

_____

_____

_____

2. What did you learn about yourself and/or others that day, and why?

_____

_____

_____

3. What would you want your readers to understand after reading about the event? _____

_____

_____

4. What specific details and examples could you use to re-create the event and vividly tell the story? _____

_____

_____

5. What critical thinking tools could you use to plan, support, organize, and develop the purpose of the narration? _____

_____

_____ ⬤

WRITING A NARRATIVE ESSAY

The structure of a narrative essay is usually less formal than for other types of essays. Often the essay tells a story about an event, or series of events, in chronological order, the order in which they occurred.

The *point of view* in narrative essays is usually *first person*. Therefore, it is perfectly appropriate to use the word "I" throughout a narrative essay. For example:

> "When I was 12 years old, I learned a valuable lesson about the dangers of playing with fire. It all started when my brother and I found a lighter in our back yard."

Cross Reference
See page 600 for more about point of view.

You should develop your narrative essay using *descriptive details*. Include specific details about the setting and detailed descriptions of the people and their actions. Choose words that conjure up vivid images, not vague descriptors like "beautiful."

Vague descriptors: The cake was *beautiful* and looked *delicious*.

Revised: The wedding cake was three layers high and snowy white, covered with fluffy whipped cream and delicate pastel pink roses made of butter cream frosting.

Use real dialogue, as far as you can remember it from the event, to make the scene(s) come alive on paper. When you use *dialogue* in a narration essay, it serves as a great way to provide supporting details in the body paragraphs to help develop the message or overall *expository purpose* of your essay. For information on how to use dialogue correctly, see page 138 later in this chapter.

The chart below provides a brief overview of the structure of a narrative essay.

BASIC STRUCTURE FOR A NARRATION ESSAY

PURPOSE

Introductory Paragraph	**Sets up background** for the event or story. **Thesis statement**: A statement that describes what you are trying to explain, show, prove, or argue in your narrative essay. What you learned from the experience.

IDEAS

SUPPORT

ANALYSIS

Body Paragraphs (Two to five, depending on assignment and purpose)	**Develop** the narration of the event using time order. **Use transitions** within and between paragraphs to emphasize time changes and/or significant turns in the narrative. **Provide concrete details** and description. **Use as many senses as possible** in your description (sight, sound, smell, touch, and taste). **Add dialogue** when appropriate. **Add commentary and analysis** about the details and descriptions to help develop the expository purpose/thesis statement. **Explain what you were thinking and feeling** as the events took place.

CONCLUSIONS

Concluding Paragraph	**Sum up and re-emphasize** the thesis: the **lesson learned** and message of the story you've told in your narration essay.

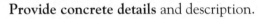

STRUCTURING A NARRATION ESSAY

Topic

If you have been assigned a narrative topic by your instructor, be sure to read the assignment carefully to determine the requirements of the assignment and how to best create your thesis and analytical purpose. If you are choosing your own topic, prewrite about possible events using a technique, or techniques, that work for you in order to generate a topic and details to include in your essay. Focus on what happened and what you learned from it. Many events stand out in people's memories as pivotal points in their lives.

A Few Topic Possibilities

Here is a list of some topics you could write a narration essay about: the birth of a child; the happiest day of your life; an accident; a tragedy; an embarrassing event; your first day on a job; the death of a loved one; the saddest day of your life; a surprise; a celebration; a proud moment; your first day at college.

Thesis Statements

The thesis statement in a narrative essay contains the lesson learned from the event. Engage your critical thinking skills to figure out why the event or story you've chosen to write about stood out to you. What can readers learn from your experience? If you have been assigned a specific narrative essay task, be sure to include key words from the assignment to fulfill the assignment's purpose. If you are generating your own topic and purpose, be sure to use the prewriting techniques from Chapter 5 to come up with ideas, details, and a purpose for telling a story about this event. For instance, if you decided to write about the death of someone you loved, you'd need to explain how you felt and what you learned about yourself, about the nature of life, and so on. Use your critical thinking and analysis skills to explain the significance of the event. Also, be sure to look back at the information on thesis statements in Chapters 4 and 5.

The easiest way to generate a meaningful thesis statement for your narrative essay is to begin with the event that is your topic, come up with a point you want to convey to your readers about the event, and then create a thesis statement that directly states the conclusion you've come to about what you learned that day. Here are some examples of that process:

Topic = My vacation to Italy

A point I want to convey = How I learned to be flexible and open minded

> **Thesis:** Last year, during my vacation to Italy, I learned to not expect everything to be the same as it is in my country and that I need to be open minded, flexible, and respectful when I travel to other countries.

Topic = Trying out for the football team

A point I want to convey = How it felt when I didn't get picked and dealing with that.

> **Thesis:** When I tried out for the football team this fall and didn't get picked, I learned a lesson about humility and carrying on.

Topic = The birth of my child

A point I want to convey = Changing priorities

Thesis: The day my daughter was born, my priorities changed completely.

Activity 7-2   Creating Thesis Statements

Directions: *For each of the following narrative topics, create a one-sentence thesis statement. Make sure the thesis statement has a clear message or lesson to convey about what you learned from the experience.*

1. **Topic:** My earliest memory

    Thesis statement: _____

    _____

2. **Topic:** My first experience with death or illness

    Thesis statement: _____

    _____

3. **Topic:** The happiest day of my life

    Thesis statement: _____

    _____

4. **Topic:** The first time I [choose an event such as "drove a car"]

    Thesis statement: _____

    _____

5. **Topic:** The most embarrassing thing that ever happened to me

    Thesis statement: _____

    _____

Introductory Paragraph

Begin your narrative essay with a general introduction to draw the reader in and set up the event you will be recounting. You may need to provide some background information to contextualize the event and its importance. End the introductory paragraph with your thesis statement.

Body Paragraphs

Body paragraphs in a narrative essay develop details and description to re-count an event vividly and support the purpose for telling the story in the first place. Often, the topic sentences in narrative essays are less formal or analyt-ical than in other types of essays. Topic sentences in narration essays often set up the next stage in a sequence of events using a clear time order and transi-tions. Sometimes, though, a topic sentence in a narrative essay can be a more traditional analytical statement that you develop with examples and details. For instance, for the thesis related to traveling to Italy, you could have topic sentences that are analytical setups for each point, or you could use time and event topic sentences that set up the next stage of what happened in the event you are writing about. For example:

> **Thesis:** Last year, during my vacation to Italy, I learned to not ex-pect everything to be the same as it is in my country and that I need to be open minded, flexible, and respectful when I travel to other countries.
>
> **Analytical statement topic sentence for this thesis:** First, I learned that day that I need to be open minded when traveling outside my own country.
>
> **Time and event topic sentence for the same thesis:** In the morning, I encountered a situation that made me rethink my previous beliefs.

Activity 7-3 Creating Topic Sentences

Directions: *Choose one of the thesis statements you developed in Activity 7-2 and write two possible topic sentences that could set up two body paragraphs in support of that thesis.*

Thesis statement: _____

Topic sentence 1:

_____

_____

Topic sentence 2:

_____

_____

Activity 7-4   Providing Examples and Details

Directions: *Now, using the two topic sentences you created in Activity 7-3, provide a specific example and a supporting detail for each.*

Topic sentence 1:

_____

_____

Supporting detail to demonstrate/develop the example:

_____

_____

Topic sentence 2:

_____

_____

Supporting detail to demonstrate/develop the example:

_____

_____

Activity 7-5   Abstract to Specific

Directions: *Translate the following abstract descriptive words bolded in each sentence into concrete, specific descriptions of the thing or person in the sentence.*

Example: It was a **big** house.
The house was three stories high and had a three-car garage, a wraparound porch, and a one-acre lawn.

1. She is a **beautiful** woman.

_____

_____

2. It was an **awesome** action scene in the movie.

_____

3. Her dress was **indescribable**.

_____

_____

4. The crowd was **unbelievable**.

_____

_____

5. The party was **fantastic**.

_____

_____ ◯

When you recount an event in time order, be sure to include transitional words and phrases to move from one point in time to another. Here are some common transitions used to convey time order:

TRANSITIONS TO SHOW TIME

after	before	in the meantime	not long after
afterwards	between	later	soon
at last	first	meanwhile	then
at length	immediately	next	while

"*After* we returned from the hospital, I went straight to bed."

"*Next*, my husband went to pick up the kids."

"*Later*, we showed them their new baby brother."

See Chapter 6 (pages 118–119) for other transitions commonly used with narration, including those that show addition of a point, summary, examples, purpose, or place.

Concluding Paragraph

The concluding paragraph for a narration essay is basic: Restate the thesis statement, focusing on the purpose for recounting the event. Be sure not to use the same sentence you used in your introductory paragraph, though. Explain what you learned from the experience and reiterate the purpose required by the specific assignment (if there is one).

Activity 7-6   Writing a Conclusion

Directions: *Using the thesis, topic sentences, and examples you chose for the last three activities, write a three- to five-sentence conclusion for the topic as if you had written the entire essay.*

_____

_____

_____

_____

DIALOGUE

As discussed earlier in this chapter, dialogue can play an important part in a narrative essay. Here are some tips to keep in mind when you include dialogue in a narrative essay.

Tips for Correct Use of Dialogue in Narration Essays

1. **Use tags and quotation marks.** When you use dialogue, you need a tag to indicate who is speaking and quotation marks around the words they are saying.

> **Tag:** Bob said,
>
> **Quotation Marks:** "I have to leave this party early."
>
> **Used Together:** Bob said, "I have to leave this party early."

Tag placement can also come in the middle or at the end of the dialogue:

> "Today," **Bob said**, "is the first day of the rest of my life."
>
> "Today is the first day of the rest of my life," **Bob said**.

Cross Reference

See page 587 for more about quotation marks.

2. **Use correct punctuation.** Start sentences of dialogue within quotation marks with a capital letter.

> Andrea sighed, "Yes, I know it's time to leave."

Punctuation goes inside the quotation marks (except when using in-text citation in documented papers).

> "The key point," Dominic said, "is to listen first."

3. Tab (indent five spaces) every time you switch speakers in dialogue.

> Mary asked Bob, "Will you change jobs too?"
> "Yes," Bob responded, "I will."
> "And how will you afford the rent until you get settled?" Mary asked sharply, unable to mask her concern.
> "I'll just figure it out as I go along," Bob responded, shaking his head and smiling at Mary's worried frown.

4. Weave descriptions of the characters and their actions into blocks of dialogue. When you have blocks of dialogue in your essay, weave in descriptions of the characters and their movements or actions as they speak. Create a "movie" of the scene by including details of what they are saying and what they are doing as they say it. Again, the key to good narrative writing is concrete description. Look again at the dialogue exchange between Mary and Bob above in tip 3 for an example of weaving description into dialogue.

5. Don't let the dialogue take over. Use dialogue as a supporting detail in your essay, not as the main vehicle for imparting your story and your story's message. Be sure to *frame your dialogue with analysis*, the realizations you came to and what you were feeling and thinking as the words were said during the incident—always re-emphasize your *analytical purpose*.

> She screamed, "No, I refuse to leave. I can't. I won't!"
> Until that moment, I hadn't realized how hard it was for her to leave the house in which she had spent her entire life.

Activity 7-7   Writing Dialogue

Directions

1. *On a separate sheet of paper, write a short dialogue between two people. Include at least two turns speaking for each person. You can use an actual dialogue that occurred between you and someone else (as best as you can remember it), or you can make up a dialogue between two fictional characters.*

2. *Be sure to include tags, start a new paragraph whenever you switch speakers, and include some physical motion or description of the characters as they speak. Review the tips on using dialogue for help.* ●

Use the following critique form to check for the basics in your narration essay draft.

Narration Essay Critique Form

Use the following critique form to check for the basics in a narrative essay draft.

Overall   Done well   Needs work

1. Does the essay tell a story using description that has a clear **purpose** (lesson(s) learned from the experience)?   _____   _____

2. Does the essay use time order in the body paragraphs?   _____   _____

3. Are the paragraphs broken up well and are they about the right length?   _____   _____

Introduction

4. Is the title interesting and in the correct format?   _____   _____

5. Is there a general introduction that gives the background for the story (the events that led up to the event/day described)?   _____   _____

6. Is there a clear thesis statement that explains the message of the story being told—the lesson learned or expository purpose?   _____   _____

Body

7. Do the **ideas** in the body paragraphs develop the story logically and flow smoothly?   _____   _____

8. Are transitions used between and, when needed, within the paragraphs?   _____   _____

9. Do the body paragraphs include **support** and descriptive details that enhance the story?   _____   _____

10. Does the writer use as many sensory details as possible in the description of what happened and how it made the writer feel?   _____   _____

11. Does the body of the paper include some dialogue to bring the action to life?   _____   _____

12. Is **analysis** woven throughout the body to emphasize the significance of the story and develop the thesis of the lesson(s) learned from the event? Are critical thinking tools engaged?   _____   _____

Conclusion

13. Does the **concluding** paragraph sum up the story with an analytical frame that reemphasizes the introductory paragraph and thesis, without adding new ideas?   _____   _____

Editing

14. Circle the following errors you think you see in this draft: spelling, fragments, run-ons/comma splices, commas, semicolon/colon use, pronoun agreement, reference fault errors, parallelism, apostrophe use, verb use/tense, and passive voice construction. (See the handbook section of the text for help in identifying and correcting these errors)

15. Other types of grammar or sentence-level errors:

_____

Comments:

_____

_____

COMPLEMENTARY MODES FOR NARRATION ESSAYS

When writing a narration essay, you can tap into several other modes described in the following chapters that combine well to create a powerful narration.

- **Description:** Description is essential in narration for adding concrete details and vivid description.
- **Illustration and example:** Most good narration essays include specific illustration and examples to develop the purpose of the writing.
- **Process:** Process focuses on narrating a series of steps to accomplish something and can be used to narrate a particular ritual or process.
- **Cause and effect:** You can describe an event in detail and employ cause and effect analysis to look at the consequences of the actions that take place.
- **Comparison/contrast:** A great way to narrate something is to compare it to or contrast it with another event.
- **Argument:** Sometimes your reason for narrating an event in detail is to persuade your readers to learn a particular lesson or feel a particular way: You are combining argument techniques within your narration.

SAMPLE STUDENT ESSAY

The dominant mode used in this student's paper is narration. Look for other modes used in this essay, such as description, illustration and example, and cause and effect analysis (marked in the essay).

Grant 1

Jamie Grant

Professor Nolan

English 100

20 April 2008

Learning Through Loss

A few years ago, my beloved grandmother, Belle, died after a

sudden and severe illness. At first I was devastated by the loss.

Thesis statement   However, after a while, I found that I could honor her life by living

my life based on her example of keeping our family connected and

being generous, and by appreciating my life and my family while I

can because life is short and therefore precious.

Topic sentence   My grandmother was beautiful to me both inside and out. She

was a tiny woman who was somewhat hunched over, her back round

from osteoporosis. Her face was lined, and the backs of her hands

were spotted and shiny, the skin fragile and paper-like. Her hair was

a stunning silver and soft and wispy. She was also the best and

Concluding sentence   wisest person I've ever known. Through her life and my times with

her, she taught me the importance of family and the importance of

giving to others.

Topic sentence   Our family has always been close, and my grandmother was

the matriarch who kept our family connected and whose life was a

model for all of us. She actively invited all of her grandchildren,

including me and my brother, to visit regularly. My brother and I

would spend long summers at my grandmother's lake property. She

made sure that my parents sent us to visit, and she invited our

cousins who we rarely saw over for visits while we were there; she

believed that connecting with family is a vital and active process.

Concluding sentence   She told us regularly that nothing is more important than family.

Topic sentence   Furthermore, my grandmother gave to her community. She

volunteered for the local Red Cross, and she helped with the local

Grant 2

food bank every week. Once, when I was eight years old and visiting her, I went with her to help give out food to the needy. I asked her, "Why do you do this every week, Grandma, even when you are tired?"

"It's important to give back to your community, to do something selfless for the good of others without expecting something in return," she said. She then winked at me as she passed her rough fingers through her silver hair.

"Oh," I said, knitting my brow in concentration. Even though I was young, I remember thinking about how wise and generous she was. Now that I'm older and she is gone, I appreciate her true wisdom and admirable character even more.

Concluding sentence

A week prior to her death, my brother and I visited her at the lake property and had a special time as usual. I didn't know it then, but that would be the last time I saw her. She became severely ill a few days later and was taken to the hospital. On September 21, 2005, at five a.m., we got a call from her doctor who told us she had passed away. We were all shocked and heartbroken. Though she was ill, we never thought she would pass away that soon. I had never experienced death before, and I didn't really know what to do. I was sad and grieving at first, but I began to understand that my grandmother had had a full life, and that she could live on in our thoughts and in our actions. I could become the kind of charitable person she was. I could help keep our family close in her absence. In addition, I began to understand that life is short and that I need to cherish my family and my life now, like my grandmother did.

Topic sentence

The death of my grandmother taught me to appreciate my life and my loved ones and to live a life that gives to others. Though she is gone and I'm sad for the loss of her physical presence, I keep her in my heart and thoughts, and I use her model of love of family and giving to others to be a better person in my life.

Restatement of thesis

This student's draft has a good basic narrative structure and organization and a strong message or lesson learned. This draft also includes some dialogue. The next draft would need more descriptive details and concrete images of the grandmother and the setting. Also, the essay would be stronger with more examples, sentence variety, and changes in style and vocabulary.

Activity 7-8   Thinking Critically About the Student Essay

Directions: *Analyze the essay to identify the features and details characteristic of the narration mode. Mark them on the essay. Then, reread the essay, and make a list of specific revisions you would make to correct any problems with content, organization, transitions, and style.* ●

PROFESSIONAL NARRATION ESSAY

Only Daughter

Sandra Cisneros

Sandra Cisneros, born in Chicago in 1954, was the only daughter raised in a Mexican-American family with six brothers. She has a B.A. in English from Loyola University and an M.F.A. in creative writing from the University of Iowa. Her first book, *The House on Mango Street* (1984), features short vignettes related to Latina women in America. Later publications include *My Wicked, Wicked Ways* (1987), *Woman Hollering Creek* (1991), and *The Future is Mestizo: Life Where Cultures Meet* (2000). "Only Daughter" is an essay first published in *Glamour*.

1   Once, several years ago, when I was just starting out my writing career, I was asked to write my own contributor's note for an anthology. I wrote: "I am the only daughter in a family of six sons. *That* explains everything."

2   Well, I've thought that ever since, and yes, it explains a lot to me, but for the reader's sake I should have written: "I am the only daughter in a *Mexican* family of six sons." Or even: "I am the only daughter of a Mexican father and a Mexican-American mother." Or: "I am the only daughter of a working-class family of nine." All of these had everything to do with who I am today.

3   I was/am the only daughter and *only* a daughter. Being an only daughter in a family of six sons forced me by circumstance to spend a lot of time by myself because my brothers felt it beneath them to play with a *girl* in public. But that aloneness, that loneliness, was good for a would-be writer—it allowed me time to think and think, to imagine, to read and prepare myself.

4   Being only a daughter for my father meant my destiny would lead me to become someone's wife. That's what he believed. But when I was in the fifth grade and shared my plans for college with him, I was sure he understood. I remember my father saying, *"Que bueno, mi'ja,* that's good." That meant a lot to me, especially since my brothers thought the idea hilarious. What I didn't realize was that my father thought college was good for girls—good for finding a husband. After four years in college and two more in graduate school, and still no husband, my father shakes his head even now and says I wasted all that education.

5   In retrospect, I'm lucky my father believed daughters were meant for husbands. It meant it didn't matter if I majored in something silly like English. After all, I'd find a nice professional eventually, right? This allowed me the liberty to putter about embroidering my little poems and stories without my father interrupting with so much as a "What's that you're writing?"

6   But the truth is, I wanted him to interrupt. I wanted my father to understand what it was I was scribbling, to introduce me as "My only daughter, the writer." Not as "This is my only daughter. She teaches." *Es maestra— teacher.* Not even *profesora.*

7   In a sense, everything I have ever written has been for him, to win his approval even though I know my father can't read English words, even though my father's only reading includes the brown-ink *Esto* sports magazines from Mexico City and the bloody *¡Alarma!* magazines that feature yet another sighting of *La Virgen de Gaudalupe* on a tortilla or a wife's revenge on her philandering husband by bashing his skull in with a *molcajete* (a kitchen mortar made of volcanic rock). Or the *fotonovelas,* the little picture paperbacks with tragedy and trauma erupting from the characters' mouths in bubbles.

8   A father represents, then, the public majority. A public who's disinterested in reading, and yet one whom I am writing about and for, and privately trying to woo.

9   When we were growing up in Chicago, we moved a lot because of my father. He suffered bouts of nostalgia. Then we'd have to let go of our flat, store the furniture with mother's relatives, load the station wagon with baggage and bologna sandwiches and head south. To Mexico City.

10   We came back, of course. To yet another Chicago flat, another Chicago neighborhood, another Catholic school. Each time, my father would seek

out the parish priest in order to get a tuition break, and complain or boast: "I have seven sons."

11   He meant *siete hijos,* seven children, but he translated it "sons." "I have seven sons." To anyone who would listen. The Sears Roebuck employee who sold us the washing machine. The short-order cook where my father ate his ham-and-eggs breakfasts. "I have seven sons." As if he deserved a medal from the state.

12   My papa. He didn't mean anything by the mistranslation, I'm sure. But somehow I could feel myself being erased. I'd tug my father's sleeve and whisper: "Not seven sons. Six! and one *daughter.*"

13   When my oldest brother graduated from medical school, he fulfilled my father's dream that we study hard and use this—our heads, instead of this—our hands. Even now my father's hands are thick and yellow, stubbed by a history of hammer and nails and twine and coils and springs. "Use this," my father said, tapping his head, "and not this," showing us those hands. He always looked tired when he said it.

14   Wasn't college an investment? And hadn't I spent all those years in college? And if I didn't marry, what was it all for? Why would anyone go to college and then choose to be poor? Especially someone who has always been poor.

15   Last year, after ten years of writing professionally, the financial rewards started to trickle in. My second National Endowment for the Arts Fellowship. A guest professorship at the University of California, Berkeley. My book, which sold to a major New York publishing house.

16   At Christmas, I flew home to Chicago. The house was throbbing, same as always; hot *tamales* and sweet *tamales* hissing in my mother's pressure cooker, and everybody—my mother, six brothers, wives, babies, aunts, cousins—talking too loud and at the same time, like in a Fellini film, because that's just how we are.

17   I went upstairs to my father's room. One of my stories had just been translated into Spanish and published in an anthology of Chicano writing, and I wanted to show it to him. Ever since he recovered from a stroke two years ago, my father likes to spend his leisure hours horizontally. And that's how I found him, watching a Pedro Infante movie on Galavision and eating rice pudding.

18   There was a glass filled with milk on the bedside table. There were several vials of pills and balled Kleenex. And on the floor, one black sock and a plastic urinal that I didn't want to look at but looked at anyway. Pedro Infante was about to burst into song, and my father was laughing.

19   I'm not sure if it was because my story was translated into Spanish, or because it was published in Mexico, or perhaps because the story dealt with Tepeyac, the *colonia* my father was raised in and the house he grew

up in, but at any rate, my father punched the mute button on his remote control and read my story.

20 I sat on the bed next to my father and waited. He read it very slowly. As if he were reading each line over and over. He laughed at all the right places and read lines he liked out loud. He pointed and asked questions: "Is this So—and—so?" "Yes," I said. He kept reading.

21 When he was finally finished, after what seemed like hours, my father looked up and asked: "Where can we get more copies of this for the relatives?"

Reading Reflection Questions

1. What are the direct or indirect (implied) messages in this story?

_____

_____

_____

2. What does Sandra Cisneros mean by her statement, "I was/am the only daughter and *only* a daughter" (paragraph 3)?

_____

_____

3. In paragraph 2, Cisneros adds details to her self-description of being one daughter among six sons. Name one of the details. What effect does her including these details have on you as a reader?

_____

_____

_____

Objective Questions

4. T/F _____ Cisneros doesn't feel there are any advantages to being a daughter.

5. T/F _____ Her father didn't want her to go to college.

6. T/F _____ Her father often announces that he has seven sons (not specifying that one of his children is a female).

7. List two examples of details Cisneros includes in this essay that illustrate how she felt treated differently by her father because she is a daughter.

_____

_____

Checking Vocabulary

Define the following in your own words, or provide a dictionary definition if you don't know the word.

8. retrospect: _____

9. philandering: _____

10. vials: _____

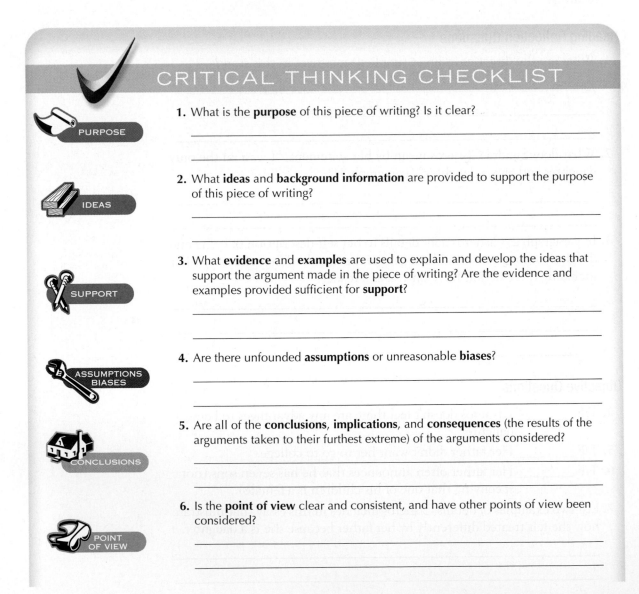

CRITICAL THINKING CHECKLIST

PURPOSE

1. What is the **purpose** of this piece of writing? Is it clear?

_____

_____

IDEAS

2. What **ideas** and **background information** are provided to support the purpose of this piece of writing?

_____

_____

SUPPORT

3. What **evidence** and **examples** are used to explain and develop the ideas that support the argument made in the piece of writing? Are the evidence and examples provided sufficient for **support**?

_____

_____

ASSUMPTIONS BIASES

4. Are there unfounded **assumptions** or unreasonable **biases**?

_____

_____

CONCLUSIONS

5. Are all of the **conclusions**, **implications**, and **consequences** (the results of the arguments taken to their furthest extreme) of the arguments considered?

_____

_____

POINT OF VIEW

6. Is the **point of view** clear and consistent, and have other points of view been considered?

_____

_____

7. Using these critical thinking tools, **analyze** the overall structure of this essay and the strength of the author's arguments, ideas, and support. Was he or she successful in accomplishing the purpose? Why or why not?

_____

_____

Essay Assignments

1. Write an essay using the thesis statement, topic sentences, supporting examples, and concluding paragraph you wrote about in the activities in this chapter.

2. Write an analytical essay about an incident that happened to you (or that you witnessed) that had a significant impact on you. Describe what happened using specific details and explain the impact. What lesson did you learn that day (about yourself, others, our culture, other)?

   a) The organization for this essay involves a general introduction that explains the incident briefly and includes a thesis statement, which tells exactly what lesson(s) you learned from the experience.

   b) The body paragraphs should use time order to tell what happened. Be sure to include some dialogue to make the event come alive for your readers; follow the tips for using dialogue correctly earlier in this chapter.

   c) When describing the incident, include specific details and descriptions, using as many senses as possible (sight, sound, touch, smell, taste). Review Chapters 4, 5, and 6 for essay writing basics and the writing process.

   d) In the conclusion, sum up the lesson(s) you learned and how you feel now about the incident.

   After you finish your first draft of this essay, use the narrative essay critique form to check for the basics. You can also have a classmate or friend check your draft using the checklist. Then review your essay.

3. Write a narrative essay about your first day of college.

4. Write a narrative essay about your first day on a job.

5. Write a narrative essay about an event that taught you something about yourself that you hadn't realized before.

6. Write a narrative essay about an occurrence related to losing trust in someone.

7. Write a narrative essay about a complex or difficult situation and how you got through it.

8

Description

"Two Part Girl," mixed media, Cindy Small.

THINKING CRITICALLY

Look at the picture above. Then answer the questions that follow.

1. Describe this mixed media piece of art in your own words using specific details that include colors, shapes, contrasts, and content.

   _____

   _____

2. Imagine how this piece feels. Add description of the texture and feel of this piece as you imagine it.

   _____

   _____

3. Why do you think concrete description is such an important part of written communication skills?

_____

_____

4. Provide some examples of when you would need to write specific descriptions in writing (school and career related).

_____

_____

5. List the kinds of descriptions and categories you can include when describing a thing, place, or person (for example, shape, color).

_____

_____

DESCRIPTION ESSAYS

Description essays describe people, places and settings, things, or whole narrative scenes using as many of the senses as possible—_sight, sound, touch, smell, and taste_—and as many concrete, descriptive words as possible.

Critical Thinking and Description

Like all essays, descriptive essays should have a clear purpose: to inform, to narrate, to convince your readers to do something or believe something, and so on. For instance, you could describe a particular computer system in order to convince your readers that it is the best buy when shopping for a new computer.

BEFORE WRITING A DESCRIPTIVE ESSAY

Before you begin to write a descriptive essay on an assigned topic, or one you have chosen, start by asking yourself these questions:

1. What exactly am I describing?

2. What kind of language and details should I include to best describe the object, place, or person I am describing?

3. How should I organize my paragraphs after my introduction and thesis, and how can I move smoothly from one descriptive detail to the next?

4. Why am I writing this description? What is my purpose for describing this person, place, or thing? What do I want my readers to learn or understand from reading this description?

5. How should I conclude this essay?

Answering these questions will lead you to an expository thesis statement, help you determine which language and details will provide vivid description and images for support, and give you a general idea of how you want to organize your essay.

Applying Critical Thinking

| PURPOSE | IDEAS | SUPPORT | ASSUMPTIONS BIASES | CONCLUSIONS | POINT OF VIEW | ANALYSIS |

Specific, or concrete, details and images provide important **support** in a descriptive essay. Use the following tips to help you write clear, vivid descriptions:

1. Choose words that conjure vivid images, not vague descriptors like "pretty" or "nice."

> **Vague descriptors:** She had a pretty face and nice hair.
>
> **Revised:** Her face was oval and pleasantly rosy, and her hair was sleek and golden.

2. Use words related to the senses (sight, hearing, touch, taste, and smell) when you describe a person, place or thing to create a picture in your reader's mind. For instance, in describing a room, include visual details (light streaming through the window), sounds (wind in the trees outside), taste (if possible—like a taste in the air), smells (of clean laundry), touch (the texture of a blanket), and the overall atmospheric feel.

3. Use similes (comparisons of one thing to another that begin with the words "like" or "as") or metaphors (comparisons in which one thing is described as being another thing). For instance, you can use a simile to help someone get a better image of your grandmother's hands by writing,

> My grandmother's hands were *as rough as a lizard's shedding skin.*

Or you can use a metaphor to describe your grandmother's hands:

> Her hands were *gentle spiders* playing with the edge of the quilt.

Be careful, though, not to resort to common clichés in your description such as, "He looked like a Greek god." Such phrases do not create vivid images because they are overused.

Cross Reference
See p. 662 for more about clichés.

Activity 8-1 Practicing Description

Directions: *Briefly describe the following topics using* concrete *language (tangible and vivid words) and specific details. Then provide a purpose for describing the object, place, or person:*

1. Briefly describe your grandmother (or a grandmother-like person).

   _____

   _____

   _____

   _____

   _____

   Purpose: _____

   _____

   _____

2. Briefly describe your bedroom.

   _____

   _____

   _____

   _____

   _____

   Purpose: _____

   _____

   _____

3. Briefly describe your car (or the car of someone you know).

   _____

   _____

   _____

   _____

Purpose: _____

_____

_____

_____

WRITING A DESCRIPTIVE ESSAY

Cross Reference

See p. 114 for more about spatial order and order of importance.

The structure of a descriptive essay is usually based on the object, place, or person you are describing. In a descriptive essay you will often use spatial order to focus on one aspect at a time. Another common pattern is order of importance, in which you list characteristics of the person, place, or thing in the order of most to least important or vice versa (for instance, starting with a description of your mother's face and eyes before moving on to her body type, voice, and other characteristics).

Be sure to include transitional words and phrases as you move from one characteristic to another. For instance, "In one corner of my room, there is a big, overstuffed chair upholstered with material with small blue flowers. In the opposite corner stands the bureau my mother used when she was a child."

Organize your descriptive essay based on the best choice for the object, place, or person you are describing (arrange spatially or by order of importance) and based on your description's purpose, the message of the essay. Engage your critical thinking skills to make a choice for the best order and plan.

The chart below provides a brief overview of the structure of a descriptive essay.

BASIC STRUCTURE FOR A DESCRIPTION ESSAY

Introductory Paragraph	**Sets up background** for describing the person, place, or thing that leads into the thesis; statement of purpose. **Thesis statement:** Presents what you are trying to explain, show, prove, or argue through the description of this subject; what you want your readers to understand about it.
Body Paragraphs	Develop the description in spatial order or order of importance. Descriptive essays often have simple **topic sentences** that introduce the next aspect being described.

(Two to five, depending on assignment and purpose)	Use **transitions** within and between paragraphs to emphasize the transition from one detail or part to the next.
	Provide concrete details and description.
	Use as many senses as possible in your description (sight, sound, smell, touch, and taste).
	Use comparisons and similes to help describe the subject.
	Add commentary about the details and descriptions to help develop the expository purpose/thesis statement.
	Create a concrete visual image that allows the readers to form a visual in their minds.

| Concluding Paragraph | **Sum up and re-emphasize** the thesis, the **purpose** for your description in the first place. |

STRUCTURING A DESCRIPTIVE ESSAY

Topic

If you do not have a topic assigned by your instructor for your descriptive essay, then brainstorm ideas for things, places, or people you might want to describe. Then come up with some ideas for a purpose for describing the topic you have chosen. What do you want your readers to understand through your description?

A Few Topic Possibilities

Here is a list of some topics you could use for a descriptive essay: your car, your family, your campus, your pet, your workplace, your favorite restaurant, your street, your room, a particular friend, your classroom, your computer, your favorite meal, your local movie theater, other ideas.

Thesis Statements

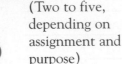

In a descriptive essay, you can reach some kind of judgment based on your detailed description, argue for a particular preference, critique an object or person, or just describe something in order to inform your readers about it. You state the purpose in your thesis statement. In order to come up with a good thesis statement for your descriptive essay, you'll need to do some form of prewriting on your subject. Try brainstorming a list of details and ideas about your topic or cluster to generate details and ideas in order to determine the purpose for your description. Here are some examples:

Cross Reference

See p. 87 for a review of prewriting techniques.

Topic: Wooden kayaks

Purpose: My goal is to describe a wooden kayak in detail in order to prove that a kayak is as much a work of art as it is a boat actually to use.

Thesis: A wooden kayak is a detailed and elaborate boat that is as much a work of art as it is a utilitarian object.

Topic: My science professor

Purpose: To describe my unusual science teacher and to show my readers how her strange outfits and eccentric personality are all part of her teaching approach.

Thesis: My science teacher is an eccentric instructor who wears elaborate and bizarre outfits every day with her lab coat and acts a bit crazy, all for the sake of improving her students' learning.

Activity 8-2   Creating Thesis Statements

Directions: *Using the topics listed below, cluster on a separate sheet of paper to generate ideas, and then create a one-sentence thesis statement for each general topic. Make sure the thesis has a* clear message or purpose to convey *about the subject you are describing.*

1.   **Topic:** Your school

    Thesis: _____

    _____

2.   **Topic:** Your street/neighborhood

    Thesis: _____

    _____

3.   **Topic:** A favorite item of clothing

    Thesis: _____

    _____

4.   **Topic:** Your best friend

    Thesis: _____

    _____

5. **Topic:** A flower garden

   Thesis: _____

   _____ ●

Introductory Paragraph

Begin your descriptive essay with a general introduction that sets up the topic of your description and intrigues your readers. End the introductory paragraph with your thesis statement.

Body Paragraphs

The body paragraphs in a description essay focus on developing specific details and concrete examples to describe your topic. They also comment about the description and your emotional or intellectual response to the subject you are describing. *Topic sentences* in a description essay focus on describing a particular quality or area of the subject you are describing.

> **Topic Sentence Example:** (based on the kayak sample thesis):
> The most important element that makes a wooden kayak a work of art is the fact that it is hand crafted from beautiful, carefully prepared wood.

Activity 8-3   Creating Topic Sentences

Directions: *Now create a topic sentence you could use to develop a body paragraph for each of the thesis statements you created in Activity 8-2.*

1. Your school: _____

   _____

   _____

2. Your street/neighborhood: _____

   _____

   _____

3. A favorite item of clothing: _____

   _____

   _____

4. Your best friend: _____

_____

_____

5. A flower garden: _____

_____

_____ ○

Details are particularly important in a descriptive essay. Details can be **objective** (factual descriptions without feelings, judgment, or bias), or they can be **subjective** (details that relate to your own biases, judgments, or emotions).

> **Sample objective detail for the kayak topic:** Any wood used to create a wooden boat must be specifically treated to ensure that it is water safe and will not warp.

> **Sample subjective detail for the kayak topic:** Though many hardwoods work well for building a kayak, the most beautiful wood to use is maple.

Activity 8-4   Providing Details

Directions: *Now provide at least three vivid, descriptive details you would use for the topic sentences you created in Activity 8-3. Then decide if your descriptions are objective, subjective, or both.*

1. Your school: _____

_____

_____

Objective, subjective, or both: _____

2. Your street/neighborhood: _____

_____

_____

Objective, subjective, or both: _____

3. A favorite item of clothing: _____

_____

_____

Objective, subjective, or both: _____

4. Your best friend: _____

_____

_____

Objective, subjective, or both: _____

5. A flower garden: _____

_____

_____

Objective, subjective, or both: _____

Activity 8-5   Abstract to Vivid Language

Directions: *Translate the abstract descriptive words that are bolded in each sentence into vivid, specific descriptions of the thing or person in the sentence. Try to include sensory description when possible (sight, touch, smell, sound, taste).*

Example: The food was **bland**.

The food tasted like cardboard mixed with mashed potatoes without salt.

_____

1. It is a **typical** house on a typical street.

_____

_____

2. My friend is **odd looking**.

_____

_____

3. It was the **ugliest** cat I had ever seen.

_____

_____

4. The room was **huge**.

_____

_____

5. The car was **old**.

_____

_____

One way to add more specific description is to use comparisons like similes and metaphors.

Activity 8-6   Creating Comparisons (Similes and Metaphors)

Directions: _Come up with a simile or metaphor for each of the objects below to help your readers get a good visual or sensory image of it. Try not to use a clichéd, commonly used simile or metaphor._

Example:

Blue eyes

Simile: _eyes as blue as a spring sky_ _____

Metaphor: _faded denim eyes_ _____

1. A nice face

Simile: _____

Metaphor: _____

2. Green

Simile: _____

Metaphor: _____

3. Happy

Simile: _____

Metaphor: _____

4. Hairy

Simile: _____

Metaphor: _____

5. Crazy

   Simile: _____

   Metaphor: _____ ●

Transitions that are useful in writing descriptive essays include those showing comparison, examples, place, or amount (see Chapter 6, pages 118–119).

Concluding Paragraph

The concluding paragraph for a descriptive essay should remind your readers what the purpose of your description was—why you described this person, place, or object in the first place.

Activity 8-7   Writing a Conclusion

Directions: *Choose one of the topics you have been developing in the previous activities and write a three- to five-sentence concluding paragraph for it.*

_____

_____

_____

_____

_____ ●

Remember, it's important to avoid using abstract descriptors in your essay: Instead, use vivid, specific descriptions, language, and examples.

Activity 8-8   Describe a Monster

Directions: *This activity requires two people, so work with a partner. It is a classic description exercise that is a fun way to practice using specific and concrete description, and it is a great way to increase your awareness of your reader's need to visualize what you are describing.*

Step One: On a sheet of paper, draw a monster. Be creative, and enjoy yourself. Don't let anyone see your monster drawing; turn it over on your desk.

Step Two: Now, on a separate sheet of paper, write a one-paragraph description of your monster using specific, concrete descriptive words.

Step Three: Exchange your written description only with your partner. Keep your monster drawing upside down so your partner doesn't see it.

Step Four: Read your partner's written description of his or her monster. Then, on a separate sheet of paper, draw the monster based on the description given.

Step Five: Compare the original drawing to the one created based on the written description.

Step Six: Answer the following questions.

1.   Did the drawings look close to the same? (Ignore drawing talent differences; focus on basic structure such as number of eyes, legs, overall shape, and so on.)

   _____

   _____

2.   What problems arose from details missing in the description?

   _____

   _____

3.   What would you do differently now if you were asked to rewrite your description of your monster?

   _____

   _____

   _____

Use the critique form on page 164 to check for the basics in your descriptive essay draft.

COMPLEMENTARY MODES FOR DESCRIPTIVE ESSAYS

When writing a descriptive essay, you can tap into several other modes described in other chapters that combine well to create a powerful description.

- **Narration:** Narration is essential in description for adding concrete details and vivid word pictures.

- **Illustration and example:** Most good descriptive essays include specific illustration and examples to develop the purpose of the writing.

Description Essay Critique Form

PURPOSE IDEAS SUPPORT ASSUMPTIONS BIASES CONCLUSIONS POINT OF VIEW ANALYSIS

Use the following critique form to check for the basics in your descriptive essay draft.

Overall   Done well   Needs work

1. Does the essay describe a person, place, or thing with an analytical
   purpose (e.g., to help clarify, narrate, inform, convince)?   _____   _____
2. Does the essay use a logical order in the body paragraphs (with an
   analytical setup and concluding paragraph)?   _____   _____
3. Are the paragraphs broken up well and about the right length?   _____   _____

Introduction

4. Is the title interesting and in the correct format?   _____   _____
5. Is there a general introduction that sets up the thesis?   _____   _____
6. Is there a clear thesis statement that explains the significance of the
   person, place, or thing being described?   _____   _____

Body

7. Do the **ideas** in the body paragraphs develop logically and flow smoothly? _____   _____
8. Are transitions used between and, when needed, within the paragraphs? _____   _____
9. Do the body paragraphs include **support** and descriptive details and
   concrete images?   _____   _____
10. Does the writer use as many senses as possible in the description?   _____   _____
11. If similes or metaphors are used, are they fresh and effective?   _____   _____

Conclusion

12. Does the concluding paragraph sum up the **purpose** and **analysis** of the
    description?   _____   _____

Editing

13. Circle the following errors you think you see in this draft: spelling, fragments, run-ons/comma splices,
    commas, semicolon/colon use, pronoun agreement, reference fault errors, parallelism, apostrophe use,
    verb use/tense, and passive voice construction. (See the handbook section for help in identifying and
    correcting these errors.)
14. Other types of grammar or sentence-level errors:

_____

Comments:

_____

_____

- **Process:** Process focuses on describing a series of steps to accomplish something and can be used to describe a particular ritual or process.
- **Cause and effect:** You can describe an event in detail and employ cause and effect analysis to look at the consequences of the actions that take place.
- **Comparison/contrast:** A great way to describe something or someone is to compare (or contrast) them to something or someone else.
- **Argument:** Sometimes your reason for describing something or someone in detail is to persuade your readers to learn a particular lesson or feel a particular way: You are combining argument techniques with your description. For instance, you could describe a particular object, like a car or computer, in order to convince your readers to purchase one.

SAMPLE STUDENT ESSAY

Hill 1

Lynne Hill

Professor Li

English 090

3 February 2008

My Husband's Guitar

My husband plays guitar everyday. I have gotten used to hearing its music move through our house, especially in the early morning and late evening. My husband's guitar is a beautiful and important part of our lives together. His guitar is a beautiful object in and of itself; however, it is more than a thing: it is also an extension of my husband himself, and the music it makes reflects his moods and serves as a tribute to our lives together.

Thesis statement

My husband's guitar is a classically styled acoustic guitar. It is made of wood and has six metal strings. The front of the guitar is a lovely honey-amber color, with fine-lined grain and a high-polish shine. The surface feels smooth, slick, and cool to the touch. There is a black plastic, kidney-shaped back plate where he strums the strings. The sides, back, and neck of the guitar are a darker colored

Topic sentence

Descriptive details

Hill 2

wood, the color of strong coffee. Also, the long neck has six metal strings, four of them copper colored and two of them the color of steel. Besides the strings, the neck has 20 fret lines and six mother-of-pearl inset dots. Both of these features help him play correct chords and guide his fingers to the right places on the strings when he plays. Finally, six knobs that look a little like keys or small handles sit at the top of the neck that the strings are wrapped around. When he turns these knobs, the stings are adjusted, and he **Concluding sentence** can get his guitar in perfect tune. As you can imagine, the guitar is a beautiful object, and even if I never heard my husband play, I would still find it admirable.

Topic sentence However, it is when my husband plays that the life and beauty of his guitar really shine. His music is rich and comforting. The sound is like a comforting humming. His songs and chords reflect the moods and best moments of his personality and of our marriage. He plays happy songs with faster, more upbeat chords, and he plays slower songs with more somber chords for the sadder or more serious **Concluding sentence** times of our lives. In fact, I can usually guess my husband's mood by the type of song or the chords he is playing on his guitar.

Restatement of thesis My husband's guitar is like an extension of himself and our relationship. It is a beautiful object with a lovely message to convey to anyone who takes the time to listen. I cherish its presence in our home and the music my husband makes with it.

Activity 8-9   Thinking Critically About the Student Essay

Directions: *Analyze the essay to identify the features and details characteristic of the description mode. Mark them on the essay. Then, reread the essay, and make a list of specific revisions you would make to correct any problems with content, organization, transitions, and style.* ●

PROFESSIONAL DESCRIPTION ESSAY

More Room

Judith Ortiz Cofer

Judith Ortiz Cofer was born in Hormigueros, Puerto Rico, in 1952 and emigrated with her family to the United States in 1954. She is the author of *The Line of the Sun*; *The Latin Deli: Prose and Poetry*; *Silent Dancing: A Partial Remembrance of a Puerto Rican Childhood*; and two books of poetry: *Reaching for the Mainland* and *Terms of Survival*. Her work has appeared in *Glamour*, *The Georgia Review*, *Kenyon Review*, and other journals. Currently, she is a professor of English and Creative Writing at the University of Georgia. Her most recent book is *An Island Like You: Stories of the Barrio*.

1   My grandmother's house is like a chambered nautilus; it has many rooms, yet it is not a mansion. Its proportions are small and its design simple. It is a house that has grown organically, according to the needs of its inhabitants. To all of us in the family it is known as *la casa de Mama*. It is the place of our origin; the stage for our memories and dreams of Island life.

2   I remember how in my childhood it sat on stilts; this was before it had a downstairs. It rested on its perch like a great blue bird, not a flying sort of bird, more like a nesting hen, but with spread wings. Grandfather had built it soon after their marriage. He was a painter and house builder by trade, a poet and meditative man by nature. As each of their eight children were born, new rooms were added. After a few years, the paint did not exactly match, nor the materials, so that there was a chronology to it, like the rings of a tree, and Mama could tell you the history of each room in her *casa*, and thus the genealogy of the family along with it.

3   Her room is the heart of the house. Though I have seen it recently, and both woman and room have diminished in size, changed by the new perspective of my eyes, now capable of looking over countertops and tall beds, it is not this picture I carry in my memory of Mama's *casa*. Instead, I see her room as a queen's chamber where a small woman loomed large, a throne-room with a massive four-poster bed in its center which stood taller than a child's head. It was on this bed where her own children had been born that the smallest grandchildren were allowed to take naps in the afternoons; here too was where Mama secluded herself to dispense private advice to her daughters, sitting on the edge of the bed, looking

down at whoever sat on the rocker where generations of babies had been sung to sleep. To me she looked like a wise empress right out of the fairy tales I was addicted to reading.

4   Though the room was dominated by the mahogany four-poster, it also contained all of Mama's symbols of power. On her dresser instead of cosmetics there were jars filled with herbs: *yerba buena, yerba mala,* the making of purgatives and teas to which we were all subjected during childhood crises. She had a steaming cup for anyone who could not, or would not, get up to face life on any given day.

5   If the acrid aftertaste of her cures for malingering did not get you out of bed, then it was time to call *el doctor.*

6   And there was the monstrous chifforobe she kept locked with a little golden key she did not hide. This was a test of her dominion over us; though my cousins and I wanted a look inside that massive wardrobe more than anything, we never reached for that little key lying on top of her Bible on the dresser. This was also where she placed her earrings and rosary at night. God's word was her security system. This chifforobe was the place where I imagined she kept jewels, satin slippers, and elegant sequined, silk gowns of heartbreaking fineness. I lusted after those imaginary costumes. I had heard that Mama had been a great beauty in her youth, and the belle of many balls. My cousins had other ideas as to what she kept in that wooden vault: its secret could be money (Mama did not hand cash to strangers, banks were out of the question, so there were stories that her mattress was stuffed with dollar bills, and that she buried coins in jars in her garden under rosebushes, or kept them in her inviolate chifforobe); there might be that legendary gun salvaged from the Spanish-American conflict over the Island. We went wild over suspected treasures that we made up simply because children have to fill locked trunks with something wonderful.

7   On the wall above the bed hung a heavy silver crucifix. Christ's agonized head hung directly over Mama's pillow. I avoided looking at this weapon suspended over where her head would lay; and on the rare occasions when I was allowed to sleep on that bed, I scooted down to the safe middle of the mattress, where her body's impression took me in like a mother's lap. Having taken care of the obligatory religious decoration with a crucifix, Mama covered the other walls with objects sent to her over the years by her children in the States. *Los Nueva Yores* were represented by, among other things, a postcard of Niagara Falls from her son Hernán, postmarked, Buffalo, N.Y. In a conspicuous gold frame hung a large color photograph of her daughter Nena, her husband and their five children at the entrance to Disneyland in California. From us she had gotten a black lace fan. Father had brought it to her from a tour of duty with

the Navy in Europe (on Sundays she would remove it from its hook on the wall to fan herself at mass). Each year more items were added as the family grew and dispersed, and every object in the room had a story attached to it, a *cuento* which Mama would bestow on anyone who received the privilege of a day alone with her. It was almost worth pretending to be sick, though the bitter herb purgatives of the body were a big price to pay for the spirit revivals of her story-telling.

8   Mama slept alone on her large bed, except for the times when a sick grandchild warranted the privilege, or when a heartbroken daughter came home in need of more than herbal teas. In the family there is a story about how this came to be.

9   When one of the daughters, my mother or one of her sisters, tells the *cuento* of how Mama came to own her nights, it is usually preceded by the qualifications that Papa's exile from his wife's room was not a result of animosity between the couple, but that the act had been Mama's famous bloodless coup for her personal freedom. Papa was the benevolent dictator of her body and her life who had had to be banished from her bed so that Mama could better serve her family. Before the telling, we had to agree that the old man was not to blame. We all recognized that in the family Papa was as an *alma de Dios,* a saintly, soft-spoken presence whose main pleasures in life, such as writing poetry and reading the Spanish large-type editions of *Reader Digest,* always took place outside the vortex of Mama's crowded realm. It was not his fault, after all, that every year or so he planted a baby-seed in Mama's fertile body, keeping her from leading the active life she needed and desired. He loved her and the babies. Papa composed odes and lyrics to celebrate births and anniversaries and hired musicians to accompany him singing them to his family and friends at extravagant pig-roasts he threw yearly. Mama and the oldest girls worked for days preparing the food. Papa sat for hours in his painter's shed, also his study and library, composing the songs. At these celebrations he was also known to give long speeches in praise of God, his fecund wife, and his beloved island. As a middle child, my mother remembers these occasions as a time when the women sat in the kitchen and lamented their burdens, while the men feasted out in the patio, their rum-thickened voices rising in song and praise for each other, *compañeros* all.

10   It was after the birth of her eighth child, after she had lost three at birth or in infancy, that Mama made her decision. They say that Mama had had a special way of letting her husband know that they were expecting, one that had begun when, at the beginning of their marriage, he had built her a house too confining for her taste. So, when she discovered her first pregnancy, she supposedly drew plans for another room, which he

dutifully executed. Every time a child was due, she would demand *more space, more space.* Papa acceded to her wishes, child after child, since he had learned early that Mama's renowned temper was a thing that grew like a monster along with a new belly. In this way Mama got the house that she wanted, but with each child she lost in heart and energy. She had knowledge of her body and perceived that if she had any more children, her dreams and her plans would have to be permanently forgotten, because she would be a chronically ill woman, like Flora with her twelve children: asthma, no teeth, in bed more than on her feet.

11   And so, after my youngest uncle was born, she asked Papa to build a large room at the back of the house. He did so in joyful anticipation. Mama had asked him special things this time: shelves on the walls, a private entrance. He thought that she meant this room to be a nursery where several children could sleep. He thought it was a wonderful idea. He painted it his favorite color, sky blue, and made large windows looking out over a green hill and the church spires beyond. But nothing happened. Mama's belly did not grow, yet she seemed in a frenzy of activity over the house. Finally, an anxious Papa approached his wife to tell her that the new room was finished and ready to be occupied. And Mama, they say, replied: "Good, it's for *you.*"

12   And so it was that Mama discovered the only means of birth control available to a Catholic woman of her time: sacrifice. She gave up the comfort of Papa's sexual love for something she deemed greater: the right to own and control her body, so that she might live to meet her grandchildren—me among them—so that she could give more of herself to the ones already there, so that she could be more than a channel for other lives, so that even now that time has robbed her of the elasticity of her body and of her amazing reservoir of energy she still emanates the kind of joy that can only be achieved by living according to the dictates of one's own heart.

Reading Reflection Questions

1. What are the direct or indirect (implied) messages in this story?

_____

_____

2. Why do you think the grandmother keeps demanding more room?

_____

_____

3. What does the extra space represent for her?

_____

_____

Objective Questions

Answer the following true/false questions by writing T for true or F for false.

4. T/F _____ The husband, Cofer's grandfather, doesn't want to grant the request for more room.

5. T/F _____ The grandmother didn't really have a temper when she was pregnant.

6. T/F _____ The author understands her grandmother's needs and reasons for more room.

7. List two specific examples of descriptive details used in this story that gave readers a vivid image.

_____

_____

Checking Vocabulary

Define the following in your own words or provide a dictionary definition if you do not know the word.

8. malingering: _____

9. fertile: _____

10. elasticity: _____

CRITICAL THINKING CHECKLIST

PURPOSE

1. What is the **purpose** of this piece of writing? Is it clear?

_____

_____

2. What **ideas** and **background information** are provided to support the purpose of this piece of writing?

_____

_____

3. What **evidence** and **examples** are used to explain and develop the ideas that support the argument made in the piece of writing? Are the evidence and examples provided sufficient for **support**?

_____

_____

4. Are there unfounded **assumptions** or unreasonable **biases**?

_____

_____

5. Are all of the **conclusions**, **implications**, and **consequences** of the arguments (the results of the arguments taken to their furthest extreme) considered?

_____

_____

6. Is the **point of view** clear and consistent, and have other points of view been considered?

_____

_____

7. Using these critical thinking tools, **analyze** the overall structure of this essay and the strength of the author's arguments, ideas, and support. Was he or she successful in accomplishing her purpose? Why or why not?

_____

_____

Essay Assignments

1. Use one of the topics you developed in this chapter, and write a complete description essay on that topic. Use the critique form to check your draft.

2. Describe a room in your house or apartment using as many senses as possible. Use specific, concrete details as opposed to abstract descriptions such as "large" or "beautiful." Create a picture of the room in your readers' heads by painting a picture with details and sensory

description. Finally, come up with an expository purpose: a conclusion you've reached upon examining this room.

3. Describe a particular spot on your college campus. Pick a space no larger than 25′ × 25′ so you can include concrete, specific descriptive details. Be sure to incorporate as many senses as possible in your description. Then create a thesis statement that has the purpose of establishing what kind of atmosphere this place has and what mood it provokes.

4. Describe one of the following people using concrete, specific nouns and adjectives and by including as many of the senses as possible. Avoid vague, abstract descriptions such as "beautiful," "handsome," and so on. Create a vivid picture of this person by developing a portrait with a description in words. Be sure to include a thesis statement that puts forth a purpose to develop: what you want to show a reader or a conclusion you have reached about this person.

your mother	your father	your best friend
your grandmother	your grandfather	a sibling

9

Process

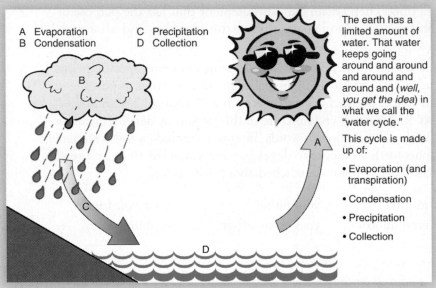

A Evaporation   C Precipitation
B Condensation   D Collection

The earth has a limited amount of water. That water keeps going around and around and around and around and (*well, you get the idea*) in what we call the "water cycle."

This cycle is made up of:

• Evaporation (and transpiration)

• Condensation

• Precipitation

• Collection

Rain and evaporation cycle chart from www.kidszone.

THINKING CRITICALLY

Look at the diagram above. Then answer the questions that follow.

1. In your own words, describe the process of evaporation, condensation, precipitation, and collection, as illustrated in the diagram.

    _____

    _____

2. If you had to write a short essay describing this process for a general audience, how would you organize the essay?

    _____

    _____

3. What are some reasons for writing a description of a specific process? Provide an example.

    _____

    _____

PROCESS ESSAYS

Process essays tell people how things work (like a combustion engine, or the digestive system), how to do something (bake a cake, get legislation through Congress, find a job), or how to analyze a process to see how efficient it is or to explain a better alternative (for example, how a traditional combustion engine works, how this contributes to pollution, and how a hybrid engine works and decreases pollution). Process writing is very common in business, in science and math classes, and in careers that involve many process-related tasks.

Critical Thinking and Process

Be sure to make the purpose of your process essay clear: to inform, to critique, to propose an alternative process after describing the status quo (the way things are now). Think carefully about the best way to describe the process and demonstrate the purpose for your essay: What do you want your readers to learn about this process besides how to do it? How can you best structure the essay to achieve your goal, and what details will you include?

BEFORE WRITING A PROCESS ESSAY

Before you begin to write a process essay on an assigned topic, or one you have chosen, start by asking yourself these questions:

1. What process am I describing?
2. What specific steps, examples, and details should I use to describe the process?
3. How should I organize my paragraphs after my introduction and thesis statement, and how can I move smoothly from one step or detail to the next?
4. What is my purpose for writing this process description (to describe how something works, to tell someone how to accomplish a task, to critique a process and provide a better alternative, other)?
5. What do I want my readers to learn and understand after reading about this process? Who is my intended audience, and how much will they already know about my topic?

Answering these questions will lead you to an expository thesis statement, help you determine what examples to use, and give you a general idea of how you want to organize your essay.

Activity 9-1   Steps in a Process

Directions: *Briefly describe the major steps in each of the following common processes. Then come up with a purpose for writing about such a process (what you would want your readers to understand or learn through your description of the process).*

1. Brushing one's teeth properly: _____

    _____

    _____

    Purpose: _____

    _____

2. Making a sandwich:_____

    _____

    _____

    Purpose: _____

    _____

3. Registering for classes: _____

    _____

    _____

    Purpose: _____

    _____

4. Grocery shopping: _____

    _____

    _____

    Purpose: _____

    _____

5. Reading a textbook chapter:_____

    _____

    _____

    Purpose: _____

    _____

WRITING A PROCESS ESSAY

The structure of a process essay is usually based on chronological order, describing one step at a time, in the order it happens. For example, if you were telling your readers how to properly make a bed, you might describe it like this:

> To make your bed in the best possible way, start by taking your fitted sheet and put one corner tightly over the top left corner of your bed. Next, put the other top corner of the fitted sheet on the top right corner of your bed. Carefully pull the bottom two corners of the sheet to the bottom of your bed, and do the same process with the two bottom corners of your mattress. Next, get your flat sheet ready . . .

A process essay can also be organized by order of importance of the individual steps if the process doesn't require a particular sequence of steps. For example, if you were describing the process of applying for a new job, you might choose order of importance to list the steps involved and include paragraphs on how to list qualifications, how to update a resumé, how to write an application letter, and how to present oneself in an interview.

Decide what your *expository purpose* or message is for writing a process description (to evaluate a process, to teach or instruct, to propose an alternative process, other). Be sure to describe the steps in chronological order or order of importance and to include *descriptive details* that explain and illustrate each one. Then make sure that your essay's conclusion reiterates the purpose of your process description or analysis. The following chart provides a brief overview of the structure of a process essay.

BASIC STRUCTURE FOR A PROCESS ESSAY

Introductory Paragraph	**Sets up background** for the process and why you are describing it.
	Thesis statement: A statement that describes what you are trying to explain, show, prove, or argue through describing a process. Do you want to instruct someone in how to perform a specific task? Do you want to explain how a process works? Or do you want to critique a process and propose an alternative?

PURPOSE

Body Paragraphs (two to five, depending on assignment and purpose)	**Develop** the process of the event using time order or order of importance. Topic sentences should clarify the type of order and the categories or major stages of the process.
	Use transitions within and between paragraphs to emphasize switching to the next step.
	Provide concrete details and description.
	Define terms when necessary, especially if your process involves parts or tools.
	Add commentary and analysis about the steps, details, and descriptions to help develop the expository purpose/thesis statement.
Concluding Paragraph	**Sum up and re-emphasize** the thesis: the **purpose** for describing this process in the first place.

STRUCTURING A PROCESS ESSAY

Topic

If you do not have a topic assigned by your instructor for your process essay, then brainstorm ideas for a process you might want to describe. Then come up with some ideas for a purpose for describing the topic. What do you want your readers to understand through your description of the process?

A Few Topic Possibilities

You could write about the following: a scientific or natural process you have learned about through other courses; a daily ritual such as getting ready for school, making your lunch, or studying for a test in order to show what you think is the best approach to accomplishing it; or the best way to accomplish a specific goal such as saving money for college.

Thesis Statements

The thesis statement in a process essay establishes what process you are describing or analyzing, and for what purpose. For instance, if you were writing a basic essay in order to explain how to do a task step by step, then the thesis statement would establish that very simply.

Example: In order to make a perfect homemade cake, complete each of the following steps in order and you will succeed.

If you were critiquing an existing process and proposing an alternative, you would set out both of these goals in your thesis statement.

Example: The combustion engine has been in use for over a century, but it is inefficient and bad for the environment; therefore, the hybrid engine's process of using gas to start and electricity for driving makes it better for the environment and an overall better choice for a new car.

The thesis statement, then, in a process essay describes the process and your purpose for writing about it: what you want your readers to understand about the targeted process after reading your essay.

Activity 9-2   Creating Thesis Statements

Directions: *Create a one-sentence thesis statement for each general topic. Make sure the thesis has a clear message or lesson to convey about why you would describe each process.*

1. **Topic:** Choosing a new wardrobe for school or work

    Thesis sentence: _____

    _____

2. **Topic:** Writing an essay

    Thesis sentence: _____

    _____

3. **Topic:** Choosing a movie to see

    Thesis sentence: _____

    _____

4. **Topic:** Finding an apartment to rent

    Thesis sentence: _____

    _____

5. **Topic:** Finding a part-time job

Thesis sentence: _____

_____

Introductory Paragraph

Begin your process essay with a general introduction that sets up the process you'll be describing. End the introductory paragraph with your thesis statement.

Body Paragraphs

The body paragraphs in a process essay can be arranged in time order or order of importance, depending on the decision you have made about the most efficient way for you to explain the purpose of your thesis statement. Topic sentences should clarify the type of order and the categories or major stages of the process. You can describe one step in each paragraph, or you can arrange the body paragraphs so you describe the process, critique it, and then propose an alternative. When you use any of these organizational patterns, you need to include specific examples and definitions as needed. Particularly useful transitions for process essays are those relating to the addition of another point (see below). Other transitions you will find useful include those used to strengthen a point and to show a summary, examples, purpose, place, and time (see Chapter 6, pages 118–119).

TRANSITIONS TO SHOW ADDITION OF ANOTHER POINT

again	but also	in addition	nor
also	equally important	last	plus the fact
and	finally	lastly	secondly
and then	first	likewise	then too
another	further	moreover	thirdly
besides	furthermore	next	too

Activity 9-3   Creating Topic Sentences

Directions: *Create one possible topic sentence for each of the thesis statements you created in Activity 9-2.*

1. **Topic:** Choosing a new wardrobe for school or work

Topic sentence: _____

_____

2. **Topic:** Writing an essay
    Topic sentence: _____
    _____

3. **Topic:** Choosing a movie to see
    Topic sentence: _____
    _____

4. **Topic:** Finding an apartment to rent
    Topic sentence: _____
    _____

5. **Topic:** Finding a part-time job
    Topic sentence: _____
    _____

Support for your topic sentences should include examples, specific details that explain the process and all of its steps, and definitions of terms when needed.

Applying Critical Thinking

| PURPOSE | IDEAS | SUPPORT | ASSUMPTIONS BIASES | CONCLUSIONS | POINT OF VIEW | ANALYSIS |

When you write a process essay, do not assume your reader will know what you mean. **Analyze** the steps involved carefully. Make sure you include them all and describe exactly how they are performed. For instance, if you are describing making a peanut butter sandwich and say, "Spread the peanut butter on the bread," you may want to add "using a knife" or the reader could use a bare hand. Obviously, most people will know you assume they will use a knife in a common process like making a sandwich, but in more complex processes, like the way a nuclear power plant works, you will need to be specific and define any technical terms you use in order for a general audience to understand you.

Activity 9-4   Using Examples, Definitions, and Other Details

Directions: *Now provide at least three possible examples or details you would include for each of the topic sentences you created in Activity 9-3.*

1. **Topic:** Choosing a new wardrobe for school or work

    Examples: _____

    _____

2. **Topic:** Writing an essay

    Examples: _____

    _____

3. **Topic:** Choosing a movie to see

    Examples: _____

    _____

4. **Topic:** Finding an apartment to rent

    Examples: _____

    _____

5. **Topic:** Finding a part-time job

    Examples: _____

    _____

Concluding Paragraph

The concluding paragraph in a process essay should restate both the process being described and the purpose for describing it: To inform the reader how to do something; to describe how a machine, experiment, or system works; to critique the way something works and propose an alternative; and so on.

Activity 9-5   Writing a Concluding Paragraph

Directions: *Choose one of the topics from the previous activities, and write a three- to five-sentence concluding paragraph for the topic. Be sure to reiterate what you set up in the thesis.*

_____

_____

_____

_____

_____

_____

Use the following critique form to check for the basics in your process essay draft.

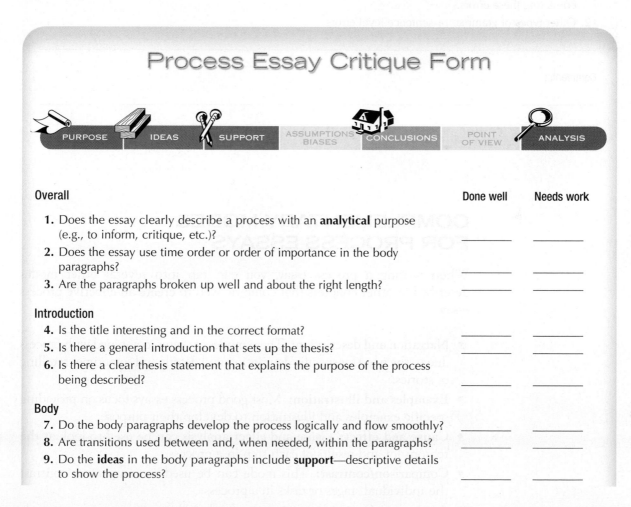

Process Essay Critique Form

PURPOSE   IDEAS   SUPPORT   ASSUMPTIONS BIASES   CONCLUSIONS   POINT OF VIEW   ANALYSIS

Overall   Done well   Needs work

1. Does the essay clearly describe a process with an **analytical** purpose (e.g., to inform, critique, etc.)?   _____   _____
2. Does the essay use time order or order of importance in the body paragraphs?   _____   _____
3. Are the paragraphs broken up well and about the right length?   _____   _____

Introduction

4. Is the title interesting and in the correct format?   _____   _____
5. Is there a general introduction that sets up the thesis?   _____   _____
6. Is there a clear thesis statement that explains the purpose of the process being described?   _____   _____

Body

7. Do the body paragraphs develop the process logically and flow smoothly?   _____   _____
8. Are transitions used between and, when needed, within the paragraphs?   _____   _____
9. Do the **ideas** in the body paragraphs include **support**—descriptive details to show the process?   _____   _____

	Done well	Needs work

Conclusion

10. Does the **concluding** paragraph sum up the process and re-emphasize the **purpose** set up in the introductory paragraph and thesis, without adding new ideas?   _____   _____

Editing

11. Circle the following errors you think you see in this draft: spelling, fragments, run-ons/comma splices, commas, semicolon/colon use, pronoun agreement, reference fault errors, parallelism, apostrophe use, verb use/tense, and passive voice construction. (See the handbook section for help in identifying and correcting these errors.)

12. Other types of grammar or sentence-level errors

_____

Comments:

_____

_____

COMPLEMENTARY MODES FOR PROCESS ESSAYS

When writing a process essay, you can tap into several other modes described in other chapters that combine well to create an effective process essay.

- **Narration and description:** These modes are often combined with process due to the need for specific description and details and sometimes retelling of stories.
- **Examples and illustration:** Most good process essays focus on providing specific examples and illustration to develop their purpose.
- **Cause and effect:** Cause and effect analysis can be used to look at the reasons for and results of each step in a process.
- **Comparison/contrast:** This mode can be used to compare or contrast the individual stages or tasks in a process.
- **Argument:** Sometimes your reason for describing a process is to persuade your readers to learn a particular process or to critique an existing process and convince your readers to use it or avoid it.

SAMPLE STUDENT ESSAY

Rooney 1

Michelle Rooney

Professor Hernandez

English 100

28 February 2007

How to Pick the Right Courses

Being a college student poses many difficult challenges. One of
the toughest parts of being in school is knowing which classes to take
and knowing how to go about registering for the right courses once
you have determined them. It is essential to plan ahead and research — Thesis statement
options, know your goals, and register on time if you want to succeed
in picking the right courses for your degree in a timely manner.

To begin with, many students make the mistake of waiting to the — Topic sentence
last minute to think about their courses for the next semester or quarter. However, it is essential to plan ahead. Choosing the right courses
for your goals and your target degree is not a matter that should be
taken lightly or put off to the last minute. Begin thinking about the
next quarter or semester's course offerings and what you might want
to take at least two weeks before your scheduled registration date.
You have to find out what the registration date is, or if it is open registration, when that begins. Then, you need to mark your calendar and
begin the next steps of getting ready to register.

The next major component to picking your classes is to — Topic sentence
research your options carefully. Get a copy of the course schedule as
soon as it becomes available. Then, research which courses you still
need to take to achieve your education or degree goals. Also, research
if any of the courses you are interested in need a prerequisite course
first. You may have to take a required course before you can take the
course you have in mind. Also, you will need to check the available

Rooney 2

times for the courses you need and make sure they do not conflict with each other or with your work schedule if you work.

Topic sentence

Finally, the last step involved in getting the courses you need is to register on time and not procrastinate. For some students, this step will first require having enough money to afford tuition, but other students who have their financial needs met still make the mistake of putting off registering and therefore risk not getting the classes they want and need. Remember, classes get full, and the longer you wait, the more you increase your chances of not getting your first choices for classes. Be sure to have some back-up courses in mind. For instance, if you plan to take a biology lab course, be prepared to take a geology lab course if biology is full.

Restatement of thesis

If you follow these steps and avoid procrastination, you should be successful in your quest for the right classes. College is stressful enough, so why make the process for registering for classes another source of tension? Prepare, be ready, and register on time.

Activity 9-6   Thinking Critically About the Student Essay

Directions: *Analyze the essay to identify the features and details characteristic of the process mode. Mark them on the essay. Then, reread the essay, and make a list of specific revisions you would make to correct any problems with content, organization, transitions, and style.*   ●

PROFESSIONAL PROCESS ESSAY

Behind the Formaldehyde Curtain

Jessica Mitford

Jessica Mitford was born in England on September 11, 1917. She wrote several books as well as articles for popular magazines such as *Life*,

Esquire, and *The Nation*. She also wrote the groundbreaking book *An American Way of Death* in 1963. The book caused a stir in the funeral business and in American's understanding of what happens to a body when it is embalmed. The following excerpt is from this book, a book that harshly critiqued the American funeral industry.

1   The drama begins to unfold with the arrival of the corpse at the mortuary. Alas, poor Yorick! How surprised he would be to see how his counterpart of today is whisked off to a funeral parlor and is in short order sprayed, sliced, pierced, pickled, trussed, trimmed, creamed, waxed, painted, rouged, and neatly dressed—transformed from a common corpse into a Beautiful Memory Picture. This process is known in the trade as embalming and restorative art, and is so universally employed in the United States and Canada that the funeral director does it routinely, without consulting corpse or kin. He regards as eccentric those few who are hardy enough to suggest that it might be dispensed with. Yet no law requires embalming, no religious doctrine commends it, nor is it dictated by considerations of health, sanitation, or even of personal daintiness. In no part of the world but in Northern America is it widely used. The purpose of embalming is to make the corpse presentable for viewing in a suitably costly container; and here too the funeral director routinely, without first consulting the family, prepares the body for public display.

2   Is all this legal? The processes to which a dead body may be subjected are after all to some extent circumscribed by law. In most states, for instance, the signature of next of kin must be obtained before an autopsy may be performed, before the deceased may be cremated, before the body may be turned over to a medical school for research purposes; or such provision must be made in the decedent's will. In the case of embalming, no such permission is required nor is it ever sought. A textbook, *The Principles and Practices of Embalming*, comments on this: "There is some question regarding the legality of much that is done within the preparation room." The author points out that it would be most unusual for a responsible member of a bereaved family to instruct the mortician, in so many words, to "embalm" the body of a deceased relative. The very term "embalming" is so seldom used that the mortician must reply upon custom in the matter. The author concludes that unless the family specifies otherwise, the act of entrusting the body to the care of a funeral establishment carries with it an implied permission to go ahead and embalm.

3   Embalming is indeed a most extraordinary procedure, and one must wonder at the docility of Americans who each year pay hundreds of millions of dollars for its perpetuation, blissfully ignorant of what it is all

about, what is done, how it is done. Not one in ten thousand has any idea of what actually takes place. Books on the subject are extremely hard to come by. They are not found in most libraries or bookshops.

4   In an era when huge television audiences watch surgical operations in the comfort of their living rooms, when, thanks to the animated cartoon, the geography of the digestive system has become familiar territory even to the nursery school set, in a land where the satisfaction of curiosity about almost all matters is a national pastime, the secrecy surrounding embalming can, surely, hardly be attributed to the inherent gruesomeness of the subject. Custom in this regard has within this century suffered a complete reversal. In the early days of American embalming, when it was performed in the home of the deceased, it was almost mandatory for some relative to stay by the embalmer's side and witness the procedure. Today, family members who might wish to be in attendance would certainly be dissuaded by the funeral director. All others, except apprentices, are excluded by law from the preparation room.

5   A close look at what does actually take place may explain a large measure of the undertaker's intractable reticence concerning a procedure that has become his major *raison d'être*. Is it possible he fears that public information about embalming might lead patrons to wonder if they really want this service? If the funeral men are loath to discuss the subject outside the trade, the reader may, understandably, be equally loath to go on reading at this point. For those who have the stomach for it, let us part the formaldehyde curtain. . . .

6   The body is first laid out in the undertaker's morgue—or rather, Mr. Jones is reposing in the preparation room—to be readied to bid the world farewell.

7   The preparation room in any of the better funeral establishments has the tiled and sterile look of a surgery, and indeed the embalmer-restorative artist who does his chores there is beginning to adopt the term "dermasurgeon" (appropriately corrupted by some mortician-writers as "demi-surgeon") to describe his calling. His equipment, consisting of scalpels, scissors, augers, forceps, clamps, needles, pumps, tubes, bowls and basins, is crudely imitative of the surgeon's, as is his technique, acquired in a nine- or twelve-month post-high-school course in an embalming school. He is supplied by an advanced chemical industry with a bewildering array of fluids, sprays, pastes, oils, powders, creams, to fix or soften tissue, shrink or distend it as needed, dry it here, restore the moisture there. There are cosmetics, waxes and paints to fill and cover features, even plaster of Paris to replace entire limbs. There are ingenious aids to prop and stabilize the cadaver: a Vari-Pose Head Rest, the Edwards Arm and Hand Positioner, the Repose Block (to support the shoulders

during embalming), and the Throop Foot Positioner, which resembles old-fashioned socks.

8   Mr. John H. Eckels, president of the Eckels College of Mortuary Science, thus describes the first part of the embalming procedure: "In the hands of a skilled practitioner, this work may be done in a comparatively short time and without mutilating the body other than by slight incision—so slight that it scarcely would cause serious inconvenience if made upon a living person. It is necessary to remove the blood, and doing this not only helps in the disinfecting, but removes the principal cause of disfigurements due to discoloration."

9   Another textbook discusses the all-important time element: "The earlier this is done, the better, for every hour that elapses between death and embalming will add to the problems and complications encountered. . . ." Just how soon should one get to embalming? The author tells us, "On the basis of such scanty information made available to this profession through its rudimentary and haphazard system of technical research, we must conclude the best results are to be obtained if the subject is embalmed before life is completely extinct—that is, before cellular death has occurred. In the average case, this would mean within an hour after somatic death." For those who feel there is something a little rudimentary, not to say haphazard, about this advice, a comforting thought is offered by another writer. Speaking of fears entertained in early days of premature burial, he points out, "One of the effects of embalming by chemical injection, however, has been to dispel fears of live burial." How true; once the blood is removed, the chances of live burial are indeed remote.

10   To return to Mr. Jones, the blood is drained out through the veins and replaced with embalming fluid pumped through the arteries. As noted in *The Principles and Practices of Embalming*, "every operator has a favorite injection and drainage point—a fact which becomes a handicap only if he fails or refuses to forsake his favorites when conditions demand it." Typical favorites are the carotid artery, femoral artery, jugular vein, subclavian vein. There are various choices of embalming fluids. If Flextone is used, it will produce a "mild, flexible rigidity. The skin retains a velvety softness, the tissues are rubbery and pliable. Ideal for women and children." It may be blended with B. and G. Products Company's Lyf-Lyk tint, which is guaranteed to reproduce "nature's own skin texture . . . the velvety appearance of living tissue." Suntone comes in three separate tints: Suntan; Special Cosmetic Tint, a pink shade "especially indicated for young female subjects"; and Regular Cosmetic Tint, moderately pink.

11   About three to six gallons of dyed and perfumed solution of formaldehyde, glycerin, borax, phenol, alcohol and water is soon circulating through Mr. Jones, whose mouth has been sewn together with a "needle

directed upward between the upper lip and gum and brought out through the left nostril," with the corners raised slightly "for a more pleasant expression. If he should be bucktoothed, his teeth are cleaned with Bon Ami and coated with colorless nail polish. His eyes, meanwhile, are closed with flesh-tinted eye caps and eye cement.

12   The next step is to have at Mr. Jones with a thing called a trocar. This is a long, hollow needle attached to a tube. It is jabbed into the abdomen, poked around the entrails and chest cavity, the contents of which are pumped out and replaced with "cavity fluid." This done, and the hole in the abdomen sewn up, Mr. Jones's face is heavily creamed (to protect the skin from burns which may be caused by leakage of the chemicals), and he is covered with a sheet and left unmolested for a while. But not for long—there is more, much more, in store for him. He has been embalmed, but not yet restored, and the best time to start the restorative work is eight to ten hours after embalming, when the tissues have become firm and dry.

13   The object of all this attention to the corpse, it must be remembered, is to make it presentable for viewing in an attitude of healthy repose. "Our customs require the presentation of our dead in semblance of normality . . . unmarred by the ravages of illness, disease or mutilation," says Mr. J. Sheridan Mayer in his *Restorative Art*. This is rather a large order since few people die in full bloom of health, unravaged by illness and unmarked by some disfigurement. The funeral industry is equal to the challenge: "In some cases the gruesome appearance of a mutilated or disease-ridden subject may be quite discouraging. The task of restoration may seem impossible and shake the confidence of the embalmer. This is the time for intestinal fortitude and determination. Once the formative work is begun and affected tissues are cleaned or removed, all doubts of success vanish. It is surprising and gratifying to discover the results which may be obtained."

14   The embalmer, having allowed an appropriate interval of elapse, returns to the attack, but now he brings into play the skill and equipment of sculptor and cosmetician. Is a hand missing? Casting one in plaster of Paris is a simple matter. "For replacement purposes, only a cast of the back of the hand is necessary; this is within the ability of the average operator and is quite adequate." If a lip or two, a nose or an ear should be missing, the embalmer has at hand a variety of restorative waxes with which to model replacements. Pores and skin texture are simulated by stippling with a little brush, and over this cosmetics are laid on. Head off? Decapitation cases are rather routinely handled. Ragged edges are trimmed, and head joined to torso with a series of splints, wires and sutures. It is a good idea to have a little something

at the neck—a scarf or high collar—when time for viewing comes. Swollen mouth? Cut out tissue as needed from inside the lips. If too much is removed, the surface contour can easily be restored by padding with cotton. Swollen necks and cheeks are reduced by removing tissue through vertical incisions made down each side of the neck. "When the deceased is casketed, the pillow will hide the suture incisions . . . as an extra precaution against leakage, the suture may be painted with liquid sealer."

15   The opposite condition is more likely to present itself—that of emaciation. His hypodermic syringe now loaded with massage cream, the embalmer seeks out and fills the hollowed and sunken areas by injection. In this procedure the backs of the hands and fingers and the under-chin area should not be neglected.

16   Positioning the lips is a problem that recurrently challenges the ingenuity of the embalmer. Closed too tightly, they tend to give a stern, even disapproving expression. Ideally, embalmers feel, the lips should give the impression of being ever so slightly parted, the upper lip pro-truding slightly for a more youthful appearance. This takes some engineer-ing, however, as the lips tend to drift apart. Lip drift can sometimes be remedied by pushing one or two straight pins through the inner margin of the lower lip and then inserting them between the two upper teeth. If Mr. Jones happens to have no teeth, the pins can just as easily be anchored in his Armstrong Face Former and Denture Replacer. Another method to maintain lip closure is to dislocate the lower jaw, which is then held in its new position by a wire run through holes which have been drilled through the upper and lower jaws at the midline. As the French are fond of saying, *il faut souffrir pour être belle.*

17   If Mr. Jones has died of jaundice, the embalming fluid will very likely turn him green. Does this deter the embalmer? Not if he has intestinal fortitude. Masking pastes and cosmetics are heavily laid on, burial garments and casket interiors color-correlated with particular care, and Jones is displayed beneath rose-colored lights. Friends will say "How *well* he looks." Death by carbon monoxide, on the other hand, can be rather a good thing from the embalmer's viewpoint: "One advantage is the fact that this type of discoloration is an exaggerated form of a natural pink coloration." This is nice because the healthy glow is already present and needs little attention.

18   The patching and filling completed, Mr. Jones is now shaved, washed and dressed. Cream-based cosmetic, available in pink, flesh, suntan, brunette, and blond, is applied to his hands and face, his hair is shampooed and combed (and, in the case of Mrs. Jones, set), his hands manicured. For the horny-handed son of toil and special care must be

taken; cream should be applied to remove ingrained grime, and the nails cleaned. "If he were not in the habit of having them manicured in life, trimming and shaping is advised for better appearance—never questioned by kin."

19   Jones is now ready for casketing (this is the present participle verb of "to casket"). In this operation his right shoulder should be depressed slightly "to turn the body a bit to the right and soften the appearance of lying flat on the back." Positioning the hands is a matter of importance, and special rubber positioning blocks may be used. The hands should be cupped slightly for a more lifelike, relaxed appearance. Proper placement of the body requires a delicate sense of balance. It should lie as high as possible in the casket, yet not so high that the lid, when lowered, will hit the nose. On the other hand, we are cautioned, placing the body too low "creates the impression that the body is in a box."

20   Jones is next wheeled into the appointed slumber room where a few last touches may be added—his favorite pipe placed in his hand or, if he was a great reader, a book propped into position. (In the case of little Master Jones a Teddy bear may be clutched.) Here he will hold open house for a few days, visiting hours 10 A.M. to 9 P.M.

21   All now being in readiness, the funeral director calls a staff conference to make sure that each assistant knows his precise duties. Mr. Wilber Kriege writes: "This makes your staff feel that they are part of the team, with a definite assignment that must be properly carried out if the whole plan is to succeed. You never heard of a football coach who failed to talk to his entire team before they go on the field. They have drilled on the plays they are to execute for hours and days, and yet the successful coach knows the importance of making even the bench-warming third-string substitute feel that he is important if the game is to be won." The winning of *this* game is predicated upon glass-smooth handling of the logistics. The funeral director has notified the pallbearers whose names were furnished by the family, has arranged for the presence of clergyman, organist, and soloist, has provided transportation for everybody, has organized and listed the flowers sent by friends. In *Psychology of Funeral Service*, Mr. Edward A. Martin points out: "He may not always do as much as the family thinks he is doing, but it is his helpful guidance that they appreciate in knowing they are proceeding as they should. . . . The important thing is how well his services can be used to make the family believe they are giving unlimited expression to their own sentiment."

22   The religious service may be held in a church or in the chapel of the funeral home; the funeral director vastly prefers the latter arrangement, for not only is it more convenient for him but it affords him the opportunity to show off his beautiful facilities to the gathered mourners. After the

clergyman has had his say, the mourners queue up to file past the casket for a last look at the deceased. The family is *never* asked whether they want an open-casket ceremony; in the absence of their instruction to the contrary, this is taken for granted. Consequently well over 90 per cent of all American funerals feature the open casket—a custom unknown in other parts of the world. Foreigners are astonished by it. An English woman living in San Francisco described her reaction in a letter to the writer:

> I myself have attended only one funeral here—that of an elderly fellow worker of mine. After the service I could not understand why everyone was walking towards the coffin (sorry, I mean casket), but thought I had better follow the crowd. It shook me rigid to get there and find the casket open and poor old Oscar lying there in his brown tweed suit, wearing a suntan makeup and just the wrong shade of lipstick. If I had not been extremely fond of the old boy, I have a horrible feeling that I might have giggled. Then and there I decided that I could never face another American funeral—even dead.

23   The casket (which has been resting throughout the service on a Classic Beauty Ultra Metal Casket Bier) is now transferred by a hydraulically operated device called Porto-Lift to a balloon-tired, Glide Easy casket carriage which will wheel it to yet another conveyance, the Cadillac Funeral Coach. This may be lavender, cream, light green—anything but black. Interiors, of course, are color-correlated, "for the man who cannot stop short of perfection."

24   At graveside, the casket is lowered into the earth. This office, once the prerogative of friends of the deceased, is now performed by a patented mechanical lowering device. A "Lifetime Green" artificial grass mat is at the ready to conceal the sere earth, and overhead, to conceal the sky, is a portable Sterile Chapel Tent ("resists the intense heat and humidity of summer and terrific storms of winter . . . available in Silver Grey, Rose or Evergreen"). Now is the time for the ritual scattering of earth over the coffin, as the solemn words, "earth to earth, ashes to ashes, dust to dust" are pronounced by the officiating cleric. This can boldly be accomplished "with a mere flick of the wrist with the Gordon Leak-Proof Earth Dispenser. No grasping of a handful of dirt, no soiled fingers. Simple, dignified, beautiful, reverent! The modern way!" The Gordon Earth Dispenser (at $5) is of nickel-plated brass construction. It is not only "attractive to the eye and long wearing"; it is also "one of the 'tools' for building better public relations" if presented as "an appropriate non-commercial gift" to the clergyman. It is shaped something like a saltshaker.

25   Untouched by human hand, the coffin and the earth are now united. It is in the function of directing the participants through this maze of gadgetry that the funeral director has assigned to himself his relatively new role of "grief therapist." He has relieved the family of every detail, he has revamped the corpse to look like a living doll, he has arranged for it to nap for a few days in a slumber room, he has put on a well-oiled performance in which the concept of *death* played no part whatsoever—unless it was inconsiderately mentioned by the clergyman who conducted the religious service. He has done everything in his power to make the funeral a real pleasure for everybody concerned. He and his team have given their all to score an upset victory over death.

Reading Reflection Questions

1. What are the direct or indirect (implied) messages in this essay?

_____

_____

2. What techniques, organizational patterns, and details distinguish this as a *process* analysis?

_____

_____

3. What tone does Mitford use in this essay? Why does she use this tone?

_____

_____

4. In your own words, what is her main message to her readers regarding the funeral industry?

_____

_____

5. List three examples from the reading that support her message.

_____

_____

6. Describe how you felt as you read about the process of embalming:

_____

_____

Objective Question

7. T/F _____ Mitford approves of the funeral industry's practices.

Checking Vocabulary

Define the following in your own words or provide a dictionary definition if you don't know the word.

8. descendent: _____

9. bereaved: _____

10. haphazard: _____

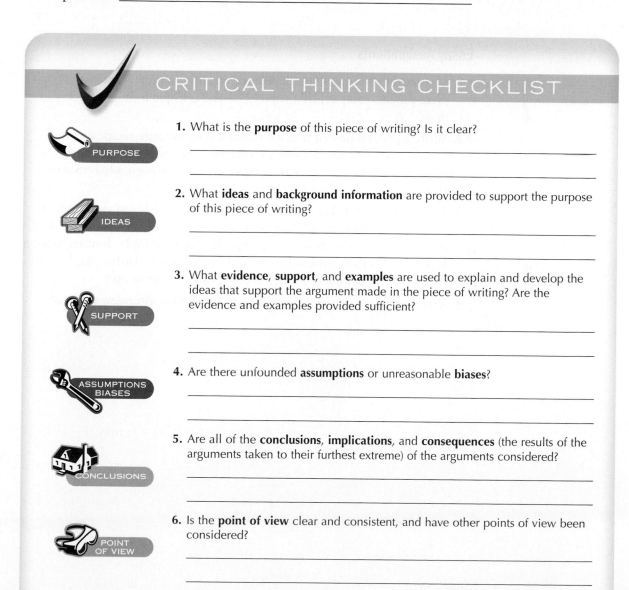

CRITICAL THINKING CHECKLIST

PURPOSE

1. What is the **purpose** of this piece of writing? Is it clear?

_____

_____

IDEAS

2. What **ideas** and **background information** are provided to support the purpose of this piece of writing?

_____

_____

SUPPORT

3. What **evidence**, **support**, and **examples** are used to explain and develop the ideas that support the argument made in the piece of writing? Are the evidence and examples provided sufficient?

_____

_____

ASSUMPTIONS BIASES

4. Are there unfounded **assumptions** or unreasonable **biases**?

_____

_____

CONCLUSIONS

5. Are all of the **conclusions**, **implications**, and **consequences** (the results of the arguments taken to their furthest extreme) of the arguments considered?

_____

_____

POINT OF VIEW

6. Is the **point of view** clear and consistent, and have other points of view been considered?

_____

_____

7. Using these critical thinking tools, **analyze** the overall structure of this essay and the strength of the author's arguments, ideas, and support. Was he or she successful in accomplishing the purpose? Why or why not?

_____

_____

Essay Assignments

1. Use one of the topics you developed in this chapter, and write a complete process essay on that topic. Use the critique form to check your draft.

2. Write a process description for making your favorite recipe or sandwich. Include all the details you can, be very specific, and use the exact order for re-creating the process you go through when making this item.

3. Pick a routine you know well from everyday experience, and write a process essay that would show someone else who has never done this activity step by step how to accomplish it (for example, how to make a bed, how to change the oil in a car, how to clean a bathroom, how to do a task you complete routinely for your job, and so on).

4. Write a process description of how to apply and interview for a job.

Classification

10

© Darrin Bell www.candorville.com

THINKING CRITICALLY

Look at the cartoon strip above. Then answer the questions that follow.

Classification is a great way to sort out the different categories within a group. For example, people classify others, at least to some extent, by gender, age, or race. Sometimes, it is appropriate to classify people by characteristics such as these, depending on your essay's purpose. At other times it can indicate bias. What kind of classification is going on in this cartoon strip? What do you think is the cartoon artist's implied message or thesis?

_____

_____

_____

_____

197

CLASSIFICATION ESSAYS

Classification (sometimes also called "division") involves grouping, or dividing items into categories. It involves using common characteristics to define categories within groups. You use classification skills all the time in your daily life. When you write a grocery list, you separate items into categories such as dairy, fruits and vegetables, frozen foods, and so on. In the academic world, classification comes in handy for subdividing larger groups in order to analyze them, or some aspect of them. Classification mode is often used in argument essays and story analysis essays (categorizing an author's techniques or characters). Classification writing is also common in the workplace: Many tasks involve sorting items or people into particular groups or classifications for marketing or analysis purposes.

Critical Thinking and Classification

Be sure you know your purpose in choosing to classify information. Decide on the criteria you are going to use, and then sort, or *classify*, items accordingly. *Division* involves specifically dividing items into distinct groupings. When dividing and classifying, look at specific qualities of the people or items being classified. Then, use those qualities as a basis for making your classification decisions. For instance, if you were classifying movies, you could sort them by their genre: horror, action, adventure, romantic comedy, and so on.

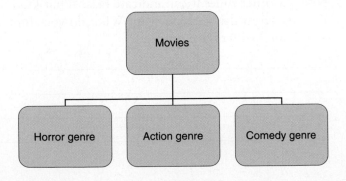

Then, you could subdivide each category, for instance,

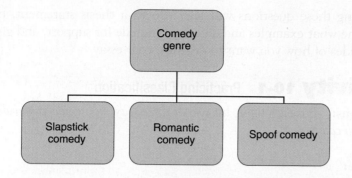

Applying Critical Thinking

| PURPOSE | IDEAS | SUPPORT | ASSUMPTIONS BIASES | CONCLUSIONS | POINT OF VIEW | ANALYSIS |

Analysis involves breaking down an idea and working out the meaning of the individual parts and how they relate to the whole. When you are classifying people or items, you want to look at the whole group and think carefully about what broad categories you could use to organize them accurately and then how you could break those categories down into more specific subgroups you can write about.

BEFORE WRITING A CLASSIFICATION ESSAY

Before you begin to write a classification essay on an assigned topic, or one you have chosen, start by asking yourself these questions:

1. What basis or principles will I use to classify the topic?
2. How can I subdivide my categories or classifications?
3. What do I want to explain or prove as a result of this classification and division?
4. Have I unfairly or inaccurately classified my subjects or oversimplified complex divisions?
5. What do I want my readers to learn or understand after reading this essay?

Answering these questions will lead you to a thesis statement, help you determine what examples and details to include for support, and give you a general idea of how you want to organize your essay.

Activity 10-1   Practicing Classification

Directions: *For each topic, list two or three ways you could subdivide or classify it into categories.*

Example:

> **Topic:** Carbohydrates
>
> Categories: _Pasta, bread, crackers_____

1. **Topic:** American cars

   Categories: _____

2. **Topic:** Dog breeds

   Categories: _____

3. **Topic:** TV shows

   Categories: _____

4. **Topic:** Sports

   Categories: _____

5. **Topic:** Types of dwellings/places to live

   Categories: _____

WRITING A CLASSIFICATION ESSAY

The paragraph structure of a classification essay is based on sorting a group into its particular parts in order to understand the whole better. For instance, you could choose to classify and divide college students based on their age, gender, race, economic backgrounds, and academic backgrounds. After classifying and studying the various parts of the college student body, you could reach a better understanding of the whole group. The purpose of a classification essay may also be to *critique* the categories set by someone else and argue against the constructions and decisions made in the process of categorizing those items or people. Often, classification essays involve a great deal of comparison and contrast, description, and narration, and they serve the purpose of making an argument to persuade a reader of the writer's point.

When you classify, think about what point you want to make about the group you've chosen for your topic and the best way to subdivide that group into categories. For instance, if you want to write about online classes, you might want to first subdivide online classes into specific types: online composition classes, online history classes, and online math classes, for instance. Be careful to avoid biased classifications that do not fairly represent the members of each subgroup or misrepresent the items, thoughts, or people within those groups. For instance, you wouldn't want to claim that online students have particular habits or faults that on-campus students don't if you didn't have legitimate support for such a claim. Also, do not oversimplify your subdivisions into groups that do not fully represent the complexities of the subjects.

Applying Critical Thinking

PURPOSE	IDEAS	SUPPORT	ASSUMPTIONS BIASES	CONCLUSIONS	POINT OF VIEW	ANALYSIS

Classification is something you do to make sense out of groups of things and people around you. When you classify, be extra careful not to overgeneralize, and be aware of your **biases** and **assumptions**.

1. A **bias** is a particular viewpoint that you have about an idea or a topic. Sometimes you are conscious of the biases in your ideas, and sometimes you are not. Having biases is not necessarily a bad thing, but when they are founded on misinformation they can get in the way of good critical thinking. When you classify people or things, think carefully about what ideas you already have about the group(s) you are discussing and whether they are based on fact.

   Example of unfounded bias: Girls are not as good at solving math problems as boys.

2. An **assumption** is a belief or claim that you take for granted. Almost everything you believe and do is based on assumptions. Some assumptions, however, are ones that you take for granted but not everyone would agree with. It is important to learn to separate the assumptions that have a solid basis in fact from ones that don't when you are making decisions about classifying information.

   Example of unfounded assumption: Computer Science majors are nerds.

In your introductory paragraph, identify your topic and explain how you will divide and classify it. For instance, you could introduce the category of online classes and then divide and classify subsets of those. Also, clearly establish your purpose for classifying this group. What conclusion did you reach through the process of subdividing the group? Then, in the body paragraphs, focus on one subgroup at a time. Be sure to use transitions that show comparisons and contrasts. You may even subdivide the subcategories using separate paragraphs. Finally, in the concluding paragraph, re-emphasize the method of classification you used, state the conclusions you reached by subdividing the group, and emphasize the point you want to express to your readers. The chart below provides a brief overview of the structure of a classification essay.

BASIC STRUCTURE FOR A CLASSIFICATION ESSAY

Introductory Paragraph

Sets up the categories/subdivisions of the larger topic you will discuss in your thesis.

Thesis statement: A statement that describes what you are trying to explain, show, prove, or argue by using classification—and what conclusions you reached by subdividing your topic.

Body Paragraphs (Two to five, depending on assignment and purpose)

Develop the separate subcategories, maybe even subdividing and classifying them— indicate with your **topic sentences.**

Use transitions within and between paragraphs to make the paragraphs flow smoothly.

Provide concrete examples/details and description about the categories.

Analyze the examples.

Concluding Paragraph

Sum up and re-emphasize the thesis: the conclusions reached by classifying your topic.

STRUCTURING A CLASSIFICATION ESSAY

Topic

To generate your topic and purpose for your classification essay, use the guidelines specified by your instructor's assignment. If you do not have a specific classification assignment, come up with a topic idea through brainstorming and decide how you could classify it into groups.

A Few Topic Possibilities

You can write a classification essay that groups together types of people, types of classes, cars, exercise, music, films, and so on. Many groups call for classification and division in order to understand nuances and complexities within them. Be sure to have a purpose in mind for categorizing: a conclusion related to the classifications you made that you want to explain to your readers.

Activity 10-2   Breaking a Topic into Categories

Directions: *For each of the topics below, use one of the ways of classifying it that you chose in Activity 10-1 and come up with a list of subcategories.*

Example:

> **Topic:** Carbohydrates
>
> **Category:** Pasta
>
> **Subcategories:** *spaghetti, lasagna, macaroni* _____

1. **Topic:** American cars

    Category: _____

    Subcategories: _____

2. **Topic:** Dog breeds

    Category: _____

    Subcategories: _____

3. **Topic:** TV shows

    Category: _____

    Subcategories: _____

4. **Topic:** Sports

    Category: _____

    Subcategories: _____

5. **Topic:** Types of dwellings/places to live

    Category: _____

    Subcategories: _____

Thesis Statements

If you have a specific classification assignment that dictates what you will be trying to explain or prove through your essay, then customize your thesis using key words from the assignment itself. For instance, if you were asked to classify colleges and universities in order to explore which options were best for you, your thesis would specify which categories you have chosen to use and what conclusion you've reached as a result of this classification.

> College students fall into certain groups when it comes to their living options—those who live in on-campus dorms, those who share an apartment or house with other students, or those who stay with their parents while in college to save money—and each category has its own advantages and disadvantages.

Activity 10-3   Creating Thesis Statements

Directions: *Using the categories and subcategories you generated in Activities 10-1 and 10-2, create a one-sentence thesis statement for three of the general topics. Make sure the thesis statement has a clear message or lesson to convey about what conclusion you reached using classification.*

1. **Topic:** _____

    _____

    _____

    _____

2. **Topic:** _____

    _____

3. **Topic:** _____

_____

_____

_____

Introductory Paragraph

In the introductory paragraph of your classification essay, provide general information about the topic, the larger group that will be classified. Then present the subcategories you will use to create your classification. Finally, in the thesis statement, explain the purpose for your classification essay: what point you want your readers to see as a result of your classification process.

Body Paragraphs

In your body paragraphs, individually develop each subcategory you created through your classification of your general topic into groups. Provide clear topic sentences that present each subcategory. Then, add specific examples and details to explain and develop the subcategories. You may need to add subcategories for your subcategories too. Use transitions when needed both within and between your paragraphs. Contrast and comparison transitions are particularly useful in classification essays; you can also use transitions that show addition of points and purpose (see Chapter 6, pages 118–119).

Transitions to Show Contrast or a Change in Idea

although	even though	instead	on the other side
anyhow	for all that	nevertheless	otherwise
at the same time	however	notwithstanding	regardless
but	in any event	on the contrary	still
despite this	in contrast	on the other hand	yet

Transitions to Show a Comparison

in like manner	in the same way	likewise	similarly

Activity 10-4   Creating Topic Sentences

Directions: *Now create two topic sentences for each of the thesis statements you created in Activity 10-3, addressing the different categories you would discuss in each paragraph.*

1. **Topic:** _____

    _____

    _____

2. **Topic:** _____

    _____

    _____

3. **Topic:** _____

    _____

    _____

Definitions and Examples

Because in classification essays you are explaining and discussing a category in each paragraph, you need to provide clear definitions and examples to illustrate the differences and similarities between the categories. For instance, if you were taking a biology class, you might be asked to classify trees into groups. You might use *evergreen* and *deciduous* as two of your subcategories, and then you would need both to define these terms and provide examples of the types of trees they refer to:

TREES

Deciduous	Evergreen
(Leaves fall off in winter)	(Leaves/needles stay on year round)
Maple	Cedar
Oak	Fir
Elm	Pine

Activity 10-5   Providing Examples

Directions: *Now provide at least three possible examples or details you would include for three of the topic sentences you created in Activity 10-4.*

1. Topic: _____

     _____

     _____

2. Topic: _____

     _____

     _____

     _____

3. Topic: _____

     _____

     _____

     _____

Concluding Paragraph

In your concluding paragraph, restate your thesis statement emphasizing what conclusions you reached by classifying your topic. Touch on the categories you used to classify your topic and the main point you want your readers to realize after they read your essay.

Activity 10-6   Writing a Conclusion

Directions: *Choose one of the topics you've been developing in the preceding activities and write a three- to five-sentence concluding paragraph that re-emphasizes the classification categories and the purpose you want to get across by using the classification process you have chosen.*

_____

_____

_____

_____

_____

    Use the following critique form to check for the basics in your classification essay draft.

Classification Essay Critique Form

PURPOSE	IDEAS	SUPPORT	ASSUMPTIONS BIASES	CONCLUSIONS	POINT OF VIEW	ANALYSIS

	Done well	Needs work
Overall		
1. Does the essay categorize two or more subjects with specific characteristics?	_____	_____
2. Does the essay use specific categories consistently and clearly?	_____	_____
3. Are the paragraphs broken up well and about the right length?	_____	_____
Introduction		
4. Is the title interesting and in correct format?	_____	_____
5. Is there a general introduction that sets up the thesis and categories?	_____	_____
6. Is there a clear thesis statement that explains the **purpose** of the classifications being made?	_____	_____
Body		
7. Do the **ideas** in the body paragraphs develop the categories and flow smoothly?	_____	_____
8. Are transitions used between and, when needed, within the paragraphs?	_____	_____
9. Do the body paragraphs include **support** (descriptive details and examples)?	_____	_____
Conclusion		
10. Does the **concluding** paragraph sum up the categories with analysis and re-emphasize the purpose developed in the introductory paragraph and thesis, without adding new ideas?	_____	_____

Editing

11. Circle the following errors you think you see in this draft: spelling, fragments, run-ons/comma splices, commas, semicolon/colon use, pronoun agreement, reference fault errors, parallelism, apostrophe use, verb use/tense, and passive voice construction. (See the handbook section for help in identifying and correcting these errors.)

12. Other types of grammar or sentence-level errors:

_____

Comments:

_____

_____

COMPLEMENTARY MODES FOR CLASSIFICATION ESSAYS

Classification mode combines well with several other modes.

- **Narration** and **description** can be used to develop the categories.
- **Illustration and examples** will further elaborate on the classifications.
- You can look at the **causes and effects** of classifications and divisions.
- You can **compare and contrast** among the categories.
- You can use classification to prove an **argument** or **persuade** your readers to a particular point of view.

SAMPLE STUDENT ESSAY

Hill 1

Lynne Hill

Professor Martinez

English 100

23 November 2007

TV People, Movie People, and Book People

Do you know people who love to watch TV, who go to the movies as much as possible, or who read books voraciously? Several of my friends fall into one of these categories, and some of them are so deeply devoted to their need for TV, movies, or books that that connection has become part of who they are. These people, let us call them the "TV people," "movie people," and "book people," have particular characteristics and particular personalities.

The TV people like to stay home on most nights, arranging their schedules as they consult the TV Guide. They hate the sound of silence if they are home. They are drawn as if by a magnet to the lure of the box in the corner, calling them like a siren: "Come turn me

Thesis statement

Hill 2

on . . . you can watch just for a little while . . . Oprah misses you. . . ." The devoted TV people will forgo housecleaning, homework, and any type of creative project to ensure they do not miss a chance for some good passive TV watching. The TV people have a master plan for avoiding engaging with their lives: They can let the shows do the thinking, and the living, for them.

The movie people are one step above the TV people when it comes to social engagement. At least they will step out of their homes in the evenings from time to time . . . to see a movie. Some movie people have even studied cinematography and consider their fascination with movies a sign of their expertise; some will even actively critique the films—true artists in their medium. There are subcategories of movie people: the loner movie people, the social movie people, and the snobby movie people versus the non-discriminating movie people. The loner movie people prefer to watch movies by themselves. They are easily irritated by friends who make comments during the show, and they are distracted by the sounds of people eating popcorn or snacks. The social movie people choose not to go to movies alone: they passively watch with someone or several people. Then, they like to engage in dialogue about the movies after-wards. The snobby movie people will see only the highly critically acclaimed, "artsy" movies, while the non-discriminating movie people will see anything—and love it! It's pricier to be a movie person than a TV person. Movies and the nearly mandatory accompanying snacks from the snack bar can set a person back $20 at a time.

Finally, the book people are often the most creative, intelligent, and self-sufficient category; however, that does not guarantee that they win in the social graces department. The book people are cre-ative: they create movies in their own heads from the books they

Topic sentence

Topic sentence

Topic sentence

Hill 3

read, casting their own actors and blocking their own scenes. They are actively engaged in the stories they read, not just passive viewers. Also, book people are smart and can be great conversationalists, if you can tear them away from whatever current book they are engaged in. In fact, book people can be downright anti-social on vacations, sneaking off to a beach or back room alone to delve back into whatever juicy book they are reading.

It's predictable that there are all levels of TV people, movie people, and book people out there. Certainly, each of these types has their own distinguishing characteristics. Which category do you fit in most closely?

Restatement of thesis

Activity 10-7   Thinking Critically About the Student Essay

Directions: *Analyze the essay to identify the features and details characteristic of the classification mode. Mark them on the essay. Then, reread the essay, and make a list of specific revisions you would make to correct any problems with content, organization, transitions, and style.*

Race in America

George Henderson

George Henderson is Dean of the College of Liberal Arts at the University of Oklahoma, where he is also a professor of human relations, education, and sociology. Henderson has served as a race relations consultant to many national and international organizations. He is author of *Our Souls to Keep: Black/White Relations in America* (1999) and coeditor with Grace Xuequin Ma of *Rethinking Ethnicity and Health Care: A Sociocultural Perspective* (1999). This essay appeared in a special issue on race in America in the spring 2000 issue of *National Forum*.

Note: Some of the vocabulary in this essay is very high level, so make sure to use context clues and consult a dictionary when you need to.

1   Because of intermarriage, most Americans have multiple ethnic and racial identities. Some persons of mixed lineage prefer to assume culturally nondescript identities. For example, they have become "white people," "black people," "Indians," "Latinos," "Asians," or just plain "Americans" in order to somehow deflect from themselves any connection with their ancestors. The task of tracing their families has become too taxing or too insignificant. Even so, the effects of ethnicity and race are pervasive: disparate patterns of community relationships and economic opportunities haunt us. At some time in their history, all ethnic groups in the United States have been the underclass. Also, at different times, all ethnic groups have been both the oppressed and the oppressors.

2   Ethnicity is the most distinguishing characteristic of Americans, where we are sorted primarily on the basis of our cultural identities or nationalities. An ethnic group is a culturally distinct population whose members share a collective identity and a common heritage. Historically, the overwhelming majority of ethnic groups emerged in the United States as a result of one of several responses to the following processes: (1) migration, (2) consolidation of group forces in the face of an impending threat from an aggressor, (3) annexation or changes in political boundary lines, or (4) schisms within a church. Hence, "ethnic minority" presupposes people different from the mainstream or dominant cultured persons.

3   But it is the erroneous belief that people who come to America can be placed in categories based on their unique gene pools that has resulted in the most blatant instances of discrimination. Races, however defined, do not correspond to genetic reality because inbreeding world populations share a common gene pool. A much more practical dictum, and one that has often been ignored throughout American history, is that all people belong to the same species. Unfortunately, too few individuals believe that the only race of any significance is the human race.

A Brief History

4   At the time of the American Revolution, the American population was largely composed of English Protestants who had absorbed a substantial number of German and Scotch-Irish settlers and a smaller number of French, Dutch, Swedes, Poles, Swiss, Irish, and other immigrants. The colonies had a modest number of Catholics, and a smaller number of Jews. Excluding Quakers and Swedes, the colonists treated Native Americans with contempt and hostility, and engaged in wars against them that bordered on genocide. They drove natives from the coastal plains in order to make way for a massive white movement to the West. Although Africans, most of whom were slaves, comprised one-fifth of the American

population during the Revolution, they, similar to Indians, were not perceived by most white colonists as being worthy of assimilation.

5   The white peoples of the new nation had long since crossed Caucasian lines to create a conglomerate but culturally homogeneous society. People of different ethnic groups—English, Irish, German, Huguenot, Dutch, Swedish—mingled and intermarried. English settlers and peoples from western and northern Europe had begun a process of ethnic assimilation that caused some writers to incorrectly describe the nation as melted into one ethnic group: American. In reality, non-Caucasian Americans were not included in the Eurocentric cultural pot.

6   During the 150 years immediately following the Revolution, large numbers of immigrants came to the United States from eastern European countries. They were the so-called "new immigrants." During the latter part of that period, slaves were emancipated, numerous Indian tribes were conquered and forced to relocate to reservations, portions of Mexico's land were taken, and Asians began emigrating to the United States. The English language and English-oriented cultural patterns grew even more dominant. Despite a proliferation of cultural diversity within the growing ethnic enclaves, Anglo-conformity ideology spawned racist notions about Nordic and Aryan racial superiority. This ideology gave rise to nativist political agendas and exclusionist immigration policies favoring western and northern European immigrants.

7   Non-English-speaking western Europeans and northern Europeans were also discriminated against. The slowness of some of those immigrants, particularly Germans, to learn English, their tendency to live in enclaves, and their establishment of ethnic-language newspapers were friction points. Such ethnic-oriented lifestyles prompted many Americanized people to chide: "If they don't like it here, they can go back to where they came from." But that solution was too simplistic. Immigrants from all countries and cultures, even those who were deemed socially and religiously undesirable, were needed to help build a nation—to work the farms, dig the ore, build railroads and canals, settle the prairies, and otherwise provide human resources.

8   Beginning in the 1890s, immigrants from eastern and southern Europe were numerically dominant. That set the stage for racist statements about inferior, darker people threatening the purity of blond, blue-eyed Nordics or Aryans through miscegenation. Intermixture was perceived as a deadly plague. Although the immigrants from eastern and southern Europe were not suitable marriage partners, their critics stated, they could be properly assimilated and amalgamated. This kind of ethnocentrism prevented large numbers of other immigrants and indigenous peoples of color from becoming fully functioning citizens. And the legacy for the children of

people denied equal opportunities was second-class citizenship. We can easily document the negative effects of second-class citizenship: abhorrent inequalities, unwarranted exclusions, and atmospheres of rejection.

9   Immigrants who lived in remote, isolated areas were able to maintain some semblance of being ethnic nations within America. But the growth of cities brought about the decline of farming populations and ethnic colonies. A short time was required for the white immigrants who settled in cities to discard their native languages and cultures. But it is erroneous to think of any ethnic group as melting away without leaving a trace of its cultural heritage. All ethnic groups have infused portions of their cultures into the tapestry of American history.

10   Early twentieth-century eastern European immigrants were a very disparate mixture of peoples. They came from nations that were trying to become states—Poland, Czechoslovakia, Lithuania, and Yugoslavia; from states trying to become nations—Italy, Turkey, and Greece; and from areas outside the Western concept of either state or nation. All of them included people such as Jews who did not easily fit into any of those categories. Through social and educational movements, laws, and superordinate goals such as winning wars and establishing economic world superiority, eastern Europeans and other white ethnic groups were able to enter mainstream America.

11   The cultures and colors of Third World ethnic groups were in stark contrast to European immigrants. Those differences became obstacles to assimilation and, more importantly, to people of color achieving equal opportunities. Nonwhite groups in the United States occupied specific low-status niches in the workplace, which in turn resulted in similarities among their members in such things as occupations, standard of living, level of education, place of residence, access to political power, and quality of health care. Likenesses within those groups facilitated the formation of stereotypes and prejudices that inhibited the full citizenship of nonwhite minorities.

12   Immigrants who held highly esteemed occupations—lawyers, artists, engineers, scientists, and physicians—became Americanized much faster than those who held less esteemed positions—unskilled laborers, farm workers, coal miners, and stock clerks. But even in those instances there were pro-European biases and stereotypes. For example, French chefs, Italian opera singers, Polish teachers, German conductors, and Russian scientists were more highly recruited than Africans, Hispanics, and Asians who had the same skills. Racial and quasi-racial groups—including American Indians, Mexican Americans, Asian Americans, African Americans, and Puerto Ricans—were not nearly so readily absorbed as various Caucasian ethnic groups. And that is generally the situation today.

Despite numerous and impressive gains during the past century, a dispro-
portionate number of peoples of color are still treated like pariahs.

What Does the Future Hold?

13 If U.S. Census Bureau population projections are correct, our nation is un-
dergoing mind-boggling demographic changes: Hispanics will triple in
numbers, from 31.4 million in 1999 to 98.2 million in 2050; blacks will increase 70 percent, from 34.9 million to 59.2 million; Asians and Pacific Is-
landers will triple, from 10.9 million to 37.6 million; Native Americans and
Alaska Natives will increase from approximately 2.2 million to 2.6 million.
During the same period, the non-Hispanic white population will increase
from 196.1 million to 213 million. Also, the foreign-born population, most
of them coming from Asia and Latin America, will increase from 26 million
to 53.8 million. The non-Hispanic white population will decrease from 72
percent of the total population in 1999 to 52 percent in 2050, and the nation's workforce will be composed of over 50 percent racial and ethnic minorities and immigrants. Who then will be the pariahs?

14   Without equal opportunities, the melting pot will continue to be an
unreachable mirage, a dream of equality deferred, for too many people of
color. This does not in any way detract from the significance of the things
minorities have achieved. Ethnic-group histories and lists of cultural con-
tributions support the contention that each group is an integral part of a
whole nation. Although all American ethnic minority groups have experienced continuous socioeconomic gains, the so-called "playing field" that
includes white participants is not yet level. Simply stated, the rising tide
of economic prosperity has not yet lifted the masses of people of color.
Whatever our life circumstances, the citizens of the United States are
bound together not as separate ethnic groups but as members of different
ethnic groups united in spirit and behavior and locked into a common
destiny.

15   There is little doubt that our nation is at a crossroads in its race relations. Where we go from here is up to all of us. We can try segregation
again, continuance of the status quo, silence in the face of prejudice and
discriminatory practices, or activism. The choice is ours.

16   Segregation of ethnic minorities is not a redeeming choice for the
United States. It did not work during earlier times, and it will not work
now. There have never been separate but equal majority-group and
minority-group communities in the United States. And the pretense of
such a condition would once again be a particularly pernicious injustice
to all citizens. Racial segregation diminishes both the perpetrators and
their victims. Preserving the status quo in education, employment, health

care, and housing, which so often is little more than codified racial discrimination, is not justice for minorities either.

17   Inaction by people who witness oppressive acts is equally unacceptable. Even though they may be shocked and frustrated by the problems,
standing in wide-eyed horror is not an adequate posture to assume. While
they may be legally absolved of any wrongdoing, these silent people must
come to terms with what others believe to be their moral culpability. Of
course, silence may be prudent. Usually, there is a high price to be paid
by those who would challenge racism in community institutions. Friends,
jobs, promotions, and prestige may be lost. Furthermore, few victories
come easily, and most of the victors are unsung heroes.

18   Individuals who choose to challenge purveyors of bigotry and unequal
opportunities must also take care that in their actions to redress racial
injustices, they do not emulate the oppressors whom they deplore. That
might makes right, that blood washes out injustices—these too are false
strategies for achieving justice. "It does not matter much to a slave what
the color of his master is," a wise black janitor once said. We, the descen-
dants of migrants, immigrants, and slaves, can build a better nation—a
place where all people have safe housing, get a top-quality education, do
meaningful work for adequate wages, are treated fairly in criminal-justice
systems, have their medical needs met, and in the end die a timely death
unhurried by bigots. This is the kind of history that should be made.

Reading Reflection Questions

1. What are the direct or indirect (implied) messages in this essay?

_____

_____

_____

_____

2. What techniques, organization patterns, and details distinguish this as a
classification essay? _____

_____

_____

3. In your own words, what is Henderson's view of people who identify
themselves by race? _____

_____

_____

Objective Questions

4. T/F _____ As early white settlers in America, the Quakers treated Native Americans badly.

5. T/F _____ The author believes that segregation by race can be beneficial to society.

6. T/F _____ Nonwhite immigrants with higher prestige jobs such as doctors or lawyers became Americanized faster.

7. Provide two examples of injustices that have happened in American society as a result of racial differences as mentioned by Henderson.

_____

_____

_____

Checking Vocabulary

Define the following in your own words or provide a dictionary definition if you don't know the word.

8. ethnicity: _____

9. migration: _____

10. ethnocentrism: _____

_____

CRITICAL THINKING CHECKLIST

PURPOSE

1. What is the **purpose** of this piece of writing? Is it clear?

_____

_____

2. What **ideas** and **background information** are provided to support the purpose of this piece of writing?

IDEAS

_____

_____

3. What **evidence** and **examples** are used to explain and develop the ideas that support the argument made in the piece of writing? Are the evidence and examples provided sufficient?

_____

_____

4. Are there unfounded **assumptions** or unreasonable **biases**?

_____

_____

5. Are all of the **conclusions**, **implications**, and **consequences** of the arguments (the results of the arguments taken to their furthest extreme) considered?

_____

_____

6. Is the **point of view** clear and consistent, and have other points of view been considered?

_____

_____

7. Using these critical thinking tools, **analyze** the overall structure of this essay and the strength of the author's arguments, ideas, and support. Was he or she successful in accomplishing the purpose? Why or why not?

_____

_____

Essay Assignments

1. Write a classification essay using any of the topics you developed in the activities in this chapter.

2. Classify college students into at least four categories (think of stereotyping them into particular *types* of students). Then come up with an analytical conclusion based on the categories or stereotypes.

3. Pick one of the following types of establishments, and then categorize the types within those establishments. Use specific examples and details. Then come to an analytical conclusion related to these categories.

   a. Fast food restaurants

   b. Coffee shops

   c. Department stores

4. Categorize your coworkers as to skill levels and efficiency. Then come to an analytical conclusion as a result of your categories and criteria.

5. Categorize teachers at your college into types. Then come to an analytical conclusion related to teachers and the categories they fall into.

6. Categorize American cars versus imported cars. Then come to an analytical conclusion related to the details and categories you come up with.

11

Definition

THINKING CRITICALLY

Look at the picture above. Then do the tasks that follow.

1. Define the object above. Use specific descriptive words, as if your audience has no idea what this thing is and cannot see it for themselves.

   _____

   _____

   _____

2. Now briefly define the symbolic significance of this object. Explain any associations and connections to its cultural identity.

_____

_____

_____

DEFINITION ESSAYS

Definition essays explain, define, and clarify items, terms, and concepts. They are used to tell the reader what something is or what something means. Though you may need to use some description in a definition essay, make sure that when you are defining an object or concept you don't merely describe the subject: _Defining_ must explain what it _is_ and what it _means_, not just what it looks like.

Applying Critical Thinking

| PURPOSE | IDEAS | SUPPORT | ASSUMPTIONS BIASES | CONCLUSIONS | POINT OF VIEW | ANALYSIS |

You define words and concepts to make it easier to communicate with others. Some definitions are straightforward and rely on facts and dictionaries, while some require more **analysis** and explanation on your part—and maybe even some creative thought and comparisons. To write an effective definition essay, you will need to consider the following questions:

1. What is my **purpose** and plan for this definition essay? What point do I want to make? How will I convey that message?

2. What **ideas** should I include to make my definition clear to my reader? What **support** (descriptive details, terms, examples, creative comparisons) will help me develop my definition and its purpose?

Critical Thinking and Definition

The purpose for a definition essay can range from providing a straightforward definition of a term or concept in order to increase your reader's understanding of it to a definition that includes the symbolic meaning or cultural and historic relevance of an item or idea. For instance, you might define a "tamale" as a type of food composed of corn masa (ground corn flour) and fillings, such as meats, vegetables, or fruit, that is popular in countries such as Mexico and El Salvador. Then you could move on to define what this particular food represents in terms of the history, culture, or traditions of these countries. Definition essays are commonly used in reports to classmates and coworkers or to define specific terms or processes in a particular field or for a particular audience.

An **extended definition** consists of one or more paragraphs that explain a complex term. In an extended definition, you might use synonyms (words that have the same or similar meanings), give examples, discuss the term's origins, provide comparisons, explain what the word is not, or create an anecdote to show the word in action. You can consult a dictionary, but do not use a dictionary quotation as the main part of your definition. You may, however, integrate information you learn from the dictionary into your extended definition (check with your instructor). Extended definitions can employ other methods of development—narration, description, process analysis, illustration, classification, comparison and contrast, and cause and effect. Often, they also define by negation, by explaining what the term *does not mean*. Extended definitions can be purely personal, or they can be largely objective. A personal definition explains how a writer is using the term and allows the reader to see a word in a different light.

BEFORE WRITING A DEFINITION ESSAY

Before you begin to write a definition essay on an assigned topic, or one you have chosen, start by asking yourself these questions:

1. What is the object or concept I want to define?
2. What general category does my subject fall into?
3. What distinguishing characteristics does it have?
4. Can I compare it to something similar to help define it?
5. Can I explain it by saying what it is not?
6. Why am I defining this subject, and what purpose can it serve?
7. What do I want my readers to learn or understand after reading this essay?

Answering these questions will lead you to an expository thesis statement, help you determine examples and details to include for support, and give you a general idea of how you want to organize your essay.

Applying Critical Thinking

| · PURPOSE | IDEAS | SUPPORT | ASSUMPTIONS BIASES | CONCLUSIONS | POINT OF VIEW | ANALYSIS |

To define your subject, you can draw on your own personal knowledge of the subject. If you are defining an object, you can have it in front of you to help create your definition. Be careful, though, not to slip into merely describing the object. Define what it is, its purpose, how it is used or what it is used for, or what relationship it has to society and human use. Use your well founded **assumptions** and **biases** to help you. Ask your instructor if you are allowed to look up definitions for an object or concept you are assigned to define. If you are allowed to include researched definitions from dictionaries, encyclopedias, or the Internet, then make sure to give credit to any outside sources you use.

Activity 11-1   Practicing Definition

Directions: *Prewrite on the following topics for a definition essay by brainstorming or clustering. Use a separate sheet of paper.*

1. Family
2. Tradition
3. Global warming
4. Discrimination
5. Globalization
6. Favoritism
7. Home
8. Logo of your choice
9. Meditation
10. Ceremony

WRITING A DEFINITION ESSAY

In your introductory paragraph, identify the topic you will be defining. Then, based on your prewriting, explain in your thesis statement how you will define the subject and what your purpose is for defining it.

In the body of your essay, you can define the item, term, or concept you have chosen by first discussing how your subject fits into a general category. Then you can write about its distinguishing features in order to define it more specifically. For instance, if you had to define a mango, you might first put it into the general category of an exotic or tropical fruit. Then you would get specific about the mango's distinguishing qualities: its taste, color, shape, size, texture, and so on.

In order to define your subject more precisely, you can also compare it to similar things. For instance, you could compare a hammer to a mallet, as they are similar kinds of tools, but emphasize how they differ. Or you could compare something unfamiliar (the item you are defining) to something familiar to your audience. For example, you could explain that bouillabaisse is like a beef stew only made from several types of fish and shellfish. You can also define a term by saying what it is not. For instance, you could define the term "obesity" by saying what it is not: It is not being just a couple of pounds overweight.

You might also want to talk about subcategories within the term you are defining. If you were defining the term *schizophrenia* for a psychology course, you might want to talk about different types of schizophrenia such as disorganized, paranoid, and catatonic. Conclude your definition essay by summing up what you have defined and your purpose for defining it. Here is a sample definition paragraph that provides a simple, clear definition of the term "flag." The topic sentence is in italics.

> *A flag is an object that is made of fabric and includes colors and possibly shapes, letters, or figures to represent a group, team, or even a country.* For example, many sports teams have flags dedicated to them that feature the team name and a picture of the team mascot. The Chicago Bulls, for instance, have a team flag that is red and black and has a picture of a bull's head along with the team name. Flags can also represent a country; for instance, the flag of the United States is red, white, and blue, with bold red and white stripes and a square shape in the corner that is dark blue with 50 white stars representing the 50 states.

If you wanted to add the dimension of cultural or symbolic significance to your paragraph, then you might make the topic sentence more analytical and add some examples of what the flag represents and what kind of symbolic weight it carries. For instance:

> *The American flag is more than just a cloth representation of the United States: It is also a symbol of our country's values, history, and identity.* The 50 stars that represent each state also represent America as a country made up of unique states that form a union. This unity is especially important symbolically, given the history of this country and the American Civil War that nearly tore the northern and southern states apart.

The chart below provides a brief overview of the structure of a definition essay.

BASIC STRUCTURE FOR A DEFINITION ESSAY

Introductory Paragraph	**Sets up background** for your definition. **Thesis statement**: States how you will define your chosen topic and your purpose for defining it.	
Body Paragraphs (Two to five, depending on assignment and purpose)	**Develop** your definition through identifying the group the item or concept belongs to and discussing its distinguishing characteristics. **Topic sentences** will set up the structure of your definition in each paragraph. **Provide concrete examples** to illustrate and define your topic. Provide definitions of any unfamiliar terms you use in your explanation of your topic. **Analyze** the examples. **Use transitions** within and between paragraphs to make the paragraphs flow smoothly.	 
Concluding Paragraph	**Sums up and re-emphasizes** the thesis statement: The **conclusions reached** through your definition.	

STRUCTURING A DEFINITION ESSAY

Topic

If you do not have a topic assigned by your instructor for your definition essay, then brainstorm ideas for things, places, or people you might want to define. Then come up with some ideas for a purpose for defining the topic. What do you want your readers to understand through your definition?

A Few Topic Possibilities

You can define a complex term or process you learned about in another class. You can define a term, position, or item from your job. Basically, anything you would need to define to your audience in order to make a point would constitute the need for an in-depth definition.

Thesis Statements

The thesis statement for a definition essay states what item, concept, or term you are going to define and establishes your purpose for writing about it. Your purpose may be simply to define an object or concept for an audience unfamiliar with your subject.

> A mitral valve prolapse is a specific type of heart murmur that exhibits several distinct characteristics.

Often, though, a definition essay's purpose is to define something in order to reach a more complex conclusion related to the subject. For instance, in the tamale example earlier in this chapter, the writer could first define what a *tamale* is and then use tamales as a cultural symbol of the tastes and traditions of the countries that prize them.

> The tamale is an important part of Mexican holiday traditions: It is more than a favorite food since it is part of a cultural tradition.

In your introductory paragraph, set up the overall topic you will be defining. Then based on your prewriting, establish how you will define the subject and what the purpose is for defining it, so as to come up with the right thesis statement for your topic and purpose.

Activity 11-2   Creating Thesis Statements

Directions: *Choose three of the topics from Activity 11-1 that you brainstormed about and two topics of your own choice (such as terms from other classes you've had), and create a one-sentence thesis statement for each. Make* *sure each thesis statement identifies the item, concept, or term being defined and your purpose for defining it.*

1. Item, concept, or term: _____

   Thesis statement: _____

   _____

2. Item, concept, or term: _____

   Thesis statement: _____

   _____

3. Item, concept, or term: _____

   Thesis statement: _____

   _____

4. Item, concept, or term: _____

   Thesis statement: _____

   _____

5. Item, concept, or term: _____

   Thesis statement: _____

   _____

Introductory Paragraph

Begin your definition essay with a general introduction to the subject or term you are defining. End with a thesis statement that sets up the purpose for your definition essay.

Body Paragraphs

After creating a strong thesis statement for a definition essay, you need to organize your body paragraphs in the best way to develop your definition. For instance, using the tamale example from earlier in the chapter, you could use the body paragraphs and topic sentences to further define the tamale and then develop the tamale's significance symbolically, giving specific details and explaining the traditions and cultural history that relate to the tamale in separate paragraphs. Comparison, contrast, and example transitions are particularly useful in definition essays; you could also use transitions to show contrast and purpose (see Chapter 6, pp. 118–119).

TRANSITIONS TO SHOW CONTRAST OR A CHANGE IN IDEA

although	even though	instead	on the other side
anyhow	for all that	nevertheless	otherwise
at the same time	however	notwithstanding	regardless
but	in any event	on the contrary	still
despite this	in contrast	on the other hand	yet

TRANSITIONS TO SHOW A COMPARISON

in like manner	in the same way	likewise	similarly

TRANSITIONS TO ILLUSTRATE OR GIVE EXAMPLES/SPECIFICS

a few include	essentially	in particular	the following
an example	for example	let us consider	specifically
especially	for instance	the case of	you can see this in

Activity 11-3   Creating Topic Sentences

Directions: *Choose three of the thesis statements you created in Activity 11-2 and write two topic sentences for each that could be used to develop two of the body paragraphs for that thesis statement in an essay.*

1. Thesis statement: _____

   _____

   Topic sentence 1: _____

   _____

   Topic sentence 2: _____

   _____

2. Thesis statement: _____

   _____

   Topic sentence 1: _____

   _____

   Topic sentence 2: _____

   _____

3. Thesis statement: _____

   _____

Topic sentence 1: _____

_____

Topic sentence 2: _____

_____ ●

Next, develop your body paragraphs by providing concrete details and examples.

Activity 11-4 Supporting Details

Directions: *Now, provide at least three possible examples or details you would include for three of the topic sentences you created in Activity 11-3.*

1. Topic sentence: _____

   _____

   Example/detail 1: _____

   _____

   Example/detail 2: _____

   _____

   Example/detail 3: _____

   _____

2. Topic sentence: _____

   _____

   Example/detail 1: _____

   _____

   Example/detail 2: _____

   _____

   Example/detail 3: _____

   _____

3. Topic sentence: _____

   _____

   Example/detail 1: _____

   _____

Example/detail 2: _____

_____

Example/detail 3: _____

_____ ⬤

Concluding Paragraph

The concluding paragraph in a definition essay should redefine the object or concept briefly and sum up your purpose for defining it to your reader.

Activity 11-5   Concluding Paragraphs

Directions: *Choose one of the topics you've been developing in the preceding activities and write a three- to five-sentence concluding paragraph that re-emphasizes the definition and your purpose for defining it.*

_____

_____

_____

_____

_____ ⬤

Use the following critique form to check for the basics in your definition essay draft.

Definition Essay Critique Form

| PURPOSE | IDEAS | SUPPORT | ASSUMPTIONS BIASES | CONCLUSIONS | POINT OF VIEW | ANALYSIS |

Overall   Done well   Needs work

1. Does the essay clearly define the subject?   _____   _____
2. Does the essay use specific details and **ideas** consistently and clearly?   _____   _____
3. Are the paragraphs broken up well and about the right length?   _____   _____

	Done well	Needs work

Introduction

4. Is the title interesting and in correct format?

5. Is there a general introduction that gives background for the subject and the **purpose** for the definition?

6. Is there a clear thesis statement that explains the **purpose** of the definition?

Body

7. Do the body paragraphs develop the definition and flow smoothly?

8. Are transitions used between and, when needed, within the paragraphs?

9. Do the body paragraphs include **support** (descriptive details and examples)?

Conclusion

10. Does the **concluding** paragraph sum up the definition with **analysis** and re-emphasize the **purpose** developed in the introductory paragraph and thesis, without adding new ideas?

Editing

11. Circle the following errors you think you see in this draft: spelling, fragments, run-ons/comma splices, commas, semicolon/colon use, pronoun agreement, reference fault errors, parallelism, apostrophe use, verb use/tense, and passive voice construction. (See the handbook section for help in identifying and correcting these errors.)

12. Other types of grammar or sentence-level errors:

_____

Comments:

_____

_____

COMPLEMENTARY MODES FOR DEFINITION ESSAYS

When definition mode is used in an essay, it is often combined with several other modes.

- **Narration** and **description** can be used to develop a definition.
- **Illustration and examples** can be further used to elaborate on the definition of a subject.
- **Classification** is usually part of the definition process itself: You have to classify items into broader groups to define them specifically.
- You can **compare and contrast** items as you define your subject.
- You can use the definition to prove an **argument** or **persuade** your readers to a particular point of view.

SAMPLE STUDENT ESSAY

Figueroa 1

Rosie Figueroa

Professor Rosen

English 100

15 March 2008

The Importance of a Quinceañera

Thesis statement

Many cultures have traditional rituals to represent a coming of age. In America, girls often celebrate their sixteenth birthday with a "Sweet 16" party. In Jewish culture, boys and girls celebrate their thirteenth birthday with a Bah or Bat Mitzvah. In my culture, which is Mexican-American, when girls turn fifteen they have an elaborate party called a quinceañera. This party and the rituals involved are a very important part of my culture and an important part of becoming a young woman.

Topic sentence

A quinceañera is a specialized birthday celebration. The word "quinceañera" comes from the Spanish word "quince" which means "fifteen"; therefore, it is literally a celebration of a girl's fifteenth birthday. In some ways, it is more like a wedding than a normal birthday party. For example, in a quinceañera, the girl wears a beautiful white dress and usually a tiara. Also, like in a wedding, she chooses friends (up to 14 of them to make a total of 15) to be part of her quinceañera. If her court is made up of girls, these girls wear special matching dresses, much like bridesmaids, and are part of the formal ceremony acknowledging her coming of age before the reception to celebrate her coming out as a young woman to society. Sometimes, the formal ceremony is held in a church with a priest who gives a bless-

Concluding sentence

ing, and sometimes it is held at a home or community hall. Always, family and friends are there to celebrate this special birthday.

Figueroa 2

The last part of the quinceañera celebrates the importance of

Topic sentence

the girl's family and friends in her transition from childhood to
adulthood and involves sharing good food, music, and dancing.
Usually, close family members and godparents contribute money
toward the celebration. Much planning goes into arranging the religious blessing part of the ceremony as well as the reception afterwards that provides food and entertainment for all the guests.
Moreover, special invitations are sent out in advance, and these parties can be huge with hundreds of guests. That's why there are websites dedicated to buying supplies for a quinceañera celebration.
Quinceañeras feature a banquet, often with rice, beans, carne asada,
tamales, and enchiladas. Also, a mariachi band usually plays traditional Mexican dance music, and everyone, young and old, dances to
celebrate the girl's coming out into society as a young adult. It's a

Concluding sentence

great chance to connect with family and friends and to celebrate
Mexican traditions, food, music, and overall culture.

The quinceañera is more than just a birthday party: it is an

Restatement of thesis

important part of my Mexican cultural identity. Young girls look forward to this special day, and family and friends see it as a way to
celebrate both the girl's birthday and their pride in their culture's
traditions and heritage. It celebrates the girl's transition into adulthood with the best combination of food, music, dancing, and family.

Activity 11-6   Thinking Critically About the Student Essay

Directions: *Analyze the essay to identify the features and details characteristic
of the definition mode. Mark them on the essay. Then, reread the essay, and make
a list of specific revisions you would make to correct any problems with content,
organization, transitions, and style.* ●

PROFESSIONAL DEFINITION ESSAY

Discrimination Is a Virtue

Robert Keith Miller

Robert Keith Miller is the author of several books, including many books on the craft of writing and handbooks for grammar and usage. He is also the author of a book called *Mark Twain*, about Twain's work and his life. Miller is an active scholar in the field of college writing.

1   When I was a child, my grandmother used to tell me a story about a king who had three daughters and decided to test their love. He asked each of them "How much do you love me?" The first replied that she loved him as much as all the diamonds and pearls in the world. The second said that she loved him more than life itself. The third replied "I love you as fresh meat loves salt."

2   This answer enraged the king; he was convinced that his youngest daughter was making fun of him. So he banished her from his realm and left all of his property to her elder sisters.

3   As the story unfolded it became clear, even to a 6-year-old, that the king had made a terrible mistake. The two older girls were hypocrites, and as soon as they had profited from their father's generosity, they began to treat him very badly. A wiser man would have realized that the youngest daughter was the truest. Without attempting to flatter, she had said, in effect, "We go together naturally; we are a perfect team."

4   Years later, when I came to read Shakespeare, I realized that my grandmother's story was loosely based upon the story of King Lear, who put his daughters to a similar test and did not know how to judge the results. Attempting to save the king from the consequences of his foolishness, a loyal friend pleads, "Come sir, arise, away! I'll teach you differences." Unfortunately, the lesson comes too late. Because Lear could not tell the difference between true love and false, he loses his kingdom and eventually his life.

5   We have a word in English which means "the ability to tell differences." That word is *discrimination*. But within the last twenty years, this word has been so frequently misused that an entire generation has grown up believing that "discrimination" means "racism." People are always proclaiming that "discrimination" is something that should be done away with. Should that ever happen, it would prove to be our undoing.

6   Discrimination means discernment; it means the ability to perceive the truth, to use good judgment and to profit accordingly. The *Oxford English Dictionary* traces this understanding of the word back to 1648 and demonstrates that, for the next 300 years, "discrimination" was a virtue, not a vice. Thus, when a character in a nineteenth-century novel makes a happy marriage, Dickens has another character remark, "It does credit to your discrimination that you should have found such a very excellent young woman."

7   Of course, "the ability to tell differences" assumes that differences exist, and this is unsettling for a culture obsessed with the notion of equality. The contemporary belief that discrimination is a vice stems from the compound "discriminate against." What we need to remember, however, is that some things deserve to be judged harshly: we should not leave our kingdoms to the selfish and the wicked.

8   Discrimination is wrong only when someone or something is discriminated against because of prejudice. But to use the word in this sense, as so many people do, is to destroy its true meaning. If you discriminate against something because of general preconceptions rather than particular insights, then you are not discriminating—bias has clouded the clarity of vision which discrimination demands.

9   One of the great ironies of American life is that we manage to discriminate in the practical decisions of daily life, but usually fail to discriminate when we make public policies. Most people are very discriminating when it comes to buying a car, for example, because they realize that cars have differences. Similarly, an increasing number of people have learned to discriminate in what they eat. Some foods are better than others—and indiscriminate eating can undermine one's health. Yet in public affairs, good judgment is depressingly rare. In many areas which involve the common good, we see a failure to tell differences.

10   Consider, for example, some of the thinking behind modern education. On the one hand, there is a refreshing realization that there are differences among children, and some children—be they gifted or handicapped—require special education. On the other hand, we are politically unable to accept the consequences of this perception. The trend in recent years has been to group together students of radically different ability. We call this process "mainstreaming," and it strikes me as a characteristically American response to the discovery of differences: we try to pretend that differences do not matter.

11   Similarly, we try to pretend that there is little difference between the sane and the insane. A fashionable line of argument has it that "everybody is a little mad" and that few mental patients deserve long-term hospitalization. As a consequence of such reasoning, thousands of seriously

ill men and women have been evicted from their hospital beds and returned to what is euphemistically called "the community"—which often means being left to sleep on city streets, where confused and helpless people now live out of paper bags as the direct result of our refusal to discriminate.

12   Or to choose a final example from a different area: how many recent elections reflect thoughtful consideration of the genuine differences among candidates? Benumbed by television commercials that market aspiring officeholders as if they were a new brand of toothpaste or hair spray, too many Americans vote with only a fuzzy understanding of the issues in question. Like Lear, we seem too eager to leave the responsibility of government to others and too ready to trust those who tell us whatever we want to hear.

13   So as we look around us, we should recognize that "discrimination" is a virtue which we desperately need. We must try to avoid making unfair and arbitrary distinctions, but we must not go to the other extreme and pretend that there are no distinctions to be made. The ability to make intelligent judgments is essential both for the success of one's personal life and for the functioning of society as a whole. Let us be open-minded by all means, but not so open-minded that our brains fall out.

Reading Reflection Questions

1. What are the direct or indirect (implied) messages in this essay?

_____

_____

_____

2. Why do you think the author began this article with the story he did (King Lear)?

_____

_____

3. How is discrimination related to prejudice according to the author?

_____

_____

Objective Questions

4. T/F _____ Discrimination means "the ability to tell differences."

5. T/F _____ Discrimination also means "racism," according to the author.

6. T/F _____ The author believes that the real purpose of discrimination—discernment—is an important and valuable skill.

7. Provide two examples the author uses to support his purpose.

_____

_____

Checking Vocabulary

Define the following in your own words or provide a dictionary definition if you don't know the word.

8. discernment: _____

9. obsessed: _____

10. prejudice: _____

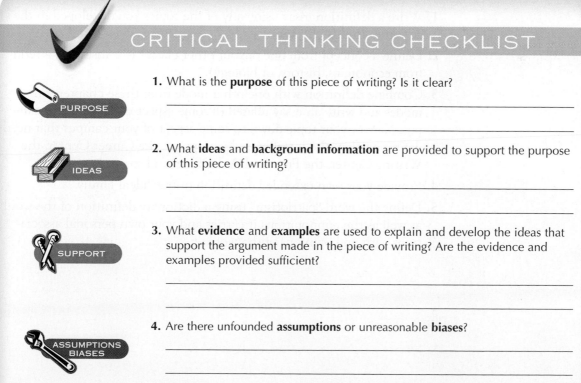

CRITICAL THINKING CHECKLIST

PURPOSE

1. What is the **purpose** of this piece of writing? Is it clear?

_____

_____

IDEAS

2. What **ideas** and **background information** are provided to support the purpose of this piece of writing?

_____

_____

SUPPORT

3. What **evidence** and **examples** are used to explain and develop the ideas that support the argument made in the piece of writing? Are the evidence and examples provided sufficient?

_____

_____

ASSUMPTIONS BIASES

4. Are there unfounded **assumptions** or unreasonable **biases**?

_____

_____

5. Are all of the **conclusions**, **implications**, and **consequences** of the arguments (the results of the arguments taken to their furthest extreme) considered?

_____

_____

6. Is the **point of view** clear and consistent, and have other points of view been considered?

_____

_____

7. Using these critical thinking tools, **analyze** the overall structure of this essay and the strength of the author's arguments, ideas, and support. Was he or she successful in accomplishing the purpose? Why or why not?

_____

_____

Essay Assignments

1. Write a definition essay using any of the topics you developed in the activities in this chapter.

2. Define a concept from one of your other classes (for instance, a term from economics, history, or biology).

3. Combine definition with one other mode from these chapters on modes and write an essay related to some aspect of your college campus. Narrow your topic down to some aspect of your campus that needs definition first: the interlibrary loan option, the Career Center, the Writing Center, the Financial Aid Office, and so on.

4. Provide your own extended definition of the "ideal family."

5. Define the word "patriotism" using a dictionary definition of the word as well as the connotations it carries and your own personal associations with and opinions of the word.

"Behold" statue, Atlanta, Georgia.

THINKING CRITICALLY

Look at the picture above. Then answer the questions that follow.

1. What is the object in this picture an example of?

_____

2. How could this picture be used to illustrate a concept?

_____

_____

EXAMPLE ESSAYS

Example/illustration essays use examples to clarify, explain, and support the purpose of the essay. Examples include facts, expert testimony, and personal experience. They can be used in combination to support a thesis; or a single, extended example can be used to develop a point.

Critical Thinking and Example

Before you begin generating examples, you need to assess your audience and determine the message you want to get across to them.

Applying Critical Thinking

One of the best ways to make a convincing point to your readers is to provide lots of examples to illustrate and prove it. To write a powerful example essay, consider the following questions:

1. What is the **purpose** of my essay? What point do I want to make through the use of examples? How will I convey that message and develop my **ideas**?

2. What **support** can I include? What are the best examples and details (descriptive details, examples, comparisons) I can include to develop my purpose?

BEFORE WRITING AN EXAMPLE ESSAY

Before you begin to write an example essay on an assigned topic, or one you have chosen, start by asking yourself these questions:

1. What point am I trying to make?
2. Which examples can I include to illustrate my purpose clearly?
3. What facts, testimony, and experiences can I tap into to develop my purpose in this essay?

4. What details should I provide to further illustrate my examples?

5. How should I organize this essay, and how should I conclude it?

Activity 12-1   Choosing Examples

Directions: *For each of the following topics, list three examples you could use to develop it.*

1. **Topic:** Diet fads _____

_____

2. **Topic:** Flowers _____

_____

3. **Topic:** A great meal _____

_____

4. **Topic:** Natural disasters _____

_____

5. **Topic:** Peer pressure _____

_____

WRITING AN EXAMPLE ESSAY

It's important to understand that all essays depend on examples and illustrations to develop and support their thesis statements. Examples are used to support topic sentences in an essay, and extended examples can be used to develop the thesis statement of an essay.

Providing concrete examples for your readers is one of the best ways to convince them about the point you want to make. In your introductory paragraph, set up the overall purpose of your essay, and in your thesis statement explain what you will be illustrating through examples, your analytical purpose. Organize your paper in a way that highlights your examples in the most powerful way to get your purpose across. For instance, you might choose to provide your examples for support in a most to least important order (or vice versa), or chronological order.

In the body paragraphs, develop several simple examples or one or more extended examples to develop your thesis. For instance, if you were explaining how American weddings usually work, you could use several different weddings you've attended as examples, or you could choose to use your own wedding—or the wedding of someone close to you—as an extended example of a typical American wedding. Your examples should be vivid and interesting but not unfamiliar to your readers. Most important, the examples must clearly demonstrate the point(s) your thesis sets out to make. Be sure to incorporate as many details and concrete images as possible into your examples. Use transitions between examples within your body paragraphs and between paragraphs for separate examples. Include key words and transitional phrases such as "for example," "to illustrate," and "for instance" to set up the examples you provide to make your points. Finally, in the concluding paragraph, re-emphasize the purpose you want to express to your readers though the examples.

The chart below provides a brief overview of the structure of an example/illustration essay.

BASIC STRUCTURE FOR AN EXAMPLE/ILLUSTRATION ESSAY

Introductory Paragraph

Sets up your subject and your purpose.

Thesis statement: A statement that defines your purpose and what example(s) you'll be using to illustrate it.

Body Paragraphs (Two to five, depending on assignment and purpose)

Topic sentences set up the organization and focus of your examples or extended example.

Develop the examples, illustrations, and details. **Analyze** their significance.

Use transitions within and between paragraphs to make the paragraphs flow smoothly.

Concluding Paragraph

Sums up and re-emphasizes the thesis.

STRUCTURING AN EXAMPLE ESSAY

Topic

If you do not have a topic assigned by your instructor for your illustration/example essay, then brainstorm ideas for things, places, or events you might want to describe. Come up with some ideas for a purpose for describing the topic. What do you want your readers to understand through your use of example?

A Few Topic Possibilities

Many topics work well for writing an example essay. You could write about the kinds of cars you can buy in America, the variety of food and interesting cuisines in this country, the types of clothing that are popular this decade, and so on.

Thesis Statements

A thesis statement for an example or illustration essay clarifies your purpose for including specific examples or illustrations. It states what you want your readers to understand after reading your examples, the message you want to impart.

> Sports fans go to many extremes to show support for their favorite teams.
>
> Technology has made being a college student easier in the last decade.

Activity 12-2   Creating Thesis Statements

Directions: *Create a thesis statement for each of the topics listed. Make sure that the thesis is something that will need to be demonstrated through examples.*

1. **Topic:** Prejudice

   Thesis sentence: _____

   _____

2. **Topic:** Interesting hobbies

   Thesis sentence: _____

   _____

3. **Topic:** Food rituals

   Thesis sentence: _____

   _____

4. **Topic:** Natural disasters

   Thesis sentence: _____

   _____

5. **Topic:** Video games

   Thesis sentence: _____

   _____

Introductory Paragraph

Begin your example/illustration essay with a general introduction to the topic for which you are providing examples to illustrate your conclusion. End with the thesis statement to set up the purpose of your example essay.

Body Paragraphs

The body paragraphs in an example/illustration essay provide specific details and examples organized to illustrate your purpose. For instance, in an essay about appropriate birthday parties for people of different ages, you could organize the examples chronologically and create topic sentences for each age-specific type of party. Or, you might choose to organize your body paragraphs based on the relevance of each example: least to most important, or vice versa. Your topic sentences should set up each specific example and its relevance to your thesis statement's purpose.

Body paragraphs can be divided into separate examples or can be parts of an extended example. For instance, the following brief outline focuses on three different age groups for birthday parties, and each topic sentence would need at least two examples and your **analysis** to illustrate it.

> **Thesis:** Birthday parties should be age appropriate.
>
> **Topic sentence 1:** Birthday parties for elementary school–aged children should have interactive games that are supervised by adults.
>
> **Topic sentence 2:** For middle school-aged children, birthday parties should skip organized games and focus on the kids just hanging out together, gifts, and food.

Topic sentence 3: For high school kids, birthday parties are usually held at a place outside the home, a get-together at a restaurant, for instance, and with a smaller group of close friends.

Activity 12-3 Creating Topic Sentences

Directions: *For three of the thesis statements you created in Activity 12-2, create topic sentences that could be used to support them.*

1. Topic: _____

   Thesis statement: _____

   Topic sentence: _____

   _____

2. Topic: _____

   Thesis statement: _____

   Topic sentence: _____

   _____

3. Topic: _____

   Thesis statement: _____

   Topic sentence: _____

   _____

Activity 12-4 Providing Examples

Directions: *Based on your answers in Activity 12-3, provide three examples that would provide support for each topic sentence.*

1. Topic: _____

   Topic sentence: _____

   Examples: _____

   _____

2. Topic: _____

   Topic sentence: _____

   Examples: _____

   _____

3. Topic: _____

   Topic sentence: _____

   Examples: _____

   _____ ⬤

Although example transitions are especially useful in example/illustration essays, other helpful transitions include those that strengthen points and show addition of points or purpose (see Chapter 6, pages 118–119).

Transitions to Illustrate or Give Examples/Specifics

a few include	essentially	in particular	the following
an example	for example	let us consider	specifically
especially	for instance	the case of	you can see this in

Concluding Paragraph

The concluding paragraph for your example essay should recap your purpose and intended message for the examples and illustrations you provided in the essay.

Activity 12-5   Writing a Conclusion

Directions: *Based on your answers to Activities 12-2, 12-3, and 12-4, write a three- to five-sentence concluding paragraph that would work for one of the topics you worked on.*

_____

_____

_____

_____ ⬤

Use the following critique form to check for the basics in your example essay draft.

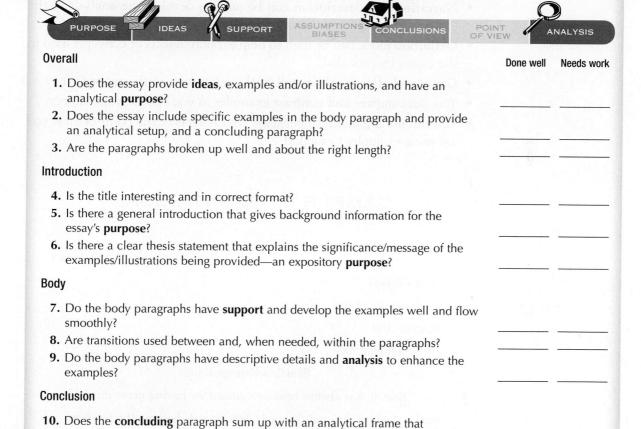

Example Essay Critique Form

PURPOSE   IDEAS   SUPPORT   ASSUMPTIONS/BIASES   CONCLUSIONS   POINT OF VIEW   ANALYSIS

Overall   Done well   Needs work

1. Does the essay provide **ideas**, examples and/or illustrations, and have an analytical **purpose**?

2. Does the essay include specific examples in the body paragraph and provide an analytical setup, and a concluding paragraph?

3. Are the paragraphs broken up well and about the right length?

Introduction

4. Is the title interesting and in correct format?

5. Is there a general introduction that gives background information for the essay's **purpose**?

6. Is there a clear thesis statement that explains the significance/message of the examples/illustrations being provided—an expository **purpose**?

Body

7. Do the body paragraphs have **support** and develop the examples well and flow smoothly?

8. Are transitions used between and, when needed, within the paragraphs?

9. Do the body paragraphs have descriptive details and **analysis** to enhance the examples?

Conclusion

10. Does the **concluding** paragraph sum up with an analytical frame that re-emphasizes the introductory paragraph and thesis, without adding new ideas?

Editing

11. Circle the following errors you think you see in this draft: spelling, fragments, run-ons/comma splices, commas, semicolon/colon use, pronoun agreement, reference fault errors, parallelism, apostrophe use, verb use/tense, and passive voice construction. (See the handbook section for help in identifying and correcting these errors.)

12. Other types of grammar or sentence-level errors:

_____

Comments:

_____

_____

COMPLEMENTARY MODES FOR EXAMPLE ESSAYS

Example mode is often combined with several other modes.

- **Narration** and **description** can be used to develop the analysis of the examples.
- **Definition** mode can be used to help explain objects or concepts used in the examples provided.
- **Cause and effect analysis** will further elaborate on the examples.
- You can **compare and contrast** examples as you analyze your subject.
- You can use **argument** to persuade your readers of the point of view you are using examples to support.

SAMPLE STUDENT ESSAY

Tobias 1

Brian Tobias

Professor Jacobson

English 100

26 September 2008

Seattle's Grunge Bands

Seattle has always been recognized for having great musicians, but in the late '80s and the early '90s, Seattle became the forefront for a new style of rock called grunge. Grunge combined elements of heavy metal, punk, and pop. The music featured screaming guitars, dissonant sounds, and wailing vocals, and it helped bring alternative rock into the mainstream. Pearl Jam, Soundgarden, and Nirvana are some of the best known grunge bands, opening the path to similar bands in the 1990s and making a name for Seattle in music history.

Pearl Jam consisted of Eddie Vedder (lead vocals and guitar), Stone Gossard (rhythm guitar), Jeff Ament (bass guitar), Mike

Thesis statement

Topic sentence

Tobias 2

McCready (lead guitar), and Dave Krusen (drummer), later replaced by Dave Abbruzzese. *Ten,* their first album, contained songs about loneliness, murder, suicide, and depression. The sound was a combination of classic rock, howling guitars, and Eddie Vedder's distinctive vocals. Pearl Jam released four other albums throughout the '90s: *Vs.*, *Vitalogy, No Code,* and *Yield.* Pearl Jam outsold Nirvana, making them the top selling grunge band. Although they were criticized for cashing in on the popularity of alternative rock, they did not play by the rules, refusing to make music videos and boycotting Ticketmaster.

Concluding sentence

Another great band formed in Seattle was Soundgarden. In 1984, Kim Thayil (lead guitar), Hiro Yamamoto (bass), Scott Sundquist (drummer), replaced in 1986 by Matt Cameron, and Chris Cornell (lead singer, drummer) formed Soundgarden. Their music was a mix of punk, heavy metal, powerful guitar riffs, clear melodies, and the extraordinary and haunting vocals of Cornell. Since 1984, the band has recorded seven albums including *Screaming Life, FOPP, Ultramega OK, Louder than Love, Badmotorfinger, Superunknown,* and *Down on the Upside.* On April 9, 1997, Soundgarden broke up due to fighting among band members. Still, they will always remain an example of one of Seattle's finest grunge bands, with a sound all their own.

Topic sentence

Concluding sentence

Finally, Nirvana is one of the best known names in the grunge world. Nirvana consisted of Kurt Cobain (singer/guitarist), Chris Novolesic (bass), and Aaron Burkhart (drummer). Burkhart was replaced by Chad Channing in 1986, who was himself replaced by Dave Grohl in 1990. Their music was a powerful combination of hard rock, high-energy pop, strong melodies, screaming guitars, and Cobain's powerful and varied vocals. The band produced several albums between 1989 and 1996 including *Bleach, Silver Dive,*

Topic sentence

Tobias 3

Nevermind, Incesticide, In Utero, and *From the Muddy Banks of the Wishkah. Nevermind* was their breakthrough album. By Christmas of 1991, 400,000 copies of the CD were being sold each week, and it became number one on the Billboard charts in January 1992. Nirvana's performances here and abroad were sold out. Then, on April 8, 1994, Kurt Cobain was found dead in his home with a self-inflicted gunshot wound. The band members disbanded in 1996.

Concluding sentence

However, Nirvana will always remain the ultimate Northwest grunge band example.

Restatement of thesis

In conclusion, Pearl Jam, Soundgarden, and Nirvana were instrumental in starting the grunge era. Each one of the bands had its own style, which laid the foundation for the bands that followed them. They put Seattle on the musical map

Activity 12-6   **Thinking Critically About the Student Essay**

Directions: *Analyze the essay to identify the features and details characteristic of the example/illustration mode. Mark them on the essay. Then, reread the essay, and make a list of specific revisions you would make to correct any problems with content, organization, transitions, and style.* ●

PROFESSIONAL EXAMPLE ESSAY

The Miseducation of Hip-Hop

Jamilah Evelyn

Jamilah Evelyn is a staff reporter at *The Chronicle* and has written several articles related to higher education. She has contributed to special reports on community colleges and guest-led a Live Colloquy on changes and needs in the community college system.

1   When Jason Hinmon transferred to the University of Delaware two years ago from Morehouse College in Atlanta, the 22-year-old senior says he almost dropped out his first semester.

2   He says that for financial reasons, he came back here to his hometown. But in many ways, he had never felt so abandoned.

3   "I came to class and my professors didn't know how to deal with me," he says, between bites of his a-la-carte lunch. "I could barely get them to meet with me during their office hours."

4   Dark-hued, dreadlocked and, well, young, he says many of his mostly White professors figured they had him pegged.

5   "They took one look at me and thought that I was some hip-hop hoodlum who wasn't interested in being a good student," he says.

6   But if Hinmon represents the "good" students with grounds to resent the stereotype, there are faculty who profess there's no shortage of young people willing to live up—or down—to it.

7   "You see students walking on campus reciting rap lyrics when they should be reciting something they'll need to know on their next test. Some of these same students you won't see back on campus next semester," says Dr. Thomas Earl Midgette, 50, director of the Institute for the Study of Minority Issues at historically Black North Carolina Central University.

8   "These rap artists influence the way they dress," he continues. "They look like hoochie mamas, not like they're coming to class. Young men with pants fashioned below their navel. Now, I used to wear bell-bottoms, but I learned to dress a certain way if I was negotiating the higher education maze. I had to trim my afro."

9   The difference between today's students and their parents, faculty and administrators is marked, no doubt. Technology's omnipresence—apparent in kids with little patience for anything less than instant meals, faster Internet information and cellular ubiquity—is certainly at play when it comes to explaining the divide.

10   But what causes more consternation among many college and university officials is a music form, a culture and a lifestyle they say is eating away at the morals, and ultimately the classroom experience, of today's college students.

11   Hip-hop—brash, vulgar, in-your-face hip-hop—is indisputably the dominant youth culture today. Its most controversial front men floss mad ice (wear lots of diamonds and other expensive jewelry), book bad bitches (usually scantily clad, less than the take home kind of girl), and in general, party it up. Its most visible females brag about their sexual dexterity, physical attributes, and cunning tactics when it comes to getting their rent paid.

12   With college completion statistics at an embarrassing low and the Black–White achievement gap getting wider by the semester, perhaps it's time to be concerned whether the culture's malevolent message is at play.

13   But can atrocious retention rates really be linked to reckless music? Or do university officials underestimate their students? Is it that young folk today have no sense of history, responsibility and plain good manners? Or are college faculty a bunch of old fogies simply more comfortable with Marvin Gaye's "Sexual Healing" than Little Kim's sexual prowess?

14   Is this no different than the divide we've always seen between young people and their college and university elders? Or do the disparities between this wave of students and those charged with educating them portend something more disparaging?

The Gap

15   At the heart of the rift between the two groups is a debate that has both sides passionately disturbed.

16   Young people say they feel pigeonholed by an image many of them don't support. They say the real rub is that their teachers—Black and White—believe the hype as much as the old lady who crosses the street when she sees them coming.

17   And they'd like their professors to consider this: They can listen to the music, even party to it, but still have a response just as critical, if not more so, than their faculty and administrators.

18   Others point out that the pervasiveness of hip-hop's immoral philosophies is at least partly rooted in the fact that the civil rights movement—the older generation's defining moment—surely did not live up to all its promises for Black America.

19   And further, they say it's important to note that not all hip-hop is irresponsible. In fact, some argue that it's ultimately empowering, uplifting and refreshing. After all, when was the last time a biology professor sat down with a Mos Def CD? How many can even pronounce his name?

20   Older faculty, administrators and parents alike respond that the music is downright filth and anyone associated with it ought to have their mouths and their morals cleansed.

21   There's a real problem when a marijuana-smoking ex-con named Snoop Doggy Dog can pack a campus auditorium quicker than Black historian John Hope Franklin; when more students deify the late Tupac Shakur and his abrasive lyrics than those who ever read the great Martin Luther King Jr.'s "I Have a Dream" speech; when kids decked out in sweats more pricey than their tuition complain that they can't afford a

semester's books; when the gains they fought so hard for are, in some ways, slowly slipping away.

22   "I think what causes us the most grief is that hip-hop comes across as heartless, valueless, nihilistic and certainly anachronistic if not atheistic," says Dr. Nat Irvin, president of Future Focus 2020, an urban futures think tank at Wake Forest University in North Carolina. "Anyone who would argue with that needs to take a look for themselves and see what images are prevalent on BET and MTV."

23   "But I don't think there's any question that the disconnect comes from the fact that old folks don't have a clue. They don't understand technology. The world has changed. And there's an enormous age gap between most faculty on college campuses and the rest of America," he says.

24   More than 60 percent of college and university faculty are over the age of 45. Meanwhile, nearly 53 percent of African Americans are under 30 and some 40 percent are under 20.

25   That means more than half of all Blacks were born after the civil rights movement and the landmark *Brown vs. Board of Education* case.

26   "There's no big puzzle why these kids are coming with a different ideology," Irvin, 49, says.

This Is What Blackness Is

27   It is universally acknowledged that rap began in New York City's Bronx borough nearly 30 years ago, a mix of Jamaican reggae's dance hall, America's funk music, the inner city's pent-up frustrations and Black folks' general propensity to love a good party.

28   Pioneering artists like the The Last Poets, The Sugar Hill Gang, Kurtis Blow and Run-DMC combined creative genius and street savvy to put hip-hop on the map. Its initial associations were with graffiti and party music, according to Dr. Robin D. G. Kelley, professor of history and Africana studies at New York University.

29   "Then in the late '80s, you begin to see more politicized manifestations of that. BDP, Public Enemy . . . In essays that students wrote that were not about rap music, but about the urban condition itself, they would adopt the language. They would quote Public Enemy lyrics, they would quote Ghetto Boys," says Kelley, 38.

30   "This whole generation of Blacks in particular were trying to carve out for themselves an alternative culture," he continues. "I saw a whole generation for the first time say, 'I don't want to go to corporate America. I don't want to be an attorney. I don't want to be a doctor. I don't want to get paid. I want to make a revolution.'"

31   "The wave that we're in now is all over the place," he explains.

32   But even hip-hop's fans stop short at endorsing some of the themes prevailing in today's music and mindset. Kevin Powell, noted cultural critic and former hip-hop journalist, says the biggest difference between the music today and the music at its onset is that "we don't own it."

33   "Corporate America completely commodified hip-hop," he says. "We create the culture and corporate America takes it and sells it back to us and tells us, 'This is what Blackness is.'"

34   And while Powell, 34, says he is disappointed in some of the artists, especially the older ones who "should know better," many students are their staunchest defenders.

35   Caryn Wheeler, 18, a freshman at Bowie State University, explains simply that "every day isn't about love." Her favorite artists? Jay-Z, OutKast, Biggie Smalls, Tupac and Little Kim, many of whom are linked to hip-hop's controversial side. "We can relate because we see what they are talking about every day," she says.

36   Mazi Mutafa, 23, is a senior at the University of Maryland College Park and president of the Black Student Union there. He says he listens to jazz and hip-hop, positive artists and those who capture a party spirit. "There's a time to party and have fun, and Jay-Z speaks to that," he says. "But there needs to be a happy medium."

37   Interrupting, senior Christine Gonzalez, 28, says a lot of artists like Jay-Z tend to be revered by younger students. "As you get older, you tend to tone down your style and find that happy medium," she says. "It's all a state of mind."

38   "People have to understand that Jay-Z is kind of like a 100-level class—an intro to hip-hop. He brings a lot of people into its fan base," Mutafa chimes in. "But then you have groups like The Roots, which are more like a 400-level class. They keep you engaged in the music. But one is necessary for the other."

39   Erick Rivas, 17, a freshman also at the University of Maryland, says he listens to Mos Def, Black Star, Mobb Deep, Wu-Tang Clan and sometimes other, more mainstream acts like Jay-Z. "Hip-hop has been a driving force in our lives. It is the soundtrack to our lives," he explains.

Keepin' It Real

40   But if hip-hop is the soundtrack to their lives, it may also mark the failure of it. De Reef Jamison, a doctoral candidate who teaches African American history at Temple University in Philadelphia, surveyed 72 Black male college students last summer for his thesis. Then a graduate student at Florida A&M State University, Jamison was interested in discovering if

there are links between students' music tastes and their cultural identity, their grades and other key indicators.

41   "While the lines weren't always so clear and distinct, I found that many of the students who had a low African self-consciousness, who overidentified with a European worldview and who were highly materialistic were often the students who listened to the most 'gangster' rap, or what I prefer to call reality rap," he explains.

42   As for grades, he says the gangster rap devotees' tended to be lower than those students who listened mostly to what he calls more conscious rap. Still, he's reluctant to draw any hard and fast lines between musical preference and student performance.

43   "I'd recommend that scholars take a much closer look at this," he says.

44   Floyd Beachum, a graduate student at Bowling Green State University in Ohio, surveyed secondary [school students to try to ascertain if there was a correlation between their behavior and the music they listened to.

45   "The more hyper-aggressive students tended to listen to more hard-core, gangster rap," he says. "Those who could identify with the violence, the drive-by shootings, the stereotypes about women—many times that would play out in their lives."

46   But Beachum, who teamed up with fellow Bowling Green graduate student Carlos McCray to conduct his research, says he isn't ready to draw any sweeping conclusions either.

47   "Those findings weren't across the board," he says, adding that he believes school systems can play a role in reversing any possible negative trends.

48   "If hip-hop and rap influence behavior and you bring all that to school, then the schools should create a very different environment and maybe we'll see more individuals go against the grain," he says.

49   Even undergraduates say they must admit that they see hip-hop's squalid influence on some of their peers.

50   "It upsets me when some young people complain that they can't get a job but when they go into that interview, they refuse to take off their do-rags, their big gold medallion and their baggy pants," says Kholiswa Laird, 18, a freshman at the University of Delaware. "But for some stupid reason, a lot of them feel like they're selling out if they wear proper clothes."

51   "That's just keepin it real," explains Darren Noble, 20, a junior at the University of Delaware. "Why should I have to change myself to get a job? If somebody wants to hire me but they don't like my braids, then either of two things will happen: They'll just have to get over it or I just won't get the job."

52   It's this kind of attitude that many in higher education see as the crux of the problem.

53   "We're not gonna serve them well in the university if we don't shake their thinking about how dress is going to influence job opportunities," says Central's Midgette.

54   Noble, from Maplewood, N.J., is a rapper. And he says that while he grew up in a posh suburb, he often raps about violence.

55   "I rap about positive stuff too, but as a Black person in America, it's hard to escape violence," he explains. "Mad Black people grew up in the ghetto and the music and our actions reflect that."

56   For sure, art has been known to imitate life. Hip-hop icon Sean "Puffy" Combs—who two years ago gave $750,000 to his alma mater, Howard University—is currently facing charges on his involvement in a Manhattan nightclub shooting last December. Grammy-winning rapper Jay-Z, also was connected with a night club dispute that ended with a record company executive being stabbed last year.

A Bad Rap?

57   A simple explanation for the boldness of much of rap's lyrics is that "artists have always pushed the limits," Kelley says.

58   But what's more, there is a politically conscious, stirring, enriching side of hip-hop that many of its fans say is often overlooked.

59   "Urban radio stations play the same songs every day," says Powell, a former reporter for *Vibe* magazine. "The media is ghettoizing hip-hop. They make it look passé."

60   Those often included in hip-hop's positive list are Lauryn Hill, Common, Mos Def, Dead Prez, Erykah Badu, Talib Kweli and other underground acts. Indeed, many of them have been active in encouraging young people to vote. Mos Def and other artists recently recorded a song in memory of Amadou Diallo, "Hip-Hop for Respect."

61   This is the side of hip-hop many young people say they'd like their faculty to recognize. This is also the side that some people say faculty must recognize.

62   "There are scholars—I've seen them do this before—who will make a disparaging remark about a whole genre of music, not knowing a dog-gone thing," NYU's Kelley says. "That's the same thing as saying, 'I've read one article on rational choice theory and it was so stupid, I dismissed the whole genre.' ... People who are trained in their own fields would never do that with their own scholarship and yet they are willing to make these really sweeping statements."

63   "And they don't know. They don't have a critical understanding of the way the music industry operates or the way in which people engage music," he says. "But they are willing to draw a one-to-one correlation between the students' failure and music."

64   Some professors argue that another correlation should be made: "My most serious students are the die-hard hip-hop fans," says Dr. Ingrid Banks, assistant professor of Black Studies at Virginia Tech. "They are able to understand politics because they understand hip-hop."

65   Banks says that more of her colleagues would be wise to better understand the music and its culture. "You can't talk about Reagan's policies in the '80s without talking about hip-hop," says the 30-something scholar. "If you start where students are, they make these wonderful connections."

Curricular Connections

66   If the augmentation of hip-hop scholarship is any indication, academe just may be coming around to at least tolerating this formidable medium.

67   Courses on hip-hop, books, essays and other studied accounts of the genre are being generated by a pioneering cadre of scholars. And while many people see that as notable, there's not yet widespread belief that academe has completely warmed to the idea of hip-hop as scholarship.

68   Banks, who has taught "Race, Politics and Rap Music in Late Twentieth Century America" at the Blacksburg, Va., school, says she's experiencing less than a speedy response to getting her course included into the department's curriculum.

69   "I understand that it usually takes a while to get a course approved, but there have been courses in bio-history that were signed off on rather quickly," she says.

70   But if academe fails to find ways to connect with hip-hop and its culture, then it essentially will have failed an entire generation, many critics say.

71   "What's happening is that administrators and teachers are faced with a real crisis. And that crisis they can easily attach to the music," Kelley says. "It's the way they dress, the way they talk. The real crisis is their failure to educate; their failure to treat these students like human beings; their failure to come up with a new message to engage students."

72   "Part of the reason why there is such a generational gap is because so few educators make an effort to understand the times in which they live. You can't apply '60s and '70s methods to teaching in the new millennium. You can't apply a jazz aesthetic to hip-hop heads," says Powell, who lectures at 70 to 80 colleges and universities a year. "You have to meet the students where they are. That's the nature of education. That's pedagogy."

73   And while Wake Forest's Irvin says he would agree with that sentiment, he also sees a role that students must play.

74   "What I see as being the major challenge that these kids will deal with is the image of young, urban America," Irvin says. "Young people need to ask themselves, 'Who will control their identity?'"

75   "If they leave it up to the media to define who they are, they'll be devastated by these images," he says. "That's where hip-hop is killing us."

Reading Reflection Questions

1. What are the direct or indirect (implied) messages in this story?

_____

_____

_____

2. Define what the author means by the term "the Gap."

_____

_____

Objective Questions

3. T/F _____ According to this article, some faculty believe hip-hop is a negative influence on students' morals as well as on their classroom behavior.

4. T/F _____ According to Jamilah, faculty often negatively stereotype students by their clothes and/or hip-hop fashion.

5. T/F _____ Rap began in New York City nearly 30 years ago.

6. T/F _____ According to this article, all students who listen to and like hip-hop never disagree with ideas promoted in the lyrics.

7. According to this article, what kinds of problems have arisen from the age gap between African-American students and faculty?

_____

_____

Checking Vocabulary

Define the following in your own words or provide a dictionary definition if you don't know the word.

8. ubiquity: _____

9. atrocious: _____

10. pervasiveness: _____

CRITICAL THINKING CHECKLIST

1. What is the **purpose** of this piece of writing? Is it clear?

_____

_____

2. What **ideas** and **background information** are provided to support the purpose of this piece of writing?

_____

_____

3. What **evidence** and **examples** are used to explain and develop the ideas that support the argument made in the piece of writing? Are the evidence and examples provided sufficient?

_____

_____

4. Are there unfounded **assumptions** or unreasonable **biases**?

_____

_____

5. Are all of the **conclusions**, **implications**, and **consequences** of the arguments (the results taken to their furthest extreme) of the arguments considered?

_____

_____

6. Is the **point of view** clear and consistent, and have other points of view been considered?

_____

_____

7. Using these critical thinking tools, **analyze** the overall structure of this essay and the strength of the author's arguments, ideas, and support. Was he or she successful in accomplishing the purpose? Why or why not?

_____

_____

Essay Assignments

1. Choose one of the topics you developed in the activities in this chapter and write a full example/illustration essay on that topic.

2. Write an essay about some type of music genre (e.g., jazz, hip-hop, rap, classical, rock, country) and provide several examples to illustrate your point about the genre. Be sure to come up with an analytical thesis you want to explain or prove in this essay.

3. Write an essay about fast-food restaurants. Include an analytical purpose and provide specific examples to illustrate your point.

4. Write an essay about a particular sport and include specific examples to illustrate the analytical purpose you set up in your introduction.

13

Cause and Effect

The Sphere, from the World Trade Center, post-9/11.

THINKING CRITICALLY

Look at the picture above. Then complete the tasks that follow.

The Sphere sculpture above used to be the centerpiece of the plaza at the World Trade Center Twin Towers. This picture is of the sculpture post–September 11, 2001, in its temporary home at Battery Park. The damage from the attack on the Twin Towers shows clearly.

In the space below, list two specific causes and two specific effects of the 9/11 attacks on New York City and Washington, D.C.

Causes (reasons)   **Effects (results)**

_____   _____

_____   _____

CAUSE AND EFFECT ESSAYS

A **cause and effect essay** analyzes causes (what led to certain results or *why* something happens) and their effects (the consequences or the *results* of an action or event). Cause and effect analysis comes in handy in many aspects of academic and workplace writing to determine what led to a particular event and the consequences of that event.

Cause and effect essays examine causes that lead to specific results. They may discuss a single cause and a single effect, a series of effects resulting from a single cause, or a series of causes that led to a particular effect. For instance, a new hair style could be the single cause that leads to a compliment (single effect) from a coworker, or overeating (single cause) could lead to several negative effects such as self-esteem issues, diabetes, back pain, and heart problems. Rainfall and dropping temperatures are two causes that lead to icy roads (single effect), and so on.

> **Language tip:** Use the word *effect* (a **noun**) when you are writing about results: She could immediately see the *effect* of her actions. Use the word *affect* (a **verb**) when you are writing about the action of the cause: The weather *affected* our travel plans. Though "effect" is sometimes used as a transitive verb too, that use is not as common, such as "The citizens *effected* a new law." In most cases, "affect" is used as a verb and "effect" is used as a noun: "When you *affect* a situation, you have an *effect* on it."

Critical Thinking and Cause and Effect

Cause and effect analysis is useful for helping your readers understand complicated events. The careful examination of the befores and afters of a specific event, for instance, can help readers understand why it happened and how it could be avoided or maybe repeated in the future. The analysis can also help convince your readers of an argument you want to get across, for instance, that they should stop smoking because of the health consequences or help stop the building of a new parking garage that will negatively affect local wetlands.

Applying Critical Thinking

| PURPOSE | IDEAS | SUPPORT | ASSUMPTIONS BIASES | CONCLUSIONS | POINT OF VIEW | ANALYSIS |

You see the causes and effects of actions and events around you all the time. You forget to put money in the parking meter (cause) and you get a ticket (effect). When analyzing a cause and effect pattern, you need to break down the parts of the cause(s) and the effect(s) of your topic. For example, maybe you forgot to put money in the meter because you saw someone fall while in a crosswalk and ran to help. Perhaps the ticket was waived because you took in the newspaper clipping applauding your rescue of the elderly woman who was almost run over by a truck. To write an effective cause and effect essay, you need to **analyze** all the *befores* and *afters* of an event.

BEFORE WRITING A CAUSE AND EFFECT ESSAY

Before you begin to write a cause and effect essay on an assigned topic, or one you have chosen, start by asking yourself these questions:

1. What process or event is the subject of my cause and effect analysis?
2. What are the benefits of doing a cause and effect analysis of my chosen topic?
3. Why did this process or event happen—what was the original cause (causes)?
4. What is the result(s) (effect/s) of this process or event?
5. What do I want my readers to learn from reading about the cause(s) and/or effect(s) of this event or process?
6. How will I conclude this essay?

Answering these questions will lead you to an expository thesis statement, help you determine the causes and effects you want to focus on, the examples and details to include for support, and a general idea of how to organize your essay.

Activity 13-1   Prewriting

Directions: *Prewrite on the following broad subjects to come up with some ideas of causes and effects that could be analyzed in relation to each.*

Example:

Topic: Discrimination
Self-esteem issues, unfair work practices, learned behavior, ignorance, school problems, therapy, cycle of discrimination, institutionalized discrimination, education.

1. **Topic:** Obesity _____

_____

_____

2. **Topic:** Eating disorders _____

_____

_____

3. **Topic:** Bankruptcy _____

_____

_____

4. **Topic:** A promotion _____

_____

_____

5. **Topic:** Being fired from a job _____

_____

_____

Activity 13-2   Cause and Effect

Directions: *For each of the topics below, create a flowchart that provides at least one* before *and after* **cause** *and* **effect** *for the subject in the middle:*

Example:

exercise	← better sleep	→	_better health_
1. _____	← exhaustion	→	_____
2. _____	← prejudice	→	_____
3. _____	← skin damage	→	_____
4. _____	← good grades	→	_____
5. _____	← tooth decay	→	_____
6. _____	← riots	→	_____
7. _____	← caffeine addiction	→	_____
8. _____	← paying bills	→	_____
9. _____	← laughing	→	_____
10. _____	← tears	→	_____

WRITING A CAUSE AND EFFECT ESSAY

The point of analyzing causes and effects is to look at the reasons why things happen and/or the results of them happening in order to understand them better and possibly to take action. When analyzing related events, you first need to make sure there is a causal relationship. Did one idea or event lead to another? What was the cause and what was the effect? After you determine there is a cause and effect relationship in your topic, then you need to determine what you want to explain to your readers about it. Do you want to explain the causes and effects in order to inform your readers of a process or to critique the effects or the causes? For example, if you were writing about health and exercise, you could explain the effects of exercise on one's health in order to convince your readers to engage in more exercise. Or you could focus on the negative effects of too little exercise to accomplish the same goal.

Be sure to organize your essay in the best way to build the analytical conclusion you establish in your thesis statement and introduction. When looking at the effects of one particular event or incident, it may help to think of the domino effect (see page 4): The dominos are lined up; then one is knocked over, and they fall one by one leading to an overall change in the structure. The initial push of the first domino is the initial cause, and the dominos that fall one by one are the effects. It is a chain reaction: cause–effect–cause–effect.

Depending on the assignment, you may analyze one cause and several effects, one effect and several causes, or several causes and several effects.

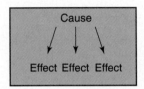

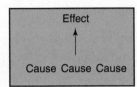

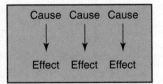

In each of the patterns diagrammed, your body paragraphs would focus on the individual causes and/or effects you have established in your introduction. Use transitional words and phrases between the causes and/or effects you are providing as examples.

The chart below provides a brief overview of the structure of a cause and effect essay.

BASIC STRUCTURE FOR A CAUSE AND EFFECT ESSAY

Introductory Paragraph

Sets up background for your cause/effect analysis.

Thesis statement: Establishes the causes and effects you will explain and your purpose for analyzing them.

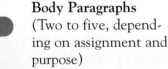

Body Paragraphs (Two to five, depending on assignment and purpose)

Topic sentences set up the cause and effect subcategories.

Develop your analysis of the causal relationship by providing specific examples of the cause(s) and effect(s) and critiquing their importance.

Provide concrete examples and details.

Use transitions within and between paragraphs to make the paragraphs flow smoothly.

| Concluding Paragraph | **Sums up and re-emphasizes** the thesis statement: the **conclusions reached** through your cause and effect analysis. |  |

STRUCTURING A CAUSE AND EFFECT ESSAY

Topic

If you do not have a topic assigned by your instructor for your cause and effect essay, then brainstorm ideas for events or processes you might want to describe. Then come up with some ideas for a purpose for describing the topic. What do you want your readers to understand through your cause and effect essay?

A Few Topic Possibilities

You can write an essay looking at the causes of pollution, a medical condition, depression, or any other cause that leads to a particular result. Or you can look at the effects of an event or condition like a hurricane or other natural disaster, a medical condition, eating habits, or any action or event that leads to a particular result. The key is to look at what caused something to occur, what happened after something occurred, or both.

Thesis Statements

The thesis statement in a cause and effect essay establishes whether you are focusing on just the causes of something, just the effects of something, or both. It also establishes the purpose for the cause and effect analysis: what you want your readers to understand. For example, if you were writing about diet and exercise, your thesis might establish both a causal relationship and an argument:

> Watching your diet and increasing your weekly exercise will create significant positive results within weeks of changing your habits.

Activity 13-3 Creating Thesis Statements

Directions: *Come up with a possible thesis statement for each of the topics you brainstormed in Activity 13-1. Be sure the thesis focuses on the causes, effects, or both related to the topic and has a purpose to convey.*

1. **Topic:** Obesity

    Thesis statement: _____

    _____

2. **Topic:** Eating disorders

    Thesis statement: _____

    _____

3. **Topic:** Bankruptcy

    Thesis statement: _____

    _____

4. **Topic:** A promotion

    Thesis statement: _____

    _____

5. **Topic:** Being fired

    Thesis statement: _____

    _____

Introductory Paragraph

Begin your cause/effect essay with a general introduction to the topic, and end your introductory paragraph with a thesis statement that sets up the purpose for your essay.

Body Paragraphs

The body paragraphs and topic sentences set up the order and the examples you will develop for your cause/effect analysis. You could arrange the causes and/or effects in separate paragraphs from least to most important (or vice versa) or arrange them in the order in which they take place (chronologically). For instance, if you were writing about Hurricane Katrina, you could look at the effects chronologically (by which place was hit first, second, and so on) or by order of importance (such as "New Orleans is the city that suffered the most loss," and so on). Use transitional words and phrases to lead your readers from one cause or effect to the next. As well as the cause and effect transitions shown here, those showing examples and purpose are also useful (see Chapter 6, pages 118–119).

Transitions to Show Result and/or Cause/Effect Relationships

accordingly	consequently	since	therefore
as a result	for this reason	so	thereupon
because	hence	then	thus

Be sure to use plenty of specific examples and details to illustrate the particular causes (high winds and torrential rainfall) or effects (such as the breaking of the levees in New Orleans, the loss of property, and so on) in your body paragraphs. Your topic sentences will indicate which causes or effects you will be explaining in each paragraph.

In New Orleans, many lifetime residents lost their homes in the floods.

Activity 13-4   Creating Topic Sentences

Directions: *Create a possible topic sentence for each of the thesis statements you generated in Activity 13-3. You will need to decide if you will focus on causes, effects, or both if you were writing this essay.*

1. **Topic:** Obesity

   Topic sentence: _____

   _____

2. **Topic:** Eating disorders

   Topic sentence: _____

   _____

3. **Topic:** Bankruptcy

   Topic sentence: _____

   _____

4. **Topic:** A promotion

   Topic sentence: _____

   _____

5. **Topic:** Being fired

   Topic sentence: _____

   _____

After you have come up with your topic sentences, you need to support them with examples and details to illustrate your points.

Activity 13-5   Providing Examples

Directions: *For three of the topic sentences you generated above, provide at least two examples that would help demonstrate your cause and/or effect analysis.*

1. **Topic:** _____

    Examples: _____

    _____

2. **Topic:** _____

    Examples: _____

    _____

3. **Topic:** _____

    Examples: _____

    _____

Concluding Paragraph

Your essay will need a concluding paragraph that briefly recaps the cause/effect analysis and the purpose for studying the causal relationship. Re-emphasize what you want your readers to realize about the cause and effect connections after they've read your essay.

Activity 13-6   Concluding Paragraphs

Directions: *Create a three- to six-sentence concluding paragraph for any one of the topics from the previous activities.*

Topic chosen: _____

Concluding paragraph: _____

_____

_____

_____

Use the following critique form to check for the basics in your cause and effect essay draft.

Cause/Effect Essay Critique Form

PURPOSE   IDEAS   SUPPORT   ASSUMPTIONS BIASES   CONCLUSIONS   POINT OF VIEW   ANALYSIS

Overall

Done well   Needs work

1. Does the essay clearly develop cause and effect **analysis** with a clear **purpose**?   _____ _____
2. Does the essay use a clear order in the body paragraphs?   _____ _____
3. Are the paragraphs broken up well and about the right length?   _____ _____

Introduction

4. Is the title interesting and in correct format?   _____ _____
5. Is there a general introduction that gives the **purpose** for the cause and effect **analysis**? Is the process clear?   _____ _____
6. Is there a clear thesis statement that explains the results of the cause(s) and effect(s) and the overall **purpose**?   _____ _____

Body

7. Do the body paragraphs develop the **ideas** and **analysis** well and flow smoothly?   _____ _____
8. Are transitions used between and, when needed, within the paragraphs?   _____ _____
9. Do the body paragraphs include **support** and descriptive details for development?   _____ _____
10. Does the essay demonstrate the relationship of the cause(s) and the effect(s) and the importance of their interrelatedness?   _____ _____

Conclusion

11. Does the **concluding** paragraph sum up the essay with an analytical frame that re-emphasizes the introductory paragraph and thesis, without adding new ideas?   _____ _____

Editing

12. Circle the following errors you think you see in this draft: spelling, fragments, run-ons/comma splices, commas, semicolon/colon use, pronoun agreement, reference fault errors, parallelism, apostrophe use, verb use/tense, and passive voice construction. (See the handbook section for help in identifying and correcting these errors)
13. Other types of grammar or sentence-level errors:

_____

Comments:

_____

_____

COMPLEMENTARY MODES FOR CAUSE AND EFFECT ESSAYS

Cause and effect mode is often combined with several other modes.

- **Narration** and **description** can be used to develop the analysis.
- **Definition** mode can be used to help explain objects or concepts used in the cause and effect analysis.
- **Illustration and examples** can further elaborate on the cause/effect analysis of the subject.
- **Classification** is usually part of the causal process itself: You have to classify items into broader groups to analyze them specifically.
- You can **compare and contrast** items or the causes or effects themselves as you analyze your subject.
- You can use **argument** to persuade your readers to accept a particular point of view related to the cause and effect analysis.

SAMPLE STUDENT ESSAY

Kunitz 1

Michelle Kunitz

Professor Archer

English 100

3 November 2007

The Dangers of Too Much TV

Television is a great invention, and it is a great element of most homes, as long as it is watched in moderation. Unfortunately, these days, too many children are watching too much TV every day. Studies show that students watch an average of two to four hours of TV a day. There are several negative effects of watching too much TV.

The first negative effect for children who watch too much TV is lack of exercise due to sitting passively in front of the tube all day. Unfortunately, many children do not spend as much time outside

Thesis statement

Topic sentence

Kunitz 2

playing with their friends as they did in the past. With the constant
availability of kid's programming, such as cartoons played 24 hours a
day, more children choose to stay on the couch watching shows than
going outside and playing with their friends. It used to be that cartoons were only available at certain times, so the fact that they are
on 24/7 may have added to the increase in TV watching.

Concluding sentence

A direct result of increased TV watching has been the increase
in childhood obesity in America. Many children are more inactive due
to increased TV watching, and, in addition, they tend to snack more
when indoors watching TV all day. Both of these reasons lead to
increased weight in a child.

Topic sentence

Concluding sentence

Another negative effect of too much TV is a decrease in reading
and imaginative play by children. When children spend hours watching TV, then they spend a lot less time reading or engaging in imaginative play. For instance, many children these days rarely play board
games or work on puzzles. These interactive types of play are much
more intellectually stimulating than passive TV viewing.

Topic sentence

Concluding sentence

Overall, the increase in TV viewing by children over the last
couple of decades has led to negative consequences for many of them.
Their health and intelligence are put in jeopardy when they watch
too much TV. Hopefully, parents will take these negative effects seriously and take action to decrease the amount of time their kids
spend in front of the tube and strongly encourage them to participate
in physical activities, imaginative play, and reading.

Restatement of thesis

Activity 13-7   Thinking Critically About the Student Essay

Directions: *Analyze the essay to identify the features and details characteristic
of the cause and effect mode. Mark them on the essay. Then, reread the essay, and*

make a list of specific revisions you would make to correct any problems with content, organization, transitions, and style. ●

PROFESSIONAL CAUSE AND EFFECT ESSAY

The Columbine Syndrome: Boys and the Fear of Violence

William S. Pollack

William S. Pollack is Assistant Clinical Professor in the Department of Psychiatry at Harvard Medical School and a clinical psychologist. He is the author of *Real Boys: Rescuing Our Sons from the Myths of Masculinity* (1999), *Real Boys' Voices* (2000), *and Real Boys Workbook* (2001). Pollack serves as an advisor to the President's National Campaign against Youth Violence. This essay appeared in the fall 2000 issue of the *National Forum*.

> "I don't want to be that type of kid who comes to school and just takes out a gun and starts shooting."—*Bobby, age 12, from a city in the West*

> "The other day I walked into school and a girl was carrying balloons and one of them popped. Everyone in the whole school got really terrified."—*Errol, age 17, from a suburb in the West*

> "I think there are people at my school who have the potential for doing something similar."—*Jules, age 17, from a suburb in the South*

> "People were coming up to me and begging me not to kill them. I felt like telling them: 'Cut it out; I'm not going to do anything.'"—*Cody, age 14, from a suburb in New England*

> "You can't say 'them' or 'you.' You have to say 'us.'"—*Jimmy, age 16, from a small town in the West*

1   Probably no risk other than violence has made America more afraid of boys and made boys more afraid of being male and living in this country. Though it has been understood for decades that the perpetrators of most violent crimes in our nation are male, the recent spate of school shootings, culminating in the heinous massacre of teachers and students recently carried out in suburban Littleton, Colorado, has made the public

even more frightened and confused about the threat of extreme violence and its connection, in particular, with boys. Boys of adolescent age, boys just like the ones who have contributed to my research, are the ones pulling the triggers and injuring, sometimes killing, their peers and school teachers. What many people do not realize—and what the media isn't following as well as they might—is that most of the victims of teenage violence, indeed the vast majority, are also boys.

Consequences of the Columbine Syndrome

2   In my travels across our country, listening to boys and doing research for my latest book, *Real Boys' Voices* (Random House, 2000), I have come to see that the effect of these terrible crimes has been immense. It has led to the "Columbine Syndrome": Across our nation students, parents, and teachers are absolutely terrified—sometimes to an extreme degree—about which boys amongst them are violent, who the next perpetrators might be, and who their victims will become. Paranoia is rampant. School children and the adults around them are constantly canvassing the student body and worrying, often inappropriately, that particular students may be murderous. Grady, age seventeen, from a school in the South says, "When a kid's wearing a trenchcoat and he's going for something in his jacket, you learn from watching the news that more than likely he might have a gun."

3   The consequence is that boys themselves are becoming increasingly afraid. They are frightened not only of being victimized by the rage and violence of other boys, but also of being accused, or falsely accused, of having the disposition it takes to snap into hyper-violent action and embark on a murderous rampage. Boys fear that despite their true nature, they will automatically, because they are boys, be seen as somehow toxic, dangerous, and culpable. As one young preadolescent boy said, "I think women like small kids. Girls like newborn babies. They don't like big people. We bigger guys scare everybody, and then we get blamed even when we've done nothing wrong."

4   Boys are also afraid of the violence they may feel inside themselves and of whether it is safe to talk with us about it. As they internalize this fear of being misunderstood—and of being charged with having a violent temperament they genuinely do not have—boys themselves are beginning to worry if maybe, just maybe, the demon is within, if lurking underneath their conscious understanding of themselves are uncontrollable urges to do depraved, violent acts. The Columbine Syndrome means that America's boys today are as confused about violence as they are afraid of it. They fear each other and they fear their own selves.

The "Boy Code"

5   While the statistics indicate that teenage boys not only commit a considerable percentage of the nation's violent juvenile crimes but also become the frequent victims of those crimes, in reality there seems to be no inherent biological factor that makes boys more violent than their female counterparts. Violence committed by and acted out upon boys seems to stem, more often than not, from what we teach (or do not teach) boys about the behavior we expect from them. It comes from society's set of rules about masculinity, the Boy Code that says, "To be a man, you must show your strength and your power. You must show that you can hold your own if challenged by another male. You can show your rage, but you must not show any other emotions. You must protect your honor and fight off shame at all costs."

6   Think of it yourself. A boy gets slightly angry as a way to express his pain, and there will be mixed emotions. Some of us may show some fear, but if the anger is in control, we are unlikely to respond in a drastic manner. So long as it is "within bounds," society tends to approve of, if not encourage, aggression by and among boys. Violence in boys is widely (although, as I have said, incorrectly) seen as inevitable, if not biologically pre-ordained. As long as nobody is seriously hurt, no lethal weapons are employed, and especially within the framework of sports and games—football, soccer, boxing, wrestling—aggression and violence are widely accepted and even encouraged in boys. Boys are constantly trying to prove their masculinity through aggression, and society is complicit; winning a game, or even a fight, helps many boys gain society's respect.

7   The corollary to this message, simply enough, is that soft, gentle, non-violent boys are "feminine" and therefore losers. While we often pay lip service to helping boys "put feelings into words" and even create multi-million dollar educational programs to address this, if you're "a big guy" and start to express your vulnerable emotions too openly, people crawl back in fear. Or imagine the boy who misses a goal and bursts into tears on the soccer field. He is not considered masculine. Peers call him a "girl," "sissy" or "fag." Parents cringe. It is precisely in this environment that even the most hearty boy soon learns to avoid showing his pain in public. He may want to cry, he may wish he could speak of his fear, sadness, or shame; but he holds it back. He resists. Instead, the boy displays anger, aggression, and violence.

8   Perhaps it should not shock us, then, when we hear from the boys who say that while they overwhelmingly condemn extreme violence, and to a large extent do not engage in it, they can understand, empathize with

the boys who hit, hurt, and even kill. They tell us about what the teasing and razzing "can do to your head," how alone and isolated some boys can become, and how rage is indeed often the only sanctioned emotion that does not bring further ridicule to them. We are all afraid of boys and violence, but boys, it turns out, are the most in fear. Gun detectors, violence screening tools or "profiles," armed guards, and "zero tolerance" only goad our sons into the very aggression we, and they, are afraid of; by expecting boys to be angry, rambunctious, and dangerous, we push boys to fulfill these prophecies. This is the essence, I believe, of the Columbine Syndrome. By living in fear and expecting danger, that is exactly what we produce.

9   To compound the risk to all of us, society is now giving boys another complex and confusing message, what I call the "No Black Shirts" response. Because the Columbine killers were outcast boys, spiteful nonconforming boys who wore dark clothing and were estranged from their peers, society has now rushed to the conclusion that adolescent boys who seem "different," especially ones who seem quiet, distant, and in pain, are the likely perpetrators of the next ghastly Columbine-like crime. Sadly, what the huge majority of outcast boys needs most—in fact what many so-called "popular" boys, boys on the "inside" often desperately need as well—is not to have their pain suppressed and disregarded, but rather to have it listened to and understood.

Curbing the Syndrome

10 Boys in pain require immediate intervention. As soon as we detect that a boy is experiencing emotional distress, we need to stop what we are doing, turn towards him, and hear him out. Whether he is wearing a black hood or Brooks Brothers sweater, whether he is well-liked or an outcast, he needs us to come toward him, embrace and affirm him, and assuage his hurt feelings before they push him to the edge. Boys are simply not inherently violent or dangerous, and the emotional distress that they may feel, in the first instance, does not make them any more so. But if we continue to give boys the message that expressing their distress is forbidden, that we will ignore their vulnerable feelings when we see them, and that we actually expect them to act out angrily and violently, we should not be surprised that the world becomes, for all of us, a mighty frightful place.

11   As the voices I heard (sampled in brief above) and published in detail in *Real Boys' Voices* exemplify, only a tiny percentage of boys are capable of egregious acts of violence. In truth, as aggressive as they can perhaps be pushed to become, most boys are quite anxious about and

revolted by the prevalence of violence in society. They feel powerless to do anything about it, though, because they simply feel too much shame, too concerned about how other people will respond to their confessions of fear.

12   The solution, I believe, is for society to commit to a whole new way of seeing boys and violence. First, as a society we need to decide, unequiv-ocally, that as much as we will not exalt boys who fight, we also will not punish or ostracize those who show their vulnerability. By defending and actually providing positive reinforcement to boys who openly exhibit their moments of fear, longing, anxiety, and despair, by telling these boys and men that they are fully "masculine" no matter what emotions they share with us, we can help them avoid the repression and resistance that may make them bottle up their emotions and then spill them out in irrational acts. Second, because society may not change overnight, we need to be on the lookout for the signs of sadness and depression that in boys and men so often seem harder to see, or more difficult to believe and accept. In my book, I outlined these many signs. If we are attentive to them, and if we help boys overcome the pain and disaffection that gives rise to them, much of the aggression and violence we now see will evaporate, or be directed towards safe, appropriate channels.

13   Finally, we must simply decide, as a society, that most boys, as angry or aggressive as they may become, are highly unlikely to become danger-ous in any way. The. boys' voices quoted at the beginning of this piece are overwhelming proof that most of our sons have a non-violent nature and that, in reality, their greater struggle is with sadness and the fear of violence rather than with violence itself. Together we must create prophe-cies that their gentle nature will triumph over old pressures to act tough and lash out. Perhaps if we hear boys' fears about violence in a new light, read their stories with a new empathy, we may be able to reach across the boundaries of fear and create a new dialogue of peace. For boys and for the rest of us, the only cure for the Columbine Syndrome, in the end, is to develop safe spaces that are friendly to boys and thereby create gen-uine security. The time is now!

Reading Reflection Questions

1. What are the direct or indirect (implied) messages in this story? _____

_____

_____

_____

2. In your own words, define what the author means by the "Columbine Syndrome." _____

_____

Objective Questions

3. T/F _____ Most of the perpetrators and victims of teenage violence are boys.

4. T/F _____ Many boys are afraid of their own potential for violence.

5. T/F _____ Many boys are afraid they will be feared just for being boys.

6. Explain what the author means by the "Boy Code." _____

_____

7. What solution does this author propose to this problem? _____

_____

_____

Checking Vocabulary

Define the following in your own words or provide a dictionary definition if you don't know the word.

8. heinous: _____

9. perpetrators: _____

10. corollary: _____

CRITICAL THINKING CHECKLIST

PURPOSE

1. What is the **purpose** of this piece of writing? Is it clear?

_____

_____

2. What **ideas** and **background information** are provided to support the purpose of this piece of writing?

IDEAS

_____

_____

3. What **evidence** and **examples** are used to explain and develop the ideas that support the argument made in the piece of writing? Are the evidence and examples provided sufficient?

_____

_____

4. Are there unfounded **assumptions** or unreasonable **biases**?

_____

_____

5. Are all of the **conclusions, implications,** and **consequences** of the arguments (the results of the arguments taken to their furthest extreme) considered?

_____

_____

6. Is the **point of view** clear and consistent, and have other points of view been considered?

_____

_____

7. Using these critical thinking tools, **analyze** the overall structure of this essay and the strength of the author's arguments, ideas, and support. Was he or she successful in accomplishing the purpose? Why or why not?

_____

_____

Essay Assignments

1. Write an essay that illustrates the negative effects of stress on a college student.

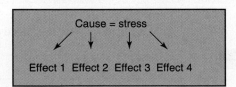

2. Write an essay that focuses on the causes of stress for college students.

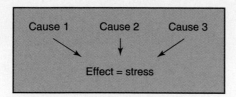

3. Write an essay that explores a chain reaction, or domino effect, where there is a sequence of one cause leading to an effect that starts a second cause that leads to a second effect, and so on.

4. Write a cause/effect essay on any of the subjects you worked on in the activities in this chapter.

14

Comparison and Contrast

THINKING CRITICALLY

Look carefully at the two photos of the same sculpture above. List some of the similarities and differences between the two pictures. Then describe briefly what effect the differences have on the way you view the sculpture.

Similarities: _____

_____

Differences: _____

_____

Overall effect of the differences: _____

_____

_____

COMPARISON AND CONTRAST ESSAYS

Comparison essays look at the *similarities* between two subjects, and **contrast essays** look at the *differences* between two subjects. A comparison *and* contrast essay looks at both the similarities and differences between two subjects.

Critical Thinking and Comparison and Contrast

There will be many instances in college and in the work world where you will need to use your comparison and contrast analysis skills. You may need to compare and contrast two politicians running for office, two periods of history, two literary characters, two theories, two formal speeches, two potential job opportunities, or two houses or apartments for rent—the possibilities are endless.

BEFORE WRITING A COMPARISON/ CONTRAST ESSAY

Before you begin to write a comparison/contrast essay on an assigned topic, or one you have chosen, start by asking yourself these questions:

1. What two objects, people, or concepts am I going to compare and/or contrast?
2. Are they in the same general category?
3. Am I going to focus on similarities, differences, or both? Are the two subjects mostly alike, mostly different, or some of each?
4. How will I set up my comparisons/contrasts, and how will I structure my paragraphs?
5. What examples and details should I include for support?
6. What do I want my readers to learn or understand after reading this comparison and/or contrast essay?
7. How will I conclude my essay?

Answering these questions will lead you to an expository thesis statement, help you determine what you will be comparing and/or contrasting, help you develop examples and details to include for support, and give you a general idea of how you want to organize your essay.

Applying Critical Thinking

We use comparisons and contrasts to make sense of the world and put things into perspective. Comparing is a way to find the familiar through looking at the similarities between things, and contrasting helps us to see the differences between things in order to better understand them. To write an effective comparison/contrast essay, you need to use your **analytical** skills to identify how things are similar and different, determine your **purpose** for writing about those similarities and differences, and decide which **ideas**, **support**, and details will best illustrate and explain the point you want to make.

For example, if you were comparing two grocery stores, what similarities would you point out? What differences? What possible conclusions could you reach? Will your comparison lead to a recommendation?

Activity 14-1   Generating Topics for a Comparison/Contrast Essay

Directions: *Generate three possible topics for a comparison/contrast essay: List the two items, concepts, people, etc. Then explain whether you would focus on similarities, differences, or both.*

1. Two subjects: _____

    Similarities, differences, or both: _____

    _____

2. Two subjects: _____

    Similarities, differences, or both: _____

    _____

3. Two subjects: _____

    Similarities, differences, or both: _____

    _____

WRITING A COMPARISON/CONTRAST ESSAY

First, make sure that the two subjects you compare and/or contrast are in the same general group or category. The old cliché "It's like comparing apples to oranges" doesn't really fit, since you could compare an apple to an orange: They are both in the "fruit" category, and they have both similarities and differences. However, you probably wouldn't want to write a compare/contrast essay about an orange and your best friend, unless your best friend is particularly orange and round: After that, there probably wouldn't be enough categories in common to make for an interesting or developed analytical comparison.

Once you have chosen your subjects, you need to decide whether you are focusing on similarities, differences, or both and determine the purpose of your essay. Then you have to choose an organizational plan for your comparison/contrast essay. There are two ways to organize comparison/contrast essays. You can choose a subject-by-subject approach, or you can choose a point-by-point approach.

Subject-by-Subject Organization Pattern

In a **subject-by-subject** organization pattern, you first present all aspects of one subject; then you transition and present all aspects of the second subject. For example:

> **Subject A = compact cars**   **Subject B = SUVs**
> > Point 1 = Size/comfort
> > Point 2 = Gas mileage/cost
> > Point 3 = Image/personality

An outline of a paper on compact cars versus SUVs, using this pattern, would look like this:

> **General introductory comments**
>
> **Thesis:** Compact cars and SUVs offer very different options for a consumer when it comes to size and comfort, gas mileage and cost, and the type of image or personality the cars project.
>
> **Subject A: Compact Cars**
> > **Point 1:** Compact cars' size and comfort
> > **Point 2:** Compact cars' gas mileage and cost
> > **Point 3:** Compact cars' image and personality

Subject B: SUVs

>   Point 1: SUVs' size and comfort
>   Point 2: SUVs' gas mileage and cost
>   Point 3: SUVs' image and personality

Conclusion: Re-emphasize thesis. Closing comments.

Point-by-Point Organization Pattern

In a **point-by-point** organization pattern, you discuss both subjects at the same time, categorized point by point. For example:

	Subject A: Compact cars	Subject B: SUVs
Point 1	Size/comfort	Size/comfort
Point 2	Gas mileage/cost	Gas mileage/cost
Point 3	Image/personality	Image/personality

An outline of a paper on compact cars versus SUVs, using this pattern, would look like this:

General introductory comments

Thesis: Compact cars and SUVs offer very different options for a consumer when it comes to size and comfort, gas mileage and cost, and the type of image or personality the cars project.

Point 1: Size and comfort for subjects A and B (compact cars and SUVs)

Point 2: Gas mileage and cost for subjects A and B (compact cars and SUVs)

Point 3: Image and personality for subjects A and B (compact cars and SUVs)

Conclusion: Re-emphasize thesis. Closing comments.

Note: These patterns do not necessarily indicate the number of paragraphs you would use in an essay. It might take more than one paragraph to develop each point.

Pick the organizational pattern that works best for your subject and purpose. Also, be sure that you give a balanced comparison and provide an equal number of details to support both subjects. Create topic sentences that will highlight the categories for comparison or contrast and the points you want to make. Provide plenty of examples and details to illustrate these points in the body paragraphs. Use transitions between paragraphs or examples when needed to help the flow of your essay.

Finally, be sure that you reach an analytical conclusion through your comparison/contrast and that your thesis and your concluding paragraph sum up that analytical conclusion.

The chart below provides a brief overview of the structure of a comparison and contrast essay.

BASIC STRUCTURE FOR A COMPARISON/CONTRAST ESSAY

Introductory Paragraph	**Sets up** your subject and your purpose. **Thesis statement:** A statement that defines your purpose and what example(s) you'll be using to illustrate it	PURPOSE
Body Paragraphs (Two to five, depending on assignment and purpose)	**Choose** subject-by-subject or point-by-point organization pattern. Create **topic sentences** to support your thesis. **Develop** the comparisons and contrasts through illustrations, details, and **analysis**. **Provide examples and concrete details** to illustrate vividly the examples. **Use transitions** within and between paragraphs to make the paragraphs flow smoothly.	IDEAS ANALYSIS SUPPORT
Concluding Paragraph	**Sums up and re-emphasizes** the thesis.	CONCLUSIONS

STRUCTURING A COMPARISON/ CONTRAST ESSAY

Topic

If you do not have a topic assigned by your instructor for your comparison/contrast essay, then brainstorm ideas for things, places, people, or ideas you might want to compare and contrast. Then come up with some ideas for a purpose for comparing/contrasting your subjects. What do you want your readers to understand through your comparison/contrast?

A Few Topic Possibilities

Any two subjects that you want to look at side by side to emphasize similarities or differences or both make for a good topic for this type of essay. You could compare and contrast two historical figures, two political figures, two people you know, two restaurants, two musicians, two paintings, two photographs, two cities, and so on. Just make sure they have enough in common in the first place to make for good explorations.

Thesis Statements

After you have done some prewriting and determined your subjects and whether you will focus on similarities, differences, or both, come up with the purpose for your comparison/contrast essay and write your thesis statement. What conclusion did you reach by comparing and contrasting these subjects? What do you want your readers to understand after reading this essay?

> The Xbox game system is very different from the Wii game system as far as style and technology are concerned.

> Home cooking and going out to restaurants to eat result in diverse dining experiences.

Activity 14-2   Creating Thesis Statements

Directions: *For each of the topics you generated in Activity 14-1, create a thesis statement.*

1. **Topic:** _____

   Thesis statement: _____

   _____

2. **Topic:** _____

   Thesis statement: _____

   _____

3. **Topic:** _____

   Thesis statement: _____

   _____

Introductory Paragraph

Begin your comparison/contrast essay with a general introduction of the two subjects you are comparing/contrasting in order to demonstrate your analytical conclusion. End with the thesis statement to set up the purpose for your comparison/contrast essay.

Body Paragraphs

The body paragraphs in a comparison and/or contrast essay are structured either by focusing on one subject at a time or on one category or point for both of the subjects one paragraph at a time. Be sure you have a clear topic sentence that spells out the subject(s) and category you are exploring for each paragraph and the point you want to make. Then, use specific evidence and examples to illustrate the comparisons or contrasts. Analyze the examples. Use comparison and contrast transitions to show your readers when you are comparing and contrasting items. (Other helpful transitions that show summary, example, and purpose are listed on pages 118–119.) Then frame your examples with a concluding sentence that ties in to your topic sentence.

TRANSITIONS TO SHOW CONTRAST OR A CHANGE IN IDEA

although	even though	instead	on the other side
anyhow	for all that	nevertheless	otherwise
at the same time	however	notwithstanding	regardless
but	in any event	on the contrary	still
despite this	in contrast	on the other hand	yet

TRANSITIONS TO SHOW A COMPARISON

| in like manner | in the same way | likewise | similarly |

Activity 14-3 Creating Topic Sentences

Directions: *Create one topic sentence for each of the thesis statements you generated in Activity 14-2.*

1. **Topic:** _____

    Topic sentence: _____

    _____

2. **Topic:** _____

    Topic sentence: _____

    _____

3. **Topic:** _____

    Topic sentence: _____

    _____

After you have created your topic sentences, develop the ideas using examples and details for support.

Activity 14-4   Providing Details

Directions: *Now, come up with at least two examples or details you could include in a body paragraph developing each of the topic sentences you came up with in Activity 14-3.*

1. **Topic:** _____

    Examples: _____

    _____

    _____

2. **Topic:** _____

    Examples: _____

    _____

    _____

3. **Topic:** _____

    Examples: _____

    _____

    _____

Concluding Paragraph

The concluding paragraph for a comparison/contrast essay should remind your readers what the purpose of your comparison/contrast was—why you compared and/or contrasted the subjects you chose.

Activity 14-5   Writing a Conclusion

Directions: *Now choose one of the topics you've been developing in the previous activities and write a three- to six-sentence concluding paragraph that could finish that essay.*

_____

_____

_____

_____

Use the following critique form to check for the basics in your comparison and contrast essay draft.

Comparison/Contrast Essay Critique Form

PURPOSE   IDEAS   SUPPORT   ASSUMPTIONS BIASES   CONCLUSIONS   POINT OF VIEW   ANALYSIS

Overall

                                                                    Done well   Needs work

1. Does the essay clearly develop comparison and/or contrast **analysis** with a clear **purpose**/analytical conclusion?   _____   _____

2. Does the essay use a clear order (subject by subject or point by point or an effective combination of the two) in the body paragraphs with an analytical conclusion drawn from the comparison or contrast?   _____   _____

3. Are the paragraphs broken up well and about the right length?   _____   _____

Introduction

4. Is the title interesting and in correct format?   _____   _____

5. Is there a general introduction that gives the purpose for the comparison and contrast analysis? Is the process and organization clear?   _____   _____

6. Is there a clear thesis statement that explains the purpose of the comparisons and/or contrasts and the overall purpose?   _____   _____

Body

7. Do the body paragraphs develop the **ideas** and **analysis** well and flow smoothly?   _____   _____

	Done well	Needs work

8. Are transitions used between and, when needed, within the paragraphs?

9. Do the body paragraphs include **support** and descriptive details for development?

10. Does the writer demonstrate the significance of the similarities and differences (both or just one of the two)?

Conclusion

11. Does the **concluding** paragraph sum up the essay with an analytical frame that re-emphasizes the introductory paragraph and thesis, without adding new ideas?

Editing

12. Circle the following errors you think you see in this draft: spelling, fragments, run-ons/comma splices, commas, semicolon/colon use, pronoun agreement, reference fault errors, parallelism, apostrophe use, verb use/tense, and passive voice construction. (See the handbook section for help in identifying and correcting these errors.)

13. Other types of grammar or sentence-level errors:

_____

Comments:

_____

_____

COMPLEMENTARY MODES FOR COMPARISON/CONTRAST ESSAYS

Compare/contrast mode is often combined with several other modes.

- **Narration** and **description** can be used to develop the analysis.
- **Definition** mode can be used to help explain objects or concepts used in the examples provided.
- **Examples** help illustrate the comparisons.
- **Cause and effect analysis** will further elaborate on the examples.
- **Classification** is usually part of the comparison itself: You have to classify items into broader groups to analyze them specifically.
- You can engage **argument** mode to persuade your readers to a particular point of view related to the comparison and contrast analysis.

SAMPLE STUDENT ESSAY

Todd White

Professor James

English 100

23 May 2008

Softball and Baseball: Serious Differences

Softball and baseball are both popular sports in America. At first glance, they seem very similar. However, there are some major differences between the two sports, not just in how they are played, but also in how much respect and attention sports fans give them.

Both sports use similar equipment, but there are differences in their design. Softball equipment is very basic. The ball is the size of a grapefruit and somewhat soft. The bats and gloves are a little larger than those used in baseball. Baseball is also played with a ball, a bat, and gloves. However, there are some differences in the equipment. To begin with, the baseball itself is smaller and harder than a softball. The baseball is the size of a small orange and it is much harder than a softball. The gloves are similar to softball gloves, but a bit smaller and the bats are a bit narrower than the ones used for softball.

In both softball and baseball, players hit the ball and run from base to base, and the goal of the game is to get as many players as possible into home base to score runs and therefore points. A major difference between these two sports is how the pitcher pitches the ball. In softball, the pitcher pitches underhand. There is slow-pitch softball and fast-pitch softball. Though both pitches are done underhand, the

Thesis statement

Topic sentence

Topic sentence

White 1

slow-pitch has a much higher arch. Moreover, in softball, there are
not different types of pitches: The throw is consistently the same. In
baseball, the pitcher throws overhand, and it is always fast-pitch.
Also, in baseball, there are many types of pitches, for instance, a

Concluding sentence — curve ball, a slider, and so on. Much of baseball depends on the speed
and unpredictability of the pitch.

Topic sentence —   Finally, the most interesting difference between softball and
baseball is the amount of recognition, popularity, and respect the
two sports receive. Though both are enjoyed and played at most
high schools and colleges, baseball is far more popular and is funded
and attended at much higher levels. Also, there are more major and
minor leagues for baseball, but there are no major leagues for softball. Most importantly, baseball is often called "America's pastime"
and is considered a major component of our American heritage.

Concluding sentence The same prestige is not attributed to softball.

Restatement of thesis —   Obviously, there are major differences between softball and
baseball, even though these two sports seem so close on the surface.
Most likely, softball will never reach the level of esteem that baseball
has earned as a beloved part of our American culture. It just doesn't
have the history. However, both of these sports are played everyday
on fields and in parks around the country.

Activity 14-6   Thinking Critically About the Student Essay

Directions: *Analyze the essay to identify the features and details characteristic
of the comparison and contrast mode. Mark them on the essay. Then, reread the
essay, and make a list of specific revisions you would make to correct any problems with content, organization, transitions, and style.* ●

PROFESSIONAL COMPARE AND CONTRAST ESSAY

American Space, Chinese Place

Yi-Fu Tuan

Yi-Fu Tuan was born in 1930 in Tientsin, China. He received his Ph.D. in 1957 from the University of California, Berkeley in geography. He is a retired professor emeritus of the University of Wisconsin, Madison. One of his most important publications is the book *Place, Art and Self*. In his book *Space and Place: The Perspective of Experience*, Tuan explores human movement from place to place and the need for a place to also have a sense of space.

1   Americans have a sense of space, not of place. Go to an American home in exurbia, and almost the first thing you do is drift toward the picture window. How curious that the first compliment you pay your host inside his house is to say how lovely it is outside his house! He is pleased that you should admire his vistas. The distant horizon is not merely a line separating earth from sky, it is a symbol of the future. The American is not rooted in his place, however lovely: his eyes are drawn by the expanding space to a point on the horizon, which is his future. By contrast, consider the traditional Chinese home. Blank walls enclose it.

2   Step behind the spirit wall and you are in a courtyard with perhaps a miniature garden around the corner. Once inside the private compound you are wrapped in an ambiance of calm beauty, an ordered world of buildings, pavement, rock, and decorative vegetation. But you have no distant view: nowhere does space open out before you. Raw nature in such a home is experienced only as weather, and the only open space is the sky above. The Chinese is rooted in his place. When he has to leave, it is not for the promised land on the terrestrial horizon, but for another world altogether along the vertical, religious axis of his imagination.

3   The Chinese tie to place is deeply felt. Wanderlust is an alien sentiment. The Taoist classic *Tao Te Ching* captures the ideal of rootedness in place with these words: "Though there may be another country in the neighborhood so close that they are within sight of each other and the crowing of cocks and barking of dogs in one place can be heard in the other, yet there is no traffic between them; and throughout their lives the two peoples have nothing to do with each other." In theory if not in practice, farmers have ranked high in Chinese society. The reason is not

only that they are engaged in the "root" industry of producing food but that, unlike pecuniary merchants, they are tied to the land and do not abandon their country when it is in danger.

4   Nostalgia is a recurrent theme in Chinese poetry. An American reader of translated Chinese poems will be taken aback—even put off—by the frequency as well as the sentimentality of the lament for home. To understand the strength of this sentiment, we need to know that the Chinese desire for stability and rootedness in place is prompted by the constant threat of war, exile, and the natural disasters of flood and drought. Forcible removal makes the Chinese keenly aware of their loss. By contrast, Americans move, for the most part, voluntarily. Their nostalgia for home town is really longing for childhood to which they cannot return: in the meantime the future beckons and the future is "out there," in open space. When we criticize American rootlessness we tend to forget that it is a result of ideals we admire, namely, social mobility and optimism about the future. When we admire Chinese rootedness, we forget that the word "place" means both location in space and position in society: to be tied to place is also to be bound to one's station in life, with little hope of betterment. Space symbolizes hope; place, achievement and stability.

Reading Reflection Questions

1. What are the direct or indirect (implied) messages in this story?

   _____

   _____

2. List two characteristics of this article that distinguish it as a contrast article. _____

   _____

   _____

   _____

3. Who do you think the main intended audience is for this article, Americans or Chinese? Why? _____

   _____

   _____

4. Provide one reason suggested in the article for the different perspectives of the Chinese and Americans toward home. _____

   _____

   _____

Objective Questions

5. T/F _____ The author suggests that Americans love open spaces.

6. T/F _____ The author suggests that Americans are more rooted to their homes than the Chinese.

7. T/F _____ The author suggests that the American desire for home is really longing for a return to childhood.

Checking Vocabulary

Define the following in your own words or provide a dictionary definition if you don't know the word.

8. ambiance: _____

9. wanderlust: _____

10. pecuniary: _____

CRITICAL THINKING CHECKLIST

PURPOSE

1. What is the **purpose** of this piece of writing? Is it clear?

   _____

   _____

IDEAS

2. What **ideas** and **background information** are provided to support the purpose of this piece of writing?

   _____

   _____

SUPPORT

3. What **evidence** and **examples** are used to explain and develop the ideas that support the argument made in the piece of writing? Are the evidence and examples provided sufficient?

   _____

   _____

ASSUMPTIONS BIASES

4. Are there unfounded **assumptions** or unreasonable **biases**?

   _____

   _____

5. Are all of the **conclusions, implications,** and **consequences** of the arguments (the results of the arguments taken to their furthest extreme) considered?

_____

_____

6. Is the **point of view** clear and consistent, and have other points of view been considered?

_____

_____

7. Using these critical thinking tools, **analyze** the overall structure of this essay and the strength of the author's arguments, ideas, and support. Was he or she successful in accomplishing the purpose? Why or why not?

_____

_____

Essay Assignments

1. Write a comparison/contrast essay on two teachers you've had. Determine at least three points you want to use for your comparison/contrast. Pick either subject-by-subject or point-by-point organization to construct your essay.

2. Compare and contrast two musicians (or musical groups). Determine at least three points you want to use for your comparison/contrast. Pick either subject-by-subject or point-by-point organization to construct your essay.

3. Compare and contrast two restaurants in your neighborhood. Determine at least three points you want to use for your comparison/contrast. Pick either subject-by-subject or point-by-point organization to construct your essay.

4. Choose any of the subjects you worked on in the activities from this chapter and write a complete comparison/contrast essay on that topic.

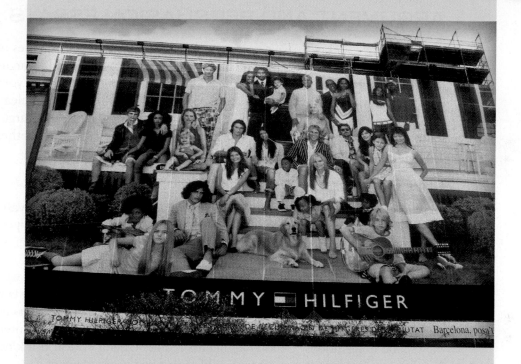

Argument and Persuasion

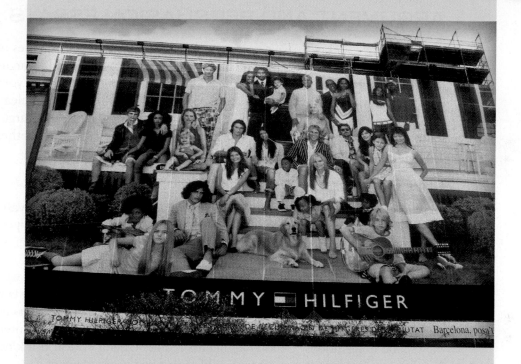

THINKING CRITICALLY

Look at the advertisment above. Then complete the task that follows.

Most advertisements have arguments embedded within them: The most common argument, of course, is "buy me!" Often other arguments are hinted at too, like if you buy a certain car you'll seem more good looking. Or, as in this Tommy Hilfiger ad, that if you wear their clothes you will be part of a large, happy, ethically diverse family of interesting people.

Choose a magazine, television, or billboard advertisement you've seen recently. Briefly describe the advertisement and what it is trying to persuade you to buy. Then list any secondary arguments the ad is suggesting.

ARGUMENT AND PERSUASION ESSAYS

Argumentative and persuasive writing is one of the most common types of writing you will be asked to do in college. You will be asked to write argumentative and persuasive pieces in the workplace too. Even a memo to your boss asking for a raise is a type of argument essay. Becoming skilled in clear, logical reasoning and arguments will help you see through the faulty arguments and logic in books, newspaper articles, political speeches, and other kinds of persuasive writing you encounter in the everyday world.

Critical Thinking and Argument

Argument essays involve stating a claim, supporting the claim with valid and fair-minded reasoning, providing examples and evidence to support your argument, and providing an even-handed presentation of counterarguments to your proposed solution.

Providing **counterarguments** (what others would say in response to your arguments) or alternative solutions to a problem shows that you are being fair-minded and not presenting an issue in a biased way. Evidence and support can include facts, statistics, detailed examples, firsthand accounts and/or interviews, and observations. Counterarguments require careful critical thinking. You have to anticipate what others would say against your argument.

Applying Critical Thinking

PURPOSE   IDEAS   SUPPORT   ASSUMPTIONS BIASES   CONCLUSIONS   POINT OF VIEW   ANALYSIS

To write an effective argument essay, you will need to consider the following questions:

1. What is my **purpose** for writing this essay? What **ideas** and point or points do I want to make to my audience?

2. What **biases** and **assumptions** do I have? What are they based on? Are they logical? What biases or assumptions might my audience have that I will need to address as I make my arguments?

3. What is my **point of view** on the subject? Is it based on credible information? How will I best present it?

4. Have I thoroughly **analyzed** my argument? How will I break it down into its basic parts, and how will I present them?

5. What **support** do I need to include? What details (descriptive details, facts, evidence, examples) can I include to develop my argument(s)?

BEFORE WRITING AN ARGUMENT ESSAY

Before you begin to write an argument essay on an assigned topic, or one you have chosen, start by asking yourself these questions:

1. What is my stand on this issue?
2. Is there a plan of action I can propose to solve a problem?
3. Who would disagree with my stand or solution and why? (What are the counterarguments?)
4. What examples and evidence can I provide to support my arguments and claims?
5. How will I organize my arguments and evidence?
6. How will I conclude my essay?

Answering these questions will lead you to an expository thesis statement, help you determine which language and details will provide vivid description and images for support, and give you a general idea of how you want to organize your essay.

Activity 15-1 Brainstorming for Potential Arguments

Directions: *Brainstorm a list of problems that exist in your neighborhood or in the country as a whole that need action to resolve them.*

Example: Need more bus routes in my town, need more stoplights in my district, neighbors need to curb their dogs, welfare reform in America.

_____

_____

_____
_____
_____
_____ ⬤

WRITING AN ARGUMENT ESSAY

Some students hear the term "argument paper" and assume that they will have to use anger and harsh tones to get their message across. However, in good argument and persuasive writing, you should use logic and fair-minded appeals to your audience in order to sway them to your point of view on a subject. The purpose of an argument/persuasion essay is to develop an *argument* or *claim* about a topic and support it with logical and valid reasons in order to persuade your readers to agree with your position.

Often, instructors will ask you to take a stand on a particular issue and then argue for the stand you take. You will need to provide reasons to support your position on the subject. You will also need to address possible counterarguments both to your overall stand and to the individual reasons or support statements and examples in your paper.

In some argument/persuasion essays, you will be arguing for a proposed *solution* to a perceived *problem*. This type of argument paper goes beyond just explaining your stand on an issue and your reasons for that stand; it also adds the element of proposing an action—arguing for a change to address a perceived problem. Often the thesis statement for an argumentative paper will include the words "should," "needs to," "ought to," or "must" as part of the proposed change.

When writing an argument paper, you must know your audience and customize your approach based on your target audience. For instance, if you were writing a position paper on the issue of gun control, your approach would need to be modified depending on your audience. How you would present your views to a parent-teacher association would be very different from how you would present them to the National Rifle Association.

Also, in all argument/persuasion essays, your tone should be respectful and fair-minded. Of course you will have a bias: That is the nature of an argument paper. Your stand on the issue must be clear from beginning to end, but do not make the mistake of oversimplifying the counterarguments or underestimating your readers' positions or knowledge on the issue. You may even point out the costs of your solution and the merits of others' arguments against it in order to convince your readers that your position is still the better solution.

ERRORS IN LOGIC WHEN CONSTRUCTING ARGUMENTS

Be careful: Argument essays are the easiest essays in which to fall prey to logical fallacies (common errors in logic that weaken your reasoning—list and definitions to follow) and the use of emotion over reason. The tone and fair-minded logic of your essay's arguments are essential to persuading your readers of your point and maintaining your credibility. Of course you are arguing based on your own opinion, but your reasoning should be detailed, logical, and free from fallacies. You need to assess your intended audience carefully in order to choose the most effective tone, approach, and evidence to provide in support of your claims and arguments. Moreover, you need to make sure you haven't oversimplified the subject, your arguments, or your opposition's arguments. You also need to engage your critical thinking skills to evaluate the assumptions and biases built into your arguments and to make sure you haven't committed any logical fallacies in your arguments or in your counterarguments.

Logical Fallacies

Here are some of the most common **logical fallacies**, or errors in reasoning, that students commit in argument essays (they are also common in speeches and debates). Check to make sure you haven't damaged your credibility by including any of these fallacies in your paper.

Ad hominem fallacy: Ad hominem is a Latin phrase that means "to the man" and involves *attacking a specific person or group of people* attached to an issue or point of view that opposes one's own position instead of arguing against their claims, reasoning, or evidence.

> **Example:** Those tree-hugging hippies should stop interfering with progress.

Post hoc fallacy: Post hoc is a Latin phrase that means "after this." This fallacy involves thinking that because one event happened first it is the cause of another event that followed it. It is an unsupported claim that something is the result of something else. One should not make a cause/effect analysis without providing evidence to support the connection between two events.

> **Example:** I decided to wear my striped shirt the day I aced my chemistry exam, so if I wear it again today, I should do great in my English test.

Hasty generalization fallacy: In this fallacy, the writer jumps to a conclusion without providing the evidence and reasoning that led to that conclusion.

> **Example:** I'm certain the students' lack of motivation is related to changes in modern music.

Begging the question fallacy: This fallacy involves stating and repeating claims but never giving support or evidence to develop them.

> **Example:** Good parenting would have prevented all of these social problems. All of our society's major problems are a direct result of bad parenting.

Equivocation: Equivocation means using vague words or phrases that mislead the reader. A writer may also use *euphemisms* (words or phrases used to soften the effect of a more direct word) to avoid addressing the severity of an issue or to soften harsher truths. For instance, the words "passed away" or "moved on" are euphemisms for "dead," and "victims of friendly fire" is a euphemism for soldiers killed by their own side.

> **Example:** There were several *casualties* as a result of *friendly* fire.

Red Herring fallacy: This fallacy occurs when a writer uses details, examples, or other language that distract the reader from the real argument.

> **Example:** I hear that many soldiers suffer from depression after returning home from Iraq. Has anyone looked into why these soldiers signed up for the military in the first place?

False dilemma fallacy: This fallacy is also known as the either/or fallacy. The writer presents only two sides to a complex issue that may have many sides. "You're either with us or against us" is a classic false dilemma: One may actually be somewhere in the middle.

> **Example:** If you don't support our request for more library funding, then you are anti–student success.

Applying Critical Thinking

PURPOSE   IDEAS   SUPPORT   ASSUMPTIONS BIASES   CONCLUSIONS   POINT OF VIEW   ANALYSIS

Besides being aware of the type of errors in logic you can make while writing a persuasive or argument essay, there are some other basic tips you should you keep in mind as you begin your essay writing process.

Ten Argument Basics

1. Clearly define your argument and **purpose**.

2. Be aware of your audience and adjust your style and tone appropriately; use tactful and fair language.

3. Provide evidence, **ideas**, examples, **support**, and **conclusions** for your claims and arguments.

4. Check for logical fallacies and oversimplifications in your reasoning.

5. Acknowledge and **analyze** differing **points or view** and present counterarguments.

6. Point out common ground, and, when appropriate, point out the merits of another view or make a concession to a well put counterargument.

7. Refute (address and disagree with) counterarguments and claims from the opposing view—again using fair and respectful language.

8. Use the Critical Thinking Checklist from Chapter 1 to check for your own **assumptions, biases,** and inferences, and for the consequences of your argument, and overall point of view.

9. Use the critique form later in this chapter to check the structure and components of your essay.

10. Revise and proofread your argument essay carefully.

STRUCTURING AN ARGUMENT ESSAY

Your argument essay will begin with a call to action or some other type of attention grabber to interest your readers in your subject and your argument. Then you will need to narrow down to your actual argument. Your thesis statement should explain exactly what you are arguing for and why. If your argument involves proposing a change in how things are, remember using the words "should" or "must" or the phrase "needs to" helps your reader know that you are arguing for a change.

> **Example:** My neighborhood needs to petition for speed bumps, and the city should respond to our neighborhood's request.

In your body paragraphs, you'll provide reasons, evidence, and examples to support your proposed argument. The topic sentences will set up those reasons and your examples for support. Also, in these paragraphs, be sure to present the major counterarguments to your point of view, what others might say against your plans or reasoning. Be fair-minded and thorough to maintain integrity and your readers' respect. Address those counterarguments and explain why you don't agree with them.

Finally, the concluding paragraph will come back and recap the argument you want to convince your readers about. The chart below provides a brief overview of the structure of an argument essay.

BASIC STRUCTURE FOR AN ARGUMENT ESSAY

Introductory Paragraph	**Sets up and background** for the problem or need.
	Thesis statement: Presents what you are arguing for, what you want to persuade your readers about
Body Paragraphs (Two to five, depending on assignment and purpose)	**Create topic sentences to develop your thesis.**
	Develop your arguments with reasoning and evidence.
	Use transitions within and between paragraphs to emphasize the transition from one argument or part to the next.

Provide examples and concrete details for support.

Present counterarguments to be fair minded.

Add analysis and commentary about the example used to help develop the arguments/thesis statement.

| Concluding Paragraph | **Sums up and re-emphasizes the thesis:** your arguments and reasons. |

STRUCTURING YOUR ARGUMENT ESSAY

Topic

The only real rule for topics for argumentative essays is that you must be trying to persuade your readers about something. You also may be arguing for a change in the status quo, so don't argue for something that already exists (though you could argue that an existing policy or situation is not effective).

A Few Topic Possibilities

Note: Be sure to narrow these broad subjects down to manageable topics.

AIDS
animal testing
assisted suicide
beauty contests
cars/auto culture
censorship
chemical fertilizers
child custody/laws
city sprawl
city housing
clearcutting
eating disorders
gender issues
genetic engineering

globalization
global warming
homelessness
hunger
infant mortality
inflation
industrial waste
illegal drugs/laws
littering/fines
loss of farmland
malnutrition
migration
multiculturalism
   issues

NAFTA
nuclear energy/
   nuclear weapons
obesity
ozone layer
police searches
pesticide use
racism
rainforests
sexism/laws
war

Activity 15-2   Narrowing Argument Topics

Directions: *Choose three of the broad subjects listed on page 307 and do a cluster or brainstorm on a separate sheet of paper to narrow them down into more manageable topics. Then choose a broad topic of your own and narrow it down in the same way.*

Subject 1: _____

Possible narrowed topics: _____

_____

_____

Subject 2: _____

Possible narrowed topics: _____

_____

_____

Subject 3: _____

Possible narrowed topics: _____

_____

_____

Subject 4, your choice: _____

Possible narrowed topics: _____

_____

_____

Introductory Paragraph

You will need an introduction of one or two paragraphs. The introduction should start with an attention grabber that introduces your topic. It can be a rhetorical question (a question you ask your readers to set up the topic) or a powerful statement. Next, you need to give a two- or three-sentence general explanation of your argument and any background information the readers would need in order to understand it. Here are some examples of attention grabbers.

Attention Grabber

1. **Rhetorical question:** "Have you ever had trouble parking in our school parking lot?"

2. **A powerful piece of information or fact:** "An average quarter's worth of books will cost a student $100–$200."

3. **An anecdote or story:** "When I started college, I only had $100 set aside for buying my books . . ."

4. **A call to action:** "It's time that students took an active part in dealing with bookstore prices."

5. **A background/explanation of the problem:** "For over twenty years, our campus bookstore has charged too high of a profit percentage on our textbooks."

Thesis Statements

Write one to three sentences that contextualize the problem and give the basic facts. Your thesis will be a plan for solving the problem (the proposed change or plan for solution you are arguing for). Try using "should," "must," or "needs to" in your plan of action to indicate the argument.

> My employer should contribute half of the cost of my family's health care.

> My local grocery store needs to offer a greater selection of organic produce.

Activity 15-3   Creating Thesis Statements

Directions: *Create a thesis statement for each of the topics you narrowed down in Activity 15-2.*

1. Subject 1: Thesis statement: _____

    _____

2. Subject 2: Thesis statement: _____

    _____

3. Subject 3: Thesis statement: _____

    _____

4. Subject 4: Thesis statement: _____

    _____

Body Paragraphs

The first body paragraph should explain in more detail the problem you see and what you are arguing for. Give specific examples and details to illustrate the problem. The following body paragraphs should explain how your plan for a solution will solve the problem, or at least be the first step toward changing the problem. Predict, evaluate, and address what people might say *against* your plan (the counterargument/s). Many counterarguments have to do with who will *pay* for the changes if the solution involves spending money. So be sure to address *who* would pay and *how* the money would be raised. If the counterarguments are about something other than money, such as a moral concern or a political difference, make sure that you present the counterargument(s) fairly and thoroughly. If you discount the real counterarguments, your paper loses credibility. Transitions showing purpose and those strengthening a point are useful in argument essays. Other helpful transitions include those that show summary or example (see Chapter 6, pages 118–119).

TRANSITIONS TO SHOW ADDITION OF ANOTHER POINT

again	but also	in addition	nor
also	equally important	last	plus the fact
and	finally	lastly	secondly
and then	first	likewise	then too
another	further	moreover	thirdly
besides	furthermore	next	too

TRANSITIONS TO SHOW PURPOSE

all things considered	for this reason	to accomplish	with this in mind
for this purpose	in order to	to this end	with this objective

Activity 15-4   Creating Topic Sentences

Directions: *Create a possible topic sentence you could use to develop a body paragraph that would provide reasons and support for each of the thesis statements you created in Activity 15-3.*

1. Subject 1: Topic sentence: _____

    _____

2. Subject 2: Topic sentence: _____

    _____

3. Subject 3: Topic sentence: _____

_____

4. Subject 4: Topic sentence: _____

_____ ⬤

Activity 15-5   Providing Support

Directions: *Provide one specific reason that provides support for each of the topic sentences you created in Activity 15-4.*

1. Subject 1: Reason to support topic sentence: _____

_____

2. Subject 2: Reason to support topic sentence: _____

_____

3. Subject 3: Reason to support topic sentence: _____

_____

4. Subject 4: Reason to support topic sentence: _____

_____ ⬤

Concluding Paragraph

The conclusion should sum up the problem and re-explain your plan for solving the problem and how effective it will be. Be sure not to introduce any new ideas, arguments, or evidence in the conclusion.

CONCLUSIONS

Activity 15-6   Writing a Conclusion

Directions: *Now choose one of the topics you've been developing in these activities and write a three- to six-sentence concluding paragraph for that topic/ argument.*

_____

_____

_____

_____

_____ ⬤

Use the following critique form to check for the basics in your argument essay draft.

Argument Essay Critique Form

PURPOSE   IDEAS   SUPPORT   ASSUMPTIONS BIASES   CONCLUSIONS   POINT OF VIEW   ANALYSIS

Overall

	Done well	Needs work
1. Is the problem chosen from school, your job, or where you live, and is it clear?	_____	_____
2. Is there a clear **purpose** and argument for change—a plan for a solution?	_____	_____
3. Is the plan for change reasonable—not too extreme? Is it specific?	_____	_____

Introduction

4. Is the title interesting and in correct format?	_____	_____
5. Is there a good attention grabber and general explanation of the problem?	_____	_____
6. Is the thesis statement a brief and specific summary of the plan for change—a solution? Are the words "should," "must," or "needs to" used to help clarify the proposed plan of action?	_____	_____

Body

7. Do the body paragraphs have clear topic sentences? Underline them.	_____	_____
8. Does the body of the paper develop, explain, and elaborate the problem with **ideas**, examples, and **support**?	_____	_____
9. Does the body explain in detail exactly how the plan for change will resolve the problem and make a positive change?	_____	_____
10. Does the solution include all details for *who, how,* and *why* the solution will work (including where the money will come from, if necessary)?	_____	_____
11. Does each body paragraph have a good concluding sentence?	_____	_____
12. Are transitions used well, both within and between paragraphs?	_____	_____

Conclusion

13. Does the **concluding** paragraph sum up well without adding new ideas?	_____	_____

Editing

14. Circle the following errors you think you see in this draft: spelling, fragments, run-ons/comma splices, commas, semicolon/colon use, pronoun agreement, reference fault errors, parallelism, apostrophe use, verb use/tense, and passive voice construction. (See the handbook sections for help in identifying and correcting these errors.)

15. Other types of grammar or sentence-level errors:

_____

Comments:

_____

_____

COMPLEMENTARY MODES FOR ARGUMENT ESSAYS

Argument mode is often combined with several other modes.

- **Narration** and **description** can be used to develop the argument(s).
- **Definition** mode can be used to help explain objects or concepts used in the examples provided.
- **Examples and illustrations** are essential to providing good reasoning and support for your argument.
- **Cause and effect analysis** will further elaborate on the arguments and reasons.
- **Description** helps explain the problem(s) and potential solutions.
- You can **compare and contrast** your arguments and counterarguments.

SAMPLE STUDENT ESSAY

Beeds 1

Julie Beeds

Professor Furness

English 101

25 January 2008

Danger Around Every Corner

Have you ever heard the screech of car tires in front of your house, the kind that makes your heart instantly skip a beat or two? We send our children out to play in our front yards. We tell

Beeds 2

them not to talk to strangers and to watch for cars. I used to think that in most neighborhoods, drivers watch for children, and they drive slower down residential streets just in case a child runs out between two parked cars. However, in my neighborhood, the number of speeding cars is staggering. My neighborhood, specifically my street, has many families with children. However, even though children are on the sidewalks at all times of the day, cars race down our street in excess of 30 mph. It is time to take action and get our neighborhood to petition for speed bumps or a round-about in order to slow cars down and increase our children's safety. Our neighborhood needs to take action to protect the safety of our families: We need to petition for speed bumps or a roundabout, and our city needs to listen to and then respond to our concerns and make the required changes.

The risk of a child on my street being hurt by a car on any given day, at any given time, day or night, is high: I hear cars speeding down my street at all hours. In reaction, some of my neighbors have walked door-to-door asking people to slow down as they drive on our street. The response seemed good at first; however, the speeding started again soon afterward. I can thankfully say that no child has been hurt yet, but there have been too many narrow escapes.

Even my own family has had a close call. Early this year when we had snow, my daughter and I were sledding down a hill half a block from our home. We had a terrific time playing in the snow until, as we were walking back to our house, a car slid around the corner almost hitting us as we were crossing the street. Even though we are very aware of the dangers on our street, the car came so fast that we had to jump out of its path. The most troubling part was that not only did we come close to getting hurt, the driver never looked back to see if we were okay.

Marginal labels:

Thesis statement

Topic sentence

Concluding sentence

Topic sentence

Concluding sentence

Beeds 3

These scary near-misses happen frequently on our block. On one sunny day this summer, my daughter and her friend were rollerblading on the sidewalk across from my house. My daughter's friend hit a rock, tripped, and fell partially into the street. At the same time, a car came down the street, swerved to miss a dog and nearly hit her. The girl's experience of nearly being hit by the car was far more traumatic than the fall she had experienced. Sadly, the driver did not look back or stop to see if there were any injuries. I asked myself, "Do people just not care anymore?"

However, several people in my neighborhood do care and are ready to take action. Some neighbors have attempted to solve the issue in less than desirable ways. Two doors down from me, my neighbor rolled a tire out into the street when a repeat offender sped down our street at what had to be 40 mph. The tire hit the car on the driver's door and the scene got ugly. A fist fight broke out on the sidewalk. When the fight ended, each man went to his corner, and, needless to say, those neighbors to this day do not speak to each other. Even though I do not agree with the tactics my neighbor used, that driver does not speed down the street any-more. However, we do not want to be vigilantes: we just want our children safe.

Instead of resorting to violent or ugly acts, we have other means of dealing with this issue. My neighbors and I have been working on getting signatures for a petition to put in speed bumps and/or a round-about on our street. The irony of getting signatures is that some of the people that are signing the petition are some of the people that are speeding down the streets in the first place. From what I have researched and been told, getting the signatures will be the easiest part. Having the petition approved and asking the city to

Topic sentence

Topic sentence

Concluding sentence

Topic sentence

Concluding sentence

Beeds 4

allocate money for this project will be the difficult part, but all of the residents are committed to this project succeeding.

Topic sentence

    In order to get the Department of Transportation to pay for a speed bump or round-about, a survey of the street or streets in question must occur. The Department of Transportation will evaluate the areas in three categories. The categories are number of accidents, volume of traffic, and average speed of the drivers. The Department of Transportation's evaluation will directly influence how much money they will allocate to the project. If the Department of Transportation allocates half, one quarter, or no money, the neighborhood will have to pay the costs to complete the project, which will be $8,000 to $14,000 depending on which speed control device the Department of Transportation advises.

Counter-argument

Many would argue that that is a lot of money, but the value of our children's lives far outweighs this cost. Also, with a neighborhood fundraiser, the price per person could be quite small.

Concluding sentence

At this stage, our neighborhood must wait its turn for the construction of the speed bumps or round-about.

Restatement of thesis

    To summarize, our goal is to keep our children safe. Our neighborhoods and our homes should be where we can feel safe, and our children need to be able to walk, run, and play outside their homes in a safe environment. Installing speed bumps and/or a round-about is an inexpensive deterrent for speeders especially when one weighs it against the possible loss of a child's life. Our lives are not that busy, nor is what we have to do that important or urgent. Do you remember the old commercial "Speed Kills"? We must take action in our neighborhood before we get to that point.

Activity 15-7   Thinking Critically About the Student Essay

Directions: *Analyze the essay to identify the features and details characteristic of the argument/persuasion mode. Mark them on the essay. Then, reread the essay, and make a list of specific revisions you would make to correct any problems with content, organization, transitions, and style.*

PROFESSIONAL SAMPLE
ARGUMENT ESSAY

The Homework Ate My Family

Romesh Ratnesar

Romesh Ratnesar is a reporter, news editor, and columnist who has worked at *The Daily* and *The New Republic*, and then *TIME*, where he worked as a foreign correspondent in London and Iraq before returning to New York to become *TIME*'s World Editor. This article originally appeared in the January 25, 1999, issue of *TIME* magazine.

1   It's a typical Tuesday afternoon in early January for 11-year-old Molly Benedict, a sixth-grader at Presidio Middle School in San Francisco. When she gets home from school at 3:30, she heads straight for the basement of her family's two-story house, flips on her computer and bangs out a one-page book report on J. K. Rowling's *Harry Potter and the Sorcerer's Stone.* After half an hour of work, Molly takes the paper upstairs and gives it to her mother Libby for proofreading. As Molly nibbles a snack of a bagel and orange-spice tea, Mom jots some corrections. "Why don't you say, 'This is the best book I ever read,'" Libby suggests. "Teachers really like strong opinions like that."

2   Time to kick back, call a few friends and get ready for *Felicity,* right? Not even close. Next Molly pulls out her math assignment: more than 100 fraction and long-division problems. Once she slogs through those, Molly labels all the countries and bodies of water on a map of the Middle East. And she's not through yet: she then reviews a semester's worth of science, including the ins and outs of the circulatory system.

3   By 5:30, after doing two hours of homework, Molly sits down at the piano and practices for an hour. She'll barely have enough time to eat

dinner and touch up that book report before crashing. "With less work I think we could learn what we're learning now," Molly says. "But I don't think it's too overwhelming." The strain of homework weighs more heavily on her mother. "I didn't feel [stressed] until I was in my 30s," says Libby, 43. "It hurts my feelings that my daughter feels that way at 11."

4   Most of us remember homework, if we remember it at all, as one of the minor annoyances of growing up. Sure, we dreaded the multiplication tables and those ridiculous shoe-box dioramas. But let's admit it: we finished most of our assignments on the bus ride to school—and who even bothered with the stuff until after the requisite hours had been spent alphabetizing baseball cards, gabbing on the phone or watching reruns of *Gilligan's Island?*

5   Kids today have scant time for such indulgences. Saddled with an out-of-school curriculum chock-full of Taekwondo lessons, ceramics work-shops and bassoon practice, America's youngsters barely have time to check their e-mail before hunkering down with homework. On the whole, U.S. students come home with more schoolwork than ever before—and at a younger age. According to researchers at the University of Michigan, 6- to 9-year-olds in 1981 spent 44 min. a week on home-work; in 1997 they did more than two hours' worth. The amount of time that 9- to 11-year-olds devoted to homework each week increased from 2 hr. 49 min. to more than 3 1/2 hr.

6   After some historical ups and downs, homework in this country is at a high-water mark. In the early decades of the century progressive educa-tors in many school districts banned homework in primary school in an effort to discourage rote learning. The cold war—specifically, the launch of Sputnik in 1957—put an end to that, as lawmakers scrambled to bol-ster math and science education in the U.S. to counter the threat of Soviet whiz kids. Students frolicked in the late 1960s and 70s, as homework declined to near World War II levels. But fears about U.S. economic com-petitiveness and the publication of *A Nation at Risk,* the 1983 government report that focused attention on the failings of American schools, ratch-eted up the pressure to get tough again. Other forces have kept the trend heading upward: increasing competition to get into the best colleges and the batteries of statewide standardized tests—starting in grade school in a growing number of states—for which teachers must prepare their pupils.

7   The homework crunch is heard loudest in the country's better middle-class school districts, where parents push their kids hard and demand that teachers deliver enough academic rigor to get students into top secondary schools and colleges. Now there's a blowback: the sheer quantity of nightly homework and the difficulty of the assignments can turn ordinary weeknights into four-hour library-research excursions, leave kids in tears

and parents with migraines, and generally transform the placid refuge of home life into a tense war zone. "The atmosphere in the house gets very frustrated," says Lynne O'Callaghan, a mom in Portland, Ore., whose daughter Maeve, 8, does two hours of homework a night. "Some days it's just a struggle. Who wants it that way?" Laura Mandel, a mother of three in Warren, N.J., feels similarly embattled. "It's ironic that politicians talk so much about family values," says Mandel, "when you can't have any family time anymore because the kids are so busy keeping their nose to the grindstone."

8   While kids grow more frazzled, parents are increasingly torn. Just how involved should they be? Should they help a son or daughter finish that geography assignment, or stay aloof and risk having a frustrated, sleep-deprived child? Should they complain to teachers about the heavy work-load or be thankful that their kids are being pushed toward higher achievement? Battles over homework have become so intense that some school districts have decided to formally prescribe the amount of home-work kids at each grade level should receive. All of which leaves open the questions of just how much and what kind of homework is best. Though there's evidence that homework does improve academic perform-ance, at least in the junior high and high school years, its true value may be more subtle. It encourages good study habits and acclimates students to self-directed work—but only when it's not so oppressive that it turns them off school altogether.

9   The war over homework is about even larger issues. Schools in the 1990s are expected to fill so many roles—and do so with often paltry resources and ill-qualified teachers—that it's no surprise more work gets sent home. For baby-boomer parents homework has become both a status gauge—the nightly load indicates the toughness of their child's school—and an outlet for nervy overbearance, so that each homework assignment is practically theirs to complete too. Yet the growth in dual-income fami-lies means less energy and shorter fuses for assisting the kids. And all the swirling arguments over homework underscore the bigger questions that confound American teachers, parents and policymakers: What should we expect from our children? What do we want them to learn? How much is enough?

10   Erica Astrove is pretty sure she knows. She's just seven—a loquacious, blue-eyed second-grader at the public Hunnewell School in Wellesley, Mass. She plays the piano, takes skating lessons and plans to add pottery and chorus. For fun Erica reads almanacs; her parents gave her a book of world maps and flags for Christmas. "My little researcher," her mother Christina says. There's not much Erica shies away from—except home-work. Recently, she told her mother she doesn't want to go to middle

school, high school or college because of homework. Asked if she might have a bit more tolerance for homework once she enters third grade, Erica shakes her head. "I'm going to keep on crying," she says.

11   Erica's mom has experience drying tears. Her homework agonies began when her eldest daughter Kate was in second grade. In addition to nightly spelling and reading assignments, Kate sometimes came home with math problems so vexing that Christina wondered whether algebra was required to solve them. Mother and daughter pored over some problems for two hours. They once scattered 200 pennies on the kitchen table in a vain attempt to get a solution. "The [problems] would be so hard," Christina says, "that I would leave them for my husband to solve when he got home from work late." Those were not happy times. "It made all our time together negative," Christina says. "It was painful for all of us."

12   The pain caused by homework isn't just emotional. Carl Glassman, father of two girls who attend public school in New York City, reports that last year his eldest daughter missed much of her first semester in sixth grade because of pneumonia, "due to the fact that she was doing homework until 11 every night." Laura Mandel, the New Jersey mother of three, found her son Jeffrey, 6, suffering homework-related nightmares this month when she tried gently to rouse him for school. "Oh, Mom," he pleaded, half asleep, "don't tell me there's another homework sheet."

13   The steady flood of homework can cause chronic weariness. Holly Manges, a high-achieving fifth-grader at the public Eastern elementary school in Lexington, Ohio, approached her mother earlier this school year close to tears. "Is it O.K. if I don't get all A's?" she asked. "I don't care anymore. I'm just too tired." Over time, that homework fatigue can pull at the fabric of families. As early as third grade, Rachel Heckelman, now 11, came home every day from her elementary school in Houston with three hours' worth of homework. The assignments were often so dizzyingly complex—one asked her to design an entire magazine—that Rachel looked for any way to procrastinate. Her mother Lissa tried banning TV for the night. When that didn't work, Lissa pleaded with increasing impatience. "I would get red in the face, and she would get defensive," Lissa says. Rachel's father typically removed himself from the fracas by repairing to the bedroom and shutting the door.

14   The frustrations that homework visits upon kids can irk their parents to the point of revolt. David Kooyman, of Covina, Calif., was so incensed about his three grade-schoolers' homework load that he exacted a pledge from their teachers not to lower his kids' grades if they didn't do assignments. When the kids found themselves lost in class discussions, Kooyman reluctantly allowed them to do the homework, but he is planning to sue the school district for violating his civil rights. "They have us

hostage to homework," he grumbles. "I'm 47, and I have 25-year-old teachers telling me what to do with my home life."

15   Other parents are ambivalent. Many resent teachers for piling on projects that cut into unstructured family time. And yet the drive of middle- and upper-middle-class Americans to keep their children at the head of the class has never been more intense. The teachers who assign mountains of homework often believe they are bowing to the wishes of demanding parents. Says Jeana Considine, a fifth-grade teacher at Elm Elementary School in Hinsdale, Ill.: "The same parents who are complaining that they don't have enough family time would be really upset if their child didn't score well." Pepperdine University president David Davenport, father of a fourth-grader who clocks two hours of homework a night, sees a chain reaction: "The pressure to get into highly selective colleges and universities backs up into high school advanced-placement courses, which backs up to elementary schools." Anxious parents can rail about what teachers do in the classroom, but homework is still one area where parents can directly improve their child's chances.

16   So even those determined to remain passive observers while their kids labor over essays and science-fair projects can find themselves getting sucked in. "It's something I never wanted to do. I hated doing homework when I was a kid," says Lizanne Merrill, a New York City artist whose daughter Gracie is in second grade. But Gracie often trudges home with elaborate assignments that all but demand Merrill's involvement. A research paper assigned to be done over Christmas vacation required Gracie, 8, to do some fieldwork on sea turtles at the American Museum of Natural History. Mom went along: "I just tell myself, if I don't help out on her homework, what kind of deadbeat mother would I be?"

17   It's hard to blame parents like Alexis Rasley of Oak Park, Ill., if they occasionally get too involved. Last fall a homework assignment for fifth-graders at the public Horace Mann School was to build a mini-space station that accounted for food, water, waste treatment, radiation shielding and zero gravity. Rasley's son Taylor, 10, spent countless maddening hours toiling at a basement countertop surrounded by cut-open soda bottles. "He just kept sitting there saying, 'I don't know what to do,'" Rasley says. "When the frustration level gets that high, you say, 'O.K., I'm going to help,' because the situation has become so hurtful."

18   Being an attentive, empathetic parent is one thing; acting as a surrogate student is another. But when pressures mount, the line can get blurred. When Susan Solomon of San Francisco saw her son bogged down last year with a language-arts paper that would help his application to an elite high school, she took matters into her own hands: she did his math homework. He later copied his mother's calculations in his own

handwriting. "He knew how to do it," Solomon shrugs. "It was just busy-work." In the affluent Boston suburb of Sherborn, Mass., parents at the public Pine Hill School tend to talk about homework in the first-person plural; and they sometimes become more than equal partners in carrying out such third-grade projects as writing up the ownership history of their house, complete with a sketch of the floor plan. Homework has been known to arrive at school two hours after the child does.

19   "So much of this is about parents wanting their kids to look good," admits psychologist Kim Gatof, mother of third-grader Jake. For an "invention convention," members of Jake's class are building contraptions of their devising. Jake wants to build a better mousetrap. "I can say, 'Just build it yourself,'" says Kim. "Or we can help with it, and it can be on the same level as the others." Jake may have a hard time topping Tucker Carter, another third-grader, who has already made his presentation. Tucker whipped up a fully functioning battery-operated alarm clock that uses a windshield pump to squirt cold water at the sleeper. The kids whooped at this bit of ingenuity, but even they were suspicious. Either Tucker is a prodigiously gifted engineer, or his dad built the clock for him. Sighed David Nihill, the school's principal: "It looks like Alexander Graham Bell made it himself."

20   Is all this homework really doing any good? Julian Betts, an associate professor of economics at the University of California, San Diego, examined surveys on the homework habits of 6,000 students over five years and found that students who did an extra 30 min. of nightly math homework beginning in seventh grade would, by 11th grade, see their achievement level soar by the equivalent of two grades. Betts argues that the amount of homework is a better indicator of how students perform than the size of class or the quality of teachers. But his study was limited to students in junior high and high school. What about younger children? In 1989 University of Missouri psychology professor Harris Cooper reviewed more than 100 studies on homework and concluded that while benefits from homework can be measured starting in junior high, the effect of home assignments on standardized test scores in the lower grades is negligible or nonexistent. "Piling on massive amounts of homework will not lead to gains," Cooper says, "and may be detrimental by leading children to question their abilities."

21   Still, some researchers make a case for elementary school homework. Carol Huntsinger, an education professor at the College of Lake County, near Chicago, compared the academic performance of local Chinese-American children with that of European-American kids. In the early grades, the Chinese-American students outperformed their white counterparts in math and mastery of vocabulary words. After examining a host of

other factors, Huntsinger concluded that homework made the critical difference. In first grade the Chinese-American children were doing more
than 20 min. of math homework a night, some of it formally assigned by
their parents, while their white classmates averaged just 5 min.

22   It may be unwise to make too much of Huntsinger's study, which
focused on a small group of families. All experts agree that weighing
second-graders down with hours of homework is pointless and probably
damaging to their self-esteem and desire to learn. But in reasonable
amounts, homework has value for students at all grade levels. "Homework has benefits that go well beyond its immediate direct impact on
what's going on in school," says Cooper. Doing homework is important
for honing organizational skills, learning how to manage time and developing the ability to learn autonomously.

23   The question of the day, of course, is what is the right amount? Cooper
recommends 10 to 20 min. nightly in first grade and an increase of
10 min. a night for each grade after that. But the point is not simply to fill
up a set amount of time. For preoccupied teachers, admits Michelann
Ortloff, a Portland school official and former elementary school teacher,
"it's always easy to pull a few things out of the workbook, give them to
students and say, 'This is your homework.'" Too many teachers send kids
home with mind-numbing math worksheets that are not even reviewed
the next day. Too many are enamored of those unwieldy "projects" that
seem to exasperate kids more than they instruct them and that lead to
excessive parent involvement. For young students, the optimal arrangement would mix skill-building drills with creative tasks closely tied to
what's being taught in the classroom—such as interviewing grandparents
as a social-studies lesson or using soccer standings to teach rudimentary
statistics.

24   Educators agree that parents should be vigilant about making sure
such a healthy blend is maintained. Everyone frowns on parents' doing
homework for their kids, but most agree that parents should monitor
homework; offer guidance, not answers, when asked for help; and give
teachers regular reports on how their kids are handling it all. Gail Block,
a fifth-grade language-arts instructor in San Francisco who feels that
homework helps overcome the limits of time in the classroom, was
nonetheless surprised to hear that her student Molly Benedict takes close
to three hours a night to finish. Pepperdine president Davenport notes the
amount of time his daughter spends on each assignment at the bottom of
her work sheet. "Sometimes," he says, "teachers are not aware of how
much time is being spent."

25   Parents could benefit from a little perspective too. American students
on the whole still work less, play more and perform worse than many of

their counterparts around the world. As Harold Stevenson and James Stigler point out in their book *The Learning Gap,* Japanese and Chinese elementary school students spend significantly more time on homework than do children in the U.S. A first-grader in Taipei does seven times as much homework as a first-grader in Minneapolis—and scores higher on tests of knowledge and skills.

26   But American parents should worry less about the precise number of minutes their students devote to homework and more about the uneven and poorly conceived way in which it is assigned. "What defines the homework problem in the U.S. today is variation," Cooper says. Less than one-third of U.S. school districts provide any guidelines to parents and teachers on how much homework children should receive and what purpose it's supposed to serve. In places that have instituted formal homework policies, a semblance of sanity has arrived. In Hinsdale, Ill., parents often complained that their children got too much homework from some teachers and too little from others. So a committee of teachers, parents and administrators spent several months devising a formal policy that requires "meaningful and purposeful" homework at all grade levels but limits the load according to age and mandates that some of it be optional. Besides helping students build their homework appetite over time, the policy aims to persuade the academically more eager parents that it's safe to back off.

27   The need for a more rational approach to homework may be one argument for establishing national standards for what all U.S. students should know. If such standards existed, teachers might assign homework with a more precise goal in mind, and parents might spend fewer nights agonizing about whether their children were overburdened or understimulated by homework. Of course, the debate over national standards is a complex one, and cramming for a national test could mean more mindless at-home drudgery for kids. But not necessarily. When Taylor Hoss, 10, of Vancouver, Wash., came home last year with packets of extra homework assigned in preparation for the state's new mandatory assessment exams, his parents shuddered. But as they worked through the test-prep material, the Hosses were pleased with the degree of critical thinking the questions required. "I was very impressed," says Taylor's dad Schuyler. "It makes you connect the dots."

28   There are other ways of soothing nerves. Both parents and students must be willing to embrace the "work" component of homework—to recognize the quiet satisfaction that comes from practice and drill, the steady application of concepts and the mastery of skills. It's a tough thing to ask of many American parents. "You want your children to be happy, and you pray for their success in the future," says Laura Mandel. "But does home-

work bring either of those goals? I don't think more homework will make a more successful adult." Maybe not, but wisely assigned homework may help make a more successful, well, child. "It is all about learning responsibility," says Janine Bempechat, an assistant professor at Harvard's Graduate School of Education. "When you have homework on a regular basis, you learn persistence, diligence and delayed gratification."

29   Molly Benedict, for one, seems to be swallowing the bad medicine with surprising equanimity. "I don't have a lot of time to do just whatever," she admits. "My friends and I think it's a lot of work. But we've adapted well." Kids like Molly have learned it's a rough world, and homework is only part of it. But who knows? If teachers and parents start approaching homework with a little less heat and a little more care, kids may still have time left to be kids. Or whatever.

Reading Reflection Questions

1. What are the direct or indirect (implied) messages in this story?

   _____

   _____

2. List two characteristics of this article that distinguish it as an argument essay. _____

   _____

   _____

3. List two reasons that justify the schools' decisions to add more homework according to Ratnesar? _____

   _____

   _____

4. Now, list two reasons that Ratnesar provides for why families are struggling with the amount and kind of homework being assigned.

   _____

   _____

Objective Questions

5. T/F _____ The author suggests that one of the main causes of the increase in assigned homework is competition for getting into the best colleges.

6. T/F _____ The author suggests that the increase in amount of homework is not related to the increase of standardized testing in American public schools.

7. T/F _____ The author suggests that some parents are getting too involved in their children's homework assignments, maybe even finishing homework for them.

Checking Vocabulary

Define the following in your own words or provide a dictionary definition if you don't know the word.

8. dioramas: _____

9. frolicked: _____

10. rigor: _____

CRITICAL THINKING CHECKLIST

PURPOSE

1. What is the **purpose** of this piece of writing? Is it clear?

_____

_____

IDEAS

2. What **ideas** and **background information** are provided to support the purpose of this piece of writing?

_____

_____

SUPPORT

3. What **evidence** and **examples** are used to explain and develop the ideas that support the argument made in the piece of writing? Are the evidence and examples provided sufficient?

_____

_____

ASSUMPTIONS
BIASES

4. Are there unfounded **assumptions** or unreasonable **biases**?

_____

_____

5. Are all of the **conclusions, implications,** and **consequences** of the arguments (the results of the arguments taken to their furthest extreme) considered?

_____

_____

6. Is the **point of view** clear and consistent, and have other points of view been considered?

_____

_____

7. Using these critical thinking tools, **analyze** the overall structure of this essay and the strength of the author's arguments, ideas, and support. Was he or she successful in accomplishing the purpose? Why or why not?

_____

_____

Essay Assignments

1. Choose one of the subjects listed on page 307 for an argument essay, and narrow that subject to a manageable topic. Then, take a stand on that issue (for or against or proposing a change). Be sure to include the opposition's view and counterarguments and address them thoroughly. Do not do any secondary research unless you are instructed to do so by your instructor. If you do include secondary research, be sure to use the research techniques and MLA documentation sections (see Chapters 18 and 19) to find and cite your sources correctly.

2. Choose a problem from the following list to create your argument (plan for change or solution):

   a. A problem you see at your school (such as parking, bookstore prices, cafeteria prices and offerings, class scheduling)

   b. A problem where you work (such as parking, scheduling of shifts, problems with coworkers, pay)

   c. A problem from your neighborhood that you'd like to see fixed (such as a needed stop sign/stoplight, parking problems, a needed park)

   After you have chosen a problem related to one of these three choices, you'll need to come up with a plan for a solution. This plan will become your thesis: It is what you'll be arguing for. Remember, using the words "should" or "must" or the phrase "needs to" helps your reader know that you are arguing for a change and helps make sure that you have developed a specific plan of action.

After you finish your draft of this essay, use the critique form for self- and peer-review of your essay draft.

3. Choose a topic from one of the activities you worked on in this chapter and write an argument essay on it.

4. Other possible subjects to narrow down and write an argument essay about:

drunken driving laws	prescription drug costs
sex offender laws	medication/medical costs
smoking laws	steroid use
gas prices	traffic problems
tuition costs	mandatory foreign language classes
immigration laws	obesity in children
overfishing	overpopulation

16

Timed In-Class Essays and Essay Exams

THINKING CRITICALLY

Look at the photo above. Then answer the following questions related to taking essay exams and writing under pressure:

1. What effect does writing with a specific time limit have on your ability to perform well?

_____

_____

2. How can you condense the writing process to make the most of your limited writing time?

_____

_____

3. What can you do to generate ideas quickly and get a focus?

_____

_____

4. How much time out of an hour of writing would you allow for generating ideas and planning?

_____

_____

_____

5. How much time would you dedicate out of that hour to proofread and revise your draft?

_____

_____

STRATEGIES FOR TAKING ESSAY EXAMS OR TIMED ESSAYS

Essay exams and timed in-class essays follow the same basic rules as take-home essays. The added pressure, of course, is the time restriction and the nervousness factor. Timed essays or in-class essay exams are great practice for writing under pressure in the real world and your future career. Often, prospective employers will ask you to write something for them during the interview process, and in many jobs, you'll need to be able to crank out a memo or other important form of writing on the spot.

Like all essays, a timed essay or a focused essay exam with a prescribed instructor prompt will ask you to narrow your focus and state a purpose. You need to stay focused and organized and provide adequate support and examples to illustrate your points. The basic structure is the same too: a focused introduction that states the purpose for your essay, body paragraphs that develop your thesis and focus on particular aspects of your topic, and a conclusion that wraps up your points in a concise way without introducing any new ideas.

Critical Thinking and Timed Essays

You'll do much better in a timed in-class essay if you engage your critical thinking skills from the moment you get your writing prompt. First you need to interpret and analyze what the writing prompt is asking you to write about. You need to assess the clues buried in the writing assignment or prompt itself: Check for specific directions as well as key words. Then you need to come up with a thesis statement (a purpose to explain in your timed essay) and a plan for writing your essay. It helps to brainstorm first and jot down a brief outline. Finally, you need to leave some time to critically assess what you've written and make needed revisions before submitting your essay.

Before the Essay Exam or Timed Essay

One of the best ways to improve your skills in writing timed essays or taking essay exams is to reduce the panic factor. For many students, the idea of a timed essay causes the same kind of test anxiety that a complicated multiple choice test conjures. In order to alleviate that panic, you need to do some of the same things you do to perform well on a regular exam.

Study and Prepare in Advance

First, be sure that you are well prepared by reading any required materials before the day of the test. If the timed essay is an analysis of assigned readings, you'll have to study them and prepare notes as you would for any exam. If the essay prompt is one that requires no prereading assignments, then prepare by reviewing your writing textbook for the basics of essay writing.

Also, be sure to get a good night's sleep the night before an essay exam or timed in-class essay. If you are exhausted, it is harder to concentrate and think clearly, and your essay will suffer. Finally, be on time to class on the day; arrive early if possible, since anxiety increases if you are running late or get behind. Sometimes instructors provide verbal directions right at the beginning of class; if you are late, you could miss crucial directions or tips.

What you will need to bring to class

1. **Pens/pencils** unless you will be writing directly on a computer. It is still a good idea to have a pen or pencil for brainstorming or in case of printer/computer problems. Most instructors prefer black or blue ink. Avoid unusual colors such as purple or green.

2. **Paper or a composition folder,** unless paper is provided by the instructor or you will be typing in a computer lab or classroom.

3. **A dictionary,** if it is allowed by the instructor; check beforehand.

4. **A memory stick or disk** if you will be writing on a computer in class—always save a copy of your work, and save regularly as you type your essay, every ten minutes or so.

5. **A watch** if there is no clock in your classroom, so you can monitor your time as you write.

During the Essay Exam or Timed Essay

If you are particularly nervous before the exam, try some relaxation techniques such as deep breathing before you go into the classroom. Use positive thinking to tell yourself you are ready. After all, you've studied, right?

The same basic writing process you learned in Chapter 5 applies to in-class essays or essay exams too. The five basic steps of the writing process still apply in an essay exam:

1. **Prewriting:** Generates ideas and your paper's purpose

2. **Organizing:** Develops a plan for presenting your purpose and ideas

3. **Drafting:** Creates a first draft of your essay based on your plan and the pattern(s) of organization you have chosen; develops support for your essay's purpose

4. **Revising:** Re-assesses the draft for content, development, organization, and support (examples and details)

5. **Editing:** Checks for sentence-level effectiveness, style, diction, grammar, and spelling errors

Remember to quickly assess your subject, purpose, and audience from the writing prompt. The **subject** of your essay is the topic you are writing about, which you need to focus into a manageable **topic** for the length of your essay. The **purpose** is what you want to explain or prove related to that topic, so your **thesis** is a statement of your overall goal. Your **audience** is the intended reader(s) for your essay—who you are addressing, so you'll need to customize both your tone (such as casual/informal or more formal/academic) and the amount and types of information you include depending on the intended audience.

Common Terms Used in Writing Prompts

As you review your writing prompt or question, check for indicator words that are clues for specific tasks your instructor wants you to accomplish in the essay. Here are some of the common terms used in writing prompts that are clues that you are being asked to provide specific information.

Analyze: Interpret the significance of something; divide the topic into individual components and analyze its parts; look at cause and effect relationships; look for purpose, messages, or meanings.

Argue: Take a stand on an issue and develop your argument with reasoning and support.

Compare/contrast: Explore similarities and/or differences among two or more subjects.

Defend: Provide evidence to support a stand or conclusion.

Define: Provide a definition (or set of definitions).

Discuss: Talk about (write!) the subject—be sure to focus on a particular purpose and not just randomly brainstorm on the topic.

Enumerate: Number off specific points, ways of doing something, steps in a process.

Examine: Analyze and explore an issue thoroughly.

Identify: Specifically list or identify what is required.

Illustrate: Show with examples, support, and analysis.

Interpret: Translate and analyze the significance of the material.

List/include: Provide a list of examples, support, and/or reasons.

Provide/support: Provide examples and details for support and explanation.

Summarize: Summarize the main ideas in your own words.

Trace: In chronological order, detail events or situations related to the subject.

Applying Critical Thinking

PURPOSE   IDEAS   SUPPORT   ASSUMPTIONS BIASES   CONCLUSIONS   POINT OF VIEW   ANALYSIS

The best way to make the most of your limited time in an exam situation is to do the following:

1. **Make sure that you understand the prompt, or question,** that has been given to you for your writing task. Read it carefully (see the list of terms that follow for clues to what you are being asked to do in the prompt). It helps to revise the given *question* into a thesis statement *answer* before you prewrite.

2. **Allow at least five minutes for brainstorming** after you get your topic or prompt. Brainstorm on paper with a pen or pencil or on the computer, depending on your preference or the instructor's directions. If you prefer, you can freewrite instead. Develop **support, purpose,** and **analysis** in your essay.

3. **Come up with a brief plan for organization:** Try a rough outline to organize your ideas.

4. **Focus more on ideas and details,** and try not to obsess about spelling and style (although do use complete sentences and paragraph structure).

5. **Allow at least five minutes for a quick review/flash revision** of glaring problems after you write your essay. Be sure to check for spelling (this is the time to use the dictionary you brought) or grammar mistakes, and check your tone and diction choices.

Use the revision checklist below as a guideline for what you should look for as you do a quick revision.

REVISION CHECKLIST

_____   Check that you have addressed the prompt and accomplished the tasks set out in the directions and in the clue words.

_____   Check for an interesting introductory paragraph that sets up your purpose and leads into your thesis.

_____   Check for purpose and a clear thesis statement.

_____   Check that you have used appropriate vocabulary, tone, and approach for your target audience.

_____   Check to make sure that you have organized your paper logically with clear topic sentences in the body paragraphs and transitions.

_____   Check to make sure you have maintained unity—all sentences and paragraphs help develop your purpose and thesis.

_____   Check to make sure you have included enough support in your essay to develop your purpose. Do you need more examples and details?

_____   Check to make sure that your sentence structure and your vocabulary choices are varied and interesting.

_____   Check for a strong concluding paragraph that sums up your analytical conclusion (purpose) established in your thesis.

_____   Check for complete sentences (eliminate fragments, run-ons, or comma splices).

_____   Check for correct punctuation throughout the paper (commas, semicolons, colons, other punctuation marks).

_____   Check for conventional rules of mechanics (spelling, capitalization, underlining, italics, abbreviations, numbering) using the grammar section of this text and a dictionary.

Activity 16-1   Identifying Word Clues in Prompts

Directions: *In each of the following sample essay prompts, identify what the italicized words are asking the writer to do in his/her essay.*

1. Write a two- to three-page essay that *defines* civic duty and *examines* why people tend to uphold it.

   _____

   _____

2. *Identify* a recurring problem in your neighborhood, and then *illustrate* why it is a problem.

   _____

   _____

3. *Trace* the events that led to the creation of NATO.

   _____

   _____

4. *Examine* the following poem, and *interpret* the meaning and messages within it.

_____

_____

5. *Summarize* a current debate or controversy in the news, and then *argue* your stand on the controversy.

_____

_____

PRACTICE WITH TIMED IN-CLASS ESSAYS AND ESSAY EXAMS

Activity 16-2 Timed Essay Practice I

Directions: *Give yourself one hour to write this essay from start to finish.*

Prompt Questions: *Write about a time when someone treated you unfairly. Explain what happened. How did it make you feel, and why? Examine your memories of the experience. Interpret this event's significance in your life and to your identity. Provide specific examples. What did you learn from this experience? (What you learned will become the thesis statement of your essay.)*
    Complete the following:

1. *Brainstorm, prewrite, and outline for five minutes to find a thesis and generate ideas.*
2. *Begin with an introductory paragraph to set up your thesis, and then provide a thesis statement that addresses the topic questions above.*
3. *Set up the rest of your paragraphs to develop your points and describe what happened. Use narration and description to develop your thesis idea.*
4. *Write a concluding paragraph that sums up your experience.*
5. *Do a quick review for needed organization and details; check quickly for spelling and grammar errors.*

Activity 16-3 Timed Essay Exam Practice II

Directions: *Write for one hour on the following prompt: Do you think that cigarette smoking should be illegal? Why or why not? Be sure to argue reasons for your position, define and analyze the counterarguments or positions, and provide support and examples for the reasons for your position on the issue.*

Activity 16-4   Self-Assessment Essay

Directions: *Write a short one- or two-page self-assessment essay. In the essay, address the following questions.*

1. *Assess your improvement over the span of this writing course in planning, drafting, and revising essays. How exactly has your essay writing improved? Be specific. Some of the categories to consider include organization, details and examples, development, flow/coherence/transitions, introductory paragraphs and thesis statements, concluding paragraphs, and, finally, grammar and editing (spelling, fragments, run-ons, comma splices, commas, semicolon/colon use, pronoun agreement, reference fault errors, parallelism, apostrophe use, verb use/tense, passive voice construction, and others).*

2. *In your opinion, what are your strengths as a writer? What do you do well in essay writing?*

3. *In your opinion, what are your weaknesses in writing essays? What do you need to continue to work on in the future?*

4. *Anything else you've noticed?*

17

Paraphrase, Summary, and Analysis

Vietnam War Memorial.

THINKING CRITICALLY

Look at the picture above. Then complete the task that follows.

In your own words, summarize what is happening in this picture. Describe the scene and the main action.

_____

_____

_____

You just wrote a summary of one picture's story. Both paraphrase and summary are tools for concisely conveying the main points made by an author. When writing about someone else's writing, you can bring in direct quotes, you can summarize the main ideas of the piece, or you can paraphrase a specific part (a couple of sentences). Most likely, you will use some combination of all three techniques.

Engage your critical thinking skills when writing about sources to make the best choices about when and how to combine summary, paraphrase, and direct quotations.

PARAPHRASE

A **paraphrase** involves using one's own words to *rephrase* a sentence or two of an original piece of writing. A paraphrase should be about the same length and contain about the same amount of detail as the original sentence(s) you are paraphrasing. Paraphrasing is like doing a phrase-by-phrase translation of an author's words into your own words. Make sure that you change both the word choice and the sentence structure of a paraphrase so you are not plagiarizing, and give the original author credit.

The purpose of a paraphrase is to provide a *detailed description or translation in your own words* of the original written material, and it should be very short. If you paraphrase more than a few sentences, you are running dangerously close to plagiarizing the author's writing. Summarize the main ideas in a general way instead and only paraphrase (rephrase) the sentences that need to be given in detail—again using only your own words, not the original author's. It is essential to be objective in your paraphrase of an author's ideas. Do not add your bias, opinion, or personal reaction to the material. A *paraphrase is much more detailed than a summary* because you are literally rephrasing a sentence or two with the same level of detail, and it may end up being the same length or longer than the original piece of writing. Here are the six steps for writing a complete and accurate paraphrase.

Six Steps for Paraphrasing Material

Step One: Read the sentences you want to paraphrase carefully before writing anything (if it is a section from a longer piece, be sure to read the whole piece before paraphrasing the passage to be sure you understand the excerpt). Use the T-KED reading system or one of the Six Steps to Active Reading from Chapter 2 to gain a thorough understanding of the work. It is essential to understand an author's main and supporting points in a work before you can paraphrase them.

Step Two: In your first sentence, provide the author's full name and the name of the work you are paraphrasing from. If it is an excerpt, provide the entire title of the story, essay, or article in quotation marks; if it is from a book or play, underline or use italics for the title, depending on your instructor's preference.

Step Three: Then paraphrase the sentence(s). You may combine two or more sentences into one concise, paraphrased sentence of your own.

Step Four: Write the paraphrase *using your own words*, not the words of the author (no direct quotations in a paraphrase). Also, be sure to use your own sentence structures and style—not too close to the original.

Tip: In order to avoid writing the paraphrase in the same words or same style as the original author, try not looking at the original and writing a sentence or two paraphrasing the sentences you have just read. Look at the text again and be sure you included all of the author's main ideas and details. It also helps verbally to explain the author's ideas and support to a friend first, using your own words, before you write a paraphrase.

Step Five: Stay objective. Do not offer your opinion in the paraphrase. Add no interpretation. Do not agree or disagree: Just paraphrase objectively. Read over your paraphrase and check for accuracy. Did you present the author's main ideas and details without adding your own bias or opinion?

Cross Reference

See Chapter 18 for more on avoiding plagiarism and Chapter 19 for correct MLA citation format.

Step Six: Include a page citation and/or publication information when needed. Even paraphrased references to a text in an essay you are writing need citations; otherwise you are guilty of plagiarism (not giving credit to the original author).

Sample Paraphrase

Paragraph excerpt from "Supersize Me" by Greg Critser, in Chapter 21.

Original Paragraph

Many franchisees wanted to take the concept even further, offering large-size versions of other menu items. At this sudden burst of entrepreneurism, however, McDonald's mid-level managers hesitated. Many of them viewed large-sizing as a form of "discounting," with all the negative connotations such a word evoked. In a business where "wholesome" and "dependable" were the primary PR watchwords, large-sizing could become a major image problem. Who knew what the franchisees, with their primal desires and shortcutting ways, would do next? No, large-sizing was something to be controlled tightly from Chicago, if it were to be considered at all.

Paraphrase of the First Two Sentences

In Greg Critser's article, "Supersize Me," he points out that many of the McDonald's franchisees decided to try offering other super-sized items after the success of super-sized fries. However, managers at the McDonald's headquarters began to worry about what the individual franchise owners were planning (Critser 1).

Use this checklist to ensure that you have accurately paraphrased the original sentence(s).

CHECKLIST FOR A GOOD PARAPHRASE

1. Check to make sure that you paraphrased the ideas in the original sentence(s) in the same order they were presented.

2. Check to make sure the paraphrase includes all of the main ideas and main examples for support from the original sentence(s).

3. Check to make sure that the paraphrase is in your own words and that there are no significant phrases that were in the original sentence(s) (no direct quotes, not even partial quotes).

4. Check to make sure that the paraphrase is accurate in its restatement of the original material and that you have not added any reaction to or opinion about the material (the restatement is objective).

5. Make sure you have included the author's name and the title of the original piece at the beginning of your paraphrase and included a citation of the source at the end.

Activity 17-1   Paraphrasing

Directions: *Pick a reading from another text or from Chapter 21 (or your instructor might assign a passage), and write a paraphrase of one to three sentences from that reading on a separate sheet of paper, following the Six Steps for Paraphrasing Material above.*

Note: *You may want to use the T-KED reading system or Six Steps for Active Reading for a thorough understanding of the passage; you must completely comprehend a reading before you can accurately paraphrase it.*

Then, explain below what effect writing your paraphrase had on your overall understanding of the ideas contained in the reading.

_____

_____

_____

_____ ●

SUMMARY

A **summary** is an objective, condensed description of an original work (an article, text chapter, story, etc.). Summarizing involves using your own words to describe the main ideas of a piece of writing. It is usually a much shorter (about one quarter or less of the original's length as a rule of thumb) presentation of the concepts of the original piece. A summary should not include direct quotations. The purpose of a summary is to provide a brief description of a longer work, and it should include the author's *main ideas* and the most prominent support for those ideas. It is essential to be objective in your summary of the author's ideas. Add no bias, opinion, or personal reaction to the material.

Here are eight steps for writing a complete and effective summary. *Be sure to read all eight steps before you begin, since some of these steps overlap.*

Eight Steps for Writing a Summary

Step One: Read the entire work (article, essay, short story, novel) at least twice before you write your summary. Be sure to use the T-KED reading system or the Six Steps to Active Reading from Chapter 2 in order to gain a thorough understanding of the work. It is essential first to understand an author's main points and supporting points in a work before you can summarize them.

Step Two: Be brief; a summary is a condensed form of the work's main ideas. Usually a summary uses about one paragraph for each two or three pages of original text. A rule of thumb is that a summary should be about one-quarter the length of the original work.

Step Three: Write the summary in your own words, not the words of the author. Do not use direct quotations in a summary. Be sure to give page citations and/or publishing information after summarized text if your summary is part of a longer paper.

Cross Reference
See Chapter 19 for how to cite sources.

Tip: To avoid writing a summary using the same words or style as the original author, reread one section of the work at a time (a couple of paragraphs to a page or so), and then, while not looking at the original work, write a few lines of summary for the section you read. Then, look at the text again, and be sure your summary includes all of the author's main ideas from that section. It also helps verbally to explain the author's ideas and support to a friend first, using your own words, before you write a paraphrase.

Step Four: Stay objective. Do not offer your opinion. Add no interpretation. Do not agree or disagree with the author: Just summarize objectively. Read over your summary and check for accuracy. Did you represent the author's main ideas without adding your own bias or opinion?

Step Five: In your first sentence, provide the author's full name and the name of the work you are summarizing. The titles of stories, essays, articles, and poems should be presented in quotation marks, and books or play titles should be italicized or underlined. Also, provide a general statement about the topic of the selection.

Step Six: State the author's main idea—the author's overall thesis—using your own words. You can identify the thesis by answering the question, What is the main message of this work?

Note: This step can be combined with Step Five above. However, your summary of the author's thesis should be in the first or second sentence of your summary.

Step Seven: Summaries longer than 200 words should be divided into two or more paragraphs. Use a natural break or change of main idea focus to decide on where paragraph breaks should occur; add a transitional word, phrase, or sentence if you break your summary into two or more paragraphs.

Step Eight: Evaluate, revise, and edit the summary. Go back and reread the work while double-checking your summary for accuracy. Check to make sure you covered all the main ideas or arguments and all the main subtopics, and that you haven't included any minor supporting details that are not needed. Check to make sure you consistently used your own words and that you did not offer any judgment or opinion in the summary. Finally, check for grammar errors, spelling errors, and overall sentence variety as well as needed transitions so your summary has a nice flow and doesn't sound choppy.

Tip: Try putting your summary away for a day or two. Then come back to it, and *read it aloud*. Listen to make sure that it flows smoothly and captures the author's main ideas in a clear and accurate way.

Note: Some instructors will ask for a summary assignment that *begins* with pure summary and then adds the element of critical analysis *after* summarizing the assigned reading. Most assignments that require analyzing an assigned reading usually require some amount of summary and then critical analysis. See the section Combining Summary and Analysis on p. 346 for further information.

Here is a sample summary of Greg Critser's article "Supersize Me" from Chapter 21. Read the selection carefully before reading this summary. Then notice how the summary keeps the same order of ideas as the article, provides the major ideas and the examples used for support of those ideas, remains objective in its presentation of the ideas, and uses transitions to flow smoothly from one idea to the next.

Sample Summary

Greg Critser's article "Supersize Me" defines and gives the history of the supersize craze and how it began as a way for fast-food executives to increase their profits and has now spread into other aspects of American society. Critser describes how David Wallerstein, a McDonald's executive, came to the realization that people want to know they are getting more for their money and would be willing to pay more for super-sized meal deals. After surveying customer behavior in a Chicago-area McDonalds's, Wallerstein presented his findings to Ray Kroc, McDonald's founder. Wallerstein's findings were that consumers were eating the entire bag of French fries and then they would look like they wanted more. Wallerstein realized that people did not want to appear gluttonous but would be happy to pay a little more and get bigger portions, so he increased the size of portions and raised the cost slightly so customers would see this move as a bargain.

Finally, Kroc agreed to serve supersized portions, and, after only months, sales were up, which meant profits were up. Then, Max Cooper, another McDonald's executive, built on Wallerstein's idea by packaging a burger, fries, and drink at a cost less than if all three were bought separately: what is called the value meal now. His original thoughts were to cut costs or prices, but, in the end, packaging a meal to make consumers think they were getting a deal is what turned a profit.

Next, the supersize meal concept spread to other fast-food chains. However, these supersized meals have had an effect on American's eating habits. Recent studies have looked at our culture and eating habits including appetite, meal size, and caloric intake. The studies are finding that appetites increased when larger portions were introduced. Finally, according to Critser, the supersize obsession has spread to other aspects of American society: The craze of buying large has spread to homes, clothes, and vehicles. Consumers now go by the adage that bigger is better.

Use this checklist to ensure that you have accurately summarized an article, essay, or textbook chapter.

CHECKLIST FOR A GOOD SUMMARY

Check to make sure that:

1. You summarized the ideas in the original work in the same order they were presented.

2. The summary includes all of the main ideas and examples for support from the passage.

3. The summary is in your own words and there are no significant phrases that were in the original passage (no direct quotes, even partial quotes).

4. The summary is accurate in its condensing of the original material's ideas and you have not added any reaction to or opinion of the material (the summary is objective).

5. You have included the author's name and the name of the original piece and included a citation at the end of your summary of the article if it is part of a paper you are writing and not a standalone summary.

Activity 17-2   Summarizing

Directions: *Pick a reading from another text or from Chapter 21 (or your instructor might assign a reading for you to summarize), and, on a separate sheet of paper, summarize it, following the Eight Steps for Writing a Summary.*

Note: *You may want to use the T-KED reading system as you read or the Six Steps for Active Reading from Chapter 2 for a thorough understanding of the material: You must completely comprehend a reading before you can accurately summarize it. Then, in the lines provided, explain what effect following this process of summarizing had on your overall understanding of the original work.*

_____

_____

_____

_____

_____

COMBINING SUMMARY AND ANALYSIS

Cross Reference
Review Chapter 1 for more explanation of the terms *analysis* and *interpretation.*

After you have mastered summarizing an original work using your own words, you are ready to analyze the meaning and significance of the piece. A **summary** explains *what* the author is saying; an **analysis** explains *what he or she means*.

Applying Critical Thinking

 PURPOSE   IDEAS   SUPPORT   ASSUMPTIONS BIASES   CONCLUSIONS   POINT OF VIEW   ANALYSIS

Summary vs. Analysis: Know Your Purpose

Summary and *analysis* are two very different skills. In a *summary* you restate in a condensed form what an author says in an article, essay, or other piece of writing using your own words without adding interpretation, commentary, or opinions on the material. *Analysis* involves using your critical thinking skills to *interpret* the important ideas in a piece of writing and to critique the techniques an author uses to present them. Some assignments only require you to summarize assigned material, while others do not require any summary and focus only on analysis and interpretation of the message in an assigned reading. Some assignments, however, require a synthesis of both skills.

To analyze a work well, you need to include some summary of the original ideas and arguments in an unbiased (fair) way. Then you add your own opinion and engage your analytical skills to interpret the direct and implied messages and to critique the author's techniques and style choices. You learned how to write an unbiased summary of an article, textbook chapter, or story earlier in this chapter using the Eight Steps for Writing a Summary (p. 342). Here are two additional steps that you would use after completing the first eight, in order to add analysis to your summary.

Steps 9 and 10 for Writing Critical Analysis

Step Nine: Interpret the language and techniques used by the author to make his or her point. Use specific examples from the text to illustrate your interpretation or to demonstrate the writing or style choices the author has made and what effect those have on the reader and on delivering the message(s) in the writing. See The Ice Cream Sandwich: Framing Facts and Sources on p. 348 for information on how to integrate paraphrases, summaries, or quotations into your analysis.

Step Ten: Analyze the author's purpose in the piece. What are his or her main messages? What are the direct messages or points made, and what indirect messages are implied? What are his or her biases?

Here is a paragraph that uses Steps 9 and 10 to add critical analysis to the end of the summary of Critser's article on page 344.

Sample Critical Analysis

Critser's argument that changing the portion size of McDonald's items has led to an increase in people's appetite is a frightening concept. He argues that, as the portions increase, so do appetites (Critser 2). The more people are offered, the hungrier they seem to be. It is a never-ending cycle. Now the super-size portions are bigger than ever, with more calories per value meal than in any time in McDonald's history. I agree that with this increase in portion size comes an increase in appetite, but more than that, there's an increase in acceptance of overeating in America. Critser's article "Supersize Me" captures a serious problem in the American fast-food industry that needs to be addressed.

Activity 17-3   Summary and Analysis

Directions: *Choose one of the readings from Chapter 21 and write a two-paragraph critique of it that includes both a summary of the main ideas and specific analysis and critical responses to the ideas in the reading (The Eight Steps Plus Steps Nine and Ten—summary plus critical analysis). After you've finished, describe below what effect the process of summarizing and analyzing this reading had on your overall comprehension of the author's ideas.*

_____

_____

_____

_____

Activity 17-4   Adding Analysis

Directions: *Review the summary you wrote for Activity 17-2 and add Steps Nine and Ten to make it a summary with critical analysis. After you finish, describe below how your thinking process was different than it was when you were writing purely summary. How did you have to think differently in order to add analysis?*

_____

_____

_____

_____

THE ICE CREAM SANDWICH: FRAMING FACTS AND SOURCES

The ice cream sandwich system that was briefly described in Chapter 4 is a great technique to help you create analytical frames for your text references. The ice cream sandwich concept is the building block for good analytical writing. Whenever you are given an assignment that involves text analysis, use this ice cream sandwich idea to ensure that each time you bring in a text reference (a paraphrase, summary, or a direct quote), you frame it with your own analytical interpretation of what is being said by the author and your analysis of the significance and the implied or directly stated message(s) of the author. You should also critique the author's technique (style, writing,

tone, and language) and choices for how his or her point(s) were developed or crafted.

The Ice Cream Sandwich at a Glance

Top Cookie: A sentence or two to introduce the point you want to make or critique

Ice Cream Filling: The text reference that supports your point. Be sure to put summaries and paraphrases into a sentence of your own:
- Summary
- Paraphrase → plus page number (in parentheses)
- Direct quote

Bottom Cookie: Interpretation and analysis
- Interpretation (what is being said—define key terms when necessary)
- Analysis (what the messages are and a critique of the author's ideas, writing style, or techniques)

Top Cookie (introduction): Start with a sentence or two that introduces the point you want to make using the author for support, or a point you want to critique using an example from the author.

> **Example:** Kim Smith feels that the influence of pop culture over young minds is unavoidable, and she doesn't hold much hope of teens breaking away from this influence.

Ice Cream Filling (paraphrase, summary, or quotation): After introducing the concept you will be discussing, bring in a specific idea or example from the author in the form of a paraphrase, summary, or direct quote from the reading. A paraphrased line or passage or a summarized idea or section from the reading can be integrated into your own sentence, but you need to put a page number citation after the part of your paragraph that was paraphrased or summarized. If you use a direct quotation from the reading, it can't float in the paper by itself: Attach it to what you are saying. There are three ways to weave a **quote** into your own sentence correctly:

1. **Use a tag line.**

   > **Example:** Kim Smith claims, "The infiltration of pop culture is inevitable" (22).

2. **Weave the quotation into a sentence of your own:**

   > **Example:** We find that the "infiltration of pop culture" (Smith 22) is destined to happen.

3. **Set up the quote with an analytical sentence of your own** and then use a colon before you list the quote to illustrate your point:

   > **Example:** The process is inevitable in American pop culture: "Teens will always be influenced by the media machine" (Smith 23).

Then be sure to add a *citation* in the assigned documentation format.

Cross Reference
See Chapter 19 for a detailed explanation of the MLA documentation format.

Note: The punctuation goes outside the parentheses.

Bottom Cookie (analysis): Analytically interpret what the paraphrased, summarized, or quoted passage from the author is saying, making sure to break down each part of a complex quote and defining terms when needed. Then, give an *analytical response* to the idea the quote is making: Agree with, disagree with, elaborate on, or critique the ideas or the logic of the arguments.

Example:

Analytical interpretation: Smith is saying that it is natural and predictable that the ideas of popular culture will seep into the tastes and values of teenagers.

Analytical response: However, she doesn't say whether or not it is a positive phenomenon or if there is a way to fight the effects of this infiltration.

Activity 17-5   Analytical Ice Cream Sandwich Exercise

Directions: *Pick a one- to two-sentence direct quotation from one of the readings included in this text and write a full analytical Ice Cream Sandwich for that quote.*

Top Cookie:

_____

_____

Ice Cream Filling (the quote itself):

_____

_____

Add the page number citation: (_____).

Bottom Cookie:

Analytical interpretation: _____

_____

Analytical reaction and/or critique: _____

_____

Activity 17-6   Creating Ice Cream Sandwiches in Essays

Directions: *Choose a reading from Chapter 21 or another article that you have found or that your instructor has assigned, and write a short essay that includes a summary of the reading and a critical analysis. Make sure that the thesis defines the main message/purpose of the reading, and make sure to include at least one "ice cream sandwich" in each body paragraph.*

THINKING CRITICALLY

Look at the picture above. Then answer the questions that follow.

1. How do you think using sources can help your essays?

_____

_____

2. What cautions do you think you need when using sources?

_____

_____

CRITICAL THINKING AND THE RESEARCH PROCESS

Often, writing for college, your workplace, or even for the general public involves conducting research and adding sources to a paper to support your thesis. Depending on your purpose and target audience, you will adjust your research process and writing style. Most documented papers include both primary and secondary sources.

Primary sources are original or firsthand materials. They include speeches, firsthand accounts of events, stories, essays, poems, novels, autobiographies, journals, blogs, and emails. If you conduct interviews, studies, or surveys, these also count as primary sources, as do poetry, fiction, or artwork you create yourself. **Secondary sources** consist of information written about primary sources. They include summaries, bibliographies, encyclopedia entries, news articles about events, commentaries such as reviews or critiques, and any other material studied and/or interpreted by others.

Using primary sources is essential in your research process as they provide direct information on your topic. Using secondary sources is also important. However, this means using information from other writers, so be especially aware of their biases and use your critical thinking skills to evaluate the credibility of their interpretations and evaluations (see Finding, Evaluating, and Integrating Sources later in this chapter).

Documented Papers and Research Papers

A **documented paper** requires you to use secondary sources to support and document your essay's arguments and conclusions. You use sources to strengthen and support your own ideas. You first write your own arguments and ideas, and then research ideas and support to illustrate them.

> **Documented paper:** Write your own arguments/conclusion → research for support → integrate sources

A **research paper**'s purpose, on the other hand, is to summarize and present secondary sources in order to draw conclusions from them or to inform your readers about a specific subject. A research paper's main purpose is to provide answers to a research question (or set of questions) designed by you or assigned by your instructor. For instance, you might begin with the question "What is acid rain, and why do we need to know about it?"

Research paper: Question(s) → research information/answers → conclusion(s)/findings

The nature of your assignment and the goals of your essay dictate the role of secondary research in your paper. Is your purpose to argue your own viewpoint and conclusions and bring in experts to back up your arguments? Or are you using secondary research to inform your audience and present facts and information? Or are you doing both? Even when your paper is research based, you need to draw conclusions based on the research you gathered. You can begin with an argument and then research for support, or begin with a question, research answers, and present your conclusions.

BEFORE STARTING RESEARCH

When you begin the process of writing a documented or research paper, spend some time thinking about what you want to accomplish and the assumptions and biases you already have on the subject. Ask yourself the following questions before you begin your research.

CRITICAL THINKING QUESTIONS

PURPOSE   IDEAS   SUPPORT   ASSUMPTIONS BIASES   CONCLUSIONS   POINT OF VIEW   ANALYSIS

Looking for Sources

1. What do I want to explain, show, or prove related to my topic? What are my goals? What is my **purpose?**
2. What information, **ideas**, and **support** do I need to develop my argument?
3. What concepts will I need to define in this paper?
4. How shall I assess the **assumptions and biases** of the sources I use?
5. Where should I look for the kinds of information I need, and how will I know if those sources are reliable? How do I **analyze** them?

FINDING, EVALUATING, AND INTEGRATING SOURCES

When you conduct research, you first need to decide how and where to find the sources you need. Then you need to evaluate whether those sources, and the information they provide, are reliable and credible. Finally, you need to integrate the sources into your paper and document them correctly.

Finding Sources

These days, students are fortunate to have easy access, at home or on campus, to an amazing source of information: the Internet. However, don't forget that some of the old-fashioned techniques for finding sources still have merit. Your campus or local library, databases, and personal interviews are all excellent resources too.

Libraries

Due to the seductive powers of the Internet and the ease of online research, many students have forgotten the value of a good library. Books and reference texts (such as specialized dictionaries and encyclopedias) as well as periodicals, magazines, and newspapers are a treasure that you'll find in any library. But libraries also hold valuable collections of DVD, CD-ROM, print, and database resources. Moreover, libraries pay for access to online databases that you might not be able to access from your home computer or would be charged for doing so.

Libraries offer two major options that can make your research easier:

1. **Web sites designed to help you efficiently search all their holdings (print, CD-ROM, database, online subscriptions, and so on).** Often, you can access your college library's Web site from home, using your student ID and password. College library Web sites also include helpful links to other online resources that you might not have found on your own. Both college and local library Web sites have search engines designed to help you customize a search through their holdings (and even the holdings of other local libraries in your area) for the topic you are writing about. Another common feature on a library Web site is an Ask a Librarian link that will allow you to post questions to the librarian on duty, who will get back to you with help.

2. **Helpful staff and trained research librarians who are expert at customized searches and can help you find what you are looking for in a fraction of the time it would take you on your own.** It's not cheating to get help from your librarians: That's what they're there for. Most of

the time they are eager, like library detectives, to help you dig for the perfect sources for your topic. They can even help you narrow and fine tune the scope of your topic and the purpose for your research. It helps to have completed your brainstorming and have a preliminary outline of ideas for your paper before you visit your local or college librarian. You can also check to see if your college or local libraries have online access to librarians so that you can email questions from home.

Databases

Databases are collections of information. They can be available on CD-ROMs and stored in libraries, or they can be online databases, accessible through your library's subscription service. Go to your local and college libraries to check which databases they subscribe to (or check online on their Web sites). The value of databases is that they are field or subject specialized and have search functions that allow for quick and easy access to reliable, credible sources for your paper. For instance, Infotrac is a database that provides articles on academic subjects either by a subject search or by author. All college libraries feature paid subscription services like Infotrac, ProQuest, EbscoHost, and CQ Researcher. These resources are the first place you should check, since they are already filtered and established credible sources (unlike what you will have to sort through on the Internet). Ask a librarian at your school which services your library subscribes to.

Interviews with Experts

You can conduct interviews in person, by telephone, or via email with experts on the subject you are writing about. Be sure to check with your instructor first to see if interviews from experts are allowed as a source in your paper. Be sure that the person interviewed is a credible expert in the field or subject. Evaluate your interviewee by asking if that person has the right credentials for the subject you are writing about: What degree does he or she hold? What has he or she published in relation to the subject? Is he or she a known authority on the subject?

The Internet and Search Engines

The Internet puts a wealth of information at your fingertips and is accessible from the comfort of your own home, your campus, or your local coffee shop. The World Wide Web has changed the way we conduct research and opened up possibilities we never dreamed of. The easiest way to navigate the Web and find sources related to your subject is to use a search engine.

A **search engine** allows you to use key words to search a database or the Web for information on specific topics. Some of the more prominent search engines include the following:

Google (www.google.com)

Google Scholar (www.scholar.google.com)

Yahoo (www.yahoo.com)

AltaVista (www.altavista.com)

Ask.com (www.ask.com)

Dictionary.com (www.dictionary.com)

You can do either a basic search using a key word or phrase, or you can do an **advanced search** that allows you to customize your search and target more specific articles for your paper. All of the sites listed, as well as more specialized discipline specific databases, provide information on how to search most effectively. For example, to the right of the search box on the Google homepage there is a link called Advanced Search that takes you to a page where you can focus your search efforts and also learn tips for using the search engine to your advantage. If you get more than 500 "hits" (articles or entries related to the key word or phrase you entered) when you do a basic search on your topic, do an advanced search to narrow the scope of the search to articles that more specifically address your topic.

Applying Critical Thinking

| PURPOSE | IDEAS | SUPPORT | ASSUMPTIONS BIASES | CONCLUSIONS | POINT OF VIEW | ANALYSIS |

Use your critical thinking and **analysis** skills when you search on the Internet. The use of the Internet for research has led to some of the most serious errors and academic offenses in student papers. The two most prominent problems that arise from students using the Internet to conduct research are:

1. **The use of sources that are not legitimate or credible.**

2. **An increase in plagiarism** (using someone else's ideas or words without giving that person credit), both "accidental" and intentional.

The Internet is a gold mine of legitimate, up-to-date, and easily accessible sources for your paper. However, there are many Web sites, articles, studies, and other sources of information available on the Internet that are

Cross Reference
See Mark Clayton's "A Whole Lot of Cheatin' Going On" in Chapter 21 for a discussion of plagiarism in colleges nationally.

not legitimate or are even false. You must be on guard particularly when evaluating a source or study online (see the questions on the next page for evaluating your sources). Throughout the country instances of plagiarism have increased in large part due to the ease of having information available at the click of a mouse (see How to Avoid Plagiarism on p. 367).

Sample Hit Page from a Google Search for "Search Engines"

Web   Images   Video^New!   News   Maps   **more »**

Sign in

search engines   Search
Advanced Search
Preferences

Web   Results **1 - 10** of about **294,000,000** for search engines. **(0.10** seconds)

Sponsored Link

All Major Search Engines
www.registereverywhere.com   Get more traffic and higher ranking in **search engines**. No monthly fees!

Search Engine Watch: Tips About Internet **Search Engines** & Search ...

Search Engine Watch is the authoritative guide to searching at Internet **search engines** and **search engine** registration and ranking issues.
searchenginewatch.com/ - 56k - Sep 8, 2006 - Cached - Similar pages

Search Engines

Offers free tips, site analysis, optimization, submission and maintenance services. Chicago, Illinois.
www.**searchengines**.com/ - 12k - Cached - Similar pages

Dogpile Web **Search** Home Page

Dogpile.com makes searching the Web easy, because it has all the best **search engines** piled into one. So you get better results from more of the web.
www.dogpile.com/ - 23k - Sep 8, 2006 - Cached - Similar pages

Wikipedia: **Search Engine**

Article in the online collaborative encyclopedia, describing the history and mechanisms of Web **search engines**.
en.wikipedia.org/wiki/**Search**_engine - 54k - Cached - Similar pages

MetaCrawler Web **Search** Home Page

MetaCrawler **Search**. **Search** the **Search Engines**. Including Google, Yahoo!, MSN **Search** and Ask. ...
www.metacrawler.com/ - 24k - Sep 8, 2006 - Cached - Similar pages

Google

Enables users to **search** the Web, Usenet, and images. Features include PageRank, caching and translation of results, and an option to find similar pages.
www.google.com/ - 5k - Sep 8, 2006 - Cached - Similar pages

GO.com - Official Home Page

Discover how GO.com can launch your online experience with **Search**, fun stuff to do, and the latest Sports, News, Entertainment, and Movies from the top ...
www.go.com/?page=Home.html - 58k - Cached - Similar pages

AltaVista

AltaVista provides the most comprehensive **search** experience on the Web! ... **SEARCH**:

Worldwide or Select a country RESULTS IN: All languages ...
www.altavista.com/ - 10k - Cached - Similar pages

Homepage HotBot Web **Search**

Offers a **search** powered by a choice of Google or AskJeeves. There are options to block offensive language, customize **search** results, and skins.
www.hotbot.com/ - 6k - Cached - Similar pages

Search Engines

Features of best **search engines** in table format. ... **Search engines** have become a little bit standardized, allowing us to use some of the same **search** ...
www.lib.berkeley.edu/TeachingLib/Guides/Internet/**SearchEngines**.html - 28k - Cached - Similar pages

Evaluating Potential Sources

Whenever you use research for a paper, you need to be very careful that the sources you have chosen are legitimate. Inaccurate, biased, or even false information is available in all forms of print or electronic material. Indeed, in the age of information we live in, with the prominence of the Internet and the seemingly limitless opportunities for information it offers, you must be more careful than ever to evaluate the sources you find and to engage your critical thinking skills to assess their accuracy and reliability. As an example, many instructors refuse to accept Wikipedia as a source because it allows anyone to add information to the entries posted on its site. Many people, intentionally or otherwise, post misinformation, and corporations have been known to add or change content to make themselves appear in a more favorable light.

Here is a set of questions to use as guidelines for evaluating whether to include specific sources in your documented or research paper. If you answer "no" to any of them, you may want to decide against using the source, or at least check with your campus's librarian to see if it is legitimate.

Questions for Checking the Reliability of a Source

1. **Is the source up to date?** Are there sources available with the same information that are more current? It is essential to use the most up-to-date and legitimate sources in your paper to support your ideas. If your sources don't have credibility, then neither do you.

2. **Is this a scholarly or academic resource?** You want to check the origin of your source and make sure the information is objective and not slanted in order to sell a product or a particular point of view on a controversial issue. Is the source privately or publicly funded? In general, you are better off using sites that end in .edu (education sites such as college websites) or .gov (government resource sites), or sites run by reputable companies or nonprofit organizations as opposed to for-profit .com sites.

3. **Does the author have the correct credentials for writing knowledgeably on this subject?** Do not assume that having an M.D. or Ph.D. automatically gives a person credibility in any field; make sure the author is writing from his or her field of expertise. Check what field the author's degree is in and see if that matches the content of the material. You can also check the job that the expert holds to see if it relates to the subject. You can even conduct a Google or Yahoo search on the author to check his or her background. If the author's background seems unrelated to the subject, then that person is probably not an expert you should use.

4. **If statistics and numbers are included in a source, who commissioned the study or conducted the research?** For instance, if you are researching the effects of tobacco industry advertising on middle school students, you should look for unbiased sources of information and carefully evaluate the accuracy of studies commissioned by the tobacco industry itself.

5. **Can you verify the information contained in a source?** If numbers and statistics are involved, double-check the facts using one or more other sources.

6. **Does the author provide secondary research of his or her own to support ideas and claims?** Are these sources credible? Choose a few key facts and run a Google search to test them against what other sources say.

7. **Does the author present different sides of an issue even if strongly advocating a particular stance?** Check your source against others that come up in an Internet search on the subject. Of course many sources will have a particular bias on a subject, but if a source or author simplifies an issue or doesn't address counterarguments, he or she could be oversimplifying his or her argument and using it would hurt your credibility.

Again, if you answered "no" to any of these questions, you may want to reject the source. You don't want the sources you've used in your paper to damage your credibility and ideas in any way. They are there to support and strengthen your claims.

Once you have determined that a source is reliable, you want to ask more specific questions about the content it contains. Here are some questions to ask in order to evaluate whether a source provides unbiased information and/or well supported arguments.

Questions for Evaluating the Content of a Source

1. What **assumptions** does the author make in his or her arguments?
2. What **biases** are evident in the author's claims and point of view?
3. Who paid for or sponsored the author's research?
4. What **point of view** is the author putting forward?
5. Has he or she included the major counterarguments and objections to the claims he or she is making?

Applying Critical Thinking

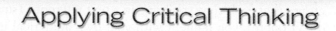

When you evaluate sources, you look at the strength of the **ideas**, reasoning, **support**, and **conclusions** provided by writers for their arguments. You want to look for examples, reasons, and details that support the points they are making. You need to be aware of their **biases**—personal opinions—and **assumptions** (information they take for granted) that might affect the reliability of their arguments. You also need to consider the counterarguments—what people who argue for a different stand might say against their conclusions on the issues.

Integrating Sources into Your Paper

As you begin to incorporate sources into your writing, be sure that they serve as backup for your own ideas and for the expository purpose of your essay. You want to let expert opinion, statistics, and other valuable nuggets of information you gleaned from your research work for you: Don't let your voice, your purpose, your ideas, and your arguments get lost in the background. The research is support; it should not speak for you.

When you synthesize ideas from sources into your arguments, you should smoothly weave together your own ideas and the quotes, summaries, and paraphrases of the other sources you use to support your ideas. When you blend your ideas with the ideas and support from other sources, you develop the purpose of your paper and the support for your ideas in the most effective way.

Every time you include a piece of information from a secondary source, whether it is a summary (a condensed statement of the author's main ideas in your own words) of an idea, a concept or argument, a paraphrase of a particular section, or a direct quotation (using an author's exact words, whether just a phrase, a whole sentence, or an entire passage) from a source, remember to frame that reference on both sides with your own analytical setup, interpretation, and conclusions.

Cross Reference
See Eight Steps for Writing a Summary, Chapter 17, for more on summary and paraphrase.

The Analytical Ice Cream Sandwich Revisited

The Analytical Ice Cream Sandwich is the building block for good analytical research and documented writing. Whenever you are given an assignment that involves secondary research and analysis of your sources, use it to ensure that each time you bring in a text reference (summary, paraphrase, or direct quote), you frame it with your own analytical interpretation of what is being said by the author and analysis of the significance of the implied or direct message(s) it contains.

Cross Reference
See the sample documented paper with integrated sources and Ice Cream Sandwiches in Chapter 19.

You can also use the Analytical Ice Cream Sandwich to critique the techniques (style, writing, tone, and language) the author uses to develop point(s). See Chapter 17, page 348.

Twelve Steps for Writing a Research or Documented Paper

The following guidelines will help you work through the process of writing a research paper.

Step One: *Select your subject.* Unless your topic is assigned, pick a subject that interests you. Remember, you'll be working with this subject for the next several weeks. Also, make sure it's a subject that can be researched with relative ease—nothing too obscure.

Step Two: *Prewrite to narrow your subject down to a manageable topic.* Most subjects are too broad to cover in a short research paper and need to be narrowed down through a process of thinking about and fine tuning one or more aspects of the general subject.

Note: If you do not know a great deal about your chosen subject, you may have to do Step Three before you can adequately prewrite.

Step Three: *Survey your topic by doing preliminary reading.* Get an overview of your topic by reading background articles and getting a sense of the issues and subtopics related to it. You may need to narrow your topic and the scope of your paper still further after you've done some preliminary research, if you find that your subject is more complex than you anticipated.

Step Four: *Write a preliminary thesis statement.* A good thesis statement presents an argument that can be proven and supported by the facts and information gathered through research. You should have an analytical purpose to prove.

Step Five: *Brainstorm, freewrite, and organize ideas, questions, and subtopics to develop your thesis statement.* Think of this stage as a chance to develop *how* you will go about structuring your paper and what kind of information you will need to find for the subtopics and categories you brainstorm based on your thesis statement.

Step Six: *Prepare a working outline.* Taking the ideas you generated in step five, create a rough outline, and determine the main subheadings for your paper. Ask yourself, *What do I want to say? How will I develop my arguments? What support will I provide?* Be sure to put your preliminary thesis at the top of your outline.

Cross Reference
See sample outline on p. 121.

Step Seven: *Conduct research and take notes.* Begin researching for sources. Be sure to record all bibliographical information in your notes for each source you locate and decide to use. A brief listing of what is required for books, newspapers, magazines, and Web pages follows. For more detailed information about a variety of sources, see Compiling a Works Cited List on page 381.

    Books: name of authors(s), title of book, place of publication, publisher, year of publication

    Newspapers: name of author(s), title of article, title of newspaper (name of city and state if local paper), date of publication (day, month, year), edition (if more than one), section and/or page number(s)

    Magazines: author(s) name, title of article, title of magazine, date (day, month, year), page number(s)

    Web pages: Note that not all this information will be available for every web page: name of author(s), page title, website title, publisher or sponsor, date of publication (day, month, year), date of access (day, month, year); if you use a database to access the page, note the name of the database.

Tip: Keep your notes sorted alphabetically by the authors' last names to make it easier to create your bibliography or works cited page later.

Step Eight: *After research, review your notes carefully* to see if you have any gaps in your research. Use your preliminary thesis and your rough outline to assess your gathered notes. *Go back to research any gaps you've discovered.*

Step Nine: *Re-outline your paper, fine tuning the structure and organization and modifying your arguments and your thesis (if necessary) based on any newly discovered information.* Add more details to your outline if necessary, noting carefully which sources you will use in which sections of your paper for support of your ideas. In addition to structuring your paper and developing a helpful Table of Contents for your major categories, you will also be planning when and how to use the sources you've found.

Step Ten: *Write the first draft of your research paper using your revised outline.* (Isn't it amazing that your first draft doesn't come until Step Ten of this process? Much of the work for a good research paper happens long before you sit down to write a draft. Procrastination is deadly in the research process.) Your introduction should lead into and then present your thesis (argument). The body of your paper should develop and support your thesis using the sources you have identified. Your conclusion should sum up and reiterate your thesis. Be sure to cite all your sources, using the documentation format required by your instructor, to avoid plagiarism (see How to Avoid Plagiarism on p. 367).

Step Eleven: *Prepare your bibliography or works cited page.* Again, check with your instructor. Follow the instructions for the documentation format assigned (see MLA documentation format in Chapter 19; for other format styles, use a handbook).

Step Twelve: *Revise, edit, and proofread your paper.* Check for unity, coherence, organization, support, and details, and then fine tune your introduction, thesis, and conclusion. Double-check format and accuracy in all references (summary, paraphrase, or direct quotes). Check especially for punctuation errors within your citations. Use a dictionary and spell-checker and consult a thesaurus to find synonyms for words you have overused. Add transitions where needed within and between paragraphs.

Tip: If you can put your draft away for at least two days before doing step twelve, you will see errors you didn't see before and get a clearer and more accurate assessment of your paper. You may want to visit your college's tutoring or writing center to get some objective feedback on your ideas, organization, and use of secondary sources for support (another good reason not to procrastinate in the research process).

Before you start work on your research paper, create a timeline using the following checklist. Write a target date for each task, and then fill in when you actually complete that stage.

TWELVE STEPS CHECKLIST

Due date for your paper (to hand in to instructor): _____

Step One: Select your subject.

Targeted date of completion: _____

Actual date of completion: _____

Step Two: Prewrite to narrow your subject.

Targeted date of completion: _____

Actual date of completion: _____

Step Three: Survey through preliminary reading.

Targeted date of completion: _____

Actual date of completion: _____

Step Four: Write a preliminary thesis statement.

Targeted date of completion: _____

Actual date of completion: _____

Step Five: Brainstorm, freewrite, and organize ideas.

Targeted date of completion: _____

Actual date of completion: _____

Step Six: Prepare a working outline.

Targeted date of completion: _____

Actual date of completion: _____

Step Seven: Conduct research and take notes.

Targeted date of completion: _____

Actual date of completion: _____

Step Eight: Review your notes and check for gaps.

Targeted date of completion: _____

Actual date of completion: _____

Step Nine: Revise your outline and fine tune content.

Targeted date of completion: _____

Actual date of completion: _____

Step Ten: Write your first draft.

Targeted date of completion: _____

Actual date of completion: _____

Step Eleven: Prepare your bibliography/Works Cited list.

Targeted date of completion: _____

Actual date of completion: _____

Step Twelve: Revise, proofread, and edit your paper.

Targeted date of completion: _____

Actual date of completion: _____

PLAGIARISM

Plagiarism is taking someone else's words, research, or even ideas and using them as if they were your own without giving credit to the original source. Some people are tempted to cheat by the ease of getting information (even full papers) written on any subject from the Internet and intentionally use someone else's work as if it were their own. By doing so, they are committing plagiarism, the most serious and damaging act possible in one's academic career. Even if a person isn't caught cheating immediately, the plagiarized work can be discovered later in his or her academic or professional career with very damaging consequences.

Some people commit "accidental" plagiarism by not correctly documenting and citing the source(s) from which they obtained information. Even if a person does not intend to cheat, however, this sloppy scholarship can seriously damage academic credibility. Penalties for plagiarism vary from course to course and campus to campus, and they range from just a failing grade for that particular paper to expulsion from the institution.

Each person's writing style and voice is as unique as one's fingerprints or handwriting. An instructor very quickly gets a sense of your style and voice (and level of writing and vocabulary ability), and when you plagiarize a phrase, sentence, passage or whole paper, red flags go up immediately in the instructor's mind. All the instructor has to do is plug a suspect phrase—even a partial sentence—into a Google search, and up pops the original source for the article or prewritten essay you plagiarized from. Moreover, most campuses have purchased software designed to spot plagiarism in student essays and automatically search for the original source on the Internet. As the possibilities for plagiarism using the Net increase, so do the methods for spotting those instances. It's just not worth risking your academic (and potentially your professional) career.

How to Avoid Plagiarism

Just buckle down and do the work and the research yourself. If you find a great source that says what you want to say, then use it well in your paper, giving a specific citation for each idea or word used from that source. Let the expert back up your own brilliant ideas and arguments; that's more impressive in the long run, anyway.

Avoiding plagiarism starts with being aware of what it is and then taking the precautions necessary to document and cite all your sources, even if you just gained an insight or idea from another person. Take careful notes and mark direct quotes as well as summarized ideas with the page numbers they came from. In the process of searching for secondary sources, especially when using the Internet, be sure to take detailed notes about the source information of any piece you are even considering using in your paper. Make sure that you use your own words and sentence constructions and even your own style when you paraphrase or summarize the ideas of others and that you credit the original source clearly to avoid plagiarism.

Here are guidelines for recording source information for print, online, and other media sources in your notes:

Guidelines for Accurately Recording Source Information

1. **Note the name of the person(s) or organization** who wrote the material or conducted the study.

2. **Write a summary of the information** you may want to use, with specific sections that are particularly relevant paraphrased in more detail (it is best to take notes on the information in your own words—noting the particular page numbers and sections where the summarized and paraphrased information came from).

3. **Write down any exact quotations** that you think you may want to use because they are worded so perfectly that you can't sum up the information better. Be sure to include the exact page number(s) for each direct quotation you record and the full name of the author or the person the author is quoting in the article. Remember if the author quotes someone else and you decide to use that quotation, then you will need to cite it as an indirect quotation in your paper—see MLA documentation format in Chapter 19.

For Internet-based sources, also,

4. **Record** where, how, and when you found the Web site.

5. **Record** the complete URL.

6. **Note** where on the site you found the information (page or section number, etc.).

> **Note:** As you search for sources, remember to consult the checklist earlier in this chapter in order to evaluate their credibility.

Activity 18-1 Avoiding Plagiarism

Directions: *Go to your library either in person or online and find an academic article or essay. First, use the Guidelines for Accurately Recording Source Information above and write in the correct source documentation on the lines below:*

_____

_____

Then on a separate sheet of paper, either summarize the article in one or two para-graphs of your own words or paraphrase one paragraph of it. After you have sum-marized or paraphrased, go back over your draft and make sure that you have used your own words, style, and sentence constructions, not those of the original author. Report your findings here.

_____

_____

_____

19

Documentation:
Using Modern Language Association (MLA) Format

THINKING CRITICALLY

Look at the picture above. Then answer the questions that follow.

1. Do you think it is important to cite sources in a paper when you use them? Why or why not?

   _____

   _____

2. Do you think it is helpful to use a consistent format for citing sources in a paper? Why or why not?

   _____

   _____

USING MODERN LANGUAGE ASSOCIATION (MLA) FORMAT

MLA style is the standard documentation format used in the United States for writing in English and the humanities (literature, philosophy, history, art, etc.). There are several other documentation styles used by various disciplines and publishers. For instance, APA (American Psychological Association) is the standard for writing in the social sciences, psychology, sociology, criminology, health sciences, business, economics, and some education departments. (For guidelines on how to use APA style, see the *Publication Manual of the American Psychological Association*, or search for APA guidelines online.) Since most English courses and courses in the humanities assign MLA style for documenting sources, this text includes an overview of that system.

Following is a brief introduction to using MLA format. For a more detailed and complete description of MLA style, consult the *MLA Handbook for Writers of Research Papers*, due out in a seventh edition in spring 2009, or a current writer's handbook that includes a full section on MLA documentation format. You can also access information on MLA format online. Go to www.mla.org or search for "MLA format" using a search engine such as www.google.com to find MLA guidelines, tips, and software that will help you format a paper using MLA guidelines and that includes templates for the Works Cited page. The description of MLA style shown here includes the updates published in the *MLA Style Manual and Guide to Scholarly Publishing,* 3rd edition (2008).

The three main principles of MLA format include the use of in-text citations, endnotes, and a Works Cited list that provides detailed publishing information for each source cited in the body of the paper.

Formatting Your Paper

Here is an outline of the general MLA guidelines for formatting a paper:

Paper: Use standard 8.5″ × 11″ paper with margins of 1 inch on all sides.

Font: The preferred font for MLA is 12 point, usually Times Roman or Courier (check with your instructor for a preference).

Spacing: Double space throughout the paper, including the title page, Works Cited list, and endnotes page.

Numbering: Number all pages, including the first page, with a heading that includes your last name and the page number, like this: Garcia 8. Place this heading in the upper right corner of each page, including the Works Cited page, 1/2 inch from the top of the page.

Note: Use the "header/footer" feature of your word processing program to set these preferences.

Titles: Italicize the titles of books when using MLA style. For shorter works such as magazine articles and short stories, use quotation marks around titles.

Title page: Do not create a separate title page when using MLA format unless your instructor requests one, in which case get specific formatting directions. In general, a basic title page should be in 12 point font, and include the title about 1/3 of the way down the page followed by your full name, the class name, the instructor's name, and the date. All of this information should be centered and double spaced.

First page: The standard MLA title page is the first page of the paper typed as follows: In the top left corner, type your full name, your instructor's name, the course name, and the date. Double space these lines. Double space again, and then center your paper's title. Capitalize the first, last, and all significant words in the title. Do not italicize your title and only use italics or quotation marks if you are including the name of another published work in your title, for instance:

Turmoil in the Minds of the Characters from *The Sound and the Fury*

Double space all titles longer than one line. If you have a title and a subtitle, separate the title from the subtitle with a colon, for instance:

Speaking Havoc: Turmoil in the Minds of the Characters from *The Sound and the Fury*

Tables and figures: Label all tables numerically (e.g., Table 1, Table 2, etc.), and always include a short caption (e.g., A Rise in Insanity Cases in the 1890s). Label all images, drawings, and other nontextual material numerically (e.g., Fig. 1, Fig. 2, etc.), and always include a short caption (e.g., A Typical View from the Asylum Window).

Incorporating Quotations

All quotations must be cited. This means you need to include the last name of the author and the page number(s) of the work the quoted information comes from in parentheses immediately after the quotation. (However, online sources often don't include page numbers. See page 381.) In general, end punctuation goes *after* the parenthetical citation, except in the case of a long quotation that is set off in a block without quotation marks. (See In-Text Citations on p. 375 for further details.)

Quotations from Prose

Four lines or less: If a quotation is four lines or less in length, include the lines within the body of the text, surrounded by double quotation marks. If the quotation includes a quotation from someone else within it, use single quotation marks to indicate where the original double quotation marks were. Provide a parenthetical citation at the end of the quotation, before the period.

Single quotation

When Daniel Meier speaks of his job as a teacher of small children, he writes, "My work is not traditional male work. It's not a singular pursuit" (91).

Quotation within a quotation

According to Greg Critser, author of "Supersize Me," the founder of McDonald's was at first reluctant to supersize: "Wallerstein could not convince Ray Kroc, McDonald's founder, to sign on to the idea. . . . 'If people want more fries,' Kroc would say, 'then they can buy two bags'" (98).

More than four lines (block quotation): If a quotation is more than four lines in length, set it off from the main body of the text in an indented block form one inch or 10 spaces from the left margin, double spaced, and do not use quotation marks. Place the parenthetical citation after the period in a long quotation.

Block quotation

George Orwell, in "A Hanging," writes,

> One prisoner had been brought out of his cell. He was a Hindu, a puny wisp of a man, with a shaven head and vague liquid eyes. He had a thick, sprouting moustache, absurdly too big for his body, rather like the moustache of a comic man on the films. Six tall Indian warders were guarding him and getting him ready for the gallows. Two of them stood by with rifles and fixed bayonets, while the others handcuffed him, passed a chain through his handcuffs and fixed it to their belts, and lashed his arms tight to his sides. (2)

Quotations from Poetry

Three lines or less: If you are quoting three lines or less from a poem, include the lines within the body of the text, with each line break indicated by a slash with a space on either side of it. The parenthetical citation should be placed *before* the final period. In the citation include the numbers of the lines you are quoting. The first time you do this, include the word *line* or *lines* before the number(s). For subsequent citations, just include the line number(s).

Example

In Madeline DeFrees's poem "Balancing Acts," she writes, "At 47, Hope's driven to find her feet in construction. / She crawls the hip roof of her house like a cat burglar" (21).

Three lines or more: If you are quoting three lines or more from a poem, set the quotation off from the main text in an indented block form one inch or 10 spaces from the left margin, double spaced, and do not use quotation marks. The parenthetical citation should follow the final period.

Example

In Edna St. Vincent Millay's poem "To Elinor Wylie (in answer to a question about her)," she writes,

> Oh, she was beautiful in every part!—
> The auburn hair that bound the subtle brain;
> The lovely mouth cut clear by wit and pain,
> Uttering oaths and nonsense, uttering art
> In casual speech and curving at the smart (1–5)

Indicating Editorial Information

Sometimes when you are quoting writers and citing information, you need to insert notes to explain some of the information or to note existing errors within the quoted material. Certain conventions for doing this are outlined below.

Indicating errors in an original source: If there is an error in a quotation you are using from a primary or secondary source (grammar, spelling, etc.), indicate you are aware of the error by placing the word "sic" (Latin for "thus") in brackets immediately after it, so your readers will know it is not your error.

Omitting words, phrases, or sentences from a direct quotation: First, be sure that the word(s), phrase(s), or even sentence(s) you are omitting from the direct quotation does not change the author's intended meaning. Then use the following guidelines for how to indicate what information has been omitted or changed.

1. To omit one or more words or a part of a sentence from an original quote, use an ellipsis (a series of three periods with spaces between them):

> "Shima deliberated on the color of her gown for the winter ball for over an hour."

becomes

> "Shima deliberated on the color of her gown . . . for over an hour."

2. To omit one or more sentences from a quotation, use an ellipsis with an extra period (a total of 4 dots):

> "Shima deliberated on the color of her gown for the winter ball for over an hour. She couldn't decide whether she wanted to be traditional or a rule breaker. Finally she decided on a very traditional cream-colored gown."

becomes

> "Shima deliberated on the color of her gown for the winter ball for over an hour. . . . Finally she decided on a very traditional cream-colored gown."

3. To insert clarifying words or information: Use brackets around words, phrases, or needed tense changes that must be added within a quotation to provide clarification for the reader or make the tense or form consistent.

> "Kyle and Emily always argue[d] about the choices for dinner."

IN-TEXT CITATIONS

For every piece of information, idea, or reference used in your paper that comes from someone other than yourself, whether you are paraphrasing, summarizing, directly quoting, or just alluding to an idea that you gained from someone else, you must include a parenthetical citation. Usually, this means including the name of the author(s) and/or the title of the work and the relevant page number(s) in parentheses immediately after the information you are using. This brief citation refers to a Works Cited list at the end of the paper, which provides the reader with detailed information on each source. However, depending on the source, the exact rules for citation vary. Consult the following list for how to include each in-text citation correctly.

> **Note:** A parenthetical citation is followed by a period, except in the case of a longer quotation that has been indented, in which case the citation follows the period.

Cross Reference
See Compiling a Works Cited List on p. 381.

Cross Reference
See Incorporating Quotations, p. 372.

Print Sources

Text by One Author

Author named in text: If you name the author in your introduction to a quotation, paraphrase, or summary, include both his or her first and last name the first time you mention him or her in your paper, and include only the page number in the parenthetical citation:

> Mary Clearman Blew describes the setting by saying, "The hills lay bare under the sweep of the galaxy, waiting from the beginning of time until the end" (33).

If you use the author's name again in the body of the text, use only the last name.

Author not named in text: If you do not name the author in the sentence in which you paraphrase, summarize, or quote him or her, then list the last name of the author and the page number of the original source from which it came in your citation:

> A writer describes the setting, saying "The hills lay bare under the sweep of the galaxy, waiting from the beginning of time until the end" (Blew 33).

Text by Two or Three Authors

Authors named in text: If you choose to use two or three authors' names in the body of your sentence to introduce source information, use their full names, in the same order of credit given in the source, and include only the page number(s) in the citation:

> The fishing crew of John Wyman, Bob Williams, and Bill Myers agreed that "There's nothing better than catching the wild Coho salmon after they have made their trek up the river" (44).

Authors not named in text: If you do not name the authors in the body of your text, include their names in the citation. Separate the names of two authors by "and" and the names of three authors by a comma and then an "and"; then add the page number(s) for the quotation or reference:

> The salmon fishers agreed that "There's nothing better than catching the wild Coho salmon after they have made their trek up the river" (Wyman, Williams, and Myers 44).

Text by More Than Three Authors

If a source has more than three authors, you can either list the authors' names in your introduction to the quotation or in the parenthetical citation. Or you can list the first author's last name and the Latin words "et al." (meaning "and others") and then the page number in the parenthetical citation:

> The return "of the wild salmon every summer in Alaska causes a boost in the local economy and a flood in the seafood market of high quality and delicious meal options" (Jordan et al. 226).

Two or More Works by the Same Author

If you use more than one work by the same author, include an abbreviated version of the specific title you are referencing in your in-text citation. Place the shortened title after the author's last name and a comma. Follow the title with the page number.

> When the character first realizes she's in love, she struggles with the emotion: "Your love is newly born, the first page in a blank notebook" (Allende, *Paula* 77).

If you use the author's name in your introductory sentence, do not include it in the parenthetical reference:

> When the character first realizes she's in love, Isabel Allende describes the girl's struggles with the emotion: "Your love is newly born, the first page in a blank notebook" (*Paula* 77).

If you use both the author's name and the title of the work in your introductory sentence, then just put the page number in the citation:

> When the character in *Paula* first realizes she's in love, Isabel Allende describes the girl's struggles with the emotion: "Your love is newly born, the first page in a blank notebook" (77).

Two Different Authors with the Same Last Name

If you are using two or more sources whose authors have the same last name, be sure to include enough additional information in your citations to distinguish between them. You can do so by using their first initials, or by using their whole first names if they share the same first initial: (B. Smith 22) or (Brenda Smith 22).

Works with No Author Listed

If you use a work whose author is not named, include the first one to three words of the title (or the whole title if it is short) in the parentheses followed by the page number(s):

> The "general notion is that people learn abuse only through modeling and there are no genetic factors" ("Abuse as a Cycle" 38).

Note: Make sure that the one to three words you use to indicate the title are alphabetized the same way in the Works Cited list.

Work from an Anthology

When you quote a selection from an anthology (a quotation from a story, article, essay, or poem from a collection of such works by various authors), cite the name of the author, not the name of the editor of the anthology. The editor and anthology information will be provided in the Works Cited list. For example, if you were quoting Linda Pastan's poem "Marks" from the anthology *Literature: An Introduction to Reading and Writing,* editors Edgar V. Roberts and Henry E. Jacobs, your citation would look like this:

> She writes, "My daughter believes / in Pass/Fail and tells me / I pass" (Pastan 814).

Works with Editors or Translators

When you use information from a work that has an editor or translator, but no named author, use the editor's or translator's name in your citation, followed by the page number(s):

> The anonymous poem encourages readers to "Live life to its absolute fullest" (Roberts and Jacobs 68).

Note: In the Works Cited entry, you will indicate that this poem is from an anthology and Roberts and Jacobs are the editors of that anthology (alphabetized by Roberts' last name in your Works Cited list).

Note: If the work has been translated into English by a translator, but the original author's name is provided, then use the original author's name and only list the translator in the Works Cited entry:

> In *One Hundred Years of Solitude,* the character Colonel Aureliano Buendia says, "We leave Macondo in your care . . . try to have it in better shape when we return" (García Márquez 105).

Works by a Corporation, Government Agency, or Other Group Author

If you are referencing a work by a group, use the name of the organization followed by the page reference in the citation. If the organization is mentioned in your introductory sentence, include just the page number(s) in parentheses:

> According to a study conducted in 2007 by the Department of Transportation, "Most people who carpool do so less than four times a week" (4).

If the organization is not mentioned in your sentence, include its name and the page number in your parenthetical citation:

> In fact, "Most people who carpool do so less than four times a week" (Department of Transportation 4).

Multiple Sources for the Same Piece of Information

If you want to indicate that you have obtained the same information from several different sources, list the last names of the authors in the citation, each followed by the relevant page number and separated by semicolons:

> Several studies have proven that child abuse is a cycle with violence passing from parents to children, who in turn abuse as parents (Smith 19; Clay 89; Misho 245).

Classic Novels

If you cite a famous literary work that is available in several versions or editions, it is helpful to add the chapter number after the page reference to help readers find the quotation in their edition of the text: (Bronte 47; ch. 6).

Verse Dramas/Plays

Instead of citing page numbers for plays, give the name of the play in your sentence, and then cite the act, scene, and line numbers, separated by periods in the parenthetical citation. Do not use Roman numerals.

> In William Shakespeare's famous play *Hamlet,* the main character, Prince Hamlet, says in apology for his somewhat-accidental murder of Polonius, "Sir, in my heart there was a kind of fighting / That would not let me sleep" (5.2.4–5).

Poetry

If you use the name of the poet in your introductory sentence, then in the citation, list the line number (or numbers):

> In T.S. Eliot's poem "The Lovesong of J. Alfred Prufrock," the opening seems like an invitation: "Let us go then, you and I" (1).

If you do not mention the author in your introductory sentence, then cite the author's last name and the line number(s) in your citation:

> The narrator in the poem says, "Let us go then, you and I" (Eliot 1).

Indirect Citations

If you use a quotation that originally came from another source (if you quote someone quoting someone else), then use the abbreviation "qtd. in" to illustrate that it is an indirect quote. Use the full name of the person you are quoting in the body of the sentence before the quote and then use the name of the author of the source you are using in the parenthetical citation, preceded by "qtd. in":

> Austin Levors argues that "we are all accountable for the future of our next generation" (qtd. in Blanchard 564).

Note: In the Works Cited page, this entry will be listed alphabetically under the name of Blanchard along with the name of his book or article and the publishing information. The purpose of a Works Cited list is to record sources *you* used, not the sources your sources used.

Reference Entry from a Dictionary or Encyclopedia

If the entry you are referencing does not credit a specific author, then use the title of the entry in your citation:

> Bioluminescence is light produced by a chemical reaction within an organism ("Bioluminescence" 203).

Note: The Works Cited entry will be alphabetized under "Bioluminescence," followed by the name of the encyclopedia or dictionary with publication information.

Sacred/Religious Texts

Since there are different versions and translations of most religious texts, you will need to identify which version you have used in your Works Cited list. In general, though, it is not mandatory to give the version of the religious text you have used in your parenthetical citation; instead, use the book, verse, and line numbers. For instance, for a quotation from the Bible, you could simply put the chapter and verse numbers: (Revelation 10.14). It is also acceptable to include an abbreviated code for the version of the Bible you are citing, for instance (KJV, Genesis 1.1–5). "KJV" stands for King James Version. See the MLA website for abbreviations of other Bible versions. Again, be sure to cite all publishing information for the religious text version you used in your Works Cited list.

Electronic Sources

Electronic sources from databases, CD-ROMs, or the Internet must be cited in your paper. Give the author's name(s) if provided; if not, give the title of the material. If the electronic source is paginated, then provide a page number.

Author Named in Source

For electronic sources, if the work has an author and uses page numbers, then use the standard rules for parenthetical citations outlined above:

> Women often forget to take care of themselves when they are pregnant (Anstor C1).

Author Not Named in Source

If the work has no author but does have a title and page numbers, then use a shortened version of the title in the citation:

> People just have a natural sense of what part of the country they should live in for their tastes ("Knowing Where" 38).

Page Numbers Not Included in Source

If the source does not include page numbers but does use paragraph numbers, include the relevant paragraph number(s) in your parenthetical citation. If there are no page or paragraph numbers, just use the author's name in the citation.

> People just have a natural sense of what part of the country they should live in for their tastes ("Knowing Where" par. 5).

No Information Available

If there is no article name, no author, no page numbers or other information and you are using just a fact or statistic from a Web site, then include the address of the Web site in your parenthetical citation:

> It is highly likely that children who were abused by their parents may abuse their own children as well, a "vicious cycle" (www.abuse.com).

Remember, all information you use from any source must be documented so that you avoid plagiarizing and provide your readers with the information necessary to view your sources. Electronic sources are the most commonly plagiarized, often unintentionally, due to a lack of knowledge about how to cite them accurately.

COMPILING A WORKS CITED LIST

Every work or idea that you cite parenthetically in your paper must also be included in the Works Cited section at the end of your paper. Here are some guidelines for formatting your Works Cited page using the MLA format.

Formatting Your Works Cited Page

1. Start your list on a new page at the end of your paper, with the title Works Cited centered one inch below the top of the page (but be sure to have your last name and the page number in the right-hand corner as in the other pages of your paper). Do not bold the Works Cited title, put it in quotation marks, or make it a larger font.

2. Double space between the title and the first entry and between and within all subsequent entries.

3. Align the first line of each entry flush with the left margin of the page, and indent each subsequent line of the entry five spaces (one tab) from the margin (sometimes called the "hanging indent format"). Do not number the entries.

4. Alphabetize the Works Cited list by authors' last names. If a work has a corporate or group author, list it alphabetically by the first word of the name of the organization. If a work does not have an author, alphabetize by the first word of the title (but ignore "A," "An," or "The").

5. If you have two or more works by the same author, then use three hyphens "---." in place of the author's name in the second and subsequent entries by the same author.

6. If a work has an editor or translator, be sure to include that information. If a work has a named author, list that name first, then the title, followed by either the abbreviation "Ed." for editor, or "Trans." for translator and then that person's first and last name, followed by a period.

> Allende, Isabel. *Paula*. Trans. Margaret Sayers Peden. Print.

If there is no author, list the name of the editor or translator first, followed by either the abbreviation "ed." or "trans." then the title and the publication information:

> Wafer, Harold, trans. *Gilgamesh*. Weston: Weston, 1969. Print.

Format for the Most Common Works Cited Entries

For source types not included here, check the *MLA Handbook*, MLA Web site, or a composition handbook with a comprehensive MLA section.

Print Sources

Print sources such as books, magazines, journals, and newspapers usually provide thorough publication information. Be sure to follow the guidelines listed below for Works Cited entries for print sources.

Books   There are six basic units of information to include for book entries:

- Names of author(s)
- Book title
- City of publication
- Publisher
- Year of publication
- Medium of publication

1. **Names of author(s):** Provide the author's full name, last name first, followed by a comma, and then the first name (followed by middle initial or name if provided). If there are two or three authors, list all of them, in the same order they appear in the source. For all authors except the first one, write their names in the usual first and last name order. Use a comma and the word "and" between the names of authors. If there are four or more authors, list the first one, last name first, and then use "et al." to identify the other authors. Follow the name of the author(s) with a period and one space.

2. **Title of book:** Provide the complete title, including the subtitle if there is one. Separate the title and subtitle with a colon and a space. Put the title in italics. Capitalize the first, last, and all principal words of the title. Follow the title with a period and one space.

3. **City of publication:** Provide the name of the city of publication (usually found on the title page or copyright page). If more than one city is listed, use the first one listed. For cities outside of the United States that are not well known, add the abbreviation for the country or province. Follow the city of publication with a colon and a space.

4. **Name of publisher:** Provide the name of the publishing company. Shorten the names of publishers by deleting "A," "An," or "The" at the beginning or "Co.," "Inc.," "Pubishers," "Press," "Ltd.," or "Books" at the end. For university presses, change the "University" to "U" and the "Press" to "P": e.g., Harvard UP or U of Oregon P. Use shortened titles for major publishers—for instance, use "Prentice" for "Prentice Hall." Follow the name of the publisher with a comma and a space.

5. **Year of publication:** Give the year of publication. If several years are listed, provide the most recent. If no publishing year is listed, then use the most recent copyright listed. End with a period after the year.

6. **Medium of publication:** Add the medium of publication at the end of the entry: Print.

Sample Entries

Book by one author:

> Sedaris, David. *Dress Your Family in Corduroy and Denim*. New York: Little, 2004. Print.

Book by two or three authors: Reverse the name of the first author only:

> McClendon, Ruth, and Leslie Kadis. *Reconciling Relationships and Preserving the Family Business: Tools for Success*. New York: Haworth, 2004. Print.

Book by four or more authors: Name only the first author listed and then add "et al." (for "and others") or you may choose to list all the authors in the order they appear in the original source:

> Durrant, Sam, et al. *Postcolonial Narrative and the Work of Mourning*. Albany: State U of New York P, 2004. Print.

Book with no author (alphabetize by the work's title):

> *New York Public Library American History Desk Reference*. New York: Macmillan, 1997. Print.

Two or more works by the same author: If you have two or more works by the same author, use ---. for the author's name for the second book. Alphabetize by the title, for example:

> García Márquez, Gabriel. *Chronicle of a Death Foretold*. Trans. Gregory Rabassa. New York: Avon, 1970. Print.
>
> ---. *One Hundred Years of Solitude*. Trans. Gregory Rabassa. New York: Ballantine, 1982. Print.

Articles from Scholarly Journals   Seven basic units of information are needed for journal articles:

- Names of the author(s)
- Title of the article
- Journal name
- Volume/issue number
- Year of publication
- Page number(s) of the article
- Medium of publication

1. **Names of the author(s):** Use the same guidelines for authors as specified in the section on books on p. 383.

2. **Title of article:** Provide the complete title of the article in quotation marks. Include the subtitle if there is one, separated from the main title by a colon and a space. Capitalize the first, last, and all principal words in the title. End the title with a period inside the quotation marks and one space after the last pair of quotation marks.

3. **Name of journal:** Give the full name of the journal, in italics. No punctuation follows (see next step).

4. **Volume (and issue) number:** Provide the volume number and, if there is one, the issue number (separated by a period): e.g., 21.7. No punctuation follows (see next step). Do not include volume and issue numbers for magazines and newspapers.

5. **Year of publication:** Put the year of publication in parentheses after the issue number. Follow the last parenthesis with a colon.

6. **Page numbers:** Provide the page numbers of the article from the journal (beginning and ending pages). End the entry with a period.

7. **Medium of publication:** Add the medium of publication at the end of each entry: Print.

   Sample Entry

   > Vasishth, Neal. "The Trouble with Pedagogy." *Pedagogical News* 28.6 (2005): 32-46. Print.

Magazine Articles   Six basic units of information are needed for magazine articles:

- Names of the author(s)
- Title of the article
- Magazine name
- Day, month, and year of publication
- Page number(s) of the article
- Medium of publication

1. **Names of the author(s):** Use the same guidelines for authors as specified in the section on books on p. 383.

2. **Title of article:** Use the same guidelines as those for the titles of scholarly journal articles above.

3. **Name of magazine:** Give the full name of the magazine, in italics. No punctuation follows (see next step).

4. **Publication date:** Provide the day first (if the magazine you are citing is published more frequently than once a month). Then provide the month and year (no punctuation between them). Months are abbreviated. Put a colon after the date. 22 Feb. 2004:

5. **Page numbers:** Provide the page numbers of the article from the magazine (beginning and ending pages). End the entry with a period.

6. **Medium of publication:** To the end of each entry, add the medium of publication: Print.

Sample Entry

Haygood, Rachel. "The Complexities of Shadow." *Speed Online* 14 Apr. 2005: 16-25. Print.

Articles, Editorials, and Letters from Newspapers   Six basic units of information are needed for newspaper articles:

- Names of author(s)
- Title of the article
- Newspaper name
- Day, month, and year of publication
- Section letter or number and page number(s) of the article
- Medium of publication

1. **Names of author(s):** Use the same guidelines for authors as specified in the section on books on p. 383.

2. **Title of article:** Use the same guidelines as those for titles of scholarly journal articles on page 385.

3. **Name of newspaper:** Give the full name of the newspaper, in italics. No punctuation follows (see next step).

4. **Day, month, and year of publication:** Provide the day first, then the month and year (no punctuation between them). Abbreviate all months except May, June, and July. Follow the date with a colon: 22 Feb. 2004:

5. **Page number(s):** Provide the section letter (such as A or F) and the page number(s) of the article from the newspaper (beginning and ending pages). End the entry with a period.

6. **Medium of publication:** To the end of each entry add the medium of publication: Print.

Sample Entry

> Haygood, Rachel. "The Complexities of Shadow." *The Monrovia
> Times* 14 Apr. 2005: A8. Print.

Note: If the entry from the newspaper is an editorial, type the word
"Editorial" after the name of the article, followed by a period and a
space. If it is a letter to the editor, type the word "Letter" after the
author's name, followed by a period and a space.

Selection from an Anthology   A selection from an anthology (a poem,
story, play, essay, or article) must include the original work's author and title
as well as the name of the anthology and the editor(s) of that anthology.
Here is the information needed in the order it should appear:

1. **Names of the author(s):** Use the same guidelines for authors as specified in the section on books on p. 383.

2. **Title of the selection:** Give the name of the selection in quotation
   marks, followed by a period (period goes inside the quotation marks)
   and a space.

3. **Title of the anthology:** Give the name of the anthology, italicized and
   followed by a period and a space.

4. **Names of the editors:** Provide the name of the editor or editors, preceded by "Ed." for one editor or "Eds." for more than one. Use the regular order for names: first and then last name. Follow with a period and a
   space.

5. **City of publication:** Provide the city of publication, followed by a
   colon and a space.

6. **Name of publisher:** Provide the name of the publisher, followed by a
   comma and a space.

7. **Year of publication:** Give the year of publication, followed by a period
   and a space.

8. **Page numbers:** Give the page numbers for the selection, followed by a
   period.

9. **Medium of publication:** To the end of each entry add the medium of
   publication: Print.

Sample Entry

> Dillon, Kim Jenice. "A Thin Neck to Snap." *Sisterfire: Black
> Womanist Fiction and Poetry.* Ed. Charlotte Watson Sherman.
> New York: Harper, 1994. 11-31. Print.

Articles in Reference Books   If the author's name is given, provide that first, then the title of the article in quotation marks, the title of the work it came from (in italics), the name of the editor(s) (preceded by Ed. or Eds.), the number of volumes, and the publication information:

> Scott, Loretta. "George Washington." *Encyclopedia of Presidents*. Ed. Campbell Kingley. 2 vols. New York: Cirius, 2005. Print.

Note: Do not include page numbers.

If the author is not named, begin the entry with the article title.

> "George Washington." *Encyclopedia of Presidents*. Ed. Campbell Kingley. 2 vols. New York: Cirius, 2005. Print.

Citing an Introduction, Foreword, Preface, or Afterword   If you cite one of these elements in your paper, start with the name of the person who wrote the part you are citing (last name first). This might be the author of the whole work, or a different author who wrote the Introduction or Foreword. Then give the name of the part (e.g., Foreword), followed by a period. Next provide the name of the book (followed by a period), the author of the book (first name first), the publishing information, and the page numbers:

Sample Entry

> Hoene, Jennifer. Introduction. *The Literary Nature of Philosophy*. Sandra Johanson. Boston: New World, 2005. v–xii. Print.

Media Sources

You have to cite information for media the same way as you do for print and electronic sources.

Paintings, Sculptures, or Photographs   State the artist's name first, putting the title of the work in italics. Follow with the year of composition and the medium of composition, such as Photograph or Watercolor. If it belongs to a museum or gallery, list the name and the city:

> Gericault, Theodore. *Raft of the Medusa*. 1819. Oil on Canvas. Musée de Louvre, Paris.

Films   Begin with the title of the film, italicized and followed by a period; then give the name of the director (followed by a period), the name of the distributor (followed by a comma), and the year of release (followed by a period). Add the medium of publication: Film.

> *Blade Runner*. Dir. Ridley Scott. Warner, 1991. Film.

Interviews   If you conduct an interview, specify whether it was an in-person or telephone interview and the date the interview took place:

> Rowling, J.K. Personal interview. 25 June 2005.

If it is a *published interview* conducted by someone else, give the name of the interviewee, the name of the interviewer, the date of the interview, and any other pertinent information (e.g., the call letters of the radio or television station the interview was originally broadcast on or the print publication it appeared in), followed by the medium of publication.

> Wiesel, Elie. Interview with Ted Koppel. *Nightline*. ABC. WABC, New York, 18 Apr. 2002. Television.

Electronic Sources

Three different kinds of electronic sources are databases supplied on CD-ROM or DVD disc, databases accessed online, and websites accessed through search engines like Google. The three sections below discuss each one. When the work you are using is an article or other piece from an online magazine, newspaper, or scholarly article, first refer to the entries for these sources when they appear in print (pages 385–387) for the basic information to include.

CD-ROM and DVD Databases   When citing CD-ROM or DVD databases that are accessible through a computer, be sure to list the author's name, if available; the title of the material; the medium of publication (e.g., CD-ROM); the vendor's name; and the date of electronic publication.

> *All Movie Guide*. CD-ROM. Ottawa: Corel, 1996.

> Anstor, Marylee. "Nutrition for Pregant Women." *New York Times* 12 Apr. 1994, late ed.: C1. *New York Times Ondisc*. CD-ROM. UMI-ProQuest. Oct. 1994.

If a CD-ROM is accessed through a periodically published database such as ProQuest, then be sure to include the name of the author, title of the material (in quotation marks), name of the print periodical the material originally appeared in (if applicable), date the material was originally published (if available), page number(s) of the original print article (if available), name of the CD-ROM, publication medium (CD-ROM), name of the database used to access the material, and electronic publication date:

> Levens, Elaine. "Telling the Stories." *Storytellers Inc*. 15 Apr. 2004: 22–26. *Story Magazines Ondisc*. CD-ROM. GRCC-Proquest. Nov. 2005.

Online Databases   When you cite sources from online databases, include as many of the following elements as possible:

1. **Names of author(s):** If the name of the author (or authors) is provided, start the citation with it, last name first.

2. **Name of article or entry:** Provide the title of the piece. Also, if no author is listed for an article, alphabetize the entry by the material's title.

3. **Name of source:** Include the name of the source—magazine, newspaper, etc. Next list the date the material was first published in print using the format day month year.

4. **Page numbers:** If the page numbers of the source are given, place them after the source name and a colon. If pages are all in one sequence of numbers, give them all: for example, 1–10. If page numbers aren't in sequence, give the first page number followed by a plus sign. No space comes between the two: 2+. If no page numbers are listed, use the abbreviation *n. pag.*

5. **Name of database and medium of publication:** Provide the name of the database in italics. Then list the medium of publication: Web.

6. **Date the source was accessed:** Include the date you accessed the source, for example 7 Dec. 2008. Abbreviate the names of all months except May, June, and July.

   Sample Entry

   > Fargo, Emmanuel. "Why Settle for Second Best?" *Education Review*
   > Mar. 2005: n. pag. *Academic Search Elite.* CD-ROM. Web. 20
   > May 2006.

Internet: Source from a Web Site   Give as much information as necessary to direct the reader to the original online source. Include all of the following information that is available:

1. **Names of the author(s):** If there is an author credited (or authors) start the citation with it, last name first.

2. **Title of the article:** Provide the full title. If there is no author listed for the material, alphabetize the Works Cited entry under this title.

3. **Name of Web site:** Provide the name of the Web site, in italics, if it is different from the title of the article.

4. **Version or edition number:** If such a number is given, provide it: Rev. ed., for instance, means "revised edition."

5. **Publisher or sponsor of the Web site:** If not given, use the abbreviation n.p. for "no publisher."

6. **Date of publication:** If not given, use the abbreviation n.d. for "no date."

7. **Medium of publication:** Web.

8. **Date of access:** Give the date you accessed the site. Use the day month year format.

9. **URL:** Only provide the URL for sources that readers won't be able to find using the information provided in the citation. For example, if you type the name of the Web site you are citing in the Google search box, you can go to that site, then use the site search feature to find the particular page you are citing. If you can find the source using a method like this, you don't need to include the URL in your citation.

Sample Entry

> Noveck, Jocelyn. "Madonna: An unlikely inspiration for 50-plus set."
> *AP News*. Associated Press, 16 Aug. 2008. Web. 18 Aug. 2008.

Again, many professional Web sites and nonprofessional, private Web sites do not provide all the information listed above. The key is to include as many of the nine elements as possible in the same order as they are listed. For complicated or difficult-to-access online sources, go to www.mla.org for more information on citing online and Internet-based sources.

ENDNOTES

In general in MLA format, it is best to avoid adding notes with supplementary information in your paper: If it's worth saying, why not put it in the body of your paper? However, you can add endnotes in MLA format (see "Content Notes" in the current edition of the *MLA Handbook* for more details). When you have additional comments or information that you want to include in your paper, but they might interrupt the flow of your ideas, include them in endnotes that have been numbered consecutively throughout your paper. Put the number for the endnote in the body of your paper at the end of the phrase or sentence containing the information you will elaborate upon in the endnote. Place the number after the punctuation mark and raise it slightly above the line, with no space before the number and no punctuation after it:

> Even before the fighting broke out, the war had started economically.[1]

Formatting Your Endnotes Page

At the end of your paper, begin a new page with the centered heading Notes (do not put the heading in quotation marks, underline it, or make the font bold or larger). The Notes page is double spaced like the rest of your paper.

For each note listed in your paper, list the number and add the note. For each note, indent five spaces from the left margin, raise the number of the note slightly above the line, leave one space, and then write the note. Any lines that carry over from the note should start at the left margin:

Notes

[1]For more details about the economic battles that were taking place at this time, see Colin Mather, *A Time of Unrest* (New York: Marigold, 2004) 64-98. Print.

For more details on using endnotes in MLA and sample Notes pages, go to www.mla.org or Section 6.5.1 in the *MLA Handbook* (6th ed.).

SAMPLE DOCUMENTED STUDENT PAPER

Bayne 1

Trina Bayne

Professor Reynolds

English 101

5 May 2008

Plagiarism: The Cost of Too Much Information and Not Enough

Do you know exactly what plagiarism is? Many students do not. Colleges agree that plagiarism, specifically using someone else's words, ideas, or original work as if they were one's own without giving proper credit, is a problem that has only gotten worse due to the ease of finding sources and pre-written term papers on the Internet. Unfortunately, too many students are not given the support they need to know what plagiarism is in the first place and how to avoid it. Colleges and universities should create specialized orientations as well as ongoing workshops to inform students of the causes and effects of plagiarism and to instruct them in the correct ways to use and document sources in their essays and other written and oral work.

Bayne 2

Numerous studies, as well as the experience of professors in the classroom, have indicated that plagiarism is on the rise. Several forms of plagiarism have been growing due to the ease of finding information on the Internet. Indeed, "Technology has made it easier for students to cheat . . . and makes the likelihood of getting caught much lower . . . professors are less likely to be able to locate the incriminating needle in the vastness of the Web's haystack" (Lee 1). Some of the types of plagiarism that students have been committing include using part or all of essays and term papers posted on free essay sites including "freeessays.com" and "cheaterhouse.com," using facts and details found through key word searches and not citing the original source, cutting and pasting passages or entire articles from Internet sources without providing citations or using quotation marks for direct quotes, re-wording quotes using students' own words, claiming the ideas as their own, and not giving the original sources credit. An article titled "Faculty Perceptions of Plagiarism" points out that the rise of Internet plagiarism has "brought these rising statistics to the forefront: 10% of students admitted to engaging in such behavior in 1999, rising to 40% in a 2001 survey in which the majority of students (68%) suggest[ed] this was not a serious issue" (Liddell and Fong 1). This increase shows that students have begun to plagiarize more and more and that their attitudes about plagiarism have become more casual.

Many students do not realize that they have committed plagiarism because they do not know exactly what it is. In general, most students realize that when they copy a passage, word for word, they are plagiarizing. In an article called "Plagiarism: Do Students Know What It Is?" professors conducted a survey asking students questions

Bayne 3

related to different types of plagiarism to see what students believed constituted cheating:

> The results indicate that students know that the act of using someone else's words as if they were their own does indeed constitute plagiarism. Students at all levels gave similar answers. However, students were less certain about the concept of using someone else's ideas, with 40% of students not acknowledging that this was plagiarism. (Dawson and Overfield 2)

Somehow, students have gotten the idea that as long as they are not using an author's exact words, then it is not cheating to use his or her ideas. In addition, "Similar uncertainty was shown with regard to the concept of using someone else's results as their own and of sharing work with someone else and pooling ideas. Getting ideas from a textbook was not seen as plagiarism" (2). Based on this study, students tend to think that as long as they are not lifting exact words, then they are not cheating using someone else's ideas or results.

Students who are not truly aware of what constitutes plagiarism need more guidance; however, intentional plagiarism is a different story. Once all students have been informed and have clear information about the different forms of plagiarism and how to avoid it, then colleges have a right to impose harsh punishments on those who plagiarize. Some people would argue that it is a student's responsibility to research and know the rules of plagiarism and how to cite sources correctly, but isn't it a college's job to inform students and teach them the rules in the first place?

Colleges and universities need to offer initial orientations to new students that go over the definitions of plagiarism and tell them explicitly how to avoid it by correctly giving credit to any sources or

Bayne 4

ideas they use. Then, colleges should offer ongoing workshops on documentation and avoiding plagiarism. Such workshops could be offered regularly in on-campus tutoring or writing centers. Predictably, some people will argue that the costs for colleges of offering such orientations and ongoing workshops is a concern. However, the need to get to students early in their college career and then reinforce the rules is evident: A 1998 study from *Who's Who Among American High School Students* found that "80 percent of college-bound students admitted to cheating on their schoolwork. Alarmingly the percentage of students actually *caught* cheating is a mere 5 percent, the study showed" (Lee 1). Students are leaving high school knowing they have cheated and not getting the guidance and rules they need to avoid doing so.

Once colleges have taken these relatively inexpensive steps to help students avoid plagiarism, the benefits will far outweigh the costs of losing students through disciplinary actions and the damage caused to colleges' reputations. Besides the orientations and work-shops, colleges will also need to invest in software that helps teach-ers spot cases of plagiarism. A number of software programs and Internet antiplagiarism sites are available to help colleges and uni-versities catch students who intentionally commit plagiarism. John Barrie, the creator of Turnitin, a program that matches student papers suspected of containing plagiarized passages or ideas with the passages or articles they have been plagiarized from, says, "What you really have here are students using the Internet like a 4.5 billion-page cut-and-paste encyclopedia" (qtd. in Lee 1). Lee responds to Barrie's insights by adding, "while he [Barrie] believes the Internet has exacerbated the problem, he also believes the Internet will solve

it, through programs such as Turnitin, which he invented in 1996"
(1). Therefore, colleges and universities will be able to take back control over this rampant problem through the very means that caused
its increase in the first place.

    The final benefit that colleges and universities will gain from
taking a proactive approach to educating students about plagiarism
and its many forms and educating them about how to avoid it will be
to their integrity as institutions. Investing the money it would take
to inform students and to go after those who blatantly break the
rules will result in the reinstatement of their reputations as insti-
tutes of higher learning and places of integrity. Matthew S. Willen
writes about the value of educating students about a moral approach
to writing and documentation and avoiding plagiarism. In his article,
"Reflections on the Cultural Climate of Plagiarism," he points out
that colleges must take an active role in creating a climate that belit-
tles the value of plagiarism. He encourages colleges to change the
way they present writing to their students by showing them how to
"value the process of writing--which includes invention, drafting, collaboration, revising, and editing--and not simply the final product as
what is essential to their learning" (1). Students need to value what
they can gain by going through all the stages of the writing process
to produce thoughtful, well-crafted papers based on their own ideas
and research. Furthermore, he emphasizes,

        We need to stress that writing doesn't simply document what
        they know on a topic; its processes enable comprehension of
        the topic. From a pedagogical perspective, the real crime of
        plagiarism is less that it is dishonest than that it precludes
        learning. (1)

Bayne 6

More than anything, as the old cliché goes, cheating only cheats the cheater. Actually, it hurts the colleges too: their reputations and their ability to offer students a chance to really learn for themselves.

Plagiarism is certainly an escalating problem at colleges and universities nationwide. Many students are not fully aware of the definitions of plagiarism and/or have lost sight of how serious an offense it is. Many do not know that plagiarizing results in loss of learning. Colleges and universities must choose to take a proactive approach to tackling this problem though educating students about it and cracking down on those who intentionally choose to cheat. Both the students and the colleges themselves will reap the benefits of a plagiarism-free learning experience.

Bayne 7

Works Cited

Dawson, Maureen M., and Joyce A. Overfield. "Plagiarism: Do

    Students Know What It Is?" *Bioscience Education Journal* 8.1

    (2006): n. pag. Web. 31 July 2008.

Lee, Grace. "Plagiarism 101." *ReadMe.* Dept. of Journalism, New

    York U, 28 Apr. 2004. Web. 28 July 2008.

Liddell, Jean, and Valerie Fong. "Faculty Perceptions of Plagiarism."

    The Journal of College and Character. NASPA, Florida State

    U, 2007. Web. 28 July 2008.

Willen, Mathew S. "Reflections on the Cultural Climate of

    Plagiarism." *Liberal Education* 90.4 (2004): n. pag. Association

    of American Colleges and Universities. Web. 26 July 2008.

Analyzing Visuals

Photo by Tim Schultz.

THINKING CRITICALLY

Look at the picture above. Then answer the questions that follow.

1. What is going on in this picture?

_____

_____

2. What are some possible messages the photograph conveys?

_____

3. What clues helped you to read these messages?

_____

4. What is your intellectual response to this photograph?

_____

5. What is your emotional response (if any)?

VISUAL COMMUNICATION AND CRITICAL THINKING

Visuals are an essential part of human communication. They are particularly important now when so many forms of visual communication abound in American culture: art, TV, movies, the Internet, advertising, and even camera phones. It is easy to overlook the importance of applying your critical thinking and analysis skills to visuals, but sometimes a visual can deliver a more effective argument or evoke a more immediate emotional response than a sentence or essay, and in a shorter amount of time. Like words, visuals represent ideas and arguments that can be thoughtful and truthful, misleading, or even deceitful. Visuals often have a clearly intended thesis, or argument, that the creator wants the viewer to infer. Artists, photographers, and advertisers employ particular visual approaches and include specific visual clues to help impart their intended messages. Therefore, reading and writing about visuals requires you to engage the same critical thinking and analysis skills you engage in writing about other authors' ideas and arguments.

Visuals *imply* the messages their creators intend, and viewers of the images *infer* these meanings from the visuals.

Visual (and sender)	**Viewer (receiver)**
↕	↕
Implies a message	*Infers* a message (based on clues)

Applying Critical Thinking

PURPOSE	IDEAS	SUPPORT	ASSUMPTIONS BIASES	CONCLUSIONS	POINT OF VIEW	ANALYSIS

Imply/implication: To imply means to hint that something is so, to say it indirectly. When artists imply what they want to say in works of art, they make choices about what they will and will not include in order to convey their message. They might present an image from an unusual angle, place contrasting images together, omit parts of an object, or add elements you would not expect to see.

Inference: To infer information from a visual involves tapping into your ability to "read between the lines" and figure out what an artist means based on clues in his or her work of art. When you are thinking critically about visuals, you need to look for clues that indicate the point the artist, photographer, or painter is making.

Use your **analysis** skills to break down all parts of the image and evaluate implications and inferences.

Visuals invite a dialogue between themselves and the viewer. An image sends a message, but the viewer creates his or her own version of the message through an intellectual and emotional response to it. Viewers bring their own personal history, knowledge, and associations to the reading of visual clues just as they do to reading written text.

When you study visuals, you must study all the clues they present. Like words, visuals can have clear **denotative,** or exact, meanings, and they can have **connotative,** or emotional, meanings and associations. You need to fill in the blanks, draw conclusions, and tap into your intellectual and emotional responses (if any) to the image. You must also study the form and conventions of the image and what choices of medium the artist has made in order to interpret its messages and implied arguments. Sometimes, you must even study what is left out and why.

THINKING AND WRITING CRITICALLY ABOUT VISUALS

There are many parallels between analyzing a visual and analyzing text:

1. Visuals have a message: a thesis or argument. They have a **purpose.**
2. Visuals express a particular **point of view** and can display the **biases** of the artist or creator.
3. Visuals include clues (or details) related to their main point and are designed to impart those clues as effectively as possible.
4. Visuals can appeal both to the viewer's intellect and emotions.
5. Visuals may need to be viewed in their historical or cultural context in order to be fully understood. You must **analyze** their parts.

The ideas of logos and pathos apply to visual arguments, just as they do to arguments made in writing. **Logos** is an appeal to reasoning and logic. For instance, most academic writing appeals to logos. Many photographs, especially documentary or news photographs, also appeal to logos. **Pathos** is an appeal to emotion. Advertisements are notorious for using visuals to appeal to our emotions in order to sell products.

Being a Visual Detective: Asking Questions

Much of the work of a good visual is done in a way that is subtle. Therefore, be sure to ask specific questions when you are analyzing visuals. Turn on your visual detective skills, and don't just look at images passively. Ask questions as you view them: *"What?" "How?" "Why?" "Who?" "When?" "Where?" "So what?"* Also, pay attention to every detail: size, color, shape, medium, approach, content, background, and historical or cultural hints within the image.

Activity 20-1   Applying Questions to an Image

Directions: *Look at the photo and answer the questions that follow. If needed, refer to the information provided earlier in this chapter for help.*

Photo by Tim Schultz.

1.   Does this photograph appeal more to your sense of logos (logic), pathos (emotion), or both? Answer and explain why:

_____

_____

2. Answer briefly (in a few words or a short sentence) each of the analytical detective questions for this photograph: *What* is this a picture of? *How* is the image organized? *Why* did the photographer arrange the picture this way? *Who* is/are the subject(s) of the picture, and who is the intended audience? *When* was this picture taken (present time, past), and what clues tell you this? *Where* was this picture taken (in general), and how do you know? *So what* is the message communicated by this image?

_____

_____

_____

3. How do the color, shapes, and background of this photograph add to its message?

_____

_____

4. What are the cultural or historical contexts of this photograph, and how do they contribute to the message this image communicates?

_____

_____

TYPES OF VISUALS

Before you can become good at critically analyzing visuals, you have to become familiar with the most common types of visuals. This chapter will focus on photos, film, TV, advertising, drawings, pictures, and sculpture, because these forms, like essays, have ideas and arguments, and they can be studied for message and technique, just like good expository writing.

Photographs

Photographs are a powerful form of visual communication. In many ways, they are like paragraphs: They pack a big message into a small space and develop the message through details and structure. It is possible to have multiple reactions to and interpretations of photographs, since a dialogue is created between them and you the viewer. It is important to keep in mind that the photographer, like a writer, determines what information you receive. He or she makes decisions about what to include and what not to include in a photograph. You are viewing an image that has been created to make a specific point or to evoke a particular emotional response. Also, digital editing and manipulation can make photographs show whatever photographers want them to. They can easily be made to lie, although we often assume they show factual truth.

Thinking Critically about Photographs

A photograph should be analyzed for its composition (the arrangement of visual elements and the decisions made in that process) and content (what's in it and the meaning evoked by it). The historical and social context of a photograph should also be carefully examined. There are specific elements of photographs you should look at and terms you should be familiar with that are used for analyzing photographs and the techniques photographers use to create their message.

Terms, Elements, and Message

Photographs convey messages and emotions through their images. The following terms and elements conventionally are used to talk about the medium of photography. Some terms deal with the composition of a photograph, and some terms deal with specific visual effects in the overall picture. Finally, the last set of terms deal with the thematic elements of a photograph—the messages.

Composition terms

Composition: The overall arrangements of all of the elements that make up the entire image

Central focus: The object or objects that are most prominent and clearly in focus

Subject: The main person or object in the photograph

Setting: The physical surroundings and background of the picture

Background: The background of the photograph may or may not be in focus

Angle: The point or angle from which the photographer took the picture, the visual point of view

Visual elements

Focus: Some objects in an image may be sharp and clear and some may be less sharp and clear, or out of focus.

Light/lighting: Some objects may be brighter than others. Some may be darker; some may be highlighted. Is the light natural or artificial? Is the light direct, harsh, or soft?

Shape: There are two types of shape to consider—the shape of the whole photograph (such as rectangular, square) and the shapes within the composition.

Texture: The feel of the paper the photograph is printed on or the appearance of texture of the image.

Theme/message terms

Theme: The main idea of a photograph

Intention: What the photographer intends to convey with this image

Audience: The target audience for the image

Social and historical context: The social and/or historical background or context for the image

Questions to Ask

When you look at a photograph, ask yourself the questions listed here. Notice that they relate directly to the terms and elements described above and ask you to consider the photographer's intentions in composing the image, the message he or she wants to convey.

1. What is my overall reaction to this image?

2. Is the photographer appealing to logos (logic), pathos (emotion), or both?

3. Is there a particular social or historical context for this picture? If so, what effect does that have on my reaction to or understanding of the message(s)?

4. Does there seem to be an intended audience for this photo or does it appeal to a broad audience?

5. Have I considered the composition elements of the photo and what effect they have on my reading of this picture?

6. Have I considered the visual effects such as lighting, setting, and focus and what effects those elements have on my reading of this picture?

7. What thesis or argument is conveyed through the image?

Activity 20-2 Analyzing a Photograph

Directions: *Look at the photograph on page 406. Then answer the questions that follow.*

Haircut. Photo by Gary Oliveira, 2006.

1. What is the theme (thesis) of this photograph? Are there any social messages? Personal messages? _____

   _____

2. What is the photographer's intention in using this image? Does he have a specific audience in mind? _____

   _____

3. Choose three of the terms from Terms, Elements, and Message above, and describe how they are used in this photograph and what effect they have on the overall message it conveys. _____

   _____

Activity 20-3   Analyzing and Writing about Photographs

Photo by Patrick Navin.

Directions: *On a separate sheet of paper, write a paragraph that provides a detailed, objective description of the photo above. Think of it as a verbal sketch, as though you were describing the photo for someone who could not see it. Summarize and describe the scene and the impression that the photograph presents. Then answer the questions that follow.*

1.   What is the theme, or controlling idea, in this picture?

   _____

   _____

2. What associations or concepts come to mind when looking at this picture?

_____

_____

3. What composition choices did the photographer make, and what visual elements did he include that influence the overall effect of this photograph? Refer to Terms, Elements, and Messages on page 404 for help in analyzing form and techniques. Be specific.

_____

_____

4. What social message or argument is suggested by this photograph?

_____

_____

5. What details helped you draw these conclusions?

_____

_____

6. Write a paragraph that develops the theme evoked by the picture but using words and written description instead. Make sure that your topic sentence states the same kind of message or point that the picture communicates.

_____

_____

_____

Activity 20-4   Themed Writing about Visuals

Directions: *Each of the photographs on p. 409 captures a moment in childhood. On a separate sheet of paper, write a brief description of these two photographs, which include what they capture about being young and how they accomplish exploring this theme visually. Afterwards, write about what childhood feelings and memories these photographs bring up for you.*

Photo by Patrick Navin.

Photo by Douglas Cole.

TV and Film

Television shows and films are complex visuals. You have to engage your critical thinking skills in order to move from being a *passive* watcher to an *active* "reader" if you want to go beyond just enjoying them to understanding the messages they convey and the techniques used to impart those messages. Television shows and films communicate important social messages and serve as "mirrors" of our society; whether in the form of documentaries, reality shows, or dramas, they reflect our values and who we are as a culture. Therefore, they should be read the same way you would read a story, article, or novel: with the intention of exploring the author's (the director's and producers') messages and techniques for delivering those messages.

Thinking Critically about Television and Film

How the camera records the scenes being acted out or happening in real life is an important part of understanding TV and films. As in photographs, the TV or movie camera limits what is shown in a particular scene. Directors intend to convey certain messages and try to evoke intellectual and emotional responses from their viewers by making decisions about what they will and will not show them. Be sure to question what you see on the screen, to think about what does not appear there, and to consider the effects on your intellectual and emotional response to the content. By looking at the techniques used and the point of view and style choices directors make, you'll get a more thorough understanding of the message being presented.

Terms, Elements, and Message

The media of TV and film use specific terms and techniques. Knowing them can help in your analysis of these types of visuals.

Composition terms

Mise-en-scene: Mise-en-scene is a French term used to describe what is in each particular scene: the lighting, costumes, sets, shapes, and characters. It is the composition that fills the frame of the screen.

Camera shots/angles: The way in which cameras are positioned in a film or show creates the point of view, the perspective from which we see everything. Each choice made in a shot creates a particular point of view and attempts to evoke a particular response from the viewer. Here are a few of the most common types of shots used in filmmaking:

> **The closeup:** An up-close shot, for instance showing a character's face only
>
> **The extreme closeup:** For instance showing just the character's eyes

Medium shot: Showing most but not all of an object or character, full or long shot, for instance, an entire person or group of people in one shot

Pan shot (panning): The camera moves across a scene, for instance, panning across a scene from left to right.

Crane shot: A scene shot from high above, usually an outdoor scene. The camera is set on a mechanical crane and moved up and down as needed.

Tracking shot: The camera moves for an extended period of time, usually following a character in motion. The camera is set on a dolly or mounted on tracks.

Editing: What is cut out of a film or show, how the scenes are cut and switched, and the decisions made after filming to make the film more powerful or effective (similar to revising a written work).

Elements

Characters: The people, animals, or fictional beings featured in the story are the characters. Pay attention to how the characters are presented, their dialogue, and what they want. Are they likable? Why or why not?

Soundtrack: Pay attention to the music in the background. What effect does the music have on your response to the scene?

Theme/message

Theme/intention/social and historical context: The themes and messages of the film or show are usually related to society and to human nature. What does this film or show reflect about its culture and the values of that culture? What is the historical context, if any? Does the film or show argue for social change? How so?

Logos and pathos: Pay attention to both your intellectual and emotional reactions as the film or show progresses. How do these reactions affect your understanding of the messages?

Audience: The target audience for the show or film

Questions to Ask

Here are some general questions to ask yourself as you watch a television show or a film. Be sure to take notes as you watch any show or film that you will write about later:

1. When was the show or film made? Does it reflect current events and values, or is it set in the past in a specific historical period?

2. What does the title mean in relation to the plot, theme, or messages of the film or show?

3. Describe the basic plot or series of events. What happens?

4. Are there any major shifts in the plot or storyline? What are they, and what do they indicate?

5. Who do you think is the intended audience for this piece? What evidence or details lead you to believe this is the intended audience?

6. How does the film or show begin? Why does it begin this way?

7. What is your intellectual response to this film or show? Why? What is your emotional response to this film or show? Why?

8. How do the settings, props, costumes, and soundtrack affect the presentation of the images and plot?

9. How do the camera angles and visual framing of the scenes affect your response to the show or film?

10. What are the messages of the film?

Activity 20-5   Analyzing a Television Show

Directions: *Watch a TV show, and take notes as you watch. Then answer the following questions. Be sure to read through these questions before you watch so you can take notes that will help you answer them.*

1. What type of show did you watch (news show, reality show, game show, sit com, and so on)?

_____

_____

2. What happened in the show? Provide a brief summary:

_____

_____

_____

_____

3. What themes or social concepts were touched on or developed?

_____

_____

4. What techniques did the director/producers use that stood out?

_____

_____

_____

5. What effect did these choices and techniques have on your intellectual and emotional response to the show?

_____

_____

6. Now, review your notes, and write a one- or two-paragraph critique of the show that explores its strengths and weaknesses and describes the messages and the techniques used to convey those messages. Be sure to incorporate specific examples and details using your notes for details. ○

Activity 20-6   Analyzing a Film

Directions: *Watch a film, and take notes as you watch. Then answer the following questions. Be sure to read through these questions before you watch so you can take notes that will help you answer them.*

1. What type of film did you watch (documentary, comedy, romance, drama, and so on)? _____

2. What happened in the film (plot or event)? Provide a brief summary:

_____

_____

_____

_____

3. What themes or social concepts were touched on or developed?

_____

_____

4. What techniques did the director/producers use that stood out?

_____

_____

5. What effect did these choices and techniques have on your intellectual and emotional response to the film?

_____

_____

6. Now write a short essay about this film focusing on one of these two options:

   a. Write a critique of the film you watched analyzing the film's social messages. Use specific terms and examples of film techniques used by the director and discuss whether or not those techniques were successful in creating a good film or conveying the intended message(s).

   b. Choose a film that is based on a book you have read. Then compare the way you saw the characters and the story in your head as you read the book to the director's vision of the same story as imparted through the film. Critique choices made by the director to recreate the story on film. Were the choices effective? Why or why not? ●

Advertisements

Advertisements come in many forms: television commercials, billboards, magazine and newspapers ads, even ads at the movie theater. All advertisements have one basic thing in common: They attempt to sell a product to a carefully targeted audience. So analyzing an advertisement is similar to analyzing an author's argument in a piece of persuasive writing. You engage the same kind of analysis skills when you look at an advertisement in order to write about it. Advertisements use various visual details and techniques to generate conscious and sometimes subconscious (below the surface) responses from viewers. They can combine text and visuals or focus solely on visuals or text.

Thinking Critically About Advertisements

In order to think critically about advertisements and analyze both their messages and the techniques used to impart those messages, you need to pay close attention to details and ask questions about everything included in the ad, as well as to what is not included. All advertisements are trying to sell something, so most of them have a direct argument, but many also have implied arguments. Most advertisements use pathos, an appeal to your emotions, to sell their product. Most are selling a particular image and are intended for specific audiences. Notice the difference in approaches in advertisements and how they target audiences by gender, social class, economic status, race, age, region, and other factors depending on the product they are selling. When analyzing advertisements, be sure to check for errors in logic or implied messages that deceive people into thinking that the product might do more than it actually can, such as a new car adding to one's sex appeal.

Cross Reference
Review Chapter 15, Argument and Persuasion, for specific types of logical fallacies.

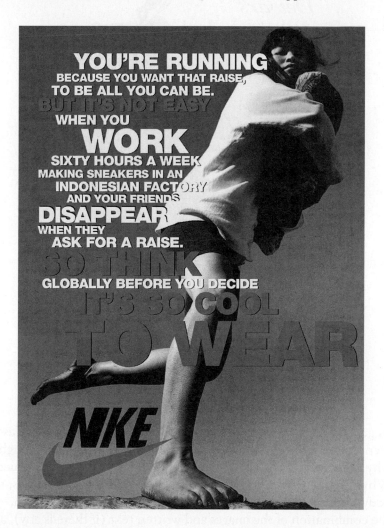

Questions to Ask

1. Who do you think the target audience is for the ad above? Men? Women? Older or younger people? Liberals or conservatives? Why?

2. Ads target particular age and economic groups. For instance, think about the differences in the commercials or print ads for the following types of alcoholic beverages: beer, malt liquor, wine, and Scotch. Who is the target audience for this ad for Dewar's "White Label" Scotch? Why did you come to this conclusion?

3. In general, what kind of ad would focus on a younger, middle class audience, one for beer or one for Scotch? If you said beer, you're right; but why? Are Scotch ads aimed at upper middle class, older white men? Why? Be sure to focus on the cultural context of ads, the details, the body language and facial expressions of people featured in them, the combination of the images and written text (if there is any), and the product placement in relation to the rest of the details.

Critical Thinking Questions to Ask About Ads

Here are some questions to ask when analyzing ads:

1. What product is this advertisement designed to sell?
2. Who is the target audience for the ad? How do you know?

3. What is the direct message of the ad?

4. What are the indirect or implied messages of the ad?

5. What are the visual details that serve as clues to the direct and/or implied messages in this ad? List them.

6. What intellectual response [logos] do you have to this ad?

7. What emotional response [pathos] do you have to this ad?

8. What arguments or appeals are embedded in this ad? Are there deceptive or illogical messages implied?

9. What cultural or historical ideas or norms does the ad tap into? Look especially for references to race, gender, age, economic class, and region.

10. In your opinion, is this an effective ad? Why or why not?

Activity 20-7   Analyzing an Advertisement

Directions: *Find an advertisement in a magazine or newspaper, and answer the Critical Thinking Questions above on a separate sheet of paper. Then, write a one- or two-paragraph analysis of the advertisement that first describes it in detail, then identifies its intended audience and direct and implied messages, and finally evaluates the overall effectiveness of its arguments for buying the product.*

Sculptures, Drawings, and Paintings

Sculptures, drawings, and paintings, like photographs, must be looked at both as a whole and in terms of their details. Look at the types of material (paper, canvas, clay, or stone) they are fashioned from, and look at what is used (ink, charcoal, pencil, paint, hammer, chisel, or mould) to create the images they convey. Sculptures, drawings, and paintings can be realistic (like a still life or a portrait of a person), abstract (based on form rather than a realistic representation of specific objects), or anything in between.

Thinking Critically about Sculptures, Drawings, and Paintings

Sculptures, drawings, and paintings try to capture some truth about life or people. When you write about these visual forms, think of them as narrative or descriptive essays, only created using a visual medium. Mine their messages through the details in their description. What themes and messages do they evoke and how? What artistic choices did their creators make, and what effects do those choices have on your intellectual and emotional responses to these works of art? Is there a particular historical or social context that adds to their messages? When analyzing a sculpture, painting, or drawing, use the following questions as guidelines for thinking critically about what you are seeing and about the techniques the artist used to create an intellectual or emotional response in the viewer.

Critical Thinking Questions to Ask About Sculptures, Drawings, and Paintings

1. What materials were used to create this sculptures, drawing, or painting? Be sure to note both the type of material (paper, canvas, cloth, wood) the visual is based on, as well as the material used to create the image.

2. How do the chosen colors, shapes, and types of materials impact the overall effect of the piece?

3. What perspective or point of view is the piece of art presented from? Why? What effect does the point of view or perspective have on your reaction to it?

4. Is the piece realistic or abstract? How does this influence your reaction to it?

5. What is your intellectual response to this piece of art?

6. What is your emotional response?

7. Is there a cultural, historical, or social context that must be considered for deeper understanding of this artwork? If so, explain.

8. What is your personal response to the piece, and what personal associations does it evoke, if any?

9. What are the direct messages and arguments conveyed in this piece?

10. What are the implied messages or arguments?

Activity 20-8   Analyzing Sculptures

Directions: *On a separate sheet of paper, write a couple of paragraphs analyzing the two sculptures on page 419 using the questions above.* ●

Carved wood, 1968. Douglas L. Cole.

Deliverance. Terra cotta/wood stain, 2006.
Paul Metivier.

Activity 20-9   Analyzing a Drawing or Painting

Directions: *Choose one of the images on page 420 or a work of art from an art book or the Internet, or a drawing or painting you have seen in a gallery or museum, and answer the questions on page 418. Then write a paragraph about what effect this process had on your viewing of the work of art and your understanding and response to it.*

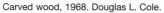

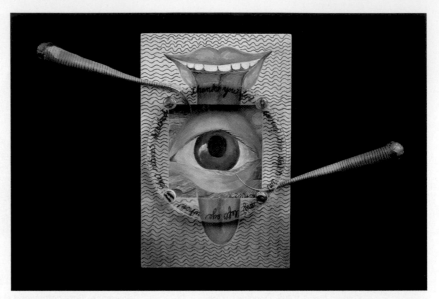

Blessing for a Detached Retina. Cindy Small, 2005.

Pierre Auguste Renoir (1841–1919), "The Luncheon of the Boating Party", 1881, oil on canvas. © Phillips Collection, Washington, DC, USA/The Bridgeman Art Library.

There are some basic questions you can ask about all types of visuals to begin your process of analysis and figure out the techniques used to convey direct and implied messages. See the Visual Detective Checklist for some general questions to get you started in analyzing various forms of visuals.

VISUAL DETECTIVE CHECKLIST

1. Who is the intended audience (general? specific? if so, list)?
2. Why did the artist use this medium to convey his or her message? Who is the intended audience (General? Specific?—if so, list.)
3. What are the strengths or advantages of the type of visual chosen?
4. What are the weaknesses or limitations, if any?
5. What are the *direct* messages of the image?
6. What are the *indirect* or implied messages of this visual?
7. What clues are present as visual evidence of the intended message(s)?
8. Ask *What? How? Why? Who? When? Where?* questions to help you check for all of the clues. Include any historical or social context you may know about the image.
9. What did you think when you first viewed this image? What did you feel?
10. Does the visual reinforce its intended theme or question it? What is the visual's overall thesis or argument?

Activity 20-10   Becoming a Visual Detective

Directions: *Choose one of the images from this chapter, and on a separate sheet of paper answer the visual detective questions on page 421. Then, write a one-paragraph analysis of the piece.*

_____

_____

_____

_____

_____

Activity 20-11   General Visual Analysis

Directions: *Choose one of the visuals from this chapter. Then follow these steps to reach analytical conclusions about the image you chose.*

1. Describe the image/visual objectively. What do you actually see (just the facts)? Don't include what you *think* and *feel* about the visual, just what is literally represented. Include details about the medium or type of visual, the format, size, shape, texture(s), colors, and so on. Describe as an observer, but add no judgment.

    _____

    _____

    _____

    _____

    _____

    _____

2. Is there any background information you can provide: historical context, cultural clues, visual type, or genre?

    _____

    _____

3. Now focus on your subjective response to the image. What thoughts are provoked by it? What feelings (if any) are evoked?

_____

_____

4. What associations come to mind when you look at this visual? Why?

_____

_____

5. Focus on the details of the image and the conscious choices made by the artist. What effects do the details and choices made have on you?

_____

_____

6. List a couple of specific examples of the details that served as visual clues that led you to a particular thought or emotion:

_____

_____

7. What ideas or concepts are represented in this image?

_____

_____

8. What is the thesis or argument implied by this visual?

_____

_____

9. After considering all of your answers so far, what do you think are the main messages of this image, and who is the intended audience?

_____

_____

_____

10. Is the visual successful in imparting its message or unsuccessful? Why?

_____

_____

Activity 20-12   Narrating a Visual

Directions: *Choose one of the following images. Describe it in detail. Then on a separate sheet of paper write a story about it (one to two paragraphs).* ●

Photo by Patrick Navin.

Photo by Patrick Navin.

Photo by Marcie Sims.

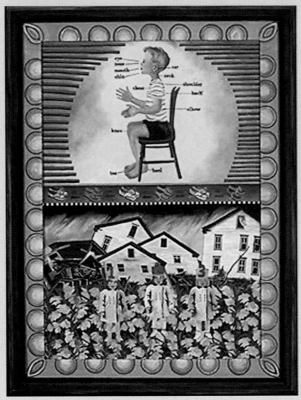

Old Shoes, New Shoes. Mixed media. Cindy Small.

THINKING CRITICALLY

Reading an essay or story requires you to engage actively in your reading, much like studying a work of art. What details and messages stand out in the mixed media picture above?

_____

_____

Be sure to engage your critical thinking skills as you read the following selections and complete the reading reflection and critical thinking questions that follow each one.

426

Applying Critical Thinking

PURPOSE — IDEAS — SUPPORT — ASSUMPTIONS BIASES — CONCLUSIONS — POINT OF VIEW — ANALYSIS

Here are some questions you can ask as you read to help you think critically about what an author is saying.

1. What is the author's **purpose** or goal in this reading selection? What does he or she set out to explain, argue, or prove?

2. What are the implied or stated questions being addressed in this reading selection?

3. What **ideas** and **support** (evidence, data, experience, or facts) does the author use to develop his or her purpose or goal for the reading? Is the support adequate? Convincing?

4. Does the author present alternative **points of view** when needed?

5. What **assumptions** does the author make in this reading selection? (Assumptions are ideas or reasons the author takes for granted and upon which he or she bases judgments or develops his or her reasoning.) Are the assumptions valid?

6. What are the implications, consequences, and **conclusions** of the author's reasoning and/or ideas and arguments (direct or implied) in this selection? Use your **analysis** skills to evaluate them.

Also, refer to the strategies for active reading in Chapter 2 on page 25 as needed.

Spudding Out

Barbara Ehrenreich

Barbara Ehrenreich was born August 26, 1941, in Butte, Montana. She is a writer and political activist. She has written articles for *The New York Times, Mother Jones, The Atlantic Monthly,* and other magazines. She has written several books, and of those, *Nickel and Dimed: On (Not) Getting by in America,* 2001, is her most famous.

1   Someone has to speak for them, because they have, to a person, lost the power to speak for themselves. I am referring to that great mass of

Americans who were once known as the "salt of the earth," then as "the silent majority," more recently as "the viewing public," and now, alas, as "couch potatoes." What drives them—or rather, leaves them sapped and spineless on their reclining chairs? What are they seeking—beyond such obvious goals as a tastefully colorized version of *The Maltese Falcon?*

2   My husband was the first in the family to "spud out," as the expression now goes. Soon everyone wanted one of those zip-up "Couch Potato Bags," to keep warm in during David Letterman. The youngest and most thoroughly immobilized member of the family relies on a remote that controls his TV, stereo, and VCR, and can also shut down the neighbor's pacemaker at fifteen yards.

3   But we never see the neighbors anymore, nor they us. This saddens me, because Americans used to be a great and restless people, fond of the outdoors in all of its manifestations, from Disney World to miniature golf. Some experts say there are virtues in mass agoraphobia, that it strengthens the family and reduces highway deaths. But I would point out that there are still a few things that cannot be done in the den, especially by someone zipped into a body bag. These include racquetball, voting, and meeting strange people in bars.

4   Most psychologists interpret the couch potato trend as a negative reaction to the outside world. Indeed, the list of reasons to stay safely tucked indoors lengthens yearly. First there was crime, then AIDS, then side-stream smoke. To this list should be added "fear of the infrastructure," for we all know someone who rashly stepped outside only to be buried in a pothole, hurled from a collapsing bridge, or struck by a falling airplane.

5   But it is not just the outside world that has let us down. Let's face it, despite a decade-long campaign by the "profamily" movement, the family has been a disappointment. The reason lies in an odd circular dynamic: we watch television to escape from our families because television shows us how dull our families really are.

6   Compare your own family to, for example, the Huxtables, the Keatons, or the peppy young people on *Thirtysomething.* In those families, even the three-year-olds are stand-up comics, and the most insipid remark is hailed with heartening outbursts of canned laughter. When television families aren't gathered around the kitchen table exchanging wisecracks, they are experiencing brief but moving dilemmas, which are handily solved by the youngest child or by some cute extraterrestrial house-guest. Emerging from *Family Ties* or *My Two Dads,* we are forced to acknowledge that our own families are made up of slow-witted, emotionally crippled people who would be lucky to qualify for seats in the studio audience of *Jeopardy!*

7   But gradually I have come to see that there is something besides fear of the outside and disgust with our families that drives us to spudhood— some positive attraction, some deep cathexis to television itself. For a long time it eluded me. When I watched television, mainly as a way of getting to know my husband and children, I found that my mind wandered to more interesting things, like whether to get up and make ice cubes.

8   Only after many months of viewing did I begin to understand the force that has transformed the American people into root vegetables. If you watch TV for a very long time, day in, day out, you will begin to notice something eerie and unnatural about the world portrayed therein. I don't mean that it is two-dimensional or lacks a well developed critique of the capitalist consumer culture or something superficial like that. I mean something so deeply obvious that it's almost scary. When you watch television, you will see people doing many things—chasing fast cars, drinking lite beer, shooting each other at close range, etc. But you will never see people *watching television.* Well, maybe for a second before the phone rings or a brand-new, multiracial adopted child walks into the house. But never *really watching,* hour after hour, the way *real* people do.

9   Way back in the beginning of the television era, this was not so strange, because real people actually did many of the things people do on TV, even if it was only bickering with their mothers-in-law about which toilet paper to buy. But modern people, i.e., couch potatoes, do nothing that is ever shown on television (because it is either dangerous or would involve getting up from the couch). And what they do do— watch television—is far too boring to be televised for more than a fraction of a second, not even by Andy Warhol, bless his boredom-proof little heart.

10   So why do we keep on watching? The answer, by now, should be perfectly obvious: we love television because television brings us a world in which television does not exist. In fact, deep in their hearts, this is what the spuds crave most: a rich, new, participatory life, in which family members look each other in the eye, in which people walk outside and banter with the neighbors, where there is adventure, possibility, danger, feeling, all in natural color, stereophonic sound, and three dimensions, without commercial interruptions, and starring . . . us.

11   "You mean some new kind of computerized interactive medium?" the children asked hopefully, pert as the progeny on a Tuesday night sitcom. But before I could expand on this concept—known to our ancestors as "real life"—they were back at the box, which may be, after all, the only place left to find it.

READING REFLECTION QUESTIONS

1. What is Barbara Ehrenreich's main message (her thesis) in this essay? Explain in your own words. _____

    _____

2. What tone does she use in this essay, and what effect does this tone have on the message she wants to convey? _____

    _____

3. List two examples Ehrenreich gives to explain why people watch TV. Are those examples humorous, serious, or both? Explain.

    _____

    _____

4. In your own words, describe what Barbara Ehrenreich means by the title "Spudding Out."

    _____

    _____

5. T/F _____ Ehrenreich discusses both the harms and the benefits of watching television.

6. _____ Which of the following best describes Ehrenreich's view toward excessive television watching? Choose the best answer:

    a. It wastes valuable time
    b. It encourages passivity
    c. It doesn't engage active critical thinking
    d. All of the above

CHECKING VOCABULARY

Define each of the following words by figuring out their meaning using context clues in the reading selection (see Chapter 30 for how to use context clues). If you cannot work out the meaning of a word, use a dictionary.

7. immobilized (paragraph 2): _____

8. infrastructure (paragraph 4): _____

9. dynamic (paragraph 5): _____

10. interactive (paragraph 11): _____

READING CRITICALLY

1. What is the author's **purpose** or goal in this reading selection?

_____

_____

2. What are the implied or stated questions being addressed?

_____

_____

3. What specific **support,** details, and examples does the author use to develop the purpose or goal for the reading?

_____

_____

4. What inferences does the author include in this reading? (Inferences imply "if this, then this" types of cause/effect analysis.)

_____

_____

5. Who is the intended audience, and how did you reach that **conclusion?**

_____

_____

WRITING ASSIGNMENTS

1. Using the Eight Steps for Writing a Summary (p. 342), write a two-paragraph summary of this reading.

2. Write an argument essay (Chapter 15) that argues for a plan to limit TV watching for families.

3. Write an argument/persuasion essay (Chapter 15) that presents the counterarguments to Ehrenreich's claims in "Spudding Out" and presents examples of the benefits of television.

4. Write a comparison/contrast essay (Chapter 14) of the benefits and harms of television. Provide specific examples to back up your analysis.

5. Write a narration/description essay (Chapters 7 and 8) about your own family's TV viewing habits. Be sure to include an analytical thesis: a conclusion or lesson learned from your analysis.

A Whole Lot of Cheatin' Going On

Mark Clayton

Mark Clayton is a writer whose research and writing about the increasing instances of plagiarism and other forms of cheating in colleges and universities have caused a stir in the academic world. Ironically, this article about plagiarism is often used and not cited in essays and summaries that can be purchased online for students to use as their own work.

1   Sitting in the glow of his computer screen at 2 a.m. on Oct. 26, 1998, John Smolik, a University of Texas freshman, fires off an e-mail message to an online debate over academic cheating on the Austin campus.

2   Many of the 100-plus student messages argue that cheaters only hurt themselves. Not so says Mr. Smolik's missive, labeled "reality check!" "Cheating is an answer," he writes. "It might not be a good answer, but nonetheless it is an answer."

3   Actually, Smolik "disagrees with cheating" and was simply playing devil's advocate, he said in a recent interview. But he allows that his provocative message put forward a widely shared view. And researchers agree.

4   Across America, college students and college-bound high-schoolers appear to be cheating like there's no tomorrow, student surveys show.

5   The Center for Academic Integrity in Nashville studied 7,000 students on 26 small-to-medium-size college campuses in 1990, 1992, and 1995. Those studies found that nearly 80 percent admitted to cheating at least once.

6   "We've seen a dramatic increase in the more explicit forms of test cheating" and illegitimate "collaboration," says Donald McCabe,

associate provost at Rutgers University in Newark, who founded CAI and did its studies.

7   He and others blame poor role models and lack of parental guidance for the growing acceptance of cheating in colleges. Easy access to the Internet, with its vast and often hard-to-trace resources, is another factor.

8   Add to that a pervasive change in societal values, and students can easily be snared if they lack a strong moral compass—as well as a campus where peers and administrators take a firm stand against dishonesty.

9   "Nobody cheated [in the 1960s] because of the peer pressure and likelihood of being turned in," claims Johan Madson, associate provost for student affairs at Vanderbilt University in Nashville. "Students of this generation are reluctant to turn their classmates in. They feel everyone ought to have their own right to do their own thing."

10   The problem is hardly limited to college campuses. Critics also point to widespread cheating in high school as a reason for colleges' current woes.

11   *Who's Who among American High School Students,* which lists 700,000 high achieving students, surveyed these top performers last year and found that 80 percent said they had cheated during their academic careers. Joe Krouse, associate publisher of the listing, says it is "the highest level we've ever seen."

12   Mr. Krouse taps adult behavior as a factor. "Because adults and role models in society do it, some students may have used those examples to rationalize cheating," he says. In a survey conducted in 1997–98, he also found that 66 percent of the parents of these top students said cheating was "not a big deal."

COLLEGES ARE WATCHING MORE CLOSELY

13   Whatever the reason for cheating, its sheer volume is capturing the attention of more than a few schools. Most, chary of their images, downplay dishonesty, unwilling to air dirty laundry in public. Yet a few are confronting cheating by making it highly public—on campus, at least.

14   The University of Texas is the nation's largest university with about 50,000 students. It has roughly 180 academic-integrity cases pop up annually, says Kevin Price, assistant dean of students. The school is trying to raise the profile of integrity issues during orientation with skits, a 10-page handout on plagiarism, and a newsletter called the *Integrity Herald* for faculty.

15   Another sign of academic stirring: the Center for Academic Integrity, founded in 1993, already has 175 member schools and is drafting a framework of principles that could be applied nationwide to lower student cheating.

16   Schools like Stanford University, Georgetown University, the University of Delaware, and a half-dozen others are also buffing up or introducing new honor codes.

17   But Mr. Madson at Vanderbilt University says what is most needed is for students themselves to take charge and reject the attitude that cheating can be justified.

18   Students say time and workload pressure are major factors spurring academic dishonesty, followed by parental pressure. "It's definitely what you get assigned—and how long you have to do it—that right there determines whether you're going to cheat," says Smolik, the University of Texas freshman.

19   Anne-Elyse Smith, another freshman at Texas, reasoned in an online debate that it may not be smart to cheat, but it could be educationally valuable.

20   "People should hold themselves accountable to a standard at which they are comfortable, and get out of the education what they can," she wrote. "If that involves looking at one answer on a quiz, I think the person is more likely to remember that one answer since they had to resort to cheating to obtain it."

A LITTLE IMAGINATION, A LOT OF HIGH TECH

21   Whether copying another student's homework, cheating on a test, or plagiarizing an essay, cheating is limited only by imagination—and technology. Some program their calculators with formulas, but rig them to show an empty memory if an instructor checks.

22   But what alarms some campus officials the most is the Internet's proven potential for explosive growth in negative areas such as pornography—and the possibility that plagiarism could be next. Web sites sporting names like "Cheater.com" and "School Sucks" offer tools for rampant plagiarism at the click of a mouse. "Download your workload" the latter site suggests, boasting more than 1 million term-paper downloads.

23   Such savvy borrowing may be lost on some educators, but others, like librarians, are catching up. "Students are finding it so easy to use these sources that they will dump them in the middle of the papers without any attribution," says John Ruszkiewicz, an English professor at Texas. "What they don't realize is how readily [professors] can tell the material isn't the student's and how easy it is for instructors to search this material on the Web."

24   Anthony Krier, a reference librarian at Franklin Pierce College Library in Rindge, N.H., is one such literary bloodhound. Last semester, he investigated nine cases of plagiarism, three of them involving the Internet. One student had downloaded and passed off as his own a morality essay, apparently unaware of the irony, Mr. Krier says.

25   Some colleges are fighting back with explicit warnings, more detailed orientations, and classes on how to cite sources—and lawsuits. Boston University sued five online "term-paper mills" in 1997. The case was rejected by a federal judge last month. School officials vow to refile.

26   Last fall, the dean of the school's College of Communication, Brent Baker, wrote a letter to students urging them to protect their "good name" by reviewing carefully the school's code of conduct. To drive home the point, he attached a listing of 13 unnamed cases and the penalties—probation, suspension, and expulsion—meted out.

27   Likewise, the 152 reports of academic dishonesty for 1997–98 at the University of Southern California in Los Angeles "is higher than previous comparable years beginning in 1991," wrote Sandra Rhoten, assistant dean in the office of student conduct, in a letter in the campus newspaper describing violations and sanctions assessed.

28   "We had a full-blown, two-year campaign [starting in 1995] to educate people about the problem," Ms. Rhoten says in an interview. "Sometimes faculty feel alone in this. We're reassuring them that we take this seriously too."

THE EXPECTATION OF HONESTY

29   Being blunt is the idea. Talking about the expectation of honesty is constant. And along with explicit warning shots, freshmen at USC are getting more intensive and detailed training in what constitutes plagiarism and other forms of cheating, Rhoten says.

30   The school passes out brochures on plagiarism, has regular coverage in the student paper on cheating cases, and has beefed up orientation courses with training to explain subtler issues like unauthorized collaboration—the largest area of student honor violation at USC and many other campuses, Mr. McCabe and others say.

31   For instance, Lucia Brawley, a senior majoring in English at Harvard University in Cambridge, Mass., does not believe cheating is a big problem at her school. But when asked about the collaboration issue, she is less sure.

32   "With people I know in the sciences, there's so much to do and so little time, they help each other," she says. "You go to a lecture today, I'll go next week. You do the reading this week, I'll do it next week. It's a gray area."

33   Ultimately, though, it is students who will have to uphold academic integrity themselves, many say.

34   The University of Virginia has a student-run honor code whose "single sanction" for violators is expulsion. It is one of the nation's strictest. Even after more than a century, it remains controversial on campus. Of 11 cheating cases last semester, five resulted in expulsion. But the code has

also created an atmosphere of trust that means students can take unproc-
tored exams. "Many of our alumni attribute their success in life to this
school's honor code," says Cabell Vest, a graduate student who chairs
UVA's honor council.

35   At Vanderbilt, which also has a strict code, 20 academic dishonesty
cases are under review, Madson says—triple the number a few years ago.
But he is confident the school is creating an atmosphere less tolerant of
cheating. "You just can't have an academic enterprise that isn't based on
integrity and honesty," he says. "Nobody wants somebody building
bridges to take shortcuts."

READING REFLECTION QUESTIONS

1. List at least three of the reasons (causes) that the author offers for the
   increase of student cheating over the past forty-five years.

   _____

   _____

2. How has technology, specifically the Internet, affected cheating/plagia-
   rism? Provide some specific examples from the article.

   _____

   _____

3. How are colleges/universities responding to this increase in cheating?
   Provide a couple of specific examples.

   _____

4. T/F _____ Clayton sees a connection to changing societal values
                 and an increase in plagiarism.

5. T/F _____ The most successful students graduating recently rarely
                 cheated (less than 10 percent of them).

6. _____   Which of the following is *not* one of the types of cheating
                 that students do that Clayton discusses?

   a. copying another student's homework
   b. cheating on a test
   c. working with a tutor
   d. plagiarizing an essay

CHECKING VOCABULARY

Define each of the following words by figuring out their meaning using
context clues in the reading selection (see Chapter 30 for how to use

context clues). If you cannot work out the meaning of a word, use a dictionary.

7. provocative (paragraph 3): _____

8. provost (paragraph 6): _____

9. plagiarism (paragraph 14): _____

10. collaboration (paragraph 30): _____

READING CRITICALLY

1. What is the author's **purpose** or goal in this reading selection?

_____

_____

2. What are the implied or stated questions being addressed?

_____

_____

3. What specific **support,** details, and examples does the author use to develop the purpose or goal for the reading?

_____

_____

4. What inferences does the author include in this reading? (Inferences imply "if this, then this" types of cause/effect analysis.)

_____

_____

5. Who is the intended audience, and how did you reach that **conclusion**?

_____

_____

WRITING ASSIGNMENTS

1. Write a classification essay (Chapter 10) that categorizes types of cheating. Use examples from Mark Clayton's essay as well as your own experience.

2. Write a cause and effect analysis essay (Chapter 13) on cheating. Be sure to look at both causes and effects and bring in references to Clayton's essay as well as to your own experience.

3. Write an argument essay (Chapter 15) that proposes possible solutions to the problem of cheating at your own campus. Come up with a specific plan of action.

Making Cell Phones in the Class a Community Builder

Alan Bloom

This article originally appeared in the March 2007 issue of *The Teaching Professor*. Alan Bloom is a professor at Valparaiso University. The following excerpt includes first an argument in favor (pro) of cell phones and their worth in the classroom and then includes an interview with an instructor who argues against (con) the worth of cell phones in the classroom.

CELL PHONES DO NOT DISTRACT IN CLASS (PRO)

1   The first time a student's cell phone rang in my class, I was angry and frustrated. With their musical ringers, cell phones that go *off* in class are rude and distracting. But how to respond? I've never been very good at playing the heavy. Was there any way I could take this annoying occurrence and twist it so that it would contribute to a more positive classroom environment?

2   I've devised a "cell phone protocol" that has enabled me to make peace with the problem. As it appears in the syllabus, the protocol reads: **"Please turn off your cell phone ringer while in class. Mind you, violation of this protocol will demand punishment—though one that clearly does not infringe on your eighth amendment rights."** I then ask someone to identify the eighth amendment, and as a history professor, I'm happy to report that someone can always explain the constitutional limits on cruel and unusual punishment. I advise students to turn off their ringers in class, and I note that if someone's phone rings, he or she will have to provide the class with food. It doesn't have to be an extravagant meal (remember the eighth amendment!), but there must be enough for everyone. In the beginning, I offered the possibility of a subsidy to economically unable students. However, I abandoned it once I realized that if students could afford a cell-phone package, they could provide treats to about 30 classmates.

3   The community-building process develops in earnest when a phone actually rings in class. During an episode that otherwise involves an

unpleasant exchange, there is now occasion for celebration, as students cheer at the prospect of their upcoming snack. The cell phone protocol, much like a kangaroo court in baseball, which exacts minor fines for small indiscretions, helps to build an esprit de corps and I push this outcome even further. When it is difficult to discern whether the cell phone rang or was in vibration mode, I encourage the students to vote as to whether or not a violation has occurred.

4   So what are the drawbacks of this policy? There are few. The biggest is that even with my policy, cell phones still ring in class and they are just as rude and distracting. I see no way around this problem. In my class, students are distracted, but we grow closer as a result of it. The other potential problem is that an instructor might not want food in the classroom, fair enough, just have the punishment be something like telling a joke or sharing a poem.

5   The policy also has produced some wonderful surprises that make me proud of my students. Once a student decided to skip the standard fare of candy and brought in dried fruit. Although most of her peers (and her teacher) were disappointed with the healthy alternative, this student took the opportunity to encourage people to eat a more healthy diet. And at the end of this past semester, one of my quietest students informed the class that she was disappointed in a classmate who still hadn't brought in food for his transgression. The chastened student, who apparently had extra money on his meal card, brought in a buffet for his dumbfounded classmates.

6   Ultimately, though, the greatest advantage of the cell phone protocol occurs when someone's phone rings in class and the other students start hooting joyously. It doesn't make the phone ringing less distracting; but on the other hand, how often do you hear students cheering in the classroom?

CELL PHONES DO DISTRACT IN CLASS (CON)

7   In case you ever had any doubts, research (reference below) now exists that verifies that both students and teachers find cell phones ringing in class distracting. The results also document strong support from students and faculty for policies against ringing cell phones. Although there was strong support against cell phones going off in class, the strength of that support was mediated by age. The younger cohort in the study was more tolerant of cell phones than the older cohort.

8   The problem, of course, is that it is virtually impossible to prevent cell phones from ringing in class. They do ring, despite strongly worded statements in the syllabus, regular announcements in class, and threats of

various sorts. Well, they don't actually ring, they beep out jingles, tunes, and other electronic sounds without pause until they are turned off or answered.

9   Ringing phones are distracting, and faculty, probably because we didn't grow up using cell phones, seem particularly annoyed when they do go off in class. If you want to generate discussion in the faculty mailroom, ask several folks standing there what they do about the problem. For many, there's something of a power issue involved here. Despite policies against cell phones in the syllabus, or announcements by the teacher that they must be turned off, right in the middle of an important point, one goes off. Every one hears the phone and watches as someone (who is usually quite embarrassed) retrieves and silences it.

10   So what should a faculty member do when the inevitable occurs? Confiscate the phone? Accost the offender? Wail and carry on about how students show no respect? The problem with these loud and powerful responses is that most of the time they don't prevent the problem from recurring.

11   It seems more prudent not to make a mountain out of a molehill. That doesn't mean molehills have to be tolerated. Their offensiveness should indeed be pointed out. But when the distraction occurs, perhaps there is silence and then an attempt to regroup. "Now, where were we?" "What's the last thing you wrote in your notes?" "Do you understand what I was trying to explain?" The disruption becomes an opportunity to review and connect with what students are (or are not) understanding. This prevents the disruption from doing even more harm when it not only distracts but results in an unpleasant exchange that threatens the climate for learning.

Reference:

Campbell, S. "Perceptions of Mobile Phones in College Classrooms: Ringing, Cheating, and Classroom Policies." *Communication Education,* 55.3 (2006): 280–294.

READING REFLECTION QUESTIONS

1. What are the main issues that arise as a result of cell phones ringing in the college classroom? _____

2. What problems do cell phones pose for teachers? For students?

_____

_____

3. How do you feel about cell phones ringing during class time?

_____

_____

4. T/F _____ The author argues that cell phones are not really a distraction.

5. T/F _____ The author argues that there are ways to make a learning lesson out of a cell phone disruption in class.

6. Provide an example of a positive way a teacher could handle a cell phone disruption as explained in the article. _____

_____

_____

7. T/F _____ According to a study cited in the article, younger students found cell phones less distracting than older ones.

CHECKING VOCABULARY

Define each of the following words by figuring out their meaning using context clues in the reading selection (see Chapter 30 for how to use context clues). If you cannot work out the meaning of a word, use a dictionary.

8. protocol (paragraph 2): _____

9. indiscretions (paragraph 3): _____

10. chastened (paragraph 5): _____

READING CRITICALLY

1. What is the author's **purpose** or goal in this reading selection?

_____

_____

2. What are the implied or stated questions being addressed?

_____

_____

3. What specific **support**, details, and examples does the author use to develop the purpose or goal for the reading?

_____

_____

4. What inferences does the author include in this reading? (Inferences imply "if this, then this" types of cause/effect analysis.)

_____

_____

5. Who is the intended audience, and how did you reach that **conclusion**?

_____

_____

WRITING ASSIGNMENTS

1. Write an argument/persuasion essay (Chapter 15) arguing for or against cell phone use in the classroom.
2. Write a narration/description essay (Chapters 7 and 8) about a time when you were annoyed or disrupted by a cell phone ringing in a class or other unsuitable place such as the movie theater or during a meeting.
3. Write a cause/effect analysis essay (Chapter 13) that explores both the causes of increased cell phone disruptions in our society and the effects of these disruptions.

"Just Walk On By": A Black Man Ponders His Power to Alter Public Space

Brent Staples

Brent Staples is an editorial writer for _The New York Times_. He has a Ph.D. in psychology from the University of Chicago. He won the Anisfield Book Award for his memoir, _Parallel Time: Growing Up in Black and White_.

1   My first victim was a woman—white, well dressed, probably in her early 20s. I came upon her late one evening on a deserted street in Hyde Park, a relatively affluent neighborhood in an otherwise mean, impoverished section of Chicago. As I swung onto the avenue behind her, there seemed to be a discreet, uninflammatory distance between us. Not so. She cast back a worried glance. To her, the youngish black man—a broad six feet two inches with a beard and billowing hair, both hands shoved into the pockets of a bulky military jacket—seemed menacingly close. She picked up her pace and was soon running in earnest. Within seconds she disappeared into a cross street.

2   That was more than a decade ago. I was 22 years old, a graduate student newly arrived at the University of Chicago. It was in the echo of that terrified woman's footfalls that I first began to know the unwieldy

inheritance I'd come into—the ability to alter public space in ugly ways. It was clear that she thought of herself as the quarry of a mugger, a rapist, or worse. Suffering a bout of insomnia, however, I was stalking sleep, not defenseless wayfarers. As a softy who is scarcely able to take a knife to a raw chicken—let alone hold one to a person's throat—I was surprised, embarrassed, and dismayed all at once. Her flight made me feel like an accomplice in tyranny. It also made it clear that I was indistinguishable from the muggers who occasionally seeped into the area from the surrounding ghetto. I soon gathered that being perceived as dangerous is a hazard in itself: Where fear and weapons meet—as they often do in urban America—there is always the possibility of death.

3   In that first year, my first away from my hometown, I was to become thoroughly familiar with the language of fear. At dark, shadowy intersections, I could cross in front of a car stopped at a traffic light and elicit the *thunk, thunk, thunk, thunk* of the driver—black, white, male, female— hammering down the door locks. On less traveled streets after dark, I grew accustomed to but never comfortable with people crossing to the other side of the street rather than pass me. Then there were the standard unpleasantries with policemen, doormen, bouncers, cabdrivers, and others whose business it is to screen out troublesome individuals *before* there is any nastiness.

4   I moved to New York nearly two years ago and I have remained an avid night walker. In central Manhattan, the near-constant crowd covers the tense one-on-one street encounters. Elsewhere, things can get very taut indeed.

5   After dark, on the warrenlike streets of Brooklyn where I live, I often see women who fear the worst from me. They seem to have set their faces on neutral, and with their purse straps strung across their chests bandolier-style, they forge ahead as though bracing themselves against being tackled. I understand, of course, that the danger they perceive is not a hallucination. Women are particularly vulnerable to street violence, and young black males are drastically overrepresented among the perpetrators of that violence. Yet these truths are no solace against the alienation that comes of being ever the suspect, an entity with whom pedestrians avoid making eye contact.

6   It is not altogether clear to me how I reached the ripe old age of 22 without being conscious of the lethality nighttime pedestrians attributed to me. Perhaps it was because in Chester, Pa., the small, angry industrial town where I came of age in the 1960s, I was scarcely noticeable against a backdrop of gang warfare, street knifings, and murders. I grew up one of the good boys, had perhaps a half-dozen fistfights. In retrospect, my shyness of combat has clear sources. As a boy, I saw countless tough guys

locked away; I have since buried several, too. They were babies, really—a teen-age cousin, a brother of 22, a childhood friend in his mid-20s—all gone down in episodes of bravado played out in the streets. I chose, perhaps unconsciously, to remain a shadow—timid, but a survivor.

7   The fearsomeness mistakenly attributed to me in public places often has a perilous flavor. The most frightening of these confusions occurred in the late 1970s and early 1980s, when I worked as a journalist in Chicago. One day, rushing into the office of a magazine I was writing for with a deadline story in hand, I was mistaken for a burglar. The office manager called security, and with the speed of an ad hoc posse, pursued me through the labyrinthine halls, nearly to my editor's door. I had no way of proving who I was. I could only move briskly toward the company of someone who knew me.

8   Relatively speaking, however, I never fared as badly as another black male journalist. He went to nearby Waukegan, Ill., a couple of summers ago to work on a story about a murderer who was born there. Mistaking the reporter for the killer, police officers hauled him from his car at gunpoint and but for his press credentials would probably have tried to book him. Such episodes are not uncommon. Black men trade tales like this all the time.

9   Over the years, I learned to smother the rage I felt at so often being mistaken for a criminal. Not to do so would surely have led to madness. I now take precautions to make myself less threatening. I move about with care, particularly late in the evening. I give a wide berth to nervous people on subway platforms during the wee hours. If I happen to be entering a building behind some people who appear skittish, I may walk by, letting them clear the lobby before I return, so as not to seem to be following them. I have been calm and extremely congenial on those rare occasions when I've been pulled over by the police.

10   And on late-evening constitutionals I employ what has proved to be an excellent tension-reducing measure: I whistle melodies from Beethoven and Vivaldi and the more popular classical composers. Even steely New Yorkers hunching toward night-time destinations seem to relax, and occasionally they even join in the tune. Virtually everybody seems to sense that a mugger wouldn't be warbling bright, sunny selections from Vivaldi's "Four Seasons." It is my equivalent of the cowbell that hikers wear when they are in bear country.

READING REFLECTION QUESTIONS

1. Explain exactly what Brent Staples means by his title to this piece. Explain how this title relates to his message in the essay.

_____

_____

2. Explain how Staples is sometimes perceived by women on the street. Then explain how Staples has adjusted his behavior and dealt with the problem. Provide specific examples from the essay.

_____

_____

3. What is the author's tone and overall viewpoint in this essay? How has he chosen to react to the stereotype he gets judged by—what is his attitude? _____

_____

4. What does Brent Staples mean by the word _victim_ when he writes "My first victim was a woman"? _____

_____

5. T/F _____ Staples' tone is angry in this essay.

6. _____   Which of the following best describes his purpose in this essay?

   a. To display his anger at the rudeness of strangers

   b. To tell readers that it's hard to get along with coworkers

   c. To explain the extra steps a black man has to take to put some white people at ease in public situations

   d. To compare and contrast living as a black person or a white person in the United States

7. What does Staples mean by the last line, "It is my equivalent of the cowbell that hikers wear in bear country"? Who would the "hikers" represent in this essay? Who would the "bears" represent? Why a cowbell?

_____

_____

_____

CHECKING VOCABULARY

Define each of the following words by figuring out their meaning using context clues in the reading selection (see Chapter 30 for how to use context clues). If you cannot work out the meaning of a word, use a dictionary.

8. impoverished (paragraph 1): _____

9. uninflammatory (paragraph 1): _____

10. vulnerable (paragraph 5): _____

READING CRITICALLY

1. What is the author's **purpose** or goal this reading selection?

_____

_____

2. What are the implied or stated questions being addressed?

_____

_____

3. What specific **support**, details, and examples does the author use to develop the purpose or goal for the reading?

_____

_____

4. What inferences does the author include in this reading? (Inferences imply "if this, then this" types of cause/effect analysis.)

_____

_____

5. Who is the intended audience, and how did you reach that **conclusion**?

_____

_____

WRITING ASSIGNMENTS

1. Write a narration/description essay (Chapters 7 and 8) that describes a time when you were stereotyped or judged based on your external appearance (e.g., race, gender, style, age, size, and so on).
2. Write a story analysis essay (Appendix A) that focuses both on how Staples uses specific writing techniques and style choices to achieve his purpose or message in this piece and analyzing his direct and implied messages in this article.
3. Write an argument essay (Chapter 15) that comes up with a specific plan of action for educating children at an early age (grade school) regarding stereotyping based on race.

One Man's Kids

Daniel R. Meier

Daniel R. Meier is a teacher and a writer. He has written articles and books related to teaching, including *Learning in Small Moments: Life in an Urban Classroom* and *Scribble Scrabble—Learning to Read and Write: Success with Diverse Teachers, Children, and Families.*

1   I teach first graders. I live in a world of skinned knees, double-knotted shoelaces, riddles that I've heard a dozen times, stale birthday cakes, hurt feelings, wandering stories, and one lost shoe ("and if you don't find it my mother'll kill me"). My work is dominated by 6-year-olds.

2   It's 10:45, the middle of snack, and I'm helping Emily open her milk carton. She has already tried the other end without success, and now there's so much paint and ink on the carton from her fingers that I'm not sure she should drink it at all. But I open it. Then I turn to help Scott clean up some milk he has just spilled onto Rebecca's whale crossword puzzle.

3   While I wipe my milk- and paint-covered hands, Jenny wants to know if I've seen that funny book about penguins that I read in class. As I hunt for it in a messy pile of books, Jason wants to know if there is a new seating arrangement for lunch tables. I find the book, turn to answer Jason, then face Maya, who is fast approaching with a new knock-knock joke. After what seems like the 10th "Who's there?" I laugh and Maya is pleased.

4   Then Andrew wants to know how to spell "flukes" for his crossword. As I get to "u," I give a hand signal for Sarah to take away the snack. But just as Sarah is almost out the door, two children complain that "we haven't even had ours yet." I stop the snack mid-flight, complying with their request for graham crackers. I then return to Andrew, noticing that he has put "flu" for 9 Down, rather than 9 Across. It's now 10:50.

5   My work is not traditional male work. It's not a singular pursuit. There is not a large pile of paper to get through or one deal to transact. I don't have one area of expertise or knowledge. I don't have the singular power over language of a lawyer, the physical force of a construction worker, the command over fellow workers of a surgeon, the wheeling and dealing transactions of a businessman. My energy is not spent in pursuing, climbing, achieving, conquering, or cornering some goal or object.

6   My energy is spent in encouraging, supporting, consoling, and praising my children. In teaching, the inner rewards come from without. On

any given day, quite apart from teaching reading and spelling, I bandage a cut, dry a tear, erase a frown, tape a torn doll, and locate a long-lost boot. The day is really won through matters of the heart. As my students groan, laugh, shudder, cry, exult, and wonder, I do too. I have to be soft around the edges.

7   A few years ago, when I was interviewing for an elementary-school teaching position, every principal told me with confidence that, as a male, I had an advantage over female applicants because of the lack of male teachers. But in the next breath, they asked with a hint of suspicion why I chose to work with young children. I told them that I wanted to observe and contribute to the intellectual growth of a maturing mind. What I really felt like saying, but didn't, was that I loved helping a child learn to write her name for the first time, finding someone a new friend, or sharing in the hilarity of reading about Winnie the Pooh getting so stuck in a hole that only his head and rear show.

8   I gave that answer to those principals, who were mostly male, because I thought they wanted a "male" response. This meant talking about intellectual matters. If I had taken a different course and talked about my interest in helping children in their emotional development, it would have been seen as closer to a "female" answer. I even altered my language, not once mentioning the word "love" to describe what I do indeed love about teaching. My answer worked; every principal nodded approvingly.

9   Some of the principals also asked what I saw myself doing later in my career. They wanted to know if I eventually wanted to go into educational administration. Becoming a dean of students or a principal has never been one of my goals, but they seemed to expect me, as a male, to want to climb higher on the career stepladder. So I mentioned that, at some point, I would be interested in working with teachers as a curriculum coordinator. Again, they nodded approvingly.

10   If those principals had been female instead of male, I wonder whether their questions, and my answers, would have been different. My guess is that they would have been.

11   At other times, when I'm at a party or a dinner and tell someone that I teach young children, I've found that men and women respond differently. Most men ask about the subjects I teach and the courses I took in my training. Then, unless they bring up an issue such as merit pay, the conversation stops. Most women, on the other hand, begin the conversation on a more immediate and personal level. They say things like "those kids must love having a male teacher" or "that age is just wonderful, you must love it." Then, more often than not, they'll talk about their own kids or ask me specific questions about what I do. We're then off and talking shop.

12   Possibly, men would have more to say to me, and I to them, if my job had more of the trappings and benefits of more traditional male jobs. But my job has no bonuses or promotions. No complimentary box seats at the ball park. No cab fare home. No drinking buddies after work. No briefcase. No suit. (Ties get stuck in paint jars.) No power lunches. (I eat peanut butter and jelly, chips, milk, and cookies with the kids.) No taking clients out for cocktails. The only place I take my kids is to the playground.

13   Although I could have pursued a career in law or business, as several of my friends did, I chose teaching instead. My job has benefits all its own. I'm able to bake cookies without getting them stuck together as they cool, buy cheap sewing materials, take out splinters, and search just the right trash cans for useful odds and ends. I'm sometimes called "Daddy" and even "Mommy" by my students, and if there's ever a lull in the conversation at a dinner party, I can always ask those assembled if they've heard the latest riddle about why the turkey crossed the road. (He thought he was a chicken.)

READING REFLECTION QUESTIONS

1. What is it that Daniel Meier loves about teaching first graders? Give some specific examples from his essay. _____

_____

2. What does Meier mean by the phrase "The day is really won through matters of the heart" (paragraph 6)? Explain. _____

_____

3. Provide some examples from the essay that prove that Meier is, as he says in his essay, "soft around the edges" (paragraph 6) with his students.

_____

4. T/F _____ The majority of first-grade teachers are male.

5. T/F _____ Meier hopes to become his school's principal.

6. List two of the "benefits" Meier sees as part of his job (see final paragraph): _____

_____

7. T/F _____ Some people question Meier's motives as a male working with young children.

CHECKING VOCABULARY

Define each of the following words by figuring out their meaning using context clues in the reading selection (see Chapter 30 for how to use context clues). If you cannot work out the meaning of a word, use a dictionary.

8. dominated (paragraph 1): _____

9. transactions (paragraph 5): _____

10. consoling (paragraph 6): _____

READING CRITICALLY

1. What is the author's **purpose** or goal in this reading selection?

_____

_____

2. What are the implied or stated questions being addressed?

_____

_____

3. What specific **support**, details, and examples does the author use to develop the purpose or goal for the reading?

_____

_____

4. What inferences does the author include in this reading? (Inferences imply "if this, then this" types of cause/effect analysis.)

_____

_____

5. Who is the intended audience, and how did you reach that **conclusion**?

_____

_____

WRITING ASSIGNMENTS

1. Write a narration/description essay (Chapters 7 and 8) about one of your favorite elementary school teachers. What makes that teacher stick out in your memory?

2. Write an example/illustration essay (Chapter 12) about what makes Meier's job more "female" or "feminine" than "male" or "masculine." Provide examples from Meier to back up your analysis.

3. Write an argument/persuasion essay (Chapter 15) that argues for the need for more male teachers in elementary school. You may want to bring in some cause/effect analysis (Chapter 13) to explain both why many men don't choose to teach younger children *and* what effects (benefits) could come from encouraging more men to enter the career of teaching young children.

The Discus Thrower

Richard Selzer

Richard Selzer was born in Troy, New York, in 1928. He is both a practicing surgeon and a writer. In 1974, after years of being a doctor, he wrote *Rituals of Surgery*, a collection of short stories. He has also published several essays and stories in magazines such as *Redbook*, *Esquire*, and *Harper's*. Many of his essays and stories are in two collections: *Mortal Lessons* (1977) and *Confessions of a Knife* (1979).

1   I spy on my patients. Ought not a doctor to observe his patients by any means and from any stance that he might the more fully assemble evidence? So I stand in the doorways of hospital rooms and gaze. Oh, it is not all that furtive an act. Those in bed need only look up to discover me. But they never do.

2   From the doorway of Room 542 the man in the bed seems deeply tanned. Blue eyes and close-cropped white hair give him the appearance of vigor and good health. But I know that his skin is not brown from the sun. It is rusted, rather, in the last stage of containing the vile repose within. And the blue eyes are frosted, looking inward like the windows of a snowbound cottage. This man is blind. This man is also legless—the right leg missing from midthigh down, the left from just below the knee. It gives him the look of a bonsai, roots and branches pruned into the dwarfed facsimile of a great tree.

3   Propped on pillows, he cups his right thigh in both hands. Now and then he shakes his head as though acknowledging the intensity of his suffering. In all of this he makes no sound. Is he mute as well as blind?

4   The room in which he dwells is empty of all possessions—no get-well cards, small, private caches of food, day-old flowers, slippers, all the usual kickshaws of the sickroom. There is only the bed, a chair, a nightstand, and a tray on wheels that can be swung across his lap for meals.

5   "What time is it?" he asks.

6   "Three o'clock."

7   "Morning or afternoon?"

8   "Afternoon."

9   He is silent. There is nothing else he wants to know.

10   "How are you?" I say.

11   "Who is it?" he asks.

12   "It's the doctor. How do you feel?"

13   He does not answer right away.

14   "Feel?" he says.

15   "I hope you feel better," I say.

16   I press the button at the side of the bed.

17   "Down you go," I say.

18   "Yes, down," he says.

19   He falls back upon the bed awkwardly. His stumps, unweighted by legs and feet, rise in the air, presenting themselves. I unwrap the bandages from the stumps, and begin to cut away the black scabs and the dead, glazed fat with scissors and forceps. A shard of white bone comes loose. I pick it away. I wash the wounds with disinfectant and redress the stumps. All this while, he does not speak. What is he thinking behind those lids that do not blink? Is he remembering a time when he was whole? Does he dream of feet? Of when his body was not a rotting log?

20   He lies solid and inert. In spite of everything, he remains impressive, as though he were a sailor standing athwart a slanting deck.

21   "Anything more I can do for you?" I ask. For a long moment he is silent.

22   "Yes," he says at last and without the least irony. "You can bring me a pair of shoes."

23   In the corridor the head nurse is waiting for me.

24   "We have to do something about him," she says. "Every morning he orders scrambled eggs for breakfast, and, instead of eating them, he picks up the plate and throws it against the wall."

25   "Throws his plate?"

26   "Nasty. That's what he is. No wonder his family doesn't come to visit. They probably can't stand him any more than we can."

27   She is waiting for me to do something.

28   "Well?"

29   "We'll see," I say.

30   The next morning I am waiting in the corridor when the kitchen delivers his breakfast. I watch the aide place the tray on the stand and swing it across his lap. She presses the button to raise the head of the bed. Then she leaves.

31   In time the man reaches to find the rim of the tray, then on to find the dome of the covered dish. He lifts off the cover and places it on the stand. He fingers across the plate until he probes the eggs. He lifts the plate in both hands, sets it on the palm of his right hand, centers it, balances it. He hefts it up and down slightly, getting the feel of it. Abruptly he draws back his right arm as far as he can.

32   There is the crack of the plate breaking against the wall at the foot of his bed and the small wet sound of the scrambled eggs dropping to the floor.

33   And then he laughs. It is a sound you have never heard. It is something new under the sun. It could cure cancer.

34   Out in the corridor, the eyes of the head nurse narrow.
"Laughed, did he?"

35   She writes something down on her clipboard.

36   A second aide arrives, brings a second breakfast tray, puts it on the nightstand, out of his reach. She looks over at me shaking her head and making her mouth go. I see that we are to be accomplices.

37   "I've got to feed you," she says to the man.

38   "Oh, no you don't," the man says.

39   "Oh, yes I do," the aide says, "after the way you just did. Nurse says so."

40   "Get me my shoes," the man says.

41   "Here's oatmeal," the aide says. "Open." And she touches the spoon to his lower lip.

42   "I ordered scrambled eggs," says the man.

43   "That's right," the aide says.

44   I step forward.

45   "Is there anything I can do?" I say.

46   "Who are you?" the man asks.

47   In the evening I go once more to that ward to make my rounds. The head nurse reports to me that Room 542 is deceased. She has discovered this quite by accident, she says. No, there had been no sound. Nothing. It's a blessing, she says.

48   I go into his room, a spy looking for secrets. He is still there in his bed. His face is relaxed, grave, dignified. After a while, I turn to leave. My gaze sweeps the wall at the foot of the bed, and I see the place where it has been repeatedly washed, where the wall looks very clean and very white.

READING REFLECTION QUESTIONS

1. What are the direct or indirect (implied) messages in this story?

_____

_____

2. Describe the conflict between the doctor and the nurse in this story in regard to the patient.

_____

_____

3. What is it about this patient that intrigues the doctor so? Provide specific examples. _____

_____

_____

4. T/F _____ The doctor is curious about this patient's unusual ritual.

5. T/F _____ The doctor is annoyed by this patient's stubbornness.

6. T/F _____ The nurse admires the patient's pride.

7. T/F _____ The patient and the doctor become good friends.

CHECKING VOCABULARY

Define each of the following words by figuring out their meaning using context clues in the reading selection (see Chapter 30 for how to use context clues). If you cannot work out the meaning of a word, use a dictionary.

8. furtive (paragraph 1): _____

9. facsimile (paragraph 2): _____

10. inert (paragraph 20): _____

READING CRITICALLY

1. What is the author's **purpose** or goal in this reading selection?

_____

_____

2. What are the implied or stated questions being addressed?

_____

_____

3. What specific **support**, details, and examples does the author use to develop the purpose or goal for the reading?

_____

_____

4. What inferences does the author include in this reading? (Inferences imply "if this, then this" types of cause/effect analysis.)

_____

_____

5. Who is the intended audience, and how did you reach that **conclusion**?

_____

_____

WRITING ASSIGNMENTS

1. Write a story analysis essay (Appendix A) that addresses both Selzer's writing technique and style as well as his analytical message (the purpose) of the story.

2. Write a narration/description essay (Chapters 7 and 8) about someone you know who displayed pride and dignity in the face of an awkward or uncomfortable event or circumstance.

3. Write a process essay (Chapter 9) that describes step by step a ritual or habit that you have or that someone you know has. Include specific details. What purpose does this ritual serve?

Supersize Me

Greg Critser

Greg Critser is a journalist who writes for *USA Today*. He has written several articles; many of them focus on medical, health, and nutrition topics. His books include *Welcome to Fat Land: How Americans Became the Fattest People in the World* and *Generation R$_x$: How Prescription Drugs* *are Altering American Lives, Minds, and Bodies.* This reading is from Chapter 2 of *Welcome to Fatland.*

1   David Wallerstein, a director of the McDonald's Corporation, hated the fifth deadly sin because it kept people from buying more hamburgers. Wallerstein had first waged war on the injunction against gluttony as a young executive in the theater business. At the staid Balaban Theaters chain in the early 1960s, Wallerstein had realized that the movie business was really a margin business; it wasn't the sale of low-markup movie tickets that generated profits but rather the sale of high-markup snacks like popcorn and Coke. To sell more of such items, he had, by the mid-1960s, tried about every trick in the conventional retailer's book: two-for-one specials, combo deals, matinee specials, etc. But at the end of any given day, as he tallied up his receipts, Wallerstein inevitably came up with about the same amount of profit.

2   Thinking about it one night, he had a realization: People did not want to buy two boxes of popcorn *no matter what.* They didn't want to be seen eating two boxes of popcorn. It looked piggish. So Wallerstein flipped the equation around: Perhaps he could get more people to spend just a little more on popcorn if he made the boxes bigger and increased the price only a little. The popcorn cost a pittance anyway, and he'd already paid for the salt and the seasoning and the counter help and the popping machine. So he put up signs advertising jumbo-size popcorn. The results after the first week were astounding. Not only were individual sales of popcorn increasing; with them rose individual sales of that other high-profit item, Coca-Cola.

3   Later, at McDonald's in the mid-1970s, Wallerstein faced a similar problem: With consumers watching their pennies, restaurant customers were coming to the Golden Arches less and less frequently. Worse, when they did, they were "cherry-picking," buying only, say, a small Coke and a burger, or, worse, just a burger, which yielded razor-thin profit margins. How could he get people back to buying more fries? His popcorn experience certainly suggested one solution—sell them a jumbo-size bag of the crispy treats.

4   Yet try as he may, Wallerstein could not convince Ray Kroc, McDonald's founder, to sign on to the idea. As recounted in interviews with his associates and in John F. Love's 1985 book, *McDonald's: Behind the Arches,* the exchange between the two men could be quite contentious on the issue. "If people want more fries," Kroc would say, "they can buy two bags."

5   "But Ray," Wallerstein would say, "they don't want to eat two bags—they don't want to look like a glutton."

6   To convince Kroc, Wallerstein decided to do his own survey of customer behavior, and began observing various Chicago-area McDonald's.
Sitting in one store after another, sipping his drink and watching hundreds
of Chicagoans chomp their way through their little bag of fries,
Wallerstein could see: People *wanted* more fries.

7   "How do you know that?" Kroc asked the next morning when
Wallerstein presented his findings.

8   "Because they're eating the entire bagful, Ray," Wallerstein said. "They
even scrape and pinch around at the bottom of the bag for more and eat
the salt!"

9   Kroc gave in. Within months receipts were up, customer counts were
up, and franchisees—the often truculent heart and soul of the McDonald's
success—were happier than ever.

10   Many franchisees wanted to take the concept even further, offering
large-size versions of other menu items. At this sudden burst of entrepreneurism, however, McDonald's mid-level managers hesitated. Many of
them viewed large-sizing as a form of "discounting," with all the negative
connotations such a word evoked. In a business where "wholesome" and
"dependable" were the primary PR watchwords, large-sizing could
become a major image problem. Who knew what the franchisees, with
their primal desires and shortcutting ways, would do next? No, large-
sizing was something to be controlled tightly from Chicago, if it were to
be considered at all.

11   Yet as McDonald's headquarters would soon find out, large-sizing was
a new kind of marketing magic—a magic that could not so easily be put
back into those crinkly little-size bags.

12   Max Cooper, a Birmingham franchisee, was not unfamiliar with marketing and magic; for most of his adult life he had been paid to conjure
sales from little more than hot air and smoke. Brash, blunt-spoken, and
witty, Cooper had acquired his talents while working as an old-fashioned
public relations agent—the kind, as he liked to say, who "got you into the
newspaper columns instead of trying to keep you out." In the 1950s with
his partner, Al Golin, he had formed what later became Golin Harris, one
of the world's more influential public relations firms. In the mid-1960s,
first as a consultant and later as an executive, he had helped create many
of McDonald's most successful early campaigns. He had been the prime
mover in the launch of Ronald McDonald.

13   By the 1970s Cooper, tired of "selling for someone else," bought a
couple of McDonald's franchises in Birmingham, moved his split-off ad
agency there, and set up shop as an independent businessman. As he
began expanding, he noticed what many other McDonald's operators
were noticing: declining customer counts. Sitting around a table and

kibitzing with a few like-minded associates one day in 1975, "we started talking about how we could build sales—how we could do it and be profitable," Cooper recalled in a recent interview. "And we realized we could do one of three things. We could cut costs, but there's a limit to that. We could cut prices, but that too has its limits. Then we could raise sales profitably—sales, after all, could be limitless when you think about it. We realized we could do that by taking the high-profit drink and fry and then packaging it with the low-profit burger. We realized that if you could get them to buy three items for what they perceived as less, you could substantially drive up the number of walk-ins. Sales would follow."

14   But trying to sell that to corporate headquarters was next to impossible. "We were maligned! Oh, were we maligned," he recalls. "A 99-cent anything was heresy to them. They would come and say 'You're just cutting prices! What are we gonna look like to everybody else?'"

15   "No no no," Cooper would shoot back. "You have to think of the analogy to a fine French restaurant. You always pay less for a *table d'hôte* meal than you pay for *à la carte,* don't you?"

16   "Yes, but—,"

17   "Well, this is a *table d'hôte* dammit! You're getting more people to the table spending as much as they would before—and coming more often!"

18   Finally headquarters relented, although by now it hardly mattered. Cooper had by then begun his own rogue campaign. He was selling what the industry would later call "value meals"—the origin of what we now call supersizing. Using local radio, he advertised a "Big Mac and Company," a "Fish, Fry, Drink and Pie," a "4th of July Value Combo." Sales, Cooper says, "went through the roof. Just like I told them they would."

* * * * *

19   Though it is difficult to gauge the exact impact of supersizing upon the appetite of the average consumer, there are clues about it in the now growing field of satiety—the science of understanding human satisfaction. A 2001 study by nutritional researchers at Penn State University, for example, sought to find out whether the presence of larger portions *in themselves* induced people to eat more. Men and women volunteers, all reporting the same level of hunger, were served lunch on four separate occasions. In each session, the size of the main entree was increased, from 500 to 625 to 700 and finally to 1000 grams. After four weeks, the pattern became clear: As portions increased, all participants ate increasingly larger amounts, despite their stable hunger levels. As the scholars wrote: "Subjects consumed approximately 30 percent more energy when

served the largest as opposed to the smallest portion." They had documented that satiety is not satiety. Human hunger could be expanded by merely offering more and bigger options.

20   Certainly the best nutritional data suggest so as well. Between 1970 and 1994, the USDA reports, the amount of food available in the American food supply increased 15 percent—from 3300 to 3800 calories or by about 500 calories per person per day. During about the same period (1977–1995), average individual caloric intake increased by almost 200 calories, from 1876 calories a day to 2043 calories a day. One could argue which came first, the appetite or the bigger burger, but the calories—they were on the plate and in our mouths.

21   By the end of the century, supersizing—the ultimate expression of the value meal revolution—reigned. As of 1996, some 25 percent of the $97 billion spent on fast food came from items promoted on the basis of either larger size or extra portions. A serving of McDonald's french fries had ballooned from 200 calories (1960) to 320 calories (late 1970s) to 450 calories (mid-1990s) to 540 calories (late 1990s) to the present 610 calories. In fact, everything on the menu had exploded in size. What was once a 590-calorie McDonald's meal was now . . . 1550 calories. By 1999, heavy users—people who eat fast food more than twenty times a month—accounted for $66 billion of the $110 billion spent on fast food. Twenty times a month is now McDonald's marketing goal for every fast-food eater. The average Joe or Jane thought nothing of buying Little Caesar's pizza "by the foot," of supersizing that lunchtime burger or super- supersizing an afternoon snack. Kids had come to see bigger everything—bigger sodas, bigger snacks, bigger candy, and even bigger doughnuts—as the norm; there was no such thing as a fixed, immutable size for anything, because anything could be made a lot bigger for just a tad more.

22   There was more to all of this than just eating more. Bigness: The concept seemed to fuel the marketing of just about everything, from cars (SUVs) to homes (mini-manses) to clothes (super-baggy) and then back again to food (as in the Del Taco Macho Meal, which weighed four pounds). The social scientists and the marketing gurus were going crazy trying to keep up with the trend. "Bigness is addictive because it is about power," commented Inna Zall, a teen marketing consultant, in a page-one story in *USA Today*. While few teenage boys can actually finish a 64-ounce Double Gulp, she added, "it's empowering to hold one in your hand."

23   The pioneers of supersize had achieved David Wallerstein's dream. They had banished the shame of gluttony and opened the maw of the American eater wider than even they had ever imagined.

READING REFLECTION QUESTIONS

1. What are the main messages of this essay (both implied and directly stated)? _____

_____

_____

2. How are statistics used in this article (see especially paragraphs 19 to 21)? What effect do these statistics have in the overall purpose for Critser's essay? _____

_____

3. According to Critser, how did the supersize craze begin, and how widely has it spread? Provide specific examples from the essay.

_____

_____

_____

4. T/F _____ Ray Kroc, McDonald's founder, was reluctant at first to increase portion sizes.

5. T/F _____ Burgers have a higher profit margin than fries and drinks.

6. T/F _____ David Wallerstein came up with the original idea of increasing portion sizes by selling popcorn.

CHECKING VOCABULARY

Define each of the following words by figuring out their meaning using context clues in the reading selection (see Chapter 30 for how to use context clues). If you cannot work out the meaning of a word, use a dictionary.

8. gluttony (paragraph 1): _____

9. pittance (paragraph 2): _____

10. franchise(s) (paragraph 13): _____

READING CRITICALLY

1. What is the author's **purpose** or goal in this reading selection?

_____

_____

2. What are the implied or stated questions being addressed?

_____

_____

3. What specific **support**, details, and examples does the author use to develop the purpose or goal for the reading?

_____

_____

4. What inferences does the author include in this reading? (Inferences imply "if this, then this" types of cause/effect analysis.)

_____

_____

5. Who is the intended audience, and how did you reach that **conclusion**?

_____

_____

WRITING ASSIGNMENTS

1. Write a cause/effect essay (Chapter 13) on the supersize phenomenon as described by Critser in "Supersize Me."

2. Write an example/illustration essay (Chapter 12) that supports Critser's view about this trend for making everything "bigger"; use examples from Critser as well as examples from your own experience. Include some narration (see Chapter 7) and cause/effect analysis (Chapter 13).

3. Write an argument essay (Chapter 15) that develops a specific plan of action for educating children at an early age regarding the supersize phenomenon and its harmful consequences.

VIEWPOINT: DEBATE ON THE CUSTOMER SERVICE MODEL IN THE COLLEGES

The following debate represents two sides of the argument about whether to run colleges using a customer service model.

Thank you for shopping at Valencia!

John Scolaro, Valencia Community College

1   A provost or regional manager of one of Valencia Community College's campuses or business centers recently sent a campus-wide e-mail to faculty and professional staff or hourly employees which infuriated me and more than a handful of my colleagues. She said that a group met last year to discuss *Unleashing Excellence: The Complete Guide to Ultimate Customer Service* (2003) by Dennis Snow and Teri Yanovitch in order to inspire those of us who work and teach at the college to create a culture of service. Our vision, she said, should be to treat each individual customer with respect, compassion, and a smile, like each of us expects to be treated when we are the customer. She also insisted that we should handle our customers like that piece of china with which our mothers once entrusted us because it was special and could easily break.

2   I couldn't believe what I had just read. My God, I thought, has academia become a business? Is education a product? Are students now consumers? Are text books like company manuals? Is a course syllabus a mere business plan? Is the college president the CEO of the corporation? Are academic deans the equivalent of department managers? And are professors and other college professionals only hourly employees?

3   If my "take" on this Provost's e-mail is accurate, then Valencia Community College like many other academic institutions has become infected with the virus of consumerism. This view of students as customers or consumers and of academia as a community of servants must be countered as nothing more than "holy crap," as Frank of the sitcom "Everybody Loves Raymond" would have called it.

4   To me and to other like-minded colleagues, we would benefit more if we returned to the literary works of the Jewish philosopher, Martin Buber, and the Lebanese poet, Kahlil Gibran. Their insights on the nature of a true education, on teaching, and on students prompt us to challenge the mentality of consumerism which has infiltrated academia today.

5   Students, according to Buber, are not consumers, who are merely shopping around for the best buy as if they truly know what they are doing. They don't! Instead, he says that students are unfurnished and unfulfilled beings who stand to gain from their teachers, whose intellectual maturity and depth of knowledge will inspire them beyond belief. Or as Gibran said, a true teacher bids his student not to enter the house of his wisdom, but leads him to the threshold of his own mind.

6   If education is only an exercise in consumerism, then perhaps colleges and universities should offer coupons, discounts, and specials so that their customers could cash in on learning as a product designed to keep them happy. However, if the objective of a true education is to challenge students to think more reflectively, to inspire them to question every thing, to nurture their creativity, and to get them to work hard to resolve diverse issues of import which plague the world today, then students, as Buber suggested, are not customers or consumers, but developing beings before mature ones. Only then will the quest for knowledge become more than a mere function of consumerism.

7   Thank you for shopping at Valencia!

The Other Side: Some Colleges Do Stress Customer Service ...

Interview by Robert Galin

8   Obviously, the idea of customer service as a general concept is not new (most of us expect a customer-service orientation at retailers, service companies like McDonald's, and government agencies). However, it apparently is new to many colleges.

9   G. David Sivak, a consultant with the League for Innovation in the Community College (www.league.org), explains that "The idea of Customer Service at community colleges is really a recent phenomenon because I know of no formal programs that exist. I wrote and have delivered a full day seminar, Customer Service and Professionalism in the Community College, for the League of Innovation in the Community College. This seminar is an outgrowth of, what I consider, the lack of good customer service in community colleges. I continue, weekly, to add more information to my research because some community colleges are starting to realize what excellent customer service can mean to their institutions in regards to image, reputation, enrollment and the bottom line. The vast majority of community colleges haven't even scratched the surface of what to do to implement a customer service program within their institution."

10   Some colleges have added their customer service orientation to their web sites. But they do not all define that orientation the same. In the same way, a number of colleges still have not gotten onto the customer service bandwagon.

11   "Most community colleges define, in my opinion, that customer service means taking care of the students and their needs while they are

attending their chosen institution. The community colleges I've visited have not implemented any programs and it shows when you walk on campus and walk through the college buildings. I've delivered customer service programs at Ivy Tech Community College in Indiana, Anne Arundel Community College in Maryland, and Alabama Southern Community College in Alabama. These colleges have seen the value of training their employees. The training heightens the awareness of what services community colleges are supposed to do for their customers (students).

12   "Moreover," Sivak says, "customer service in a community college compared to commercial enterprises is not quite on the same level. Community colleges are just starting to realize how many services are dispensed to their clientele. Historically, community colleges have not been in existence as long as other businesses and services have been around, hence, the comparison is somewhat lopsided. The fundamental purpose of a business is to attract a customer, keep a customer, and attract more customers. Community colleges are just starting to understand how they can impact individuals who seek to attend their respective institutions."

13   Implementing a customer service orientation doesn't necessarily take care of all ills. In fact, Sivak says, some colleges don't quite do it the right way.

14   "The only downside of customer service in a higher education setting is when customers (students) are not valued, not respected, and DO NOT receive value for the fees they have paid for and were promised by the institution." In other words, Sivak explains, "higher education 'has not gotten it' when it comes to having a program of customer service and dispensing it. Just think of any other entity that you patronize and you don't receive added value from them. You would be very upset to pay a fee and not get equal value from that organization. For example, if you pay for a computer service and it goes down for two days and you can't use it. You would expect compensation, an apology and some kind of assistance to keep you as a customer."

15   Just as there is accountability and evaluation in the classrooms and administrative offices, there needs to be some understanding of the effectiveness of the customer service program a college implements, Sivak says.

16   "There is a way of unofficially judging the success or lack of success with a customer service program at a community college. People frequent establishments that tend to meet or exceed their needs," he says. "If an institution has poor service, rude employees, poor coordination, no teamwork, and a general sense of not meeting customer needs, you can rest

assured people will 'vote with their feet' and walk away from the college. Also, 'word of mouth' is one of the most powerful ways of advertising something. People WILL tell their friends about poor services and facilities and it will deter people from enrolling at the college.

17   "Conversely," Sivak explains, "a community college that employs a friendly, well trained staff, keeps a well manicured campus, stresses a clean and healthy environment, and goes the 'extra mile' for their students, will reap the benefits of a well satisfied and proud student body."

18   Sivak says that the sign of a good program, such as those at the colleges mentioned above, are that they are a "fluid, continuing, and ever-evolving program of commitment to the student, your ultimate customer."

19   Because the idea of formal customer service programs is new to many colleges, there is no "research or statistics on customer service programs that haven't worked," Sivak explains. However, "It is, in my opinion, an overlooked portion of a student's overall experience at a community college. Customer service needs to be exemplary in a community college to help allay any fears or situations for the traditional student or for an older returning student who needs reassurance that they will be given every support to succeed in their educational journey. We owe students the finest of service we can possibly render to them," Sivak emphasizes. "They are our life blood and we need them or we don't have jobs as administrators, instructors, and support staff."

READING REFLECTION QUESTIONS

1. In your own words, what is the main question, the main concept being debated, in this article? _____

_____

2. What does John Scolaro argue in the section titled "Thank you for shopping at Valencia!"? _____

_____

3. Provide one of the counterarguments to Scolaro's points presented in the second section of the reading which features an interview with G. David Sivak titled "The Other Side: Some Colleges Do Stress Customer Service": _____

_____

_____

4. T/F _____ Problems with the economy have had a big impact on community colleges.

5. T/F _____ John Scolaro thinks the customer service model does not work for higher education.

6. Do you think colleges should stress customer service? Why or why not?

_____

_____

_____

_____

7. T/F _____ According to the interview, Sivak thinks students should receive a full refund if they are not happy with a class (the product).

CHECKING VOCABULARY

Define each of the following words by figuring out their meaning using context clues in the reading selection (see Chapter 30 for how to use context clues). If you cannot work out the meaning of a word, use a dictionary.

8. consumerism (paragraph 3): _____

9. phenomenon (paragraph 9): _____

10. exemplary (paragraph 19): _____

READING CRITICALLY

1. What is the author's **purpose** or goal in this reading selection?

_____

_____

2. What are the implied or stated questions being addressed?

_____

_____

3. What specific **support**, details, and examples does the author use to develop the purpose or goal for the reading?

_____

_____

4. What inferences does the author include in this reading? (Inferences imply "if this, then this" types of cause/effect analysis.)

_____

_____

5. Who is the intended audience, and how did you reach that **conclusion**?

_____

_____

WRITING ASSIGNMENTS

1. Write an argument/persuasion essay (Chapter 15) in favor of or against colleges moving to a customer-service based philosophy.

2. Write a narration essay (Chapter 7) about a class you took in college or high school that did not provide the kind of service you expected.

3. Write a cause and effect essay (Chapter 13) that explores the potential positive and negative effects that moving to a more customer-based outlook in the classroom would have.

The Lottery

Shirley Jackson

Shirley Jackson (1916–1965) wrote several stories and novels, including _The Sundial_, _We Have Always Lived in the Castle_, and _The Haunting of Hill House_. Her story "The Lottery" is her most famous work and was originally published in a 1948 issue of _The New Yorker_.

1   The morning of June 27th was clear and sunny, with the fresh warmth of a full-summer day; the flowers were blossoming profusely and the grass was richly green. The people of the village began to gather in the square, between the post office and the bank, around ten o'clock; in some towns there were so many people that the lottery took two days and had to be started on June 27th, but in this village, where there were only about three hundred people, the whole lottery took less than two hours, so it could begin at ten o'clock in the morning and still be through in time to allow the villagers to get home for noon dinner.

2   The children assembled first, of course. School was recently over for the summer, and the feeling of liberty sat uneasily on most of them; they tended to gather together quietly for a while before they broke into boisterous play, and their talk was still of the classroom and the teacher, of books and reprimands. Bobby Martin had already stuffed his pockets full of stones, and the other boys soon followed his example, selecting the smoothest and roundest stones; Bobby and Harry Jones and Dickie Delacroix—the villagers pronounced this name "Dellacroy"—eventually made a great pile of stones in one corner of the square and guarded it against the raids of the other boys. The girls stood aside, talking among themselves, looking over their shoulders at the boys, and the very small children rolled in the dust or clung to the hands of their older brothers or sisters.

3   Soon the men began to gather, surveying their own children, speaking of planting and rain, tractors and taxes. They stood together, away from the pile of stones in the corner, and their jokes were quiet and they smiled rather than laughed. The women, wearing faded house dresses and sweaters, came shortly after their menfolk. They greeted one another and exchanged bits of gossip as they went to join their husbands. Soon the women, standing by their husbands, began to call to their children, and the children came reluctantly, having to be called four or five times. Bobby Martin ducked under his mother's grasping hand and ran, laughing, back to the pile of stones. His father spoke up sharply, and Bobby came quickly and took his place between his father and his oldest brother.

4   The lottery was conducted—as were the square dances, the teen club, the Halloween program—by Mr. Summers, who had time and energy to devote to civic activities. He was a round-faced, jovial man and he ran the coal business, and people were sorry for him because he had no children and his wife was a scold. When he arrived in the square, carrying the black wooden box, there was a murmur of conversation among the villagers, and he waved and called. "Little late today, folks." The postmaster, Mr. Graves, followed him, carrying a three-legged stool, and the stool was put in the center of the square and Mr. Summers set the black box down on it. The villagers kept their distance, leaving a space between themselves and the stool, and when Mr. Summers said, "Some of you fellows want to give me a hand?" there was a hesitation before two men, Mr. Martin and his oldest son, Baxter, came forward to hold the box steady on the stool while Mr. Summers stirred up the papers inside it.

5   The original paraphernalia for the lottery had been lost long ago, and the black box now resting on the stool had been put into use even before Old Man Warner, the oldest man in town, was born. Mr. Summers spoke frequently to the villagers about making a new box, but no one liked to upset even as much tradition as was represented by the black box. There

was a story that the present box had been made with some pieces of the box that had preceded it, the one that had been constructed when the first people settled down to make a village here. Every year, after the lottery, Mr. Summers began talking again about a new box, but every year the subject was allowed to fade off without anything's being done. The black box grew shabbier each year: by now it was no longer completely black but splintered badly along one side to show the original wood color, and in some places faded or stained.

6   Mr. Martin and his oldest son, Baxter, held the black box securely on the stool until Mr. Summers had stirred the papers thoroughly with his hand. Because so much of the ritual had been forgotten or discarded, Mr. Summers had been successful in having slips of paper substituted for the chips of wood that had been used for generations. Chips of wood, Mr. Summers had argued, had been all very well when the village was tiny, but now that the population was more than three hundred and likely to keep on growing, it was necessary to use something that would fit more easily into the black box. The night before the lottery, Mr. Summers and Mr. Graves made up the slips of paper and put them in the box, and it was then taken to the safe of Mr. Summers' coal company and locked up until Mr. Summers was ready to take it to the square next morning. The rest of the year, the box was put way, sometimes one place, sometimes another; it had spent one year in Mr. Graves's barn and another year underfoot in the post office, and sometimes it was set on a shelf in the Martin grocery and left there.

7   There was a great deal of fussing to be done before Mr. Summers declared the lottery open. There were the lists to make up—of heads of families, heads of households in each family, members of each household in each family. There was the proper swearing-in of Mr. Summers by the postmaster, as the official of the lottery; at one time, some people remembered, there had been a recital of some sort, performed by the official of the lottery, a perfunctory tuneless chant that had been rattled off duly each year; some people believed that the official of the lottery used to stand just so when he said or sang it, others believed that he was supposed to walk among the people, but years and years ago this part of the ritual had been allowed to lapse. There had been, also, a ritual salute, which the official of the lottery had had to use in addressing each person who came up to draw from the box, but this also had changed with time, until now it was felt necessary only for the official to speak to each person approaching. Mr. Summers was very good at all this; in his clean white shirt and blue jeans, with one hand resting carelessly on the black box, he seemed very proper and important as he talked interminably to Mr. Graves and the Martins.

8   Just as Mr. Summers finally left off talking and turned to the assembled villagers, Mrs. Hutchinson came hurriedly along the path to the square, her sweater thrown over her shoulders, and slid into place in the back of the crowd. "Clean forgot what day it was," she said to Mrs. Delacroix, who stood next to her, and they both laughed softly. "Thought my old man was out back stacking wood," Mrs. Hutchinson went on, "and then I looked out the window and the kids was gone, and then I remembered it was the twenty-seventh and came a-running." She dried her hands on her apron, and Mrs. Delacroix said, "You're in time, though. They're still talking away up there."

9   Mrs. Hutchinson craned her neck to see through the crowd and found her husband and children standing near the front. She tapped Mrs. Delacroix on the arm as a farewell and began to make her way through the crowd. The people separated good-humoredly to let her through: two or three people said, in voices just loud enough to be heard across the crowd, "Here comes your Missus, Hutchinson," and "Bill, she made it after all." Mrs. Hutchinson reached her husband, and Mr. Summers, who had been waiting, said cheerfully. "Thought we were going to have to get on without you, Tessie." Mrs. Hutchinson said grinning, "Wouldn't have me leave m'dishes in the sink, now, would you, Joe?" and soft laughter ran through the crowd as the people stirred back into position after Mrs. Hutchinson's arrival.

10   "Well, now." Mr. Summers said soberly, "guess we better get started, get this over with, so's we can go back to work. Anybody ain't here?"

11   "Dunbar." several people said. "Dunbar. Dunbar."

12   Mr. Summers consulted his list. "Clyde Dunbar," he said. "That's right. He's broke his leg, hasn't he? Who's drawing for him?"

13   "Me. I guess," a woman said, and Mr. Summers turned to look at her. "Wife draws for her husband," Mr. Summers said. "Don't you have a grown boy to do it for you, Janey?" Although Mr. Summers and everyone else in the village knew the answer perfectly well, it was the business of the official of the lottery to ask such questions formally. Mr. Summers waited with an expression of polite interest while Mrs. Dunbar answered.

14   "Horace's not but sixteen yet," Mrs. Dunbar said regretfully. "Guess I gotta fill in for the old man this year."

15   "Right," Mr. Summers said. He made a note on the list he was holding. Then he asked, "Watson boy drawing this year?"

16   A tall boy in the crowd raised his hand. "Here," he said, "I'm drawing for my mother and me." He blinked his eyes nervously and ducked his head as several voices in the crowd said things like "Good fellow, lad." and "Glad to see your mother's got a man to do it."

17   "Well," Mr. Summers said, "guess that's everyone. Old Man Warner make it?"

18   "Here," a voice said, and Mr. Summers nodded.

19   A sudden hush fell on the crowd as Mr. Summers cleared his throat and looked at the list. "All ready?" he called. "Now, I'll read the names—heads of families first—and the men come up and take a paper out of the box. Keep the paper folded in your hand without looking at it until everyone has had a turn. Everything clear?"

20   The people had done it so many times that they only half listened to the directions: most of them were quiet, wetting their lips, not looking around. Then Mr. Summers raised one hand high and said, "Adams." A man disengaged himself from the crowd and came forward. "Hi. Steve." Mr. Summers said, and Mr. Adams said, "Hi, Joe." They grinned at one another humorlessly and nervously. Then Mr. Adams reached into the black box and took out a folded paper. He held it firmly by one corner as he turned and went hastily back to his place in the crowd where he stood a little apart from his family not looking down at his hand.

21   "Allen," Mr. Summers said. "Anderson. . . . Bentham."

22   "Seems like there's no time at all between lotteries any more," Mrs. Delacroix said to Mrs. Graves in the back row.

23   "Seems like we got through with the last one only last week."

24   "Time sure goes fast," Mrs. Graves said.

25   "Clark. . . . Delacroix."

26   "There goes my old man." Mrs. Delacroix said. She held her breath while her husband went forward.

27   "Dunbar," Mr. Summers said, and Mrs. Dunbar went steadily to the box while one of the women said, "Go on, Janey," and another said, "There she goes."

28   "We're next." Mrs. Graves said. She watched while Mr. Graves came around from the side of the box, greeted Mr. Summers gravely and selected a slip of paper from the box. By now, all through the crowd there were men holding the small folded papers in their large hands, turning them over and over nervously. Mrs. Dunbar and her two sons stood together, Mrs. Dunbar holding the slip of paper.

29   "Harburt. . . . Hutchinson."

30   "Get up there, Bill," Mrs. Hutchinson said, and the people near her laughed.

31   "Jones."

32   "They do say," Mr. Adams said to Old Man Warner, who stood next to him, "that over in the north village they're talking of giving up the lottery."

33   Old Man Warner snorted. "Pack of crazy fools," he said. "Listening to the young folks, nothing's good enough for them. Next thing you know,

they'll be wanting to go back to living in caves, nobody work any more, live that way for a while. Used to be a saying about 'Lottery in June, corn be heavy soon.' First thing you know, we'd all be eating stewed chick-weed and acorns. There's always been a lottery," he added petulantly. "Bad enough to see young Joe Summers up there joking with everybody."

34   "Some places have already quit lotteries," Mrs. Adams said.

35   "Nothing but trouble in that," Old Man Warner said stoutly. "Pack of young fools."

36   "Martin." And Bobby Martin watched his father go forward. "Overdyke. . . . Percy."

37   "I wish they'd hurry," Mrs. Dunbar said to her older son. "I wish they'd hurry."

38   "They're almost through," her son said.

39   "You get ready to run tell Dad," Mrs. Dunbar said.

40   Mr. Summers called his own name and then stepped forward precisely and selected a slip from the box. Then he called, "Warner."

41   "Seventy-seventh year I been in the lottery," Old Man Warner said as he went through the crowd. "Seventy-seventh time."

42   "Watson." The tall boy came awkwardly through the crowd. Someone said, "Don't be nervous, Jack," and Mr. Summers said, "Take your time, son."

43   "Zanini."

44   After that, there was a long pause, a breathless pause, until Mr. Summers, holding his slip of paper in the air, said, "All right, fellows." For a minute, no one moved, and then all the slips of paper were opened. Suddenly, all the women began to speak at once, saying. "Who is it?," "Who's got it?," "Is it the Dunbars?," "Is it the Watsons?" Then the voices began to say, "It's Hutchinson. It's Bill," "Bill Hutchinson's got it."

45   "Go tell your father," Mrs. Dunbar said to her older son.

46   People began to look around to see the Hutchinsons. Bill Hutchinson was standing quiet, staring down at the paper in his hand. Suddenly, Tessie Hutchinson shouted to Mr. Summers. "You didn't give him time enough to take any paper he wanted. I saw you. It wasn't fair!"

47   "Be a good sport, Tessie," Mrs. Delacroix called, and Mrs. Graves said, "All of us took the same chance."

48   "Shut up, Tessie," Bill Hutchinson said.

49   "Well, everyone," Mr. Summers said, "that was done pretty fast, and now we've got to be hurrying a little more to get done in time." He con-sulted his next list. "Bill," he said, "you draw for the Hutchinson family. You got any other households in the Hutchinsons?"

50   "There's Don and Eva," Mrs. Hutchinson yelled. "Make them take their chance!"

51   "Daughters draw with their husbands' families, Tessie," Mr. Summers said gently. "You know that as well as anyone else."

52   "It wasn't fair," Tessie said.

53   "I guess not, Joe." Bill Hutchinson said regretfully. "My daughter draws with her husband's family; that's only fair. And I've got no other family except the kids."

54   "Then, as far as drawing for families is concerned, it's you," Mr. Summers said in explanation, "and as far as drawing for households is concerned, that's you, too. Right?"

55   "Right," Bill Hutchinson said.

56   "How many kids, Bill?" Mr. Summers asked formally.

57   "Three," Bill Hutchinson said. "There's Bill, Jr., and Nancy, and little Dave. And Tessie and me."

58   "All right, then," Mr. Summers said. "Harry, you got their tickets back?"

59   Mr. Graves nodded and held up the slips of paper. "Put them in the box, then," Mr. Summers directed. "Take Bill's and put it in."

60   "I think we ought to start over," Mrs. Hutchinson said, as quietly as she could. "I tell you it wasn't fair. You didn't give him time enough to choose. Everybody saw that."

61   Mr. Graves had selected the five slips and put them in the box, and he dropped all the papers but those onto the ground where the breeze caught them and lifted them off.

62   "Listen, everybody," Mrs. Hutchinson was saying to the people around her.

63   "Ready, Bill?" Mr. Summers asked, and Bill Hutchinson, with one quick glance around at his wife and children, nodded.

64   "Remember," Mr. Summers said, "take the slips and keep them folded until each person has taken one. Harry, you help little Dave." Mr. Graves took the hand of the little boy, who came willingly with him up to the box. "Take a paper out of the box, Davy." Mr. Summers said. Davy put his hand into the box and laughed. "Take just one paper." Mr. Summers said. "Harry, you hold it for him." Mr. Graves took the child's hand and removed the folded paper from the tight fist and held it while little Dave stood next to him and looked up at him wonderingly.

65   "Nancy next," Mr. Summers said. Nancy was twelve, and her school friends breathed heavily as she went forward switching her skirt, and took a slip daintily from the box "Bill, Jr.," Mr. Summers said, and Billy, his face red and his feet overlarge, near knocked the box over as he got a paper out. "Tessie," Mr. Summers said. She hesitated for a minute, looking around defiantly, and then set her lips and went up to the box. She snatched a paper out and held it behind her.

66   "Bill," Mr. Summers said, and Bill Hutchinson reached into the box and felt around, bringing his hand out at last with the slip of paper in it.

67   The crowd was quiet. A girl whispered, "I hope it's not Nancy," and the sound of the whisper reached the edges of the crowd.

68   "It's not the way it used to be," Old Man Warner said clearly. "People ain't the way they used to be."

69   "All right," Mr. Summers said. "Open the papers. Harry, you open little Dave's."

70   Mr. Graves opened the slip of paper and there was a general sigh through the crowd as he held it up and everyone could see that it was blank. Nancy and Bill Jr. opened theirs at the same time, and both beamed and laughed, turning around to the crowd and holding their slips of paper above their heads.

71   "Tessie," Mr. Summers said. There was a pause, and then Mr. Summers looked at Bill Hutchinson, and Bill unfolded his paper and showed it. It was blank.

72   "It's Tessie," Mr. Summers said, and his voice was hushed. "Show us her paper, Bill."

73   Bill Hutchinson went over to his wife and forced the slip of paper out of her hand. It had a black spot on it, the black spot Mr. Summers had made the night before with the heavy pencil in the coal company office. Bill Hutchinson held it up, and there was a stir in the crowd.

74   "All right, folks." Mr. Summers said. "Let's finish quickly."

75   Although the villagers had forgotten the ritual and lost the original black box, they still remembered to use stones. The pile of stones the boys had made earlier was ready; there were stones on the ground with the blowing scraps of paper that had come out of the box. Delacroix selected a stone so large she had to pick it up with both hands and turned to Mrs. Dunbar. "Come on," she said. "Hurry up."

76   Mrs. Dunbar had small stones in both hands, and she said, gasping for breath. "I can't run at all. You'll have to go ahead and I'll catch up with you."

77   The children had stones already. And someone gave little Davy Hutchinson few pebbles.

78   Tessie Hutchinson was in the center of a cleared space by now, and she held her hands out desperately as the villagers moved in on her. "It isn't fair," she said. A stone hit her on the side of the head. Old Man Warner was saying, "Come on, come on, everyone." Steve Adams was in the front of the crowd of villagers, with Mrs. Graves beside him.

79   "It isn't fair, it isn't right," Mrs. Hutchinson screamed, and then they were upon her.

READING REFLECTION QUESTIONS

1. What are the implied and direct messages of this story? _____

_____

2. What was the *original* purpose for the lottery? Write the quotation that explains it:

_____

3. T/F _____ The children are exempt from participating in the lottery.

4. T/F _____ "The Lottery" involves winning money.

5. T/F _____ Most of the people in the village understand the purpose and agree with the need for continuing the lottery.

6. T/F _____ During the lottery drawing, a black dot indicates that a person has "won" the lottery.

7. Explain exactly what happens to someone who wins this lottery:

_____

CHECKING VOCABULARY

Define each of the following words by figuring out their meaning using context clues in the reading selection (see Chapter 30 for how to use context clues). If you cannot work out the meaning of a word, use a dictionary

8. interminably (paragraph 7): _____

9. disengaged (paragraph 20): _____

10. gravely (paragraph 28): _____

READING CRITICALLY

1. What is the author's **purpose** or goal in this reading selection?

_____

_____

2. What are the implied or stated questions being addressed?

_____

_____

3. What specific **support**, details, and examples does the author use to develop his or her purpose or goal for the reading?

_____

_____

4. What inferences does the author include in this reading? (Inferences imply "if this, then this" types of cause/effect analysis.)

_____

_____

5. Who is the intended audience, and how did you reach that **conclusion**?

_____

_____

WRITING ASSIGNMENTS

1. Write a story analysis essay (Appendix A) that addresses both Jackson's writing technique and style as well as her analytical message (the purpose) of the story. Be sure to use Six Steps to Active Reading (p. 25) to increase your comprehension and improve your analysis.

2. Write an argument essay that argues against some tradition or ritual that has been kept up in our society (or in your own family or community) merely for the sake of tradition and that you think should be ended. First, explain what the tradition or ritual is; then, argue to end the tradition or ritual, and be sure to provide your reasons and support for your proposal to end the tradition. Finally, be sure to address the main counterarguments from your family, community, or society (Chapter 15).

3. Write a description essay (Chapter 8) that describes in detail a tradition or ritual that your family practices.

A Hanging

George Orwell

George Orwell, a famous British writer and journalist, was born Eric Arthur Blair on June 25, 1903, in Motihari, India. He died in London in 1950. He wrote many essays and stories, but he is most famous for his two novels that critique fascism: *Animal Farm* and *1984*. This story was written in 1931 and relates to his life in Burma before he left for England.

1   It was in Burma, a sodden morning of the rains. A sickly light, like yellow tinfoil, was slanting over the high walls into the jail yard. We were waiting outside the condemned cells, a row of sheds fronted with double bars, like small animal cages. Each cell measured about ten feet by ten and was quite bare within except for a plank bed and a pot of drinking water. In some of them brown silent men were squatting at the inner bars, with their blankets draped round them. These were the condemned men, due to be hanged within the next week or two.

2   One prisoner had been brought out of his cell. He was a Hindu, a puny wisp of a man, with a shaven head and vague liquid eyes. He had a thick, sprouting moustache, absurdly too big for his body, rather like the moustache of a comic man on the films. Six tall Indian warders were guarding him and getting him ready for the gallows. Two of them stood by with rifles and fixed bayonets, while the others handcuffed him, passed a chain through his handcuffs and fixed it to their belts, and lashed his arms tight to his sides. They crowded very close about him, with their hands always on him in a careful, caressing grip, as though all the while feeling him to make sure he was there. It was like men handling a fish which is still alive and may jump back into the water. But he stood quite unresisting, yielding his arms limply to the ropes, as though he hardly noticed what was happening.

3   Eight o'clock struck and a bugle call, desolately thin in the wet air, floated from the distant barracks. The superintendent of the jail, who was standing apart from the rest of us, moodily prodding the gravel with his stick, raised his head at the sound. He was an army doctor, with a grey toothbrush moustache and a gruff voice. "For God's sake hurry up, Francis," he said irritably. "The man ought to have been dead by this time. Aren't you ready yet?"

4   Francis, the head jailer, a fat Dravidian in a white drill suit and gold spectacles, waved his black hand. "Yes sir, yes sir," he bubbled. "All iss satisfactorily prepared. The hangman iss waiting. We shall proceed."

5   "Well, quick march, then. The prisoners can't get their breakfast till this job's over."

6   We set out for the gallows. Two warders marched on either side of the prisoner, with their rifles at the slope; two others marched close against him, gripping him by arm and shoulder, as though at once pushing and supporting him. The rest of us, magistrates and the like, followed behind. Suddenly, when we had gone ten yards, the procession stopped short

without any order or warning. A dreadful thing had happened—a dog, come goodness knows whence, had appeared in the yard. It came bounding among us with a loud volley of barks, and leapt round us wagging its whole body, wild with glee at finding so many human beings together. It was a large woolly dog, half Airedale, half pariah. For a moment it pranced round us, and then, before anyone could stop it, it had made a dash for the prisoner, and jumping up tried to lick his face. Everyone stood aghast, too taken aback even to grab at the dog.

7   "Who let that bloody brute in here?" said the superintendent angrily. "Catch it, someone!"

8   A warder, detached from the escort, charged clumsily after the dog, but it danced and gambolled just out of his reach, taking everything as part of the game. A young Eurasian jailer picked up a handful of gravel and tried to stone the dog away, but it dodged the stones and came after us again. Its yaps echoed from the jail wails. The prisoner, in the grasp of the two warders, looked on incuriously, as though this was another formality of the hanging. It was several minutes before someone managed to catch the dog. Then we put my handkerchief through its collar and moved off once more, with the dog still straining and whimpering.

9   It was about forty yards to the gallows. I watched the bare brown back of the prisoner marching in front of me. He walked clumsily with his bound arms, but quite steadily, with that bobbing gait of the Indian who never straightens his knees. At each step his muscles slid neatly into place, the lock of hair on his scalp danced up and down, his feet printed themselves on the wet gravel. And once, in spite of the men who gripped him by each shoulder, he stepped slightly aside to avoid a puddle on the path.

10   It is curious, but till that moment I had never realized what it means to destroy a healthy, conscious man. When I saw the prisoner step aside to avoid the puddle, I saw the mystery, the unspeakable wrongness, of cutting a life short when it is in full tide. This man was not dying, he was alive just as we were alive. All the organs of his body were working— bowels digesting food, skin renewing itself, nails growing, tissues forming—all toiling away in solemn foolery. His nails would still be growing when he stood on the drop, when he was falling through the air with a tenth of a second to live. His eyes saw the yellow gravel and the grey walls, and his brain still remembered, foresaw, reasoned—reasoned even about puddles. He and we were a party of men walking together, seeing, hearing, feeling, understanding the same world; and in two minutes, with a sudden snap, one of us would be gone—one mind less, one world less.

11   The gallows stood in a small yard, separate from the main grounds of the prison, and overgrown with tall prickly weeds. It was a brick erection

like three sides of a shed, with planking on top, and above that two beams and a crossbar with the rope dangling. The hangman, a grey-haired convict in the white uniform of the prison, was waiting beside his machine. He greeted us with a servile crouch as we entered. At a word from Francis the two warders, gripping the prisoner more closely than ever, half led, half pushed him to the gallows and helped him clumsily up the ladder. Then the hangman climbed up and fixed the rope round the prisoner's neck.

12   We stood waiting, five yards away. The warders had formed in a rough circle round the gallows. And then, when the noose was fixed, the prisoner began crying out to his god. It was a high, reiterated cry of "Ram! Ram! Ram! Ram!", not urgent and fearful like a prayer or a cry for help, but steady, rhythmical, almost like the tolling of a bell. The dog answered the sound with a whine. The hangman, still standing on the gallows, produced a small cotton bag like a flour bag and drew it down over the prisoner's face. But the sound, muffled by the cloth, still persisted, over and over again: "Ram! Ram! Ram! Ram! Ram!"

13   The hangman climbed down and stood ready, holding the lever. Minutes seemed to pass. The steady, muffled crying from the prisoner went on and on, "Ram! Ram! Ram!" never faltering for an instant. The superintendent, his head on his chest, was slowly poking the ground with his stick; perhaps he was counting the cries, allowing the prisoner a fixed number—fifty, perhaps, or a hundred. Everyone had changed colour. The Indians had gone grey like bad coffee, and one or two of the bayonets were wavering. We looked at the lashed, hooded man on the drop, and listened to his cries—each cry another second of life; the same thought was in all our minds: oh, kill him quickly, get it over, stop that abominable noise!

14   Suddenly the superintendent made up his mind. Throwing up his head he made a swift motion with his stick. "Chalo!" he shouted almost fiercely.

15   There was a clanking noise, and then dead silence. The prisoner had vanished, and the rope was twisting on itself. I let go of the dog, and it galloped immediately to the back of the gallows; but when it got there it stopped short, barked, and then retreated into a corner of the yard, where it stood among the weeds, looking timorously out at us. We went round the gallows to inspect the prisoner's body. He was dangling with his toes pointed straight downwards, very slowly revolving, as dead as a stone.

16   The superintendent reached out with his stick and poked the bare body; it oscillated, slightly. "He's all right," said the superintendent. He backed out from under the gallows, and blew out a deep breath. The moody look had gone out of his face quite suddenly. He glanced at his

wrist-watch. "Eight minutes past eight. Well, that's all for this morning, thank God."

17   The warders unfixed bayonets and marched away. The dog, sobered and conscious of having misbehaved itself, slipped after them. We walked out of the gallows yard, past the condemned cells with their waiting prisoners, into the big central yard of the prison. The convicts, under the command of warders armed with lathis, were already receiving their breakfast. They squatted in long rows, each man holding a tin pannikin, while two warders with buckets marched round ladling out rice; it seemed quite a homely, jolly scene, after the hanging. An enormous relief had come upon us now that the job was done. One felt an impulse to sing, to break into a run, to snigger. All at once everyone began chattering gaily.

18   The Eurasian boy walking beside me nodded towards the way we had come, with a knowing smile: "Do you know, sir, our friend (he meant the dead man), when he heard his appeal had been dismissed, he pissed on the floor of his cell. From fright.—Kindly take one of my cigarettes, sir. Do you not admire my new silver case, sir? From the boxwallah, two rupees eight annas. Classy European style."

19   Several people laughed—at what, nobody seemed certain.

20   Francis was walking by the superintendent, talking garrulously. "Well, sir, all hass passed off with the utmost satisfactoriness. It wass all finished—flick! like that. It iss not always so—oah, no! I have known cases where the doctor wass obliged to go beneath the gallows and pull the prisoner's legs to ensure decease. Most disagreeable!"

21   "Wriggling about, eh? That's bad," said the superintendent.

22   "Ach, sir, it iss worse when they become refractory! One man, I recall, clung to the bars of hiss cage when we went to take him out. You will scarcely credit, sir, that it took six warders to dislodge him, three pulling at each leg. We reasoned with him. 'My dear fellow,' we said, 'think of all the pain and trouble you are causing to us!' But no, he would not listen! Ach, he wass very troublesome!"

23   I found that I was laughing quite loudly. Everyone was laughing. Even the superintendent grinned in a tolerant way. "You'd better all come out and have a drink," he said quite genially. "I've got a bottle of whisky in the car. We could do with it."

24   We went through the big double gates of the prison, into the road. "Pulling at his legs!" exclaimed a Burmese magistrate suddenly, and burst into a loud chuckling. We all began laughing again. At that moment Francis's anecdote seemed extraordinarily funny. We all had a drink together, native and European alike, quite amicably. The dead man was a hundred yards away.

READING REFLECTION QUESTIONS

1. In your own words, what is the main message of this story that George Orwell wanted his readers to understand? _____

_____

2. T/F _____ According to the narrator, the prisoner's crime was murder.

3. T/F _____ This hanging was the first hanging that the soldier/ narrator had witnessed.

4. _____   Which of the following best describes the mood or atmosphere of the characters and story?

   a. Light and humoroous
   b. Somber and serious at first with relief and laughing at the end
   c. Outraged and angry throughout

5. Which sentence in the story best sums up Orwell's main thesis? Write it here:

_____

6. T/F _____ The prisoner is a Hindu.

7. Why is the dog important in this story? What function does the dog serve for the plot? _____

_____

8. Why is the fact that the prisoner stepped around the puddle important? What does it signify for the soldier who witnessed this action? _____

_____

_____

CHECKING VOCABULARY

Define each of the following words by figuring out their meaning using context clues in the reading selection (see Chapter 30 for how to use context clues). If you cannot work out the meaning of a word, use a dictionary.

9. sodden (paragraph 1): _____

10. pariah (paragraph 6): _____

READING CRITICALLY

1. What is the author's **purpose** or goal in this reading selection?

_____

_____

2. What are the implied or stated questions being addressed?

_____

_____

3. What specific **support**, details, and examples does the author use to develop the purpose or goal for the reading?

_____

_____

4. What inferences does the author include in this reading? (Inferences imply "if this, then this" types of cause/effect analysis.)

_____

_____

5. Who is the intended audience, and how did you reach that **conclusion**?

_____

_____

WRITING ASSIGNMENTS

1. Write a story analysis essay (Appendix A) that addresses Orwell's writing technique and style as well as his purpose for writing the story. Be sure to use Six Steps to Active Reading (p. 25) to increase your comprehension and ability to analyze the story effectively.

2. Write a narration/description essay (Chapters 7 and 8) about a traumatic or uncomfortable incident you witnessed and what you learned from the experience. Be sure to frame your essay with an introduction and conclusion that explains what lessons you learned about yourself and others from that incident. Also, be sure to include some dialogue in correct dialogue format.

3. Write an argument essay (Chapter 15) that argues for or against capital punishment. Be sure to define your stand clearly, including when and how capital punishment is or isn't justified. Present clear counterarguments to your stand and address those counterarguments fully. Check with your instructor whether you should or should not conduct and include secondary research on capital punishment. If you do include research, then be sure to cite all sources correctly (see MLA section and Research/Documented Paper information in Chapter 19).

I Wonder: Was It Me or Was It My Sari?

Shoba Narayan

Shoba Narayan has written several articles about travel, food, and life. She holds a B.S. in Psychology and an M.A. in Journalism. Also, her book, *Monsoon Diary: A Memoir with Recipes* (2003) describes growing up in South India. This essay originally appeared in *Newsweek* in March 2000.

1   A sari for a month. It shouldn't have been a big deal but it was. After all, I had grown up around sari-clad women in India. My mother even slept in one.

2   In India, saris are adult attire. After I turned 18, I occasionally wore a sari for weddings and holidays and to the temple. But wearing a sequined silk sari to an Indian party was one thing. Deciding to wear a sari every day while living in New York, especially after 10 years in Western clothes, sounded outrageous, even to me.

3   The sari is six yards of fabric folded into a graceful yet cumbersome garment. Like a souffle, it is fragile and can fall apart at any moment. When worn right, it is supremely elegant and unabashedly feminine. However, it requires sacrifices.

4   No longer could I sprint across the street just before the light changed. The sari forced me to shorten my strides. I couldn't squeeze into a crowded subway car for fear that someone would accidentally pull and unravel my sari. I couldn't balance four grocery bags in one hand and pull out my house keys from a convenient pocket with the other. By the end of the first week, I was stumbling around my apartment, feeling clumsy and angry with myself. What was I trying to prove?

5   The notion of wearing a sari every day was relatively new for me. During my college years—the age when most girls in India begin wearing saris regularly—I was studying in America. As an art student at Mount Holyoke, I hung out with purple-haired painters and rabble-rousing

feminists wearing ink-stained khakis and cut-off T shirts. During a languid post-graduation summer in Boston, when I sailed a boat and volunteered for an environmental organization, I wore politically correct, recycled Salvation Army clothes. After getting married, I became a Connecticut housewife experimenting with clothes from Jones New York and Ann Taylor. Through it all, I tried to pick up the accent, learn the jargon and affect the posture of the Americans around me.

6   Then I moved to New York and became a mother. I wanted to teach my 3-year-old daughter Indian values and traditions because I knew she would be profoundly different from her preschool classmates in religion (we are Hindus), eating habits (we are vegetarians) and the festivals we celebrated. Wearing a sari every day was my way of showing her that she could melt into the pot while retaining her individual flavor.

7   It wasn't just for my daughter's sake that I decided to wear a sari. I was tired of trying to fit in. Natalie Cole had never spoken to me as eloquently as M.S., a venerable Indian singer. I couldn't sing the lyrics of Ricky Martin as easily as I could sing my favorite Hindi or Tamil songs. Much as I enjoyed American cuisine, I couldn't last four days without Indian food. It was time to flaunt my ethnicity with a sari and a bright red bindi on my forehead. I was going to be an immigrant, but on my own terms. It was America's turn to adjust to me.

8   Slowly, I eased into wearing the garment. Strangers stared at me as I sashayed across a crowded bookstore. Some of them caught my eye and smiled. At first, I resented being an exhibit. Then I wondered: perhaps I reminded them of a wonderful holiday in India or a favorite Indian cookbook. Grocery clerks enunciated their words when they spoke to me. Everywhere, I was stopped with questions about India as if wearing a sari had made me an authority. One Japanese lady near Columbus Circle asked to have her picture taken with me. A tourist had thought that I was one, too, just steps from my home.

9   But there were unexpected advantages. Indian cabdrivers raced across lanes and screeched to a halt in front of me when I stepped into the street to hail a taxi. When my daughter climbed high up the Jungle-Gym in Central Park, I gathered my sari and prepared to follow, hoping it wouldn't balloon out like Marilyn Monroe's dress. One of the dads standing nearby watched my plight and volunteered to climb after her. Chivalry in New York? Was it me or was it my sari?

10   Best of all, my family approved. My husband complimented me, my parents were proud of me. My daughter oohed and aahed when I pulled out my colorful saris. When I cuddled her in my arms, scents from the vetiver sachets that I used to freshen my sari at night escaped from the

folds of cloth and soothed her to sleep. I felt part of a long line of Indian mothers who had rocked their babies this way.

11   Soon, the month was over. My self-imposed regimen was coming to an end. Instead of feeling liberated, I felt a twinge of unease. I had started enjoying my sari.

12   Saris were impractical for America, I told myself. I would continue to wear them, but not every day. It was time to revert to my sensible khakis. It was time to become American again.

READING REFLECTION QUESTIONS

1. What are the direct or indirect (implied) messages in this story?

_____

_____

_____

_____

2. List the main reason Narayan chose to wear a sari for one month:

_____

_____

_____

3. _____   Which of the following was *not* presented as a *disadvantage* of her wearing a sari?

   a. Unable to dart quickly across a street

   b. Indian cabdrivers reactions to her hailing a cab

   c. Riding a crowded subway with worries about the sari unraveling

   d. No pocket for house keys

4. T/F _____ Saris are important to Indian culture and heritage.

5. T/F _____ The author decided to wear a sari every day for the rest of her life.

6. _____   Which of the following was *not* presented as an *advantage* of her wearing a sari?

   a. Her husband complimented her.

   b. Her parents were proud.

    c. She could move more quickly while wearing a sari.

    d. Her daughter liked her sari.

CHECKING VOCABULARY

Define each of the following words by figuring out their meaning using context clues in the reading selection (see Chapter 30 for how to use context clues). If you cannot work out the meaning of a word, use a dictionary

7. languid (paragraph 5): _____

8. jargon (paragraph 5): _____

9. venerable (paragraph 7): _____

10. sashayed (paragraph 8): _____

READING CRITICALLY

1. What is the author's **purpose** or goal in this reading selection?

_____

_____

2. What are the implied or stated questions being addressed?

_____

_____

3. What specific **support**, details, and examples does the author use to develop the purpose or goal for the reading?

_____

_____

4. What inferences does the author include in this reading? (Inferences imply "if this, then this" types of cause/effect analysis.)

_____

_____

5. Who is the intended audience, and how did you reach that **conclusion**?

_____

_____

WRITING ASSIGNMENTS

1. Write a narration essay (Chapter 7) based on a time that you were treated better or worse than usual based on what you were wearing.

2. Write a description essay (Chapter 8) about a particular item of clothing or object that you or your family owns that illustrates your heritage or your family heritage.

3. Write an argument essay (Chapter 15) arguing for or against adding a mandatory cultural diversity course at your campus.

Still Hungry, Still Homeless

America Magazine Editorial

America magazine describes itself as a journal of opinion on current events, historical events, spiritual events, family, books, film, and television for Catholic people. This editorial appeared in the magazine's February 5, 2001, issue.

1   One might think that last year's particularly strong economy would have led to a reduction in the number of requests for emergency food and shelter. In fact, however, the year 2000 actually saw a rise in both areas. This was among the sad findings of the United States Conference of Mayors' annual survey of 25 cities around the country, which was released in late December.

2   Officials in the survey cities estimated that requests for emergency food assistance jumped by 17 percent—the second highest rate of increase since 1992. Over half of the people seeking help were children and their parents: a particularly disturbing finding, given the need for parents to be able to provide adequate and nutritious food for their children. A third of the adults, moreover, were employed. This reflects the fact that minimum wage jobs at $5.50 an hour cannot cover the cost of living for most Americans. Mirroring the conclusions of the mayors' report, Catholic Charities USA found in its own year-end survey that its agencies had seen what it termed "a startling 22 percent increase in the use of their emergency services."

3   How could this be, in the face of what many politicians have trumpeted as our unprecedented level of prosperity? Ironically, the mayors' report points out that the very strength of the economy has been partly to blame. Seeing that the earnings of middle-class Americans have risen, landlords have been quick to realize that they can charge much higher rents. But for families at the bottom of the economic ladder, whose

earnings did not increase, the consequence has been an ever more desperate search for housing within their income range; it is a search that has sometimes ended in homelessness. Even those lucky enough to have Section 8 vouchers have discovered that apartment owners often refuse to accept them, knowing that they can command higher prices than the government's reimbursement rate for the vouchers. Thus, in nearly half the survey cities, the report cites housing costs as a primary reason for the increase in requests for emergency food and shelter.

4   Welfare reform has played its part in this bleak scenario. People leaving Temporary Assistance for Needy Families (T.A.N.F.) may indeed have full-time jobs that pay above the minimum wage and yet still not be making enough to lift them above the poverty line. And all too frequently, they are unaware that despite being employed, they may still be eligible for the food stamps (and Medicaid) that could tide them over from one month to the next. Government agencies are not as aggressive as they should be in promoting these programs among the working poor. True, the number of food assistance facilities has increased, but the strain on their limited resources is so great that half the cities report that these facilities must either send people away or reduce the amount of what they can provide.

5   The same situation applies to emergency housing requests. Nearly a quarter of them, says the mayors' report, went unmet. Turned-away families in San Antonio, for instance, found themselves obliged to sleep in cars or parks, under bridges or in already doubled- or tripled-up substandard housing. Even when they can be accommodated, in 52 percent of the cities homeless families may have to break up, with older male youths and fathers sent elsewhere.

6   The outlook for the future is not bright. Almost three-fourths of the survey cities expect a rise in the demand for emergency food. As the officials in Boston put it, "the number of pantries increases every year, and [yet] the requests for assistance have increased by as much as 40 percent." Nor, they add, do they "see any relief in the near future." Again, there as elsewhere, high housing costs, along with low-paying jobs, lead the list of causes for more hunger and homelessness. The answer is implied in the comments of the respondents from Burlington, Vt.: "Without a significant commitment to building a significant number of new and affordable housing units, homelessness will continue to rise." The new secretary-designate of the Department of Housing and Urban Development, Mel Martinez, said at his Senate confirmation hearing that he would try to make more housing available to low-income Americans. We hope that he will act on his words. For many years, however, Congress has shown little interest in this neglected area of American life.

7   In releasing its annual report in December, Fred Kammer, S.J., president of Catholic Charities USA, spoke of its findings as "a story about . . . escalating need in a land of skyrocketing wealth." He recalled Bill Clinton's promise to "end welfare as we know it." That has happened, but the rise in requests for emergency food and housing calls into question the effectiveness of welfare reform. The real goal, Father Kammer concluded, should be to "end poverty as we know it." Now is the time for Congress to take the strong measures needed to assist the most vulnerable members of society.

READING REFLECTION QUESTIONS

1. What are the direct or indirect (implied) messages in this article?

_____

_____

2. What tone does the editorial have? What effect does it have on the reader?

_____

_____

3. According to this article, where does action need to take place?

_____

4. T/F _____ The homeless people this article describes are solely single males.

5. T/F _____ Homelessness has been increasing since the 1990s.

6. T/F _____ There has been an increase in the need for emergency food aid.

7. T/F _____ When a homeless person gets a job, he or she no longer needs assistance with food or housing.

CHECKING VOCABULARY

Define each of the following words by figuring out their meaning using context clues in the reading selection (see Chapter 30 for how to use context clues). If you cannot work out the meaning of a word, use a dictionary

8. unprecedented (paragraph 3): _____

9. escalating (paragraph 7): _____

10. vulnerable (paragraph 7): _____

READING CRITICALLY

1. What is the author's **purpose** or goal in this reading selection?

_____

_____

2. What are the implied or stated questions being addressed?

_____

_____

3. What specific **support**, details, and examples does the author use to develop the purpose or goal for the reading?

_____

_____

4. What inferences does the author include in this reading? (Inferences imply "if this, then this" types of cause/effect analysis.)

_____

_____

5. Who is the intended audience, and how did you reach that **conclusion**?

_____

_____

WRITING ASSIGNMENTS

1. Write an argument/persuasion essay (Chapter 15) about what could be done in your local community to help with the food and shelter shortage.
2. Write a one- or two-paragraph summary of this editorial (see Eight Steps for Writing a Summary, p. 342).
3. Write an example essay (Chapter 12) about another prominent social problem besides homelessness that you've witnessed in your community.

All the Rage

Dave Barry

Dave Barry, born July 3, 1947, in Armonk, New York, has worked over 25 years as a syndicated humor columnist. His work has appeared in more than 500 newspapers internationally. He has also written several books and had a sitcom called *Dave's World* that aired for four seasons (based on his life and two of his books). In this essay, he explains Parking Lot Rage, Shopping Cart Rage, and other sources of anger that are all the rage.

1   If you do much driving on our nation's highways, you've probably noticed that, more and more often, bullets are coming through your windshield. This is a common sign of Road Rage, which the opinion-makers in the news media have decided is a serious problem, ranking just behind global warming and ahead of Asia.

2   How widespread is Road Rage? To answer that question, researchers for the National Institute of Traffic Safety recently did a study in which they drove on the interstate highway system in a specially equipped observation van. By the third day, they were deliberately running motorists off the road.

3   "These people are *morons!*" their official report stated.

4   That is the main cause of Road Rage: the realization that many of your fellow motorists have the brain of a cashew. The most common example, of course, is the motorists who feel a need to drive in the left-hand lane even though they are going slower than everybody else.

5   Nobody knows why they do this. Maybe they belong to some kind of religious cult that believes the right lane is sacred and must never come in direct contact with tires. Maybe one time, years ago, these motorists happened to be driving in the left lane when their favorite song came on the radio, so they've driven there ever since.

6   But whatever makes these people drive this way, there's nothing you can do. You can honk at them, but it will have no effect. People have been honking at them for years: It's a normal part of their environment. They've decided, for some mysterious reason, wherever they drive, there is honking.

7   I am familiar with this problem because I live and drive in Miami, which bills itself as the Inappropriate-Lane-Driving Capital of the World, and where the left lane is thought of not so much as a thoroughfare as a public recreational area, where motorists feel free to stop, hold family

reunions, barbecue pigs, play volleyball, etc. Compounding this problem is another common type of Miami motorist, the aggressive young male whose car has a sound system so powerful that the driver must go faster than the speed of sound at all times, or else the nuclear bass notes emanating from his rear speakers will catch up to him and cause his head to explode.

8   So the tiny minority of us Miami drivers who actually qualify as normal find ourselves constantly being trapped behind people drifting along on the interstate at the speed of diseased livestock, while at the same time being tailgated and occasionally bumped from behind by testosterone-deranged youths who got their driver training from watching "Star Wars." And of course nobody ever signals or yields, and people are constantly cutting us off, and *after a while we start to feel some rage, OK? You got a problem with that,* mister opinion-maker?

9   In addition to Road Rage, I frequently experience Parking Lot Rage, which occurs when I pull into a crowded supermarket parking lot, and I see people get into their car, clearly ready to leave, so I stop my car and wait for them to vacate the spot, and . . . nothing happens. They just stay there! *What the hell are they doing in there?? Cooking dinner???*

10   When I finally get into the supermarket, I often experience Shopping Cart Rage. This is caused by the people—and you just know these are the same people who drive slowly in the left-hand lane—who routinely manage, by careful placement, to block the entire aisle with a shopping cart. If we really want to keep illegal immigrants from entering the United States, we should employ Miami residents armed with shopping carts; we'd only need about two dozen to block the entire Mexican border.

11   What makes the supermarket congestion even worse is that shoppers are taking longer and longer to decide what to buy, because every product in America now comes in an insane number of styles and sizes. For example, I recently went to the supermarket to get orange juice. For just one brand, I had to decide between Original, Homestyle, Pulp Plus, Double Vitamin C, Grovestand, Calcium or Old Fashioned; I also had to decide whether I wanted the 167-ounce, 32-ounce, 64-ounce, 96-ounce or six-pack size. This is *way* too many choices. It caused me to experience Way Too Many Product Choices Rage. I would have called the orange juice company and complained, but I probably would have wound up experiencing Automated Phone Answering System Rage (". . . For questions about Pulp Plus in the 32-ounce size, press 23. For questions about Pulp Plus in the 64-ounce size, press 24. For questions about . . .").

12   My point is that there are many causes of rage in our modern world, and if we're going to avoid unnecessary violence, we all need to "keep our *cool.*" So let's try to be more considerate, OK? Otherwise I will kill you.

READING REFLECTION QUESTIONS

1. What are the direct or indirect (implied) messages in this story?

_____

_____

2. What tone does the author use, and what effect does this tone have on the ideas he presents? _____

_____

3. T/F _____ The official report on Road Rage listed that drivers have the brain the size of a cashew.

4. T/F _____ The author thinks Road Rage is appropriate.

5. T/F _____ Barry pretends to be a person who supports Road Rage for the sake of humor.

6. List two examples of other types of rage that Barry discusses:

_____

7. In your own experience, what is the worse type of rage and why?

_____

_____

CHECKING VOCABULARY

Define each of the following words by figuring out their meaning using context clues in the reading selection (see Chapter 30 for how to use context clues). If you cannot work out the meaning of a word, use a dictionary.

8. emanating (paragraph 7): _____

9. testosterone (paragraph 8): _____

10. congestion (paragraph 11): _____

READING CRITICALLY

1. What is the author's **purpose** or goal in this reading selection?

_____

_____

2. What are the implied or stated questions being addressed?

_____

_____

3. What specific **support**, details, and examples does the author use to develop the purpose or goal for the reading?

_____

_____

4. What inferences does the author include in this reading? (Inferences imply "if this, then this" types of cause/effect analysis.)

_____

_____

5. Who is the intended audience, and how did you reach that **conclusion**?

_____

_____

WRITING ASSIGNMENTS

1. Write a description (Chapter 8) and illustration (Chapter 12) essay about a type of rage you have encountered (you witnessed or you have been involved in).

2. Write an argument essay (Chapter 15) where you propose possible solutions for dealing with Road Rage more efficiently.

3. Write a cause and effect essay (Chapter 13) on the subject of road rage.

Barbie Madness

Cynthia Tucker

Cynthia Tucker is a syndicated columnist whose work appears in newspapers internationally. She is editorial page editor for *The Atlanta Journal-Constitution*. She is a member of the International Women's Media Foundation and the National Association of Black Journalists.

1   When I was 9 or 10, I was steeped in Barbie madness. So much so that I joined the Barbie fan club. My mother still has the membership document displaying my careful cursive writing alongside the scrawled block letters of a younger sister.

2   Too old to play with baby dolls, I was developing a vicarious interest in high fashion—a world to which Barbie allowed me access. Her over-priced collection of clothes included everything from bridal gowns to swimsuits, all accented by stiletto heels. In fact, her feet were perma-nently arched so that she could not wear sensible shoes.

3   She wore sheath dresses, capri pants, long gowns. She never got dirty; she never burst a seam (she never bent, of course); she never tripped over those heels.

4   Nor did she ever cause me to believe I would see many real women in the real world who looked or dressed like that. I had never seen a grown woman on the beach in high heels, and if I had— even at 10—I would have thought her nuts. Barbie was fantasy, one of the joyous escapes offered by childhood. My Barbie, white and brunette, never symbolized what I thought anyone ought to look like.

5   After nearly four decades of building a doll with a figure that, by one estimate, gives her measurements of 38-18-34, Mattel is preparing to release a new Barbie of less fantastic proportions. Many parents are breathing a sigh of relief that their daughters will no longer be subjected to such an unrealistic—and possibly damaging—cultural icon. Well, I have good news and bad news for those parents.

6   The bad news is, there will always be damaging cultural icons, plenty of unrealistic representations of women that emphasize youth and a weird voluptuousness/thinness, the combination of which defies physiology. If you think Barbie is the last of them, check out the *Sports Illustrated* swim-suit issue. Check out *Baywatch*. (The syndicated show sells well around the world. Sexism needs little translation.)

7   Now, for the good news: Parents will always have more influence over their children than any doll, any model, any magazine, any movie. Per-haps even more than their children's peers. Don't take my word for it— scientific research has confirmed it.

8   A recent study found that no matter a teenager's economic back-ground, a close-knit family helps prevent risky behavior and encourages educational excellence. Might not attentive parents also provide protec-tion against the sexist influences that permeate the culture?

9   Children learn not just from their parents' rhetoric, but also from their behavior. When a father leaves his family for a younger and more glam-orous trophy wife, he gives his children a much more profound lesson

about the value of women than Barbie ever could. So does the mother who constantly applauds her adolescent daughter's popularity with boys.

10   Years ago, Barbie's wardrobe evolved beyond *haute couture* to include professional attire. She also became more ethnically diverse. Now, the doll will get a little nip-and-tuck that widens her waist and de-emphasizes her chest (a bit).

11   But no matter what she looks like, Barbie will never be as important a role model as Mom and Dad are. When Dad coaches his daughter's soccer team or helps her build a treehouse, he gives her a measure of her worth that overshadows even Barbie's bustline.

READING REFLECTION QUESTIONS

1. What are the direct or indirect (implied) messages in this story?

_____

_____

2. What are the two main criticisms made about Barbie, according to this article? _____

3. _____ The main message of "Barbie Madness" is:

   a. Barbie is a harmful toy.

   b. Barbie has no effect on girls' self esteem.

   c. Parental influence is more important for children's development than toys like Barbie's influence.

   d. The author wanted to grow up to look just like Barbie.

4. T/F _____ Barbie will soon be changed in proportions (including an enlarged waist).

5. T/F _____ Barbie is available in various ethnic types.

6. T/F _____ The author thinks Barbie should be banned.

7. T/F _____ The male version of Barbie, Ken, is also discussed in this article.

CHECKING VOCABULARY

Define each of the following words by figuring out their meaning using context clues in the reading selection (see Chapter 30 for how to use context clues). If you cannot work out the meaning of a word, use a dictionary.

8. steeped (paragraph 1): _____

9. cursive (paragraph 1): _____

10. vicarious (paragraph 2): _____

READING CRITICALLY

1. What is the author's **purpose** or goal in this reading selection?

_____

_____

2. What are the implied or stated questions being addressed?

_____

_____

3. What specific **support**, details, and examples does the author use to develop the purpose or goal for the reading?

_____

_____

4. What inferences does the author include in this reading? (Inferences imply "if this, then this" types of cause/effect analysis.)

_____

_____

5. Who is the intended audience, and how did you reach that **conclusion**?

_____

_____

WRITING ASSIGNMENTS

1. Write an argument essay (Chapter 15) about whether or not Barbie's proportions should be changed to be more realistic. Provide specific reasons for your arguments.

2. Define (Chapter 11) and describe (Chapter 8) a favorite childhood toy of yours.

3. Write a narration essay (Chapter 7) about a particular childhood memory of yours that involves playing with a toy/s.

4. Write a cause and effect essay (Chapter 13) related to the images of dolls like Barbie to a child's body image.

Our Tired, Our Poor, Our Kids

Anna Quindlen

Anna Quindlen began her journalism career at the *New York Post* and then became metropolitan editor of the *New York Times*. Currently she contributes to *Newsweek*'s prestigious back page column, *The Last Word*, every other week. Her columns are collected in *Living Out Loud* (1988) and *Thinking Out Loud* (1992). She has written three best-selling novels, *Object Lessons* (1991), *One True Thing* (1994), and *Black and Blue* (1998), and an advice book, *A Short Guide to a Happy Life* (2000). This essay appeared in the March 12, 2001, issue of *Newsweek*.

1   Six people live here, in a room the size of the master bedroom in a modest suburban house. Trundles, bunk beds, dressers side by side stacked with toys, clothes, boxes, in tidy claustrophobic clutter. One woman, five children. The baby was born in a shelter. The older kids can't wait to get out of this one. Everyone gets up at 6 A.M., the little ones to go to day care, the others to school. Their mother goes out to look for an apartment when she's not going to drug-treatment meetings. "For what they pay for me to stay in a shelter I could have lived in the Hamptons," Sharanda says.

2   Here is the parallel universe that has flourished while the more fortunate were rewarding themselves for the stock split with SUVs and home additions. There is a boom market in homelessness. But these are not the men on the streets of San Francisco holding out cardboard signs to the tourists. They are children, hundreds of thousands of them, twice as likely to repeat a grade or be hospitalized and four times as likely to go hungry as the kids with a roof over their heads. Twenty years ago New York City provided emergency shelter for just under a thousand families a day; last month it had to find spaces for 10,000 children on a given night. Not since the Great Depression have this many babies, toddlers and kids had no place like home.

3   Three mothers sit in the living room of a temporary residence called Casa Rita in the Bronx and speak of this in the argot of poverty "The land-lord don't call back when they hear you got EARP," says Rosie, EARP being the Emergency Assistance Rehousing Program. "You get priority for Section 8 if you're in a shelter," says Edna, which means federal housing programs will put you higher on the list. Edna has four kids, three in foster care; she arrived at Casa Rita, she says, "with two bags and a baby." Rosie has three; they share a bathroom down the hall with two other fam-

ilies. Sharanda's five range in age from 13 to just over a year. Her eldest was put in the wrong grade when he changed schools. "He's humiliated, living here," his mother says.

4   All three women are anxious to move on, although they appreciate this place, where they can get shelter, get sober and keep their kids at the same time. They remember the Emergency Assistance Unit, the city office that is the gateway to the system, where hundreds of families sit every day surrounded by their bags, where children sleep on benches until they are shuffled off dull-eyed for one night in a shelter or a motel, only to return as supplicants again the next day.

5   In another world middle-class Americans have embraced new-home starts, the stock market and the Gap. But in the world of these displaced families, problems ignored or fumbled or unforeseen during this great period of prosperity have dovetailed into an enormous subculture of children who think that only rich people have their own bedrooms. Twenty years ago, when the story of the homeless in America became a staple of news reporting, the solution was presented as a simple one: affordable housing. That's still true, now more than ever. Two years ago the National Low Income Housing Coalition calculated that the hourly income necessary to afford the average two-bedroom apartment was around $12. That's more than twice the minimum wage.

6   The result is that in many cities police officers and teachers cannot afford to live where they work, that in Las Vegas old motels provide housing for casino employees, that in shelters now there is a contingent of working poor who get up off their cots and go off to their jobs. The result is that if you are evicted for falling behind on your rent, if there is a bureaucratic foul-up in your welfare check or the factory in which you work shuts down, the chances of finding another place to live are very small indeed. You're one understanding relative, one paycheck, one second chance from the street. And so are your kids.

7   So-called welfare reform, which emphasizes cutbacks and make-work, has played a part in all this. A study done in San Diego in 1998 found that a third of homeless families had recently had benefits terminated or reduced, and that most said that was how they had wound up on the street. Drugs, alcohol and domestic abuse also land mothers with kids in the shelter system or lead them to hand their children over to relatives or foster homes. Today the average homeless woman is younger than ever before, may have been in foster care or in shelters herself and so considers a chaotic childhood the norm. Many never finished high school, and have never held a job.

8   Ralph Nuñez, who runs the organization Homes for the Homeless, says that all this calls for new attitudes. "People don't like to hear it, but

shelters are going to be the low-income housing of the future," he says. "So how do we enrich the experience and use the system to provide job training and education?" Bonnie Stone of Women in Need, which has eight other residences along with Casa Rita, says, "We're pouring everything we've got into the nine months most of them are here—nutrition, treatment, budgeting. By the time they leave, they have a subsidized apartment, day care and, hopefully, some life skills they didn't have before."

9   But these organizations are rafts in a rising river of need that has roared through this country without most of us ever even knowing. So now you know. There are hundreds of thousands of little nomads in America, sleeping in the back of cars, on floors in welfare offices or in shelters five to a room. What would it mean to spend your childhood drifting from one strange bed to another, waking in the morning to try to figure out where you'd landed today, without those things that confer security and happiness: a familiar picture on the wall, a certain slant of light through a curtained window? "Give me your tired, your poor," it says on the base of the Statue of Liberty, to welcome foreigners. Oh, but they are already here, the small refugees from the ruin of the American dream, even if you cannot see them.

READING REFLECTION QUESTIONS

1. What are the direct or indirect (implied) messages in this story?

_____

_____

2. How does the title get featured in the conclusion of the article, and for what purpose? _____

_____

3. According to Quindlen, how much has the number of homeless families and children who need shelter at night increased in the last 20 years?

_____

_____

4. According to the article, what is the "simple" solution to the homelessness problem? _____

5. T/F _____ Homeless kids are twice as likely as nonhomeless kids to repeat a grade.

6. T/F _____ The author argues that welfare reform has actually increased the homeless problem.

7. T/F _____ The average cost of an apartment, according to Quindlen, requires nearly twice the current hourly wage.

CHECKING VOCABULARY

Define each of the following words by figuring out their meaning using context clues in the reading selection (see Chapter 30 for how to use context clues). If you cannot work out the meaning of a word, use a dictionary.

8. claustrophobic (paragraph 1): _____

9. flourished (paragraph 2): _____

10. supplicants (paragraph 4): _____

READING CRITICALLY

1. What is the author's **purpose** or goal in this reading selection?

_____

_____

2. What are the implied or stated questions being addressed?

_____

_____

3. What specific **support**, details, and examples does the author use to develop the purpose or goal for the reading?

_____

_____

4. What inferences does the author include in this reading? (Inferences imply "if this, then this" types of cause/effect analysis.)

_____

_____

5. Who is the intended audience, and how did you reach that **conclusion**?

_____

_____

WRITING ASSIGNMENTS

1. Write an argument essay (Chapter 15) that poses a solution to combating homelessness in your city or town.

2. Write a one- to two-paragraph summary of this essay using Eight Steps for Writing a Summary (p. 342).

3. Write a narration/description essay (Chapters 7 and 8) describing an incident you were part of or that you witnessed related to poverty and the effects on the youth in our society.

Sentence Parts

22

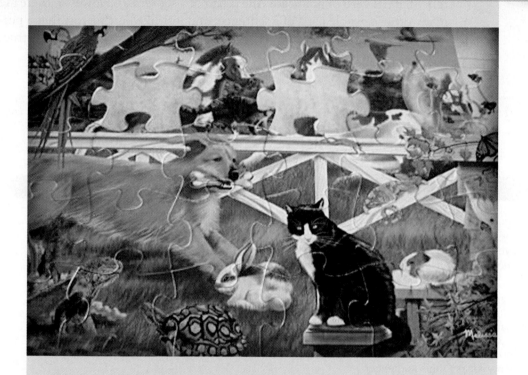

THINKING CRITICALLY

Sentence parts are like puzzle pieces: They have to fit together in the right order in order to make a coherent whole. What sentence parts do you already know before reading this chapter? List all possible sentence parts you can think of here.

_____

_____

_____

_____

_____

_____

THE BUILDING BLOCKS OF SENTENCES

The building blocks are the individual components of sentences. For instance, all sentences must have at least a **subject** (the *what* or *who* of a sentence) and a **verb** or **predicate** (the *action* of a sentence). However, there are many other possible parts of a sentence, and just like putting together a puzzle or building with blocks, you need to make choices in order to construct the best possible sentences to express your purpose.

Applying Critical Thinking

 PURPOSE   IDEAS   SUPPORT   ASSUMPTIONS BIASES   CONCLUSIONS   POINT OF VIEW   ANALYSIS

When you are making choices about which elements to include when **constructing a sentence,** you need to ask yourself the following questions:

1. What is my **purpose** for this particular sentence? What do I want to say?

2. What **ideas** and information do I need to include in this sentence?

3. Who is my target audience? How can I best put the parts of the sentence together to convey my ideas to this audience?

Then, use your **analysis** skills to break the sentence back down into its parts and make sure that you have constructed it correctly. Check that the sentence contains a verb and a subject, expresses a complete thought, and is written in the correct tense.

SUBJECTS AND PREDICATES

A **sentence** is a group of words that expresses a complete thought. Every sentence contains at least a subject (a noun or a noun plus its modifiers) and a predicate (a verb or a verb plus its modifiers). When the modifiers are stripped from the subject and predicate, leaving only the noun and verb, the noun is called the **simple subject** and the verb is called the **simple predicate.** The simple subject and simple predicate are the two most basic building blocks of the sentence.

SUBJECT   PREDICATE

The three-year-old cell **phone / started dialing** numbers randomly on its own.

The Subject

Cell describes the type of phone. *Three-year-old* describes the particular cell phone. *The* describes the rest of the words in the subject. When a word describes another word, we call it a modifier.

The Predicate

What did the phone do? It *started dialing*. That action is the verb and the simple predicate. How did it start dialing? *Randomly, on its own*. These words describe how the dialing happened.

SIMPLE SUBJECT	SIMPLE PREDICATE
phone	started dialing

Activity 22-1   Simple Subjects and Predicates

Directions: *Underline the simple predicate (the verb) in each sentence and mark it with a V. Then underline the simple subject and mark it with an S.*

1. The old dog slept peacefully.

2. His snoring sounded throughout the house.

3. His legs were stretched out behind him.

4. In his dream, a rabbit must have run by.

5. Suddenly, his whole body jerked.   ○

Subjects

The subject is the word or words that indicate *who* or *what* is doing the action of the verb. The subject can be a noun or noun phrase, a pronoun, or the implied *you* of a command. In the following sentences, the subjects are in *italics* and the verbs are in **boldface.**

> *Rachel* **left** the house at dawn. [Noun as subject]
>
> *She* **didn't look** carefully where she was going. [Pronoun as subject]
>
> *The school building* **loomed** out of the darkness. [Noun phrase as subject]
>
> *Its long shadow* **looked** like a huge monster. [Noun phrase as subject]

"Run!" her legs **seemed** to scream to her. [Implied *you* as subject]

The urge to run **was** almost irresistible. [Noun phrase as subject]

1. **The subject can be a noun, noun phrase, or an infinitive.**

   - A **noun** can be a person, place, thing, idea, or state of existence.

Nouns at a Glance

Common nouns name general categories or types: buildings, person, professor

Proper nouns name specific people or items: the Wrigley Building, Sharon Thornton, Professor Delhart

Abstract nouns are not related to specific details: peace, joy, sorrow, belief, certainty

Concrete nouns are related to specific sensory details: hat, face, sidewalk, river

Singular nouns name one of something: Nancy, Snake Mountain, dog, liberty, peacefulness

Plural nouns name more than one of something: women, mountains, dogs, dreams, feelings

Collective nouns name several items grouped as one collective item: family, team, police

Count nouns can be counted as individual units: cat, boy, grains, chairs

Noncount (mass) **nouns** cannot be counted as individual units in English: rice, water, furniture, salt

---

   - **Noun phrases** (a **phrase** is a group of related words without a subject and a predicate) are phrases that include nouns plus their modifiers, the words that describe them. Noun phrases can be subjects.

     Almost all children **love** chocolate. [The noun is *children*. The words that describe it are *almost all*.]

   - **Infinitives** can also be the subject: "to" phrases as the subject, for instance, *To live* is the greatest gift of all.

   Nouns and noun phrases can be joined to form a compound subject. A **compound subject** is made of two or more nouns or noun phrases joined with the word *and* or *or*.

     Li and Tinh **took** the test early. [Compound subject]

     Rachel's classmates, Maria and Rosie, **arrived** before Rachel did. [Subject]

>   *Either the homeroom teacher or the two girls* **were** there first.
>   [Compound subject]

2. **The subject can be a pronoun.** A **pronoun** is a word that replaces a noun that was mentioned previously: words like *I, you, he, she, it, we, they, this, that, these, those,* and so on. Pronouns can also be indefinite: for example, *everyone, someone, anybody, both, few,* and *many.*

>   The owner of the store and her husband had left the door open for a moment. *They* never **dreamed** the shop could be robbed so quickly, in broad daylight.

3. **All sentences must have a subject, but in commands the subject *you* is implied.** The subject *you* is implied in a command or request directly stated to someone.

>   Stop! [Subject = *you*—implied; *Stop* is the verb]

>   Grab the phone. [Subject = *you*]

4. **The subject doesn't always come first in the sentence.** Sometimes other words come before the subject of a sentence. For instance, the second sentence in the example below starts with a **transition**, that is, a word that shows the relationship between the two sentences. The subject follows it. To find the subject, look for the verb and then ask who or what performed the action of the verb.

>   *The mask* **hung** on the wall. Above it, *the mirror* **glittered.**

5. **The subject can be a gerund phrase** (an *-ing* phrase that serves as the subject of the sentence).

>   *Knowing who you are* **is** important in life. [*Knowing who you are* is a gerund as subject; *is* is the main verb of the sentence.]

Activity 22-2   Spotting Subjects

Directions: *Underline the subjects in the following sentences. Be careful not to underline all nouns—only the part of the sentence functioning as the subject. If the subject is implied, write "implied" at the end of the sentence.*

1. Matt likes to mow the lawn in the spring.

2. He says mowing in the spring can be more difficult when the grass gets longer.

3. My friends, Mary and Mike, like to mow their lawn once a week.

4. However, Bart and Chris mow their lawn once every two weeks.

5. Just to be safe, be sure to mow the lawn at least semiregularly. ⬤

Predicates

All sentences must have at least one verb or verb phrase. A verb is the action of a sentence—it can be a physical action, a mental action, or a state of being.

Physical action: Dean **ate** the pizza. [*Ate* is the simple predicate; *the pizza* describes what he ate. The complete predicate is *ate the pizza*.]

Dean **ate** the pizza and **slurped** his root beer. [Compound predicate; the two verbs are in bold. The complete compound predicate is *ate the pizza and slurped his root beer*.]

Mental action: I **thought** about it, too. [*Thought* is the simple predicate]

State of being: I **exist**. I **am**. [Simple predicates]

1. **Some verbs can stand on their own as the main verb of a sentence.** Here are some examples.

   My family **eats** dinner together regularly. [Simple present tense verb]

   Marshall's sisters **spent** all their money before noon. [Simple past tense verb]

   The town council member **was** angry about the new rules. [Simple past tense verb]

2. **Some verb forms need auxiliary, or helping, verbs to complete them.** A **verb phrase** is two or more words working together to create the action (verb) for the sentence. Here are some examples:

   My baby sister **was born** yesterday. [*Born* can't be a main verb on its own.]

   She **has been crying** ever since. [*Crying* can't be a main verb on its own.]

   When **will** she **stop?** [*Will* adds the meaning of "the future" to the verb *stop*.]

   I **am praying** she **will start smiling** soon. [*Am* adds the meaning of "the present" to the verb *praying*.]

   That **would improve** my mood tremendously! [*Would* adds the idea "if . . . then" as in "If the baby starts smiling soon, then my mood will improve tremendously." Since the speaker isn't sure when that might happen, *would* is used instead of *will* to indicate that it depends on a condition being met.]

There are three verb forms that can't be the main verb of a sentence without some helping verbs. They are the *to* form, the *-ed* form in certain cases, and the *-ing* form.

> My parents *should have informed* me about how annoying new babies can be.

- **To + verb (infinitives).** In an infinitive, the word *to* comes before the plain form of the verb: *to return, to call, to fight.* The infinitive can't be used alone as the main verb of a sentence—you couldn't write, *The artist to paint here.* Infinitives don't give enough information about when something is happening to be used as the main verb. In predicates, they normally follow the main verb.

> I **had promised to arrive** on time. [*Had promised to arrive* is the whole verb phrase.]

> The plane **was scheduled to land** at nine o'clock.

Note: Avoid *splitting your infinitive* by putting a word in between.

> **Incorrect:**   Jack decided *to eagerly charge* toward the sales rack.

> **Correct:**   Jack decided eagerly *to charge* toward the sales rack.

To verbs can also act as the subject of a sentence; here is an example:

> *To lift the car* **is** a great show of strength.

- **-ed verbs (past participles).** To indicate the past tense of most verbs, *-ed* or *-d* is added to the plain form. If there is no helping verb (such as *is, was, has,* or *had*), then the verb is in simple past tense form. A verb in the simple past can act as the main verb of a sentence. In other cases, the *-ed* form of a verb must be helped by an auxiliary verb. A helping verb plus an *-ed* verb forms a perfect tense.

> **Simple past tense:**   He **looked** handsome. So **did** his father.

> **Present perfect:**   She **has wanted** that car for years. [*Has* adds the meaning of "the present" to *wanted*.]

> **Past perfect:**   She **had planned** to buy it by the time she was 25. [*Had* adds the meaning of "the past" to *planned*.]

- **-*ing* verbs (gerunds).** Verbs that end with -*ing* are called gerunds. An -*ing* form is never a complete verb by itself—you wouldn't say *My roommate drying her hair.* In predicates, a form of the verb *to be* is needed before the gerund to indicate an action that was, is, or will be continuing. An -*ing* word can also serve as a subject, without the auxiliary verb.

    Auxiliary + gerund in the predicate:

    She **is having** the time of her life. [*Is* adds the meaning of "the present" to the gerund.]

    Before, she **was dreading** the party. [*Was* adds the meaning of "the past."]

    She **will be dancing** all night long. [*Will be* adds the meaning of "the future."]

    Remember: Gerunds can also serve as the subject of the sentence— see subjects above.

3. **Verb tense indicates time—past, present, and future.** Think of tense as a timeline that starts on the left, in the past, and moves to the right, into the future.

Applying Critical Thinking

| PURPOSE | IDEAS | SUPPORT | ASSUMPTIONS BIASES | CONCLUSIONS | POINT OF VIEW | ANALYSIS |

Analysis involves breaking down an idea and working out the meaning of the individual parts and how they relate to the whole. Use your analysis skills to help you choose the correct tense to use as you write. Ask the following questions to identify when the action of the sentence is taking place, and then check that you have used the tense that correctly conveys what you want to say:

1. "Am I writing about something that happened in the past and then stopped?" If so, use the simple past: Marguerite **read** the book *The Secret.*

2. "Am I writing about something that happened and stopped before another past event?" If so, use the past perfect: Although she **had considered** buying *Sharp Objects,* in the end she **chose** *No Country for Old Men.* (*Considering* happened before *choosing.*)

3. "Am I writing about something that started before but still happens?" If so, use the present perfect tense: She **has thought** many times that she would like to read more great novels.

4. "Am I writing about something that is happening now?" If so, use the present or present progressive tense. She **is reading** now, out on the porch, wearing her new sunglasses.

5. "Am I writing about something that hasn't happened yet but will happen in the future?" Use the future: By the time I finish this novel, I **will know** who did it!

6. "Am I writing about something that will start in the future, continue, and then stop at a particular time?" If so, use the future perfect tense: She **will have stopped** reading by dinnertime.

Verb Tense at a Glance

Picture a timeline like the one below to figure out which tense you want to use:

	Past	Present	Future	

◄——————I already had breakfast —— I am hungry —— I will eat lunch soon ——————►

X---------present progressive---------- Y -----------future progressive----------Z

past   **present**   **future**

Here's a chart that demonstrates past, present, and future tenses.

Tense	Past	Present	Future
Simple	She ate.	She eats.	She will eat.
Perfect	She was eating.	She has eaten.	She will be eating.
Progressive	She was eating.	She is eating.	She will be eating.
Perfect progressive	She had been eating.	She has been eating.	She will have been eating.

Note: Most verbs in the present tense use the base form (as found in the dictionary) for the first person subjects *I* and *we*, the second person subject *you*, and the third person plural subject *they*. For third person singular subjects *he*, *she*, and *it*, add *-s* or *-es*.

Example: base form *talk*.

First person: I talk.

Second person: You talk.

Third person singular: He talk**s**. She talk**s**. It talk**s**.

Third person plural: They talk.

Base Forms: *To Be* Verbs

Since there are many irregular verbs in English that don't follow this pattern, be sure to consult a dictionary and/or grammar handbook for correct verb forms. Here are the three most common irregular verbs and a key for how to change them.

Base Verb	Present Singular	Present Plural	Past Singular	Past Plural
Be	I am	We are	I was	We were
	You are	You are	You were	You were
	He/she/it is	They are	He/she/it was	They were
Have	I have	We have	I had	We had
	You have	You have	You had	You had
	He/she/it has	They have	He/she/it had	They had
Do	I do	We do	I did	We did
	You do	You do	You did	You did
	He/she/it does	They do	He/she/it did	They did

Irregular Verbs

Below is a list of some of the most common irregular verbs in English.

Base Form	Simple Past Tense	Past Participle
awake	awoke	awoken
be	was, were	been
bear	bore	born
beat	beat	beat
become	became	become
begin	began	begun
bend	bent	bent
beset	beset	beset
bet	bet	bet
bid	bid/bade	bid/bidden
bind	bound	bound
bite	bit	bitten
bleed	bled	bled
blow	blew	blown
break	broke	broken
breed	bred	bred

Base Form	Simple Past Tense	Past Participle
bring	brought	brought
broadcast	broadcast	broadcast
build	built	built
burn	burned/burnt	burned/burnt
burst	burst	burst
buy	bought	bought
cast	cast	cast
catch	caught	caught
choose	chose	chosen
cling	clung	clung
come	came	come
cost	cost	cost
creep	crept	crept
cut	cut	cut
deal	dealt	dealt
dig	dug	dug
dive	dived/dove	dived
do	did	done
draw	drew	drawn
dream	dreamed/dreamt	dreamed/dreamt
drive	drove	driven
drink	drank	drunk
eat	ate	eaten
fall	fell	fallen
feed	fed	fed
feel	felt	felt
fight	fought	fought
find	found	found
fit	fit	fit
flee	fled	fled
fling	flung	flung
fly	flew	flown
forbid	forbade	forbidden
forget	forgot	forgotten

Base Form	Simple Past Tense	Past Participle
forgive	forgave	forgiven
forsake	forsook	forsaken
freeze	froze	frozen
get	got	gotten
give	gave	given
go	went	gone
grind	ground	ground
grow	grew	grown
hang	hung	hung
hear	heard	heard
hide	hid	hidden
hit	hit	hit
hold	held	held
hurt	hurt	hurt
keep	kept	kept
kneel	knelt	knelt
knit	knit	knit
know	knew	know
lay	laid	laid
lead	led	led
leap	leaped/leapt	leaped/leapt
learn	learned/learnt	learned/learnt
leave	left	left
lend	lent	lent
let	let	let
lie	lay	lain
light	lighted/lit	lighted
lose	lost	lost
make	made	made
mean	meant	meant
meet	met	met
misspell	misspelled/misspelt	misspelled/misspelt
mistake	mistook	mistaken
mow	mowed	mowed/mown

Base Form	Simple Past Tense	Past Participle
overcome	overcame	overcome
overdo	overdid	overdone
overtake	overtook	overtaken
overthrow	overthrew	overthrown
pay	paid	paid
plead	pled	pled
prove	proved	proved/proven
put	put	put
quit	quit	quit
read	read	read
rid	rid	rid
ride	rode	ridden
ring	rang	rung
rise	rose	risen
run	ran	run
saw	sawed	sawed/sawn
say	said	said
see	saw	seen
seek	sought	sought
sell	sold	sold
send	sent	sent
set	set	set
sew	sewed	sewed/sewn
shake	shook	shaken
shave	shaved	shaved/shaven
shear	shore	shorn
shed	shed	shed
shine	shone	shone
shoe	shoed	shoed/shod
shoot	shot	shot
show	showed	showed/shown
shrink	shrank	shrunk
shut	shut	shut
sing	sang	sung

Base Form	Simple Past Tense	Past Participle
sink	sank	sunk
sit	sat	sat
sleep	slept	slept
slay	slew	slain
slide	slid	slid
sling	slung	slung
slit	slit	slit
smite	smote	smitten
sow	sowed	sowed/sown
speak	spoke	spoken
speed	sped	sped
spend	spent	spent
spill	spilled/spilt	spilled/spilt
spin	spun	spun
spit	spit/spat	spit
split	split	split
spread	spread	spread
spring	sprang/sprung	sprung
stand	stood	stood
steal	stole	stolen
stick	stuck	stuck
sting	stung	stung
stink	stank	stunk
stride	strode	stridden
strike	struck	struck
string	strung	strung
strive	strove	striven
swear	swore	sworn
sweep	swept	swept
swell	swelled	swelled/swollen
swim	swam	swum
swing	swung	swung
take	took	taken
teach	taught	taught

Base Form	Simple Past Tense	Past Participle
tear	tore	torn
tell	told	told
think	thought	thought
thrive	thrived/throve	thrived
throw	threw	thrown
thrust	thrust	thrust
tread	trod	trodden
understand	understood	understood
uphold	upheld	upheld
upset	upset	upset
wake	woke	woken
wear	wore	worn
weave	weaved/wove	weaved/woven
wed	wed	wed
weep	wept	wept
wind	wound	wound
win	won	won
withhold	withheld	withheld
withstand	withstood	withstood
wring	wrung	wrung
write	wrote	written

Activity 22-3   Verb Spotting

Directions: *Underline the verbs in the following sentences. If there is an auxiliary verb, be sure to underline that as well.*

1. In grade school, dodge ball is a popular schoolyard game.

2. Dodge ball can be fun too.

3. My friends, Mary and Mike, like dodge ball the most.

4. However, Bart and Chris say dodge ball is a mean sport.

5. Just to be safe, be sure not to try to hit someone at his or her feet.

Activity 22-4   Correct Forms and Tenses of Verbs

Directions: *Choose the correct forms and tenses of the verbs in brackets to fill each space in the following paragraph.*

Last summer, I [to go] _____ to the Grand Canyon. The views from the top [to be] _____ amazing. I [to feel] _____ overwhelmed by the sheer size of the canyon. I remember I [to be] _____ a little queasy because I [to be] _____ afraid of heights. Having a fear of heights [to be] _____ normal in my family. Almost all of us [to have] _____ it. I didn't [to realize] _____ how bad my fear [to be] _____ until I [to look] _____ down into that immense canyon. I must [to admit] _____ that I [to be] _____ a bit intimidated. Finally, when it was time to leave, I [to think] _____ about the importance of taking the opportunity [to see] _____ this amazing natural wonder. ●

Inside the Predicate: Objects

1. Some verbs describe an action that doesn't include a receiver:

   The sun **rises.** The moon **sets.**

2. Other verbs do require (or can have) a receiver:

   The European Space Agency **sent** the spacecraft Rosetta into space in 2004.

   The verb *sent* needs a receiver, which is called the **object of the verb.** What did the European Space Agency send? A spacecraft. *Spacecraft* is the object of the verb *sent*.

3. As you know, pronouns can take the place of nouns. So a pronoun can also be the object of a verb.

   Rosetta **will orbit** a comet in 2015.
   Rosetta **will orbit** it.

   In the second sentence, *it* replaces *comet*. *It* is the object of the verb *will orbit*.

4. Sometimes the subject acts on an object *to* or *for* someone or something else. That someone or something else is called the **indirect object**.

> Prescription sleeping pills **can cause** problems for people.

To find the direct object, you would ask "What can sleeping pills cause?" The direct object is *problems*. To find the indirect object, ask "Problems to or for whom?" In this case, the word *for* is in the sentence. The indirect object is *people*.

In English, the indirect object may come before the direct object in the sentence. In that case, the word *to* or *for* does not appear, although it is implied.

> Sleeping pills **can cause** people problems.

Problems is still the direct object, and *people* is still the indirect object. The word order has changed, and the word *for* has been removed.

Activity 22-5   Spotting Direct Object and Indirect Objects

Directions: *Underline the direct objects and indirect objects in the following sentences. Mark DO over the direct objects and IO over the indirect objects.*

1.   Martha tossed the magazine to the floor.

2.   Manny gave her a cake.

3.   Sandy provided an argument in favor of the proposed bill.

4.   Angelo kissed her suddenly.

5.   Jen gave the old dress to her.

PHRASES

A **phrase** is a group of related words without a subject and a predicate. You saw at the beginning of the chapter that a subject can be a noun phrase, which includes a noun and all its modifiers: *The smelly cheese* looked blue and green. A noun phrase can also act as the object of a verb: She decided to try *the smelly green cheese*. Two of the verbals that you studied earlier can also be considered noun phrases: one is the gerund phrase (*The eating of cheese after dinner* is a European custom), and the other is the infinitive phrase (*To live for the peace of others* is noble). A noun phrase can also be the object of a preposition, which is discussed in the next section.

Prepositional Phrases

Prepositions are words that connect their objects (nouns and pronouns) to other parts of the sentence. Taking out the prepositional phrases from a sentence doesn't affect the basic meaning, and prepositions cannot serve as subjects or verbs. A preposition is like sentence glue, connecting sentence parts together.

> **Example:** The <u>subject</u> *of the essay* **is** the trouble *with plagiarism* and the ease *of finding* free essays *on the* Internet.

The prepositional phrases italicized above help guide the readers through the meaning of the sentence. The subject of the sentence above is underlined, and the verb is in bold.

Visualization/memory tip: Think of a cat and a set of two large tubes or pipes: The prepositions are anything that cat can do related to those two tubes (for instance, the cat can go *around* the tubes, *toward* the tubes, *over* the tubes, *on* the tubes, *in* the tubes, *between* the tubes, and so on).

Of course, there are many prepositions that don't work with the cat/tubes example; for instance, can a cat be "of" the tubes? The cat/tubes idea is just a memory trick (mnemonic device) to help you recognize many common prepositions.

The Most Common Prepositions in English

about	against	around
above	along	as
according to	along with	at
across	among	because of
after	apart from	before

behind	inside	respecting
below	in spite of	round
beneath	instead of	since
beside(s)	into	than
between	like	through
beyond	near	throughout
by	next	till
concerning	of	to
considering	off	toward
despite	on	under
down	onto	underneath
during	on top of	unlike
except	opposite	until
except for	out	unto
excepting	out of	up
for	outside	upon
from	over	up to
in	past	with
in addition to	plus	within
in case of	regarding	without

Note: Try not to end your sentences with a preposition.

> **For example:**   She is the one he is going to the movies with.
>
> **Rearranged:**   She is the one with whom he is going to the movies.
>
> **Or even better:** He is going to the movies with her.

Some informal writing allows for prepositions used at the end of a sentence. Also, there are cases where one can't avoid ending in a preposition—there is no way to rearrange the sentence.

> **For example:** It was something he couldn't stop thinking *about*.
>   The cat wants to come *in*.

Prepositional phrases include a preposition, the object of the preposition, and any modifiers of the object. The entire prepositional phrase functions as a modifier in the sentence.

> **For example:** That silly cat *of hers* is always looking *for more food*.

Of hers modifies *cat* and so is part of the subject; *for more food* modifies *is looking* and is part of the predicate. Put another way, *of hers* modifies a noun, so it is an adjective. *For more food* modifies a verb, so it is an adverb. Adjectives and adverbs are discussed later in the chapter.

Activity 22-6   Spotting Prepositions

Directions: *Underline all the prepositions and prepositional phrases in the following sentences.*

1. Carrie came along with the girls because she was fast becoming one of the group.

2. She arrived at the back door of his house looking for food.

3. Aubrey changed her mind because of the reasons that Brandon gave her.

4. She had thought differently before he spoke to her.

5. She decided to stay instead of leaving for the week.   ●

Participles and Participial Phrases

Participles are verb forms that can either be part of the main verb or can function as adjectives or adverbs. Present participles end in *-ing: singing, breathing, enjoying.* Past participles usually end in *-ed* or *-d: cheated, loved, said.* However, some participles are formed irregularly with endings such as *-n* and *-t: forgiven, taken, spent, brought.*

Part of main verb: Mary **was** *focusing* on the assignment.

Karen **was** *defeated* from the first moment due to her attitude.

As adjective: The *defeated* wrestler **shook** hands with his opponent.

As adverb: I **saw** Darci *looking at* my new set of magazines.

Participial phrases use the *-ing* form for present participle, and the past participle phrase usually ends in *-ed, -d, -n,* or *-t: elected, deleted, chosen,* and sen*t.*

For example: I *saw* Don *trying* to understand my point.

The *chosen* delegate *would begin* her term in May.

Activity 22-7   Spotting Participles/Participial Phrases

Directions: *Underline the participles and participial phrases in the following sentences.*

1. Ranjit was exhausted after the race.

2. Gurpreet was encouraging him to keep it up.

3. I saw Latara asking for advice from Miwa.

4. Miwa watched Omar spending so much time trying to get the answer.

5. Midori was wondering if she could solve the problem. ⬤

Adjectives and Adjective Phrases

Adjectives are words that modify nouns and pronouns (the adjectives below are italicized; the nouns they modify are underlined).

> Modifying nouns: The *red* <u>house</u> looked a little like a barn.

> Modifying pronouns: <u>They</u> were very *beautiful*.

Descriptive adjectives can take three forms:

1. **The positive form,** used to express simple descriptions like *blue, shiny, large, bumpy, unattractive:*

> The *shiny* <u>apple</u> looked appetizing.

2. **The comparative form,** used to compare two things such as *brighter, cleaner, more lovely, less attractive:*

> She had a *cleaner* <u>room</u> than her sister.

3. **The superlative form,** used to compare three or more things such as *brightest, cleanest, most lovely, least attractive:*

> She had the *cleanest* <u>room</u> in the house.

> It was the *least attractive* <u>dog</u> in the whole competition.

An **adjective phrase** is a phrase that modifies a noun or pronoun:

> The <u>woman</u> *eating the cheese* is the hostess.

The adjective phrase describes *woman*, a noun.

Activity 22-8   Spotting Adjectives

Directions: *Underline all the adjectives and adjective phrases in the following sentences.*

> **Tip:** *It might help to circle all the nouns first.*

1. The old clock on the antique dresser kept time like a reliable friend.

2. The moldy cheese from Gina's refrigerator smelled like a wet sock.

3. The happy child sitting in the worn leather chair looked pleased with her tiny furry puppy by her side.

4. The large blue luxury car pulling into the station took only expensive premium gas.

5. The loud, obnoxious buzzing was coming from inside the stranger's handbag, and we were sure it was an overactive and overly loud cell phone.

Adverbs and Adverb Phrases

Adverbs are words that modify verbs, verb forms, adjectives, and other adverbs. Many adverbs end with *-ly*, but not all. The adverbs below are in italics; what they are modifying is underlined.

> **Modifying verbs:** She <u>laughed</u> *loudly*.
>
> **Modifying verb forms:** She had *barely* <u>recovered</u> from the surgery.
>
> **Modifying adjectives:** It was a *very* <u>expensive</u> handbag.
>
> **Modifying other adverbs:** The child ate *very* <u>quickly</u>.

Adverbs indicate how, where, when, or how much. Like adjectives, they have three forms:

1. **Positive:** *slow, quick, clumsy, happily, intently*

   She <u>moved</u> *slowly*.

2. **Comparative:** *slower, quicker, more clumsily, more happily, more intently*

   She <u>moved</u> even *slower* than her pet turtle.

3. **Superlative:** *slowest, quickest, most clumsy, most happily, most intently*

   She <u>moved</u> the *slowest* of the whole third-grade class.

An **adverb phrase** is a phrase that begins with a preposition and functions as an adverb:

> The party was full *of the host's colleagues*.

The adverb phrase *of the host's colleagues* modifies *full*, an adjective.

Activity 22-9   Spotting Adverbs/Adverb Phrases

Directions: *Underline the adverbs in the following sentences.*

1. The hamsters dashed happily through the see-through tubes.

2. Knowing the crowd was really hungry, the wait staff served the customers extremely quickly.

3. The ants fought mightily and valiantly against the attack of the termites.

4. The fish swam sporadically and hastily in the tank.

5. The hungry bird gulped greedily at the dangling worm.

Activity 22-10   Spotting Adjectives and Adverbs

Directions: *Underline the adjectives and adverbs in the following sentences. Then circle the nouns, verbs, verb forms, adjectives, or adverbs they are modifying.*

1. The sleek, spotted cheetah slunk stealthily through the tall grass.

2. The fast-paced and exciting world of racing keeps the fans coming.

3. The old green turtle walked slowly over the wet grass.

4. The red rubber ball bounced quickly on the hot pavement.

5. The ice-cold watermelon dripped juice sloppily down her chin.

ARTICLES AND NOUN DETERMINERS

The **articles** *a, an,* and *the* come before a noun and are determined by the context and type of noun that follows them.

A and *an* are **indefinite articles** used for general description words:

• Use *a* when the word that follows starts with a consonant or a consonant sound: *a toy, a kid, a choice, a unified country* (the "u" sounds like a consonant "y," so use the "a").

• Use *an* when the word that follows has a vowel or a vowel sound: *an Egyptian, an apple, an onion, an honor* (the *h* is silent; the word begins with a vowel sound of "o," so use "an").

The is a **definite article:** Use *the* when the word that follows is a specific noun (not a general descriptor): *the* only one in town, *the* winner, *the* chapter to read.

Cross Reference
See ESL Tips, Appendix B, for more about when to use an article.

Other Noun Determiners

Other words besides articles that signal that a noun is about to follow include the following:

- **Demonstratives:** *this, that, these, those*
- **Possessives:** *my, our, your, his, her, their, its*
- **Cardinal numbers:** *one, two, three, etc.*
- **Miscellaneous noun determiners:** *all, another, each, every, much, etc.*

Activity 22-11   Spotting Article and Noun Determiners

Directions: *Underline the articles and noun determiners in the following sentences.*

1. The math teacher in Room 5 held a set of keys.

2. Spotting every type of error that is common in writing is difficult.

3. That chair over there is broken.

4. One of these will work better.

5. Your sister is a very nice person.

CONJUNCTIONS

A **clause** is a group of words containing a finite verb. A clause can be dependent, which means it cannot stand on its own as a complete sentence, or independent, which is a complete sentence. *Coordinating conjunctions, subordinating conjunctions,* and *conjunctive adverbs* help correctly join two clauses. If the clauses are both independent (two complete sentences, each with its own subject and verb), use a coordinating conjunction with a comma or a conjunctive adverb with a semicolon. If one of the clauses is dependent on the other, use a subordinating conjunction.

Coordinating Conjunctions

Coordinating conjunctions connect two independent clauses using a comma and a coordinating word. The **only seven words** that can be used along with a comma to connect two independent clauses are the following coordinating conjunctions:

For   And   Nor   But   Or   Yet   So

A simple mnemonic device for remembering these seven words is to remember the acronym **FANBOYS** that consists of the first letter of each.

> **Note:** Be careful not to assume that whenever you use these seven words in a sentence that they are serving as coordinating conjunctions. You may be using the word "and," for instance, in a list of items such as *bread, cheese,* **and** *mustard,* in which case the word "and" is not coordinating two independent clauses.

Cross Reference
See Chapter 26 for more about coordination versus items in a series.

Activity 22-12   Spotting Coordinating Conjunctions

Directions: *Underline the coordinating conjunctions in the following sentences. Check to make sure that the word you underline is functioning as a coordinating conjunction.*

1. *It must be one of the seven words listed on p. 526.*
2. *It must be preceded by a comma.*
3. *It must be between two independent clauses.*

If the word is one of the seven words listed above but does not fulfill one of the other two criteria needed to be a coordinating conjunction, do not underline it.

1. The boys came to the party, and they left with lots of prizes.

2. The boys and girls all went fishing and camping, but later only the girls made a campfire.

3. Several of the campers hiked in the hills, but the whole group marched along the beach.

4. The youngest campers headed back with the headmaster, for it was getting late.

5. The directors wouldn't let the kids climb the trees, nor would they let them throw rocks.

Subordinating Conjunctions

Subordinating conjunctions connect dependent (or subordinating) clauses to independent clauses. If the dependent clause is first, be sure to use a comma after it. If it follows the independent clause, do not use a comma.

> **Example with dependent clause first:** *Since* the bus was usually on time, Kris was sure that she'd make it to her appointment.

> **Example with dependent clause second:** Kris was sure that she'd make it to her appointment *since* the bus was usually on time.

Here are the twenty most common words used for subordination.

after	before	though	whether
although	if	unless	which
as	once	until	while
as though	since	when	who
because	that	whereas	whose

Conjunctive Adverbs

Conjunctive adverbs are words that can also connect two independent clauses using correct punctuation, but they are not coordinating conjunctions: They are adverb transitions. Conjunctive adverbs can also be used at the beginning of a sentence to help connect it to a preceding sentence or paragraph.

Here are the most common conjunctive adverbs:

consequently	however	nevertheless	therefore
furthermore	moreover	otherwise	thus

When the conjunctive adverb appears between two clauses, a semicolon sets it off from the clause that comes before it, and a comma sets it off from the clause that comes after it.

> **Examples:**
> Clara wanted the best cake; *consequently*, she decided to make it herself.
>
> David wanted to have a piece of cake; however, he was late to the party, and it was all gone.

Activity 22-13   Spotting Subordinating Conjunctions and Conjunctive Adverbs

Directions: *Underline the subordinating conjunctions and/or conjunctive adverbs in the following sentences.*

1. When the sequel comes out in the theaters, I will be the first one in line.

2. Although Emma wanted to see the play, Debbie had her heart set on seeing the baseball game.

3. The school track team had a great season; however, they did not win the championship.

4. She wanted to buy a new umbrella because the old one was coming apart.

5. I have decided to run for office; furthermore, I want you to be my campaign manager. ●

Activity 22-14 Spotting Coordination and Subordination

Directions: *In the blanks provided, label the word bolded in each sentence as either a CC (a coordinating conjunction), a SC (a subordinating conjunction), or a CA (a conjunctive adverb).*

_____ 1. Halloween is an unusual American holiday, **yet** it is one of American children's favorite holidays.

_____ 2. Parents usually warn children about taking candy from strangers; **however,** on this holiday, taking candy from neighbors, and sometimes even strangers, is acceptable.

_____ 3. Many American children are not familiar with the origins of this holiday, **but** usually their parents don't know the history either.

_____ 4. **Although** there are some traditions, like carving pumpkins, that have carried over from the Celtic All Hallow's Eve, most of the old traditions are not practiced.

_____ 5. The Mexican holiday Dia de Los Muertos (Day of the Dead) shares some similarities with Halloween; **nevertheless,** many customs are different. ●

Activity 22-15 Create Your Own Sentences Using Coordination and Subordination

Directions: *Create five sentences of your own on the **subject of music** using both coordination and subordination. Three should include either a coordinating conjunction, a subordinating conjunction, or a conjunctive adverb. The other two are your choice. Refer to the tables earlier to help you identify possibilities.*

1. Use a **coordinating conjunction:**

_____

_____

2. Use a **subordinating conjunction**:

_____

_____

3. Use a **conjunctive adverb**:

_____

_____

4. Your choice:

_____

_____

5. Your choice:

_____

_____

After you have created your sentences, re-read them, and using the tips from this chapter, make sure you haven't made any of the common errors that occur when using coordination and subordination. Fix any errors you see. ●

Activity 22-16   Identifying Parts of Speech

Directions: _In the following excerpt from Shoba Narayan's "I Wonder: Was it Me or Was it my Sari?" from Chapter 21, mark the various parts of speech or connecting words in this manner: Circle all subjects; underline all verbs and double-underline all prepositions or prepositional phrases._

The notion of wearing a sari every day was relatively new for me. During my college years—the age when most girls in India begin wearing saris regularly—I was studying in America. As an art student at Mount Holyoke, I hung out with purple-haired painters and rabble-rousing feminists wearing ink-stained khakis and cut-off T shirts. During a languid post-graduation summer in Boston, when I sailed a boat and volunteered for an environmental organization, I wore politically correct, recycled Salvation Army clothes. After getting married, I became a Connecticut housewife experimenting with clothes from Jones New York and Ann Taylor. Through it all, I tried to pick up the accent, learn the jargon and affect the posture of the Americans around me. ●

Sentence Variety

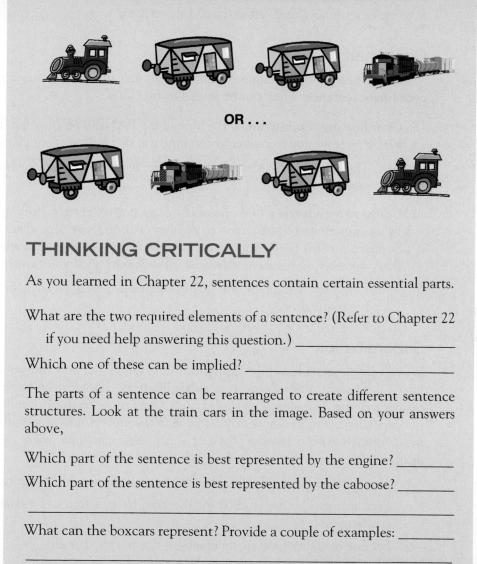

23

THINKING CRITICALLY

As you learned in Chapter 22, sentences contain certain essential parts.

What are the two required elements of a sentence? (Refer to Chapter 22 if you need help answering this question.) _____

Which one of these can be implied? _____

The parts of a sentence can be rearranged to create different sentence structures. Look at the train cars in the image. Based on your answers above,

Which part of the sentence is best represented by the engine? _____

Which part of the sentence is best represented by the caboose? _____

_____

What can the boxcars represent? Provide a couple of examples: _____

_____

Cross Reference
See Chapter 22, p. 526, for more on coordination and subordination.

COORDINATION AND SUBORDINATION

In order to achieve sentence variety in your writing, you must fully understand the functions of coordination and subordination. They are crucial, because they allow you to combine independent clauses in different ways so as to make sentences more effective and interesting.

Coordination

When two independent clauses of equal importance are joined, they form a **coordinate sentence**. They can be joined in two ways.

1. **Coordinating conjunctions:** Use one of the **FANBOYS** (*for, and, nor, but, or, yet, so*) and a **comma** to combine the two independent clauses.

   The pain that Marcus felt was intense, *but* his increasing feeling of panic was worse.

2. **Conjunctive adverbs:** Use one of the conjunctive adverbs (followed by a comma) after a semicolon to combine two independent clauses. Some commonly used conjunctive adverbs include *however, therefore, thus, moreover, furthermore, otherwise, nevertheless,* and *consequently*.

   Karen knew that she was losing the match; *consequently,* she lost her motivation.

Subordination

When one clause is less important (needs less emphasis) and can be made into a dependent clause, then it is **subordinate** or *dependent* on the independent clause. Use subordinating conjunctions to mark the beginning of the dependent or subordinate clause. Some of the most common subordinating conjunctions are *because, since, if, after, although, until, while, as, as though, before, once, that, who, whose, which,* and *whereas*.

   The math test was difficult *although* it was not impossible to figure out.

   Even though Thomas studied for the test, he still found it extremely challenging.

   Because he didn't give up, he managed to get a good grade.

Activity 23-1   Sentence Combining Using Coordination and Subordination

Directions: *Combine each of the following pairs of sentences into one grammatically correct sentence using either coordination or subordination as indicated.*

The Capitol dome, Washington, D.C.

Example: **a)** The Capitol building is located in Washington, D.C.
                 b) The Capitol building is a beautiful and symbolic building.

Coordination: The Capitol building is located in Washington, D.C., **and** it is a beautiful and symbolic building. *[coordinating conjunction]*

Coordination: The Capitol building is located in Washington, D.C.**; moreover,** the Capitol building is a beautiful and symbolic building.   *[conjunctive adverb]*

Subordination: The Capitol building is a beautiful and symbolic building, **which** is located in Washington, D.C. *[subordinating conjunction]*

1. The U.S. Capitol building was designed in 1792.

   The designer, Dr. William Thornton, created the original notion of the dome.

Use **coordination:**

_____

_____

2. Dr. Thornton submitted his design in a contest for the Capitol building design.

He was only an amateur architect.

Use **subordination:**

_____

_____

_____

3. The first cornerstone was laid by George Washington on September 18, 1773.

The original north wing wasn't fully constructed until November 17, 1800.

Use a **conjunctive adverb with a semicolon:**

_____

_____

_____

4. The British troops were marching on Washington, D.C., during the War of 1812.

Unfortunately, on August 23, 1814, British troops set fire to the building.

Use **coordination:**

_____

_____

_____

5. The new architect, Benjamin Latrobe, used the opportunity to make interior changes, since most of the exterior was spared.

He added more marble and a more ornate interior design.

Use a **conjunctive adverb with a semicolon:**

_____

_____

_____

6. Charles Bulfinch took over as head architect in 1818.

Bulfinch worked on the restoration and the Senate and House chambers until his position was terminated in 1829.

Use **coordination:**

_____

_____

_____

7. By 1850, the Capitol needed to be expanded to accommodate the growing number of senators.

Another competition was held offering $500 for the best expansion design.

Use **coordination:**

_____

_____

_____

8. In 1856, the old dome was removed.

Work began on a new dome that was cast-iron and fireproof.

Use **subordination:**

_____

_____

9. In 1861, construction was halted due to the Civil War.

In 1862, construction was resumed as a symbol of the strength of the Union.

Use **coordination:**

_____

_____

10. The work on the dome and extensions was completed in 1868 under the new architect, Edward Clark.

Clark held the post of Architect of the Capitol until his death in 1902.

Use **coordination:**

_____

_____

_____ ◯

SENTENCE TYPES

A sentence is a group of words that expresses a complete thought and contains at least one independent clause. An independent clause includes, at a minimum, an implied or stated subject and a main verb; it expresses a complete thought. Sentences can have distinct purposes and different structures.

Sentence Purposes

Sentences can have one of the following four purposes (the verbs are bolded, and the subjects are underlined in the sample sentences below):

Declarative: They make a statement or declaration.

The chicken enchiladas **are** delicious.

The chicken enchiladas and the quesadillas **taste** delicious and **are** spicy.

Interrogative: They ask a question.

Do you **like** the enchiladas and quesadillas?

Imperative: They give a command.

Try the enchiladas and quesadillas. [Subject is the implied _you_]

Exclamatory: They express a strong emotion or sentiment.

These enchiladas and quesadillas **are** out of this world!

Activity 23-2   Sentence Types

Directions: _Write one sentence of your own for each of the sentence types. Be sure to punctuate them correctly._

Declarative: _____

Interrogative: _____

Imperative: _____

Exclamatory: _____ ◯

SENTENCE STRUCTURES

There are four basic sentence structures. The subjects in the following sentences are underlined, and the verbs are bolded.

Simple sentences: Simple sentences have one independent clause.

The crime <u>rate</u> **is** rising.

Compound sentences: Compound sentences have two or more independent clauses.

The crime <u>rate</u> **is** rising, and <u>people</u> **are** moving out.

Complex sentences: Complex sentences have at least one independent clause and at least one dependent clause (in any order).

The city <u>council</u> **is** concerned since the citizens are moving to other cities.

Compound-complex sentences: Compound-complex sentences have at least two independent clauses and at least one dependent clause (in any order).

The <u>mayor</u> of the city **decided** to hold a special meeting, and the <u>leaders</u> of the community **were all invited** because all concerned voices needed to be heard.

Activity 23-3 Practicing Sentence Structures

Directions: *Create each sentence using the sentence structure indicated.*

Simple sentence: _____

Compound sentence: _____

_____

Complex sentence: _____

_____

Compound-complex sentence: _____

_____

To vary the sentence constructions in your writing, you can combine dependent clauses with independent clauses (coordination and subordination) in various patterns to achieve a variety of sentence types. Think back to

Cross Reference
Review Chapter 22 for definitions and examples of types
of clauses and phrases.

the train metaphor at the beginning of the chapter. You can create a variety of train types (of different lengths) using combinations of independent and dependent clauses (boxcars) hooked together with their appropriate coordination or subordination hook.

Engage your critical thinking skills to decide on the best sentence type to express your ideas in the context of your writing assignment. The types of sentences you use will depend on what you are discussing and who you are writing for. Here are a few possible combinations (DC = dependent clause, IC = independent clause).

Two independent clauses (joined by a coordinating conjunction):

IC   +   IC

I love apples, *and* I know that they are good for me

A dependent clause in front of an independent clause:

DC   +   IC

When I eat apples, pieces of the peel can get caught in my teeth.

Independent clause followed by a dependent clause:

IC   +   DC

Pieces of the peel can get caught in my teeth when I eat an apple.

A dependent clause followed by an independent clause and a dependent clause:

DC   +   IC   +   DC

When I eat apples, pieces of the peel can get caught in my teeth *because* they tend to get lodged in the crevices.

See how many types of sentences you can create as you experiment with coordination and subordination (review Chapter 22 for more on coordination and subordination).

Activity 23-4   More Sentence Combining Practice

Directions: *Step One: Write a paragraph that describes where you live using 8–15 simple sentences.* **Step Two:** *Go back and revise your original paragraph, and combine some of your sentences using coordination and subordination to achieve sentence variety.*

Original version:

_____

_____

_____

_____

_____

_____

Revised version:

_____

_____

_____

_____

_____

_____

SENTENCE VARIETY

When crafting longer pieces of writing, such as paragraphs and essays, you should vary your sentences in length, type, and rhythm. Don't ask readers to understand a series of short, choppy sentences when you could have made the relationships between them clear. Similarly, readers become bored if all the sentences in an essay are similar, with a monotonous tone and rhythm. Include a variety of sentence types, structures, and lengths in your writing.

One way to achieve sentence variety is to go back to some of your simple sentences and add more details and examples. For instance, if you had a sentence that read *I love pizza*, you could vary this sentence in length and style simply by adding more details: *I love sinking my teeth into an oozing, hot cheese and mushroom pizza.*

Another way is to combine sentences through coordination and subordination to create more complex sentences, as you have been practicing in this chapter and the preceding one.

> **Before:** I love pizza. Veggie pizza is my favorite.
>
> **Revised with coordination:** I love pizza, and veggie pizza is my favorite.
>
> **Revised with subordination:** Though I love all pizza, veggie is my favorite.
>
> **Before:** This class is challenging. I heard astronomy is even harder.

Revised with coordination: This class is challenging, but I hear astronomy is even harder.

Revised with subordination: Though this class is challenging, I hear astronomy is even harder.

You can also achieve more sentence variety by varying your sentence types: declarative, interrogative, imperative, and exclamatory.

I love pizza. Don't you think it is the perfect food? Try Pietro's famous veggie pizza. It is the best pizza ever!

Applying Critical Thinking

PURPOSE	IDEAS	SUPPORT	ASSUMPTIONS BIASES	CONCLUSIONS	POINT OF VIEW	ANALYSIS

In order to achieve sentence variety in the revision stage of your writing, engage your **analysis** skills. Go back through your draft and read each sentence carefully. Make sure you have expressed your thoughts clearly, using correct grammar, and that all the parts of the sentence work together to express what you want to say. Then see if you can incorporate some of the following suggestions for making your sentences more interesting and expressive.

Five Tips for Achieving Sentence Variety

1. Double check your whole piece to make sure you have a good balance of shorter and longer sentences and sentence types.
2. Try adding some additional information (words or phrases) to your shorter, simpler sentences.
3. Try using some different types of sentences: statements (declarative), questions (interrogative), commands (imperative), and exclamations.
4. Try combining some of your sentences to create compound, complex, or even compound-complex sentences using coordination and subordination.
5. Vary the style and rhythm of your sentences. Read them aloud to check whether they sound interesting or could benefit from some of the changes listed above.

Before and After Revising for Sentence Variety

Before—no sentence variety:

I really enjoy going to local fairs. It's a great way to get a look at the local culture. Also, I can try many of the local specialties. Fairs feature everything from specialty foods to hand-crafted items. The food available at local fairs is usually amazing. One of my favorite items to try is the local jams. Also, the local honey is usually something worth trying. Some nonfood items to see at fairs include wood carvings, paintings, and other work by local artists. Local fairs provide an insight into regional produce and art.

After—revised using the five tips from the critical thinking box:

Do you ever go to county fairs? *[Change in sentence type for variety]* I really enjoy going to local fairs. A local county fair is usually a great way to get a look at the local culture, and I get the opportunity to try many of the local specialties. *[Use of coordination to combine two sentences]* Fairs feature everything from specialty foods to hand-crafted items. Because vendors usually feature the best of the fresh local produce, the food available at local fairs is usually amazing. *[Use of subordination to combine two sentences]* One of my favorite items to try is the local jams; however, the local honey is usually even more unique to a particular region. *[Subordination]* Because I can't spend the whole time just eating, some nonfood booths I like to frequent at fairs include the art booths. *[Subordination]* Some booths sell wood carvings, paintings, and other work by local artists. If you haven't been to your local fair lately, you should make the trip. *[Subordination]* Local fairs provide an insight into regional produce and art.

Activity 23-5   Practicing Sentence Variety

Directions: *Using the five tips on page 540, rewrite the following paragraph to achieve more sentence variety.*

Washington, D.C., in the springtime is a wonderful place for visitors. The cherry blossoms are in bloom throughout the city. The blooming trees create a wonderful, pink and white scene. There are many interesting places to visit. These include the Jefferson Memorial, the Mall, and the White House. The Jefferson Memorial is especially beautiful in the springtime when the trees are in blossom. The blossoms float in the air like snow when the wind picks up. Anyone lucky enough to see this sight is amazed by the beauty of this memorial. Springtime is certainly the best time to visit Washington, D.C., and enjoy the sights.

_____

_____

_____

Correcting Major Sentence Errors

24

THINKING CRITICALLY

Look at the picture above. Then answer the questions below.

Can you spot the sentence error in this fortune cookie's message? The answer is that there are really two complete thoughts in this message, and thus, two sentences. Based on what you learned in Chapters 22 and 23, what are the two sentences?

First sentence: _____

Second sentence: _____

The two sentences of the fortune cookie message are linked with only a comma, creating a sentence error called a *comma splice*. A comma is not a strong enough mark of punctuation to separate two sentences. A period should end each of the two sentences. Along with two other sentence construction errors, the sentence fragment and the run-on, comma splices are a serious yet all too common error. All three errors make it difficult for readers to understand where sentences begin and end. Learning to spot and fix fragments, comma splices, and run-ons will strengthen your writing immediately.

543

FRAGMENTS

A **sentence fragment** is exactly that: a fragment, a piece of a sentence posing as a complete sentence. It starts with a capital letter and ends with a period, but it does not express a complete thought. Though we often use fragments in everyday speech and when reporting the speech of others in written dialogue, college essays generally requires the use of grammatically complete sentences.

See the following box for a list of errors that cause fragments.

Common Errors That Create Fragments

1. **Missing a subject:** leaving out the *subject* of the sentence
2. **Missing, incomplete, or incorrect form of verbs:** leaving out the *verb,* using an incomplete verb, or using the wrong form of a verb.
3. **A subordinate word or phrase before the subject and verb:** adding a word or phrase which makes a clause *dependent* on another clause for meaning.

Check carefully for these three common errors that lead to sentence fragments.

1. Missing a subject:

> Leaves the towels on the bathroom floor.
> [Subject missing: *Who* leaves the towels on the floor?]
>
> *Kalil* leaves the towels on the bathroom floor.

2. Missing the verb, using an incomplete verb, or the wrong form of a verb:

> Colorful flowers in a garden.
> [No verb. Add one to make a complete sentence.]
>
> Colorful flowers *bloomed* in the garden.
>
> Jesse leaving the towels on the bathroom floor.
> [Incomplete verb: add the helping verb *is* or *was* before *leaving*]
>
> Jesse *is* leaving the towels on the bathroom floor.

Or you could see this error as resulting from the wrong form of the verb being used and you could change *leaving* to *leaves* or *left:*

Jesse *leaves* the towels on the floor.

Here is another example of the wrong form of the verb:

The blanket covering the table.

Corrected: The blanket *covers* the table.

3. **Subordinate word or phrase before the subject and verb (makes the word group a dependent clause):**

Because Jesse leaves towels on the bathroom floor.

[Subordinating word: The word *because* makes this a dependent clause, a sentence fragment. To fix it you could either delete the word *Because* or add an independent clause before or after it.]

~~Because~~ Jesse leaves towels on the bathroom floor.

His mother is shouting because Jesse leaves towels on the bathroom floor.

Because he leaves towels on the bathroom floor, *his mother has told him she will not wash them for him.*

Identifying Sentence Fragments

A complete sentence contains a subject and a verb and does not have a subordinating word or phrase before the subject. Here are three steps you can use to identify sentence fragments.

Three Steps for Identifying Sentence Fragments

1. Find the verb
2. Find the subject
3. Check for a subordinating word or phrase

1. **Find the verb:** Since the verb is usually easy to find because it denotes the action or state of being (physical action or mental/emotional "action") in a sentence, find it first. If there is no verb (or an auxiliary verb is needed), then you have a sentence fragment. Ask yourself, "What is happening in this sentence?" For example:

Cross Reference
See p. 508 for more on verbs.

Martin downstairs to the kitchen.
[What is Martin doing? How did he get downstairs? The sentence needs a verb.]

Martin *walked* downstairs to the kitchen.

If the verb is an *-ing* form (verbal), make sure there is an auxiliary or helping verb (a *to be* verb such as *is*, *was*, *are*, or *were*) in front of it. For instance:

Cleo *working* on a new letter.
[The above sentence needs a helping verb.]

Cleo *is* working on a new letter.

OR, change the *-ing* form to a regular verb:

Cleo worked on a new letter.

Cross Reference
See p. 505 for more on subjects.

2. **Find the subject:** Ask yourself, "*Who* or *what* is the subject of the action/verb I found?" If there isn't a noun that serves as the subject, then the word group is a sentence fragment. For example:

Walked into the room, to the astonishment of the assembled crowd.
[Who walked into the room? Who is the subject of this sentence?]

The presidential candidate walked into the room, to the astonishment of the assembled crowd.

Exception: The one exception is when the subject is implied, as in the word *you* in a command. For example:

Don't ask me again.
[Although not stated, the subject of this sentence is the implied *You*.]

Cross Reference
See p. 507 for more on the "implied you" subject.

3. **Check for a subordinating word or phrase that creates a dependent clause:** When you put a subordinating conjunction such as *because* in front of the subject of a sentence, the sentence becomes a dependent clause. It is incomplete because it now depends on the addition of more information to make sense. For example:

Whenever I go away.
[The word *whenever* makes this a dependent phrase. You need either to delete the subordinating word *whenever*, or add an independent clause before or after the phrase.]

~~Whenever~~ I go away.

I *always pack too much*, whenever I go away.

Whenever I go away, *I look for interesting rocks*.

Here are a few of the most common words that indicate the beginning of a dependent clause or subordinate phrase:

because, since, when, whenever, if, as, on, in, every time, knowing that, believing that, hoping that, and especially

Cross Reference
See Chapter 22, p. 527, for a more complete list of subordinating words and a more in-depth explanation of using subordination.

Correcting Sentence Fragments

When you have spotted a fragment caused by one or more of the errors listed above, use that error or set of errors as a key to fixing the problem.

Fragment: Does a poor job with the dishes. [Missing a subject—so add one]

Revised: *Simon* does a poor job with the dishes.

Fragment: A pile of unwashed clothes on the counter. [Missing a verb—so add one]

Revised: A pile of unwashed clothes lay on the counter.

Fragment: Maria singing like a bird. [Not a complete verb—add an auxiliary verb or change the verb form]

Revised: Maria *was* singing like a bird.

OR

Maria sang like a bird.

Fragment: Since he has not returned.
[Dependent clause due to the word *since*—follow it with a comma and an independent clause, precede it with an independent clause or delete the word *since*]

Revised: Since he has not returned, I will keep his security deposit.

I will keep his security deposit since he has not returned.

He has not returned.

Activity 24-1   Identifying and Correcting Fragments

Directions: *Using the three-step test for fragments, look at the fragments below and list which type or types of error created each fragment. Some items may have more than one error.*

1. *Missing a subject*
2. *A missing, incomplete, or incorrect form of verb*
3. *Subordinate word or phrase before the subject and verb*

Then, add or delete words to fix the fragment and rewrite it as a complete sentence. You may need to add more information for the sentence to make sense.

Example: Caught the ball.   Error type(s) _____1_____

Corrected: *Sue caught the ball.* _____

1. Several fish in one tank.   Error type(s) _____

    Corrected: _____

2. Because the fabric was textured.   Error type(s) _____

    Corrected: _____

    _____

3. The grass growing strong and tall.   Error type(s) _____

    Corrected: _____

4. Since the bird was in a large cage.   Error type(s) _____

    Corrected: _____

    _____

5. Marty singing at the top of his lungs. Error type(s) _____

    Corrected: _____

    _____

Activity 24-2 Identifying and Correcting Fragments

Directions: *Review the following word groups. If a word group is a complete sentence, write S on the line provided. If it is a fragment, write F, and then revise it to make it a complete sentence. You may add or delete words to fix the fragments.*

_____ 1. San Francisco's Golden Gate Bridge, a miraculous engineering achievement.

    _____

    _____

_____ 2. The bridge, completed in 1937, spanning 1.7 miles, linking Marin County and San Francisco.

_____

_____

_____ 3. The bridge's two famous towers are 746 feet high.

_____

_____

_____ 4. Making the towers 191 feet taller than the Washington Monument.

_____

_____

_____ 5. Featuring an art deco design.

_____

_____

Activity 24-3   Identifying and Correcting Fragments

Directions: *Add the needed words, information, or even a complete additional independent clause to the following fragments to make them into complete sentences. You can also change the tense of the verb to correct a sentence.*

1. Knowing it was the third Monday of the month.

_____

_____

2. Running as fast as she could.

_____

_____

3. Believing in something strongly.

_____

4. Finding his keys in the nick of time.

_____

_____

5. Deciding it was too late after all.

_____

_____

Activity 24-4   Identifying and Correcting Fragments

Directions: *In the spaces provided below the paragraph, mark F for a fragment and S for a complete sentence for each of the numbered word groups.*

[1]The famous Golden Gate bridge is a beautiful sight. [2]A long suspension bridge, spanning 4,200 feet. [3]It is a stunning sight in the skyline. [4]Because of the spectacular view. [5]Visitors will travel over the bridge to see it from the other side as well. [6]Fort Point, built at the beginning of the Civil War, sitting at the south end of the bridge. [7]The fort designated a National Historic Monument in 1970. [8]It is built of brick. [9]The bridge and its surrounding areas are some of the most photographed spots of California. [10]Lighthouses visible from the bridge in the distance.[11]One of the lighthouses situated on Alcatraz Island. [12]Alcatraz Island also was home to a famous prison.[13]It, too, a famous tourist attraction. [14]Every day, boats take tourists from the mainland to the island. [15]The boats loading at the waterfront. [16]Then they take people to Alcatraz. [17]It's a short ride. [18]Once there, tourists exploring the old prison. [19]However, the Golden Gate Bridge is the most defining San Francisco site. [20]Its beautiful orange towers raised to the sky in beauty.

1. _____	6. _____	11. _____	16. _____
2. _____	7. _____	12. _____	17. _____
3. _____	8. _____	13. _____	18. _____
4. _____	9. _____	14. _____	19. _____
5. _____	10. _____	15. _____	20. _____

RUN-ONS AND COMMA SPLICES

A **run-on**, sometimes called a *fused sentence*, occurs when you combine two or more independent clauses (complete sentences) with no punctuation to separate them. See Chapter 22, "Sentence Parts," for more about what makes an independent clause or complete sentence. Use your analysis skills to check for the necessary parts of a sentence and to make sure you don't have two or more independent clauses that need stronger punctuation to join them.

Sample run-on/fused sentence:

I like cake he likes ice cream.
[This group of words is a run-on because there are two full sentences, each with a subject and verb.]

I	like	cake	he	likes	ice cream
(SUBJ)	(VERB)	(OBJ)	(SUBJ)	(VERB)	(OBJ)

A **comma splice** is a particular type of run-on that occurs when you combine two or more independent clauses (complete sentences with two subjects and two verbs) with just a comma.

Sample comma splice:

I like cake, he likes ice cream.
[This word group is a comma splice because there is a full sentence, with its own subject and verb, on both sides of the comma.]

Correcting Run-ons or Comma Splices

Here are four ways to fix run-ons or comma splices.

Four Ways to Fix a Run-on or Comma Splice at a Glance

1. , + Coordinating conjunction (FANBOYS)

2. . or **!** or **?** (add a final punctuation mark)

3. ; and sometimes a **:**

4. Make a sentence into a dependent clause by adding a subordinating word.

---

1. **Add a coordinating conjunction** (FANBOYS—*for, and, nor, but, or, yet, so*) after the comma. A comma with a coordinating conjunction is equal to a period.

    I like cake, and he likes ice cream.

2. **Change the comma into a period** (or an exclamation point or a question mark if the first independent clause is a question).

I like cake. He likes ice cream.

3. **Change the comma into a semicolon or a colon.** A semicolon can be used to combine two independent clauses that have a strong content connection, but use semicolons sparingly to indicate a powerful connection between two complete thoughts.

I like cake; he likes ice cream.

A colon can also be used between two independent clauses if the second clause *answers* or *explains* the first one.

I like cake for one reason: It satisfies my sweet tooth completely.

4. **Turn one of the independent clauses into a dependent clause by adding a subordinating word.** See page 527 for more on subordination.

Since I love movies, I go to see a film once a week.

Cross Reference

See Chapter 26 for more on using semicolons and colons.

Activity 24-5   Correcting Run-Ons

Directions: *Fix the following run-on (fused) sentences by (1) adding a comma and a coordinating conjunction (For And Nor But Or Yet So), (2) adding a period, or (3) adding a semicolon or colon.*

1. The airplane was made of wood it also had painted wings. _____

   _____

2. The cat saw the mouse she immediately ran to catch it. _____

   _____

3. At first, the children were scared of the snake after a while, they became more comfortable handling it. _____

   _____

4. The store owner wanted to attract new customers he added a big new sign out front. _____

   _____

5. It's amazing the trick is to believe it. _____

   _____

Activity 24-6   Correcting Comma Splices

Directions: *Fix the following comma splices by (1) adding a coordinating conjunction (For And Nor But Or Yet So) after the comma, (2) changing the comma to a period, or (3) changing the comma to a semicolon or colon.*

1.   The air was calm, the wind wasn't blowing at all.

   _____

2.   Middle school is a tough time for kids, many of the students are uncomfortable at this age.

   _____

   _____

3.   The dog ate the last of the cookies, they had been sitting on the counter.

   _____

4.   The job interview was tough, Karla didn't think she would get the position.

   _____

   _____

5.   My friend Neal has applied for a new job, he'll hear if he got it soon.

   _____

   _____

Activity 24-7   Run-ons and Comma Splices

Directions: *Mark each sentence RO for run-on (no punctuation between two independent clauses), CS for comma splices (two independent clauses joined with only a comma), or C if it is a correct sentence. Then fix any run-ons and comma splices on the lines below, using one of the methods listed in Four Ways to Fix a Run-on or Comma Splice at a Glance.*

_____   1.   The Eiffel Tower is one of the most famous monuments in the world it is the most well known monument in Europe.

   _____

   _____

_____ **2.** The Eiffel Tower was built in 1889, its first year it hosted two million visitors.

_____

_____

_____ **3.** From 1889 to the present, more than 200 million people have visited the Eiffel Tower.

_____

_____

_____ **4.** The Eiffel Tower was built for the Universal Exhibition in celebration of the French Revolution it has come to symbolize the heart of France.

_____

_____

_____ **5.** The architect of the Eiffel Tower was Stephen Sauvestre, the construction took two years, two months, and five days.

_____

_____

_____ **6.** The total weight of the Eiffel Tower is 10,100 tons, the height is 324 meters.

_____

_____

_____ **7.** The Eiffel Tower contains more than 18,038 pieces of metal, and there are 2,500,000 rivets.

_____

_____

_____ **8.** The Tower is open 365 days a year more than 6 million visitors come each year.

_____

_____

_____ **9.** There are several elevators servicing different levels of the Tower, one elevator is exclusively for guests dining at the famous Jules Verne Restaurant at the Tower.

_____

_____

_____ **10.**   The Eiffel Tower is under surveillance 24 hours a day, security is essential for a world-class monument such as this.

_____

_____ ⬤

Activity 24-8   Run-ons and Comma Splices

Directions: *In the spaces provided below the paragraph, mark RO for run-ons, CS for comma splices, and C for correct sentences for each of the numbered word groups.*

[1]According to a survey hosted by the Eiffel Tower website, visitors from five countries (Italy, England, Spain, Germany, and the United States) all listed the Eiffel Tower as the most well known European monument. [2]The Italian responses listed three other popular European monuments after the Eiffel Tower, they were the Coliseum, the Dome of Milan, and the Louvre. [3]The British respondents listed several other monuments the Tower of Pisa, the Arc de Triomphe, Big Ben, and the Tower of London were among their answers. [4]Similarly, the Spanish respondents listed other monuments, but none were above the Eiffel Tower. [5]Spanish tourists included the Tower of Pisa as a monument that was high on their list. [6]Similarly, German visitors listed the Eiffel Tower as number one, they also mentioned the Tower of London and the Tower of Pisa. [7] The German tourists included a few lesser known sites including the Cologne Dome they further listed the Brandenburg Gate and the Atomium. [8]The American respondents listed the most monuments of all, they, like the other tourists, put the Eiffel Tower at the top of their list. [9]They included the Tower of Pisa and Big Ben on their list the Tower of London ranked high as well. [10]Like the British, the Americans also listed the Arc de Triomphe; it is interesting to see how people around the world view Europe's most famous landmarks.

1._____   5._____   9._____

2._____   6._____   10._____ ⬤

3._____   7._____

4._____   8._____

Commas, Semicolons, and Colons

25

Coconut in sand.

THINKING CRITICALLY

Punctuation is essential to imparting meaning. A well used comma, semicolon, or colon can be as dramatic as this image of a coconut in the sand. What do you think it would be like to read a paragraph with no punctuation marks? Why?

_____

_____

_____

_____

_____

_____

COMMAS

Commas (,) are the most common form of punctuation. They serve several functions in writing and help your readers understand your ideas and sentences. Commas clarify, make distinctions, or create the pauses needed to let your readers follow your sentences and ideas.

Five Comma Rules

There are five basic rules of comma use, and if you keep them in mind, the mystery of comma usage will be solved. Try not to use the "comma by instinct" approach: There really are consistent rules for comma use.

When you are editing your writing, check to see if the commas you have used fall into one of these categories, and if they do not, then remember the old comma saying: "When in doubt, leave it out." A comma where it doesn't belong usually causes more problems than leaving it out does.

Rule 1

Use a comma in front of a coordinating conjunction in order to combine two independent clauses to create a compound sentence.

> Independent clause + , + FANBOYS + independent clause
> ▼
> (Coordinating conjunctions)

Here are the seven coordinating conjunctions: **F**or **A**nd **N**or **B**ut **O**r **Y**et **S**o. Remember the mnemonic device (memory trick) of FANBOYS to recall them. They are the only seven words in English that can be used after a comma to combine two independent clauses (use any other word and you have a comma splice).

College students often work while in school, and it makes their lives very busy.

Many of them would like to attend classes without having to work, but college costs are just too high.

Tip: The comma comes *before* the coordinating conjunction. Also, be careful not to put a comma in automatically as soon as you see one of the FANBOYS. These words need to have an independent clause (with a subject and a verb) on *both* sides in order to use the comma. Otherwise, they are part of a compound subject or compound predicate, and you don't use a comma:

Abdul goes to school full time and works 20 hours a week.

There is only one subject in this sentence: *Abdul.* There are two verbs that both relate to the subject Abdul: *goes* and *works.* The word *and* links two parts of a compound predicate, and no comma is needed.

Rule 2

Use a comma to separate the items in a series (a list of three or more items) or a list of coordinate adjectives.

1. **Using commas with items in a list.** Commas help separate distinct items within a list of items:

> Item + , item + , item + , and item

> Marcus took several courses, including math, English, history, and sociology.

Placing the last comma before the "and" is one of the comma rules currently in debate. Some people argue that a comma replaces the word "and" so the last comma before an item in a series isn't necessary. However, there are cases when a reader could get confused by the lack of a comma before the last item in the series, so it's usually a good idea to put it in. Consistency and clarity are the rules of thumb. For example:

> Levi brought a variety of sandwiches to the picnic, including peanut butter and jelly, bologna, ham, and cheese.

Without the comma, the reader might think "ham and cheese" is one sandwich type instead of two separate ones.

2. **Coordinate adjectives versus cumulative or compound adjectives**

   - **Coordinate adjectives:** If you have two or more adjectives listed before a noun that indicate separate qualities, then use a comma between them. In other words, you are listing the separate qualities:

     Katharine is a loyal, affectionate, forgiving friend.

     Tip: If you can change the order of the adjectives and replace the commas with the word *and,* then you are dealing with coordinate adjectives:

     Katharine is an affectionate and forgiving and loyal friend.

   - **Cumulative adjectives:** If the adjectives are working together in order to describe something or modify each other in stages, then *do not* use commas:

     Marcia brought over a sweet apple pie for dessert.

Tip: If you cannot add the word *and* between the adjectives or reverse the order of the adjectives without changing the meaning of the sentence, do not use a comma. For example, no comma should come between "sweet" and "apple" because they are cumulative adjectives:

> Marcia brought over a sweet *and* apple pie.

> Marcia brought over a *apple sweet* pie.

The order can't be changed: They work together to describe the pie.

> The ancient Chinese tradition of serving tea at social events is still evident in America today.

Again, you wouldn't want to change the order of "ancient" and "Chinese" in this sentence.

Tip: Cumulative adjectives should sound right in the particular order they are in—they are not interchangeable. You wouldn't say "apple sweet pie" or "Chinese ancient tradition."

- **Compound adjectives:** If two adjectives are used together to make one descriptor, then they become a compound adjective, and you should use a hyphen between them instead of a comma.

  Coordinate adjectives: The blue, green, and gray house sits at the top of the hill. [Three separate qualities/colors: Use commas.]

  Compound adjective: The blue-green and gray house sits on the top of the hill. [Blue-green is one color: Use a hyphen, not a comma.]

  Coordinate adjectives: The fat, furry cat ran slowly. [Two separate qualities: Use a comma.]

  Compound adjective: The fat-faced cat ran slowly. [One quality: Use a hyphen.]

Rule 3

Use a comma after introductory material (an introductory dependent clause, an introductory prepositional or participial phrase, or just a word for emphasis or transition).

Dependent clause		
Introductory phrase	+ , +	independent clause
Introductory word		

A comma sets off the introductory word, phrase, or clause from the main sentence. To find introductory material, look for the main subject and verb and see if anything comes before them.

1. Introductory dependent clause

Use a comma between the end of an introductory dependent clause and the independent clause that follows it. A dependent clause has a subordinating word in the front of it such as *because*, *since*, *when*, and *if*.

> *Since Jeb is allergic to shellfish,* I won't serve shrimp cocktail at the party.

However, if a dependent clause comes after an independent clause, then *do not* use a comma:

> I won't serve shrimp cocktail at the party *since Jeb is allergic to shellfish*.

Cross Reference
See p. 527 for more about subordinating words.

2. Introductory prepositional phrase

Use a comma after a prepositional phrase that comes before the independent clause. A prepositional phrase begins with a preposition such as *on*, *in*, *after*, and so on:

> *On every other weekend,* I visit my brother Nick.

However, if a prepositional phrase comes after the independent clause, then *do not* use a comma:

> I visit my brother Nick *on every other weekend*.

Cross Reference
See p. 520 for more about prepositions.

3. Introductory participial phrase

Use a comma after a participial phrase that comes before an independent clause. A participial phrase begins with a word ending in *-ing*:

> *Thinking she was late,* Di drove too quickly to work.

4. Word for emphasis or transition

Use a comma after a transitional or emphatic word used in front of your independent clause:

> *However,* I try to visit my mom and dad every weekend.

5. Direct address

Use a comma when you directly address someone by name or title:

> *Darci,* do you visit your parents regularly?

Tip: You still need a comma if the direct address comes at the end of the sentence, or two commas around the person's name or title if it comes in the middle of your independent clause:

> Do you visit your parents regularly, *Darci?*

> Will you, *Mr. President,* visit Portugal in the coming year?

> Dear Kim, I've been thinking about you lately. [Also used in an informal letter greeting]

6. Yes and no statements

Use a comma after a yes or no answer that begins a sentence:

> Yes, I do visit my parents regularly.

7. Tag lines for dialogue or quotations

Use a comma after a tag word or phrase that comes before a quotation or dialogue in your sentence:

> He said, "No, I will not be able to attend."

> William Shakespeare wrote, "Life is but a walking shadow . . ."

Note: Sometimes the comma can be omitted after introductory material if there is a short adverb clause or phrase that causes no danger of misreading.

> In any case we weren't confused.

However, it's acceptable to use the comma there too.

> In any case, we weren't confused.

Rule 4

Use a comma to set off interrupters—words, phrases, or clauses that "interrupt" a sentence between the beginning and the end of an independent clause (IC):

> | Beginning of IC   +   ,   +   interrupter   +   ,   +   end of IC |

1. Dependent clause interrupter

Use commas to set off a dependent clause that interrupts an independent clause:

> Thomas realized, *after he took a good look at his things,* that he had forgotten his backpack.

Tip: Imagine taking the middle clause out of the sentence, using the two commas like two handles you can grab to remove it. The sentence should still make sense without the clause you removed.

> Thomas knew that he had forgotten his backpack.

2. Transitional words and phrases or parenthetical interrupters

Use commas to set off transitional words or parenthetical interruptors:

> Levi told us, *however,* about the difference between fruit bats and vampire bats.

Tip: You can also imagine these commas as handles you can use to remove this transition and test to make sure your sentence still makes sense.

Levi told us about the difference between fruit bats and vampire bats.

Note: Use commas around parenthetical or side information instead of using parentheses when the information is still fairly important and when you are using parenthetical citations in more formal writing (see Chapter 19 for more on parenthetical citations).

3. Appositive interrupters

Use commas to set off appositive interrupters (nouns or phrases that rename or categorize nearby nouns):

Jaspar Wyman, *a famous geologist,* was eager to climb Mt. Rainier.

4. Nonrestrictive clauses

A nonrestrictive adjective clause starts with a relative pronoun (*who, whom, whose,* or *which*) or with a relative adverb (*where* or *when*). The information it conveys is not essential for identifying the subject of the sentence. That is, it doesn't *restrict* the noun.

Winston, *who loves to collect rocks,* headed straight for the riverbed.

The "who" relative pronoun statement is nonrestrictive since you do not need the information to identify the subject, Winston. It is extra, nonrestrictive information.

Note: Restrictive clauses. When the information in the relative pronoun or adverb statement is necessary in order to *restrict* or identify the noun/subject, then *do not* use commas:

The students who work hard in this class will receive a good grade.

The clause *who work hard* is necessary to identify which students will get the good grades—it *restricts* the noun.

5. Tag lines that interrupt dialogue or quotations

Two commas are used to set off these tag lines because they appear in the middle of the sentence.

"It's too bad," he said, "that I will not be able to attend."

Tip: You even need a comma if the tag comes at the end:

"It's too bad that I will not be able to attend," he said.

Note: Notice the comma comes *inside* the quotation marks in both cases. Do not use quotation marks or a comma with an indirect quotation:

Neal said that he would not be able to attend either.

Rule 5

Use commas according to conventions for dates, times, titles, and so on, and to avoid confusion. Here are some examples of commas used to indicate time, place, and title:

1. **Dates:**

    Charlie was born May 21, 1972.

    Geoffrey was born on January 6, 1981, in Gainesville, Florida.

    [Notice the comma is required after the year, as well, if more information follows, as in this example.]

2. **Addresses/locations:**

    Samuel grew up in Berkeley, California.

    She was born in Columbus, Ohio, in 1855.

    [Notice the required comma after *Ohio*.]

3. **Numbers:**

    Jerith has collected more than *50,000* trading cards in his lifetime.

4. **Formal titles:**

    Josie McQuail, *PhD*., will be visiting our college next month.

Use commas to prevent confusion and to distinguish between repeated words or phrases:

    Those students who can speak, speak frequently in class.

    What we were afraid would disappear, disappeared.

When Not to Use a Comma

- Do not use a comma to separate a subject from its verb.
- Do not use a comma to separate verbs that share the same subject.
- Do not automatically put a comma before every *and* or *but*. Check to be sure that they have a subject and verb on both sides (in other words, that they link two independent clauses).
- Do not put a comma between the verb and the direct object.
- Do not put a comma before a dependent clause that follows an independent clause (unless the comma is necessary for reading clarity).
- Do not put a comma after *especially* or *such as*.

Activity 25-1   Practice Spotting Misused Commas

Directions: *Delete the misused or unnecessary commas in the following sentences.*

1. Springtime in the Northwest, brings a lot of amazing spring flowers.
2. The crocuses are the first to pop from the ground, and then the daffodils.
3. The tulips grow, out of the ground in March.
4. Other flowers are common in the spring, such as, narcissus, lilacs, and lilies.
5. The Northwest is beautiful in the spring, because of all the beautiful, and colorful flowers. ●

Activity 25-2   Adding Commas and Their Rules

Directions: *Each of the ten sentences below needs one or more commas. Place the commas where they belong in the sentence. Then write the number of the rule that applies for each added comma or commas.*

1. The Space Needle in Seattle Washington, is a famous landmark and tourist attraction.

   Rule(s) _____

2. The Space Needle was built in 1961 and it was designed by Edward Carlson for the 1962 World's Fair.

   Rule(s) _____

3. The Space Needle has a 120-foot concrete foundation massive steel beams and a flying saucer-shaped structure on top.

   Rule(s) _____

4. The Space Needle designed to withstand a strong earthquake has a reinforced foundation that is as heavy as the structure itself.

   Rule(s) _____

Space Needle, Seattle, Washington. Douglas Cole, 2007.

5. When the 1962 World's Fair was held in Seattle the Space Needle was opened to the public.

Rule(s) _____

6. There are three levels to the Space Needle, including the Pavilion Level the Restaurant Level and the Observation Deck.

Rule(s) _____

7. Knowing that Seattle can be a windy city the engineers designed the Space Needle to withstand a wind velocity of 200 miles per hour.

Rule(s) _____

8. The Space Needle is 605 feet tall so its presence in the Seattle skyline is unmistakable.

Rule(s) _____

9. The grounds of the Space Needle include green areas for gathering a valet or drop-off area and a gateway to the Seattle Center Amusement Park.

Rule(s) _____

10. The Legacy Light a light that shines skyward from the top of the Space Needle was first illuminated on New Year's Eve 1999 as a celebration of the new millennium.

Rule(s) _____

Activity 25-3   Add, Delete, and Move Commas, Part I

Directions: *Add, delete, and move commas as necessary in each sentence. Then, in the space provided, explain the reason and/or the comma rule involved in your decision.*

1. We knew that Charlie would be late, and that he would have an excuse.

Reason for change: _____

2. Chica always got her food last and, she wanted it that way.

Reason for change: _____

3. In the third week of class Julio decided to change his major.

Reason for change: _____

4. Sylvia on the other hand knew what she wanted to do and stuck with it.

Reason for change: _____

5. Matthew said "I don't care either way."

Reason for change: _____

6. Jerith even though he did care said that it didn't matter to him.

Reason for change: _____

7. We knew that all of us would need pencils paper and a notebook.

Reason for change: _____

8. Katrina wanted to get a cup of coffee but she was afraid to miss her bus.

Reason for change: _____

9. Jen who never drinks plain coffee ordered a vanilla latte.

    Reason for change: _____

10. Christopher said, that it is not a good idea to drink coffee after dinner.

    Reason for change: _____

Applying Critical Thinking

PURPOSE   IDEAS   SUPPORT   ASSUMPTIONS BIASES   CONCLUSIONS   POINT OF VIEW   ANALYSIS

When you are constructing sentences and making choices about using commas, ask yourself the following questions:

- What is my **purpose** for this particular sentence, and how can I best construct my sentence and use commas to achieve my purpose?
- How can punctuation make my meaning clearer?

  Then *break down the particular parts* of the sentence, using your **analysis** skills to make sure that you have constructed the sentence correctly and used comma(s) correctly.

SEMICOLONS AND COLONS

The Semicolon

The semicolon (;) is one of the most abused, misused, and neglected punctuation marks in English. However, when used correctly (and not too often), it is also one of the most specific and powerful punctuation marks.

There are only two rules for using the semicolon.

Rule 1

Use a semicolon between two independent clauses when the second one has a strong connection to the first one, and they are equally important. Choose a semicolon over a period or over a comma and a coordinating conjunction when you want to emphasize to your reader the connection between the two independent clauses.

> | Independent clause   +   ;   + independent clause |
> | --- |

Julie loves to shop; she   hits the department stores at least once
(subj)(verb)   (subj) (verb)
a week.

Both of these clauses are complete sentences with a subject and verb; however, the semicolon emphasizes their connection more than a period or coordinating conjunction would. Here is another example:

We love to take exotic family vacations; last year, we went to Hawaii, and the year before that, we went to Tahiti.

Often, students add commas to sentences like these because they don't want the hard stop of a period, creating a comma splice. They either need to add a coordinating conjunction or in cases where the second independent clause connects directly to the first, use a semicolon.

Often, semicolons are followed by either a transitional expression or word (see p. 118 for a list of common transitional words or expressions) or a conjunctive adverb, followed by a comma.

We love to eat apples; however, we prefer pears when they are in season.

Cross Reference
See p. 550 for more about comma splices.

CONJUNCTIVE ADVERBS OFTEN USED AFTER A SEMICOLON
(AND FOLLOWED BY A COMMA)

however	therefore	furthermore	moreover	consequently
also	finally	certainly	next	then
besides	conversely	likewise	subsequently	similarly
otherwise	indeed	meanwhile	thus	specifically

Tip: The semicolon should be used sparingly for maximum effect. It is a gem, so use it when it is the perfect punctuation mark, not when a period would do.

Rule 2

Use a semicolon to separate complex items in a series. That is, when items already have commas in them, use semicolons to separate the items:

> | Item 1, with internal punctuation ; item 2, with internal punctuation ; and item 3, with internal punctuation. |
> | --- |

Remember Rule 2 for commas separating items in a series (see p. 559)? This semicolon rule is very similar except that you use semicolons when the items you are listing have subcomponents separated by commas:

> Last year, Dolly went to Honolulu, Hawaii; Mallorca, Spain; Puerto Vallarta, Mexico; Florence, Italy; and Tacoma, Washington.

If only commas had been used, a reader might become confused and think Dolly had visited ten places instead of five.

> **Tip 1:** Notice that you include a semicolon before the "and" that comes before the final item listed.

> **Tip 2:** If there was just a list of the cities, you would use only commas: Honolulu, Mallorca, Puerto Vallarta, Florence, and Tacoma.

Here's another example:

> I like lots of musical groups such as The Beatles, a classic rock group; OutKast, a hip hop group; The Dixie Chicks, a country and western group; and The Dave Brubeck Quartet, a jazz group.

When Not to Use a Semicolon

- Do not use a semicolon after the phrases *especially* or *such as*.
- Do not use a semicolon after a coordinating conjunction (FANBOYS).
- Do not use a semicolon before the words *because* or *since* if they are beginning a dependent clause at the end of a sentence.
- Do not use a semicolon before a list of words or items after an independent clause (use a colon).

Activity 25-4   Semicolon Practice

Directions: *Add semicolons where they belong in the following sentences.*

1. We knew that it was early we decided to head out anyway.

2. Several faculty members attended the meeting, including Sandy Johanson, Professor of Philosophy Jennifer Hoene, Professor of English Frank Wilson, Professor of Mathematics and Gary Oliviera, Professor of Art.

3. I love scary movies watching them late at night is the best.

4. My sister knew it was a lost cause she decided to let her son go to the movies.

5. The realization was a strong one she had it while she was dreaming.

Activity 25-5   Add or Delete Semicolons

Directions: *Add or delete semicolons or change a semicolon to a comma if needed in the following sentences.*

1. The marriage was beautiful the ceremony went perfectly.

2. The bride cried during the ceremony; because she was so happy.

3. The cake was delicious; and the music was lovely.

4. The DJ played "Lady," by the Commodores "I Just Called to Say I Love You," by Stevie Wonder and "Time of Your Life," by Green Day.

5. There was other music for dancing too; such as "Hey Ya," by OutKast. ●

Applying Critical Thinking

| PURPOSE | IDEAS | SUPPORT | ASSUMPTIONS BIASES | CONCLUSIONS | POINT OF VIEW | ANALYSIS |

When you are constructing sentences and making choices about using semicolons, ask yourself the following critical thinking questions:

- What is my **purpose** for this particular sentence, and how can I best construct my sentence and use a semicolon to achieve my purpose?
- Will a semicolon make my meaning clearer and add emphasis to a cause and effect relationship between two clauses?

Then *break down the particular parts* of the sentence using your **analysis** skills to make sure that you have constructed the sentence correctly and used a semicolon correctly.

The Colon

There are several rules for using a colon (:), but it basically indicates that a list or explanation is to follow.

Rule 1

Use a colon between two independent clauses when the second clause explains, summarizes, or answers the first one:

> Barry wanted only one thing from life: he wanted to make lots
> (SUBJ) (VERB)   (SUBJ) (VERB)
>
> of money.

Both clauses are complete sentences. The second clause explains the first one. It's true that a period or a comma followed by a coordinating conjunction would work here, and even a semicolon would work between these two clauses. However, the colon is the *best choice* because it is the most specific and exact form of punctuation in this case and helps the reader see the answer-explanation relationship between the two clauses. Here's another example:

> Erin knew there were two options left for her: She could finish school, or she could join the army.

Note: When a colon separates two independent clauses, the second independent clause usually begins with a capital or lowercase letter (He wanted . . .).

Rule 2

Use a colon after an independent clause that is followed by a word or phrase that answers or explains the idea set up in the independent clause.

> Barry wanted only one thing from life: to make lots of money.
> [Colon followed by a phrase]

> Barry wanted only one thing from life: lots of money.
> [Colon followed by a phrase]

> Barry wanted only one thing from life: money.
> [Colon followed by a single word]

> Two options were left for her: finishing school or joining the army.
> [Colon followed by a phrase]

Tip: An independent clause must come before the colon.

Correct: The test was assessing two things: the students' understanding of the reading and their use of examples.

Incorrect: Assessing two things: the students' understanding of the reading and their use of examples.

Rule 3

Use a colon after an independent clause that introduces a list of items.

Vik and Seema bought several household items at the street fair: art, rugs, dishes, and linens.

To get good grades, you will have to focus on the following tips: getting enough sleep, reading all homework assignments, finishing homework tasks on time, and doing professional work in and out of class.

Tip 1: Be sure that the clause that comes before the colon and the list is independent. It should have both a subject and a verb and not be introduced by a subordinating conjunction.

To learn karate, you will need: discipline, time, patience, and a sensei. [Incorrect use of the colon—delete it]

Tip 2: Don't use a colon after words and phrases such as *for example, such as,* and *including.* Think of these words as replacements for a colon; they serve the same function.

Examples: Many birds frequented Jen's feeder such as: finches, chickadees, sparrows, and starlings. [Incorrect use of the colon—delete it]

Rule 4

Use a colon before a quotation if an independent clause is used to set up the quotation:

Richard Bach wrote the following words of wisdom in *Illusions:* "Disappointment requires adequate planning."

Miscellaneous Uses

There are several miscellaneous uses for colons.

- **In greetings:**

  To the Director of Personnel:

  Dear Mr. Sanders:

- **To show hours and minutes:**

  3:24 PM

- **In titles and subtitles:**

  Changing Economics: A Study of Spending in Our Current Times

- **To show ratios:**

  The odds were 3:1 against him.

- **In bibliography or works cited formats:**

  Boston: Bedford, 2004.

Cross References
See Chapter 19 for documenting sources.

When Not to Use a Colon

- Do not use a colon after *especially, such as, consisted of, including,* and other words or phrases that indicate a list will follow.

- Do not use a colon after a verb that sets up a list of objects.
- Do not use a colon between book and verse or act and scene (in MLA style). Use periods instead:

Correct: Bible: John 2.5   Plays: *Romeo and Juliet*, 1.3 (or I.III)

Incorrect: Bible: John 2:5   Plays: *Romeo and Juliet*, 1:3 (or I:III)

Activity 25-6   Colon Practice

Directions: *Add colons where they belong in the following sentences.*

1. There was one obvious reason for the fire The faulty wiring started a spark on the old wood walls.

2. The name of the textbook was *Fundamentals of Math An Introduction to College Mathematics.*

3. The following cars are the most popular Hondas, Toyotas, and Fords.

4. Marcia and Hugh have two lovely daughters They are Page and Eliza.

5. He had two things he wanted to say He loved her, and he wanted to marry her. ◯

Activity 25-7   Add or Delete Colons

Directions: *Add or delete colons where needed in the following sentences.*

1. Isabelle likes: eating macaroons, playing on the beach, and swimming in the pool.

2. She wanted one thing from this vacation to get lots of rest.

3. There are several activities to do on the beach, such as: swim, snorkel, build sandcastles, or read a book.

4. She was told to order the book titled *Geography An Introduction to the Field* in the school bookstore.

5. To get ready for the camping trip, she needed to buy the following items coffee, beans, candles, matches, bottled water, and granola. ◯

Activity 25-8   Semicolon and Colon Practice

Directions: *Add colons or semicolons to the following sentences when needed. Choose the best, most specific choice for each.*

1. The coach told the players to do one thing to have fun while playing.

2. The game is always exciting it is most exciting when the crowd gets involved.

3. The kids came up with cool superhero names and matching titles including Marvoman, Defender of the Universe BrilliaWoman, Protector of the World AquaGoddess, Matron of the Sea and TerraMan, Keeper of the Earth.

4. At 330 in the afternoon, we decided to hit the road.

5. I like to swim he prefers to jog.

6. I know the key ingredient to delicious curries high-quality and fresh cumin.

7. If the odds were only 21, then we might have had a chance of winning.

8. Red wine goes well with red meats and red or hearty sauces white wine is better for chicken, fish, and delicate sauces.

9. The essay was titled "Nonsensical A Study of Unusual Lyrics."

10. That outfit is unusual the one she wore last week was even more so.

Activity 25-9   Comma, Semicolon, and Colon Practice

Directions: *Commas, semicolons, and colons are three punctuation marks that are often incorrectly interchanged. Choose the best punctuation mark listed below to complete each of the blanks in the following passage. Be sure to review the rules if you get stumped.*

, (Comma)   ; (Semicolon)   : (Colon)

The Thomas Jefferson Building _____ one of the three buildings that make up the Library of Congress _____ is one of the loveliest buildings on Capitol Hill _____ its architecture and the art within its walls help contribute to the beauty of this magnificent building.

Of course _____ the Library of Congress is mostly famous for one thing _____ its incredible collection of books. However _____ visitors should not underestimate this building's other charms _____ it's full of surprises. The Library of Congress acquires more than 10 _____ 000

Library of Congress, Jefferson Building.

new items per working day _____ that's an incredible number at the end of each year. Actually _____ as mentioned previously _____ there are three buildings that make up the Library of Congress _____ the Thomas Jefferson Building _____ named after Thomas Jefferson _____ The Adams Building _____ named after John Adams _____ and the Madison Building _____ named after James Madison.

Though all three of these buildings are visually distinct _____ all of them have the same primary purpose _____ to house books _____ films _____ maps _____ and other forms of information for the United States. ◯

Applying Critical Thinking

 PURPOSE | IDEAS | SUPPORT | ASSUMPTIONS BIASES | CONCLUSIONS | POINT OF VIEW | ANALYSIS

When you are constructing sentences and making choices about using colons, ask yourself the following critical thinking questions:

- What is my **purpose** for this particular sentence, and how can I best construct my sentence and use a colon to achieve my purpose?
- Am I using a colon to list individual items after a clause or between two clauses where the second answers the first?

Then, *break down the particular parts* of the sentence using your **analysis** skills to make sure that you have constructed the sentence correctly and used a colon correctly.

26

Other Punctuation

Sunglass Rock.

THINKING CRITICALLY

Punctuation can add character to a sentence (like this face on a rock). How do you think choices you make in punctuation affect the meaning of your sentences?

_____

_____

_____

_____

_____

END PUNCTUATION

As its name implies, end punctuation comes at the end of a sentence. There are three types of end punctuation: the period, the question mark, and the exclamation point.

Period

A period (.) is used to end a statement. You should use a period under the following circumstances:

1. **Use a period at the end of a complete sentence (independent clause).**
   The sentence can be a statement or an indirect question:

   > She is my best friend. [Statement]

   > She asked him when the homework was due. [Indirect question]

2. **Use periods with some abbreviations (not all abbreviations require periods; check a dictionary if you are unsure).**

   Mr.   Ms.   etc.   e.g.   R.S.V.P.   B.C.   A.D.

   A.M. (or a.m.)   P.M. (or p.m.)   Dr.   Ph.D.

   Note: Some of these abbreviations are acceptable without the periods: AM, PM, BC, AD.

Activity 26-1 Period Practice

Directions: *Add periods where needed in the following passage:*

Mrs Murphy told us her son was in trouble I decided that I better find out what was wrong He had been acting strangely, howling at night, and so on I didn't know what I should do to help. Mr Murphy was at a loss, too. I guess we'll have to wait and see what Dr Shepard has to say. ●

Question Mark

A question mark (?) is used at the end of a sentence to indicate that a question is being asked. Use a question mark when a sentence is a direct question.

> Do you like to eat Indian food?

Do not use a question mark if the sentence is an indirect question:

> Neal asked Katharine if she liked to eat Indian food. [Period, not a question mark]

Using Question Marks with Quotations or Dialogue

Be sure to check if a question mark is part of a quotation or a piece of dialogue (whether you are quoting a question or a person is asking a question) or if you are asking a question about a quotation. If it is part of a quotation or piece of dialogue, the question mark goes inside the quotation marks.

> Dorothy asked, "Will you be able to join me later?"

If you are asking a question about a quotation, the question mark comes after the closing quotation marks:

> Who was it that said, "I have a dream"?

Activity 26-2   Question Mark Practice

Directions: *Add question marks, move question marks, or change question marks to another form of punctuation as necessary in the following passage.*

"Do you know what time it is " I asked. However, he didn't answer me. Later he asked me if I knew what time it was? I wonder if he was paying attention at all? What do you think? Also, who wrote, "Time is a winged chariot?"

Exclamation Point

Use an exclamation point (!) to show emphasis, to express strong emotion—excitement, surprise, disbelief—or to indicate a strong command.

> Stop it now!
>
> No way!
>
> Of course I do!
>
> Great!

Note: Try not to overuse exclamation points or they will lose their power! See what I mean?! Too much!

Activity 26-3   Exclamation Point Practice

Directions: *Add exclamation points or replace exclamation points with a different type of punctuation mark as needed in the following passage.*

"Fire" he shouted. We all panicked, but we knew we had to stay calm! So we gathered our things quietly! However, right when I got to the front door, I heard someone yell "Run" That's when I knew I'd better get out of there quickly.

APOSTROPHES

Apostrophes (') are used to indicate contractions (words in which certain letters have been omitted) and to show possession (who or what owns something).

Apostrophes and Contractions

Use an apostrophe to indicate the omission of one or more letters when words are combined to form a contraction. Put the apostrophe where the missing letter(s) would be: *it's (it is)* or *haven't (have not)* or *would've (would have)*. Contractions may not be appropriate for formal, academic writing. See Chapter 29 for more about tone and word choice.

Common Contractions

aren't	are not	**it's**	it is	**'twas**	it was
can't	cannot	**let's**	let us	**wasn't**	was not
could've	could have	**mightn't**	might not	**we'll**	we will
couldn't	could not	**might've**	might have	**we're**	we are
didn't	did not	**mustn't**	must not	**weren't**	were not
doesn't	does not	**she'd**	she had/	**what'd**	what had/
don't	do not		she would		what would
hadn't	had not	**she'll**	she will	**what's**	what is
hasn't	has not	**she's**	she is	**won't**	will not
haven't	have not	**shouldn't**	should not	**wouldn't**	would not
he'd	he had/he	**should've**	should have	**would've**	would have
	would	**there'd**	there had/	**you'll**	you will
he'll	he will		there	**you're**	you are
he's	he is		would		
I'm	I am	**there'll**	there will		
isn't	is not	**they're**	they are		
it'd	it had/it				
	would				
it'll	it will				

Note: Be careful when you use the following contractions. They sound like other words that have different meanings (see Chapter 28, Commonly Confused Words section, p. 628):

they're = they are	vs.	there	= adverb
you're = you are		your	= possessive pronoun
who's = who is		whose	= possessive pronoun
it's = it is		its	= possessive pronoun

Simple test: If the word can be said aloud as two words, then it is probably the contraction you want.

> **Correct:** It's a beautiful day. [*It is* a beautiful day.]

> **Incorrect:** It's paws were muddy. [*It is* paws were muddy—oops, wrong word; use "Its"—possessive pronoun—instead.]

Apostrophes and Possession

Add an apostrophe to a noun or indefinite pronoun to indicate possession. (But don't add an apostrophe to a pronoun that is already possessive, such as *his, hers,* or *its.*)

> Tony's cat got into my yard again last night.
> [The apostrophe indicates the cat belongs to Tony.]

> Everyone's legs were shaking as the tornado approached.
> [The apostrophe indicates the legs belonging to everyone were shaking.]

1. **Singular possession.** Use an apostrophe before the added *s* to indicate possession.

   > The *cat's* food is smelly.
   > [The apostrophe indicates the food belongs to one cat.]

   > *Today's* society is more complex.
   > [The apostrophe indicates that it is the society of today that is more complex.]

   > *Someone's* dog is barking loudly.
   > [The apostrophe indicates the dog belongs to someone.]

   Singular nouns that end in *s*: If the singular noun already ends with the letter *s*, then add an apostrophe and another *s*.

   > My *boss's* office is tiny.
   > [The singular word boss ends with an *s*, so add an apostrophe and another *s*.]

Did you find *James's* notebook?
[The name *James* already ends with an *s*, so add an apostrophe and another *s*.]

Note: Don't use apostrophes with pronouns that are already possessive.

Correct: Is it *yours* or mine? *Its* face was dirty.

Incorrect: Is it *your's* or mine? *It's* face was dirty.

2. **Plural possession.** Use an apostrophe after the *s* that indicates a plural, possessive noun.

The *cats'* food is smelly.
[Refers to two or more cats—the only way to know this is by the placement of the apostrophe.]

My *bosses'* offices are tiny.
[The placement of the apostrophe indicates there is more than one boss.]

Note: If the form of the noun is already plural, add an apostrophe and an *s*.

The *children's* books are scattered everywhere.

Note: Don't use an apostrophe to make nouns plural.

Correct: She eats two *cookies* every day.

Incorrect: She eats two *cookie's* every day.

3. **Possessive and compound nouns.** Place apostrophes at the end of compound nouns in order to indicate possession.

My *sister-in-law's* tamales are the best.
[Apostrophe goes at the end of the compound noun; you do not write *sister's-in-law*.]

With two sisters-in-law, you make the word "sister" plural by adding an *s*; then just use apostrophe and an *s* after "law" (only one law but two sisters).

My *sisters-in-law's* recipes for tamales came from their mother.

4. **Possession and proper names.** Add an apostrophe and an *s* to single proper names to show possession, even if the name already ends in *s*.

Mary *Johnson's* cat is nice.
[There is only one Johnson, so the apostrophe goes before the *s*.]

James's sister is visiting from Chicago.
[Usually, you add an *s* after a proper name ending in *s*.]

Have you ever read John *Keats's* poetry?

However, if the pronunciation would be awkward with the added *s*, it is acceptable to omit the extra *s* (both ways are acceptable).

Socrates' writings still intrigue us today.

If the proper name is plural, put the apostrophe after the *s*.

The *Johnsons'* dog is nice.
[Adding the *s* makes the name *Johnson* plural to indicate a whole family, not one person, and the apostrophe after it indicates their joint possession of the dog.]

5. **Joint possession.** If two or more people share a possession, then only use an apostrophe and an *s* after the last noun.

Are you going to *Keiko* and *Toshio's* house?
[The house belongs to both of them, so the apostrophe goes after *Toshio*.]

If people individually (separately) possess things, use an apostrophe and an *s* for each one.

Are you going to *Walter's* house, *Kate's* house, or *Louis's* house?
[There are three separate houses, so the apostrophes are used to indicate individual possession.]

Apostrophes and Plurals

Use an apostrophe to indicate plural numbers, letters, and symbols and to indicate the plurals of words used as an item. (Due to the dynamic nature of grammar—rules change with use and word processing has also affected them—it is now acceptable to use an apostrophe or to omit the apostrophe in many of these cases. You may choose to add the apostrophe or leave it out, but be consistent in your choice.)

We will have to find lots of number *6's* to finish this game.
[It's okay to use *6s*.]

He has three *A's* in his report card.

We'll have to look at all the *+'s* and *—'s* in the chart.

Mothers like to say a lot of *maybe's* and *we'll see's*.

Apostrophes and Missing Letters or Numbers

You can use apostrophes to indicate letters or numbers that are missing from words in dialogue, slang, or colloquial speech. Remember, you should only include slang or colloquial words like this in dialogue; otherwise, these words are inappropriate in academic writing.

Ralph shouted, "The train is comin', Mama!"

My mom said, "The '50s were a time of harmony."

When Not to Use an Apostrophe

- Do not use an apostrophe with possessive pronouns (*his, hers, its, ours, yours, theirs, whose*).
- Do not use an apostrophe to form plurals that do not indicate possession.

Activity 26-4 Apostrophe Practice, Part I

Directions: *Add, delete, or move apostrophes in the following sentences as needed. Write C for correct if the use of apostrophes is correct.*

_____ 1. "Theyre only bugs," his mother said. "Don't be afraid of a bugs presence."

_____ 2. My required textbooks were too expensive. Were your's that expensive?

_____ 3. The Edmundsons house was finally being sold.

_____ 4. The childrens shoes were lined up and didn't look dirty.

_____ 5. The cats were hungry.

_____ 6. The bosses memos were posted in the hallway.

_____ 7. Todays car prices are higher than ever.

_____ 8. The 6s and 7s from the game were missing.

_____ 9. Anna's report card was full of As.

_____ 10. Its a shame that we cant see all the leaves colors yet.

Activity 26-5 Apostrophe Practice, Part II

Directions: *Place apostrophes where they are needed in the following passage. There are **25** apostrophe-related errors.*

The Ye Olde Curiosity Shoppe in Seattle, Washington, is a famous tourist attraction. The shop opened first in 1899. It was originally an Indian trading post. Now it is mostly a tourist spot, but collectors and locals visit regularly

Ye Olde Curiosity Shop, Seattle, Washington. D. Cole, 2006.

to buy unique gifts and even artifacts. Its like a museum too. Many of its ar-tifacts are not for sale. The shops owners know that the rare and bizarre items in the shop draw its crowds. Theres something for everyone. In fact, the shops most famous artifact is named "Sylvester." Sylvester is a mummy. Though Sylvesters real identity and full story arent known, it is known that he was dis-covered half-buried in the sands of the Gila Bend Desert, naturally mummi-fied by the hot sand and wind. Sylvesters age at death is estimated to be 45. Hes been featured in the National Geographics TV show *The Mummy Road Show,* and hes featured in several books about Americas mummies.

Sylvesters death was the result of a gun shot to the stomach, and the bul-let hole is still clearly visible. Most mummies deaths were natural, and their mummification was intentional: not so in Sylvesters case.

Incidentally, Joe Standley was the original founder and owner of Ye Olde Curiosity Shoppe. Andy James, the current owner of the shop, still features Sylvester prominently in the back of the shop in a glass case. James grandfather started the tradition. The shop sells every type of item imaginable from A to Z. The Zs have it in this case, since much of the shops charms lean toward the bizarre, macabre, and even joke gifts, like fake spilled sodas and soap that blackens ones skin. The shop does feature real art and crafts too. James commitment to selling genuine artifacts includes featuring art from around the world: Eskimo figurines, Russian dolls, distinctive Northwest jewelry, and beautiful Native American art are all part of the shops collection. Many locals, proud of the shops growing popularity, will say that "Folks have been comin to Seattles waterfront to visit the Shoppe for as long as Ive known." Visitors can visit the shop on Seattles famous waterfront, or they can read more about it in the shops website or in several books that feature this unique shop. ●

QUOTATION MARKS

Quotation marks (" ") are used to indicate direct quotations or dialogue (written or spoken), to indicate some types of titles, and to define words or to use them ironically.

1. **Use quotation marks around direct quotations** (when you are directly quoting someone else's words in your writing).

   - **Double quotation marks:** Enclose all words that are quoted directly from another source in a pair of double quotation marks, one set at the beginning of the quotation and one set at the end:

     Cox notes, "Members of Congress have been eager, in an election year, to make a show of throwing away their perks" (76).

     Note: Remember to include a page citation for sources. See Chapter 19 for correct MLA citation format.

   - **Single quotation marks:** When there is a quotation within a quotation, use single quotation marks around the internal quotation:

     My philosophy teacher said, "Do not forget the advice of Kathy Parrish, animal activist, who said, 'We humans need to remember our connections to the animals who co-inhabit the Earth.'"

- **How to quote prose or poetry**
  - **Introducing quotations.** If you are quoting a complete sentence, use a tag to introduce the quotation followed by a comma. If, however, you are introducing the quotation using a complete sentence of your own, use a colon. Be sure to start the quotation with a capital letter.

    Tag: Parrish said, "We humans need to remember our connections to the animals who co-inhabit the Earth" (28).

    Introductory sentence: We should pay attention to the words of wisdom from animal activist Kathy Parrish: "We humans need to remember our connections to the animals who co-inhabit the Earth" (28).

  - **Quoting partial sentences.** If you quote only part of a sentence, then don't start the quotation with a capital letter.

    We should "remember our connections to the animals who co-inhabit the Earth" (Parrish 28).

  - **If you leave part of the quotation out,** use an ellipsis (three spaced dots) where the omitted word or words were deleted.

    Dr. Martin Luther King, Jr. said in his famous "I Have a Dream" speech, "Five score years ago, a great American, in whose symbolic shadow we stand today, signed the Emancipation Proclamation . . . It came as a joyous daybreak to end the long night of their captivity" (25).

  - **If you add a word or phrase** for clarification within the direct quotation, put brackets around the insertion.

    She said, "The doctor spoke of it [the operation] as if it were a casual event."

  - **If you quote lines of poetry** in your own sentences, use slashes to indicate where the original line breaks were.

    John Keats wrote the following lines in his poem "Ode on a Grecian Urn": "'Beauty is truth, truth beauty,'—that is all / Ye know on earth, and all ye need to know" (1).

  - **If you quote four or more lines of poetry** or prose, set the quotation off in a block by indenting ten spaces from the left margin and omit quotation marks.

Toni Morrison, in her novel *Jazz*, wrote,

> I know that woman. She used to live with a flock of birds on Lenox Avenue. Know her husband, too. He fell for an eighteen-year-old girl with one of those deepdown, spooky loves that made him so sad and happy he shot her just to keep the feeling going. (1)

2. Use quotation marks with dialogue. Quotation marks are used in writing to indicate when someone is speaking. Here are some tips for using quotation marks with dialogue.

- Put the actual words spoken by the person in quotation marks.
- Use commas to set off tags at the beginning, middle, or end of the dialogue.
- Start a new paragraph whenever you switch speakers or characters in dialogue, even if the line is only one word.

> He said, "I'd like to take you to lunch sometime."
>
> "Okay," she replied. "I like that idea." She looked him directly in the eye with a slight smile shaping in the corners of her mouth.
>
> "Great, it's a date, then," he said, obviously happy that she had accepted.

3. Use quotation marks for specific types of titles. Short story titles, short poems (not book-length epic poems, though), chapter titles, essay titles, magazine article titles, television episodes from series, and song titles.

> Story title: "A Hanging" by George Orwell
>
> Poem title: "The Grammar Lesson" by Steve Kowit
>
> Magazine title: "The Rise of Consumerism" by Bev Beeker
>
> Television episode title: "Changes"
>
> Song title: "Imagine" by John Lennon

Note: Titles of books, epic poems, plays, movies, CD/albums, TV shows, and magazines are all italicized.

4. Use quotation marks around words that are being singled out for definitions or to indicate irony.

> The word "oblivious" means to be completely unaware.
>
> She said she found the "special treat" her cat left for her on the front porch. The poor bird never had a chance.

Punctuation and Quotation Marks

Put commas and periods inside quotation marks if you do not include a page citation.

> "Living in Exile," an article about expatriates, was in the local paper last week.

> The author wrote, "We will rise to a higher consciousness."

However, if you include a citation, the punctuation goes after the citation.

> "Living in Exile," an article about expatriates, was in the local paper last week, and in that article, the author wrote, "We will rise to a higher consciousness" (Brown A2).
>
> [The period should not go inside the closing quotation: Place the period after the citation and after the last parentheses.]

> **Note:** When you use semicolons and colons in your own sentences, they come after quotation marks. For instance:

> > We were fighting the "battle of the bulge": We had to lose five pounds in one month.

> See Chapter 19 for details about correct citation format. Also, review the rule for when to put a question mark inside or outside of the quotation marks on p. 580.

Activity 26-6   Quotation Marks Practice

Directions: *Put quotation marks where needed in the following sentences. Write a C if the sentence is correct without quotation marks.*

_____ 1. William Shakespeare wrote the play *Hamlet* in which the famous To be or not to be soliloquy appears.

_____ 2. Really, said Riley, trying to sound convincing, I think you should come to the party.

_____ 3. She asked her new police chief, When is it appropriate to use the word Halt or the word Stop?

_____ 4. Which famous Shakespeare character said Out, out brief candle, life is but a walking shadow?

_____ 5. Sylvia Plath's poem Daddy is a powerful piece dealing with her mixed feelings about her father.

_____ 6. He asked her where he could find the person in charge.

_____ **7.** Living the Lawyer's Life Large was the title she picked for her article featured in *Legal Issues* magazine.

_____ **8.** One of the most famous American poems ever written is Robert Frost's poem Stopping by Woods on a Snowy Evening.

_____ **9.** T.S. Eliot's poem The Love Song of J. Alfred Prufrock is also very well known and claimed as both an American and British poem.

_____**10.** Do I dare? is something Prufrock asks several times in the poem. ●

PARENTHESES

Parentheses as used for setting off information or citations. Here are some examples of uses for parentheses.

1. Use parentheses [( )] to set off nonessential information or side comments in the middle of a sentence. If the information in a side comment is relatively important, it is preferable to use parenthetical commas to set it off (see Commas, Rule 4, p. 562).

> The owner of the shop (who loves cats) had lots of merchandise that featured cats.

> The owner of the shop, which sells lots of cat merchandise, is a cat lover.

> **Tip:** You can test to see if parentheses or commas work best around a word or phrase by reading the sentence without them to see if it still makes sense.

2. Use parentheses to set off numbers or letters in a list or series.

> The main things to remember for a good marriage are (1) communication, (2) respect, and (3) trust.

> The test contained several tips, including (A) pointers for filling out boxes, (B) directions for submitting the final results, and (C) a partial answer key.

> **Note:** Only certain style formats, for instance, writing for business or science, encourage the use of numbers or letters with parentheses. Writing in the humanities usually involves using full words to list items (such as "first," "second," "next," and so on).

3. Use parentheses in formal citations when documenting sources. See Chapter 19 for correct MLA format.

MLA format:

> The aging process "is often harder for women in American society" (Smith 26).

4. Use parentheses around the letters serving as an abbreviation of a full name. Use the full name and follow it with the abbreviation in parentheses, so readers know what the initials stand for when you use them again:

> The Modern Language Association (MLA) helps explain the style format for writing in the humanities.

Activity 26-7   Parentheses Practice

Directions: *Add or delete parentheses as needed in the following passage:*

The order (of steps) for an emergency evacuation was easy to remember. I like lists for memory tips. The order was listed out to us as follows: 1 gather all our books, 2 head for the exits calmly, 3 do not push or shove, and 4 wait outside for further directions. I read that most injuries in an emergency incident like this are the result of people panicking Markos 26. These rules will soon be posted in the halls thanks to the Parent Teacher Association PTA.

HYPHENS

Hyphens are used to combine or divide words. Here are some examples of the uses for hyphens.

1. Use hyphens (-) to form compound words. Check your dictionary to be sure that the compound word you're using is usually hyphenated. Some are not. Here are some commonly hyphenated compound words.

> Fractions such as *one-third, two-thirds, one-fourth*
>
> Numbers that are spelled out between twenty-one and ninety-nine
>
> Compound nouns such as *mother-in-law* or *brother-in-law*

2. Use hyphens with compound modifiers, usually adjectives that are used together as one descriptor before a noun.

> Her long-term job ended up being torturous.
> [Here *long-term* is a modifier for the word *job*—a compound adjective with hyphens.]
>
> The state-of-the-art laptop computers were smaller than ever.

Note: If a compound modifier is not followed by a noun, then omit the hyphens.

The job was long term and torturous.

[Here *job* is the actual noun and *long term* is the object so there are no hyphens.]

The new laptop computers were *state of the art*.

3. **Use hyphens to join letters, prefixes, and suffixes to a word.** Here are some examples of common prefixes that require hyphens:

Letters before words: T-shirts, U-turn, A-team, C-mart

Self- before words: self-expression, self-serving

All- before words: all-powerful, all-encompassing

Ex- before words: ex-wife, ex-governor

Usually the prefixes *anti-, pro-, co-,* and *non-* do not require hyphens unless the prefix ends in a vowel and so does the root word, for example, *anti-inflammatory, co-owner, non-union, de-emphasize, re-cover* (to cover again), *re-create,* and *co-ed*.

4. **Use a hyphen when dividing words at the end of a line.** It is preferable not to divide words at all, but if you do, be sure to follow these guidelines:

   • Divide words at syllable breaks

   • Don't leave less than three letters at the end of a sentence before the hyphen or have two or less letters only on the next line.

   Dividing words is rare these days since computers automatically wrap words over to the next line. Some textbooks still divide words at the end of a line, but in your papers, you should avoid dividing words and let the computer format them for you.

Activity 26-8 Hyphen Practice

Directions: *Add hyphens where needed in the following sentences. If the sentence is correct, then write C on the line provided.*

_____ 1. I really want to reemphasize my commitment to my family.

_____ 2. She had a reputation for always taking an antiestablishment stance on politics.

_____ 3. Charles wanted to write a new preamble to his college's constitution.

_____ 4. Breanna has the most striking bluegreen eyes.

_____ 5. Kimiko's sixyearold sister is always copying her big sister's style.

DASHES

Dashes are used to help information stand out. Here are some examples. If your keyboard doesn't include a dash (—), use two hyphens together to create one.

Use a dash to add emphasis. Dashes can be used around a phrase in the middle of a sentence or at the end of a sentence. They enclose material like parentheses do, but dashes are used to emphasize the material inside them, not de-emphasize it. At the end of a sentence, a dash can work much like a colon, but it is more informal.

> **Note:** Dashes are considered an informal punctuation mark. In more formal writing, use commas or colons instead of a dash. Dashes should be used rarely in any writing.

> She wanted only a few things from her mother—love was not at the top of the list.

> Flowers—red roses are the most romantic—are a special gift for a date.

> **Note:** Material enclosed by dashes can be removed, and the sentence will still make sense.

Activity 26-9   Dashes Practice

Directions: *Add or delete dashes in the following passage:*

The tennis racket an essential element of a professional tennis players' game has many traits that affect the way the ball moves. One trait—is the tension of the strings. Also—it's important to get a grip that fits the size of your hand a grip too big for you can ruin a shot.

SLASHES

A slash (/) is a diagonal line slanting from right to left. Here is a list of how to use it correctly.

1. **Use slashes between two words to indicate there is a choice:**

   yes/no   and/or   either/or

2. **Use slashes to indicate line breaks when you quote two or three lines of poetry within your own sentence.**

   > Madeline Defrees' poem "Phobias Incorporated" features two lines that say, "Father Giuliano, the drama instructor, fainted / every time he saw blood" (2).

Activity 26-10   Slashes Practice

Directions: *Write a sentence that uses words sometimes combined with slashes to show they are a choice.*

Example: *The test featured a yes/no answer format.*

_____

_____

_____ ⬤

ELLIPSES

An ellipsis is used to omit information. Here are some examples. An ellipsis (. . .) consists of three periods with spaces between them, but no space before or after them.

1. **Use an ellipsis to signify omitted words when you are quoting.** An ellipsis is used to indicate where you have omitted words within material you are quoting. Be careful not to change the author's intent when omitting a word or words in the middle of a phrase or sentence. An ellipsis is not needed at the beginning or end of a quotation if you are quoting part of a sentence or a phrase.

     Here is an original passage from Toni Morrison's novel *Jazz*:

> In this scene, the energy between the characters is obvious: "They laughed, tapped the tablecloth with their fingertips and began to tease, berate and adore him all at once. They told him how tall men like him made them feel, complained about his lateness and insolence, asked him what *else* he had in his case besides whatever it was that made Sheila so excited. They wondered why he never rang *their* doorbells, or climbed four flights of double-flight stairs to deliver anything to them, they sang their complaints, their abuse, and only Alice confined herself to a thin smile, a closed look, and did not join the comments with one of her own" (Morrison 70).

     Here is the same passage with some of the contents removed as indicated by the use of an ellipsis:

> In this scene, the energy between the characters is obvious:
> They laughed, tapped the tablecloth with their fingertips and began to tease, berate and adore him all at once . . . sang their compliments, their abuse and only Alice confined herself to a thin smile, a closed look, and did not join the comments with one of her own. (Morrison 70)

2. Use an ellipsis to indicate a cutting off or trailing off of a sentence in dialogue.

> She looked nervous when she mumbled, "But I thought you . . ."
>
> OR
>
> Anna said, "I want to come to the park with . . ."
>
> "Wait . . ." Tom interrupted, "I can't hear the radio."

Activity 26-11   Ellipses Practice

Directions: *Choose one of the readings from Chapter 21 and copy five sentences from it. Then remove at least five words from one of the sentences using an ellipsis and without changing the original meaning of the passage.*

_____

_____

_____

_____

BRACKETS

Brackets ([ ]) are similar to parentheses, only square as opposed to curved. They are used to set off information.

1. Use brackets to add a word or comments to a direct quotation.

> She said, "The use of this punctuation tool [brackets] is a great way to clarify your quotations."
>
> She wrote, "The need for a clear dicision [sic] at this time is essential."

Note: The word *sic* (Latin for "as is") in brackets is used to show that a word in a quotation has been quoted exactly, even if it is incorrect or misspelled.

2. Use brackets when you need to set off material that is already in parentheses.

> The labors of Hercules included the slaying of the Nemean lion (so called because Hera [Juno] sent it to destroy the Nemean plain).

Activity 26-12   Brackets Practice

Directions: *Choose one of the reading selections from Chapter 21 and quote two sentences from it, adding a word or phrase of your own in brackets.*

_____

_____

_____

_____ ⬤

Applying Critical Thinking

 PURPOSE   IDEAS   SUPPORT   ASSUMPTIONS BIASES   CONCLUSIONS   POINT OF VIEW   ANALYSIS

When you are constructing sentences and making choices about punctuation, ask yourself the following critical thinking questions:

- How can punctuation make my meaning and **purpose** clearer?
- What are the best choices I can make for punctuation in this sentence? A period? An apostrophe? Quotation marks? A colon or semicolon?
- Am I sure I've used this punctuation correctly?

   Then, *break down the particular parts* of the sentences using your **analysis** skills to make sure that you have constructed the sentence correctly.

Activity 26-13   Practicing Other Forms of Punctuation

Directions: *In the paragraph below, choose the appropriate punctuation mark from the list below to fill in each of the blanks.*

( ) parentheses	/ slash
- hyphen	... ellipsis
— dash	[ ] brackets

The Library of Congress is the largest library in the world. The Library of Congress _____LOC_____ is located on Capitol Hill in Washington, D.C. The world _____ famous library consists of three buildings named after U.S. presidents: Thomas Jefferson, John Adams, and James Madison. The first and most famous building _____ now called the Thomas Jefferson building _____ opened in 1897.

According to a brochure from the Library of Congress, "After its founding in 1800, the Library was housed in the U.S. Capitol _____ it had to be moved later _____. The Jefferson building opened in 1897 [omitted words from the quote here] _____ the Adams building opened in 1939. The Madison Memorial Building in 1980."

A poet once wrote the following lines about the beautiful Jefferson Building: "Within your walls are more than books _____ more than knowledge and history _____ Indeed, within your walls the heart of a nation, the tuffest _____ sic _____ stuff that 'dreams are made of.'" ◯

Activity 26-14   Punctuation Practice

Directions: *In the paragraph below, choose the appropriate punctuation mark from the box to fill in each of the blanks.*

?	()	-	—	/	...
,	!	" "	'	;	:

Taking a successful family vacation requires a great deal of planning and creativity. The whole family _____ including the children _____ should have a part in the decision _____ making process. A family meeting long in advance is a good idea _____ it's important to start the brainstorming process early. Knowing what each family member_____s preferences are early will make the negotiations go smoothly. Each parent will contribute ideas too and will record answers using a yes_____ no score-card. If someone feels left out of the process, then he or she may say something inaudible, with his or her voice trailing off at the end. For instance, he or she might say, _____ Oh _____ I thought you said we would all get a chance to _____ _____ And, if someone gets angry _____ the kind of angry that leaves no room for repair _____ the family will have to scrap the whole process and be left with only one choice _____ They will have to start over completely _____ Who would want that _____ ◯

27

Common Shift and Construction Errors

Delray Beach palm trees.

THINKING CRITICALLY

Look at the photo above. Then answer the questions that follow.

A shift in point of view, unusual construction, or sudden change in the structure of a sentence can interfere with a reader's understanding of it. What point of view is this picture taken from?

_____

_____

What effect did looking at these trees from this angle have on your understanding of what you saw?

_____

_____

This chapter covers some of the most common shift and construction errors that writers make, explaining what they are and how to fix them so readers don't get lost and confused.

Note: Changing tense is another kind of shift that can occur, and it is covered in Chapter 22 in the section on verbs (p. 511).

POINT-OF-VIEW [POV] SHIFTS

In Chapter 1, the term *point of view* was used to refer to a writer's perspective on a subject. In grammar, however, **point of view** means specifically what voice you use in your paper. There are three point-of-view voices you can employ in essay writing: first, second, and third person. While it is possible to switch among points of view within an essay, you generally write using one particular point of view.

The Three Points of View

1. **First person**

   Singular: I, me, my, mine

   Plural: we, ours, our, us

   First person point of view is most commonly used in narrative writing.

   Example: I went on a vacation with my family this summer. We took our favorite car. However, two days into the trip, our car broke down.

2. **Second person**

   Singular and plural: You, yours, or implied you/imperative (command form)

   Second person point of view is most commonly used for rhetorical questions (a question you ask to interest your readers) in an essay introduction. However, in general, avoid using second person point of view when writing essays except in rhetorical questions. Be careful not to use the pronoun *you* to mean "a person" or "one." Even though in common speech we use the generic *you* to mean "people," in writing, use third person point of view when referring to people in general.

   Example: Do you think you pay too much for your college textbooks?

3. Third person

> **Singular:** He, she, one, a person, an individual, his, her, it, its
>
> **Plural:** They, them, their, people, human beings, humanity, humankind

> **Note:** Avoid using the words *man* or *mankind* to represent people in general. These terms are no longer used to refer to both men and women (but of course you can use *man* if you are talking about one particular man). (See Chapter 29, Avoiding Sexist Language.)

Third person is the preferred point of view for most essays.

> **Example:** The student body president decided it was time to do something about the campus's cafeteria prices. People were concerned about unfair practices and overpricing.

Avoid Unwarranted Point-of-View Shifts

Though it is possible to employ more than one point of view in an essay, be sure that the switch is logical and needed grammatically. The most common point-of-view shift error involves switching to second person point of view (*you*) from first or third person point of view. In this type of error, the writer switches to *you* instead of using *I, one, a person,* or another third-person singular noun. In casual speech, people often use a generic *you* to mean "one." However, in formal writing this substitution is not acceptable.

> **Example:** When a person is walking along the beach, you will see several seashells and lots of sand.

The words *a person* are in third person singular and the word *you* is second person. This switch creates a point of view shift error.

> **Note:** Many teachers recommend using the third person plural to avoid both point of view shifts or other agreement errors.

> **Example:**
>
> **POV shift (singular to plural):** A student can get their classes paid for by financial aid.
>
> OR
>
> **POV shift (third person to second person):** One can get your classes paid for by financial aid.
>
> **Both fixed by making the subject plural:** Students can get their classes paid for by financial aid.

Activity 27-1   POV Shifts

Directions: *Correct the POV shift errors in the following sentences. Be sure to stay in the point of view that is used first in the sentence. You may need to change other words to match singular or plural form.*

1. When I see a chocolate donut, you can't resist the temptation.

2. Students should eat a wide variety of fruits and vegetables because you know the benefits of healthy eating.

3. One would not be wise to plagiarize: you can jeopardize your college career.

4. I like to see movies when they first come out because otherwise you hear too much about what happens from others.

5. People should be careful when crossing the road; you can't trust drivers to yield the right of way to pedestrians.

6. Human beings have a need for interconnection; you just need other people.

7. We love to go camping. They love the fresh air.

8. The teacher had a great deal of material to cover. You had to listen very closely to get all the information needed.

9. People should respect their parents. You will need that connection for all of your life.

10. Students love to go to the movies on the weekend. We love the chance for escape.

Many students switch point of view from third to first and back to third in the same paragraph. If you are writing for a general audience, for most subjects, you should stick to the third person, only switching to first person when you provide a personal example to support a more general point you make. For instance:

Most people tend to eat healthier foods in the summertime than they do in the winter. For instance, people usually eat more fruit in the summer because it is so readily available. I, for example, can hardly wait each year for the summer strawberries. People tend to eat more salads in the summer too and do not tend to crave starchier foods like potatoes when it's hot.

This passage is mostly written in the third person, with the exception of the personal example about strawberries in the first person. However, it would not be acceptable in this passage to switch to second person and say something like "When you eat lighter, you feel better." Instead you would write, "When people eat lighter, they feel better."

SUBJECT–VERB AGREEMENT [S-V agr]

A verb must agree with its subject in number. A singular subject requires a singular verb, and a plural subject requires a plural verb.

- Collective nouns (words that include a group but can act as a singular noun) take singular verbs:

    The *band* **plays** during halftime.

- Singular nouns ending in *s* take singular verbs:

    Physics **is** a field that demands skills in math.

    Measles **is** an awful illness for children.

- Words referring to measurements, such as time, weight, and money, usually take singular verbs:

    The twenty *dollars* **goes** to Beth.

    The extra five *pounds* **looks** good on her.

A **subject–verb agreement** error occurs when a writer switches from a singular noun to a plural verb or from a plural noun to a singular verb. For a subject and verb to "agree," both must be in singular form or both must be in plural form.

Errors often occur in subject–verb agreement in the following situations:

- When a verb comes before the subject
- When words come between the subject and the verb
- When the subject is an indefinite pronoun
- When there is a compound sentence.

Here's how to avoid these errors.

1. Verb before the subject (verb is in bold and subject is in italics).

   Incorrect: There **is** many *birds* in our yard.

   Corrected: There **are** many *birds* in our yard.

2. Words that come between the subject and the verb (usually prepositional phrases).

> **Incorrect:** *One* of the students **were** in the bookstore this morning.

The subject of the sentence is the word *one*, and, since the subject *one* is singular, the verb should also be singular. The subject is not *students*, which would require the verb *were*. A noun at the end of a prepositional phrase, such as *students*, can never be the subject of a sentence.

> **Corrected:** *One* of the students **was** in the bookstore this morning.

Cross Reference

See p. 520 for more on prepositions.

> **Tip:** To avoid mistaking part of a prepositional phrase for the subject, try crossing out all the prepositional phrases in a sentence to help you find the subject in order to check if the verb agrees with it.

One ~~of the students~~ **was** in the bookstore this morning.

3. Subjects that are indefinite pronouns usually take singular verbs. Indefinite pronouns usually take singular verbs, but students often make the mistake of using plural verbs with these types of pronouns. Here are some of the indefinite pronouns that take singular verbs: *anybody, anyone, anything, each, either, everybody, everyone, everything, neither, nobody, nothing,* and *one*.

> **Incorrect:** *Everyone* **like** to eat good food.
>
> *Each* of the customers **order** food from the menu.
>
> **Corrected:** *Everyone* **likes** to eat good food.
>
> *Each* of the customers **orders** food from the menu.

Some indefinite pronouns such as *all* and *both* take the plural verb:

> **Incorrect:** *Both* **is** tired.
>
> *All* **is** tired.
>
> **Corrected:** *Both* **are** tired.
>
> *All* **are** tired.

4. Compound subjects take plural or singular verbs. Compound subjects can take either singular or plural verbs, depending on the subject.

Subjects joined by *and* generally take a plural verb:

> **Incorrect:** *Peanut butter* and *bread* **makes** a good afternoon snack.
>
> **Corrected:** *Peanut butter* and *bread* **make** a good afternoon snack.

When subjects are joined by *either . . . or, neither . . . nor,* or *not only . . . but also,* the verb agrees with the subject closer to the verb:

Incorrect: Neither the kids nor *William* **want** to leave late.

Neither William nor the *kids* **wants** to leave late.

Neither Hank nor *Jim* **order** decaf in the morning.

Corrected: Neither the kids nor *William* **wants** to leave late.

Neither William nor the *kids* **want** to leave late.

Neither Hank nor *Jim* **orders** decaf in the morning.

Activity 27-2   Subject–Verb Agreement Practice

Directions: *Underline the correct verb in each of the following sentences. Remember to try crossing out all prepositional phrases to help you spot possible errors.*

1. The Eiffel Tower is quite a climb: The number of steps (is/are) 1,665.

2. Each of the visitors (is/are) up for a challenge if the elevators (is/are) broken.

3. One of the many interesting facts about the Tower (is/are) that it took only two years, two months, and five days to build.

4. The tower's website (boast/boasts) that the Eiffel Tower is a site that is recognized throughout the entire world.

5. Parisians (claim/claims) this monument as part of their cultural identity.

6. The structure (contain/contains) 18,038 pieces.

7. The 2,500,000 rivets in the structure (is/are) all along the beams.

8. The weight of all the pieces together (is/are) more than 10,000 tons.

9. The engineers who built it (was/were) Maurice Koechlin and Emile Nouguier.

10. Neither of the architects (is/are) famous for any other major work.

PRONOUN AGREEMENT (Pro agr)

Pronoun agreement errors occur when a pronoun does not have an **antecedent** (a word it refers to) or does not match the antecedent to which it clearly refers. (Remember that an antecedent can be a noun or another pronoun, but not usually a possessive form.) Agreement errors can also arise when there is no clear antecedent, or when the pronoun does not "agree" with the antecedent as far as **number** (singular/plural), **gender** (male, female), or **person** (first, second, or third).

Often writers create pronoun agreement errors in an attempt to avoid using gender-specific language. However, the rules of pronoun usage relate to the logic of singular and plural balance. If the subject is singular, then the pronoun must be singular. If the subject is plural, then the pronoun must be plural.

Example: A <u>student</u> can get *their* books at the campus bookstore.

The subject *student* is singular; therefore, using the pronoun *their* (which is plural) creates a pronoun error. There are two ways to fix this error.

1. Make the pronoun singular:

> A <u>student</u> can get *his or her* books at the campus bookstore.

2. Make the subject plural:

> <u>Students</u> can get *their* books at the campus bookstore.

Cross Reference
See p. 664, Avoiding Sexist Language.

Note: Making the subject plural helps avoid two problems related to sexist language: using unnecessarily gender-specific language, and using the split pronoun *his/her*.

Note: If the singular subject *is* gender-specific, then be sure to use a gender-specific pronoun.

> A <u>Boy Scout</u> must keep *his* uniform clean.

> A <u>ballerina</u> must have *her* shoes custom made.

It's a matter of logic: When gender *is* specific, use a gender-specific pronoun. When gender *is not* specific, don't use a gender-specific pronoun.

Activity 27-3   Pronoun Agreement Practice

Directions: *Correct any pronoun agreement errors in the following sentences. Cross out errors and write corrections over them.*

1. A kindergartner must learn their ABC's.

2. Dogs must get his shots to be safe.

3. A mother should take his or her responsibilities seriously.

4. Parents should take his or her responsibilities seriously.

5. A student can pay her tuition via the Internet. [On a co-ed campus]

6. A goldfish can eat their food while swimming.

7. A Girl Scout can sell their cookies in front of local stores.

8. A musician can get their instruments online now.

9. Chefs can order his or her utensils online too.

10. Teachers can get her raises by performing their jobs well. ⬤

Activity 27-4   Combined Practice: Point-of-View Shifts, Subject–Verb Agreement, and Pronoun Agreement

Directions: *Fix errors in POV, S-V, and pronoun agreement. Cross out errors and write corrections above them. You will find a total of six errors.*

The Tower of Pisa in Italy is known as the "Leaning Tower of Pisa." Visitors flocks to the tower to admire its beauty. The tower, which is actually the bell tower of the adjoining cathedral, have become more and more inclined over the years. The architect for the tower is unknown; their design is now famous, though. The tower's construction began in 1173 and took more than 200 years (with long interruptions) to complete. Sightseers like to pose near the famous tower. You can lean like the tower for a humorous photo. One of the damaged parts of the tower are the columns. These columns are slowly being replaced. When one visits now, you can be sure the tower is being conserved for the pleasure of future visitors. ⬤

PRONOUN REFERENCE ERRORS [Pro ref]

Pronoun reference errors occur when a pronoun does not have a clear connection to its antecedent (the noun it refers to). The antecedent can be ambiguous (it is unclear which noun is the antecedent), vague (the antecedent is often completely missing), or too broad (there is no specific antecedent).

Types of Pronoun Reference Errors

1. **Ambiguous pronoun reference** errors occur when there are two or more possible antecedents for the pronoun. To fix this type of reference error, revise the sentence to distinguish which antecedent you meant to refer to.

   Example: Julie told Mayra that she needed to take her test at the Testing Center. [Who is taking the test, Julie or Mayra?]

   Corrected: Julie told Mayra that she *was planning* to take *the* test at the Testing Center.

2. **Vague pronoun reference** errors occurs when the antecedent for the pronoun is completely missing. To fix this type of reference error, you need to fill in the missing noun or subject.

   Example: At coffee shops, *they* never provide enough free coffee refills. [Who does *they* refer to? *Coffee shops* is not the antecedent]

   Corrected: At coffee shops, *the servers* never provide enough free coffee refills.

3. **Broad pronoun reference** errors occur when a relative pronoun (most commonly *who, whom, whose, which, these, those, that,* and *this*) is used without a clear noun to refer to or when a pronoun is used to refer to a whole group of words or even a whole sentence instead of referring back to one clear noun antecedent. To fix this type of pronoun reference error, supply the missing noun or replace the relative pronoun with a noun.

   Example: A dog ran in front of my car, *which* caused me to slam on my brakes. [The relative pronoun *which* refers to the entire situation of the dog running across the road. In order to correct this broad pronoun reference error, an antecedent for *which* must be supplied or the sentence restructured to indicate a clear subject.]

   Corrected: A dog ran in front of my car, *a situation* which caused me to slam on my brakes.

   OR

   The dog running in front of my car caused me to slam on my brakes.

The pronouns *this, that, these,* or *those* can cause pronoun reference errors when they are used to refer to a whole sentence or a situation described in a previous sentence. When this happens, the pronoun has no clear, specific noun antecedent. Usually, this type of reference error requires you to insert a noun or a noun phrase after the pronoun.

Examples:

This is the reason for our trouble.
[This what is the reason for our trouble?]

That is the one I want.
[What is the that?]

These (or *those*) are the ones I want.
[What are the these?]

Corrected: *This* <u>lack of funding</u> is the reason for our trouble.

That <u>puppy</u> is the one I want.

These (or *those*) <u>puppies</u> are the ones I want.

Tip: When a reference error is caused by using a pronoun like *this* or *that*, think of adding a "fill in the blank" answer after it. Answer the question, "This *what?*" or "That *what?*"

Activity 27-5   Pronoun Reference Error Practice

Directions: *Rewrite the sentences below to correct pronoun reference errors. You may need to fill in nouns or rewrite sentences completely to fix the errors.*

1. Dan was annoyed with Terrill because he lost his phone.

   _____

   _____

2. This is just too hard for me.

   _____

   _____

3. I went to my favorite store, but they were closed.

   _____

   _____

4. That is one she wanted.

_____

_____

5. The clock stopped suddenly, and I was late to work, which is why I'm grumpy.

_____

_____ ●

FAULTY PARALLELISM [//]

Parallel structure involves using a consistent grammatical form or word form in sentences that have a series of verbals or phrases in order to keep them in balance. Faulty parallelism occurs when the same grammatical form or structure is not used throughout. When this happens, the form changes and the sentence becomes unbalanced.

Example: She likes _to swim_ in the ocean, _to run_ on the beach, and _hiking_ in the mountains.

The last verb in this list of three verbs is _hiking,_ which uses an _-ing_ form of the verb, while the first and second verbs use the infinitive form. To correct this error, simply change _hiking_ to _to hike._ Or, if you prefer to use _-ing_ verbs, then change _to swim_ and _to run_ to _swimming_ and _running._

Correction: She likes _to swim_ in the ocean, _to run_ on the beach, and _to hike_ in the mountains.

OR

She likes _swimming_ in the ocean, _running_ on the beach, and _hiking_ in the mountains.

Sometimes, problems with parallelism occur with whole phrases, especially when comparisons are being made.

Example: Page didn't know _whether to give_ Eliza her new toy or _if she should keep_ it for herself.

The phrases _whether to_ . . . and _if she should_ . . . are not parallel constructions. Choose one or the other to create the comparison.

Corrected: Page didn't know _whether to give_ Eliza her new toy or _to keep_ it for herself.

Page didn't know *if she should give* Eliza her new toy or *if she should keep* it for herself.

Page didn't know *if she should give* Eliza her new toy or *keep* it for herself.

Activity 27-6   Faulty Parallelism Practice

Directions: *Rewrite the following sentences to correct errors in parallelism.*

> **Example:** Baseball players love *to throw, to catch,* and *running* around the bases.
>
> **Revised:** Baseball players love *to throw, to catch,* and *to run* around the bases.

1. The position of Union Secretary involves taking the meeting minutes, typing the minutes, and to send the minutes via email to the Union Board.

   _____

   _____

   _____

2. To do well in your classes, be sure to study often, to arrive on time, and keeping a good attitude.

   _____

   _____

3. Leslie wasn't sure whether to run for president or if she should run for vice president.

   _____

   _____

4. Painting on canvas, throwing clay pots, and to take photographs were all artistic skills that Paul practiced.

   _____

   _____

5. To live, to love, and learning from one's mistakes are all part of a rich life.

   _____

   _____

6. Choosing if you should live with a roommate or whether to rent an apartment alone is an important decision for your college experience.

_____

_____

7. Marilou loves to cook Filipino dishes, to eat Indonesian food, and ordering take-out of all types.

_____

_____

8. Living in the mountains, to live at the beach, or to live in the country all reflect one's taste and values.

_____

_____

9. Aliya and Robynne studied all week for the test, checking with their friends for alternative viewpoints, and decided to take a practice test to be especially ready.

_____

_____

_____

10. Cameron applied to four colleges, sent out ten resumes, and chooses to search for both colleges and jobs at the same time.

_____

_____

DANGLING AND MISPLACED MODIFIERS [DM and MM]

A **modifier** is a word or word group that *refers to* or *modifies* a nearby word or word group. Errors in modifiers occur when the nearby word or word group is not directly stated (so the modifier is "dangling" without anything to connect to) or the modifier is in the wrong place and therefore isn't close enough to the word or word group it is suppose to modify (a misplaced modifier).

Dangling Modifiers

Dangling modifiers are missing a home base: The word they intend to modify is missing in action. As a result, dangling modifiers are often unintentionally funny. This example illustrates the dangers, and the humor, of dangling modifiers:

> **Example:** Wearing my pajamas, the dog chased me down the street.

Okay, it's bad enough to be chased by a dog, but it adds insult to injury if he's wearing my pajamas! The modifier is dangling because the subject *I* is missing.

> **Revised:** The dog chased me down the street as I was wearing my pajamas.
>
> OR
>
> Wearing my pajamas, I was chased down the street by the dog. [This switch creates a passive voice construction—see pp. 618–619 for help.]

Note: Dangling modifiers often occur due to an introductory phrase not followed by a needed subject.

Activity 27-7   Fixing Dangling Modifiers

Directions: *Rewrite the following sentences to correct dangling modifiers. You may need to add a subject, change words, or rearrange the sentence.*

1. While having a romantic dinner, the candles flickered in the dimly lighted restaurant.

   _____

   _____

2. At the age of ten, my grandfather took me fishing for the first time.

   _____

   _____

3. Upon walking through the door, Rita's designer quilts lit up the room.

   _____

   _____

4. Though it was her first cooking class, the chicken turned out wonderfully.

   _____

   _____

5. While visiting New York, the yellow taxicabs were a charming sight.

    _____

    _____

6. Winning the lottery, the winning numbers were held high overhead.

    _____

    _____

7. Taking a bath with glee, the birdbath provides a nice haven for the birds.

    _____

    _____

8. Upon learning about the accident, the news hit like a kick in the stomach.

    _____

    _____

9. To find a new way to their house, the map was consulted at least twice.

    _____

    _____

10. While walking through a forest, the trees impress with their ancient beauty.

    _____

    _____

Misplaced Modifiers

A **misplaced modifier** occurs when there is a word in the sentence that is being modified, but it is too far away from the modifier for the reader to figure out what is being modified:

Example: I chased a dog wearing my pajamas.

The modifier *wearing my pajamas* is in the wrong spot: it is closer to *dog* than to *I*.

Revised: Wearing my pajamas, I chased the dog.

Single-word modifiers, such as *often* and *almost,* are often misplaced:

Example: I almost made $200 for the lawn-mowing job.

So did the job not happen? If the writer means that he or she made almost $200 for the job, then the modifier needs to be placed immediately before the word (or words) being modified:

Revised: I made almost $200 for the lawn-mowing job.

Activity 27-8 Spotting Misplaced Modifiers

Directions: *Rewrite the following sentences to correct misplaced modifiers. You may need to completely restructure the sentences.*

1. John showed the children how to make paper airplanes out of a magazine article that demonstrated the steps.

   _____

   _____

2. Ashley almost ate an entire chocolate cake by herself.

   _____

   _____

3. The professor said that complete research papers will only be graded.

   _____

   _____

4. She nearly threw away every magazine in the house.

   _____

   _____

5. Tom proposed to Marta on a cruise ship smoking a cigarette.

   _____

   _____

6. Buzzing loudly, I turned off the alarm clock.

   _____

   _____

7. The report said there were traces of toxins in the boxed cereal in the newspaper.

_____

_____

8. There was concern about the toxins discovered on campus from the parents.

_____

_____

9. Parents are already almost all banning the cereal in question.

_____

_____

10. The near removal of all boxes from the store shelves has been a consequence.

_____

_____

Activity 27-9 Identifying Dangling and Misplaced Modifiers, Part I

Directions: *On the line before each numbered sentence, mark DM if the sentence includes a dangling modifier and MM if it includes a misplaced modifier. Then revise the sentences to correct the modifier errors.*

_____ 1. Running to make the plane, the luggage carts got in the way.

_____

_____

_____ 2. She nearly created 100 designs for the cover contest.

_____

_____

_____ 3. The team almost won all the games in the competition.

_____

_____

_____ **4.** To make a living, jobs must offer a good base salary.

_____

_____

_____ **5.** Small and wrapped in only a blanket, I held the newborn baby.

_____

_____

The Washington Monument.

Activity 27-10   Identifying Dangling and Misplaced Modifiers, Part II

Directions: *Underline misplaced and dangling modifiers in the following paragraph. Then write MM over the underlined word or phrase if it is a misplaced modifier or DM over the phrase if it is a dangling modifier. You should find seven modifier errors.*

The Washington Monument is one of our most impressive national monuments. It nearly stands 555 feet high. Made entirely of marble, visitors are impressed by both its height and its simple beauty. On one visit, my mother almost climbed all 896 steps to the top of the monument. Two-thirds of the way through the climb, exhaustion got the better of her. My brother and I made it all the way to the top, and we could almost see the entire city. Flashing intermittently, we also saw the light at the top that helps keeps planes from getting too close to the monument. Waving my arms wildly after coming back down the stairs, climbing the Washington Monument is certainly an achievement. ●

Applying Critical Thinking

| PURPOSE | IDEAS | SUPPORT | ASSUMPTIONS BIASES | CONCLUSIONS | POINT OF VIEW | ANALYSIS |

Once you have drafted and revised your work, use your **analysis** skills to break your sentences down into their particular parts to make sure you have constructed them correctly and haven't made any of the errors discussed in this chapter. Ask yourself the following questions:

- Have I switched point of view when I shouldn't have (from first person [I, me us] to second person [you] or to third person [he, she they])?
- Does each verb agree with its subject (are the verb and the subject both singular or both plural)?
- Do pronouns agree with my subjects (are both the pronoun and the subject both singular or plural)?
- Are pronoun references clear (is it clear to which noun a pronoun refers)?
- Are my sentence structures parallel (do they stay consistent throughout the sentence)?
- Are my modifiers attached and in the right place (are the words they modify included in the sentence)?

PASSIVE VOICE CONSTRUCTION [Pass]

Passive voice includes a form of the verb "to be" and a past participle. Whenever possible, avoid using *passive* voice construction and opt for *active* construction to write clear, powerful sentences. An active verb construction is easier for readers to understand because the active voice places the emphasis on *who* is doing the action:

> **Passive voice construction:** The ball *was thrown by* Thomas.

> **Revised to active voice construction:** Thomas *threw* the ball.

Not only does the active voice construction sound cleaner, it is also clearer since the "doer" of the action (Thomas) is emphasized and not buried at the end of the sentence. Here is another example of passive voice construction:

> **Passive:** The color that was picked by the owners was unpopular with the renters.

> **Changed to active:** The owners picked a color that was unpopular with the renters.

Activity 27-11   Passive Voice Construction

Directions: *Change the following sentences to the active voice.*

1. The vote that was made by the Board of Trustees was to support the proposed fee.

   _____

   _____

2. The meal was cooked by Katharine.

   _____

   _____

3. The job was taken by Russ.

   _____

   _____

4. The clubhouse was designed and constructed by Alex and Beyla.

   _____

   _____

5. The hot stew was eaten by Amelia and Tamasin.

   _____

   _____

Activity 27-12   Passive Voice Construction

Directions: *Rewrite the following paragraph using an active voice.*

Making a mushroom and cheese omelet is easy. First the eggs must be whipped. A wire hand whisk can be used by the old-fashioned cook. The whipping action must be done by a swift hand. After the eggs are whipped and then added to a pan with a little sizzling butter, sliced mushrooms can be added to the mixture. The cheese should be added last since it melts quickly. The flipping of the omelet should be done in a very delicate manner. Scrambled eggs are always an option to be chosen if the flipping stage goes badly.

_____

_____

_____

_____

_____

28

Spelling and Mechanics

Frank and Ernest

EXPRESS CHECKOUT

10 ITEMS OR LESS
FOR ENGLISH MAJORS: 10 ITEMS OR FEWER

THAVES

© 2004 Thaves. Reprinted with permission. Newspaper dist. by NEA, Inc.

THINKING CRITICALLY

Look at the comic strip above.

Explain what this comic is about. What is funny about it?

_____

_____

_____

_____

_____

_____

_____

_____

_____

_____

_____

_____

This chapter will give you tips on how to choose the right word and how to use a dictionary or thesaurus for help in spelling it correctly. It will also provide tips on how to abbreviate words and how to use numbers and capitalization correctly in your writing.

TEN TIPS FOR SPELLING IMPROVEMENT

Though not everyone is a "natural born speller," correct spelling is important in your writing. If you make spelling mistakes in a final draft, your readers may still understand what you mean, but they may lose respect for your ideas and find your arguments less credible. If you want to be taken seriously as a writer, then you have to take correct spelling seriously too. My friend Walter, who teaches composition, always says to his students, "I don't take off for spelling in essays, but I do take off for misspelling!"

Spelling Tip 1

During the revision and editing stage of your writing process, use a dictionary to double check any word that you are not 100 percent sure is spelled correctly. *When in doubt, look it up.*

Spelling Tip 2

Some spelling errors occur because words are not spelled the way they sound or are pronounced. Here are a few examples of words that are commonly mispronounced and, consequently, misspelled: *accidentally* (not "accidently"), *athletics* (not "atheletics"), *disastrous* (not "disasterous"), *February* (not "Febuary"), *government* (not "goverment"), *mathematics* (not "mathmatics"), *publicly* (not "publically"), *temperament* (not "temperment"), and *wondrous* (not "wonderous").

Spelling Tip 3

Some spelling mistakes occur as the result of confusing two homophones (words that sound alike or nearly alike).

affect/effect

complement/compliment

lead/led

right/write/rite

See Commonly Confused Words later in this chapter (p. 628) for a more complete list of homophones, and use it to help you avoid spelling errors.

Spelling Tip 4

Some plural forms of words are commonly misspelled. Watch for them. Here are a few rules to help you spell plurals correctly:

1. Most nouns are made plural by adding a final s: *cat/cats*, *dog/dogs*, and *apple/apples*.

2. Nouns ending with s, x, ch, or sh need an *es* to form the plural: *boss/bosses*, *ax/axes*, *crutch/crutches*, and *dish/dishes*.

3. If a noun ends in y with a consonant in front of it, then change the y to an i and add *es* to form the plural: *beauty/beauties* and *city/cities*. If the y is preceded by a *vowel, then keep the y and add an s: boy/boys* and *ray/rays.* However, be sure to always keep the y when you are making plural a family's name: *the Murphys.*

4. If the noun ends in o, add either an s or an *es*. It's best to check a dictionary if you're not sure which one is right for the word you are spelling: *solo/solos*, *piano/pianos*, *hero/heroes*, and *tomato/tomatoes*.

5. If a noun ends in f or an f followed by a silent e, then change the f to a v and add an *es*. However, some words ending directly in f just take a simple s, so use a dictionary if you are not sure: *chief/chiefs*, *proof/proofs*, *leaf/leaves*, *knife/knives*, *wife/wives*, and *self/selves*.

6. There are many irregular plurals in English, and most of them are well known from regular usage. As always, when in doubt, consult a dictionary: *child/children*, *man/men*, *woman/women*, *tooth/teeth*, *mouse/mice*, *deer/deer*, *moose/moose*, *sheep/sheep*, *datum/data*, and *medium/media*.

Spelling Tip 5

Distinguish between *ei* and *ie*. Pay attention to the previous letter and the sound of the word to figure out whether "i" goes before "e" or vice versa. There are some simple rules you can use.

1. When the sound you want to make is *ee* as in *see*, then use the i before e to form *ie*: *believe, chief, grief,* and *yield*.

2. When the combination is preceded by a c, the spelling is almost always *ei*: *receive, deceiving, ceiling,* and *conceit*.

3. When the sound produced sounds like *ay* as in *bay* or *way*, then the spelling is almost always *ei*: *neigh/neighborhood*, and *weigh/weight*.

Tip: Remember the famous saying taught in grammar school: "'i' before 'e' except after 'c' or when it sounds like an 'a' as in 'weigh' or 'neighborhood.'"

Even this rule has exceptions: *caffeine* and *seize*, for example. So remember to consult that dictionary when you have any doubts.

Spelling Tip 6

Learn the basic rules for adding suffixes (endings such as *–ing, -er, -est ,-ed, -ence, -ance, -ible, -able,* and *–ened*) and prefixes (beginnings such as *anti-, bi-, de-, dis-, pre-, mis-, co-,* and *un-*).

Adding Suffixes

1. When adding the *-ing* suffix, in general drop the silent *e* at the end of a word: *become/becoming, come/coming, hope/hoping, scare/scaring* and *surprise/surprising.* However, there are a few exceptions: *dye/dyeing* and *shoe/shoeing.*

    When the word ends with a *y,* then retain the *y: cry/crying, enjoy/enjoying, lay/laying,* and *study/studying.*

2. When adding the *-ible* suffix, drop the silent *e: force/forcible.*

3. When adding the *-able* suffix, sometimes you drop the silent *e* and sometimes you keep it, so be sure to check a dictionary if you are unsure: *advise/advisable, argue/arguable, manage/manageable,* and *change/changeable.*

4. A final silent *e* that is preceded by another vowel is always dropped when adding any suffix: *argue/arguable* and *true/truly.*

5. When a word ends with *y* and is preceded by a consonant (and the suffix added is not *-ing*), then change the *y* to an *i: happy/happiest/ happier, pity/pitiful,* and *ugly/uglier/ugliest.* However, when the *y* is preceded by a vowel, keep the *y* and add an *s: delay/delays, enjoy/enjoys, toy/toys,* and *valley/valleys.*

6. When you are adding a suffix to a word that ends in a consonant, often you need to double the consonant first: *cancel/cancelled, grip/gripping, grip/gripped, sad/saddest, occur/occurrence, refer/referred,* and *scar/scarring.* But there are exceptions: *deep/deepened, cancel/canceling,* and *crawl/crawler,* so check your dictionary.

Adding Prefixes

Adding a prefix does not require you to change the spelling of a word, but if the word you're adding the prefix to starts with a vowel, it may or may not require a hyphen. Again, when in doubt, consult your dictionary.

appear/disappear	eminent/preeminent
operate/cooperate	educate/re-educate

spell/misspell   emphasize/re-emphasize
usual/unusual

Spelling Tip 7

Keep a list of your own repeat offenders—frequently misspelled words—in a spelling log or journal. Just being aware of your most frequent errors will help you to eradicate them.

Spelling Tip 8

Consult the following list for some of the most commonly misspelled words in college essays: *believe, conceive, curiosity, definitely, disastrous, environment, forty, friend, interrupt, irrelevant, license, mathematics, medieval, necessary, occasion, precede, professor, receive, tendency, themselves, thorough,* and *weird.*

Spelling Tip 9

Be aware of common letter groupings such as *qu, ei, ie, au, ch, ou, th, sh,* and *gh.* Notice patterns and remain aware of them: *quiet, quite, receive, diet, launch, those, should,* and *tough.* Use those patterns as spelling tips.

Spelling Tip 10

Use the spell-check function on your computer, but be careful. See the Rewards and Dangers of Spell-check on the next page.

Activity 28-1 Trying Out the Spelling Tips

Directions: *Correct the spelling errors in the following paragraph. Refer to the ten spelling tips above for help. You should find 12 spelling errors in this paragraph.*

Tyson finally recieved the news he'd been waiting for. He would have known the results of his test sooner, but their was some kind of mix up in the male. It had allready been almost fourty days since he sent in the test: He sent it back in Febuary. He knew that at least 100 other man and woman had taken the test too. Still, he couldn't understand why it took so long to get his results. When the results still hadn't arrived after a month, this fact lead to his worrying even more. Its a good thing his results finaly came in and that they were good. Now he is quiet happy. ⬤

THE REWARDS AND DANGERS OF SPELL-CHECK

The computer age has made it much easier for students to get quick help with spelling and grammar. Spell-check is certainly a gift to writers. However, don't fall into the habit of always believing what spell-check suggests. You need to be sure you are using the right word in the right context. Spell-check will always suggest a correctly spelled word, but it might not be the word you intended, and it may mean something completely different. Many spell-check programs automatically indicate a misspelled word as soon as you've finished typing it (indicated by a red underline). You can use your computer mouse to right-click the word, and spell-check will offer possible correct spellings. When in doubt, though, use your dictionary to double-check. Here is a list of the rewards and dangers of using spell-check programs.

The Rewards

1. The spell-check function can help you spot many of your spelling errors.
2. The spell-check function requires just the click of an icon or is an automatic function for some word processing programs or computer systems.
3. The spell-check function has a fairly thorough collection of words and their correct spellings.

The Dangers

1. Spell-check cannot distinguish the meaning of words, so it may not point out words in your essay that are spelled correctly but not used correctly. For example, spell-check would not identify these two errors:

   Incorrect: The school *principle* balanced the annual budget as a matter of *principal*.

   These two italicized words should be reversed.

   Corrected: The school *principal* balanced the annual budget as a matter of *principle*.

   Tip: The princi*pal* is the one with whom you hope to be "pals."

2. Spell-check can suggest a word or words to replace your misspelled words that are still incorrect:

> **For instance:** I do not <u>wrecomend</u> the procedure.

> **Spell-check suggestion:** I do not <u>wreck amend</u> the procedure.

> **Intended correct spelling:** I do not <u>recommend</u> the procedure.

> **Note:** Be careful not to automatically click Replace for suggested words—look carefully, and, when in doubt, use a dictionary to make sure you are choosing the right word for the context of your sentence.

3. Spell-check does not include every word you might use. Sometimes correctly spelled words might get signaled as being spelled incorrectly. Again, check a dictionary.

As you can see, spell-check is a wonderful tool. However, far too often, students rely completely on spell-check and run into trouble. Use this tool with caution and critical thinking and have a good dictionary handy as a backup.

Activity 28-2   Testing Spell-Check

Directions: *Using a computer with spell-check installed, write a paragraph and purposely misspell five words (try to make them more difficult words to make the most of this exercise). Then, use spell-check to fix the spelling of the words. Be sure to use a dictionary to double check the spelling and meaning of the words. Then answer the following questions.*

1. Was the first spell-check suggestion for each of your misspelled words the correct spelling of the word you wanted? If not, list the suggestions that were wrong and explain why.

   _____

   _____

2. When you mistyped the word, did spell-check automatically underline it in red? Did you try right-clicking on the word for instant correction? If so, how did that go? _____

   _____

3. How did looking up the words in a dictionary help?

   _____

   _____

COMMONLY CONFUSED WORDS

Often, spelling mistakes result from writers confusing one word with another that sounds like it (a homonym). Some confusion also results from using the wrong form of a word, using slang, or misusing a word that is spelled correctly.

Here is a list of some of the commonly confused words that most often show up in student writing. Consult this list to make sure that you haven't used a word that sounds like the word you want but is incorrectly spelled.

a/an   Both of these words are indefinite articles (see p. 525 for more on articles). Use **a** when the word following it starts with a consonant sound, and use **an** when the word following it starts with a vowel sound (a, e, i, o, u) or a silent *h*.

> Lil ate *an* apple from Hallie's fruit bowl, and Hallie thought it was *an* honor to provide her with a treat. Neither was interested in eating *a* banana.

a lot/allot/alot (misspelling)

a lot is two words (an article and a noun) that mean "a great deal" or "many." It is best to use them only in informal writing.

allot is a transitive verb meaning "to divide something up" or "to portion" or "to allow."

alot is a common misspelling of "a lot." It is not a word.

> Marge didn't want *a lot* from life: She just wanted what was *allotted* to her.

accept/except

accept is a transitive verb (see p. 508 for more on verb forms) that means "to agree" or "to receive."

except is either a verb meaning "to exclude" or "leave out" or a preposition meaning "other than" or "apart from."

> Sandy decided to *accept* all the gifts from Sam *except* the new pet lizard.

adapt/adopt

adapt is a verb meaning "to adjust" or "to fit or make suitable."

adopt is a verb meaning to make something or someone one's own.

> Martin had to *adapt* his viewpoint to match his wife's state of mind so they could *adopt* the newborn kittens.

advice/advise

advice is a noun meaning "a suggestion or recommendation."

advise is a verb meaning "to suggest, give a recommendation."

> I *advise* you not to listen to all of your parents' *advice* when you have a new baby.

affect/effect

affect is a verb meaning "influence" (think "a" for action).

effect is a noun meaning a "result" (think "e" for "ending"), or it can be a verb if used to mean "to bring about."

> Monique's strong academic goals *affected* her success and created long-lasting, positive career *effects*. The new rules *effected* a change in policy.

afraid/frightened

afraid is an adjective, usually followed by the preposition *of* or the word *that* and means "filled with fear, regret, or concern."

frightened is an adjective too, usually followed by the prepositions *at* or *by* and means "filled with fear" or "alarmed."

> Will was more *afraid of* spiders than *frightened by* the prospect of entering the dark basement.

aggravate/irritate

aggravate is a verb meaning "to make worse."

irritate is a verb meaning "to annoy, anger, inflame, or to chafe."

> Winston was *irritated* by the rash on his arm, but he *aggravated* the itching by constantly scratching it.

all ready/already

all ready is an adjective phrase meaning "prepared."

already is an adverb used in expressions of time.

> We were *all ready* to leave for the airport, but we realized that our ride had *already* left.

all right/alright (misspelling)

all right is an adjective or an adverb depending on its context and means "agreeable, satisfactory."

alright is a misspelling of "all right" and should not be used.

Kelly was *all right* after she found out that lots of students confused words and their spellings.

allude/refer

allude is a verb meaning "to call attention to something *indirectly*."

refer is a verb meaning "a *direct* indication to something."

Susan didn't directly *refer* to the Bible in her speech, but she *alluded* to it.

allusion/illusion

allusion is a noun meaning "an indirect or casual reference" or "a specific reference to a well-know artistic or literary work."

illusion is a noun meaning "an unreal perception" or a "visual trick."

Houdini often included *allusions* to famous lines from Shakespeare before he performed one of his famous *illusions*.

among/between

among is a preposition used for referring to *more than two* people or things.

between is a preposition used for referring to *two people or things*.

The money was divided *among* the nieces and nephews, but the furniture was divided equally *between* the son and the daughter.

bad/badly

bad is an adjective used as a negative attribute of a person or a thing.

badly is an adverb used to describe a verb or action in a negative light.

It was a *bad* idea to act *badly* on the first day on the job.

beside/besides

beside is a preposition meaning "by the side of" or "next to."

besides is an adverb meaning "in addition to."

Besides waiting for him for over two hours, she had to stand *beside* a smelly Dumpster.

board/bored

board is a noun meaning "a wooden plank."

bored is a verb meaning "a disengaged mindset, uninterested."

Sharif was so *bored* by the lecture that he wanted to hit his head against a *board*.

brake/break

> **brake** is a noun meaning "an instrument for stopping a vehicle" or a verb meaning "to stop a vehicle."
>
> **break** is a noun meaning either "a rest period" or "a fractured bone or object," or a verb meaning "to separate something(s) into two or more pieces" or "to exceed a record or violate a rule."
>
> > Mohammad decided to *brake* suddenly so he didn't *break* the bumper on his car or any of his bones as a result.

can/may

> **can** is a verb meaning "to be able to."
>
> **may** is a verb meaning "permission to do" or "possible to do."
>
> > Since Valeriy *can* eat anything he wants, he *may* ask you if he *may* have more cookies.

cannot/can not/can't

> **cannot** is the correct spelling of the negative form of "can."
>
> **can not** is a common misspelling of "cannot."
>
> **can't** is a contraction—less formal—for "cannot."
>
> > Marisela *cannot* believe her ears whenever her daughter Soroa says, "I *can't* do it, Mom."

capital/capitol

> **capital** is a noun meaning "the location or seat of a government (states and countries)," or wealth, or the first letter of a sentence or proper noun, or the death penalty (capital punishment).
>
> **capitol** means the actual building where the state or country's government meets.
>
> > When Jane visited an elementary school in Washington, D.C., she learned that students had taken a tour of the U.S. *Capitol* building and had also memorized all of the *capital* cities of the United States.

coarse/course

> **coarse** is an adjective used to describe "rough" either in texture or attitude.
>
> **course** is a noun that can mean "a class," "a curriculum," "a direction for a journey," or "one part of a several-part meal."
>
> > Lee didn't accept *coarse* language in his workshop. He did let people work with *coarse* material like sandpaper though.

Ilona took a special *course* on French cooking and learned to make a full five-*course* meal. She now wants to continue on her *course* to receive a full culinary degree.

complement/compliment

complement is a noun meaning "something that completes or coordinates with something else" or a verb meaning "to complete."

compliment is a noun meaning "a positive statement about something or someone" or a verb meaning "to give a positive statement about something or someone."

Craig gave Joan a *compliment* about the way her aqua-colored blouse *complemented* her eyes.

conscious/consciousness/conscience/conscientious

conscious is an adjective meaning "able to feel, think, or be aware."

consciousness is the noun form meaning "awareness" or "knowledge."

conscience is a noun meaning "a person's sense of right or wrong, morals."

conscientious is the adjective form of "conscience" used to describe a person.

Lily had a guilty *conscience* about what she had done, but Shima wasn't even *conscious* of her inappropriate behavior.

Mikhail's acute *consciousness* allowed for him to become a more *conscientious* student.

could have/could've/could of

could have is the helping verb *could* meaning either "might" or "having the ability to" plus the plain form of the verb *to have*.

could've is the correct contraction form of "could have"—use in informal writing only.

could of is a misuse/misspelling of "could have"—do not use.

Kate decided her students needed a reminder not to use "*could of*" in their papers instead of "*could have*." However, Marta declared after class, "I *could've* done without that lesson!"

desert/dessert

desert is a noun meaning "a dry, arid place, usually with sand and little vegetation" and it is a verb meaning "to leave or abandon."

dessert is a noun meaning "the last course in a meal, usually sweet."

The Mojave *Desert* is probably the most prominently featured *desert* in Hollywood movies. Often, the hero is *deserted*—wounded and horseless—in the *desert* by the enemy.

Bev remembered the memory trick for how to spell *"dessert"*: It's the one you want two helpings of after dinner, so remember to include *s* twice when you spell it.

device/devise

device is a noun that means "an object, usually high-tech."

devise is a verb meaning "to create a plan or think up something."

The spy *devised* a way to escape that involved creating a *device* that would blow up the lock on his cell door.

effect/affect (see **affect/effect**)

either/neither

either is an adjective or pronoun meaning "one of two people, things, or concepts" and also an adverb introducing "the first of two alternatives."

neither is the negative version of "either": "not one of . . ."

Nguyen was told to choose *either* a taco or a burrito for lunch. However, Nguyen decided to have *neither* and asked for a hamburger.

Note: If more than two things or people are involved, use *any* instead of *either*—Nguyen wasn't sure she liked *any* of the choices on the menu.

except/accept (see **accept/except**)

explicit/implicit

explicit is an adjective meaning "directly expressed."

implicit is an adjective meaning "implied but not directly expressed."

The rules of board games are usually very *explicit*, but the rules of life tend to be more *implicit*.

farther/further

farther is an adjective, adverb, or noun meaning "more distance."

further is an adjective or noun meaning "more."

Francisca needed *further* proof to fully understand how it benefited her heart to walk a little bit *farther* every day.

fewer/less

fewer is an adjective or noun meaning "less" and is used only for things that can be counted.

less is an adjective or noun that refers to an "amount" or "specific value or degree." It is used with more abstract nouns that cannot be counted.

To diet successfully, it helps to consume *fewer* calories and take in *less* fat.

good/well

good is an adjective used to describe a person or thing in a positive way, and it is a noun meaning "positive."

well is an adverb, noun, or adjective used to describe positive attributes.

When used to describe a person, "well" focuses on health or state of being and feelings while "good" focuses on character or personality.

Sibyl is a *good* person. She is feeling *well* now, after her long bout with pneumonia. She dances *well*, too.

hanged/hung

Both *hanged* and *hung* are past tense forms of *hang*.

Use hanged only as a past-tense of the verb *hang* when referring to an execution.

Use hung for all other past-tense forms of "hang."

The prisoner was *hanged*, and, afterwards, a sign was *hung* over the gallows that stated his crimes.

hear/here

hear is a verb meaning the physiological act of *hearing*.

here is a noun that indicates a physical or symbolic place.

Eduardo, did you *hear* that loud noise? I think it is coming from behind *here*.

Tip: Remember that the word "hear" has the word "ear" in it.

hole/whole

hole is a noun that means "an opening."

whole is a noun or an adjective that means "complete."

Pedro, there must be a *hole* in Napoleon's stomach because I can't believe he ate the *whole* pie.

imply/infer

imply is a verb meaning "to suggest a secondary meaning, to indirectly suggest."

infer is a verb meaning "to deduce, or to draw a conclusion."

I didn't mean to *imply* that he was stingy, but I did *infer* from his comments that he won't be joining us on the trip.

its/it's

its is a possessive pronoun indicating ownership.

it's is a contraction for the words "it is."

It's a fact that that dog loves *its* bone.

lay/lie

lay is a transitive verb meaning "to put or place." It is followed by a direct object.

lie is a noun meaning "false statement" or an intransitive verb meaning "to recline or rest" or "to be placed."

The police officer told the suspect to *lay* down his gun and then to *lie* on the ground with his hands behind his back.

lead/led

lead has two pronunciations and two meanings: (1) pronounced *led*, it is a noun meaning a "type of metal" and (2) pronounced *leed*, it is a noun or verb meaning to "show the way" or "to have follow."

led (rhymes with *bed*) is a verb and is the past tense form of definition 2 of *lead* above.

David asked Traci to *lead* the way to the kitchen so he could inspect the *lead* pipes, so Traci *led* him there.

loose/lose

loose (pronounced *loohs*, with a final s sound) is a noun or adjective meaning "not attached," "roomy, unbinding," or "not exact."

lose (pronounced *loohz*, with a final z sound) is a verb meaning "to fail" or "to not be able to keep or to find something."

We knew we would *lose* the match since Iliana managed to *lose* her lucky socks and her confidence the day before the match.

She must have a *loose* interpretation of sports fashion to wear such *loose* shorts on top of everything else.

passed/past

passed is a past tense verb meaning "to go by" or "to have achieved," such as a goal or test.

past is a noun or adjective used with time meaning "in a previous time, not current."

Sophia *passed* Brad on the way to take her last test. Later, she told him that she had *passed* the exam. Now her *past* fears related to passing the test have been laid to rest.

precede/proceed

precede is a verb or adjective meaning "something that comes before."

proceed is a noun or a verb meaning "to go forward" (action).

The winter *precedes* the spring, but when spring arrives, we will *proceed* with wearing lighter clothing.

principal/principle

principal is a noun for "the head position of a school" or an adjective meaning "first, most important."

principle is a noun meaning "a basic truth, moral law, or assumption."

Andy always acts on the *principles* he learned from his parents. Because of his good moral sense, he would make a great *principal* for my son's elementary school.

quiet/quit/quite

quiet is a noun, verb, adjective, or adverb meaning "silent, or with little or no sound."

quit is a verb meaning "to stop or give up."

quite is an adverb meaning "very, entirely, completely."

The crowd suddenly went *quiet* as the band walked onstage. Saito *quit* talking to Dolly and turned toward the stage, and it was all *quite* magical.

raise/rise

raise is a noun or a verb. The noun *raise* means "an increase in salary." The transitive verb *raise* means "to move or lift something up to a higher position."

rise is a noun meaning "an increase," and it is an intransitive verb meaning "to go (or come) up."

After Val decided to *raise* her expectations and work her hardest, she finally got her *raise*.

We *rise* at sunrise and hope not to see another *rise* in gas prices.

right/rite/write

right is a noun meaning "a moral," "guaranteed condition," or "the opposite of left"; it can also be an adjective meaning "appropriate" or "correct"; it can even be a verb meaning "to make something correct, fix."

rite is a noun for a "ritual or ceremonial act, literal or symbolic."

write is a verb meaning "the creation of words or symbols on a surface."

Lisa knew she had the *right* to make the *right* choice for her own life and to set things *right* with Sam, so she made a sharp *right* turn onto back streets to go talk with him yet again.

In California, learning to surf is a *rite* of passage for many teens.

The textbook title *The Write Stuff* is a pun on the idea of being "right" when one *writes* an essay.

than/then

than is a conjunction used for comparison of two or more unequal items.

then is an adverb related to a particular period in time or a conjunction meaning "therefore."

Becky first asked if Cindy was smarter than Allen. Then she asked if Allen was smarter than Dave.

that/which/who

See the discussions of restrictive versus nonrestrictive clauses on p. 563 and pronouns on p. 507 for more help on these.

that is a pronoun used before a word or word group when it is necessary to distinguish the noun (restrictive).

Did you try *that* new pen that Will told us about?

which is a pronoun used when a group of words is not necessary to distinguish the noun or the meaning of the sentence (nonrestrictive).

Washington, D.C., *which* is lovely in the fall, is not really a state or a city: It's a district.

who is a pronoun used to refer to a person for both essential and non-essential information (restrictive and nonrestrictive).

Restrictive: Maria is the one *who* knows how to make perfect Mexican wedding cookies from scratch.

Nonrestrictive: Maria, *who* grew up in Mexico, knows how to make perfect Mexican wedding cookies from scratch.

their/there/they're

their is a plural possessive pronoun.

there is a noun, an adverb, or an impersonal pronoun. Use it to indicate a place or direction and as a pronoun to start sentences.

they're is a contraction for the words "they are."

Did Anna and Liz finish *their* paperwork so we can go to lunch?

Do you want to go *there* with me for lunch? *There* is an excellent lunch menu.

Cindy and Allen are my cousins; *they're* the ones who live in Mount Vernon, Virginia.

threw/through/thru

threw is the past tense form of the verb "throw."

through is a preposition indicating passage or movement, often from one side to another; and it is also an adverb meaning "finished" or "done."

thru is a common misspelling of "through," and it should not be used in formal writing.

Heather *threw* the pen to Abby.

Sothera is *through* with love since she has gone *through* the rocky passage of heartbreak too many times.

to/too/two

to is a preposition used to indicate direction or movement.

too is an adverb meaning "also," "in addition," or "very."

two is a noun or adjective used to indicate the number that comes after one and before three.

Jim went *to* his new classroom.

After Emma and Dominic moved to Arizona, Ann and Dale moved there, *too*. Carlene and John were *too* happy to complain about them all coming at once.

It was lucky that Becky was able to get *two* weeks of vacation during the busiest time of the year.

waist/waste

waist is a noun meaning the middle part of a person's body.

waste is a noun or a verb. The noun means "garbage," and the verb means "to squander something."

Juliette, even though she has had two children, has a tiny *waist*.

Annika knew it was a *waste* of time to try and get her bored cousin excited about Eliot's poem, "The *Waste*land," so she threw the extra copy in the *waste* basket.

weather/whether

weather is a noun used to indicate climate conditions.

whether is a conjunctive adverb used in clauses to indicate conditions, similar to "if."

The *weather* conditions for the Labor Day weekend in Lake Chelan were favorable.

Whether he liked it or not, Josh's parents made him stick with his piano lessons.

were/we're/where

were is a past-tense form of the verb *to be* (the plural form of *was*).

we're is a contraction for the words "we are" or "we were."

where is a noun indicating a direction or a place.

The kindergarteners *were* eager for snack time.

We're ready to serve the milk and cookies now.

Where do you want us to set the cookies?

Home is *where* the heart is.

who/whom

Both *who* and *whom* are used to refer to people (in restrictive clauses) Use **who** when you can substitute the word "he" (subject/noun) and **whom** when you can substitute "him."

Who was William Shakespeare really?   [He was . . .]

To *whom* does this book belong?   [To him]

Tip: Remember the "m" in *whom* like the "m" in *him*.

who's/whose

who's is a contraction for "who is" or "who has," and **whose** is used to indicate possession.

Who's ready to read *Hamlet*? *Whose* book is this?

would have/would of (misuse)

would have is the correct spelling for this verb tense phrase and **would of** is an incorrect usage of the verb tense.

Caroline *would have* been sad if she had missed the concert.

your/you're

your is the second person possessive pronoun.

you're is the contraction for the words "you are."

Did you take *your* medicine yet?

You're not looking too well.

You're welcome.

Activity 28-3   Commonly Confused Words Practice

Directions: *Underline the correct word for each bracketed choice below.*

The Library of Congress is [a/an] amazing place. It has more holdings [then/than] any other library. However, the Library of Congress also has [alot/allot/a lot] of other things besides books in [its/it's] collection. The LOC has practically everything [accept/except] books from other planets! If you know [whose/who's] book [your/you're] looking for, [then/than] you can search by author. If you know the title but not the author, you can search [threw/through/thru] the holdings by title. If you've forgotten the title [to/two/too], you can search by subject. Some people don't realize the benefits of a computer search and so [waist/ waste] [allot/alot/a lot] of time. They [could of/could have] saved a great deal of time if they had started at the computer. This [device/devise] was [deviced/ devised] for making one's job easier. Why [loose/lose] precious time?

In the [past/passed], before computers, patrons of the LOC used card catalogs. Going [through/thru/threw] these cards would [precede/proceed] going to the shelves. This process was not [quite/quiet] as efficient as a modern computer search. Also, the reader would have to [write/right/rite] the call number and location on a piece of paper.

Most readers now have [already/all ready] become used to the ease of computer searches. You can find some of the most savvy computer users [among/between] the people [that/who/which] frequent the Library of Congress. These smart searchers of information may find a way to [lead/led] the way in research. The Library of Congress is known for [it's/its] incredible and comprehensive collection. The pleasant [affects/effects] of finding a rare book can [affect/effect] even the most seasoned reader. It is a [good/well] place to search for information [weather/whether] [your/you're] an avid reader or an occasional one. ●

TIPS FOR USING A DICTIONARY

A **dictionary** is a reference text (or online version of a reference text) that gives the pronunciation and definitions of words. There are specialized dictionaries for particular subjects or areas of expertise. There are also dictionaries that give a word in one language and then the word in another language, for instance a Spanish–English dictionary (be careful not to depend on these for accurate translations). It is a good idea to own your own copy of a college dictionary that specializes in the kind of words you use most in college.

During the writing process it is best to save using the dictionary until the revision and editing steps. If you are writing your first draft and you stop to look up words (for spelling or for word choice), you may lose your train of thought, and the delay may lead to a stall in generating ideas and details. Instead, after you have written at least one full draft, go back and use a dictionary to check your word choices. See if the words you're using are appropriate in terms of their denotations (exact meanings) and connotations (associated meanings), spelling, tone and style, and context.

Be sure that your dictionary is no more than five years old and that it features American spellings and usage.

Anatomy of a Dictionary Entry

A dictionary entry has three main parts: The word's pronunciation, the forms or parts of speech the word can take, and the word's meaning(s). Here is an example of a typical dictionary entry from dictionary.com.

Dictionary.com Unabridged (v 1.1) - *Cite This Source*

punc·tu·ate 🅟 🔊 ˈpʌŋk tʃuˌeɪt - Show Spelled Pronunciation[**puhngk**-choo-eyt]
Pronunciation Key - Show IPA Pronunciation *verb,* **-at·ed, -at·ing.**
–verb (used with object)
1.   to mark or divide (something written) with punctuation marks in order to make the meaning clear.
2.   to interrupt at intervals: *Cheers punctuated the mayor's speech.*
3.   to give emphasis or force to; emphasize; underline.
–verb (used without object)
4.   to insert or use marks of punctuation.

[Origin: 1625–35; < ML *pūnctuātus* (ptp. of *pūnctuāre* to point), deriv. of L *pūnctus* a pricking; see
PUNCTUAL]

—Related forms
punc·tu·a·tor, *noun*
Dictionary.com Unabridged (v 1.1)
Based on the Random House Unabridged Dictionary. © Random House, Inc. 2006.

TIPS FOR USING A THESAURUS

A **thesaurus** is a reference text (or an online version of a reference text) that provides **synonyms** (words that mean the same as each other) and sometimes **antonyms** (words that mean the opposite of each other) for words.

When revising your writing, you may find that you have used certain words too often in your essay or that you need a better, more precise, or just more interesting word than the one you have used. At those times, a thesaurus can be a great help.

When using a thesaurus, you have to be particularly careful to check the connotations (associated or more subtle meanings) of a word to make sure you have used the *best* word for your intended meaning. It's a good idea to use a dictionary in tandem with a thesaurus to check the synonyms listed and make sure the one you choose has the right meaning.

Anatomy of a Thesaurus Entry

A thesaurus entry lists the word in bold, names its part of speech, and then lists its synonyms and sometimes also its antonyms. The entry will usually give you one or more words at the end to check that are close in meaning to the original word but have slightly different nuances or connotations. Here is an example of a typical thesaurus entry.

> **Goal,** n [noun] object, end, aim, ambition, (in games) finish line, home, end zone, point, marker. See DESIRE.

A thesaurus can come in very handy on those days when you are writing your essay draft and several of the same words come up again and again. For instance, consider the following synonyms for the word *said*.

acknowledged	cried	lectured
added	debated	maintained
addressed	decided	mentioned
admitted	declared	moaned
advised	denounced	mumbled
advocated	described	murmured
affirmed	dictated	muttered
agreed	directed	narrated
alleged	disclosed	noted
announced	divulged	objected
answered	droned	observed
argued	elaborated	petitioned
asserted	emphasized	pleaded
assured	entreated	pled
attested	exclaimed	pointed out
avowed	explained	predicted
began	exposed	proclaimed
called	expressed	professed
claimed	indicated	ranted
commented	inferred	reassured
complained	implied	refuted
confided	instructed	related

repeated	sneered	threatened
replied	solicited	told
responded	specified	urged
resumed	spoke	uttered
retorted	stated	vowed
returned	stressed	whispered
revealed	suggested	yelled
snapped	thought	

Each of these words conveys a particular connotation for *how* a person *said* something.

Activity 28-4 Using Synonyms

Directions: *Fill in each blank using the most appropriate synonym for* said *listed above.*

1. "Get out of my house!" she _____.

2. "Please," Meredith _____, "please let me go."

3. "It must happen," Tom _____. "There's no doubt about it."

4. "Shhh. I'll tell you what happened," Amy _____, putting her finger to her lips.

5. "Never again," Theresa _____. "I won't let it happen again." ●

Activity 28-5 Using a Dictionary and Thesaurus in Combination

Directions: *First use a thesaurus to look for an alternative word for each of the words listed below. Then use a dictionary to provide the meaning for the new word you chose. Write your findings in the spaces provided.*

1. Premature

    Thesaurus word: _____

    Dictionary meaning: _____

    _____

    _____

2. Deceive

Thesaurus word: _____

Dictionary meaning:

_____

_____

3. Ridiculous

Thesaurus word: _____

Dictionary meaning:

_____

_____

4. Positive

Thesaurus word: _____

Dictionary meaning:

_____

_____

5. Intention

Thesaurus word: _____

Dictionary meaning:

_____

_____

CAPITALIZATION

Capital letters are used for the first word of a sentence, of course, but there are other capitalization basics that you should know.

Capitalization Basics

The basic rule is that capital letters are needed when you are using a specific name or label. So, if it describes a general object or category, a word is not capitalized, but if it describes a specific person, place, or thing—one particular, named object—the word will be capitalized. That is, common nouns are not capitalized, and proper nouns are capitalized. (For a review of nouns, see p. 505.)

Here are some general categories of words that need to be capitalized.

1. **Capitalize the first word of a sentence and the first word of a sentence used in a direct quotation:**

> The human will is a powerful tool.

> Jim said, "The human will is a powerful tool."

> **Note:** Do not capitalize the first word of an interrupted or continuing quotation—the second part: "The human will," according to Jim, "*is* a powerful tool."

2. **Capitalize all proper nouns including specific persons, proper names, as well as the pronoun *I*:**

> Fumitaka Matsuoka, Octa Belle Hill, Thomas Cole, Joe, I

3. **Capitalize the names of specific groups of people and their languages:**

> French, English, American, Spanish, African, Swahili, Philippine, Tagalog

4. **Capitalize formal and informal titles for specific persons or positions:**

> President John F. Kennedy, Aunt Donna, Senator Alan Cranston, Mother and Father, Grandmother

> **Note:** But do not capitalize the title if it follows the proper name— John Kennedy, president; Alan Cranston, senator; Donna, my aunt.

Also, do not capitalize the general nouns *mother, father, grandfather,* and *grandmother* if they are being used as proper names:

> Isn't it nice to have a grandmother? Do you know my mother?

> Then Dad said we could do it.

> I love my uncle, Nick.

> I just heard that Aunt Annie moved to Florida.

5. **Capitalize the names of specific places (including countries, cities, continents, regions, counties, specific addresses, and buildings) and famous objects:**

> Japan, Seattle, Asia, the Northwest, North America, Canada

New York City, New York Street, Central Park, Brooklyn Ave.

The Hancock Building, the Hope Diamond, Haley's Comet, Monrovia High School, Santa Fe Middle School

Note: High school and middle school are not capitalized if they are not part of a specific name: Next year, I will be going to high school.

6. **Capitalize the names of days, months, holidays, and holy days:**

Saturday, February, Fourth of July, Thanksgiving, Martin Luther King, Jr. Day, Passover, Ramadan

Note: In general, do not capitalize the seasons (summer, winter, spring, and fall). However, if they are part of a specific event or title, they are capitalized: the Spring Festival, Fall Quarter Marathon, and so on.

7. **Capitalize the names of religions and religious members:**

Buddhism/Buddhists, Hinduism/Hindus, Christianity/Christians, Judaism/Jews, Islam/Muslims, the Dalai Lama, Reverend Smith

8. **Capitalize the names of specific cultures and members of ethnic and political groups:**

Indonesians, Vietnamese, African Americans, Latin Americans, Cuban Americans, Hawaiians, Chinese, Japanese, Korean, Democrats, Republicans, Marxists, Green Party members

Note: If a prefix comes in front of a word that is usually capitalized, keep the formal name capitalized: un-American, anti-American, etc.

9. **Capitalize the names of specific organizations or institutions and their abbreviations:**

Greenpeace, the Republican Party, Camp Fire Boys and Girls, Boy Scouts, Girl Scouts, the Seattle Art Museum (SAM), the New York Yankees, and so on.

Note: Capitalize abbreviations (or acronyms) for companies, institutions, and organizations: ABC, CIA, IBM, FBI, and so on (see Abbreviations later in this section for more examples).

10. **Capitalize the names of historical periods, events, or historical documents and holy texts:**

The American Revolution, the Middle Ages, the Battle of Gettysburg

The Declaration of Independence, the Constitution, the Magna Carta

Bible, Koran, Bhagavad-Gita, the Tao Te Ching

Note: Do not capitalize *centuries*: the seventeenth century, etc.

Note: *Lord* and *God* are usually capitalized and so are pronouns that go with particular supreme beings: the *Lord* and *His* teachings, the *Goddess* and *Her* ways.

11. **Capitalize the names of specific brands or trademarks:**

    Nabisco, Volkswagen, Hershey, Microsoft, Microsoft Office

12. **Capitalize the titles of books, plays, films, TV shows, magazines, articles, stories, poems, albums, tapes, CDs, songs, and works of art.** In titles, capitalize the first and last word and all significant words in between except articles (*the*, *a*, and *an*) and prepositions (*of*, *in*, *on*, and so on):

    The Sound and the Fury, Othello, The Wizard of Oz, Sesame Street, People Magazine, "Four Days to Improved Sleep," "A Good Man Is Hard to Find," "Stopping by Woods," *The White Album,* "Let It Be," and the *Mona Lisa*

Activity 28-6 Capitalization Practice

Directions: *Correct the capitalization errors in the following sentences. Underline the error(s) in each sentence, and then write the correct form(s) in the space provided at the end. If the sentence has no capitalization errors, write "correct" in the space provided.*

1. Rachael checked her class schedule again: She was taking history, spanish, and biology. _____

2. When I was growing up, we lived on Elm street. _____

3. My favorite Shakespeare play is *The merchant of Venice.* _____

4. I asked my Mother if we could visit for the holidays. _____

5. I bought Dad a sweater for his birthday. _____

6. I love the Fall and all the colors it brings. _____

7. My aunt and uncle will be joining us for Thanksgiving. _____

8. When I went to High School, my teachers were strict. _____

9. Liza graduated from Monrovia high school in California. _____

10. The band U2 features Joshua Tree national park on one of the band's CDs. _____

NUMBERS

Rules for using the correct format for numbers vary according to context. The following standards will work for most academic writing.

1. **Spell out numbers zero through ten and numbers that can be written using one or two words.**

> Chelsey has two cats and one dog.
>
> There were fifteen hundred fans.

> **Note:** For business or technical writing, use numbers for all numerals above ten.

2. **Spell out numbers that begin a sentence, no matter how large the number**—but see if you can revise the sentence so you don't need to start with the number. Be sure to use commas correctly in numbers over 1,000.

> Ten thousand and twelve soldiers were deployed.
>
> In the conflict, 10,012 soldiers were deployed.

3. **For extremely large numbers, use a combination of figures and words:**

> The school's budget for the next five years is $46 million.

> However, if it is not a round number, you'll have to use all figures.

> Our rival school spent $43,625,012 in a three-year period.

4. **Use figures for dates, years, and times.**

> December 10, 1995, 8:03 AM.

5. **Use figures in addresses:**

> 302 E. Maydee St., Los Angeles, CA 98110

6. **Use figures for exact measurements and specific identifications:**

> The rug is 8 feet long and 6 feet wide.
>
> Room 222, Interstate 101, Queen Elizabeth II, Channel 13, Chapter 14, page 202, Act 2, Scene 3, 2:1 ratio, 75% (or 75 percent), 3.8 GPA, 32°, $16.50, 144 hours, 4,521, 1/4

Activity 28-7   Numbers Practice

Directions: *Correct the errors in numbers usage in the following sentences.*

1.   The teacher went over 3 grammar rules in one hour.

_____

_____

2. My neighbor has one hundred and twenty different types of plants in her yard.

_____

_____

3. The entire estate was worth more than one hundred and forty-two thousand dollars.

_____

_____

4. She spent six dollars and seventy five cents on the book.

_____

_____

5. He asked us to read page sixty-six in Chapter Twelve of our text.

_____

_____

6. Queen Elizabeth the first was an historical leader and a woman.

_____

_____

7. Martha was ninety-eight % sure she would pass the test.

_____

_____

8. 12 months of the year I will have homework.

_____

_____

9. I have two siblings, 7 cousins, and five aunts.

_____

_____

10. She sold 200000 copies of her novel.

_____

ABBREVIATIONS

Though abbreviations are common in casual writing, they are less acceptable in academic writing. These are a few of the categories of acceptable abbreviations.

1. Titles or academic degrees:

- Mr., Mrs., and Ms. are acceptable abbreviations used as titles **before** a person's last name.
- Abbreviated academic titles and/or degrees are used **after** a person's name:

  B.A. (Bachelor of Arts), M.A. (Master of Arts), B.S. (Bachelor of Science), M.F.A. (Master of Fine Arts), Ph.D. (Doctor of Philosophy), R.N. (Registered Nurse), M.D. (Doctor of Medicine), C.P.A (Certified Public Accountant), and so on.

  Suzu Ozaki, Ph.D.; James Bader, C.P.A.; Carolin Dillon, M.F.A.

  Note: The title *Professor* is usually spelled out: Professor George C. Gross.

- Abbreviate governmental, military, and religious titles when they are used **in front** of someone's complete name. If only a person's **last name** is given, then use his or her full title.

  Sen. Patty Murray spoke at the luncheon in downtown Seattle. Senator Murray discussed port security in the city.

  Rev. Jesse Jackson addressed a crowd of labor workers at the largest sports arena in the city. Reverend Jackson traced the history of the civil rights movement.

2. Countries, states, or cities:

- In addresses, abbreviate the state and country. In sentences, spell out the names of cities and states.

  She lives at 201 Clinton St., Princeton, NJ, USA. Her other address is 1402 Pennsylvania Ave., Washington, D.C.

  The conference will be held in Princeton, New Jersey.

  Note: Abbreviate United States only when used in an address or used as an adjective.

  The U.S. Capitol building is located on Capitol Hill. The United States is proud of its historical buildings.

3. Common acronyms:

- Acronyms are composed of the first letters of each word of a name that includes two or more words. Acronyms using the first letters of the name of an agency, business, or institution are commonly used in writing and speech. These types of acronyms do not require periods between the letters.

> CIA (Central Intelligence Agency), FBI (Federal Bureau of Investigation), NAACP (National Association for the Advancement of Colored People), NASA (National Aeronautics and Space Administration), PTO (parent/teacher organization), CD (compact disc), DVD (digital video disc), IBM (International Business Machines), NEH (National Endowment for the Humanities), SDSU (San Diego State University), ABC (American Broadcasting Corporation), NBC (National Broadcasting Company), CBS (Columbia Broadcasting System), SUV (sport utility vehicle)

Use these abbreviations when using the following terms with **numbers**: A.M., or a.m. (ante meridian), or P.M. or p.m. (post meridian), or MPH or mph (miles per hour)

4. Latin expressions:

> e.g. (for example), etc. (and so forth), et al. (and all others), i.e. (that is), and vs. or v. (versus)

Note: These standard Latin terms are abbreviated only when they appear inside parentheses. In the main body of a sentence, use complete words and/or their English equivalents.

> I ate all kinds of ice cream: chocolate, vanilla, strawberry, fudge ripple, praline, green tea, *and more*.

> All flavors of ice cream (chocolate, vanilla, *etc*.) are good in my opinion.

5. Documentation formats such as MLA or APA:

> vol. or vols. for "volume" or "volumes," or trans. for "translator" or "translated by"

See Chapter 19 for specific MLA documentation information.

Activity 28-8 Abbreviation Practice

Directions: *In the blanks provided, write the appropriate abbreviations of the words given in parentheses. Refer to the rules above for help.*

1. At 10 _____ (post meridian/P.M.), we have to leave for the airport.

2. The _____ (U.S./United States) is a country that thrives on a market economy.

3. We were hoping that _____ (Sen./Senator) Cantwell would attend the luncheon as well.

4. We heard that _____ (NBC/N.B.C.) has a great fall lineup ready.

5. _____ (Mister/Mr.) Coleman is a fair and conscientious employee. ●

Activity 28-9   More Abbreviation Practice

Directions: *Underline any mistakes in the use of abbreviations in the following paragraph. You should find five errors.*

When visiting Washington, dc, be sure to make a trip to the United States Supreme Court building. Also, the U.S. Capitol across the street is a location that can't be missed. The Senate may be in session, so you may see Senator Edward Kennedy. Sen. Kennedy is the brother of the late John F. Kennedy. Don't drive too quickly near these important sites. It's best to go no more than 25 miles per hour, as there are frequent illegal street crossings by star-struck tourists. Also, be sure to follow all rules related to national security. You wouldn't want to be followed by the F.B.I. for acting suspiciously. ●

Active Spelling

You need to be active in your spelling choices:

- If you are not sure how a word is spelled, use the spelling the tips in this chapter and/or consult a dictionary.
- If the word you are using is a homophone (a word that sounds like another word) check that you have used the correct spelling so that readers will know what you mean. Consult a dictionary or the list of commonly confused words in this chapter to be sure.
- Be aware of the spelling errors you most commonly make (keep a list of corrections received from instructors) and check for them when you proofread your writing.
- Use the spell-check feature on your computer. Remember: If a word is spelled correctly but used incorrectly, spell-check will not indicate this.

Tone, Style, Word Choice, and Usage

29

THINKING CRITICALLY

Look at the words on the fortune above.

Something's wrong here. Can you spot what kind of error is in this sentence from the fortune cookie?

_____

_____

_____

_____

_____

_____

_____

Cross Reference
See p. 667 for tips for ESL students.

When you write, you should use the right tone for your audience and be careful to avoid usage mistakes, like the common error demonstrated on page 653 that ESL (English as a Second Language) writers often make—skipping the definite article.

THINKING CRITICALLY ABOUT TONE AND STYLE

Tone and style are important elements in writing essays. Tone and style together create your writing "voice." **Tone** reflects your manner or attitude, and **style** includes the choices you make about language, diction, and sentence structure. The way you employ these elements helps establish your voice in writing. Writing styles can be as distinct as fingerprints. In fact, some teachers say that after a few weeks of class, students could turn in their essays without names on them, and they would be able to figure out who wrote each paper based on the distinctive voices evident in each of the essays.

The tone and style choices you make affect the way a reader hears or responds to your ideas and the credibility and effectiveness of your ideas. Some writers create style, tone, and voice patterns in their essays unconsciously; they don't think about the distinctive voice they have created through their choices. However, it's important to become aware of these choices and *evaluate critically* whether they are the best choices for your assignment and audience.

When deciding on a particular tone for an assignment, remember that the tone you use reflects your attitude toward the subject and the arguments you are making. Also, be sure to think about your audience when choosing the most effective and appropriate tone for your essay. Your tone may be formal, serious, informal, playful, mocking, sarcastic, or impartial and removed. For instance, the tone that Barbara Ehrenreich develops in "Spudding Out" in Chapter 21 is mocking, playful, and a bit sarcastic even though she is serious about the negative effects of watching too much TV. The tone in Mark Clayton's "A Whole Lot of Cheatin' Going On" is more formal and serious and works well for his use of statistics and his academic audience. Both authors made these style and tone choices consciously based on their subject matter and their intended audience.

Applying Critical Thinking

| PURPOSE | IDEAS | SUPPORT | ASSUMPTIONS BIASES | CONCLUSIONS | POINT OF VIEW | ANALYSIS |

Consider the following questions before you begin writing and then make conscious choices about tone and language as you write your drafts:

1. What is my topic, and what kind of tone would be most appropriate for the subject matter, **ideas**, and arguments that I want to make?

2. What attitude do I want to portray in this essay (for example, serious/formal, playful/informal, sarcastic/mocking, and so on)?

3. Who is my intended audience? What tone would be most effective for getting my message across to my intended audience?

4. What is my **purpose** in this essay? What tone and style choices would be most effective for the messages and arguments I want to convey?

As you revise your essay draft, check again to make sure that the style and tone of your writing is appropriate and is the most effective choice for your topic, your audience, and your arguments and conclusions. For instance, a formal research paper on breast cancer would require a serious tone. However, a personal narrative essay about your first time snowboarding might be more casual and informal.

Here is an example of inappropriate tone.

> Barbara's article talked about fat losers who sit on their cans and watch TV all day.

Revised:

> Barbara Ehrenreich's article "Spudding Out" explores the reasons why Americans like to spend so much time in front of the TV.

Formal Style and Tone vs. Academese

Even when you are writing a more formal academic paper, avoid academese: writing that uses pompous multisyllabic words and unnecessarily complicated sentence structures. Academese is filled with passive voice constructions (see page 618 for more on passive construction) and contains overly complex language or jargon. Here is an example:

> Being that the particle removal machinery had been malfunctioning for several days, we made the decision to modify our strategy and investigate a replacement unit.

Translation into a more reasonable tone and style:

> Our vacuum was not working well for several days, so we decided to buy a new one.

The bottom line is that academese doesn't make you sound smarter if your audience doesn't understand what you are trying to say—and sometimes even when they do. Successful writing communicates ideas clearly. Strengthen your tone and style by consciously choosing the best voice and language for your arguments and your intended audience.

Note: Using a complex vocabulary word in and of itself is not a bad idea. Just be sure that the word you choose conveys your intended meaning best and that the overall passage you write is not too complex for your intended audience. See the vocabulary-building section on p. 674 for more on using complex words and expanding your vocabulary.

Activity 29-1   Appropriate Tone and Style

Directions: *Revise the following sentences so they have a more appropriate tone for a general audience.*

1.   That dance was happening and totally outrageous.

   _____

2.   He was an ugly guy with an ugly dude haircut.

   _____

3.   She better get outta that life before it eats her up.

   _____

4. The idea of that philosopher is just stupid.

_____

5. It was a lame excuse for a party.

_____

Activity 29-2   Academese Tone and Vocabulary Revision

Directions: *Revise the following passage, and change the overly formal and distant tone to a more readable tone for a general audience. You may need to look up some of the words in a dictionary in order to translate them.*

    Being that the consequences of the aforementioned action were disastrous, the committee made the premeditated decision to halt all deliberations on the project. Therefore, the potential for disruption of the habitual rituals of the afternoon may be affected.

_____

_____

_____

WORD CHOICE

Word choice, sometimes referred to as **diction**, is exactly that: You make a conscious *choice* when you are selecting each word. Pick the best word for the message or idea you are expressing based on the content of the sentence and where the word will appear. Think about your intended audience as you choose the right words. Will you need a formal or informal word? Will you need to use language that a general audience can understand or should you use discipline-specific terms for a specialized audience? Is your tone more academic or casual? How should that affect your word choices?

Many words have both literal and suggested or implied meanings. Primary or more literal meanings are **denotations**, and secondary or more implied meanings are called **connotations**. Think of the denotation of a word as the exact or surface meaning of a word, and think of connotations as the "baggage" or associations that come with that word. The denotation of a word then is like the tip of an iceberg that shows on the surface of the water, and the connotations, which often impart the most meaning, are the base of the iceberg under the water's surface. Some words have very few connotations, while others are rich with connotative associations. For instance, consider the following two signs:

Which language is more effective? Both signs are advertising the selling of a residence, but "house" is a more denotative word while "home" is full of connotations. Home is where the heart is; it's apple pie, mom, comfort, and everything we associate with the bigger concept of "home." So make word choices carefully in order to mine their full effect and to make sure they are conveying (both on the surface and more subtly) exactly what you mean to say.

Choose the language (or specific word) that achieves clarity and accuracy in both your sentence and your overall essay. When you use effective diction, your ideas are communicated successfully.

For example:

Intended audience: The faculty at your campus

Inappropriate diction: The old faculty on this campus are clueless. They just don't get what younger students are like. They are totally lost and into old school rules.

Revised: The older generation of faculty on this campus do not understand the new generation of students. Social rules are different.

Slang

Slang is casual language consisting of informal words that are not listed as "genuine" words in the dictionary (though they might be listed as slang). The old saying "*Ain't* ain't a word 'cause it ain't in the dictionary" is partially true: It isn't a real word, but it is listed in most dictionaries—as slang. It's fine to use slang in casual social speech or emails between friends, or even in dialogue in narration essays. However, in most cases in essay writing, you should convert slang into more conventional word choices.

Slang: She wore some serious bling to the concert, and she brought her honey too.

Revised: She wore elaborate jewelry to the concert, and she brought her boyfriend too.

Slang: Dude, my terminator gym teacher like seriously messed with my groove. He was too harsh.

Revised: My gym teacher was very demanding.

Jargon

Jargon is the language used in a specific field. Jargon has its place, and if one is writing for an audience familiar with the jargon of that field, then it's fine to use it. Otherwise, it needs to be translated into more general language. For instance, if you worked in a computer repair store, you could leave a list of instructions for your coworkers that would be filled with jargon that they would understand but a new computer owner would not.

Jargon: The search engine allowed him to download jpegs loaded with megapixels onto his hard drive.

Revised: The Internet search engine he used allowed him to save extremely large picture files onto his computer.

Dialect

Dialect is language that reflects the speech (word choice and accent) of a certain region or culture. Dialect can reflect a specific region of a country such as a Southern dialect in the United States or it can reflect a particular economic group or cultural heritage.

Dialect: If y'all are fixin' to come to the picnic, bring your gear.

Revised: If all of you are planning on attending the picnic, be sure to bring what you will need.

Although you would not use dialect in an academic paper, it would certainly be appropriate to use it in dialogue to communicate information about a person or character speaking.

Foreign Words

Foreign words that are used without a specific purpose can be confusing. If you decide to use a foreign term in your sentence, be sure it is one your intended audience will recognize. Otherwise, use the English version of the term, or define it in parentheses:

Foreign term: She had a *laissez faire* attitude about the upcoming test.

Revised: She had little concern about the upcoming test.

With definition: She had a *laissez faire* (unconcerned) attitude about the upcoming test.

There are times when it is appropriate to use slang, dialect, technical jargon, and foreign words, in dialogue or in direct quotations, but in general, you should not use them in formal academic writing.

Activity 29-3 Slang, Dialect, Foreign Words, and Tone Practice

Directions: *Revise the following paragraph so it has a more appropriate tone and more appropriate word choices, and rewrite it below. Be sure to translate slang into more formal alternatives.*

My teacher really blew it last semester. His assignments were really lame, and his attitude really sucked. He totally played favorites too. He handed out A's like candy to the teacher's pets, claro que si! In the meantime, the rest of us got screwed and treated like dirt. I think he was just lazy and mean. He never told us what he wanted us to do. It's like we had to be psychic to get an assignment done. Then, he'd rag about how bad the assignments were. Overall, this dude and this class really blew.

_____

_____

_____

_____

Idioms

Idioms reflect the customary speech patterns of a given language. They are particular ways of saying things that develop in a specific region or in a language that don't translate directly or easily into another language. Idioms are learned over time through immersion in a language, and the incorrect use of an idiom is often an indicator that the writer is not a native speaker. Many mistakes in idiom usage come from the misuse of prepositions (see p. 520) or verbs (see p. 505).

Cross Reference
Also see p. 667 for ESL tips and idioms.

Preposition-based idioms:

We leave *on* Saturday.
[Not *in* Saturday]

The book is *on the table*.
[Not *in the table*]

Particle-based idioms:
They *made up* their minds.
She *backed up* her car.
Bob *made off with* the keys to the cabin.

Activity 29-4   Practice with Idioms

Directions: *Revise the italicized idioms in the following sentences. See ESL Tips, p. 667, if you need help with common idioms in English.*

1. She had to *back off* to the beginning of the problem to figure it out.

   _____

2. *In the weekend*, we will go to the carwash.

   _____

3. She put her books *in the table* and left.

   _____

4. Sharon knew that Jessica *had made out with* her car keys.

   _____

5. *In the day* she was born, John Lennon was killed.

   _____

6. She wanted to find a good *substitute of* coffee to drink in the morning.

   _____

7. She discovered there were several *alternatives of* drinking coffee.

   _____

8. She asked Barry to *take a stab in* doing the exercise.

   _____

9. *At a typical day*, students will have to focus for many hours.

   _____

10. *Arriving of another country*, visitors can get confused in American airports.

_____

Clichés

Clichés are expressions that have been used so often they have become stale and no longer communicate their intended meaning. Originally, they effectively conveyed a powerful image or idea to readers, but through extensive use, they have lost their effectiveness, no longer conjuring images at all.

Most clichés are metaphors or similes that make implied or direct comparisons between two things in order to convey an idea. **Metaphors** are implied comparisons to other things.

> Imagination is a camel's hump, a reserve of water for a troubled and thirsty mind.

Similes are comparisons that use the specific words *like* or *as:*

> Robert Burns wrote, "My love is *like* a red, red rose."

Many famous metaphors and similes from literature pop up in student writing. However, many have lost their power and should be avoided. Instead, create a fresh comparison of your own. Who knows, maybe it will be so good that everyone will want to use it, and it too will become a cliché one day. Here are some of the most overused clichés.

> That goldfish is *as dead as a doornail.*
>
> My roommate *sleeps like a log.*
>
> My cat is *as dumb as a post.*
>
> Her hair is *as black as the night.*
>
> Her eyes are *as blue as the sea (or sky).*
>
> Her lips are *as red as a rose.*
>
> This soufflé is *as light as a feather.*
>
> His eyelids felt *as heavy as lead.*
>
> She had to *face the music.*
>
> My father *worked like a dog* and *kept his nose to the grindstone* five days a week.
>
> Betty was *green with envy* over Sarah's new coat.

There's no use *crying over spilled milk.*

Avoid clichés *like the plague.*

In the revision stage of your writing process, check to make sure that clichés haven't crept into your writing—they can be automatic and hard to spot. Here is a list of some of the most common clichéd phrases in English—be sure to look again at the very common clichés used in the sentences above, too.

Common Clichés

add(ing) insult to injury	drunk as a lord	right as rain
better half	face the music	rise and shine
beyond a shadow of a doubt	few and far between	rise to the occasion
blind as a bat	flat as a pancake	sharp as a tack
bottom line	green with envy	sink or swim
brave as a lion	heavy as lead	smart as a whip
brown as a nut	hit the nail on the head	sneaking suspicion
cold, hard facts	in this day and age	straight and narrow
come to grips with	last but not least	tears streamed down
cool as a cucumber	nose to the grindstone	tried and true
crazy as a loon	nutty as a fruitcake	ugly as sin
cute as a button	paint the town red	untimely death
dead as a doornail	pale as a ghost	walk the line
deaf as a post	pass the buck	wax eloquent
deep, dark secret	pretty as a picture	white as a ghost
	quick as a flash	white as a sheet
		worth its weight in gold

Activity 29-5   Cliché Revision

Directions: *Rewrite the clichés in the following sentences using fresh imagery.*

Example: Her lips were as red as cherries.

Revised: Her lips were dark red, like the nail polish of a 1940s starlet.

1. I knew what was going on because I could *read him like a book.*

_____

2. Our meeting went badly because *too many cooks spoil the broth.*

_____

3. Tina was *playing with fire* by choosing that outfit.

_____

4. Erin decided not *to stick her neck out* for that promotion.

_____

5. We'll just have to *go with the flow* to do well on this project.

_____

6. Sharon said her mother was *as sharp as a tack* even at the age of 95.

_____

7. Midori was *as pale as a ghost* after watching the horror flick.

_____

8. Lisa and Maria thought their English teacher was *as nutty as a fruitcake.*

_____

9. Nick tried to *pass the buck* when asked to do his chores.

_____

10. Matt *hit the nail on the head* when he said that the homework was hard.

_____

AVOIDING SEXIST LANGUAGE

Language is dynamic: It evolves with culture. It used to be acceptable to use gender-specific terms such as *man* or *mankind* to stand for all people, but due to political and societal changes of the last 30 to 40 years, the use of such language is now considered sexist.

Use Gender-Specific Terms Only When Appropriate

The key to avoiding sexist language is to use logic: Use gender-specific terms only when the subject really is gender specific. **Gender-specific terms** are words that refer to a specific gender. For instance, the terms *men* and *he* refer to males, and the terms *women* and *her* refer to females.

> Each Girl Scout and Brownie can pick up *her* sash at Tuesday's meeting.

> The student at the all-boys academy had to order *his* books online.

If your subject is not gender specific, then use inclusive (non–gender specific) language.

> Students across the nation are beginning to order *their* books online.

Non–gender specific terms are neither male nor female; they are neutral and therefore include both sexes. Some examples of gender-neutral terms are *people, one, humanity,* and *humankind.* Plural pronouns such as *their* are also gender neutral. When you use terms like *people* or *humans,* you can use the plural pronoun *their.* If you use singular terms such as *a person* or *one* as your subject, then you'll need to use a *he or she* instead of *their* in the place of the pronoun to avoid a different type of mistake (a pronoun agreement error, see p. 606 for more on pronoun agreement). In general, the easiest way to avoid a pronoun agreement error is to use the plural forms of non–gender specific terms and the corresponding plural pronouns.

> **Singular:** A person addicted to technology needs his or her new toys the way some people need shelter.

> **Plural:** Humans are more in love with technology than ever. They need their technological advances like they need shelter.

Don't Assume an Occupation Is Exclusively Male/Female

Another kind of sexist language arises from stereotyping certain occupations as being primarily for women or for men.

> When a nurse graduates with *her* R.N. degree, *she* can then look into a career in either a hospital or a private practice.

> When a doctor chooses where *he* will work, *he* will consider whether *he* prefers the fast pace of a large hospital or the more intimate conditions of a private practice.

Both sentences stereotype either men or women. Of course men can be nurses, and women can be doctors. Careers are not limited to a single gender. Along the same lines, be careful not to write *male nurse* or *woman doctor*—just say *nurses* or *doctors,* and then use the plural pronoun *their.*

Use Parallel Terms for Men and Women

Be careful not to have double standards. For instance, if you are writing about high school students, don't call the males *men* and the females *girls.*

Instead call them *boys and girls* or *men and women*. Be consistent and fair in your use of terms.

Here are some gender-specific terms that are already obsolete and some non–gender specific terms that can be used to replace them.

Gender-Specific Term	Inclusive Term
man or mankind	humans, humanity, people, humankind, human beings
fireman	firefighter
policeman	police officer
mailman	mail carrier, postal carrier
weatherman	meteorologist, weather forecaster
salesman	sales associate
congressman	representative, senator, legislator
foreman	supervisor
chairman	chairperson, chair
businessman	business person or exact title (e.g., sales manager)
manpower	staff, personnel, workers
to man	to operate, to staff
man-made	handcrafted, human-made
male nurse	nurse
female doctor	doctor

Activity 29-6   Revising Sexist Language

Directions: *Rewrite any of the following sentences that contain sexist or inappropriately gender-specific terms. Remember, you can also correct sentences by making the pronouns plural. (If you choose to do this, you may need to change the verb and make some nouns plural.) If the sentence is correct, write "correct" on the answer line.*

1.   A clever student of science will know how to move forward in his classes and in his career. _____

_____

_____

2. A student majoring in dance will have to monitor her diet and exercise routine. _____

_____

_____

3. The scientist who does not know his chemical formulas may run into trouble in the lab. _____

_____

_____

4. In the 1960s, mankind entered the space age. _____

_____

_____

5. The secretary of the union is responsible for taking accurate notes for her fellow union workmen. _____

_____

_____ ●

TEN USEFUL ESL TIPS FOR NON-NATIVE SPEAKERS

Here are ten grammar tips that are useful for both non-native speakers and those students who need to brush up on their grammar usage.

Tip 1: Check for Count vs. Noncount Nouns

Count nouns name items that can be counted as individual units:

> **Example:** dog/dogs, cat/cats, boy/boys, girl/girls, flower/flowers, window/windows, cracker/crackers, street/streets, nut/nuts

Noncount (or mass) nouns name items that cannot be counted as individual units:

> **Example:** food, rice, flour, water, sugar, peace, life, death, furniture, milk, wood, cotton, leather, beauty, chess, evidence

Tip 2: Check for Article Use and Definite vs. Indefinite Articles

Articles (sometimes called determiners) are divided into two categories: **definite** (or specific) = *the,* and **indefinite** (or nonspecific) = *a* or *an, some,* or no article at all.

1. **Definite articles:** Use *the* with common nouns, singular or plural, and noncount nouns that are specific because the noun was previously mentioned:

> *The* new book that will come out in the spring will be better.

OR, because the noun is a particular one, not a general descriptor:

> *The* book's index is at *the* end.

OR, because the noun is identified by a modifier:

> *The* new book is *the* best choice.

Also, use the definite article *the* with proper nouns, singular or plural:

> *The* Wards have been collecting vases for years.

> I used to live in *the* Northwest.

> Many different races live in *the* United States.

> He swam in *the* Pacific.

> *The New York Times* is a great newspaper.

2. **Indefinite articles:** Use *a* or *an* with singular countable nouns that are generic or are nonspecific because the noun was not mentioned previously:

> Ordering *a* book from the library is easy.

OR, because the noun's identity is not important to the context:

> The chef will be planning *a* new menu.

OR, because the noun has no restricting modifier:

> Buying *a* book will be more costly than borrowing.

Use *some* with plural nouns or noncount nouns that refer to a particular or specifiable quantity:

> Can you lend me *some* money to buy my books?

Do not use any articles with noncount common nouns that are generic and nonspecific and have no particular quantity or identity:

> Go buy *milk* at the store so we can have breakfast.

OR, if they are singular proper nouns:

> *Mary* has a nice car.

> *People* is a fun magazine to read.

Tip 3: Choose the Right Preposition or Prepositional Phrase

Getting prepositions right is difficult since many are learned through use and familiarity with a language, but some logical rules do apply for using some prepositions. The most easily confused prepositions are those related to *space* and *time*.

1. **Space:** Think location vs. direction.

    Location: Use *at, on,* or *in*

    We will meet *at* [location] the car.

    We will sit *on* [surface] the car while we wait for the rest of the group.

    We will sit *in* [enclosed] the car.

    Direction: Use *to, onto,* or *into*

    We walked *to* [direction] the car.

    We let our books fall *onto* [surface] the floor.

    We walked *into* [enclosed] the house.

2. **Time:** Use *at* for an exact point in time, *on* for a particular day, and *in* for an unspecified time or particular general period of time.

    At 3:30 AM *on* a Monday *in* the spring of 1972, he was born.

3. **Prepositional phrases:** A prepositional phrase cannot be used as the subject of a sentence. Instead, use a noun or add a subject pronoun after the prepositional phrase.

    Incorrect: *In my city* is a low crime rate.

    Correct: My city has a low crime rate. OR, *In my city,* there is a low crime rate.

Tip 4: Avoid Mixing Subordination and Coordination

Use a subordinating clause with a comma, or connect two clauses with a coordinating conjunction, but do not use both (see Chapter 23 for more on sentence combining).

Incorrect: *Although* Thomas liked tennis, *but* he decided to play soccer instead.

Correct: *Although* Thomas liked tennis, he decided to play soccer instead. OR, Thomas liked tennis, *but* he decided to play soccer instead.

Tip 5: Be Sure to Use Subject Pronouns

If you have used a noun subject in a sentence and don't want to repeat the subject in the next sentence, be sure to use a pronoun to represent the original noun in your second sentence.

> **Incorrect:** The Chihuahua is a small dog breed. *Is* a cute dog. [no subject pronoun]

> **Correct:** The Chihuahua is a small dog breed. *It is* a cute dog. [subject pronoun added]

Tip 6: Use *It* or *There* Correctly with Deferred Subjects

In English, when a subject is deferred (placed later in the sentence than is usual), the usual subject spot has to be filled with *it* or *there*.

> **Incorrect:** *Is* not good to eat too much sugar. *Are* health risks involved.

> **Correct:** *It is* not good to eat too much sugar. *There are* health risks involved.

Tip 7: Be Familiar with Verbal Phrases and Idioms

Verbal phrases are formed when a verb is combined with an adverb or preposition to create a new meaning. Most verbal phrases are idioms, and they are used more in informal conversation or informal writing than in formal essays. However, even when used in informal writing, verbal phrases are written in a particular order.

Here's a list of some of the most commonly used verbal phrases in English.

Commonly Used Verbal Phrases

ask out	call off	cut (it) out
break down	call up	cut up
break up (with)	catch up (with)	drop in
bring up	check in	drop off
burn down	check out	drop out (of)
burn out	check up (on)	figure out
burn up	come out	fill in
call back	cross out	fill out

fill up	keep on/out/up	stay in/off/up
find out	leave out	stop up
get along (with)	look after/into/out/over/up	take after/in/off/out/over
get away (from or with)	make up	take care (of)
get back in/on	pass out	tear down/up
get out/over/up	pick out/up	think on/over
give back/in/up	put away/back/off/on/	throw out/up
go out (with)	out/up	try on/out (for)
go over	quiet down	tune in/out/up
grow up	run across/into/out	turn down/off/on/out/up
hand in/out	show off/up	wake up
hang out/up	shut off/up	watch out (for)
have on	speak out/up	
help out	stand up (for)	

Tip 8: Check Your Infinitive and Gerund Verb Uses

An **infinitive** is a verb with the word *to* in front of it. It indicates action *after* the time of the main verb, indicates an *effort*, or indicates a *purpose*:

> **Infinitive (action after):** I decided *to eat* the whole pie.

> **Infinitive (indicates effort):** Try *to eat* a whole pie yourself.

> **Infinitive (indicates purpose):** I shopped *to buy* two whole pies.

A **gerund** uses an *-ing* verb form and indicates action *before* the time of the verb or indicates an experiment:

> **Gerund (action before):** I plan on *eating* that whole pie.

> **Gerund (experiment):** Try *eating* a whole pie in two minutes.

Check to make sure you've used the infinitive and gerund forms of verbs correctly.

Tip 9: Be Careful About Commonly Confused Words

Be careful not to use a word that sounds like another one (a homonym) but isn't the right word for what you want to say. Use the correct spelling. See p. 628 for a list of some of the most commonly confused words in English.

> **Incorrect:** *Your* the one *whose* always worried about the *whether*.

> **Correct:** *You're* the one *who's* always worried about the *weather*.

Tip 10: Use a Good Second-Language Dictionary and Use It Well

Travel or minimal translation dictionaries tend to oversimplify a word's meaning or give minimal choices. Instead, choose a good, complete English as a Second Language dictionary. A complete dictionary will give you more specific meanings and connotations so you can pick the best English word for the context of the sentence you are writing. Check a word's meaning carefully. Also see if there is a list of idioms so you can check your verb phrases to make sure they are correct.

Activity 29-7   Fixing ESL Errors

Directions: *Rewrite this paragraph with the ESL errors corrected on the lines provided. Refer to the ten tips in this section for help.*

Yesterday I had weird experience. I look at my neighbor's yard and saw that there was many dog in their yard. I knew they have several childs in that home also, so I become worried at the dog behaviors. The life is strange thing sometime: You have to carry all the evidences and decide what to do. I decide to tell the childs in the yard to look out for dogs because these dogs was growling and had drools dripping from their mouth. The one dog is the one who's face looked so scared, so I was afraid for that children. I yell, "Look out!" The childs then look on the dogs and see that one with it's mean face and the growls, so kid got away from dog right then. I am relieve after that.

_____

_____

_____

_____

_____

_____

_____

_____

_____

30

Vocabulary in Context

THINKING CRITICALLY

Look at the comic strip above. Then answer the following questions.

1. Do you think having a good vocabulary is important? If so, why?

_____

_____

2. When in life will you need to rely on your verbal and written communication skills? Provide a couple of examples of situations when you will need to tap into these skills.

_____

_____

3. What impression do you get when you hear someone who has an accurate and impressive command of vocabulary give a speech?

_____

_____

4. In your opinion, what do words represent? Explain.

_____

_____

5. Why does having a command of several options for word choices increase your power as a speaker and a writer?

_____

_____

VOCABULARY BUILDING

Did you know that the average educated person knows about 20,000 words and uses about 2,000 different words a week? William Shakespeare, arguably the greatest author in English, had a vocabulary of between 18,000 to 25,000 words, back when people were happy to have an average of 5,000 words. Why is having a better vocabulary important? Studies have shown that having a better vocabulary increases your success in school and in your career. Also, understanding other people's ideas and arguments in verbal and written form becomes easier for you as well. Having a command of language is a form of power. Most highly successful business and political leaders have impressive vocabularies and a clear command of the English language.

The best way to increase your vocabulary is to make a conscious decision to work on building it up daily. Write new words and their definitions in a notebook as you learn them and then use them when you speak and write. The more you use new words in your day-to-day life, the faster your personal vocabulary will grow. Don't be afraid to take some risks and make some mistakes as you try out new words. However, try not to use an awkward or overly formal or complex word where a simpler one would be better. As Mark Twain once said, "Never use a five dollar word when a ten cent one will do." However, using too many simple words won't successfully generate more complex arguments and reasoning. Find the right balance for your purpose and audience.

Five Tips for Building Your Vocabulary

1. **Keep a Vocabulary Log or Vocabulary Journal.** Every time you read or hear a new word , write it in your log, note where it came from (a textbook, lecture, the radio, and so on), look it up in a dictionary (right then or as soon as you get a chance), and write down the definition. Try writing the definition using your own words first; then add the dictionary definition. Using a new word helps you to remember its

meaning, so after the definition write a sentence using the new word. Be sure to review your log regularly to brush up on your new words list.

Sample entry:

labyrinth: I heard this word in my English class when my teacher was talking about a character lost in the forest. I looked it up, and it means a maze-like situation, someone going through a confusing place, path, or journey.

Dictionary definition: lab•y•rinth (lăb′ə-rĭnth) NOUN:

1. An intricate structure of interconnecting passages through which it is difficult to find one's way; a maze.
2. Something highly intricate or convoluted in character, composition, or construction: *a labyrinth of rules and regulations.*

Used in a sentence: I was winding through the *labyrinth* of hallways at my new school.

---

2. **Make a conscious effort to use new words.** If you use a word more than a few times, it becomes "yours" and a natural part of your own vocabulary. Again, be sure that you are using the word correctly.

3. **Make friends with your dictionary and your thesaurus.** Consult the dictionary and thesaurus regularly to learn new words and to find substitutes for words you tend to use all the time so you can add variety and volume to your vocabulary.

Cross Reference
See Chapter 28 for tips on how to use a dictionary and thesaurus and sample entries for each.

4. **Learn the Latin roots, prefixes, and suffixes for words.** A large percentage of words in English are derived from Latin word parts. Becoming familiar with the meanings of these common **prefixes** (word beginnings), **roots** (common word bases), and **suffixes** (word endings) makes it easier to understand new words. For instance, the Latin prefix "de" meaning "away" or "from" is used all the time, as in words like *derail* (go off the tracks) and *depart* (go away from); the Latin root "tact" means "touch" as in *tactile*; and the Latin suffix "ism" means "belief" as in *pacifism* (belief in settling disputes peacefully).

5. **Use the Internet.** The Internet puts a world of vocabulary tools and information at your fingertips. Besides the numerous vocabulary-building sites available, you can also look up roots, prefixes, and suffixes as well as definitions of words and homonyms (words that sound alike but don't mean the same thing), synonyms (different words that mean the same thing), and antonyms (words that mean the opposite

of each other) in various online dictionaries and thesauruses. Just use your favorite search engine (such as Google, Ask, or Yahoo), and punch in a word to see what happens!

Activity 30-1   Keeping a Log

Directions: *Begin your own vocabulary log. Keep track of new words that you hear or read this week. Look up the meanings of the new words in your dictionary, and then use them in sentences of your own. Use a separate notebook for your vocabulary log and try to keep it with you throughout the day: You never know when a good word will come along.* ●

Activity 30-2   Vocabulary Practice

Directions: *Write down two words that appear somewhere in this chapter that you did not know before reading this section.*

    1. _____

    2. _____

Look up their meanings in a dictionary (online or hard copy):

    1. _____

    2. _____

Use each word in a sentence of your own:

    1. _____

    2. _____ ●

Activity 30-3   Vocabulary-Building Techniques

Directions: *Do the following for the listed vocabulary words:*

1. *Look up their meanings using an Internet search engine, such as Google, Ask, or Yahoo.*
2. *Define them using your own words.*
3. *Create a sentence of your own using each word.*
4. *Try to use each of the words in conversation or writing this week.*

    1. Incendiary

    Meaning: _____

    Defined in your own words: _____

    Used in a sentence: _____

2. Obsequious

Meaning: _____

Defined in your own words: _____

Used in a sentence: _____

3. Phenomenal

Meaning: _____

Defined in your own words: _____

Used in a sentence: _____

4. Disposition

Meaning: _____

Defined in your own words: _____

Used in a sentence: _____

5. Irradiate

Meaning: _____

Defined in your own words: _____

Used in a sentence: _____

SYLLABLES

Syllables are the number of sounds in a word. For instance, "dog" is only one syllable, but the word "Labrador" has three syllables: lab-ra-dor. Syllables help you pronounce words correctly. When you look up a word in the dictionary, you will see the syllables broken down correctly for you. For example, "irritable" would be broken down like this: ir-it-a-ble (use hyphens, dots, or slashes).

PRONUNCIATION

Pronouncing words correctly isn't just about breaking a word into syllables. Dictionaries provide pronunciation guides for words that use phonetics (spelling by how a word sounds). The following pronunciation guide will help you identify the most common consonant and vowel sounds in English.

PRONUNCIATION GUIDE

Consonant sounds		Short vowel sounds		Long vowel sounds	
b	bed	a	ham	a	say
d	dog	e	ten	e	she
f	fur	i	if	i	hi
g	goat	o	lot	o	go
h	her	oo	look	oo	school
j	jump	u	up	u (yoo)	use
k	kick				
l	leaf				
m	man				
n	no				
p	power				
r	row				
s	saw				
t	tea				
v	vase				
w	way				
y	yes				
z	zero				
ch	channel				
sh	shop				
th	that				
th	thick				

Activity 30-4 Practicing Pronunciation

Directions:

1. *Pronounce* the following words aloud.
2. *Mark the individual syllables* with slashes or dots between each syllable.
3. *Check a dictionary* to make sure you have pronounced each word correctly and have divided the syllables correctly.
4. *Write down the definition* of each word in your own words.

   1. Undeniable _____

     Definition: _____

_____

2. Predicate _____

Definition: _____

_____

3. Enunciate _____

Definition: _____

_____

4. Beneficial _____

Definition: _____

_____

5. Inconceivable _____

Definition: _____

_____

CRITICAL THINKING AND CONTEXT CLUES

Sometimes when you are reading it's not possible to stop and look up a word you don't know in a dictionary or on the Internet. Also, it may be impractical to look up *every* word you don't know at first glance. At those times, it is best to figure out a word's meaning as best you can by reading the context clues that surround it.

Figuring out vocabulary from context clues is not really just "guessing": More accurately, you are using the clues that come before and after the word and engaging your reasoning and critical thinking skills to put the clues together and figure out the word's meaning.

Critical Thinking and Visualization

Think of a jigsaw puzzle that is missing a piece. Based on the pieces surrounding the missing piece, you can figure out pretty accurately what that missing piece should look like.

Cross Reference

See Chapter 22 for help with parts of speech.

When you come across a word you don't know as you read, don't skip over it or get frustrated. Instead, use context clues and your critical thinking skills to figure out the word's meaning.

Figuring out a word using context clues is a skill that you get better at with practice. Moreover, you'll remember the new word longer if you have to figure it out for yourself, which helps you to build your personal vocabulary as you read. Therefore, make the time commitment needed to build your vocabulary: It pays off in the long run.

Using Context Clues

To figure out the meaning of a word, ask yourself the following questions:

1. Does the word have a prefix, root, or suffix I know that will give me a partial clue to its meaning?

2. What part of speech is the word functioning as in the sentence? Is it a noun? A verb? An adverb? An adjective?

3. Is the word followed by a secondary explanation or an example?

4. Is there a word used near the word that may mean the same (synonym) or opposite thing (antonym) that I can use as a clue?

5. What details or descriptive words are used in the sentence that I know? Do they give me clues to this word's meaning?

6. What idea or specific content is being developed in the individual sentence that this word belongs to?

7. What is the subject of the whole reading? How does the sentence that this word is part of develop the subject?

8. What purpose is being developed in this piece of writing? Does the word in question relate to the overall theme? Does it make sense in that context? Does it serve the essay's purpose?

9. If I guess the meaning now, can I read the next few sentences and then come back to the word and try again?

10. Do I still need to look up this word in the dictionary after I have tried to figure it out from context clues?

Activity 30-5   Using Context Clues

Directions: *Use the context clue questions to figure out the meanings of the words that are bolded in the following paragraph. Write the meanings below, and indicate which types of context clues you used to figure them out. Then double-check your answers using a dictionary.*

Gretchen is downright (1) **malicious** when it comes to on-the-job competition between departments. She says nasty things and becomes (2) **irate,** so irate her face turns red, with anyone who is beating her sales numbers. She always has been a bit (3) **eccentric**, dressing in strange outfits and riding a bike-for-two by herself to work. Some say her personality is too strong anyway; she's (4) **obnoxious** and loud in the break room every day. Some people think it's funny to (5) **provoke** her, but one time she was so upset after a teasing (6) **episode** that she was (7) **inconsolable** for hours, sad and moping on her own. Her level of competitive spirit is (8) **ludicrous**; she loses sleep during competitions and stops talking to her coworkers. She is (9) **obsessive** about every competition, not giving up or stopping to think about it for a moment. I hope we (10) **discontinue** the competitions for everyone's sake, especially Gretchen's.

1. Malicious: _____

    Context clues used: _____

2. Irate: _____

    Context clues used: _____

3. Eccentric: _____

    Context clues used: _____

4. Obnoxious: _____

    Context clues used: _____

5. Provoke: _____

    Context clues used: _____

6. Episode: _____

    Context clues used: _____

7. Inconsolable: _____

    Context clues used: _____

8. Ludicrous: _____

    Context clues used: _____

    9. Obsessive: _____

       Context clues used: _____

  10. Discontinue: _____

       Context clues used: _____

Note: The reading selections in Chapter 21 include more practice for figuring out the meanings of words using context.

Typing and Word Processing Tips

31

The correct typing format for documents varies from field to field and purpose to purpose. For instance, in business letters, a change in paragraphs is indicated not by indenting the first line but by adding an extra space *between* paragraphs. In essay writing, though, an indent of five spaces (hit the tab button) is used to indicate a new paragraph. No extra spaces are used between the paragraphs of an essay. The format explained in this chapter is the standard typing format for essays.

WORD PROCESSING

Typing Format for Essays

Paper	8½ × 11 inch white paper.
Line spacing	Use double spacing throughout the entire paper, including heading and title—no extra spaces between them or between paragraphs.
Margins	One-inch margins at the top, bottom, and both sides of the paper. Justify left margins, but, unless otherwise requested, do not justify right margins.
Titles	Modern Language Association (MLA) format does not require a title page (if your instructor requests a title page, get instructions for desired format). If your instructor does not want a title page, then leave a one-inch margin at the top of the first page, and on the left-hand side at the top, put your full name, your instructor's name, the course name and number, and the date submitted. Start each item on a separate line. See the sample paper in correct MLA format at the end of this chapter (p. 689). Then press the return button once (remain in double space), and center the title. In the title, capitalize the first word, last word, and all words in between, unless they are an article or a preposition. If you have a title and a subtitle, use a colon between the title and subtitle. Do not make the title bold or increase the font size. Do not underline your title or use italics or quotation marks unless citing the title of another work (see Italics on next page). See the sample title format in the model paper at the end of this chapter.
Page numbering	Page numbers should be in the upper right corner of each page, one-half inch from the top of your page and flush with the right margin. Include your last name, a space, and then the page number. Use the headers and footers function on your computer if using word processing. Do not put a comma or *p.* or *page* between your last name and the page number; just one space should separate them.
Fonts	Use 10- to 12-point type and a standard-style font (fonts most commonly used include Times New Roman, Arial,

Cross Reference
See Chapter 19 for a detailed introduction to MLA format.

Helvetica, Courier, and Palatino). Check with your instructor for particular preferences.

How to use . . .

Italics	Use italics for the titles of the following sources: books, films, journals or magazines, book-length poems, websites, online databases, television and radio broadcasts, CDs, record albums, performances, and works of art.
Tabs/ indentations	Indent five spaces (one tab) every time you start a new paragraph (including in dialogue), with no extra spaces between paragraphs. Indent ten spaces when inserting a block quotation of more than four lines (see page 373).
Spacing/ punctuation	**End punctuation** (periods, question marks, and exclamation marks): Use no space before the mark and type one space after. **Commas, semicolons, colons:** Use no space before the mark and type one space after it. **Parentheses, brackets, and quotation marks**: Use one space before the opening mark and one space after the closing mark. **Hyphens and dashes:** Do not use a space on either side. **Ellipses:** Use one space before the first period. The exception is when a complete sentence is followed by an ellipsis. In that case, the period that ends the sentence is placed before the ellipsis, with no space before it (since it is end punctuation). Put one space between each of the three periods that form the ellipsis. After the ellipsis, use one space. The only time you don't use a space afterward is when a closing quotation mark comes next. In that case, there is no space after the last period in the ellipsis. **Slashes:** When using a slash to separate lines of poetry, use a space on both sides of the slash. When using a slash between two words (e.g., either/or), do not use any spaces.
Visuals in your document:	Some papers, especially papers written for non-English courses across the curriculum, will require you to add visuals such as charts, graphs, or even photographs. If so, be sure to lay out the visuals in a clear format with a text explanation below the visual. See Chapter 20, Analyzing Visuals, for types of visuals and techniques for writing about them.

Five Word Processing Tips

Make friends with your computer! The best way to make typing your documents on a computer easier is to practice and take advantage of the many shortcuts computers offer. Here are five tips to help make your experience go more smoothly.

1. **Save often and back up your files.** Back up your files! Save them on your hard drive and on a separate disk, memory stick, or CD. You may even want to send them to yourself as an email attachment in case of an emergency. Be sure to *save your document every five minutes* or so to keep from losing it in case of a power outage or other disaster.

2. **Label all documents carefully.** *Create an effective folder system* to store your files, and label them as specifically as possible. Create a folder for each of your classes. Then label each document for each assignment, and even assignment drafts, that you've created for that course:

   Folder: English 101
   > **Document 1:** Narration Essay Draft, 5-23-08
   > **Document 2:** Final Narration Essay Draft, 5-28-08

   Include a brief description of the assignment and the draft date of each document.

3. **Control AutoFormat.** You can decide if you want to use AutoFormat or if you want to turn it off. It is there to work for you, not to work against you (check in the Format drop-down menu for the AutoFormat function). Go to your Edit button and click Undo Autoformat if it is doing things you don't want it to do.

4. **Get to know your toolbar.** Take the time to take a thorough tour of your toolbar—it's designed to help you.

5. **Use spell-check and grammar check.** However, don't completely trust these tools; they are not perfect, so double-check anything you're not certain about in a dictionary and a grammar handbook. Remember, spell-check will always give you a correctly spelled word, but it may not be the word you want at all.

   Example: I took a *brake* from work today.
   [The italicized word should be "break."]

Cross Reference
See Chapter 28 for more tips on using spell-check.

Finally, always print an extra copy of your final draft and keep a spare copy for yourself (even the most dedicated instructors have lost essays—it is your responsibility to have a backup copy). Before you submit your work, check through the hard copy for last-minute spelling and typo errors, overall format, and the quality of the printing before submitting the essay.

Basic Word Processing Shortcuts

1. **How to select spacing:** Go to **format,** select **paragraph,** choose **spacing,** then choose single or double.

2. **How to cut or copy:** Cut and Copy both put a copy of an image or text onto the computer's clipboard. The difference between the two is that Cut will remove the selected item from the document it is in, and Copy will not. You must then paste right away because whatever you next cut or copy will replace the current item on the clipboard.

   - **Select the text or image you want to cut or copy:** Press Ctrl + A to highlight the whole text or, for a specific section of the text, drag the mouse across the words you want to copy, so they are highlighted. For an image you want to copy, right-click on it. You should see some sign that it is selected—either small boxes at the corners or a heavier line around the edge.

   - **To cut or copy selected text:** Click Edit from your top screen menu and then select Copy OR press Ctrl + C. To cut, click Edit from your top screen menu and then select Cut OR press Ctrl + X.

   - **To paste text:** Left click where you want the copied material to go. Click on Edit and then select Paste OR Ctrl + V.

3. **How to align words left, right, or center:** Do not use the space bar or tab key. Instead, look for a menu that says Text Alignment or for these **buttons:**

   The button on the left aligns words flush left (aligning them evenly down the left margin). The next button centers text. The third button aligns words flush right (aligning them evenly down the right margin). The last button on the right will justify type, which means it will force text to spread out to both margins and be flush left and right (aligning words flush left is the preference for essays and MLA style).

4. **How to keep your text on one line:** Every once in a while you need to keep related text from splitting awkwardly at the end of a line. A common example of such a need is keeping phone numbers and their area codes together on the same line or keeping someone's full name on one line (e.g., Dr. Kim Abson). The trick is putting in a special kind of space so your word processor will recognize that it is not to start a new line. If you are a WordPerfect® user, this special space is called a "hard space." If you are a Word® user, it is called a "nonbreaking space."

   - **Word Perfect** users must press *Ctrl + Spacebar* to enter a hard space after the area code (to use the telephone number example).

Visually, this inserts a space at the proper point, but it is in fact a hard space. WordPerfect interprets a hard space as a text character and keeps the entire string together.

- **Word** users must press *Ctrl + Shift + Spacebar* to enter a nonbreaking space. Again, visually it appears the same, but it is treated differently if that space ends up at the end of a line.

5. **How to make paragraph breaks:** Do not type spaces to mark the beginning of a paragraph. Indent the first line one tab stop or use a style with a first-line indent.

6. **How to grab text:** Pressing *Ctrl + A* is a simple way to select an entire document. If you need to select an entire sentence in Word, hit F8 three times in quick succession. Pressing F8 a fourth time will select the entire current paragraph, pressing it a fifth time will select the entire document. These F8 shortcuts do not work in WordPerfect, but the *Ctrl + A* to select the entire document does.

7. **How to use the mouse:** In WordPerfect, you can use a mouse to select text by word, sentence, paragraph, or entire document by right-clicking in the left margin and selecting your choice. As an alternative, in WordPerfect you can use a mouse to select text by word, sentence, or paragraph, respectively, by double-clicking, triple-clicking, or quadruple-clicking with your left mouse button anywhere within the text you want to select.

   In Word you can use a mouse to select text by word and paragraph by either double-clicking or triple-clicking with your left mouse button anywhere within the text you want to select.

8. **How to insert bullets:** Both Word and WordPerfect allow you automatically to number or bullet a list of items. That is, each time you hit enter, you get a new number or bullet. Just click on the *numbered list* or *bullet* buttons to start such a list:

   Sometimes you find yourself wanting to enter an unnumbered item within a numbered item list or two points under the same bullet. To do so, press *Shift + Enter* instead of just *Enter*. *Shift + Enter* is recognized as a line break and not a paragraph break, and it won't insert a new automatic number or bullet. When you want to move on to your next numbered item or bullet, just press *Enter* as you would normally.

STUDENT ESSAY IN CORRECT TYPING FORMAT

David Hubbard

Professor Mendoza

English 100

4 April 2008

The Smoking Must Stop

Imagine sitting in a room filled with unwanted second-hand smoke every day. Such conditions could ruin your work environment. I work for a large company that is, for the most part, a great employer. Unfortunately, there are mandatory meetings every morning in which people smoke. The company needs to adopt a firm no-smoking policy for all mandatory meetings so that the health of non-smokers is not placed at risk and their right to work in a smoke free environment is respected.

Every morning I attend a required meeting that is thirty minutes long. During this time, multiple employees spend the duration of the meeting smoking cigarettes. I am surrounded by dangerous and unpleasant tobacco smoke. Tobacco is toxic, smells bad, and causes health problems. A person's decision to smoke is his or her own personal choice, just as someone makes the choice *not* to smoke. However, my supervisors have taken my choice away from me at these meetings. The smoke from tobacco carries many toxins, known to cause ailments such as cancer, birth defects, and emphysema. It also smells terrible and clings to one's clothing and hair. For a company whose number one concern is safety, this condition is unacceptable. A new policy should be implemented.

Hubbard 2

A second reason to discourage smoking in these meetings is because it is distracting. Many workers pay more attention to their lighters and cigarettes than to what is being said in the meetings. In addition, management does not allow us to eat, drink, or talk on cell phones in these meetings, so why do they allow smoking? Smoking must be restricted to break times to increase employee attention during meetings.

Many people feel they have a right to smoke whenever and wherever they want. However, their right should stop being a right as soon as someone else's right is affected by it. Smokers should lose their right to smoke in public or workplaces when there are other workers who want to exercise their right not to smoke and not to breathe someone else's smoke.

Therefore, something needs to be done at my workplace to stop the infringement on non-smokers' rights. I have brought up the need for change, but nothing has happened. I believe this is partly due to the fact that members of management also smoke, and perhaps they are reluctant to implement change. However, I think they need to see beyond their own desires and do what is best for the company. The company needs to move the meeting to a non-smoking area and make it a new rule that no one can smoke during the morning meetings. I realize smokers will be upset and voice their opinions about their right to smoke. However, I have a right to not smoke. Smokers can still smoke at other designated places at the proper time. Furthermore, smokers can use their break times to smoke instead of meetings. This change needs to happen if we are to have a fair and safe workplace.

Hubbard 3

In addition to my personal dislike of secondhand smoke, Washington state recently passed a law making it illegal to smoke indoors in public places. I feel this law is a reflection of the growing awareness of the dangers of secondhand smoke. My company needs to follow the lead of our state government and implement similar policies. Using the state law as guidance would also help alleviate any bad feelings that the smokers might have and would keep the company from looking like "the bad guy."

After these mandatory changes are made, everyone will be happier because smokers can smoke with other smokers in designated places at specific times without being harassed by non-smokers, and non-smokers will be able to do their jobs and attend mandatory meetings without having to breathe unwanted cigarette smoke. People will be more attentive in the meetings because they won't be distracted by smoking or by trying to avoid other people's smoke.

Appendix A

Writing About Stories and Essays

THINKING CRITICALLY

When critics review a play, they not only talk about whether the play was enjoyable, they also talk about the classic elements it should contain and whether they were executed well, including the writing, the acting, the sets, the costumes, the lighting, and so on.

How is a critic's job of reviewing a play similar to a student's job of critiquing another writer's story or essay? What do you think is similar? What kinds of things do you think you would look at when writing about an author's writing?

_____

_____

_____

_____

WRITING ABOUT STORIES AND ESSAYS

Analysis essays written about a story or essay go beyond just a summary of what happened. Instead, you interpret and analyze what the author's intended messages are and the techniques the author used to get his or her message across to the reader. Engage your critical thinking skills when you write about stories and essays. The skill of analysis is particularly essential in writing about fiction.

If you are writing an analysis essay for your instructor and classmates that is on an essay or story you have all read, then do not *summarize* the story or essay, since your audience has already read it. Instead, focus on interpreting the story's meaning. Show what the author's main messages are, and analyze the techniques and style choices the author made to convey those messages.

Applying Critical Thinking

| PURPOSE | IDEAS | SUPPORT | ASSUMPTIONS BIASES | CONCLUSIONS | POINT OF VIEW | ANALYSIS |

Inference involves tapping into your ability to "read between the lines" and figure out, or infer, what someone means based on clues in what they say or write. For instance, in a short story you would use information about the setting, the characters, the plot, and maybe repeated images as clues to *infer* the message and **purpose** the author means to convey through telling the story.

Interpretation involves decoding an idea so you understand its meaning. When you interpret an author's ideas, you explain them using your own words. You need to interpret and understand an author's ideas before you can **analyze** their importance and evaluate them. When you read a short essay, you need to be sure that you clearly understand the **ideas** the author is discussing before you can evaluate whether they are valid or important.

However, if your analysis essay is for a broader audience who may not have read the original work, you may need to include a brief summary of the story first (see Chapter 17, p. 342, Eight Steps for Writing a Summary).

Before you begin writing your analysis of an assigned or chosen essay or story, ask yourself the following questions:

1. What is the most important message the author wants to get across to the reader?
2. What are some of the secondary messages or ideas developed in this piece?
3. Are there any implied messages or ideas? If so, what are they?
4. How does the author's tone affect the overall impression made by the essay or story?
5. What specific writing techniques did the author use?
6. Are the style and writing techniques used effective or not? Why or why not?

Further questions to ask if you are analyzing a fictional story include:

1. What is the plot? What happens, and how does the action build and resolve, or not?
2. Who is the main character (protagonist)? Is there something he or she wants?
3. Is the setting (physical place and/or historical setting) of the story significant?
4. Is there any symbolism in the language or in the action of the story?

STRUCTURE OF AN ANALYSIS ESSAY

Introductory Paragraph

In the first paragraph of your analytical essay, begin with a general introduction to the subject and to the direct or implied message(s) (two to four sentences). Then add an analytical thesis statement that presents your opinion of what are the main messages of the piece.

If you are writing about fiction, it helps to include a plan in your thesis statement that outlines how you will organize your essay. For instance, you could focus on individual characters (one paragraph at a time), or you could discuss the progression of the story and its themes in the order events occur, or you could examine the author's writing style and techniques (such as symbolism, diction, and so on).

Body Paragraphs

Each body paragraph should have an analytical topic sentence based on your thesis and elements of the essay or story you are analyzing. For instance, if your essay focuses on analyzing the main characters, you could have a topic sentence for each main character that relates to the thesis statement. If you are writing an analysis based on the progression of events in the story, you could explain how the author leads up step by step to an analytical message. Then again, if you are focusing on the writing techniques used by the author, you could discuss style and language choices, such as the use of particular words or symbols, in order of their importance.

After the topic sentence, you should provide support statements, examples from the essay or story, and analysis of those examples. Each example from the essay or story needs to be interpreted (translated by you to explain what this part of the essay or story illustrates) and analyzed for its meaning (the direct and implied messages in the story).

In general, you need about two quotations from an essay or story for each body paragraph in order to provide adequate support for your thesis. Every time you use a quotation from the essay or story, you need to structure it in the following way.

The Ice Cream Sandwich Technique for Framing Quotations

- **Top cookie:** First, you need a general analytical statement, one or two sentences, to set up the quotation.

  Example: In "The Discus Thrower," by Richard Selzer, the doctor in the story is intrigued by his patient's sense of pride.

- **Ice cream filling:** Next, you need to incorporate the quotation, and then a citation.

  Use a colon: You may connect a quotation of one to three sentences in length to your general analysis sentence (top cookie) by using a colon and then the quotation. To use a colon to set up a direct quotation, the sentence in front of the colon must be a complete sentence and must set up the idea(s) within the quotation to follow:

  Example: In "The Discus Thrower," by Richard Selzer, the doctor in the story is intrigued by his patient's sense of pride: "His face is relaxed, grave, dignified" (96).

  Use a tag: You may use a simple tag:

  Example: Selzer writes, "His face is relaxed, grave, dignified" (96).

Cross Reference
See Chapter 17, p. 348,
The Ice Cream Sandwich:
Framing Facts and Sources.

Cross Reference
The following examples are in
MLA citation format—see
Chapter 19 for how to integrate quotations correctly.

Weave the quotation: Or, you may weave a piece of a quotation from the story or essay into your own sentence:

> **Example:** The doctor describes the patient's face as "relaxed, grave, dignified" (96).

- **Bottom cookie:** Finally, you need one or two sentences that interpret what the quotation is saying and analyze its significance (what this excerpt demonstrates, why it's important).

> **Example:** This description of the patient creates an image of dignity and grace. The doctor realizes this poor patient still has dignity and pride and a need for respect, even though there is little left to him physically.

Again, it's a good rule of thumb to include at least two full ice cream sandwiches (with specific references to the story, essay, or article) for support of your thesis in each body paragraph.

Concluding Paragraph

You will need a concluding paragraph that restates your thesis (not the same words, though; say it a different way) and sums up and concludes your essay's main points.

Use the following critique form to check that you have included all the elements of a good analytical essay.

Analytical Essay Critique Form

Overall

	Done well	Needs work

1. Is the essay analytical (does it include interpretation, commentary, and analysis of the message/s)?

2. Does the essay avoid merely summarizing the story or essay?

3. Does the essay stay focused on proving the thesis?

Introduction

4. Is the title interesting, appropriate, and typed in correct format?

5. Does the general introduction lead smoothly into the thesis?

6. Is the thesis statement clear (is it a clear presentation of the story's message)?

7. Is a plan of development included in the thesis (e.g., did you organize your paragraphs by themes or ideas, characters, the author's style and writing techniques, and so on)?

Body

8. Do the body paragraphs have clear topic sentences?

9. Does each body paragraph include support, examples and quotes from the story or essay (about two quotations per body paragraph)?

10. Is each quotation tagged or woven into your own sentence?

11. Is each quotation framed with your analysis—set up and then interpreted (ice cream sandwich technique)?

12. Are quotation marks and punctuation handled correctly?

13. Is there a concluding analytical sentence in each body paragraph?

14. Are transitions used well, both within and between paragraphs?

Conclusion

15. Does the concluding paragraph sum up your points well without introducing new ideas or analysis?

Citation Format (MLA)/Grammar/Spelling

16. Citation format: Every time a quotation is used, is it followed by parentheses containing the author's name and/or a page number and a period outside the parentheses?

17. **Circle grammar errors you see in this paper:** spelling, fragments, run-ons/comma splices, pronoun agreement, reference fault errors, verb use, commas, semicolons/colons, quotation marks, apostrophes, point-of-view shifts, faulty parallelism, passive voice constructions.

18. Other types of grammar or sentence-level errors you noticed in this draft:

_____

Comments:

_____

_____

SAMPLE STUDENT STORY ANALYSIS ESSAY

Read the original essay "'Just Walk on By': A Black Man Ponders His Power to Alter Public Space" by Brent Staples in Chapter 21 first, in order to fully understand this student's analysis of the piece.

Smith 1

Martin Smith

Professor Johnson

English 090

11 October 2007

Judged by Appearance Only

People view each other based on a variety of factors, including race and gender, and sometimes they act in ways that are judgmental and prejudiced. Brent Staples, a black man, focuses on how he is seen by others and how he solves the problem of discrimination in "'Just Walk On By': A Black Man Ponders His Power to Alter Public Space." In this story, Staples explains why some people are scared of

Thesis

him and what steps he takes to prevent people from seeing him as a threat.

Smith 2

Throughout the story, Staples focuses on the subconscious, and sometimes conscious, behavior that people exhibit. This behavior involves acting differently toward and being afraid of those who look different. This behavior reflects the biased nature of all humans. People often focus first on the differences of others before they look for common ground. So, people tend to choose to be close to people who are like them, and they often choose to think the worst of people who are different.

Staples' first encounter with prejudice was with a 20-year-old white woman on a deserted street in Hyde Park, Chicago. Staples writes, "As I swung onto the avenue behind her, there seemed to be a discreet, un-inflammatory distance between us. Not so. She cast back a worried glance" (88). Even before Staples says a word or makes a move, the woman reacts to him in a negative and worried manner. This reaction shows that she fears him based solely on his appearance. However, the fact that it was night and a lonely street is important too. She probably felt scared even before seeing Staples. However, Staples goes out of his way to alleviate this woman's fear. He has gotten into the habit of crossing to the other side of the street just to help women feel safer at night if he is around them.

In another instance of being judged by his skin tone, Staples brings up a time when he was rushing to work: "One day, rushing into the office of a magazine I was writing for with a deadline story in hand, I was mistaken for a burglar" (89). Since Staples was moving quickly, it gave the appearance that he was going to do something bad or had already committed a crime. Like "the speed of an ad hoc posse" (89), security chased him. And as Staples says, they "pursued me through the labyrinthine halls, nearly to my editor's door . . .

Topic sentence

Concluding sentence

Topic sentence & top cookie

Quotation = ice cream

Bottom cookie

Analysis

Topic sentence & top cookie

Quotation = cream filling

Bottom cookie

Smith 3

Analysis

I had no way of proving who I was" (89). In the first place, Staples should have acted more professionally by not running, and he should have stopped when he realized he was being pursued. However, he was an employee at this place, and it's not all that unusual for people to run in the halls when they are in a hurry. Staples implies that he was pursued because he was black. A white man or woman running down the hall probably would not have gotten security's attention. These types of unfair and unpleasant experiences happened to Staples on a regular basis, just for being a black man.

Concluding sentence

Topic sentence & top cookie

Therefore, staying in the shadows or modifying his own behavior to appear non-threatening became Staples' way of dealing with the prejudice of people who feared him. Choosing to avoid problems before they happen, he says, "I now take precautions to make myself less threatening. I move about with care, particularly late in the evening" (89). This decision to stay in the shadows and appear less threatening seems to work well for Staples; he discovers quickly what puts the people who are frightened by his appearance at ease. He avoids uncomfortable situations whenever possible, and, when he does come across unsuspecting "victims," he whistles tunes from Beethoven or Vivaldi (89). By whistling classical tunes, he puts frightened white people at ease. Staples demonstrates a strong ability to adapt to the situations he encounters.

Quotation = ice cream

Bottom cookie

Analysis

Concluding sentence

Restatement of thesis

In this story, Staples demonstrates some everyday instances of prejudice and brings to light the unkind and biased ways in which some people act. He also shows that he has chosen to respond to prejudice thoughtfully and with grace and humility instead of bitterness and anger. A man's power to alter public space can come from within him, despite the way he is viewed by others.

Activity 1   Story Analysis Assignment

Directions: *Choose one of the stories or essays from Chapter 21 or a different story or essay that your instructor assigns or that you have chosen. Then, use the Six Steps to Active Reading in Chapter 2, and read the piece. Next, write an analytical essay using the suggestions in this section for structuring and developing your analysis. Finally, use the critique form in this chapter for self- and peer-review of your essay draft.* ○

Activity 2   Analysis Essay Assignment

Directions: *Choose one of the stories or essays from Chapter 21, and complete one of the essay assignments listed at the end of it.* ○

Appendix B

Grammar Practice for Nonnative Speakers

NOUNS

Nouns name persons, places, things, or ideas. They can be *concrete* (such as *man*, *park*, *table*) or *abstract* (such as *friendship*, *love*, *freedom*). Nouns that you can count can be singular or plural and usually end in *s* in their plural form (such as *parks*, *tables*), or they can be irregular (such as *children*, *men*, *women*).

Noncount nouns are singular, not plural, and take a singular verb. They include words like *love*, *advice*, *freedom*, *knowledge*, or *information*. In fact, the words *homework* and *vocabulary* are noncount.

> *Homework* <u>takes</u> time.   *Vocabulary* <u>is</u> important to learn.

Activity 1a

Directions: *Underline all of the nouns in the following sentences. Then identify them as count or nouncount by writing C or NC under each.*

1. One student in my class likes to climb mountains and write about her experience.

2. Students who read her writing comment that nature brings her peace.

3. Most people agree that safety is important when someone is climbing in the mountains.

Activity 1b

Directions: *Now go back and circle the verbs that follow the noncount nouns. Are they singular (S) or plural (P)?* ⬤

ARTICLES

The **articles** *a, an,* and *the* are determiners that signal a noun will follow. Some languages do not have articles. In English, *a* or *an* is usually placed before nonspecific nouns to mean *any,* and *the* is placed before specific nouns that are clearly identified (or are the only one).

> We went on *a* vacation to *the* Rocky Mountains.
> [a = any; the = specific and plural count noun]
>
> Henry wants *a* pizza. He likes *the* pizza I make.
>
> I want *an* egg for breakfast. Please fry *the* egg.

Note: The examples above show how a general statement uses *a,* but a specific statement uses *the.* In addition, *a* is used for first mention and *the* for second mention of the same noun.

> I bought *a* new car last week.   *The* new car gets very good gas mileage.

However, noncount or abstract nouns and nonspecific plural nouns do not require articles.

> I drink *coffee* for breakfast.   *Coffee* gives me energy for daily activities.

Activity 2

Directions: *Write the correct article:* a, an, *or* the *(or* X *for no article) in the space provided.*

1. Many families turn on _____ national news when they get out

   of bed in _____ morning.

2. _____ adult may watch _____ news and _____

   weather, but _____ child may watch _____ cartoons.

3. Although _____ adults enjoy _____ television, they

   often have _____ work to do around the house. ⬤

SINGLE WORD MODIFIERS

Single word modifiers help clarify the meaning of nouns.

Rules for Modifiers

1. Before singular count nouns, use *this*, *that*, *another*, *every*, *each*, *neither*, *either*

2. Before plural count nouns, use *these*, *those*, *some*, *any*, *a lot of*, *many*, *a few*, *other*

3. Before nouncount nouns, use *much*, *any*, *some*, *a little*, *lots of*, *a lot of*, *this*, *that*

4. Use *any* in questions and negative statements.

5. Use *other* to mean different ones, and use *another* to mean one more or additional ones.

6. Use *the other* to mean a specific different one (or ones).

7. Before nouns, to show possession, use possessive adjectives: *my*, *your*, *his*, *her*, *its*, *our*, or *their*

> I don't understand *this* assignment we have today; *every* student is confused.
>
> *These* homework questions are difficult, but we have *many* days to complete them.
>
> One classmate doesn't have *much* trouble with *his* homework; *another* classmate has *lots of* trouble. I'm not sure about *the other* students.

Activity 3

Directions: *Write an appropriate modifier in each of the blanks in the following passage, using the rules listed above.*

_____ people prefer to read books about historical events. _____ people don't. _____ people might prefer books about scientific discoveries or current social problems. Of course, a person's age can affect _____ choices for reading topics. _____ thing that can affect such choices is a recommendation from a friend, but _____ person has his or her own interests. Interested readers don't have _____ problems finding good books. ●

Activity 4

Directions: *Write* this, that, these *or* those *in the following blanks.*

1. I have _____ computer right here. You have _____ one
   over there.

2. I am using _____ pencils on my desk. Can you use
   _____ instead?

Write another *or* the other, other *or* the others *in the following blanks.*

3. This sentence has two errors, and the next sentence has _____
   error.

4. That student registered for summer school, but _____ student
   with her did not.

5. That college doesn't offer cooking classes, but _____
   colleges do.

   Note: If there is no noun following, you can use *other* + *s:* (*#5* . . . but
   others do.)

Write much *or* many *in the following blanks.*

6. The counselor gave the new student _____ information about
   the campus.

7. The registration forms had _____ blanks to complete.

8. Does your instructor take _____ time to correct your
   papers?

ADJECTIVES AND ADVERBS

Adjectives

Adjectives describe or clarify nouns, pronouns, and groups of words that
function as nouns. Usually, words that end in *-ful* (helpful), *-ish* (selfish), or
-less (careless) are examples of adjectives.

Rules for Adjectives

1. Adjectives come before nouns they describe:

   The *tall, yellow* flower is blooming.
   NOUN

   > **Note:** Where two or more adjectives come before a noun, use a comma or commas between them.

2. Adjectives follow a *be* verb:

   The flower near the door **is** *tall and yellow.*

3. Adjectives do not have a plural form even with a plural noun:

   They are *serious* students.

Activity 5

Directions: *Underline the adjectives that modify (describe) the italicized words.*

New *students* often need a lot of information about current *schedules* on campus. They might not know where to go to see *counselors* who are available to help them. In addition, they might not understand lab *hours* or parking *rules.* They need helpful *staff* and *classmates.* ●

Adverbs

Adverbs describe or clarify verbs, adjectives, or other adverbs.

Roles of Adverbs

1. Adverbs describe or clarify verbs (for example, *usually* clarifies the frequency of an action: *usually* sleeps).
2. Adverbs describe or clarify adjectives (for example, *very* clarifies the adjective *good or helpful*).
3. Adverbs describe or clarify other adverbs (for example, *very* or *really* clarify the adverb *quickly*).

> **Note:** Many adverbs end in *-ly,* but others have no special ending. Adverbs can be moved in a sentence, as follows:
>
> **Beginning:** *Quietly,* Mother opened the door to the baby's room.
> **End:** Mother opened the door to the baby's room *quietly.*

Between subject and verb: Mother *quietly* opened the door to the baby's room.

Between helping verb and main verb: She has *quietly* opened the door to the baby's room.

Some words have both an adverb and an adjective form:

Correct use: (Adverb) Mother <u>speaks</u> *quietly*.

ACTION VERB

Incorrect use: Mother speaks quiet.

Correct use: (Adjective) Mother is a *quiet* <u>person</u>.

NOUN

Incorrect use: Mother is a quietly person.

Activity 6

Directions: *Choose an adjective or adverb from the list below and write it in the correct blank.*

stressful   always   important   clearly   strong

1. Exercising provides _____ benefits.

2. A _____ heart works efficiently.

3. Cells _____ need oxygen.

4. Exercise helps relieve a _____ day.

5. Exercising can help students think more _____. ●

PRONOUNS

Pronouns replace nouns or noun phrases and must agree with nouns in usage, gender, and number.

Subject Pronouns

Subject pronouns identify the doer of the action. They include *I, you, he, she, it, we, you, they.*

My *parents* bought a house near the mountains. *They* really like the house.

The *mountain* near my house is beautiful. *It* is covered with snow in the winter.

Note: English, unlike some other languages, always requires a subject before a verb, even a pronoun subject. However, remember not to repeat the subject.

Correct: *John* has some plans for tonight. *He* is going bowling.

Incorrect: *John* has some plans for tonight. Is going bowling. [subject *He* is missing.]

Correct: *Erika's* hobby is swimming. *She* goes to a pool every day.

Incorrect: *Erika's* hobby is swimming. *Erika she* goes to a pool every day.

Activity 7

Directions: *Write the missing subject pronouns in the blanks.*

During the first five years that Mom and Dad lived in Puerto Rico, _____ traveled to some Caribbean Islands. Mom felt sad because many of the people were poor. _____ said, "In our country, _____ have so much, but these people don't." Dad could speak the language in the Dominican Republic, but he couldn't understand the languages in Haiti. Dad likes languages. _____ says, "_____ great to understand people in other cultures." ⬤

Object Pronouns

Object pronouns identify the receiver of the verb action. They include *me, you, him, her, it, us, you,* and *them.* Notice the positions in each sentence below where an object pronoun must be used. Objects follow verbs and also follow prepositions.

The teacher *asked* me to give back the papers. She had already *corrected* them.

Theresa *helps* her friends, and they *help* her.

Friendship is important *to* us. We *appreciate* it.

Activity 8

Directions: *Fill in the blanks with a correct subject or object pronoun.*

While my parents lived in another country, _____ did not see _____ for several years. Finally, my brother and I took a vacation to visit _____. While _____ were away from home, our friends wrote letters to _____ at my parents' address. The mail was slow. We didn't get _____ until after returning home. _____ missed my friends as much as I had missed my parents. _____ both mean a lot to _____. ⬤

Possessive Pronouns

Possessive pronouns answer the question *whose?* They include *mine, yours, his, hers, its, ours, yours,* and *theirs.*

> Some new books are at the bookstore now. *Ours* came in today, but *theirs* haven't arrived yet.

Note: Do not confuse *its* (no apostrophe/not a contraction) with *it's* (contraction of *it is* or *it has.*)

Activity 9

Directions: *Fill in the blanks with a correct object or possessive pronoun.*

1. Both individuals in a marriage must work at communication. The responsibility is _____.

2. Both partners want their spouse to pay attention to _____.

3. Researchers in the U.S. are studying this communication problem and trying to solve _____.

4. Hopefully new research will help all of us improve relationships. I want to improve _____. ⬤

Reflexive Pronouns

Reflexive pronouns refer to their noun antecedent for clarification or emphasis. Reflexives include *myself, yourself, himself* (not *hisself*), *herself, itself, ourselves, yourselves,* and *themselves* (not *theirselves*).

> He hurt *himself* when he fell off his bike. The children saw *themselves* in the mirror.

Activity 10

Directions: *Fill in the correct reflexive pronoun for each blank; refer to the list of examples above.*

1. I have been dressing _____ since I was four years old.

2. She told _____ she would not cry at the movie.

3. He married so that he didn't have to live by _____ anymore.

4. The caregiver cooked for the old man and woman because they couldn't cook for _____.

5. My wife and I don't ask for others' opinions. We trust _____ when making decisions. ⬤

Relative Pronouns

Relative pronouns are used to join sentences, making two sentences come together as one. Relative pronouns describe a noun that comes just before them. In the following example, *who* describes John, a noun.

> John likes to play baseball. John is my friend.
>
> John, *who* is my friend, likes to play baseball. [The relative pronoun *who* is used to join the two sentences.]

Note: The clause starting with a relative pronoun cannot stand alone.

> **Incorrect:** John is my friend. Who likes to play baseball.
>
> **Correct:** John is my friend *who* likes to play baseball.   OR   John, *who* is my friend, likes to play baseball.

Note: *who* = people; *which* = animals, things, or ideas; *that* = people, animals, or things.

In the following examples notice how the relative pronoun is used to combine two ideas:

Two clauses joined into one with *which:*

> The book on Kennedy is so heavy. I bought it.
>
> The book on Kennedy, *which* I bought, is so heavy.

Two clauses joined into one with *that:*

> The book on Kennedy is so heavy. I bought it.
>
> The book on Kennedy *that* I bought is so heavy.

Two clauses joined into one with *whose:*

> The author is famous. *His* book is on Kennedy.
>
> The author *whose* book is on Kennedy is very famous.

Activity 11

Directions: *Underline the correct relative pronoun for each blank.*

1. Florida is a state (who/that) has many residents who are retired.

2. Florida tourists are people (who/which) like warm weather attractions.

3. People (who/whose) income is low don't have money for entertainment.

4. Florida is a state (whose/that) has a very warm climate.

5. Tourists are people (which/whom/that) every state needs for added income.   ○

> **Note:** *Whom* (object pronoun) can be used as a relative object pronoun, but *that* is now more common.

Punctuating Relative Clauses

There are two kinds of relative clauses, restrictive and nonrestrictive. **Restrictive (essential)** relative clauses are needed to identify a noun clause and have no commas. **Nonrestrictive (nonessential)** relative clauses are *not* needed to give meaning to the sentence and identify a noun. They are set off by commas on both sides as shown in the following example:

> John likes to play baseball. John is my friend.

> John, *who* is my friend, likes to play baseball.

In this example, the relative clause starting with *who* is not needed to give the sentence meaning.

> **Note:** Nonrestrictive (unnecessary) clauses cannot use *that*; therefore, *which* is used instead:

> My neighbor's house, *which* needs a new coat of paint, is older than mine.

Activity 12

Directions: *Put commas around the relative clause if the clause is not important to give the sentence meaning; otherwise, do not punctuate a necessary clause that is needed to identify or describe the noun. Instead, write C for correct.*

_____   **1.**   This exercise which I started late is helping me understand relative clauses.

_____ **2.** Grammar which often requires us to study is important in learning a language.

_____ **3.** Our teacher told us to study the grammar review section that is at the end of the chapter.

_____ **4.** I am interested in the early morning Spanish I class which begins on January 16.

_____ **5.** The instructor whose class I took last fall is Mr. Jones.

_____ **6.** Mr. Jones who is going to retire next year was my favorite teacher.

PREPOSITIONS

A **preposition** is a word that helps show a relationship between two ideas in a sentence. Common prepositions include: *at, for, from, in, on, of, to, with, through, between,* and *by*. A preposition followed by a noun or pronoun becomes a prepositional phrase. A prepositional phrase must not be separated from the rest of the sentence by punctuation.

Correct: He lives alone in a small apartment.

Incorrect: He lives alone. In a small apartment.

Preposition Rules

1. Some prepositions indicate location, as shown in the prepositional phrases below:

on his father's farm   *in* the country   *at* school
by the bus stop   *on* Main Street

- Use *in* for inside a specific place (*in* his pocket) and *on* for on top of (*on* the table)
- Use *on* for a street without a house or building number (*on* Main St.)
- Use *at* with a house or building number (*at* 1258 Main St.)
- Use *in* for the city and state (*in* San Francisco; *in* California)

2. Some prepositions indicate time, as shown in the prepositional phrases below:

in May   *in* the spring   *on* December 1
at night   *after* school   *by* noon

- Use *in* for months and years (*in* May; *in* 2008)
- Use *on* for dates (*on* Dec. 1) and days of the week (*on* Thursday)
- Use *at* for specific times (*at* 9:00 am)
- Use *from . . . to* for a specific time period (*from* 10:00 *to* 2:00) and *for* for duration (*for* 2 days)

Activity 13

Directions: *Read the following paragraph. Underline all prepositional phrases, and circle the prepositions. You will find 12 prepositional phrases in all.*

I began studying English in 1999. The English class I took was offered by the public school in the evening. Many of the students in my class were from other countries. The class met on Tuesday and Thursday evenings from 7 to 10 pm. I went to class with my husband because he was also learning English. Now the school has grown and moved to a new building at 1650 Compass Boulevard. I am proud that our English has improved. ◉

SENTENCE STRUCTURE

Basic Building Blocks

1. We build a sentence from word to phrase to clause:

   Word + Word = Phrase: Eating lunch. [Not a sentence; there is no subject.]

   Subject + Verb = Clause: He knows.   They are coming.   I study.

   Note: An **independent clause** (like *He knows* above) must have a subject and verb to be complete, no matter how long it is. A long group of words that is missing a verb or missing a subject (or both) is not a sentence.

2. Two independent clauses make a compound sentence. These sentences are joined with connectors, such as *and, or, but,* and *so.*

   He knows, *but* she doesn't.

   I study, *and* you work.

   They are coming, *so* he is leaving.

3. Not all clauses with a subject and a verb are sentences. They may depend on an independent clause to form a complete thought because they begin or end with a subordinator, such as *if, since, because, when, before, after, while, although, even though,* and so on.

- A **dependent clause** is an incomplete idea. The following clauses are not complete sentences:

> *If* I have time . . .   *Because* I want good grades . . .
> *When* I get home . . .   *Even though* I might be tired . . .
> *After* the class . . .   *Since* I am sick . . .

Note: A **fragment** (a broken or incomplete thought) happens when you put a period between a dependent and independent clause.

> **Incorrect:** Even though I might be tired**.** I study. [Use a comma, not a period between ideas.]
> **Correct:** Even though I might be tired**,** I study.

Note: A fragment can, in fact, occur when a sentence is missing *any* of its parts.

- A dependent clause and an independent clause make a complex sentence and a complete thought:

> *If* I have time, <u>I study.</u>   OR   <u>I study</u> *if* I have time.

Note the comma when the dependent clause comes first.

> *Even though* I might be tired, <u>I study.</u>
> OR   <u>I study</u> *even though* I might be tired.

Activity 14

Directions: *Underline any incomplete idea (dependent clause), and correct the punctuation if needed. One of the examples is correct.*

1. If I loved you. We would be happy.

2. I love you. Because of all the nice things you do.

3. I love you. Although I wonder if you love me.

4. When you tell me you love me, I will be happy.

5. While I am waiting for your answer. I am worrying about our relationship. ⬤

    Note: Relative pronouns can also begin an incomplete idea.
    Incorrect: He is the person. Who helped me with my registration.
    Correct: He is the person *who* helped me with my registration.

    Incorrect: That is the newest section of the campus. Which is more crowded.
    Correct: That is the newest section of the campus, *which* is more crowded.

Other Sentence Structure Points to Remember: Gerunds and Infinitives

Gerunds

A gerund is a verb + -ing:

> **Gerunds follow prepositions:** interested *in* learn*ing*; tired *of* study*ing*
>
> **Gerunds can be the subject of a sentence:** <u>Study*ing*</u> is important.
>
> **Gerunds can be the object of a sentence:** They avoided <u>study*ing*</u>.
>
> **Gerunds can be used as modifiers, also called participles:** <u>Study*ing*</u> hard, the student passed.

Note: Certain verbs require gerunds, not infinitives, for the verb following: I *enjoy* learn*ing*. I *avoid* study*ing*.

Infinitives

An infinitive is *to* + a verb. Infinitives separate verbs. Often infinitives are used after verbs expressing feelings.

> I want **to** *travel*.   I like **to** *meet* people.   I didn't need **to** *leave*.

Infinitives are also used in place of *that* in sentences showing the will of one person over another:

> **Correct:** They want us *to come* to the party.
>
> **Incorrect:** They want that we come.

Do not use infinitives with modal auxiliary verbs (helping verbs like *must*, *should*, *will*, *could*, and so on).

> **Correct:** He *should listen* to that advice.
>
> **Incorrect:** He *should to listen* to that advice.

Activity 15

Directions: *Write a gerund (verb + -ing) or infinitive (to + base verb) for each blank, using verbs from the list below.*

> arrive   improve   see   take   register   manage   attend

1. Maria: I am interested in _____ a computer class this year.

2. Thuy: I can see why you are interested. It would be helpful. I hope _____ my skills also.

3. Maria: Have you thought about _____ a class in the day or evening?

4. Thuy: I want to avoid _____ at work late, so I think I will take a morning class.

5. Maria: That would work for me too. Let's plan _____ for the same course this time.

6. Thuy: Ok. I'll ask my husband _____ my daughter to school if the class time conflicts.

7. Maria: _____ time is always a challenge.

8. Thuy: Yes, and the family expects _____ us too. ⬤

VERBS

Function of Verbs

Verbs are words that show action or join the subject to the rest of the sentence.

1. Verbs indicate the time the action took place—for example, present, past, or future.

2. Verbs begin with a **base** form, which doesn't show time (tense) or person. This is part of the infinitive:

to understand   to know   to read   to write   to come   to go

> **Note:** An infinitive = *to* + base form of verb. The base form is not the present tense. Never change the base verb in an infinitive by adding an ending.
>
> **Incorrect:** to learning

3. Some tenses and verb forms are followed by base verbs:

> **Present tense questions and negatives:** *Does* he <u>*know*</u>? No, he *doesn't* <u>*know*</u>.
>
> **Past tense questions and negatives:** *Did* she <u>*know*</u>? No, she *didn't* <u>*know*</u>.
>
> **Modal verbs:** *Could* they <u>*come*</u>? No, they *couldn't* (<u>*come*</u>). *Should* you *call*?

Commands (the **imperative**) also use base verbs:

(You) *Come.*   (You) Don't *call.*

4. A few verbs require base verbs to follow (*make, let, have*):

The teacher *let* him *leave*.

5. Questions can be either "yes/no" type or "information questions" with the words *who, what, where, when, how,* and *why.*

Did you *understand?* (Yes/No)   OR   *What did* you *understand?*

Activity 16   Base Verbs

Directions: *Write in any appropriate verb form for each blank.*

Responsibility in college involves not only completing assignments but also how a student should _____ them. With their busy lives, students often let time _____ without getting homework finished. Some students have their classmates _____ their homework for them. For example, if a student doesn't _____ time to study, he or she may feel pressure and decide to complete the assignment any way possible. Even if a student can _____ help from another person, the other person could _____ mistakes also. Worst of all, copying another person's work can make you _____ your class and give you a bad reputation. Did you ever _____ of this problem? Don't _____ it! ⬤

Simple Present Tense

Present tense is used for routines (actions that happen anytime or regularly).

Note: Time words (such as *always, sometimes, once a week*) should help you know when to use the present tense.

Action Verbs

Use the base verb for all persons, but add *s* for *he, she,* and *it.*

I learn, you learn, he learns, we learn, you learn, they learn

Insert *do* or *does* only for questions or negative answers before a base verb.

Does he always *eat* breakfast?

Yes, he always *eats* at 8 am. [Note *s* for affirmative answer.]

No, he *doesn't* always *eat* breakfast. [No *s* with negative helping verb.]

Note: Remember, do not use *do* or *does* for affirmative statements, only for questions and negatives.

Correct: *Do* they always *eat* breakfast?

Yes, they usually *eat* at 8:30 am.   OR   No, they *don't*.

Activity 17

Directions: *Fill in a present tense verb to complete each statement or question.*

1. Every day my mail _____ at 1 pm.

   Question: When _____ your mail _____?

2. Often the mail carrier _____ me a package.

   Question: What _____ he _____?

3. When I'm away, I _____ my neighbor for help.

   Question: Whom _____ you _____ for help when you are away?

4. My neighbor never _____ to help me.

   Question: _____ your neighbor _____ you? ●

Be Verbs

The **be verb** (*is, are, was, were, have/has been*) is followed by nouns, adjectives, and locations. Questions require a form of *be* before the subject, and statements require a form of *be* after the subject.

Is he a student?   Yes, he's a student.   OR   No, he *isn't* a student.

Is he happy?   Yes, he's happy.   OR   No, he *isn't* happy.
                                                  [adjective after *be*]

Where *is* he?   He *is* at school.   He's in the library.
He *isn't* at home. [location]

Note: *Be* verbs are also followed by the gerund form (verb + *-ing*), but that is the progressive, not the simple present tense. Use it to show an action in progress. The tense of the *be* verb shows the time, not the main verb + *-ing*: I *am* learning, I *was* learning, I *have been* learning, and so on.

Remember that simple present tense is used for routine actions, not actions in progress.

Activity 18   **Directions:**   *Underline the correct action verbs or be verbs in the sentences that follow.*

1. Austin (is/are) hot but beautiful in the summer.

2. Flowers (blooms/bloom) on many plants.

3. The hotel (has/have) a lovely dining area.

4. My family (likes/like) visiting other places.

5. The attractions of this city (offers/offer) relaxation and good food.

6. Austin (was/were) much smaller when I went there as a child. ⬤

Activity 19

Directions: *Form questions with action verbs (Do/Does + base verb) and be verbs using the sentences in Activity 18.*

1. Austin/hot in summer: _____

2. Flowers/bloom: _____

3. Hotel/have/dining area: _____

4. Family/visiting other places: _____

5. Attractions of this city/offer: _____

6. Austin/smaller/when you went as a child: _____

_____ ⬤

Present Progressive Tense

In comparison to the simple present tense, the present progressive shows action in progress or temporary actions happening at this time. The present progressive (also called the *present continuous*) is formed with *be* + verb *-ing*.

He *is* study*ing*.   We *are* listen*ing*.   You *are* writ*ing*.   They *are* learn*ing*.

Be Verb

The *be* form (*is, are, was, were, has* or *have been*) is called the *helping verb* and combines with the main verb. Continuous temporary actions in the past or present perfect use *be* + verb *-ing*:

Past continuous: He *was* study*ing* when I called.
He *has been* study*ing* hard all year.

Future continuous actions also use *be* + verb *-ing*:

> He *will be* study*ing* until he graduates in June.

Questions

Questions are formed as in the *be* present tense. Move the *be* form in front of the subject.

> *Are they* eating breakfast now?   When *is he* eating breakfast?
> *Was* he study*ing?*

Negatives

Negatives are formed by putting *not* after the appropriate form of the helping verb *be*.

> They *are not* (*aren't*) eating breakfast now.
> They *have not* (*haven't*) *been* studying long.

Activity 20

Directions: *Write the correct form of the verb in parentheses for each sentence.*

1. He (like) _____ to play soccer.

2. She (teach) _____ tennis to beginning players

3. I (take) _____ a test right now.

4. She (talk) _____ to the teacher about today's homework assignment.

5. Answer the following question: When should you use present tense, and when should you use present continuous? _____

_____ ⬤

Simple Past Tense

The simple past tense is used for actions that began and finished in the past.

Rules for Simple Past Tense

1. Often a specific time in the past is given, indicated by a time word, such as *ago* or *last* (*week, month, year*).

2. Simple past verbs are regular (add *-ed* to base verb) or irregular (no *-ed* but spelling change). Refer to an irregular verb list for study of these past forms.

> He *cooked* breakfast an hour ago.   The flowers *bloomed* last month.
> [completed action]

3. To form questions in the simple past tense, use *did* before the main verb, which takes the base form.

> *Did* he <u>cook</u> breakfast?   *Did* the flowers <u>bloom</u>?   *Did* you <u>call</u>?

4. To form negatives in the simple past tense, use *didn't* + the base form of the main verb.

> He *didn't* <u>cook</u>.   The flowers *didn't* <u>bloom</u>.   I *didn't* <u>call</u>.

Note: Remember that *was* and *were* (*be* verbs) are used for simple past statements and questions as well.

Activity 21

Directions: *Fill in the correct form of the past tense, including questions and negatives.*

1. He (have) _____ to choose a new line of work last year.

2. Working at the automobile factory (be) _____ difficult.

3. Last summer his wife (tell) _____ him to consider college.

4. When you were a child, (do) _____ your family (speak) _____ to you about college?

5. Unfortunately, my parents (not have) _____ the opportunity to attend college. ⬤

Present Perfect Tense

Present perfect tense is used to indicate an action that began in the past but continues into the present and even could continue into the future.

> **Note:** Like the simple past, the present perfect has both regular endings (with *-ed*) and irregular forms.

> **Rules for Present Perfect Tense**

1. Do not add *been* before the past participle. The present perfect has just two parts.

> **Have or has + past participle:** He *has* worked here for 5 years.
> The company *has* grown a lot.

2. Use *has* for *he/she/it* and *have* for all other forms. As with other verbs, the negative is formed by placing *not* after the verb—in this case, after the helping verb, *has* or *have*.

> He *has* cooked breakfast since he was a teenager.   They *have not eaten* yet.

3. Sometimes you use the present perfect for completed actions that are still important.

We *have* already *eaten*.   They *have never been* to that restaurant before.

4. You also use the present perfect for actions that stop and start (re-peated actions) from past to present.

He *has cooked* for his friends every Tuesday since last year.

Note: Time words, such as *always*, *never*, *already*, and so on go between the helping verb and past participle.

5. To form a question, put the helping verb before the subject.

Has he cooked? [subject is *he*]

Activity 22

Directions: *Underline the correct form in each sentence (compare present perfect to simple past, finished actions).*

1. Yesterday I (cleaned/have cleaned) the garage.

2. I (didn't clean/have not cleaned) the garage for two years.

3. We (never used/have never used) the shelves in the back of the garage.

4. We (bought/have bought) our house in 2002.

5. Have you (worked/work) on home improvement yet? (Note the help-ing verb position for questions.) ●

Past Perfect Tense

In contrast to the present perfect tense, the **past perfect tense** indicates a past action that occurred before another action in the past. In this case, two verb actions are involved; for the first action that happened, use *had* + past participle.

Note: It makes no difference which action comes first in the sentence.

Before I studied this grammar, I *had not understood* the difference in verb tenses.

After I *had practiced* the verb tenses, I improved my writing.

Activity 23

Directions: *Write in the correct answer.*

_____   1. The present perfect uses a helping verb, which is:
a. have or has
b. had
c. had or has

_____ **2.** The past perfect uses a helping verb, which is:
  a. have or has
  b. had
  c. had or has

_____ **2.** In the sentence, "I came here after I (action)." use:
  a. had + past participle
  b. have + past participle ○

Present Perfect Continuous Tense

The present perfect continuous tense emphasizes actions in progress, continuing from past into the present time without interruption. It uses the same helping verbs as present perfect (*have* or *has*) but adds two other changes: the helping verb *been* and *-ing* on the base form instead of using a past participle.

She *has been taking* Spanish since the tenth grade.

Passive Voice

Sentences with action verbs that focus on the action, not the subject, are called *passive*. For example, we can say "The letter *was sent*" instead of "*John sent* the letter." Use a form of *be* + past participle. The *be* verb controls the time, not the past participle.

Note: If you learn past participles for present perfect with *have/has,* you will know the past participle form to use with a form of *be* in the passive voice.

John *is sending* the letter.   becomes   The letter *is being sent*.
                                            [present progressive passive]

John *has sent* the letter.   becomes   The letter *has been sent*.
                                            [present perfect passive]

My friends *send* letters.   becomes   Letters *are sent* by my friends.
                                            [simple present passive]

Do not confuse passive voice sentence construction with active voice sentences.

Incorrect: My friend has been sent a letter. [passive voice]

Correct: My friend has sent a letter. [active voice]

Credits

Index

725